AF225730

U.S. ARMY HELICOPTER NAMES IN VIETNAM

John Brennan

Mini Power: *F Troop 4 Cav, OH-6A, 1971*. Inscriptions on a Loach's minigun housing were an extremely rare sight. Photo by Carl Betsill.

HELLGATE PRESS • ASHLAND, OREGON

U.S. ARMY HELICOPTER NAMES IN VIETNAM

©2011 JOHN BRENNAN

Published by Hellgate Press
(An imprint of L&R Publishing, LLC)

Hellgate Press
PO Box 3531
Ashland, OR 97520
www.hellgatepress.com

Editing: Harley B. Patrick
Cover design: L. Redding
Cover art: Geoff Liebrandt

Author photo, back cover: John Brennan beside *Death's Little Angel*, 114 AHC, Cobra Platoon AH-1G (sn 66-15322), Vinh Long, 1970.

Library of Congress Cataloging-in-Publication Data

Brennan, John, 1948-
U.S. Army helicopter names in Vietnam / John Brennan.
p. cm.
Includes bibliographical references and index.
ISBN 978-1-55571-694-3 (alk. paper)
1. Military helicopters--United States--Registers. 2. United States. Army--History--Vietnam War, 1961-1975. 3. Nicknames--United States.
4. Military helicopters--Vietnam. 5. Vietnam War, 1961-1975--Aerial operations, American. I. Title.
UG1233.B746 2011
959.704'348--dc23
2011019482

Printed and bound in the United States of America
First edition 10 9 8 7 6 5 4 3 2

One June day at South Vietnam's Vinh Long Army Airfield in 1970, an Army buddy snapped a photo of me leaning against the nose of a 114 AHC slick that had been christened "THE IRON BUTTERFLY." A few months later the Crew Chief that named this ship, SP5 Frank Akana, was Killed In Action. Nowhere among this young man's official records would "THE IRON BUTTERFLY" be mentioned. Outside of a small group of buddies, friends and family this entitled bit of Army aviation history had but all been neglected and forgotten… until now.

An Khe Annie: *B Troop 1/9 Cav, UH-1B, April 1967.* An Khe was 1st Air Cav Div Hdqs; the UH-1B gunship in foreground has a "frog" configuration weapons system as opposed to the UH-1B gunship in background which has a "hog" configuration. Standing (*left to right*): Jim Bennett CP, Dick Hale AC. Front (*left to right*): CE and DG, names unknown. Photo courtesy Dick Hale.

TABLE OF CONTENTS

How Do We Look?: 68 Avn Co, UH-1B, 1965-66. You just gotta love the in-country humor of the everyday soldier. Photo by Dan Telfair.

PREFACE

The personal naming of military aircraft in the Vietnam War is not unique in American history. What is unique is the near total lack of documentation on file of their existence. Not any longer. Unseen and nearly forgotten for over forty years, 3,100 Army helicopter names from the VN War have been rescued from history's cutting room floor and respectfully restored to their rightful place of importance, ending forever a societal estrangement that has lasted these many years.

Against a backdrop of censorship, political correctness, and military directives to the contrary, in-country Army helicopter nose art and fanciful names flourished in Vietnam. Understand, by no means does this imply anything approaching the scale of artistic expression exhibited on Army Air Force bombers and fighter aircraft of WWII. Yet the tradition was carried on, the baton was passed forward, and the legacy continued, borrowing some from the old, manufacturing others that were new, and gleefully composing for levity's sake enough cockeyed artwork and names to counterbalance the weight of war on the psyche of the war weary G.I. in Vietnam.

Between 1962-1973, stretching from the Delta to the DMZ, affixed to every helicopter model from the AH-1G through the UH-1M, and crewed/piloted by Army aviators from the 1st Aviation Detachment to the UTT (Utility Tactical Transport), there materialized in non-OD colors a veritable smorgasbord of personalized names and art. It is important here to be clear on the elements that DO NOT figure into this project's definition of personalized markings, these being: pilot/crew nicknames and call-signs, and unit/platoon names, call-signs, insignia, and slogans. The job of tracking down and recovering helicopter names would be a big enough challenge all in itself.

Although considered by the military to be of an unofficial and transient nature, personalized names and art represent an unbroken tradition dating back to WWI, with one little wrinkle. Because hearts and minds were part of our military strategy, and Vietnam being the first TV war, the Army decided to buckle down on any inscriptions and art that contained lewd, crude, vulgar, or pornographic overtones. For many Army brats any thoughts of carrying on dear old dad's WWII nose art legacy to Vietnam were sadly put to rest.

Over time and under scrutiny many new details would emerge in the wake of America's military presence in Vietnam. With over 3,100 helicopter names thus documented, one of the last remaining unexplored goldmines of Army aviation history will have been excavated and brought to light. Consequently, what is revealed after sorting out the collected data are four basic marking patterns as they appeared on in-country Army helicopters: *name only, name and artwork, artwork only, name as artwork*. Additionally, because some units adhered to a strict "no-personal markings policy," it was common practice for these crews to assign a *verbal name* to their aircraft; thus, a fifth classification of names will be honored that includes these as well. Furthermore, this fifth class will also take into account the VN War practice of naming one's helicopter according to the configuration of the aircraft serial numbers. For example, BALLS THREE (66-15003), DEUCE + A DIME (65-19210) and DOUBLE ACE (66-16011).

From the beginning the intended goal of this project was to document that quintessential and unmistakable American war custom of embellishing one's assigned military aircraft with personalized markings. As with any challenge worth its weight, such an undertaking would serve to be nothing less than daunting. Factor in the degrading nature of time upon memory and the declining veteran population, and the odds looked far from promising.

But a historical void needed to be filled, the personal computer and the Internet made the task achievable, and my own curiosity needed to be satisfied. In addition, any study of Army aviation history in this particular conflict would be considered incomplete without including an overview of this project's findings, for that which was deemed inconsequential at the time now offers a significant insight into the state of mind of Army helicopter crews during those nights and days of Vietnam flying between 1962-1973.

Before this project was initiated very little was known about the in-country practice of painting individualized names and nose art on Army helicopters. The fact that it was tolerated by most local commanders on the ground and was visible throughout the course of the war in all four Corps Tactical Zones begged a couple of questions, chief among them, What happened to it all? and secondly, Does anyone know the who, what, and why behind these artistic creations? The fact that the UH-1 Huey possessed a detachable nose panel, which doubled as a natural canvas for artwork and names, was in itself a unique fuselage amenity among in-country helicopters. It also offered a viable keepsake for a lucky few who courted fate and faith to see it home.

Any in-depth analysis of a post-war collection such as helicopter nose art and names is dependent on a healthy database of information. Let's suppose other than helicopter names, someone wanted to study similar by-products of the war—like Zippo lighter art, flight helmet art, or short-timer calendar art. Here too, because of their "unofficial" military status, one might find it completely justified to bypass the Army and government altogether and appeal directly to the veterans themselves for help. With over 10,000 emails received to date that's precisely how this very project gained transitional lift and completed its mission. To break it down further, roughly two-thirds of the names obtained were from email correspondence and photos attached. The other third were acquired via websites, published print media, interviews, and reunions. It's a storied road to becoming a worded entity. First, the manufacturer gives it a serial number, then the assigned unit gives it a platoon slot number, and finally the crew gives it a name. Soon afterwards, brushes and paint become the next order of business.

Crossword puzzles and patchwork quilts can best describe the challenge inherent in documenting the history of any single crew and helicopter in the VN War. Take it up another notch to that of uncovering the actual painter of STRANGE DAZE and its accompanying giant eyeball (C/229 AHB), and the task nearly equals that of the mythological bucket of prop wash and fifty feet of flight line that in-country newbie pilots were instructed to collect as part of their initiation. With helicopter serial numbers and crew names in the runner-up positions, the single most elusive component to pin down is the not-so-simple identity of a particular nose art artist. Curiously, what might contribute to this dilemma is the fact that a fair amount of nose art was commissioned and performed by civilian contractors, Vietnamese artisans, and Korean personnel. However, aside from this small cottage industry that developed in and around helicopter air fields, there's no doubt that the bulk of painted names and art applied to helicopters were carried out by self-taught G.I.'s who took brush in hand and did their utmost to craft an additional identity for a certain ship, and its CANNED HEAT personality.

Unquestionably, and to the credit of my generation, what I experienced in assembling this book mirrored what I witnessed in the Mekong Delta as exemplified by Army-crewed helicopters in their rapid and decisive response whenever the need arose. They got the job done then, and they helped in getting the job done today. Merely calling it a group effort would be a gross injustice, for it was an outpouring beyond expectation to an appeal that resonated with each contributor who also recognized the need to validate and correct an historical omission before it was too late. What became a massive outpouring of information and images was equally reinforced by tons of positive messages of genuine encouragement, support, and brotherly goodwill. Simply put, describing it as an anthology authored by 2,000 narrators is far from being an exaggeration.

Enough time has elapsed for the Vietnam War to have reached its peak historical interest, which offers, at last, an opportunity to showcase a unique assortment of re-discovered epigrams of the expressive American spirit. Once estranged and thought lost, these 3,100 in-country Army helicopter names have been fittingly repatriated, to assume their rightful place alongside previous combat seasoned names from generations past. The appearance of this subject material, in essence, strips away some of the enigma of that war by providing an essential puzzle piece in helping to understand our warrior brothers, fathers, uncles, sons, and friends who manned these "mostly" military green flying machines for the U.S. Army in S.E. Asia.

Pandora's Box*: B Co 123 Avn Bn, OH-6A, (sn 69-15997), 1971, Chu Lai.* An exclusive seventeen-month B-123 in-country tour netted 1,034 total flight hours before returning stateside. Photo by Jim Barnett.

ADVISORY NOTES

The search for Army helicopter names of the Vietnam War is predominately first a people search of those intimately familiar with an event that spanned eleven years. The process brings with it both challenges and triumphs, and hard-won knowledge. Whenever new ground is broken in any research project it is customary for the researcher to share his findings and educated conclusions. Here then are the highlights of what was discovered, what was not discovered, what anomalies cropped up, and what shortcomings were detected.

The absence of official Army aircraft flight records (they simply don't exist) that spanned the period of November 1961 through August 1966 greatly hampered any attempt in obtaining a detailed in-country accounting on any single aircraft or of a unit's fleet of aircraft for the early years of the war.

Approximately half of the listed 3,100 Army helicopter names are without an accompanying serial number. Such a deficiency greatly reduced the possibility of successfully tracing a particular helicopter's in-country history.

Helicopter names that were obtained via an in-country photo versus other alternate means (email, verbal, text) have an extra-ordinary reliability rating when it comes to spelling. All other alternate sources pale in comparison. For example, was it ROAD RUNNER or ROADRUNNER? Was it SUZY Q or SUSIE Q? Was it THE JINX or merely JINX? Sometimes, the weight of evidence validates a certain spelling if no photo exists. Yet, there will always be a certain percentage of names garnered from former crew members whose true spelling will have fallen victim to that affliction commonly known as old age.

Depending on the angle of the photo and whether it is a close-up or not, will determine how much supplemental information is obtained besides the painted name. If it's a gunship, is it a B, C or M model Huey? If it's a slick, is it an A, B, D or H model Huey? If the photo is an extreme close-up of the name or artwork blocking out any other identifying markers on the copter nose, much more investigative work will be necessary. Is it possible to determine if the nose is riding high or low (slick vs gunship)? Can the location of the pitot tube be a reliable tell-tale sign for identifying the model and year of the helicopter? Trust me, it's never a surefire clue. Remember also, early in the war before the arrival of the UH-1D slick the B model Huey served in the role of both slick and gunship.

For the researcher, a series of challenges begins immediately upon the discovery of a helicopter name or artwork: pinning down a specific date when the helicopter acquired the name and its duration on the ship, identifying its author, learning the definition of the name, and identifying the artist. Next is the task of identifying the assigned crew and their occupations on the ship. A lot of detective work ensues with much needed help from former unit members and Internet webmasters. When it comes to identifying Medevac and Dustoff crews it helps to know that because of their standby status and quick reaction posture oftentimes regular crew and ship assignments were intermixed.

When a "II" is added to a copter name, it, strange as it sounds, doesn't necessarily symbolize the second in a series of helicopters with the same name. If this is the case then the usual reason that the "II" is the first incarnation of the copter name is that the origin for the name is something other than a helicopter, usually a loved one back home.

There are a few instances where helicopters have been documented showing a high range of Roman Numerals after the name, and in all likelihood, although some of the middle numbers have never been documented, represent a true reincarnation of the original copter name. Under a deductive evaluation process, which I label "calculated assumption," these missing originators receive full recognition and get added to the database. WITCH DOCTOR I-VIII of the 128 AHC and SNOOPY I-VIII of the 175 AHC quickly come to mind.

On the spreadsheet is a column labeled "Unit #1." All those copter units that changed names or unit designation get recognized here. Those TC's that became AVN, those AVN's that were re-designated AHC, those AHC's that became AWC, etc. For reasons of simplicity and orderliness you will also notice that a single unit designator, AHC, has been assigned to the majority of the helicopter aviation companies, even though their in-country tenure might have included them performing in the capacity of an AML (Air Mobile Light) or AVN CO (Aviation Company).

Identifying exactly who among a helicopter crew was the AC, CP, CE, FE, or DG is easy if the photograph or email generously provide that kind of factual information. However, if faces and rank go un-captioned, or are lumped together without details, there is little one can do but record the crew names without specified occupation. Unfortunately, the regular occurrence of this particular omission is quite evident among the entries in the spreadsheet CREW column. The temptation at guess work here runs a high risk for error, and is not recommended. Querying the unit's webmaster for assistance oftentimes would prove successful.

During the later war years of 1970-73, in what author Lawrence Johnson called the "Air Cavalry Shell Game," the task of tracking certain Cav helicopters that carried personalized names take on a whole new challenge. A certain political technicality allowed several Air Cav units to merely change names instead of leaving Vietnam, which by itself bought extra time for our side, but admittedly plays havoc with anyone keenly interested in the status of a particular helicopter, its pseudo new management policies, and newly re-designated unit markings. That being said, one big question remains to be answered: did the personalized helicopter names and artwork remain intact after transition? Without conclusive evidence to change an assumption to a fact, I've decided that any known "shell game" participant helicopter that sported a name before the change-over goes into the spreadsheet database affiliated to a single unit only—the former.

You will obviously notice in the spreadsheet FATE column that only a small percentage of data has been posted. The upshot of this is the lack of documentation. For the majority of names that were collected there is no beginning and there is no end when going about determining their calendar lifespan. Let's say a contributor sends me a name which he had spotted on a Chinook at LZ Judy during his1968-69 tour. No more specifics and no other details. With a little detective work the unit gets identified, a serial number becomes known, a door gunner's name comes to light via the Association's webmaster, and this "hook's" official flight records are consulted. However, during further research all trails leading to the potential author of the CH-47 name turns cold. What must be considered also is that subsequent crew changes carry a huge potential for aircraft name changes. What was observed at LZ Judy in 1968-69 would most likely have been renamed on our sample Chinook in 1969-70, especially if the name was a female flame of a former crewman.

Here's what you need to know in order to avoid any misunderstandings regarding the contents of the chapter titled, INDIVIDUAL CONTRIBUTOR'S UNITS—NUMERICAL: unit members, authors, and anyone else credited with furnishing a copter name are included here.

ADVISORY NOTES

The "INDIVIDUAL CONTRIBUTORS A-Z" chapter contains 2,093 names, of which only 1,988 are actually in alphabetical order. Those names that fall between #1,989 thru #2,093 were late additions that were received while the book was being finalized for publication. Consequently, the last 104 names are not listed in A-Z order.

I encourage all readers to forward me any corrections, additions, or omissions that would lend a better understanding of these data filled pages. Please send all queries and comments to the following email address: johnmailman@yahoo.com

It was during the course of this project's research that a surprising bit of historical curiosity was uncovered which gave reason for further examination. Comparative findings would reveal that among the favorite bomber names of WWII (re: Wallace Forman) and favorite helicopter names of the VN War, resides but one single name that coexists on both eras' top ten names list. That's 16,000 versus 3,100 documented names respectively. On solving its identity one will immediately understand the reason for its seemingly dual nature among military aircraft types, and its adaptability as a relevant name across generations. I'll leave it to the reader to perform the necessary additions and subtractions towards revealing the celebrated answer.

200 ASHC, 1968, Bear Cat: Displayed on the company board that SGT David Seibert is leaning against is a listed register of individual Chinook names for all fifteen unit aircraft. After the 101st Airborne Div absorbed the 200th in July and renamed it "A Co 159 ASHB," all art and names vanished. Photo courtesy David Seibert.

ARMY HELICOPTER NAMES

A - Z

Copter Name	Unit	Unit #1	Aircraft	Circa	Function	Serial #	Config	Location	Artist	Crew	Contributors
"A" Modified	200 ASHC		CH-47A	67-68	cargo	66-00108	N+A	front fuselage	Larry Dumford	Daryl Garrett FE, R. Grusheski CE, Bill Bray DG	190, 995, 1195, 1585,1703
#1	129 AHC		UH-1H	68-69	slick	67-17465	NO	nose		Lloyd Robinson DG, A. Noble CE, J.M. Rau AC, M.J. Solar CP	1495,
#1 Boom Boom	A Co 227 AHB		UH-1D	66-67	slick	65-09713	N+A	nose	Tom Rose	Carl Barnett DG, Tom Rose CE, Ed Turner AC, Tom Loughlin CE	237, 959, 1039, 1512
#1 Du Me Mi	F Trp 4 Cav		AH-1G	1972	gun	68-15012	NO	doghouse		Ken Mick	120, 134, 422, 439, 888, 1266, 5450, 5700
? (question mark)	81 TC	119 AHC	CH-21C	1962	lift	51-15898	NAA	fuselage		Al Doucette DG	431,
007	240 AHC		UH-1H	1970	C+C	66-16007	NAA	nose		Richard Tierney AC, Bob Cooper CP	340, 1748, 2009, 8625
007 *	498 Med Co		UH-1H	1968	dustoff	66-17007	v-nn			Pappy Richardson CE	1974,
1%	176 AHC		UH-1M	70-71	gun	66-00618	NO	nose	Garry Roberts	Garry Roberts CE	301, 395, 439, 504, 696, 1486, 1930, 5150, 5675, 5725, 5900, 6275, 9450
2%er	176 AHC		UH-1C	1969	gun		NO				1595,
2nd Try	335 AHC		UH-1H	1968	slick	66-16649	NO	nose		George Jennings CE	847, 9600
3-5 Pig	F Trp 4 Cav		UH-1H	1972	slick	68-16358	N+A	nose		J. Dan Keirsey AC	888, 1851
4 More Shooting Days Til Xmas	71 AHC		UH-1D	66-67	slick		N+A	cargo door window			1241, 9210
5th Dimension	C Trp 1/9		OH-6A	1971	scout	68-17252	NO	doghouse		Randy Kerkar, D. Findley	271, 890, 1266, 1592, 6250, 9805
7-11	B Co 4 Avn Bn		UH-1C	1967	gun		N+A	doorpost		Jerry Polman DG	1407, 9060
10 Thou *	161 AHC		UH-1D	1967	slick	65-10000	v-nn				710, 7125
11th ARM. CAV. Recovery	11 ACR		UH-1H	68-69	maint		NO	nose			1703,
11th Commandment (The)	134 AHC		UH-1H	67-69	slick	66-16326	NO			Bill Harrison AC, Bob Monniger CE, Bill Ogden DG	352, 1818
15 Cents	187 AHC		UH-1H	68-69	slick	67-17555	NO	pilot door			1002,
76	A Trp 7/17		AH-1G	68-69	gun	67-15576	NO	bpw		Maxwell AC, Castlema CE	1602, 4825
96 Tears	A Trp 7/1		AH-1G	71-72	gun	69-16434	NO	bpw	Oscar from downtown Vinh Long	Mel Hinton AC, Free CE, Ken Larcher CE	755, 971, 4825

Copter Name	Unit	Unit #1	Aircraft	Circa	Function	Serial #	Config	Location	Artist	Crew	Contributors
744's Revenge	176 AHC		UH-1C	1969	gun	66-15233	NO	nose		Phil Varnum CE	742, 901, 1595, 9450
9,000 Lbs Of Romp + Stomp	F Btry 79 AFA		AH-1G	71-72	gun		NO	bpw		Bruce Stotler CE	1711,
A Shau Express	B Co 159 ASHB		CH-47B	68-69	cargo	66-19134	NO	fuselage		John Maddock FE, Wayne Clarke DG	310, 1068, 8025, 8250
A Slight Touch Of Death	B Co 227 AHB		UH-1H	70-71	slick	68-16171	NO	nose		Bobby Mullinax DG	1025, 1258
AA/G	A Trp 3/17		OH-58A	1970	scout	68-16935	NO	doghouse		Bill Sager CE, Paul Clergy	1976, 9720
Ace High	335 AHC		UH-1H	1967	slick	66-16621	NO	pilot door			301,
Ace Of Spades	114 AHC		UH-1H	1970	slick		NO				1704,
Ace Of Spades	162 AHC		UH-1H	71-72	slick	67-17649	NO			George Bell CE	122, 9390
Ace Of Spades **	174 AHC		UH-1C	69-71	gun	64-14170	AO	quarter panel		Hawkins CE '69, Parker CE '71, Manuel CP, Harter AC, Wade DG, Jansen CE	130, 233, 278, 316, 469, 592, 1611, 1770, 6050, 9430
Ace Of Spades	175 AHC		UH-1C	1967	gun		N+A	pilot door			301,
Ace Of Spades **	191 AHC		UH-1D	67-68	slick	66-00821	AO	pilot door	door gunner unk name	Art Almaraz CE, Richard Inskeep AC	27, 9500
Ace Of Spades **	205 ASHC		CH-47A	68-69	cargo		AO	fuselage			1834, 1836, 8325
Ace Of Spades II **	174 AHC		UH-1C	1971	gun	65-09470	AO			B. Wilder CE, F. Thompson, P.J. Roth, B. Holmes	130, 1907, 9430
Adkinson's Reb Raiders	116 AHC		UH-1B	67-68	gun		N+A	pilot door		Mike Adkinson AC	290,
Advengers (The)	48 AHC		UH-1B	1967	gun		NO	nose			531, 1451, 4050
Aeroplane	335 AHC		UH-1H	70-71	slick	68-16373	NO	nose			69,
Aimless Lady	117 AHC		UH-1M	70-71	gun	66-00667	NO	cargo door frame top		Dennis Lemons AC, Lee Bradley CE, Frank Alverez DG	92, 127, 177, 1006, 1654, 9250
Ain't It A Bitch	175 AHC		UH-1D	1968	slick	65-09791	NO			Mike Haley AC, Joe Wisneski CE, Steve Smith DG, Ronnie Walsh DG, Eddie McGuire DG	682, 1926
Ain't War Hell	B Co 25 Avn Bn		UH-1C	68-69	gun hog	66-15567	NO	nose		Potter, Sal	1060, 3950, 9120
Airhorne	C Co 159 ASHB		CH-47C	1971	cargo	67-18510	NO	rear pylon		David Holdings FE	776,
Alabama	187 AHC		UH-1H	1970	slick	66-16406	NO	nose		Tommy Nigh, Mike Mann	1932,

Copter Name	Unit	Unit #1	Aircraft	Circa	Function	Serial #	Config	Location	Artist	Crew	Contributors
Alaskan (The)	C Trp 1/9		AH-1G	69-70	gun	67-15752	N+A	rocket pod	Grover Wright	Grover Wright AC, Ed Scheurer CE	1963,
Alerquin	187 AHC		UH-1D	1968	slick	66-00834	NO	pilot door		Al Duquette AC, Imants Celtnieks CE	454, 1451, 1908, 4050, 4600
Alfi	128 AHC		UH-1D	1967	slick		NO	pilot door		Charles Decker AC	402,
Alfred E. Neuman **	20 TC		UH-1D	1967	recovery	66-01008	AO	nose		William McGowan AC	1145,
Alfred E. Neuman **	57 AHC		UH-1C	1968	gun		AO	doorpost			696, 5900
Alfred E. Neuman **	121 AHC		UH-1D	1968	slick	66-16098	N+A	nose		Beaver AC	1593, 6975
Alfred E. Neuman	283 Med Det		UH-1H	67-68	dustoff	66-17005	N+A	jump door			1638,
Alfred E. Neuman	C Co 228 ASHB		CH-47B	68-70	cargo	67-18480	N+A	front fuselage	Mel Chappell	Mel Chappell FE, Steve Keller CE, Steve Bolton CE	297, 347, 1571
Alfred E. Wall **	178 ASHC		CH-47A	66-67	cargo	66-19002	AO	front fuselage	Bob Means	Bob Means FE, Wall AC	841, 1167
Ali Baba	92 AHC		UH-1H	1968	slick	66-16502	NO	nose		Jim Heyn CE, Rocco Colucci DG	745, 9220
Alice In Wonderland	114 AHC	Avn Co	UH-1B	1965	slick	62-01960	NO	nose		R. Zehr, L. Greenly, T. Gallagher	1984, 6700
Alice's Restaurant	C Co 229 AHB		UH-1H	68-69	slick	66-16565	NO	nose			1466, 6805
Alive + Kickin'	45 Med Co		UH-1H	70-71	dustoff	69-15296	NO	nose		Thom Hall CE, John J. Koss MD, Ron Willy MD	683, 938, 2066, 7725
Alive N' Kickin'	45 Med Co		UH-1H	1970	dustoff		NO	nose		David Phillips CE, Richard Parmenter MD	2066, 2070
Alive N' Kickin'	57 Med Det		UH-1H	1971	dustoff		NO				7550,
Alive N' Kickin' II	57 Med Det		UH-1H	1972	dustoff	69-15083	NO	nose		David Freeman	561, 7550
AlJan	134 AHC		UH-1H	68-71	slick		NO				352, 1818
All American Frog **	128 AHC		UH-1M	71-72	gun	65-12741	AO	M-5 turret		Jim Taylor CE, Mike Honara AC	785,
Aloha	A Trp 7/1		OH-6A	70-71	scout	67-16630	NO	doghouse			1908, 4600
Aloha	D Trp 1-1		OH-6A	69-70	scout	68-17161	NO	doghouse			670,
Aluminum Butterfly (The)	B Co 25 Avn Bn		UH-1H	1970	slick	66-16257	N+A	nose		Bill Osthagen DG	9120,
Always In Good Hands ^^	339 TC	339 TC	UH-1	1967	maint		NO	nose			2021, 9450

America Love It Or Leave It: *C Troop 7/1 Cav, AH-1G (sn 66-15342), Vinh Long, 1968-69*. Topical sentiments of the day. Including time in the 334 AWC, she flew a total of 2,448 in-country hours. Photo by Mike Peterson; art by Owen Hamiel.

Copter Name	Unit	Unit #1	Aircraft	Circa	Function	Serial #	Config	Location	Artist	Crew	Contributors
Amazing Spiderman (The) ^	A Co 158 AHB		UH-1H	1969	slick	67-17678	N+A	doorpost		Eugene Franck AC	556,
America Love It Or Leave It	C Trp 3/17		UH-1H	1971	slick		N+A	nose		R. Chapman CE, Hosmer AC, Rex Gooch CP	296, 625, 4825
America Love It Or Leave It	C Trp 7/1		AH-1G	68-69	gun	66-15342	NO	turret	Owen Hamiel		1382,
America Love It Or Leave It	D Trp 3/5		UH-1H	1971	slick		N+A	nose		Hosamer AC, Chapman CE	296, 9860
American Dream	B Co 25 Avn Bn		UH-1C	1968	gun	65-09459	NO				1011,
American Flag **	57 AHC		UH-1H	69-70	slick		AO	nose			923,
American Sportsmen	C Trp 7/1		AH-1G	71-72	gun	68-15166	NO	bpw		James Drury AC, Dayne Smith CP	1382, 1634, 1906
American Woman	48 AHC		UH-1C	1970	gun		NO	nose	Al Meadows	Gary Winchester CE	1165, 1813, 9150
American Woman	117 AHC		UH-1C	1971	gun	65-09458	NO	cargo door frame top		Cid Allen CE, Gary Allen DG '70-'71, T. Standsbury, F. Herbert, C. Behm, R. Ricks	92, 117, 127, 8650
American Woman	135 AHC		UH-1M	70-71	gun	65-09438	N+A	cargo door frame top		Larry Ritchie CE, Bob Bratkovic AC	187, 1250, 1381, 6805, 9330
American Woman	162 AHC		UH-1H	71-72	slick		NAA	nose		James Lewis CE, Jackie Tibbets CE	190, 1018, 1782, 1908, 9390
American Woman	174 AHC		UH-1H	1971	slick		NAA	nose			1770, 9430
American Woman	B Co 227 AHB		UH-1H	70-71	slick		N+A	nose		Glen Teague CE	629, 1171, 6805
AMF	92 AHC		UH-1H	1968	slick	66-16502	NO	belly		Jim Heyn CE	745,
An Khe Annie	B Trp 1/9		UH-1B	66-67	gun		NO	pilot door		Dick Hale AC, Jim Bennett CP	679,
Anachronistic Bummer	A Trp 7/17		AH-1G	70-71	gun		NO			Orville Davidsmeyer AC	40,
Anacronistic	A Trp 3/17		OH-6A	69-70	scout		NO	doghouse			1181, 6050
Ancient Age	114 AHC		UH-1D	67-68	slick	65-10131	NO	nose		L. Sanford	6700, 6775
Andy Capp	121 AHC		UH-1D	67-68	slick		N+A	nose		Smith AC	477, 1593, 4825, 6975, 9290
Angel Babe	D Trp 3/5		UH-1C	68-69	gun		NO			Bruce Mitchell CE	1211,
Angel Baby	135 AHC		UH-1H	67-68	slick		NO	pilot door			1249,

Copter Name	Unit	Unit #1	Aircraft	Circa	Function	Serial #	Config	Location	Artist	Crew	Contributors
Angel Of Death	11 ACR		AH-1G	71-72	gun	67-15501	NO	bpw			1467, 1674
Angel Of Death	336 AHC		UH-1C	69-70	gun		N+A	nose			1825, 9610
Angel Of Death II	11 ACR		AH-1G	71-72	gun		NO	bpw			1467,
Angel Of Mercy	15 Med Bn		UH-1H	70-71	medevac		NO			Monty Halcomb AC	608,
Angel Of Mercy	45 Med Co		UH-1H	67-68	dustoff	66-16433	NO	nose	Greg Tibbetts	Greg Tibbetts CE, Ken Rucker MD, Joe Gorge CE	378, 700, 1412, 1783, 7450, 7775
Angel Of Mercy *	237 Med Det		UH-1H	70-71	dustoff	69-15617	v-nn			Tim Boyd CE, Geoff Morris MD, Ed Iacobacci MD	171,
Angel Of Mercy	247 Med Det		UH-1H	70-71	dustoff		NO	nose		Dave Flaten CE	707, 869, 1780, 7650
Angel Of The Mourning	11 ACR		AH-1G	68-69	gun		NO	bpw			1448, 8625
Anheuser-Busch **	A Co 101 AHB		UH-1	67-71	slick / gun		NAA	nose			1633, 1727, 9680
Anka	71 AHC		UH-1H	70-71	slick		N+A	nose		James Arno AC, Norm Pruett CE	1429, 1754
Ann	170 AHC		UH-1C	1969	gun		NO	nose			1729, 9400
Ann	189 AHC		UH-1H	68-69	slick		NO	nose			1053, 1686
Anna B	188 AHC		UH-1H	67-68	slick		NO	pilot door			1621,
Anna Marie	114 AHC	Avn Co	UH-1B	1965	slick		NO	nose		E.Hunt	14, 1326
Apache Flash	A Trp 1/9		OH-6A	1969	scout	67-16494	NO	fuselage		Bill Donics AC	9690,
Apocalypse	175 AHC		UH-1C	67-68	gun		N+A	pilot door		Dick Koenig AC, Al Zanetti DG	932,
Apocalypse (The)	A Trp 7/1		AH-1G	70-71	gun		NO	bpw		Will Gibbons AC	606,
Aquarian Effort	117 AHC		UH-1C	70-71	gun	66-00588	NO	cargo door frame top		Jim Barrie DG	92,
Aquarius	71 AHC		UH-1H	70-71	slick / C+C	69-15762	N+A	nose	Taylor	Ron Taylor CE, Hathaway	1754,
Arbitrator (The)	C Trp 16 Cav		AH-1G	1970	gun		NO	bpw			1250, 1450, 9810
Archangel (The)	118 AHC	Avn Co	UH-1D	1965	slick		NO	pilot door			1508, 9260

Arizona Gambler*: D Co 227 AHB, AH-1G, 1968-69*. Coiled Cobra superimposed over unit designator; extra large name lettering was gunship trademark in D-227. Front seat pilot has been identified as Martin Beckam. Photo by Terry Moon; art by Bill Muncey.

Copter Name	Unit	Unit #1	Aircraft	Circa	Function	Serial #	Config	Location	Artist	Crew	Contributors
Ares	155 AHC		UH-1C	69-70	gun	65-12739	NAA	nose		Herman Hedrick CE	301, 696, 724, 878, 1053, 1187, 5900, 9360
Arfunt Annie II	121 AHC	Avn Co	UH-1B	64-65	gun		NO	nose			2071,
Arizona Gambler	D Co 227 AHB		AH-1G	68-69	gun		N+A	bpw	Bill Muncey painted snake	Martin Beckman	1, 34, 113, 120, 229, 1226, 1318, 4825,4850, 9825
Arizona Gambler	D Co 227 AHB		UH-1B+C	68-69	gun		NO			Guy McMahan DG/CE	1156, 8525
Arkansas Highway Patrol	D Trp 3/5		AH-1G	71-72	gun	67-15802	NO	bpw		Hugh Mills AC, John Bryant CP	1205, 4450
Arleen's Clown	118 AHC	Avn Co	UH-1D	1965	slick		NO	pilot door		William Stewart CE, Alley CE, John Boyce DG	167, 603, 9260
Armageddon's Child	54 Med Det		UH-1H	1971	dustoff		NO	nose			1709,
As Ye Sow So Shall Ye Reap	E Trp 1/9		OH-6A	69-71	scout	68-17270	N+A	clamshell			280, 1053, 1205, 1266, 1497, 6025, 6250
Asassins Inc	188 AHC		UH-1C	67-68	gun		NO				1178, 1322
Assassin (The)	68 AHC		UH-1C	67-68	gun		NO				2076, 9200
Assassin (The)	118 AHC		UH-1C	1970	gun		NO	nose		J. D. Badgley AC	63, 1360
Assassins (The)	48 AHC		UH-1B	66-67	gun		NO	nose			1488, 9640
Auggie	45 Med Co		UH-1H	1969	dustoff	66-16410	NO	nose		Rominger AC, Clark CP, Collins MD	328, 7725
Autobus	203 ASHC		CH-47A	71-72	cargo		NO			Bill Clingon FE	1233,
Autumn Mist *	162 AHC		UH-1H	69-70	slick		v-nn			William Seward CE	1590, 9390
Ava's Darlin	335 AHC		UH-1H	1969	slick		N+A	nose		Larry Morrison AC	1243,
Avenger	114 AHC		UH-1C	1967	gun		NO	pilot door		D. Wickman, B. Gunn, J. Alday	666, 1569, 3100, 6700
Avenger	118 AHC		UH-1C	67-68	gun		NO				9260,
Avenger	240 AHC		UH-1H	1968	slick	66-16185	NO	pilot door		John Thrift CE, Warren Espig DG, Mark Webb AC	919, 1781
Avenger	B Trp 1/9		AH-1G	1969	gun		NO	bpw			898,
Avenger	B Trp 3/17		UH-1H	1969	slick		NO				9790,
Avenger	C Btry 2/20 ARA		AH-1G	70-71	gun	68-15183	NO	bpw			730, 1627
Avenger	D Co 227 AHB		UH-1C	1967	gun	64-14176	NO	nose			301, 696, 1266, 1876, 5900, 6075

Copter Name	Unit	Unit #1	Aircraft	Circa	Function	Serial #	Config	Location	Artist	Crew	Contributors
Avenger	F Btry 79 AFA		AH-1G	71-72	gun	68-15183	NO	bpw			82, 518, 730
Avenger (The)	175 AHC		UH-1	1970	slick		NO				1926,
Avenger (The)	192 AHC		UH-1C	1970	gun		NO	nose			7050,
Avenger II	118 AHC		UH-1C	68-69	gun		NO				9260,
Avenger II	B Trp 3/17		UH-1H	1969	slick		NO	doorpost		Ron Jones AC	446, 1395, 9260
Avenger III	118 AHC		UH-1C	1969	gun		NO	nose		G. Ronning AC, John Flynn CE, Tom Monroe DG	1507, 9260
Avenging Angel	187 AHC		UH-1H	71-72	slick		NO			Greg Monroe CE	1222,
Ba Moui Ba	175 AHC		UH-1C	1967	gun		N+A	nose	Oscar from downtown Vinh Long	Terry Holley AC, Tom Kennedy CE	461, 900, 982, 1316, 5775, 5775
Baby Hewey	81 TC	119 AHC	CH-21C	63-64	lift		N+A	fuselage		David L. Edwards CE	188,
Baby Huey	11 GS		UH-1B	1968	slick		NO	nose	Ainslie	Charles Richardson AC, Dan Ainslie CP	1469,
Baby Huey	119 AHC	Avn Co	UH-1B	65-66	gun		N+A	nose			1856,
Baby Huey	162 AHC		UH-1H	68-69	slick		NO	pilot door		Gary Calderon DG	44, 262, 428, 652, 1908, 9390
Baby Huey	180 ASHC		CH-47C	1971	cargo	68-16019	NO		Michael Neally	Michael Neally	1276,
Baby Huey **	191 AHC		UH-1H	67-68	slick		AO	pilot door	Richard Weske	Bob Walker CE, Don Nicholas AC	86, 1847, 9500
Baby Huey	339 TC		UH-1D	67-68	slick	64-13532	N+A	nose			105,
Baby Huey	A Co 1 Avn Bn		UH-1B	1966	gun		N+A	doorpost			1352, 9460
Baby Huey	C Btry 2/20 ARA		UH-1B	1968	gun		NO	nose			221, 4325
Baby Jo	155 AHC		UH-1H	1969	slick		NO	nose		Al Bollens AC	157,
Baby Jo	B Co 229 AHB		UH-1H	1969	slick		NO	nose			157,
Baby Snooks	B Trp 1/9		UH-1H	67-68	slick	66-16645	NO	pilot door		John Flanagan AC	535,

Ball's Deuce: *B Co 159 ASHB, CH-47C, (sn 68-16002), 1970-72.* Despite severe damage by a 122mm rocket, she remains active in Army inventory; 1,036 total VN hours.

Right: Norm Bass FE standing next to fuselage artwork. Photos courtesy of Norm Bass.

Copter Name	Unit	Unit #1	Aircraft	Circa	Function	Serial #	Config	Location	Artist	Crew	Contributors
Baby Snooks II	B Trp 1/9		UH-1H	67-68	slick		NO	nose		John Flanagan AC	535,
Bac Si	45 Med Co		UH-1H	1968	dustoff		NO	nose			2067,
Bad (The)	371 RRC		UH-1H	68-69	slick		NO	nose			1286,
Bad Ass	191 AHC		UH-1C	1971	gun	66-15217	NO	nose		Steve Armas CE, Jerry Schafer DG, Bill Fryant AC, Gordon Gosch DG	301, 565, 633, 1999, 9500
Bad Breath	C Trp 1/9		AH-1G	1969	gun		NO	nose			1686,
Bad Lady	117 AHC		UH-1H	69-70	slick		NO	nose			128, 4825, 8650
Bad Man Jose	C Co 229 AHB		UH-1H	69-70	slick	68-15667	N+A	nose		Cashner CE	73, 1466, 1816, 6900
Bad Moon	92 AHC		UH-1H	69-70	slick	68-16509	NO	nose		Jerry Valentine DG	1820,
Bad Moon Risin	240 AHC		UH-1H	1971	slick		NO				1266,
Bad News	1 Bn 50 Inf		UH-1H	1968	slick / C+C		NO	nose			137, 9010
Bad News	119 AHC		UH-1H	69-70	slick		NO	nose			1797,
Bad News	175 AHC		UH-1B	1966	gun	63-08702	NO			Dan Hudgins CE, David Huereca DG, Larry Jackson AC	1926,
Bad News	187 AHC		UH-1H	70-71	slick	68-16305	NO	nose		R. Daniels CP, E. Guynn CE, R. Bellerue CE, W. Kirkpatrick DG	125, 389, 652, 671, 1954, 9470
Bad News	335 AHC		UH-1H	68-69	slick		NO				897,
Bad News	B Btry 2/20 ARA		AH-1G	70-71	gun	67-15490	NO	bpw			439, 804, 1474, 5700
Bad News II	335 AHC		UH-1H	68-69	slick		N+A	nose			897,
Bad News!	56 TC		CH-37B	65-66	recovery		N+A	front fuselage		Foster AC	688, 1921, 2058
Bah Humbug	unk		UH-1H	1967	slick		NO	cargo door			1123,
Baja Bush Bandit	227 AHB		UH-1H	69-70	slick		NO				2,
Ball Buster	A Trp 3/17		UH-1C	67-68	gun	66-15030	NO	nose			1421,
Ball's Deuce ***	B Co 159 ASHB		CH-47C	70-72	cargo	68-16002	pv-nnp	fuselage		Rip Masselli FE, Larry Buffington CE, Norman Bass DG	100,
Balls Deuce *	A Co 159 ASHB		CH-47C	1971	cargo	70-15002	v-nn			John Keller AC, Fluharty, Resch	891, 7850

Copter Name	Unit	Unit #1	Aircraft	Circa	Function	Serial #	Config	Location	Artist	Crew	Contributors
Balls Eight *	180 ASHC		CH-47C	71-72	cargo	68-16008	v-nn			Mike Molish AC	1220,
Balls Five *	192 AHC		UH-1H	70-71	slick	66-16005	v-nn			Mike Pederson DG/CE, Martinez CE	1365, 9510
Balls Five *	242 ASHC		CH-47A	70-71	cargo	65-08005	v-nn				1199,
Balls Nine *	C Co 159 ASHB		CH-47C	70-71	cargo	68-16009	v-nn			Pop Briggs CE	179,
Balls Niner *	173 AHC		UH-1D	68-69	slick	66-01009	v-nn			Jay Reigel DG, Leroy Avery CE, Max Taylor	1455, 1752, 4425
Balls One *	178 ASHC		CH-47C	1971	cargo	70-15001	v-nn			Mark Baird FE	68, 7875
Balls Seven *	188 AHC		UH-1C	1968	gun	007	v-nn			G. Dean Murphy AC	1262, 6475
Balls Three *	92 AHC		UH-1C	68-69	gun	66-15003	v-nn				538,
Balls Two *	178 ASHC		CH-47A	67-68	cargo	66-19002	v-nn			Bob Means FE	841, 1167
Balls Two *	243 ASHC		CH-47A	68-69	cargo	66-19002	v-nn			Bryon Wilson FE	111, 1483
Band-Aid Machine (The)	326 Med Bn		UH-1H	70-71	dustoff		NO				1926,
Band-Aid Special	45 Med Co		UH-1H	68-71	dustoff		NO	nose		John J. Koss MD, Bruce McCartney MD	683, 938, 1040, 2068, 7725
Bandit	175 AHC		UH-1D	68-69	slick		NO				1926,
Banshee	48 AHC		UH-1B	68-69	gun		NO	nose			1000, 9150
Banshee	132 ASHC		CH-47B	68-69	cargo	67-18454	NO	front fuselage			303, 1162, 1588, 7800
Barbara	170 AHC		UH-1H	1970	slick		NO	nose			1041, 1839, 4150
Barbara	C Trp 16 Cav		AH-1G	1972	gun		NO	bpw		Bob Jackson AC	1205,
Barbara II	C Trp 16 Cav		AH-1G	1972	gun		NO	bpw		Bob Jackson AC	1205, 5000
Barbie	189 AHC		UH-1H	1968	slick	67-17272	NO	nose		Bob Steinbrunn AC, Paul Stoddard CP	1053, 2049, 6025, 6450
Bare Chicken	A Co 227 AHB		UH-1H	1971	slick	69-15033	N+A	nose			1232,
Barking Dog *	117 AHC		UH-1H	69-70	slick	66-16772	v-nn			Patrick Tooke CE	2092,
Baron Von Lemon	D Trp 1/4		AH-1G	69-70	gun		N+A	bpw			195,

Copter Name	Unit	Unit #1	Aircraft	Circa	Function	Serial #	Config	Location	Artist	Crew	Contributors
Baroness	336 AHC		UH-1H	69-70	slick		N+A	nose	either 336 or 121 VN artist		1908, 4600
Bastard Cav	D Trp 3/5		UH-1H	1971	slick		N+A	nose		Joe Sheeran AC, Russ Marsden CE, Art Heile	1091, 1982, 4825
Bat Masterson	175 AHC		UH-1D	66-67	slick	65-09976	NO	nose		Mike Kidd CE, Jerry Bly DG	906, 1269
Batmobile	187 AHC		UH-1H	1970	slick		NO	nose			652,
Batmobile II	187 AHC		UH-1H	70-71	slick	66-16446	NO	nose		Meyers CE, Randy Smith DG, Ray Kingsbury AC	652,
Batship **	191 AHC		UH-1D	67-69	slick		AO	pilot door	Richard Weske	Don Sandrock AC, Richard Weske CE	86, 1544, 1570, 1913, 9500
Batship	B Co 25 Avn Bn		UH-1C	1967	gun / smoker	65-09435	N+A	nose		Francis Paradise DG, Jim Montana CE	242, 301, 909, 1011, 1060, 1223, 2046, 9120
Batship II **	B Co 25 Avn Bn		UH-1C	1968	smoke	66-15210	AO	nose			502, 9120
Battlin Bitch	48 AHC		UH-1B	1969	gun	64-14012	NO	nose			75, 1053, 1187, 1266, 6025, 6225, 6275, 9150
Battlin Bitch **	174 AHC		UH-1C	1971	gun hog	65-09507	AO	quarter panel	Harter	McGaffick AC, Klindt DG	1342, 1770, 1908, 9430
Be Nice Or I Will Kill You	191 AHC		UH-1C	67-68	gun	66-15076	N+A	belly		Stan Cherrie AC, Skip Waugh CE	302,
Beach Boy	114 AHC		UH-1C	66-67	gun		NO		Don Lenning	Don Lenning DG	1008,
Bean Bandit (The)	192 AHC		UH-1C	69-70	gun		NO				560,
Beantown Bandit (The) *	117 AHC	Avn Co	UH-1B	64-65	slick	62-04567	v-nn			Carl Vogel CE	1840,
Bear (The)	D Trp 1/1		AH-1G	67-68	gun	22474	N+A	bpw		Mike Bauman AC	104,
Bear's Pig	C Trp 3/17		AH-1G	1972	gun		NO	bpw		Loran Bryant AC	121,
Beast (The)	A Trp 3/17		OH-6A	69-70	scout	67-16202	NO	doghouse		Elcard CE	503, 1630, 8625
Beats Walkin	114 AHC		UH-1D	67-68	slick	64-13620	NO	nose		R. Scott DG, S. McFarlan, A. Jensen, J. McLeod	41, 696, 1577, 3100, 4650, 6700
Beautiful Balloon	162 AHC		UH-1D	1968	slick	65-09730	N+A	pilot door	Larry Tiebay - PA+E employee	Carl Weddle CE	1884,
Beaver's Abortion	B Co 229 AHB		UH-1H	69-70	slick	67-17314	NO			Ron Carr CE, Wayne Eggert DG	283, 468, 9780
Bed Of Roses	D Co 227 AHB		UH-1C	67-68	gun	65-09713	N+A	nose		Ron Charmichael AC	425, 1876, 9700

Copter Name	Unit	Unit #1	Aircraft	Circa	Function	Serial #	Config	Location	Artist	Crew	Contributors
Bee Keeper ^	116 AHC	392 TC	UH-1D	1967	maint		N+A	nose			252, 852, 1623, 9120, 9240
Bee Keeper ^	116 AHC	392 TC	UH-1D	1969	maint	55	N+A	nose			1048, 1196, 1451, 1539, 1996, 4050
Beelzebub	B Co 123 Avn Bn		AH-1G	1970	gun	69-16438	N+A	bpw		Ray LaPointe AC, Walter Lynn CE	968, 1059
Beep Beep Ya Ass	271 ASHC		CH-47B	69-70	cargo	66-19129	N+A	interior - center console		Dan Lampman	964,
Beep Beep Yuass	242 ASHC		CH-47A	67-68	cargo	66-19024	N+A	nose		R. Merryman DG, Moranville FE, G. Mahoney	1074, 1199, 4300
Beep Beep Yur Butt	A Co 159 ASHB		CH-47A	1968	cargo	66-00100	NO	fuselage		Boxley FE, Lenny Breeden DG/CE, Chico DG	166,
Beep Beep Yurass	200 ASHC		CH-47A	67-68	cargo	66-00100	N+A	front fuselage	Larry Dumford	Garry Ledbetter FE, Jim Hennessey CE, Joe Boxley DG, L. Breeden	166, 995, 1195, 1585, 7950, 8275
Beer, Bullt + Blood	121 AHC		UH-1D	1968	slick	65-09967	N+A	nose		Mike Shakocius AC, Jim Noblin CP	1593, 6975, 9290
Beer Wagon (The)	335 AHC		UH-1B	69-70	gun	62-04592	N+A	nose			453, 1201, 1696, 1926, 1941, 9590
Behemoth	B Co 228 ASHB		CH-47A	68-69	cargo		NO				933,
Belle Star	175 AHC		UH-1D	1967	slick		NO	nose		John Savelli AC, Jerry Jackson CE	461, 9440
Bell's Lemon	282 AHC		UH-1D	65-66	slick	65-09954	N+A	nose		Tom Adams CE, Theron Talbot AC, C. Smith DG	8, 9560
Bell's Misfit	283 Med Det		UH-1H	1970	dustoff		NO	nose			438, 9950
Beloved	D Trp 3/4		UH-1H	70-71	slick		NO	doghouse	Gary Schmidt		1559, 8400
Bennie's Bomb	unk		UH-1D	1965	slick		N+A	nose			812,
Betty K	C Trp 1/9		AH-1G	1970	gun	69-16437	NO	bpw		John Craig, Dick Skaaden	134, 5450
Betty Lee (The)	B Co 25 Avn Bn		UH-1C	1967	gun	66-00603	N+A	nose	Bob Moorhead	Bob Moorhead CE, Charles Burnett DG	242, 909, 1234, 9120
Betty Boobs	D Trp 3/4		AH-1G	70-71	gun	67-15776	NO			Dan Coles CE, Bruce Sikkema AC	324, 1282
Beverly	C Trp 2/17		OH-6A	1970	scout	67-16236	NO	nose		Darrell Hunt AC, A.K. Middlebrook DG, R.D. Alexander CE	1908, 1992
Biere 33 Export	147 ASHC		CH-47A	67-68	cargo		N+A	fuselage			264, 461, 573, 7825

Copter Name	Unit	Unit #1	Aircraft	Circa	Function	Serial #	Config	Location	Artist	Crew	Contributors
Biere 33 Export	175 AHC		UH-1C	68-70	gun	66-15194	N+A	pilot door	Oscar from downtown Vinh Long	Farr AC, Von Schwedler DG, Terry Holley AC	15, 107, 461, 932, 1670, 1926, 5775, 9520
Big Bad John	478 Avn Co		CH-54A	1965	recovery	64-14205	NO	access door			1053, 1181, 1717, 4825, 6025, 6050
Big Bertha	A Trp 7/1		AH-1G	1970	gun	69-16422	NO	bpw		Rob Nelson AC, Paul Cupp CE	1281,
Big Bertha	B Co 228 ASHB		CH-47A	68-69	cargo	64-13137	NO	fuselage	Lloyd A. Judd	Cliff Morley FE	1239,
Big Bertha	UTT		UH-1B	1964	gun		NO	M-3 rocket box			1975, 6500
Big Boob (The)	A Co 228 ASHB		CH-47A	69-70	cargo		NO				996,
Big Bright Green Pleasure Machine	162 AHC		UH-1D	67-68	slick		NO	pilot door	Larry Tiebay - PA+E employee		1884,
Big Brother	179 ASHC		CH-47A	68-69	cargo		NO			Edward Finke FE	527, 8525
Big Brother	180 ASHC		CH-47C	69-70	cargo		NO			Edward Finke FE	527, 8525
Big Brother	191 AHC		UH-1C	1969	gun	66-15156	NO	nose		Bill Flores CE, Bill Grebe AC	539, 1416, 9500
Big Brother	242 ASHC		CH-47A	68-69	cargo	66-19023	N+A	fuselage		Jack Label FE, Don Ross CE, Tom Doyle DG	1199, 1515, 4300
Big Brother	A Trp 7/1		AH-1G	1970	gun	67-15457	N+A	bpw		Paul Cupp CE	381,
Big Daddy	116 AHC		UH-1D	67-68	gun 20mm		N+A	nose		Dennis Slate DG, Rick Morhland CE, Mike Cheney AC, Ray Caudle CE, Laurie Linder	290, 852, 1023, 1238, 1273, 1506, 1625, 2046, 9120, 9240
Big Daddy ^	611 TC		CH-37B	1964	recovery		NO	nose			1046, 1915, 4280
Big Daddy	D Co 227 AHB		UH-1C	67-68	gun		NO				164, 1015, 1876, 8525
Big Ed	611 TC		CH-37B	1965	recovery		NO	nose		Brooks CE, Anderson DG, Chaney AC	1398, 3650, 5025
Big Fanny	C Co 227 AHB		UH-1H	1969	slick	66-16809	NO	nose			112,
Big Gun	129 AHC		UH-1B	66-67	gun hog	63-08666	N+A	nose		David Sale, John Redmon	1446, 1537
Big Iron	A Co 1 Avn Bn		UH-1B	65-67	gun	64-13914	NO	nose + M-3 rocket box		Danny Breckenridge CE	301, 1181, 1973, 5275, 6050

Copter Name	Unit	Unit #1	Aircraft	Circa	Function	Serial #	Config	Location	Artist	Crew	Contributors
Big Kahuna	271 ASHC		CH-47B	69-70	cargo	66-19117	NO	fuselage			256,
Big Leroy	116 AHC		UH-1B	67-68	gun		NO	pilot door		Bob Lanegan CE, Clayton Hazelbaker DG	290,
Big Mac	132 ASHC		CH-47B	1968	cargo		NO	front fuselage			1822, 7800
Big Mack	178 ASHC		CH-47A	66-67	cargo	64-13165	N+A	front fuselage		Steve Niedbala FE, Randy Wilson CE, Ted Kus DG	1294,
Big Mother	478 Avn Co		CH-54A	1968	10,000 bomb	67-18418	NO	pilot door		James Oden AC, Johnson CE, Wilson (bombardier)	1053, 1181, 1319, 4850, 6050, 8450
Big Nick ^	611 TC		CH-37B	64-65	maint		NO	nose			583, 1451, 4050
Big Train	A Co 82 Avn Bn		UH-1B	1965	gun hog	64-13978	NO	doorpost		Harold Woody DG, Lawrence Ashton CE, Karl Schultz DG, Dwayne Ginter AC, David Blevin AC, D. Smith AC	52, 301, 439, 800, 1266, 1567, 1958, 5575, 5725, 6225
Big Tuffy	242 ASHC		CH-47A	1970	cargo	66-00076	NO	nose			754, 1199, 4300
Big Zilch	147 ASHC		CH-47C	1970	cargo		NO	front fuselage		Al Fitzgerald	532,
Billy The Kid	128 AHC		UH-1B	1967	gun		N+A	quarter panel			98,
Billy The Kid	175 AHC		UH-1D	66-67	slick		NO	nose		Mike Kidd CE, John Myhre AC	461, 1652
BIOYA	162 AHC		UH-1D	1968	slick	65-12775	NO	doorpost		Bill Greenhalgh AC	652,
Bird Of Pray	336 AHC		UH-1C	1968	gun		N+A	pilot door		Sweet CE	1108,
Bird Shippers (The)	611 TC		CH-47A	67-68	recovery		NO				2035, 6835
Bird Watcher	118 AHC	573 TC	UH-1D	1967	maint	66-01032	NO	vertical stabilizer			1189, 1908, 4600
Bird Watcher ^	118 AHC	573 TC	UH-1D	66-67	maint	65-09909	NO	nose + vertical stabilizer		Elsinger CE, Williams AC, Clark CP,Tauer, Ryal, Hawkin	1029, 1189, 9260
Bird Watcher ^	118 AHC	573 TC	UH-1H	69-70	maint	68-15490	NO	nose + vertical stabilizer		Robert Springer CE	1673, 9260
Birdie Num Num	B Trp 3/17		AH-1G	1969	gun		NO	bpw		George Berthel CE	136, 728, 1503, 9790
Birdie Num Num Jr	B Trp 3/17		AH-1G	1969	gun		NO	bpw		Doug Gray AC, George Berthel CE	643, 9790

Copter Name	Unit	Unit #1	Aircraft	Circa	Function	Serial #	Config	Location	Artist	Crew	Contributors
Birth Control	1 Avn Det		ACH-47A	66-68	gun	64-13154	N+A	fuselage			301, 395, 566, 903, 959, 1266, 1898, 4600, 4825, 5200, 5675, 6300, 8025, 8275, 8300
Birth Control	11 ACR		AH-1G	71-72	gun	68-15131	NO	bpw		Rock Rhoades AC	1467, 1674
Birth Control	53 Avn Det		ACH-47A	1966	gun	64-13154	N+A	doorpost		L. Webb, J. Arroyo, J. Ely, R. Durrett, R. O'Connor, D. Rivera	301, 395, 959, 1053, 1726, 1898, 4600, 4825, 5200, 6300, 8025, 8275, 8300
Birth Control	68 AHC		UH-1C	67-69	gun		NO	revetment art			69, 1304, 1683, 1883, 9200
Birth Control	118 AHC		UH-1C	1967	gun	65-09551	NO	doorpost plaque		Little CE, Ellzey DG	1029, 9260
Birth Control	119 AHC		UH-1C	69-70	gun	66-00639	NO	nose		Jim Saufley AC	3125, 1549, 1797, 1800, 9270
Birth Control	134 AHC		UH-1C	67-70	gun hog	66-15151	NO	nose		Jerry Berg CE, Bruce Porter AC, Terry Buttram DG, Don McNeely CP, David E. Jones	131, 352, 979, 1818, 9320
Birth Control	176 AHC		UH-1C	1970	gun	66-00715	NAA	nose			901, 9450
Birth Control	336 AHC	A/101	UH-1B	65-66	gun hog		NO	M-3 rocket box			1354, 9680
Birth Control	A Co 25 Avn Bn		UH-1H	1968	slick	66-17086	NO	nose		Sal Cannizzaro DG, Bob Frazier CE, Ed Behne AC	272, 519
Bismarck (The)	135 AHC		UH-1C	71-72	gun		NO	pilot door			1381, 9330
Bitch (The)	68 AHC	Avn Co	UH-1B	65-66	gun	64-14088	NO	nose		Ed Harris AC, John Kanakaris CE	701,
Bitch (The) **	170 AHC		UH-1H	69-70	slick	68-15262	v-nnp			Dave Baker AC, Ron Sanders CE	1543,
Bitch (The)	335 AHC	A/82	UH-1B	66-67	gun	64-13978	NO			John Hoza AC	800,
Bitch (The) *	B Co 228 ASHB		CH-47A	66-67	cargo	64-13139	v-nn			Robert Rex FE	1462,
Bitches Brew	240 AHC		UH-1D	1971	slick		NO	nose		Wheaton CE	652,
Bite + Strike ^^	129 AHC		UH-1H	1969	slick		NO	nose			18, 1908, 4600
Bits + Pieces	128 AHC		UH-1H	1970	slick		NO	nose		Ed Zubrinic DG, Shoemaker CE, Vic Brimmer AC	200, 395, 439, 754, 989, 1988, 5675, 5725
Bits And Pieces	unk		UH-1B		gun		NO	pilot door			1705, 4825
Bits N Pieces	134 AHC		UH-1H	69-70	slick	67-17549	NO	nose			352, 1818

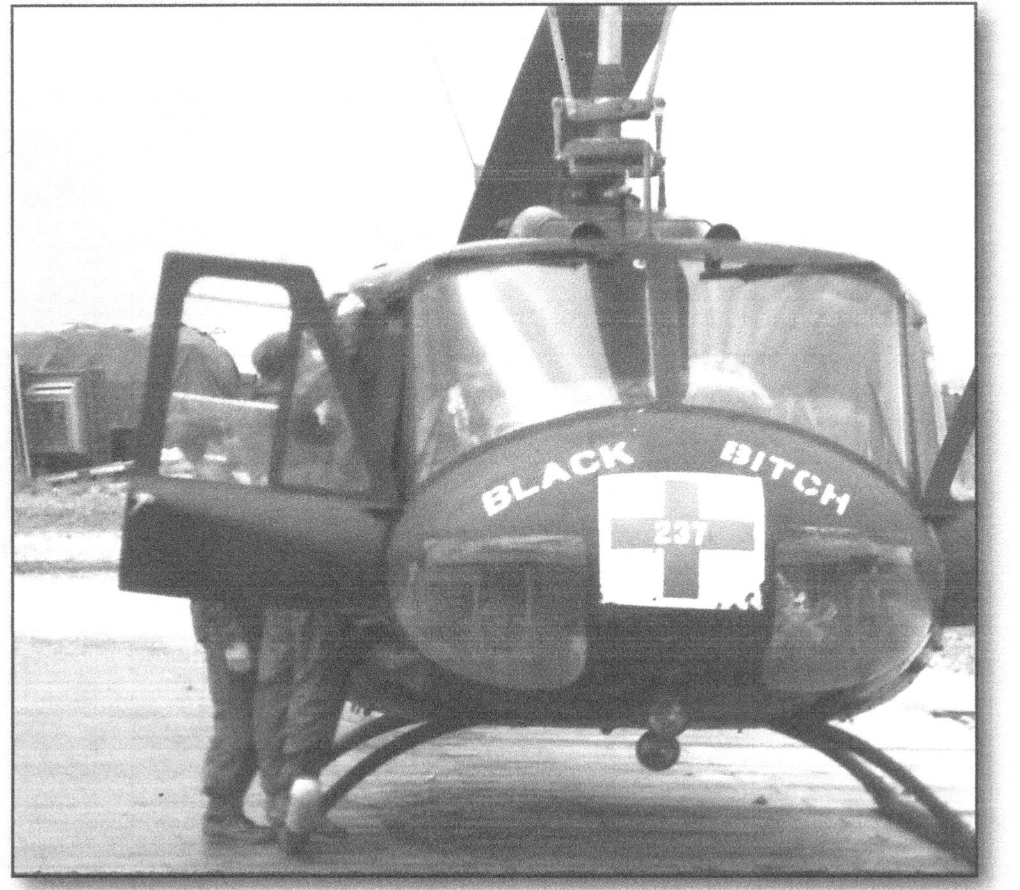

Black Bitch: *237 Med Det, UH-1H, (sn 66-01125), Phu Bai, 1970-71.* Name refers to black paint job and "hangar queen" reputation. Survived VN with 1,876 hours after serving with four different units. Photo by Robert Hill via Bruce Hill.

Copter Name	Unit	Unit #1	Aircraft	Circa	Function	Serial #	Config	Location	Artist	Crew	Contributors
Black Bicth	175 AHC		UH-1H	70-71	slick		NO	nose		Terry Straub AC, Frank Effenberger CP	467, 1926
Black Bitch	175 AHC		UH-1H	70-71	slick		NO	nose		Terry Straub AC, Frank Effenberger CP	467, 1926
Black Bitch	237 Med Det		UH-1H	70-71	dustoff	66-01125	NO	nose		Mike Bradley, Robert Hill, Walt Adams, Ken Hillman, Paul Simcoe MD, Dennis Fuji MD	638, 690, 749, 945, 1094, 1468, 2069
Black Bitch	571 Med Det		UH-1H	1970	dustoff	66-01125	NO	nose		John Moore CE	945, 1229, 1468
Black Jack **	174 AHC		UH-1H	70-71	slick	68-15458	AO	nose		Rex Schumacher CE	1568, 9430
Black Knight **	174 AHC		UH-1C	1970	gun	65-09507	AO	nose			184, 278, 1770, 9430
Black Label	189 AHC		UH-1C	1968	gun	66-00649	N+A	rocket pod		Carl Spofford AC, Pat Leary CP	993, 1170, 9490
Black Power	A Co 1 Avn Bn		UH-1B	67-68	gun		NO				1973,
Black Sheep	188 AHC		UH-1H	67-68	slick		NO				414,
Black Stallion **	D Trp 1/4		OH-6A	1970	scout		v-nnp			Rod Willis	1923,
Black Widow (The)	68 AHC		UH-1B	65-66	gun	64-14088	NO	nose		G. Kanakaris CE, J. Taylor DG, Ed Harris AC, Al Smith	881,
Blackhorse Recovery	11 ACR		UH-1H	68-69	maint		NO	nose			1703,
Black Jack Dealer	175 AHC		UH-1H	70-71	slick		NO			Jay Klein AC, Jim McAllister CE, Jim Cowart AC	354, 1370, 1926, 9440
Blacksmith ^	11 ACR		UH-1H	71-72	maint		NO				1467,
Blacksmith ^	176 AHC	411 TC	UH-1H	1971	maint	67-17834	N+A	nose		Pearson AC, Erdkamp CP	901, 1930, 9450
Blenda's Rage	335 AHC		UH-1B	70-71	gun	62-02025	NO	nose			69, 1926
Blind Faith	116 AHC		UH-1D	1970	slick		NO	nose		Tommy Kyle CE	90,
Blind Faith	B Co 123 Avn Bn		UH-1H	70-71	slick		NO				1731,
Blind Faith	C Trp 1/9		OH-6A	69-70	scout		NO	fuselage			407, 9805
Blitz Krieg	121 AHC		UH-1B	1967	gun	63-08669	NO	pilot door			301,
Blivet	282 AHC		UH-1H	70-71	slick	66-16537	NO	nose		Jim Bush CE, Kent Gabriel DG	249, 569

Copter Name	Unit	Unit #1	Aircraft	Circa	Function	Serial #	Config	Location	Artist	Crew	Contributors
Blood, Sweat + Tears	15 Med Bn		UH-1H	70-71	medevac		NO	nose		R. Huether AC, T. Triffero CP, J. Hodges CE, M. Parsons DG	152, 178, 513, 608, 777, 808, 1171, 1345, 1837, 2037, 7375, 9030
Blood, Sweat + Tears	45 Med Co		UH-1H	69-70	dustoff		NO	nose			1308,
Blood, Sweat + Tears	48 AHC		AH-1G	1972	gun		NO	bpw		John Hiemstra	1053, 1187, 6025
Blood, Sweat + Tears	54 Med Det		UH-1H	1971	dustoff	68-xxxxx	NO				421, 1934
Blood, Sweat + Tears	82 Med Det		UH-1H	69-70	dustoff		NO			David Cahill MD	258,
Blood, Sweat + Tears	175 AHC		UH-1C	1970	gun		N+A	pilot door		Guillermo Dorame CE	467, 696, 1926, 5900
Blood, Sweat + Tears	175 AHC		UH-1H	69-70	slick		NO			Hans-Peter Naegele CE	1370, 1926
Blood, Sweat + Tears	179 ASHC		CH-47C	69-70	cargo		NO			Roger Boyd FE	170, 943
Blood, Sweat + Tears	180 ASHC		CH-47C	68-69	cargo	68-15847	N+A	fuselage		Rodger Faddis FE, Kessler	110, 247, 495, 7925, 8800
Blood, Sweat + Tears	203 ASHC		CH-47A	71-72	cargo		NO			Mike O'Connell FE	1233,
Blood, Sweat + Tears	215 Composite Svc Bn		UH-1H	71-72	medevac		NO	nose		Eric Traub	2031,
Blood, Sweat + Tears	243 ASHC		CH-47A	68-70	cargo		NO				550,
Blood, Sweat +Tears	247 Med Det		UH-1H	70-71	dustoff		NO	nose		Hartman AC, J. Jones CE, Hogan	707, 869, 1780, 7725
Blood, Sweat + Tears	254 Med Det		UH-1H	69-70	dustoff		NO	nose		Jack Wolfe CE, Jim Miller MD, Doc Dinsmore MD	421, 1934
Blood, Sweat + Tears	271 ASHC		CH-47B	70-71	cargo	66-19127	NO				1106, 8100
Blood, Sweat + Tears	498 Med Co		UH-1H	69-71	dustoff		NO	nose		Don Jones CE	143, 337, 863
Blood, Sweat + Tears	B Btry 2/20 ARA		AH-1G	69-71	gun	68-15063	NO	bpw		Mike Cole CE	154, 318, 804
Blood, Sweat + Tears	B Co 159 ASHB		CH-47B	1969	cargo		NO	fuselage		Albert Holland FE, Wayne Clarke DG	310,
Blood, Sweat + Tears No 2	498 Med Co		UH-1H	1970	dustoff		NO	cargo door window panel			143, 7700
Blood, Sweat And Lead	134 AHC		UH-1C	68-71	gun		NO				352, 1818

Blue Angel: *8 TC, CH-21C, (sn 56-02087), Nha Trang, 1962-63*. Named by Crew Chief Hiawatha Oakes. Photo by Jim Woodward.

Copter Name	Unit	Unit #1	Aircraft	Circa	Function	Serial #	Config	Location	Artist	Crew	Contributors
Blood, Sweat N Tears	D Trp 2/1		AH-1G	69-70	gun	67-15654	NO	nose			369, 4000
Blood, Sweat 'N Tears	173 AHC		UH-1H	68-70	slick		NO	nose			374, 1461, 1862, 9420
Bloody Mary	119 AHC		UH-1H	1968	slick	66-16536	NO	nose		Mike Murry AC, Larry Hayes CE	717, 9270
Bloody Mary	C Co 101 AHB		UH-1H	67-68	slick	67-17833	NO			Lacey, Kennett, Freeman	414, 1024
Bloody Mary	C Co 101 AHB		UH-1H	71-72	slick	67-17833	NO			Lacey AC, Kennett CE, Freeman DG	414,
Blow It Out Your Ass **	162 AHC		UH-1D	1968	slick	65-12775	v-nnp			Bill Greenhlagh AC	652,
Blue Angel	8 TC	117 AHC	CH-21C	62-63	lift	56-02087	NO	fuselage		Bill Bogges DG, Hiawatha Oakes CE	1317, 1956, 2093, 9620
Blue Ass Buzzard	114 AHC		UH-1C	1967	gun	66-00568	NO			R. Munro, D. Schuster, E. Fielding, T. Demski	301, 6700
Blue Lu	A Trp 7/17		OH-6A	1967	scout	65-12973	NO	doghouse		Bright, Ehrhardt, Young	1972, 9730
Blue Max (The)	114 AHC		UH-1C	66-67	gun		N+A	pilot door			1641, 1652
Blue Max (The)	114 AHC		UH-1C	67-68	gun		NO	pilot door		Bruce Gunn, W. Lightfield	301, 666, 6700
Blue Max (The)	336 AHC		UH-1H	68-69	slick		NO	nose			1970, 9610
Blue Womb	B Co 229 AHB		UH-1H	68-69	slick	66-16698	NO			Larry McMillin DG/CE, Bob Raviera CE	1158, 9780
Body By Fisher	243 ASHC		CH-47A	1968	cargo	66-19058	NO	fuselage		Tom Moser FE, Bob Hines CE	1245,
Body Snatcher	539 TC		CH-47A	1970	cargo		N+A	fuselage		Bud Hinson DG	77, 754, 9660, 9925
Body Snatcher (The)	45 Med Co		UH-1H	69-70	dustoff	66-16515	NO				1318, 1533
Body Snatcher II (The)	45 Med Co		UH-1D	1970	dustoff	66-16793	NO			John Smith AC, Don Marlow CE, K. Keleher MD	1308, 7725
Boeing 707 *	F Trp 9 Cav		UH-1H	1972	slick	70-15707	v-nn			Mark F. Hostetler CE	795,
Boeing's Blunder	180 ASHC		CH-47C	1970	cargo		NO	front fuselage			7925,
Bond	498 Med Co		UH-1D	67-69	dustoff	66-17007	NO	nose		Copeland AC, Ewing CP, Pappy CE, Ferg MD	511, 1465
Bones 11 ^	282 AHC		UH-1H	70-71	slick	68-16117	N+A	pilot door		Larry Hickerson AC	746,

Copter Name	Unit	Unit #1	Aircraft	Circa	Function	Serial #	Config	Location	Artist	Crew	Contributors
Boneyard Special (The)	93 TC	121 AHC	CH-21C	1963	lift		NO	fuselage			1828, 9290
Bonita	128 AHC		UH-1H	1971	slick		NO	nose		Sanchez	989,
Bonnie	135 AHC		UH-1M	69-70	gun	66-00708	NO	rocket pod arm		Joe Ralph CE	1439,
Bonnie G	162 AHC		UH-1D	68-69	slick	66-00798	NO			H. Wetzel CE, M. Gallagher DG, H. Schiebe AC	575, 9390
Bonny's Baby	162 AHC		UH-1H	1971	slick		NO	nose		Dan Scott	325, 9390
Bonzai Boss **	213 ASHC		CH-47A	1967	cargo	65-08021	AO	fuselage		Mike Brown FE	219, 1053, 8000
Boo	D Trp 3/5		OH-6A	68-69	scout	67-16071	NO	doghouse		Newkirk AC, Grose CE, Frady	554, 823, 9860
Boo-Boo-A-Go-Go	119 AHC		UH-1	66-67	slick		NO			Don Scalf	,9270
Boo-Boo-A-Go-Go II	119 AHC		UH-1H	67-68	slick	66-16376	NO	nose		R. Harrison CE, Cal Brown DG, Don Scalf AC, Pilat AC	705, 1399, 4125, 9270
Boom Boom #6	15 Trans Bn	HHC	UH-1H	67-68	slick		N+A	nose		Jimmy Shows CE, Ron Dowling DG, Grant Curtis, Albert Schlim, John Deperro	411, 1607, 2056
Boom Boom A-Go-Go	188 AHC		UH-1H	1968	slick	66-16122	N+A	pilot door	Dick Detra	Robet Sadouski AC, Jim Trueblood CE, Dick Detra DG	414,
Boony Bus	132 ASHC		CH-47B	70-71	cargo	67-18452	N+A	front fuselage	SP4 Davis did all '70-'71 a/c art	Francis Wadginski CP, Justen FE	1162, 1588, 1744, 1843, 2062, 7800, 8275
Boot (The)	71 AHC		UH-1H	1970	slick		N+A	nose			1424,
Boot Hill	B Trp 7/1		AH-1G	71-72	gun	67-15522	NO	bpw			1634,
Boots	188 AHC		UH-1H	67-68	slick		NO				1024,
Born Free	11 ACR		AH-1G	1971	gun	67-15662	NO	bpw			712, 1051, 1417, 1674, 4825
Born Free	92 AHC		UH-1H	1970	slick	66-16507	N+A	nose		Dave Furches CE, Dave Harmon DG	697, 1492, 1811
Born Free	121 AHC		UH-1D	66-68	slick		NO	nose			831,
Born Free	173 AHC		UH-1D	66-68	slick	65-09588	NO	nose		Kevin Hathaway CE	2001,
Born Free	200 ASHC		CH-47A	67-68	cargo	66-00096	NO	front fuselage	Larry Dumford	John Murley FE	995, 1195, 1585, 7950, 8275
Born Free	B Trp 1/9		OH-6A	67-68	scout		NO	fuselage			1392,

Copter Name	Unit	Unit #1	Aircraft	Circa	Function	Serial #	Config	Location	Artist	Crew	Contributors
Born Free II	92 AHC		UH-1H	1970	slick	66-17097	N+A	nose		Dave Harmon CE, Dave Cline DG, Rocco DG, Colluci DG	697, 1811
Born Free III	92 AHC		UH-1H	1968	slick	67-17460	N+A	nose	Mr. Turner	Joe Calaway DG/CE, Ken DeVore DG, Dave Harmon CE	261, 697, 931, 1811, 9220
Born To Raise Hell	57 TC	120 AHC	CH-21C	1963	lift		N+A	fuselage			1975, 6525
Borrowed Time	196 ASHC		CH-47A	69-70	cargo	66-00082	NO			Stan Kluge FE	925, 8250
Borrowed Time	D Trp 3/4		OH-6A	1970	scout	69-16019	NO	doghouse		David Atkinson DG	55, 1266, 9855
Boss (The)	A Co 228 ASHB		CH-47A	1970	cargo		N+A	fuselage			475, 1451, 4050
Boss Hoss	271 ASHC		CH-47B	68-69	cargo		NO			Tom Blazina CE	150, 3775
Boss's Hoss (The)	135 AHC		UH-1C	67-68	gun	66-15124	N+A	pilot door		Rick Coleman DG, Bill Weeks CE, Madison AC	322, 1249, 9330
Boss's Hoss II (The)	135 AHC		UH-1C	1968	heavy hog	66-15029	N+A	pilot door		Rick Coleman CE	322, 9330
Boston Patriot	176 AHC		UH-1H	1971	slick		NO	nose		Tim Boettger DG/CE	153, 9450
Bouncy **	213 ASHC		CH-47A	1967	cargo	65-07973	AO			James Stanley CE, Lancaster FE	790, 1684
Bounty Hunter	170 AHC		UH-1C	1969	gun		NO				9400,
Bounty Hunter	A Trp 3/17		OH-58A	1971	scout		NO			Marvin Swinford	1740,
Bounty Hunter II	170 AHC		UH-1C	1969	gun		NO	nose			1519, 1543, 9400
Boxcar	unk		CH-47	68-69	cargo		NO				652,
Boxcars *	119 AHC	Avn Co	UH-1B	1963	slick	62-02012	v-nn				188,
Brain Bucket (The)	B Trp 1/9		UH-1B	66-67	gun		NO	nose		Stanley Nash AC	1274,
Brat (The)	114 AHC	Avn Co	UH-1B	1965	slick	62-01915	NO			N. Pennington, B. Basinger, E. Owens, D. Dilday, D. Guswell, J. Poppert	1047, 6000, 6700
Bret And Bart	175 AHC		UH-1B	66-67	gun	63-08712	NO			Bob Michalic CE, Brown DG	1926,
Broken Bull	68 AHC	391 TC	UH-1B	65-66	maint		NO	pilot door			1402,
Brother Bird	A Co 227 AHB		UH-1H	69-70	slick	66-16471	N+A	nose		Munday CE	562,

Copter Name	Unit	Unit #1	Aircraft	Circa	Function	Serial #	Config	Location	Artist	Crew	Contributors
Brother Bird	A Co 227 AHB		UH-1H	70-71	slick	66-16936	N+A	nose			132, 1232
Brother Love's Travelin' Salvation Show	48 AHC		UH-1C	70-71	gun	66-00520	NO	nose	Winchester 1970	J. Winchester CE, C. Haws DG, R. Lester AC, R. Cowley CP	355, 716, 832, 1014, 1053, 1165, 4460, 9150
Brotherhood (The)	48 AHC		UH-1H	70-71	slick	66-01206	NO	nose		Bud Dunlap CE, Bill Martin AC, Rick Hickman DG	449,
Bubbles	134 AHC		UH-1C	68-69	gun		NO	nose		Milton Omlid CE, David Root CE, Don Elliott	352, 1818, 9320
Buck Shot	A Co 227 AHB		UH-1D	1967	slick	63-08742	N+A	nose		Bill Foster	547, 733, 9630, 9700
Buckaroo	175 AHC		UH-1D	66-67	slick	65-09805	NO			Durham, Dale Vernon	461,
Bucket Of Blood *	15 Med Bn		UH-1D	66-67	medevac		v-nn			Bill Louche DG, John Moyer CE	1038,
Buckeye	335 AHC	A/82	UH-1D	65-66	slick		NO				800,
Buddha	174 AHC		UH-1C	1968	gun	66-15138	NO	right cargo door	door gunner	Don Richardson CE	1471, 8425
Budweiser	92 AHC		UH-1C	68-69	gun	66-15113	N+A	rocket pod	Denny Turner	Tom Tucker CE, John Horn DG, Brice	538, 1053, 1359, 1492, 1772, 1806, 1811, 6300, 9220
Buffy	271 ASHC		CH-47B	70-71	cargo		NO			Tom Hope CE	791, 8025, 8250
Bug	114 AHC		UH-1D	67-68	firefly / smoke	65-09717	N+A	nose		Lew Hudspeth AC, Ron Thacker CP	807,
Bull Frog	60 AHC		UH-1H	1972	slick		NO	nose		Don Bullis CE, John McGuire DG	1148,
Bull Of The Woods	271 ASHC		CH-47B	1971	cargo		NO				1199, 8100
Bunny Bird **	57 AHC		UH-1H	71-72	slick	69-15361	AO	nose		Don Terry CE, Mason AC	167, 395, 420, 1266, 1761, 5675, 6275
Buschwacker	335 AHC		UH-1H	69-70	slick	66-16572	N+A	nose	CW2 Dale Dilts, 1st plt	Tom Gould AC, Rene Visscher CE, Angelo Rodriguez DG	635, 1926
Bush Rat	176 AHC		UH-1H	1968	slick	67-17516	N+A	nose	Ron Williams	Ron Williams CE, Harry Sweeney CE	1919,
Business Has Been Good	B Trp 1/9		OH-6A	1969	scout	67-16351	N+A	doghouse		Ken James, Ted Lofton, Tom Weigle	898, 9905
Busy Boy	unk		CH-21C	1962	lift		N+A	beside pilot window			877, 4850
Buzz Off	121 AHC		UH-1D	67-68	slick		N+A	nose		Smith AC	477, 1593, 4825, 6975, 9290

Copter Name	Unit	Unit #1	Aircraft	Circa	Function	Serial #	Config	Location	Artist	Crew	Contributors
Buzzard	498 Med Co		UH-1H	69-70	dustoff		NO	nose			863, 1357, 7700
Buzzards	147 ASHC		CH-47A	1968	cargo		N+A	fuselage			264,
Buzzards ^	E Co 704 Maint Bn	571 TC	UH-1H	1970	maint	67-17320	NO	nose		Danny Brown CE	209, 1451, 4050
C Ration Sall	147 ASHC		CH-47A	67-68	cargo		N+A	removable panel			264, 1272, 7825, 8275
C. C. Rider	45 Med Co		UH-1H	67-68	dustoff		NO			Clarence Crim CE	5,
C. C. Rider	187 AHC		UH-1H	70-71	slick	68-16357	NO	nose		Pedelewitz, R. Smith	125, 1954, 3300
Cajun Lady	D Co 229 AHB		AH-1G	69-70	gun		NO	bpw			280,
Cajun Queen	175 AHC		UH-1B	1966	gun	64-13984	NO			E.P. Shreve DG, Matlock CE, Ringenberg AC	1926,
Cajun Queen	335 AHC		UH-1B	70-71	gun	83	NO	nose	Ron Corb	Ron Corb DG	69, 767, 1646, 1926, 9600
Cajun Queen	C Co 227 AHB		UH-1H	1968	slick		N+A	nose		Milton Lesemann CP	656, 1013
Calico Cat *	D Trp 1/10		AH-1G	69-70	gun	67-15528	v-nn				119, 463, 1659, 9840
Calif	147 ASHC		CH-47A	67-68	cargo		N+A	removable panel	SP4 Davis did all '70-'71 a/c art		307, 392, 1272, 7825, 8275
Calif. Dreamer	335 AHC		UH-1B	70-71	gun	62-04594	N+A	nose	Robert Smith	Robert Smith DG, John Enos CE, Juan Hernandez CE	1646, 1926, 9590
California	336 AHC		UH-1H	1970	slick		N+A	nose		Mike Leslie, Jim Deb	1305, 4825
California Beachboy (The)	155 AHC		UH-1D	66-69	slick		N+A				9360,
California Beachboy II (The)	155 AHC		UH-1D	66-69	slick		N+A	nose			911, 9360
California Dreamer	15 Med Bn		UH-1D	1966	medevac		NO				263, 7375
California Dreamer	119 AHC		UH-1H	1967	slick	66-16373	N+A	nose	CE painted CA state outline	Ron Corbin AC, Jim Daniels CP, D. W. Kelmick CE, J. N. Allen DG, Jim Bosley CP	345, 6835, 9910
California Dreamer	155 AHC		UH-1H	68-69	slick	352 ?	NO	nose		Ken Brown CE	216, 9360
California Dreamin'	45 Med Co		UH-1H	1968	dustoff		NO	nose			2067,
California Dreamin'	117 AHC		UH-1H	70-71	slick		NO	nose + cargo doors			1552,

Copter Name	Unit	Unit #1	Aircraft	Circa	Function	Serial #	Config	Location	Artist	Crew	Contributors
California Dreamin'	128 AHC		UH-1D	69-70	slick	65-09612	NO			Gerry Martin CE	613,
California Dreamin'	135 AHC		UH-1H	67-68	slick	66-01112	N+A	pilot door		Robert Mounts CE	1249,
California Dreamin'	571 Med Det		UH-1H	71-72	dustoff	69-16651	NO	CE jump door		Ken Warner AC, Ken Bohrman CE, R. Clabby MD	155,
California Dreamin'	D Trp 3/4		AH-1G	70-71	gun	68-15135	NO	doghouse	Gary Schmidt	Rudy Paris AC, Don Vaughn CE	1559, 8400
California Dream'n	21 Signal Group		UH-1H	70-71	slick		NO	nose		D. Baggott AC	64,
California Dremin'	B Co 228 ASHB		CH-47A	69-70	cargo	66-19008	NO			Scott Sheridan CE, Gary Trimble FE	1604, 8025
California Flash	116 AHC		UH-1H	70-71	slick	66-16292	NO	nose		Bill Chavez CE, John Hazelwood DG, John Pepe AC, Ed Hughes AC	300, 9240
California General (The) **	147 ASHC		CH-47A	67-68	cargo		AO	removable panel	SP4 Davis did all '70-'71 a/c art		307, 392, 7825, 8275
California Girl	B Co 229 AHB		UH-1H	68-69	slick	67-17785	NO			Larry McMillin DG, John Divett CE	1157, 9780
California Republic	335 AHC		UH-1H	69-70	slick		N+A	nose			635, 695, 3350, 9590
Cambodian Clearwater Revival	147 ASHC		CH-47C	71-72	cargo		NO			Randy Rushing DG	1355, 3775
Can Do	A Co 227 AHB		UH-1H	69-71	slick	66-16610	NO			H.C. Lovelace CE	1043, 8075
Canadian Club	176 AHC		UH-1H	69-70	slick	67-17441	N+A	nose		Ralph Bigelow AC	72, 141, 901, 1595, 1987, 9450
Cannabis Sativa	C Btry 2/20 ARA		AH-1G	1970	gun	67-15508	N+A			Don Mather CE, Perez AC	1111,
Canned Heat	B Btry 2/20 ARA		AH-1G	70-71	gun	68-17028	NO	bpw			439, 804, 1474, 5700, 6325
Canned Heat	B Trp 1/9		UH-1H	69-70	slick	67-17555	NO	nose		Roger Snow DG	898, 1656, 4825
Cannibal (The)	121 AHC		UH-1D	1968	slick	078 ?	N+A	nose		Urguhart AC, D. Radabaugh CE, Carl Purvis DG	1435, 4975, 6975
Canuck	68 AHC		UH-1B	1966	gun		NO	doorpost			1402,
Capt Zig Zag **	B Trp 3/17		UH-1H	1971	slick		AO	nose			1581,
Capt. Crude	C Co 227 AHB		UH-1D	1967	slick	62-12367	N+A	nose		Dick Buehler CE, Gerry Caputo DG	231,
Captain America	57 AHC		AH-1G	71-72	gun		NO				314,

Copter Name	Unit	Unit #1	Aircraft	Circa	Function	Serial #	Config	Location	Artist	Crew	Contributors
Captain America	129 AHC		UH-1C	69-71	gun		NO			Jay Hillon CE	1415,
Captain America **	187 AHC		UH-1H	70-71	slick	69-15515	AO	tailboom end cap			1932,
Captain America	191 AHC		UH-1D	1967	slick	65-10019	NO				268,
Captain America	271 ASHC		CH-47B	69-70	cargo	67-18462	N+A	front fuselage	Rick Ferrell	Pete Hodges FE, Craig Markovich FE	256, 964, 1089, 8100, 8950
Captain America	B Co 123 Avn Bn		OH-6A	1970	scout	69-16023	N+A	fuselage			184, 1266, 6275, 9430
Captain Klutz	205 ASHC		CH-47A	68-69	cargo		N+A				1836,
Captain Zig Zag	A Co 227 AHB		UH-1H	69-70	slick	68-15624	N+A			Wayne Jackson CE, Bill Rogers	562, 836, 1500, 9700
Cara Mia	C Trp 1/9		UH-1B	66-67	gun	64-14015	NO	nose		George Gavaria CE	893,
Carol	81 TC	119 AHC	CH-21C	62-63	lift	57072	NO	fuselage		Buddy McGarrett CE	1144,
Carol	129 AHC		UH-1H	69-70	slick	68-15664	NO	gun mount		John Sartor CE	1547,
Carol Ann	129 AHC		UH-1D	65-66	slick	64-13745	NO	nose		Joe Nicolich DG	1293,
Carolina Kid	116 AHC		UH-1H	1970	slick		NO	nose		Dennis Piper CP	69, 1401
Caroline	189 AHC		UH-1H	68-69	slick	66-01111	NO	nose		David Munsell CE	760, 1260, 9490
Carolyn	174 AHC		UH-1H	69-70	slick	68-15644	NAA	nose		Robert Chipley AC, Guy Martin CP, Holder CE	184, 2084, 9430
Casper Night Hawk	173 Abn Bde		UH-1H	69-70	nighthawk		N+A	nose		Jerry Brown CE, Dale Morrison AC	214, 9410
Cassie	117 AHC		UH-1H	1971	slick	67-17382	NO	cargo door		Ken Scales CE	1552,
Cassy	A Co 1 Avn Bn		UH-1D	66-67	slick	767 ?	NO	cargo door		Harry Myers CE, Johnson DG	1268, 9000, 9925
Cat Ballou	117 AHC		UH-1H	68-69	slick		NO	nose			21,
Cat Ballou	175 AHC		UH-1D	66-67	slick	65-09800	NO	nose		Dave Eastman AC, MacDougal CE	461, 5775, 9130
Cat Doctor ^	282 AHC	484 TC	UH-1H	68-70	maint	67-17457	NO	nose		L. Johnson CE, J. Mathews DG, Michaud AC, Hill AC, Geer AC	172, 856, 1551, 9560
Cat In The Hat **	213 ASHC		CH-47A	67-68	cargo	65-07968	AO	fuselage			1410, 8000

Copter Name	Unit	Unit #1	Aircraft	Circa	Function	Serial #	Config	Location	Artist	Crew	Contributors
Cathy's Clown	116 AHC		UH-1D	1970	slick		NO	nose			90,
Cathy's Clown	118 AHC	Avn Co	UH-1D	1965	slick		NO				167,
Cathy's Clown	178 ASHC		CH-47	71-72	cargo		NO				1541,
Cathy's Clown	191 AHC		UH-1D	68-69	slick	66-00820	NO	pilot door		L. Arnold AC, T. Jens CP, J. Wilson CE, A. Moniton DG	245,
Caution: This Box Contain FOD	B Co 9 Avn Bn		AH-1G	68-69	gun		NO	turret			1710,
Cav Heart **	B Co 228 ASHB		CH-47A	1969	cargo		AO	fuselage			475,
Cav Jester	C Co 229 AHB		UH-1H	69-70	slick	67-17779	N+A	nose		Lawrence Shemley AC, McNutt CE, Bob Bastian DG	1601, 1767, 9830
CBS Special	1 Sig Bde		UH-1H	1970	slick		NO	nose		Tom Crews CE, Brown CE, Stringum CE	331, 366, 8525
Challenger	B Co 123 Avn Bn		OH-6A	70-71	scout	67-16524	NO	fuselage			184, 1266, 6275, 9430
Challenger	C Btry 2/20 ARA		AH-1G	69-71	gun	66-15345	NO				850,
Challenger	F Btry 79 AFA		AH-1G	71-72	gun	66-15345	NO			Hinch CE, Bogue AC, Hoult AC	2000,
Charla II	A Trp 1/9		UH-1H	69-70	slick		NO		Glen Senkowski	Glen Senkowski AC	1589,
Charlie Chaser	48 AHC		UH-1B	66-67	gun		NO			Oscar Hale CE	680, 9150
Charlie Chaser	162 AHC		UH-1C	1966	gun		NO	pilot door			9390,
Charlie Chopper	180 ASHC		CH-47C	1969	cargo		N+A	front fuselage			8275,
Charlie Chopper	D Trp 1/4		AH-1G	69-70	gun		N+A	bpw			195, 1053, 1205
Charlie Lima Express	178 ASHC		CH-47B	70-71	cargo	67-18459	NO	front fuselage		Mark Baird DG/FE	68, 841, 1541, 1946, 7875
Charlie Tuna	174 AHC		UH-1C	1971	gun	65-09470	NAA	quarter panel		Bill Wilder CE, F. Thompson AC, Gary Halter CP	1770, 1907, 9430
Charlie's Chow	120 AHC		UH-1B	1967	gun	64-14091	N+A	M-3 rocket box			210, 301, 5225
Charriot (The)	121 AHC		UH-1D	1970	slick		N+A	nose		Ray Burke CE, Schoenfelder	240,
Chartwriter (The)	240 AHC		UH-1H	1967	slick		NO	pilot door		Bob Wessel DG, Gary Land CE, Bill Armstrong AC, James Fussell CP	1781,

Copter Name	Unit	Unit #1	Aircraft	Circa	Function	Serial #	Config	Location	Artist	Crew	Contributors
Chattanooga Choo-Choo	57 TC	120 AHC	CH-21C	1962	lift		NO	fuselage			1975, 6500
Cheap Charlie	114 AHC	Avn Co	UH-1B	1964	gun	62-01965	NO			R. Lilly, A. Apel, Burner, E. Sipe, R. Stringer, L. Simonis	674, 6700
Cheap Thrills	11 ACR		OH-6A	71-72	scout	67-16470	NO	clamshell			1264,
Cheap Thrills	15 Med Bn		UH-1H	70-71	medevac	68-16459	NO	nose		Mark "Doc" Holiday CE	50, 152, 513, 608, 777, 7375, 9030
Cheap Thrills	92 AHC		UH-1C	1970	gun		NO	nose			931,
Cheap Thrills	118 AHC		UH-1H	1970	slick		NO	nose			69, 1061, 8650
Cheap Thrills	162 AHC		UH-1H	1969	slick		NO	pilot door		Floyd Stringer	1718, 9390
Cheap Thrills	175 AHC		UH-1D	1969	slick	63-13002	NO	nose		Robert Moran DG, Tim Cox CE, Florian	358, 467, 1926, 8650
Cheap Thrills	176 AHC		UH-1H	69-71	slick	68-16468	NO	nose		Henry Lipscomb DG	1027, 1390, 9450, 9885
Cheap Thrills	242 ASHC		CH-47A	68-71	cargo		NO				1056, 1199
Cheap Thrills	A Co 158 AHB		UH-1H	1969	slick	67-17643	NO	doorpost		John Reasoner AC, Robert Gates CE, Stephen Stahl DG	1443,
Cheap Thrills	A Co 227 AHB		UH-1H	69-70	slick		NO				197,
Cheap Thrills	D Co 229 AHB		AH-1G	70-71	gun		NO	bpw		Linder AC, Charles Covert CE	280, 351, 9850
Cheap Thrills	unk Cav		AH-1G	1970	gun		NO	bpw			1174,
Checker Cab	175 AHC		UH-1D	1966	slick		NO				461, 5775
Checkmate	114 AHC	Avn Co	UH-1B	64-65	gun		NO	cargo door window panel			6700, 6775
Checkmate ^	C Co 229 AHB		UH-1H	69-72	slick	68-15226	NO	nose			1816,
Cherry	175 AHC		UH-1H	69-70	slick		NO				1419,
Cherry	178 ASHC		CH-47A	67-68	cargo	66-19087	N+A	front fuselage		Jerry Balmer FE	80, 841, 9925
Cherry	282 AHC		UH-1D	66-68	slick	65-09736	NO	nose		Tom Pullen	1430,
Cherry Boy	57 TC	120 AHC	CH-21C	1963	lift	56-02061	NO	fuselage			1953, 1181, 6025, 6050

Copter Name	Unit	Unit #1	Aircraft	Circa	Function	Serial #	Config	Location	Artist	Crew	Contributors
Cherry Boy	128 AHC		UH-1D	1967	slick		N+A	pilot door			402,
Cherry Buster	57 AHC		AH-1G	71-72	gun		NO				1841,
Cherry Buster	121 AHC		UH-1B	67-68	gun hog		NO	hardpoint dust shield		Taylor, Brinnon, Beard	395, 439, 5675, 5725
Cherry Buster	C Co 229 AHB		UH-1H	69-70	slick	68-15648	NO		Roger Baker	Dave Holte CE, Roger Baker AC, Painter DG	73, 784, 9830
Cherry Girl	57 TC	120 AHC	CH-21C	1963	lift		NO	fuselage			3600, 8925
Cherry Picker	132 ASHC		CH-47B	1971	cargo	67-18446	N+A	front fuselage			1162, 7800
Cherry Picker	B Trp 1/9		OH-6A	69-70	scout	67-16556	N+A	doghouse		Chandler	758, 8650, 9740
Cherry Popper	1 Bde 101 Abn	HHC	UH-1H	1969	slick		NO	nose			2059, 4825
Chi Town	B Co 228 ASHB		CH-47A	69-70	cargo	66-00124	NO	nose		Juan Gozier CE	637, 1239, 8025
Chi Town Hustler	B Btry 2/20 ARA		AH-1G	69-70	gun	67-15490	NO	bpw			1601,
Chicago II	117 AHC		UH-1H	71-72	slick	68-16563	NO	nose		Paul Goodwin CE	628, 936, 5325
Chicago Police Dept	unk		AH-1G	1971	gun		N+A	bpw + belly			1581,
Chicago Transit	114 AHC		UH-1H	1971	slick	69-15433	NO	nose			3100, 6700
Chicago Transit	179 ASHC		CH-47C	70-71	cargo	67-18528	NO	fuselage		Tom Messenger FE, Byron Raney DG, Ben Hodges CE	1182,
Chicken Coop	175 AHC		UH-1D	1969	slick	65-09871	NO			Ed McGuire CE, Vernon Bernard, Summers	1147, 1891, 6805, 9440
Chicken Coupe	A Co 227 AHB		UH-1H	1970	slick	68-16172	N+A	nose		Joe Paranal CE	1340,
Chicken Heart	71 AHC		UH-1C	1967	gun		NO	nose			1579, 9210
Chicken Little	175 AHC	A-502	UH-1D	65-66	slick		NO	nose			1908, 4600
Chicken Little	A Co 227 AHB		UH-1H	1971	slick	66-16064	N+A	nose		Dennis Howell CE	798,
Chicken Runner	57 TC	120 AHC	CH-21C	1963	lift	55-04143	NO	fuselage			301, 1053, 1181, 1975, 5575, 6025, 6050, 6500
Chicken Ship	A Co 227 AHB		UH-1H	69-70	slick	68-15650	N+A	nose		Mike George AC, Roy Moore AC, Phil Meskinnis CE, Rollin Monter DG	102, 197, 1793, 9700

Chi Town Hustler: *B Btry 2/20 ARA, AH-1G, (sn 67-15490), 1969-70.* "49k2" fuselage call-sign is clever algebraic equivalent to sn '490. Served in five different units and survived VN with 1,928 total flying hours. Photo by Larry Shemley.

Copter Name	Unit	Unit #1	Aircraft	Circa	Function	Serial #	Config	Location	Artist	Crew	Contributors
Chicken Slick	A Co 227 AHB		UH-1H	69-71	slick	66-16825	N+A	nose			102,
Chicken Wagon	129 AHC		UH-1H	72-73	slick	71-20067	NO			Larry Stokes CE, Joe Abarelli CP	1705, 9310
Chickenest Chicken	A Co 227 AHB		UH-1H	70-71	slick	68-16479	N+A	nose	Joe Paranal		1340,
Chickenman America	A Co 227 AHB		UH-1H	69-71	slick	68-15284	N+A	nose		Robert Douglas AC, Tim O'Connor CE	1310, 1789, 9700
Chickenman Chicken	A Co 227 AHB		UH-1H	1971	slick	68-16477	N+A	nose		John Green CE	649, 9700
Chickenman's Magnet Ass	A Co 227 AHB		UH-1H	69-70	slick	68-15735	N+A			Ed Friday CE, George Puta AC, Ken Massa AC, Bruce Sinkey AC	562, 9700
Chickenman's Rotary Connection	A Co 227 AHB		UH-1H	70-71	slick	69-15277	N+A	nose	Joe Paranal	Roger Reid AC	101, 1340
Chief	336 AHC		UH-1B	1967	gun	64-13905	NO	vertical stabilizer			301, 927, 1190, 1212, 5275
Chief Smoke	175 AHC	A-502	UH-1B	65-66	slick	63-0870?	NO	nose		Sam Vincent AC, Enoc Sturgill CE, Chastine DG, Fair CE	1724, 1926
Chi-Town Hustler	117 AHC		UH-1H	71-72	slick	67-17777	NO			Paul Goodwin CE	127, 628, 1377, 9250
Chi-Town Hustler	B Trp 3/17		UH-1H	1971	slick		NO	pilot door		Roger Searcy	1581, 6475
Choo Choo's Train	unk		UH-1H		slick		N+A	nose			4350,
Christine	174 AHC		UH-1H	1971	slick	69-15763	N+A	nose	local VN artist	Randy Godbold CE, Don Peterson AC	619, 623, 9430
Chu Lai Express *	178 ASHC		CH-47B	1971	cargo	67-18459	NO			Mark Baird FE, Frank Sorenson FE	68, 7875
Chubby Cheeks	179 ASHC		CH-47A	66-67	cargo		NO	fuselage			1058,
Chuck Crusher	114 AHC		UH-1C	1967	gun	66-00514	NO	pilot door		R. Brooks, R. Bentson, G. Slingerland, D. Griffin, S. Hunt	41, 947, 1569, 1628, 6700, 8950
Chuck Crusher	281 AHC		UH-1C	69-70	gun		NO				66,
Chuck Crusher II	114 AHC		UH-1C	1968	gun		NO	pilot door		H. Rand, J. Cahill, B. LaVoque, R. Swart, E. Krumbiegel	634, 666, 848, 947, 1053, 1266, 1569, 3100, 6075, 6700
Chuck You Farlie	1 Bde 1 Cav Div		OH-6A	68-69	scout	67-16272	NO	fuselage		Sam Estes DG	486,
Chuck You Farlie	3 Bde 1 Cav Div		UH-1H	1969	slick		N+A	nose			1226,
Chuck You Farlie	170 AHC		UH-1D	1969	slick		NO	nose			1266, 1724, 6125

Copter Name	Unit	Unit #1	Aircraft	Circa	Function	Serial #	Config	Location	Artist	Crew	Contributors
Chuck You Farlie	A Co 228 ASHB		CH-47A	69-70	cargo		NO	nose			475, 1451, 4050
Chug A Lug	2 Signal Group		UH-1D	66-67	slick	65-10021	NO	pilot door		Oliver Ridgway CE	265, 1041, 1266, 6125
Chunky	238 AWC	AHC	UH-1C	69-70	gun		NO	M-5 turret			9530,
Cindy Ann	C Trp 1/9		AH-1G	1971	gun	68-15068	NO	bpw		Zahn AC, Marshall H. Maring CE	306, 120, 134, 838, 1086, 1963, 1978, 5450, 5625, 6550
Circus Wagon	C Btry 4/77 ARA		AH-1G	1969	gun		NO	nose		Robert Smith CP, Ed Miller AC	1647,
Cisco Kid	128 AHC		UH-1B	1968	slick	64-14010	N+A	quarter panel		Johnny Garza CE	913, 1376
City Of Eufaula	271 ASHC		CH-47B	68-69	cargo	66-19110	N+A	front fuselage		Willie B. Williams	144, 1087, 1896
City Of Nha Trang	339 TC		CH-37B	63-64	recovery		N+A	fuselage			889,
Clark Bar	187 AHC		AH-1G	1971	gun	67-15652	N+A	nose		Rodney Woods AC, Dan Clark CE	1954,
Climax	188 AHC		UH-1C	1968	gun hog	65-09471	N+A	pilot door	Dick Detra	Soares AC	414, 1660, 9480
Cloud 9	179 ASHC		CH-47C	69-70	cargo	68-15821	N+A	front fuselage	Mike Rubalcava	T. Miller FE, M. Rubalcava FE, Burris FE, D. Lujan DG	1203, 1277, 1522, 7900
Cloud 9	A Co 227 AHB		UH-1H	69-70	slick	68-15626	NAA	nose		Bill Hess AC	102, 562, 197
Cloud Dancer	A Trp 7/1		OH-6A	71-72	scout		NO				217,
Cobra **	174 AHC		UH-1M	70-71	gun	64-14140	AO	quarter panel	Bud Vann	Bud Vann CE	184, 9430
Cobra Lead ^	114 AHC		UH-1C	67-68	gun	66-00599	NO	pilot door		Robin Miller, Eugene Schwanebeck, J. Popin, G. Connally, O. Kershaw	301, 696, 1266, 1569, 3100, 5900, 6075
Cobra Surprise	114 AHC		UH-1H	1972	lightship	69-15031	NO			Bob Hoffman AC, William Gay CP	768, 6700, 6835
Cobra's Kill	114 AHC		UH-1C	1968	gun		NO	M-3 rocket box		H. Rand, J. Cahill, B. LaVogue, R. Swart, E. Krumbiegel	634, 848, 947, 1266, 1569, 3100, 6075
Coffin (The)	117 AHC		UH-1D	70-71	slick		NO	nose			78, 9250
Coffin Dodgers (The)	170 AHC		UH-1H	1970	slick		NO	jump door			1839, 4150
Cold Sweat	188 AHC		UH-1C	1968	gun frog	66-15087	NAA	pilot door	Dick Detra	Wright, Johnson, Smalley, Parrish, Searles, Clark, Kim, Burton	414, 9480
Colleene	A Co 227 AHB		UH-1D	66-67	slick	62-12355	NO	nose		Dennis Burden CE	237, 9700

City of Eufaula: *271 ASHC, CH-47B, (sn 66-19110), Can Tho, 1968-69*. Renamed "Magnet Ass" after attracting unwanted enemy attention; survived VN with 2,633 hours, all with the 271st. Standing near artwork is Woody Whitaker, Flight Plt Sgt. Photo courtesy Woody Whitaker.

Copter Name	Unit	Unit #1	Aircraft	Circa	Function	Serial #	Config	Location	Artist	Crew	Contributors
Color Me Bad	175 AHC		UH-1H	69-70	slick	63-08745 ?	NO	nose		Joe Wisneski CE, Mike Haley AC	467, 682, 1926, 8650
Color Me Bad News	121 AHC		UH-1B	1968	gun	64-14022	NO	pilot door			3600,
Color Me Death	114 AHC		AH-1G	1970	gun		NO	bpw			282, 8625
Color Me Death	118 AHC		UH-1C	1971	gun		NO	cargo door window panel			191, 9260
Color Me Gone	187 AHC		UH-1D	66-67	slick		NO	pilot door			1908, 4600
Color Me Gone	498 Med Co		UH-1H	68-69	dustoff	66-17020	NO	nose		Bill Allen	22,
Color Me Peace	134 AHC		UH-1H	69-70	slick	68-15464	NO	nose		Mike Koehler DG, Jim Radke CE	352, 1818
Colorado	336 AHC		UH-1H	69-70	slick		N+A	nose		J. Leandro AC, D. Cram CE, J. Dean CP, G. Penia DG	992, 1305, 4825
Colt 45	68 AHC		UH-1B	66-67	gun	64-14086	NO	rocket pod		Woody AC, Jim Poston CE, Reynolds DG	2075,
Comanche	114 AHC		UH-1D	1967	slick	65-09865	NO			L. Custer, J. Faltynski, S. Kline, G. Artis, N. Gray, R. Calkins	301,
Combattre Chien	57 TC	120 AHC	CH-21C	63-64	lift		N+A	fuselage			1975, 6525
Comely Cock (The)	A Co 227 AHB		UH-1H	70-71	slick	66-16150	N+A	nose	Joe Paranal		1232, 1340
Comin' On Strong	117 AHC	Avn Co	UH-1D	66-67	slick		NO	nose			57, 8650
Condemned	200 ASHC		CH-47A	67-68	cargo	66-00099	N+A	front fuselage	Larry Dumford	Jim Thalacker FE, Dennis Wilson CE, Fred Silva CE, Ralph DG	995, 1195, 7950, 8275
Cong Stalkers	A Trp 7/17		UH-1H	68-69	slick		NO			Walter Lyons DG	1062,
Cong Stomper	191 AHC		UH-1D	67-68	slick	65-10019	NO	pilot door		Dick Calton DG	268, 6950
Connie	174 AHC		UH-1H	68-71	slick	67-17471	NO	nose			3250, 9430
Connie	A Trp 3/17			69-70			NO				1747,
Coon's Ass	C Co 228 ASHB		CH-47B	1970	cargo		NO				1239,
Coors	92 AHC		UH-1C	68-69	gun	66-15113	N+A	rocket pod	Denny Turner+Tom Tucker + Bob Johnson	Tom Tucker CE, John Horn DG	207, 306, 698, 931, 1053, 1492, 9220
Coors Special	A Trp 3/17		OH-58A	70-71	scout		NO			Dave Nickel AC	1292,
Corsair	D Co 227 AHB		AH-1G	69-70	gun	68-17077	N+A	bpw			113, 120, 1674

Copter Name	Unit	Unit #1	Aircraft	Circa	Function	Serial #	Config	Location	Artist	Crew	Contributors
Cosa Nostra	114 AHC		UH-1H	69-70	slick	64-13771	NO	nose		E. Pinther, Brown, T. Desimone, S. Walbridge	413, 1400
Cost Of Living	1 Avn Det		ACH-47A	66-67	gun	64-13145	N+A	fuselage		David Knight DG	301, 566, 903, 1266, 1726, 1898, 4600, 4825, 6275, 6300, 8025, 8275, 8300
Cost Of Living	53 Avn Det		ACH-47A	1966	gun	64-13145	N+A	fuselage		David Knight DG	1723, 4600, 4825, 8025, 8275
Cougar's Revenge ^	57 AHC		UH-1H	70-71	nighthawk		NO			Charles Brainerd AC, Calvin Blankenship	147, 183, 314, 6475, 9180
Country Boy	117 AHC	Avn Co	UH-1B	64-65	gun		NO			George Collins AC	329, 9250
Courier Of Death	B Trp 3/17		AH-1G	1972	gun		NO	bpw		Hendricks CE	459, 1942, 6850
Cowboy Joe	188 AHC		UH-1H	67-68	slick		NO				414, 1024
Crap Shooter	188 AHC		UH-1C	67-68	gun hog	66-00711	NO		Dick Detra	Staley, Lamb, Pierpoint	414, 9480
Crap Shooter	A Co 228 ASHB		CH-47A	1968	cargo		N+A	fuselage		Garry Daniel AC	388, 8300
Crash's Mistake	A Co 227 AHB		UH-1H	1971	slick	67-19523	N+A	nose		LaFrancouis DG, T. Moore CE, Dennis Wheatley AC	1232,
Crater Creator	129 AHC		UH-1B	66-67	gun		NO	nose			1452,
Crazy 8	53 Avn Det		ACH-47A	1966	gun	64-13145	NO	doorpost			653, 1266, 6275, 6300, 6275, 8300
Crazy Horse	11 ACR		AH-1G	68-69	gun		NO	bpw			713, 1703, 4500, 9040
Creature Of Death	B Trp 3/17		AH-1G	1971	gun	67-15852	NO				1674,
Creeping Ginnie	unk		UH-1B	1965	slick		N+A	fuselage			1908, 4600
Creeping Jesus	F Trp 4 Cav		UH-1H	71-72	slick	69-15108	NO	nose		William Cooper AC, John Schilinski DG	339, 422
Crimson And Clover	188 AHC		UH-1H	67-68	slick		NO				414,
Crimson King (The)	178 ASHC		CH-47B	70-71	cargo		N+A	front fuselage			1946,
Cross Ways Breezer	unk		UH-1B	1965	gun		NO			Walter Sarratt DG, Mike O'Connell DG	1546,
Crum Snatcher	B Trp 1/9		UH-1H	68-69	slick	66-16924	NO	nose		C. Burgess AC, O'Toole CE, Ross DG, Rago DG, Holland DG	193, 238, 779, 1312, 1436, 9740
Cry Of The Banshee	B Trp 3/17		AH-1G	1971	gun		NO	bpw		Larry Witte CE	1942,

The Crystal Ship*: 187 AHC, UH-1H, (sn 66-16574), Tay Ninh, 1968-69*. Flew 1,537 VN hours in three different units before crashing on 4-14-73 with the VNAF. Door Gunner Alan Wise standing beside pilot's door flashing peace sign. Photo courtesy Alan Wise.

Copter Name	Unit	Unit #1	Aircraft	Circa	Function	Serial #	Config	Location	Artist	Crew	Contributors
Crystal Blue Persuasion	336 AHC		UH-1C	69-70	gun	66-15034	NO	nose		Jim Beddingfield AC, Tim Allen CP, Jim Elliott CP	114,
Crystal Ship	189 AHC		UH-1C	67-70	gun	65-09552	NO	nose		Jimmy Benka CE, Gordon Cockrell AC, Tom Freis CE, Jack Lokin DG	126, 313, 9490
Crystal Ship	254 Med Det		UH-1H	67-69	dustoff		NO			Jerry Schneider CE	664,
Crystal Ship	335 AHC		UH-1B	1970	gun		NO			Mark Schmipf AC	1557,
Crystal Ship	C Co 229 AHB		UH-1H	68-69	slick		NO	nose			230, 1466, 6805
Crystal Ship (The)	11 ACR		UH-1H	68-69	slick		NO	pilot door			1703,
Crystal Ship (The)	179 ASHC		CH-47B	68-69	cargo		NO	front fuselage		Ron Kessler FE, Ron Swift CE	1739,
Crystal Ship (The)	187 AHC		UH-1H	68-69	slick	66-16574	NO	pilot door		Alan Wise DG, J. Ron Longoria CE	1940,
Crystal Ship (The)	196 ASHC		CH-47A	68-69	cargo	66-00122	NO				883, 925
Crystal Ship (The)	C Trp 1/9		AH-1G	70-71	gun	68-15062	NO	bpw	Glen McCloy	Walker Jones AC, Ross Rainwater CP, Glen McCloy CE, Joel Hageman AC, Van Joyce CP	134, 360, 873, 1438, 1592, 1963, 2025, 4825, 5450, 9805
Cucaracha	unk		CH-21C	63-64	lift		NO	fuselage			4350,
Cuddles	A Trp 7/1		AH-1G	70-71	gun		NO			Ron Matthews	291,
Cupid's Quiver	178 ASHC		CH-47B	70-71	cargo	66-19125	NO			Marty Eckelson FE	464,
Curious Yellow	237 Med Det		UH-1H	1971	dustoff	69-16656	N+A	nose		David Hansen AC, Milton Kreger CP, Ed Hopper CE, Ed Iocabacci MD, George Shaughnessy DG	631, 638, 690, 824, 1085, 1742, 1865, 2069, 3890, 7780
Curse You Red Baron	175 AHC		UH-1C	67-68	gun		N+A	M-3 rocket box			982,
Cutlass Mundir (The)	121 AHC		UH-1D	67-68	slick		NO	nose			1135,
Cyclops	271 ASHC		CH-47B	68-69	cargo	66-19107	N+A	fuselage + front pylon		Mark Bjurstrom FE, Mike Budka CE, Jim Morton DG, Synder	144, 1087, 1805, 1896, 8100, 8950
Cyclops	D Trp 3/5		OH-23G	1968	scout		NO	nose			9130,
D. J.	134 AHC		UH-1C	68-69	gun		NO	nose			352, 1818
D. B. (The) *	E Btry 82 Arty Bn		OH-13S	1965	scout	63-09105	v-nn			Ed Lemp CE	1007,

Copter Name	Unit	Unit #1	Aircraft	Circa	Function	Serial #	Config	Location	Artist	Crew	Contributors
D. B. II (The) *	E Btry 82 Arty Bn		OH-13S	1965	scout	64-15391	v-nn			Ed Lemp CE, Rockne AC	1007,
D. B. III (The)	E Btry 82 Arty Bn		UH-1B	65-66	slick	64-14051	NO	nose		Ed Lemp CE, Hussey CP, Jim Lashley DG, Dickson AC	1007, 1020, 4400, 6275
Da Judge	178 ASHC		CH-47B	68-70	cargo	67-18463	N+A	front fuselage		Lionel Caeton	267, 367, 497, 1946, 2061, 3850
Da Judge	C Co 229 AHB		UH-1H	70-71	slick / nigthawk	68-16082	N+A	nose	Roger Baker	R. Peatross DG, Brouwers DG, Bargala CE, Zennie CE, Ron Sites DG, Todd Troll CE	73, 85, 199, 208, 803, 1364, 1601, 1622, 1816, 8450, 9830
Daddy Rabbit	134 AHC		UH-1H	1971	slick	66-16177	NO	nose			69, 1908, 4600
Daddy Rabbit	175 AHC		UH-1B/D	1966	slick	745?	NO	nose		Daniel Last AC, Terry McDowell AC	461, 478, 682, 976, 1141, 1266, 1926, 6275, 9440
Daisy Mae	45 Med Co		UH-1H	69-70	dustoff		NO			Jerry Abrams CE	1533, 1831, 7475
Dale	B Co 229 AHB		UH-1H	1967	slick		NO	nose		Dale Fillmore AC, Dennis Osborne DG, Pete CE	173, 1331
Damn You Charlie	243 ASHC		CH-47A	1969	cargo		N+A	front fuselage			111, 157, 8075
Dark Death	C Trp 16 Cav		OH-6A	72-73	scout	68-17365	NO	doghouse		Rod Willis AC	576, 1205, 1763, 1923
Darkhorse Air Maintenance	D Trp 1/4		OH-6A	69-70	maint	67-16516	NO	clamshell			195,
Darlin Jenny	B Trp 1/9		UH-1D	1966	slick		NO				1418,
Darlin Jenny II	B Trp 1/9		UH-1D	66-67	slick		NO	pilot door		Don Lewis AC, Ray Cluff DG, John Sater CE	535, 652, 1418, 1909, 9740
Das Leichte Katzchen	D Co 229 AHB		UH-1B	1965	gun	63-08700	NO	doorpost		John Holt CE	783,
Day Tripper	82 Med Det		UH-1H	69-70	dustoff		NO			F. Ruckhaber MD, Keith Carpenter CE, Terry Mullins CE, David Cahill	258, 1523
Day Tripper	173 AHC		UH-1H	70-71	slick	66-16155	NO	nose		Dick Crow AC, Tom Sutton CE	374,
Day Tripper	178 ASHC		CH-47B	67-68	cargo		N+A	front fuselage			497, 841
Day Tripper	192 AHC		UH-1H	69-70	slick	67-17476	NO	nose		Jon Freel CE, Williams AC, Collins CP, Fensky DG	560, 621
Day Tripper	C CO 229 AHB		UH-1D	1967	slick	66-16144	NO			Ron Pritchett CE	1427,
Day Tripper II	82 Med Det		UH-1H	69-70	dustoff	68-16204	NO			Fred Ruckhaber MD, Keith Carpenter CE, James Duncan AC	1523,
DDAP ^^	D Trp 1/1		AH-1G	1969	gun	67-15686	NO	bpw		Leo Huber, Mike Henry, Elliott	91, 134, 1391, 5450, 9835

Copter Name	Unit	Unit #1	Aircraft	Circa	Function	Serial #	Config	Location	Artist	Crew	Contributors
DDAP ^^	D Trp 1/1		OH-6A	1969	scout	68-17207	NO	doorpost			470, 670, 9835
De Judge	174 AHC		UH-1H	1971	slick		N+A	nose	Abe Jones	Abe Jones CE	623, 1770, 9430
Deacon (The)	281 AHC		UH-1C	1967	gun		NO				946, 9550
Dead Dinks Are Pacified **	D Trp 1-1		OH-6A + AH-1G	1969	scout / gun		v-nnp				91, 134, 470, 670, 1391, 5450
Deadbone **	498 Med Co		UH-1H	69-70	dustoff		AO	nose			1357, 7700
Dean Fixer ^	120 AHC	98 TC	UH-1B	65-66	maint		NO	nose		George Kanakaris DG, John McDougal CE	881, 1140, 9280
Death American Style	114 AHC		UH-1H	1971	slick	66-01036	NO	nose		M. Gilpin, T. Johnson, O'Brien	611, 3100, 6700
Death Angel	B Trp 7/17		AH-1G	1969	gun		NO	nose			1076,
Death Before Dishonor	C Trp 1/9		UH-1H	1970	slick		NO	nose		Lamont, Hobson, Hinch, Mahaffey, Atkins	205, 873, 4825, 9805
Death Committee	D Trp 3/5		UH-1H	1971	slick		NO	pilot door		Joe Zavis CE, Russ Marsden	1982, 9860
Death Dealer	48 AHC		UH-1B	66-67	gun	64-14093	NO	nose		Oscar Hale CE, Dan Crance DG, Ray Chan CE	79, 362, 580, 680, 9150
Death Dealer	281 AHC		UH-1C	69-70	gun		NO			Tom Smyrl	66,
Death Destruction	129 AHC		UH-1C	71-72	gun	66-15212	NO	nose		Kim LaVoie CE, Mike Mckinney DG	1053, 1131, 9310
Death Express	281 AHC		UH-1C	69-70	gun	520	NO				66,
Death From Above	135 AHC		UH-1H	1971	slick	69-15374	NO			James Wingrove CE	1936,
Death From Above	170 AHC		UH-1C	68-69	gun		NO	nose			2079,
Death From Above	A Co 227 AHB		UH-1D	66-67	slick		NO	nose			667,
Death Merchant	281 AHC		UH-1C	1969	gun	66-15004	NO	nose	John Gachich	Daryl Evangelho CE, John Gachich DG, Jerry Krueck CE	66, 488, 570, 1053, 1677, 9550
Death N Destruction	unk		UH-1C	68-69	gun		NO	nose			813,
Death On Call ^^	240 AHC		UH-1C	70-71	gun		NO	nose			2048, 5575, 5725, 6050, 6125
Death On Call ^^	281 AHC		UH-1C	1969	gun		NO	nose		Daryl Evangelho CE	488,
Death On Call	B Trp 1/9		AH-1G	1969	gun	66-15324	NO	bpw		Russell P. Smith AC	898, 1650, 9905

Delta Rat: *271 ASHC, CH-47B, Can Tho, 1968-69*. Crew Chief Perry reacting to being clubbed by the painted rat. Photo by Dan Markell.

Copter Name	Unit	Unit #1	Aircraft	Circa	Function	Serial #	Config	Location	Artist	Crew	Contributors
Death Rides A White Horse	114 AHC		UH-1H	70-71	slick	67-17461	NO	nose		Marvin Tabaka AC, Richard Lunceford CE, Lee Smith DG	782, 1644, 6700
Death Trap	118 AHC	Avn Co	UH-1B	1965	gun		NO			Chip Austin DG	58, 9260
Death Trap (The)	C Co 227 AHB		UH-1H	69-70	slick		NO	pilot door			656, 770
Death Trap II	C Co 227 AHB		UH-1H	1969	slick	68-15469	NO	pilot door			112,
Death's Little Angel	114 AHC		AH-1G	1970	gun	66-15322	NO	bpw			192, 1926, 6700
Death's Orgasm	117 AHC		UH-1M	70-71	gun	65-09458	NO			Tom Stansbury AC, Fred Hebert CP, Chris Behm CE, Ron Ricks DG	1654, 2010, 2036, 4500, 7300, 9250
Debbie	174 AHC		UH-1H	68-69	slick	68-15223	NO	nose	Ben Kennedy	Gauby CE, Sours CE, Upton CE, W. Price DG	598, 1137, 1423, 9430
Debbie	242 ASHC		CH-47A	1971	cargo		NO	nose			989,
Debbie II	187 AHC		UH-1D	67-68	slick		NO				1882,
Debbie Jo	242 ASHC		CH-47A	68-71	cargo		NO	nose			1225, 8350
Dee Dee Mow M. F.	A Co 1 AVN Bn		UH-1D	1969	slick	66-01167	N+A	pilot door			195,
Deer Slayer	240 AHC		UH-1H	1967	slick	66-16630	NO	pilot door		John Thrift DG, Troy Willis CE, Don Brown AC	1781,
Dee's Delight	187 AHC		UH-1H	1970	slick	68-15411	NO	nose		Eugene Moats CE	441, 765, 1932, 9470
Deho	A Trp 1/9		AH-1G	68-69	gun		NO	bpw		Joe Bowen AC, Rick Rowe	304, 500, 9740
Déjà Vu	175 AHC		UH-1H	71-72	slick	68-16070	NO	nose		Norm England AC, Larry Lane CE, Gonzales DG, Steve Mullinex CP	478, 1926
Delta Air ^^^	281 AHC		UH-1H	69-70	slick	66-00923	NO	nose		Paul Swol CE	1741, 9550
Delta Rat	271 ASHC		CH-47B	68-69	cargo		N+A	fuselage		Bill Hutson FE, Perry FE	819, 1087, 1896
Delta Rat II	271 ASHC		CH-47B	69-71	cargo		NO			Dewey Hood FE	787, 2002, 5433
Delta Rebel (The)	175 AHC	A-502	UH-1B	65-66	slick	63-0870?	NO	nose		Sam Vincent AC, Enoc Srurgel CE, Chastine DG, Fair CE	1724, 1926
Delta Sweetheart	114 AHC	Avn Co	UH-1B	64-65	slick		N+A	cargo door window panel		R. Patton AC, Mitchell CE	1356, 6700
Delta To DMZ	235 AWC		AH-1G	1971	gun	67-15656	NO	doghouse			1674, 5425, 5427

Copter Name	Unit	Unit #1	Aircraft	Circa	Function	Serial #	Config	Location	Artist	Crew	Contributors
Delta Yank	114 AHC	Avn Co	UH-1D	1966	slick		NO	nose		Frank McChesney	1128, 1926, 6700
Denise	189 AHC		UH-1H	68-69	slick		NO			Don Torres CE	1796,
Dennis The Menace **	B Co 25 Avn Bn		UH-1C	66-69	gun	66-15111	AO	nose	Charles Edwards DG '69	A. Asberry CE, J. Mosley DG, G. Rushing CE, R. Rodriquez CE, Gayle Williams CE, Horton CE	49, 909, 1060, 3950, 9120
Desert Rat (The)	200 ASHC		CH-47A	67-68	cargo	66-00103	NO		Larry Dumford		995, 1585
Destroyer (The)	173 AHC		UH-1C	66-67	gun	65-09418	NO	pilot door		Ron Salmon DG, Ed Compton CE '67-'68	708, 1981
Deuce + A Dime *	195 AHC		UH-1H	1970	slick	69-15210	v-nn			McFarland AC, Tom Nadeau CP, Cole	1271, 4530, 4825
Deuces Wild	175 AHC		UH-1H	69-70	slick		NO				1891, 6805
Devastator (The)	121 AHC		UH-1B	66-68	gun		NO	nose			1135,
Devil Or Angel	117 AHC	Avn Co	UH-1B	65-66	gun		NO	nose		Norbert Murray DG	1263,
Devil Or Angel	155 AHC		UH-1B	66-67	gun		NO	nose			255, 9360
Devil Or Angel II	155 AHC		UH-1B	66-67	gun		NO	nose		Ken Byrnes CE	255, 9360
Devil's Advocate	A Co 227 AHB		UH-1H	69-70	slick		NO			Gary Bridges CP	197,
Devil's Advocate (The)	235 AWC		UH-1H	69-70	slick		N+A	nose			1996, 3725, 8450
Devil's Anger	175 AHC		UH-1C	70-71	gun		N+A	pilot door		Gary Klutting CE, Tommy Ivey DG	467, 1370, 1493, 8650
Devil's Delight	48 AHC		UH-1B	66-67	gun		NO	nose			79, 9640
Devil's Disciple	114 AHC		UH-1H	1970	slick	69-15085	NO	nose		Peter Smalley, Law, Frank Stroebel, Pascual Mantanona	408, 1719, 6700, 9230
Devil's Disciple	134 AHC		UH-1C	68-69	gun	66-15019	NO	nose		Eugene Molek CE, D. L. Schindler AC, N. E. Lawrence CP, R. L. Defrenn CE, R. E. Bernard DG	352, 923, 1405, 1818, 1908
Devil's Disciple	B Co 229 AHB		UH-1H	67-68	slick		NO	nose		Dennis Osborne CE	1331, 4350
Devil's Disciple	D Trp 1/4		UH-1B	1965	gun	074	NO	doorpost		Colin Kelley DG, Larry Dickerson CE, John McLeod AC	894, 4425
Devil's Disciple (The)	68 AHC		UH-1C	67-68	gun	66-00657	NO	revetment art			69, 1304

Copter Name	Unit	Unit #1	Aircraft	Circa	Function	Serial #	Config	Location	Artist	Crew	Contributors
Devil's Disciple's	187 AHC		UH-1D	67-68	slick		N+A	pilot door		Shann, Havemann	652,
Devil's Sister (The)	B Trp 3/17		AH-1G	1971	gun	68-17042	NO	bpw		Bobby J. Turner CE	1674, 1942
Dial L	114 AHC		UH-1C	1968	gun		NO	nose		J. Kaltchthaler, R. Brodt, J. Juhrs, J. Kowalczyk	491, 941, 1569
Diana	117 AHC		UH-1H	70-71	slick		NO	nose			1908, 4600
Diane	A Co 229 AHB		UH-1H	1968	slick	641	NO	nose			4350,
Diane	A Trp 1/9		UH-1H	69-70	slick		NO	doorpost	Glen Senkowski	Glen Senkowski AC	145, 1589, 9690
Di-Di	50 Med Det		UH-1H	1968	dustoff		NO	pilot door		Woody Nesbitt AC	1284,
Die Goldene Rose	162 AHC		UH-1H	71-72	slick		NO	nose		Don Nicholson AC, Len Malick CE	1077, 1291, 1908, 9390
Dike Runner Beep Beep	121 AHC		UH-1D	1966	slick		N+A	nose			831, 1908, 4600
Dirty D	117 AHC	Avn Co	UH-1B	63-64	gun	103 or 611	NO			Daily Dalton CE	383,
Dirty Dozen	175 AHC		UH-1D	1968	slick	66-16051	NO			Bill Julius CE, Bob Rosar AC, Francis Schmitt CP, Ray Hensley DG	1535, 9440
Dixie	D Trp 1/1		UH-1H	68-69	slick	67-17330	NO	nose		Al Brittingham CE, Walt Ferrell CP, Eiss AC, Michko CE	203, 9835
Dixie Bell	B Trp 1/9		OH-13S	67-68	scout		N+A	nose			1266, 6275
Dixie J	C Co 227 AHB		UH-1H	1969	slick	66-16912	NO	nose		Howie Belkin DG	120,
Docter Copter	45 Med Co		UH-1H	1968	dustoff	66-17101	NO	nose		Clif Adams CE	5, 2067
Doctor 570	F Trp 8 Cav	570 TC	UH-1H	1969	maint		NO	nose	Carl Mumaw	Carl Mumaw	1259, 9870
Doctor Death	A Trp 1/9		OH-6A	70-71	scout		NO				1266, 1497, 6250
Doctor Death	E Trp 1/9		OH-6A	70-71	scout		NO				1266, 1497, 6250
Doctor Oldsmobile	E Trp 1/9		AH-1G	70-71	gun	442	NO				1497,
Dog (The)	D Trp 1/1		OH-6A	1970	scout	67-16251	N+A	doghouse			670, 1804, 9835
Dog (The)	F Trp 8 Cav		OH-6A	70-71	scout	67-16251	N+A	doghouse			69, 949, 9870

Copter Name	Unit	Unit #1	Aircraft	Circa	Function	Serial #	Config	Location	Artist	Crew	Contributors
Don Juan	611 TC		CH-37B	1965	recovery	55-00625	NO	nose			1975, 6525
Donna	5 Trans Bn		UH-1H	1968	slick		NO	nose			870,
Donna	A Co 229 AHB		UH-1H	1968	slick	66-16797	NO	nose		Dan Noonan CE	1300, 6805
Donna	B Trp 1/9		OH-13S	1967	scout		NO	doorpost		Black, Myers	855, 5925
Donna	C Trp 1/9		AH-1G	70-71	gun		NO	bpw			1003, 9805
Donna Sue	254 Med Det		UH-1H	66-67	dustoff		NO	jump door		Charlie Webb AC, Jim Bynum CP	664, 2063
Donna Sue II	254 Med Det		UH-1H	1967	dustoff		NO	jump door		Barry Grubbs MD, James Ihli	664, 2063, 2077
Doris	282 AHC		UH-1B	1967	gun		NO	nose		John Swiney CE	279,
Double Ace *	A Trp 1/9		UH-1H	70-71	slick	66-16011	v-nn			Ken Lockhart CE	1031,
Double Deuce	281 AHC		UH-1H	69-70	slick	66-00923	NO	nose		Paul Swol CE	1741, 9550
Double Deuce	A Co 228 ASHB		CH-47A	1970	cargo	65-08022	N+A	front fuselage		Frank Steele FE	1819, 1908, 2014
Double Duce	C Co 228 ASHB		CH-47B	70-71	cargo	66-19122	N+A	front fuselage		Mike Goodknight FE	626,
Double Eagle	498 Med Co		UH-1H	69-70	dustoff		N+A	nose			1357, 7700
Double Nothing *	119 AHC	Avn Co	UH-1B	1963	slick	62-02002	v-nn			David Braum CE	188,
Double O Pig *	335 AHC		UH-1B	69-70	gun	62-02028 ?	v-nn				1926,
Double O Pig *	B Trp 3/17		UH-1H	70-72	slick	66-17006	v-nn			Jay Ward CP	1863,
Double O Soul	173 AHC		UH-1D	66-67	slick	00	NO	pilot door			1931,
Double O Soul	B Trp 3/17		UH-1H	1971	slick	66-17006	NO			Roger Searcy	1581,
Double Ought Duce *	128 AHC		UH-1D	68-69	slick	63-13002	NO	pilot door		Ed Ewing AC, Tom Bresnahan CE	494,
Double Trouble	121 AHC		UH-1	68-69	slick		N+A	nose		Mike Koone AC	935,
Double Trouble	200 ASHC		CH-47A	67-68	cargo	66-00105	N+A	front fuselage	Larry Dumford	Bennie Birch FE	995. 1195, 1585, 7950, 8275

Copter Name	Unit	Unit #1	Aircraft	Circa	Function	Serial #	Config	Location	Artist	Crew	Contributors
Double Trouble *	334 AWC	AHC	UH-1D	67-68	slick	65-09947	v-nn			Greg Spratt CE	1672, 9580
Douche Bag (The) *	E Btry 82 Arty Bn		OH-13S	1965	scout	63-09105	v-nn			Ed Lemp CE	1007,
Douche Bag II (The) *	E Btry 82 Arty Bn		OH-13S	1965	scout	64-15391	v-nn			Ed Lemp CE, Rockne AC	1007,
Douche Bag III (The) **	E Btry 82 Arty Bn		UH-1B	65-66	slick	64-14051	v-nnp	nose		Ed Lemp CE, Hussey CP, Jim Lashley DG, Dickson AC	1007, 1266
Dove Of Peace	187 AHC		UH-1H	69-70	slick	67-17778	NO	nose	VN artist who worked on base		1700, 1727
Down In The Boondocks	D Trp 1/4		UH-1D	1969	slick		NO	pilot door			1053, 1205
Dr. Chicken Chickenman	A Co 227 AHB		UH-1H	1971	slick	27	N+A	nose			1232,
Dr. Know	82 Med Det		UH-1H	69-70	dustoff		NO			Gregg Randall MD, Tom Rich CE	1523,
Dr. Strangelove	82 Med Det		UH-1H	69-70	dustoff		NO				1523,
Dragnet	92 AHC		UH-1H	68-69	slick	67-17714	NO			Bill Thoma CE, Steve Lee DG	931, 9220
Dragon Ass	8 TC	117 AHC	CH-21C	1963	lift		N+A	fuselage		Barc Boyd AC	168,
Dragon Fly	242 ASHC		CH-47A	68-69	cargo		NO			Bud Cauley DG	292, 3750
Dragon Wagon	8 TC	117 AHC	CH-21C	63-64	lift	56-02087	NO	fuselage		Bill Bogges CE	1317, 2093
Dreadnaught	336 AHC		UH-1H	69-70	slick		N+A	nose			1305, 1825, 4825, 9610
Drinking Problem	unk		CH-47		cargo		N+A	fuselage			1908, 4600
Droopy	93 TC	121 AHC	CH-21C	1962	lift	51-15903	NO	near pilot's window			1975, 6500
Dry Place Dry Time	147 ASHC		CH-47A	67-68	cargo		N+A	fuselage			573, 7825
Drydock ^	170 AHC	405 TC	UH-1H	1969	maint		NO	nose			1543, 9400
Dud (The)	242 ASHC		CH-47A	70-71	cargo	64-13150	NO			Rickey D. Wittner CE	1944,
Duff And Dilly's	197 AHC		UH-1B	1965	gun		NO	nose		John Duff AC	652,
Duit Tuit-Sir	C Trp 3/17		AH-1G	68-69	gun		NO	bpw			212, 4025, 9120

The Dynamic Duo: *571 Med Det, UH-1H, (sn 69-15629), 1972.* Medic Scott Hanson, pictured, crewed a big chunk of '629's total VN hours of 1,314. Photo courtesy Scott Hanson.

Copter Name	Unit	Unit #1	Aircraft	Circa	Function	Serial #	Config	Location	Artist	Crew	Contributors
Dumb Bunny III (The) **	E Btry 82 Arty Bn		UH-1B	65-66	slick	64-14051	NO	nose		Ed Lemp CE, Hussey CP, Jim Lashley DG, Dickson AC	1007, 6275
Dutch	119 AHC		UH-1H	69-70	slick	69-15345	NO	nose		Merlin Holland AC	1325,
Dynamic Duo (The)	571 Med Det		UH-1H	1972	dustoff	69-15629	N+A	nose		Scott Hanson MD, Jerry Green CE, Boyd AC	103, 693
Earth Wind + Fire	116 AHC		UH-1D	1970	slick		NO				501, 8625
Easy Flyer	170 AHC		UH-1H	1970	slick		NO	nose			1839, 4150
Easy Money	1 Avn Det		ACH-47A	66-68	gun	64-13149	N+A	fuselage		Garry Daniel CP, M. Alan Matthews AC	301, 566, 903, 1266, 1898, 4600, 4825, 5200, 5575, 6300, 8025, 8275
Easy Money	53 Avn Det		ACH-47A	1966	gun	64-13149	N+A	front fuselage			301, 652, 1266, 1726, 1898, 6300, 4600, 4825, 5200, 5575, 5700, 6300, 8025, 8275
Easy Rider	15 Med Bn		UH-1H	70-71	medevac	68-16491	NO			Pat Martin CE	608,
Easy Rider	21 Signal Group		UH-1H	70-71	slick	68-16138	NO	nose		Mattern CP, D. Baggott AC, Mike Kerr DG	64, 2003, 7125
Easy Rider	48 AHC		UH-1C	70-71	gun		NO	nose			832, 9150
Easy Rider	132 ASHC		CH-47B	70-71	cargo	67-18456	N+A	front fuselage	SP4 Davis did all '70-'71 a/c art	Matlack AC, Stanness FE	392, 1162, 1588, 2062, 7800, 8275
Easy Rider	173 AHC		UH-1H	69-70	slick		NO	nose		Larry Johnson AC	374, 593, 854, 9420
Easy Rider	174 AHC		UH-1C	1970	gun	66-15045	NO	quarter panel		Hodges CE, Budd Vann DG, Bob Hackett, Greg Manuel	130, 184, 439, 592, 762, 896, 1514, 1770, 5275, 5725, 6050, 6300, 9430
Easy Rider	175 AHC		UH-1H	70-71	slick		NO			Robert Moran DG	1926,
Easy Rider	242 ASHC		CH-47A	1970	cargo		NO	nose			308, 4825, 9200
Easy Rider	271 ASHC		CH-47B	70-71	cargo	116 or 125	NO	front fuselage		Tom Hope DG/CE, Decattorb FE	192, 791, 1266, 6100, 8025, 8250
Easy Rider	498 Med Co		UH-1H	69-70	dustoff		N+A	nose			1357, 7700
Easy Rider	B Trp 1/9		OH-6A	69-70	scout	67-16537	NO		Mike Jones	Mike Jones CE, Scott AC, Marc Abel DG	758, 872, 9905
Easy Rider	B Trp 1/9		OH-6A	1970	scout	67-16434	N+A	doghouse		Bill Hankinson AC, Mike Jones CE, Ron Klus	26, 758, 872, 9740

Copter Name	Unit	Unit #1	Aircraft	Circa	Function	Serial #	Config	Location	Artist	Crew	Contributors
Easy Rider	C Co 228 ASHB		CH-47B	1970	cargo	67-18443	NO	fuselage		Phillip Duke FE	448, 1239, 8025
Easy Rider	D Co 229 AHB		AH-1G	69-70	gun		NO	bpw			280,
Easy Rider (#2)	174 AHC		UH-1M	70-71	gun	66-15242	NO	quarter panel		Fred Thompson AC, P. J. Roth CP	301, 439, 1055, 1181, 5275, 5725, 6050
Easy To Be Hard	175 AHC		UH-1H	71-72	slick		NO				1926,
Eight Ball	242 ASHC		CH-47A	70-71	cargo	65-08008	N+A	fuselage		Roger King	74, 96, 119, 1225, 4825
Eight Balls *	B Trp 3/17		AH-1G	71-72	gun		v-nn				1613,
Eighter From Decatur	187 AHC		AH-1G	1971	gun	66-15297	N+A	bpw		Rodney Woods AC, Dan Clark CE	1954,
El Bandito	271 ASHC		CH-47A	70-71	cargo		NO			Ron Creamer CE	365, 8025, 8100
El Bandit-O	155 AHC		UH-1B	65-66	gun		NO	nose			939, 9360
El Cid	A Co 1 Avn Bn		UH-1B	1967	gun	64-13924	NO	cargo door			301,
El Culo Malo	D Co 229 AHB		UH-1B	65-66	gun hog	62-01935	N+A	doorpost		Sidney Reeder CE	783,
El Devastator	118 AHC		UH-1C	67-70	gun		NO	nose + doorpost		Donaldson, Little, Crawford, Boehm, Payne, Erwin	1029, 9260
El Diablo	A Trp 3/17		OH-6A	69-70	scout		NO	doghouse			1976, 8625, 9720
El Gato	11 ACR		OH-6A	68-69	scout	67-16346	NO	clamshell			1181, 6050
El Loch-O	D Co 227 AHB	166 TC	OH-6A	69-70	maint	66-14388	NO	clamshell			113, 1053, 1205, 1315, 4825
El Taco	C Co 227 AHB		UH-1H	68-69	slick	67-17469	NO	nose		Frank Parra CE	1346,
El Toro	117 AHC.	Avn Co	UH-1B	64-65	gun		N+A	gun pod			1840, 5025
Electric Banana	498 Med Co		UH-1H	69-70	dustoff	66-17007	N+A	nose		Tim Coogan MD, Paul Coleman CE	337, 863, 923
Electric Banana (The)	A Co 4 Avn Bn		UH-1H	69-70	slick	67-17352	NO	cargo door window panel		Bill Wells CE, William Bellis AC, C. A. Howard DG	1886,
Electric Butterfly	A Trp 7/1		OH-6A	71-72	scout		NO	doghouse			1053, 1205

Electric Banana*: 498 Med Det, UH-1H, (sn 66-17007), 1970.* Joe Kline of B Co 101 Avn Bn in the 540 TC copter yard at Qui Nhon. It survived VN with 1,150 total hours, all with the 498th. Photo courtesy Joe Kline.

ARMY HELICOPTER NAMES: A-Z

Copter Name	Unit	Unit #1	Aircraft	Circa	Function	Serial #	Config	Location	Artist	Crew	Contributors
Electric Ladyland	116 AHC		UH-1C	69-71	gun		NO				820,
Electric Olive	A Trp 7/1		OH-6A	70-72	scout	68-17331	NO	doghouse			1266, 8650
Electric Olive	C Trp 16 Cav		OH-6A	71-72	scout	67-16310	NO			Bob Todd AC	1266, 1923, 6250
Electric Olive II	C Trp 16 Cav		OH-6A	71-72	scout	68-17365	NO	doghouse		Rod Willis AC, Ken Stormer DG, Terry Davis DG	439, 1205, 1266, 1923, 5700, 6275
Electrical Egg	11 ACR		OH-6A	1969	scout	67-16418	NO	clamshell		Guy Ballou AC	1070, 4825
Eli Is Coming	C Co 227 AHB		UH-1H	71-72	slick		NO	nose		Phil Williams CE	1917, 5446
Eliminator (The)	120 AHC		UH-1B	1968	gun	64-14017	NO	rocket mount		Pete Iglesias CE, Fagan DG	827,
Eliminator	48 AHC		UH-1B	1967	gun		NO	nose			830, 9150
Elizabeth Ann	18 CAC		UH-1H	71-73	slick	70-15836	NO	nose		Jim Lorenzo DG/CE	870, 4825
Elmira	162 AHC		UH-1D	1967	slick		NO	pilot door			1125, 9390
Elusive Butterfly	17 AHC		UH-1C	67-68	gun		NO	pilot door		Brad Owens CE	1159,
Elusive Butterfly (The)	128 AHC		UH-1H	68-69	slick		NO	pilot door		Pinkston DG, Russell Layton CE, Osborne AC	989,
Elvira	48 AHC		UH-1H	68-69	slick	66-16351	NO	nose		Logan Weiler AC, John Penley CE, Harry Bledsoe DG, Weiler AC, Craig Osborne CE, Ernie Borbee	1885, 9150
Elvira	116 AHC		UH-1B	1967	gun		NO	pilot door			290, 301, 5575
Elvira II	116 AHC		UH-1B	1968	gun		NO	pilot door		Dan Johnson CE	852,
Enforcer (The)	C Trp 16 Cav		OH-6A	1972	scout	68-17365	NO	doghouse		Rod Willis AC	1053, 1205, 1923
Eradicator	188 AHC		UH-1C	1968	gun	66-00713	NAA	pilot door		John Soares AC, Cain CE, Pierpoint DG	1660,
Erinaala I	187 AHC		UH-1H	1971	slick	69-15905	NO	nose		Whittikind	9470,
Ethyl's Ambulance	159 Med Det		UH-1H	69-70	dustoff		NO			James Seal AC, Eitler AC, I. Moy MD	139, 1251, 7725, 9080
Eve Of Destruction	175 AHC		UH-1C	69-70	gun		N+A	pilot door		Ed Timmers CE	467, 1787, 8650
Eve Of Destruction	178 ASHC		CH-47A	66-67	cargo	64-13160	N+A	front fuselage		Johnny Jones FE, Jim Druin CE	1294,

Copter Name	Unit	Unit #1	Aircraft	Circa	Function	Serial #	Config	Location	Artist	Crew	Contributors
Eve Of Destruction	B Trp 2/17		AH-1G	1969	gun	67-15744	NO	bpw		Scott Kerr	588, 910, 1528, 4825
Eve Of Destruction	C Trp 2/17			69-70			NO	nose			587, 4825
Eve Of Destruction (The)	114 AHC		UH-1C	1968	gun		NO	pilot door			491, 666, 817, 1266, 6275, 6700, 8750
Every Man A Tiger ^^	68 AHC		UH-1D	65-66	slick	64-13873	N+A	pilot door			69, 1499, 9200
Everyday People	11 ACR		AH-1G	1969	gun		NO				645,
Evil Ways	92 AHC		UH-1C	1971	gun		NO	nose		Larry Fowler CE	169, 551, 9220
Evil Woman	117 AHC		UH-1M	1970	gun	66-00667	NO	rocket pod			69, 1061, 1908, 8650
Executioner	118 AHC		UH-1C	66-68	gun		N+A	nose			1029, 1037, 2080, 9260
Executioner	B Co 1 Avn Bn		AH-1G	1970	gun	67-15762	N+A	bpw		Lou Bouault AC	134, 1513, 5450
Executioner (The)	129 AHC		UH-1B	69-70	gun		NO				1042,
Executioner (The)	187 AHC		UH-1H	1972	slick	68-16568	NO	nose			1700,
Executioner (The)	192 AHC		UH-1C	1971	gun	66-00597	N+A	nose		John Arthur CE, Fred Solis DG, Whitney AC, Prince CP	343, 1901
Executioner (The) *	195 AHC		UH-1C	1970	gun		v-nn			Joey Bishop CE, Chuck Croley DG	368,
Executioner (The)	281 AHC		UH-1C	67-68	gun		N+A	nose		Don Digenova CE, Larry Williams DG, Harry Wetmore, Wally Kirchmeier	570, 1017, 1893, 9550
Exhibit A	116 AHC	Avn Co	UH-1B	66-67	gun	64-13956	NO	pilot door		Santos Garcia CE	585, 9240
Exodus	200 ASHC		CH-47A	67-68	cargo	66-00106	NO		Larry Dumford		995, 1195, 1585
Experience (The)	D Co 227 AHB		AH-1G	1969	gun		NAA	bpw			1226, 4350
Exterminator	82 Med Det		UH-1H	68-69	dustoff		NO	nose	CE painted it	Del Livingston AC	1030, 7575
Exterminator	176 AHC		UH-1C	1969	gun		NO				1595,
Exterminator (The)	155 AHC		UH-1C	66-68	gun	66-00583	NO	nose		Cherry DG, Paul Fadz CE, David McGillian DG, John Ganns	59, 496, 533, 663
Exterminator (The)	B Trp 1/9		AH-1G	1970	gun		NO	bpw			8925,
Fabulous Blue 7 (The) *	118 AHC		UH-1H	69-70	slick	66-16521	v-nn			Dave Norton CE, Lyman Sramek AC, Brian Willard DG, Fred Lilly DG, Domke DG	1302,

Copter Name	Unit	Unit #1	Aircraft	Circa	Function	Serial #	Config	Location	Artist	Crew	Contributors
Family Car (The)	165 TC		UH-1H	1971	slick	69-15165	NO	jump door	Pat Lund	Pat Lund	1051,
Family Car (The)	C Trp 1/9		UH-1H	70-71	maint		NAA	cargo door	Larry Verner	Mike Smith AC, Larry Verner CE	1266, 1438, 1497, 1645, 1832, 2051, 5560, 6250
Family Car (The)	unk		UH-1H	1968	slick		NO	cargo door			652,
Fancy's Boy	A Trp 3/17		OH-58A	69-71	scout	68-16934	NO	doghouse		Gary Swartz CE	1737, 1908, 1991, 3875
Fang	A Co 229 AHB		UH-1H	71-72	slick		NO	nose			604, 803, 9710
Fannie C (The)	unk		UH-1H	68-69	slick / C+C		NO	pilot door			1908, 4600
Fantastic Plastic Machine	335 AHC		UH-1H	69-70	slick		NO				695, 1926
Far Far Eastern Airways	178 ASHC		CH-47C	70-71	cargo	68-15997	NO	interior - center console		Marty Eckelson FE, Pruitt CE	464, 7875
Fat Albert *	114 AHC		AH-1G	1970	gun		v-nn				1527,
Fat Albert	134 AHC		UH-1H	1970	slick	65-10055	NO	nose	Frank Snyder	Jerry Spoon CE, Mike Barth DG	352, 1658, 1818, 1895, 9320
Fate Is The Hunter	48 AHC		UH-1C	1971	gun	66-00627	NO	nose	Al Meadows was unit artist	Al Meadows CE, H. Forsythe DG, E. Peterman AC, J. Giles	1165,
Faye's Love	191 AHC		UH-1D	1968	slick		NO	pilot door			452, 5750
Feelin' Groovy	128 AHC		UH-1D	1969	slick		N+A	pilot door		Vic Brimmer AC	200, 989
Fighting Fifth	117 AHC	Avn Co	UH-1B	1964	slick		N+A	doorpost			1266, 6125
Filthy Few	132 ASHC		CH-47B	68-69	cargo	67-18438	NO	front fuselage			303, 1162, 1289, 2002, 3175, 7800
Fireball	F Btry 79 AFA		AH-1G	71-72	gun	028	NO			McBride CE	850, 2000
Firebird	B Btry 2/20 ARA		AH-1G	68-69	gun	67-15769	NO	bpw			154, 804
FireFly	334 AWC	AHC	UH-1C	1967	gun	64-14187	NO	nose		Ray Bradley AC, Mike Uhlig CP, Dom Escalante CE	1683, 9200
First American (The) *	128 AHC		UH-1H	1971	slick	69-15534	v-nn			Johnson Tracey CE, Hoskie Etsitty DG, S. Tillotson AC	1801,
First Hoss	11 CAG	HHC	UH-1H	71-72	slick		NO	nose		Bob Bruce AC, Hill CE, Mason DG, CP James Hamlet	225, 1105, 1908, 4600

Copter Name	Unit	Unit #1	Aircraft	Circa	Function	Serial #	Config	Location	Artist	Crew	Contributors
Fixer (The)	498 Med Co		UH-1H	70-71	dustoff		NO	nose			184, 9430
Flaming Mime	116 AHC		UH-1H	1969	slick		NO	pilot door			1869, 9240
Flight To America	188 AHC		UH-1H	1968	slick	66-16221	NAA	pilot door		Geoff Handel AC, Wolfe CE, Moore DG	115, 686, 1266, 1849, 6275
Flintstone Flyer	B Co 25 Avn Bn		UH-1C	66-68	gun	66-15174	N+A	nose		Don Taylor DG, Earl Schmuck DG, Ed Lyons CE, Mark Kimm CE	49, 502, 909, 1060, 1562, 1751, 9120
Flower Power	45 Med Co		UH-1H	67-69	dustoff	66-16429	NO	nose		John Casper CE, Mark Kimm CE, Richardson	288, 378, 916
Flower Power	48 AHC		UH-1D	67-68	slick		N+A	nose			226, 9150
Flower Power	173 AHC		UH-1C	1968	gun	66-15169	N+A	pilot door		Richie Wolk CE	1461, 1908, 1948, 8450
Flower Power	176 AHC		UH-1H	1969	slick		NO				1595,
Flower Power	188 AHC		UH-1H	67-68	slick		NO				1024,
Flower Power	A Co 228 ASHB		CH-47A	67-69	cargo	66-19066	N+A	front fuselage		Robert Bartlett FE, Wade Kane DG, Foster CE, Bill Hughes	96, 813, 8025
Flower Power	A Trp 1/9		AH-1G	1969	gun		N+A	bpw		Swede Erickson AC	482, 9905
Flower Power	unk		UH-1C	68-69	gun		N+A	M-5 turret		J. O'Connor, Chuck Saunders	1908, 4600
Flower Power *	A Co 9 Avn Bn		UH-1D	1968	slick	66-16047	v-nn			Dennis McCullough CE	1134, 8525
Fly Delta's Big Jets	336 AHC	A/101	UH-1D	65-66	slick		NO	pilot door	Delta Airlines promo sticker	Jerry Turner	1812,
Fly Me	362 ASHC		CH-47A	1972	cargo	64-13157	NO	below DG window			1264,
Fly The Friendly Skies	B Co 159 ASHB		CH-47B	1968	cargo		NO	nose			1842, 7850
Fly The Friendly Skys	162 AHC		UH-1H	1971	slick		NO	nose		Boyter, Slay..	988, 6850
Flyin' Coffin	48 AHC		UH-1B	66-68	gun	64-14084	NO	nose		Oscar Hale CE	624, 680, 9150
Flying Alone (The)	B Trp 7/17		UH-1H	1970	slick		NO	nose		Purdum CE	681,
Flying Circus	B Trp 3/17		UH-1H	1970	slick		NO				728,
Flying Circus **	C Btry 2/20 ARA		AH-1G	70-71	gun	68-15183	AO	bpw		Jet Jackson AC, Wetsel CE, Bill Baskett AC	833, 1236, 1476, 1627, 1674, 9880

Copter Name	Unit	Unit #1	Aircraft	Circa	Function	Serial #	Config	Location	Artist	Crew	Contributors
Flying Circus **	F Btry 79 AFA		AH-1G	71-72	gun	68-15183	AO	bpw		Ernie Rickenbacker AC	833, 1236, 1476, 1627, 1674, 2010, 9880
Flying Circus (The)	21 Signal Group		UH-1H	69-70	slick		NO	nose		D. Baggott AC, Tom Higgerson DG, Doug Escher CE	331, 483, 748
Flying Coffin (The)	114 AHC		UH-1D	69-70	slick	64-13831	NO	nose		F. Stroebel, J. Sine, F. Akana	192, 1719, 6700, 9430
Flying Coffin (The)	174 AHC		UH-1D	67-68	slick	65-09621	N+A	doorpost		Whelan CE, Messinger AC, Pelliccia CE, Wheeler	1184, 1368, 9230
Flying Coffin (The)	A Co 228 ASHB		CH-47A	69-70	cargo		N+A	fuselage			475, 1451, 4050
Flying Conex (The)	147 ASHC		CH-47A	66-67	cargo		N+A	front fuselage			563, 1199, 7825
Flying Doily *	243 ASHC		CH-47A	68-69	cargo	002 or 008	v-nn				1722,
Flying Dutchman	A Co 227 AHB		UH-1H	1969	slick	68-15354	NO	nose		Dirk Appel	43, 1841, 9700
Flying Dutchman II	A Co 227 AHB		UH-1H	69-70	slick	68-15626	NO	nose		Dirk Appel, Hanna	43, 1841, 9700
Flying Fool	114 AHC		UH-1H	70-71	slick		NO	nose		Joe Akin	12,
Flying Hemorrhoid (The)	227 AHB	HHC	OH-6A	1968	scout	67-16286	NO	fuselage		Dennis Beckler CE	112,
Flying Jackass (The)	114 AHC		UH-1H	1970	slick	66-01036	NO	pilot door		O'Brien	1114,
Flying Leak *	147 ASHC		CH-47A	67-69	cargo	66-19034	v-nn	fuselage		Larry Smith FE, Paul Michelson CE, Helgason DG	1640,
Flying Miss Gail	A Trp 7/1		OH-6A	1971	scout		NO	doghouse			1426, 3375
Flying Nunn	C Btry 2/20 ARA		AH-1G	70-71	gun		NO	bpw			1236,
Flying Pig **	174 AHC		UH-1C	69-70	gun	66-15137	AO	cargo door window panel			69, 8450
Flying Scotsman (The)	117 AHC		UH-1D	68-69	slick		NO	nose			435, 1903, 9250
Flyin' Soul	C Co 227 AHB		UH-1H	1969	slick	67-17412	NAA	nose			112,
Flying Tank (The)	unk	Avn Co	UH-1B	64-65	gun		N+A	pilot door			2071,
For A Few Dollars More	114 AHC		UH-1H	1971	slick	67-17289	NO	nose		J. Arends, E. Espinoza, R. Perez, J. Stogner	484, 6700
For God, Country + Body Count	D Trp 3/4		OH-6A	1970	scout	68-17359	NO	doghouse		Carnathan AC, Steve Dobry DG, J. McGlothien CE, Dan Lohwassen AC	146, 194
For God, Country + Body Count	D Trp 3/4		OH-6A	71-72	scout	69-16003	NO	doghouse			422, 1117, 1282, 9855, 9865

Copter Name	Unit	Unit #1	Aircraft	Circa	Function	Serial #	Config	Location	Artist	Crew	Contributors
For God, Country + Body Count	F Trp 4 Cav		OH-6A	71-72	scout	69-16003	NO	doghouse			140, 422, 1117, 9855, 9865
For Sale	179 ASHC		CH-47A	68-69	cargo	65-08005	N+A	fuselage	Sam Smith	Sam Smith FE	1651,
For Sale	A Co 101 AHB		UH-1H	1971	slick		NO	windshield			1785, 9760
For Sale	B Co 158 AHB		UH-1H	1971	slick	67-17650	NO	nose	Brian Bailey	Tom Taylor CE, Holger Renken CE, Don Turney CE	1756, 7100
For The Love Of Freedom	F Trp 4 Cav		OH-6A	71-72	scout	67-16563	N+A	doghouse			422,
Foreign Aid	117 AHC	Avn Co	UH-1B	65-66	gun		NO	nose		P. Ron Hudak AC	805,
Forget Hell	335 AHC		UH-1H	69-70	slick		N+A	nose		Dennis Dupuis	453, 9590
Fornicator 44	188 AHC		UH-1H	67-68	slick		NO				414,
Four Balls *	189 AHC		UH-1H	1970	slick	69-15400	v-nn			Harold MacDonald DG	1065,
Foxey Lady	134 AHC		UH-1H	69-70	slick	68-16222	NO	nose		Dee Sessions CE, Roger Pierce CE	352, 1296, 1583, 9320
Foxey Lady	236 Med Det		UH-1H	1970	dustoff		NO	nose			490, 2044, 5025
Foxie Lady (The)	B Co 229 AHB		UH-1H	69-70	slick	68-16229	NO			Ron Carr CE	283, 9780
Foxy Lady	45 Med Co		UH-1H	1970	dustoff	66-17101	NO			D. Williams CE, Best MD, Ross MD, Crump MD	288, 1308, 1912, 7725
Foxy Lady	116 AHC		UH-1D	1969	slick		NO	nose		Kirk Farrell CP, Greg Fox CE	501, 8625
Foxy Lady	132 ASHC		CH-47B	69-70	cargo	67-18456	N+A	front pylon		Gordon Aleshire FE	395, 729, 2002, 2054, 3175, 5675, 7800
Foxy Lady	162 AHC		UH-1H	68-69	slick		NO	pilot door		Daniel Nieto CE, Harold Carden DG	275, 1295, 1666, 9390
Foxy Lady	190 AHC		UH-1H	69-70	slick	67-19528	NO	doorpost		Eugene Petra DG, Von Kenner CE	1385,
Foxy Lady	240 AHC		UH-1H	68-69	slick	66-16630	NO	nose	Leslie Higa	Dave Fox DG, Leslie Higa CE	552,
Foxy Lady	326 Med Bn		UH-1H	68-69	dustoff		NO	nose			288,
Foxy Lady	A Trp 3/17		UH-1H	69-70	slick	67-17841	NO	doghouse		McCalister CP, Charles Stutzman AC, Mike Scott CE	719, 1093, 1124, 9720
Foxy Lady II	116 AHC		UH-1H	1970	slick		NO	nose		Kirk Farrell AC, Greg Fox CE	501, 8625, 9240

Copter Name	Unit	Unit #1	Aircraft	Circa	Function	Serial #	Config	Location	Artist	Crew	Contributors
Fred's Flying Fool	93 TC	121 AHC	CH-21C	62-63	lift		NO	fuselage			1314,
Free And Easy	129 AHC		UH-1H	1969	slick		NO	nose			1266, 1451, 1451, 4050, 6275, 9310
Free Huey	116 AHC		UH-1H	1971	slick		NO	nose			8425,
Free Huey	C Btry 2/20 ARA		AH-1G	70-71	gun		NO				154,
Freedom Bird *	135 AHC		UH-1H	1971	slick	70-15747	v-nn			James Wingrove DG, Harry Douglas CE	1936,
Freedom Bird	335 AHC		UH-1H	69-70	slick	66-16704	N+A	nose			695, 897, 1926
Frenchie	B Co 228 ASHB		CH-47A	66-67	cargo	66-00069	NO			James Kee FE	885, 8025
Frenchy's Folly	188 AHC		UH-1H	1967	slick		NO	pilot door			1322,
Friar Tuck ^	173 AHC	408 TC	UH-1D	67-68	maint	65-09598	NO	pilot door		John Jackson CE Frank Gabean CE, Durska AC, French (test pilot)	232, 834, 2001, 8675, 8925
Friar Tuck (#2) ^	173 AHC	408 TC	UH-1D	69-70	maint	66-00958	NO			Frank Prevost CE, Wayne Perrin	232, 593, 1266, 1375, 1422, 4125, 6125
Friday's Child	117 AHC		UH-1H	67-68	slick		NO			Butch LaRoue AC	127,
Friday's Child	188 AHC		UH-1H	67-68	slick		N+A	pilot door			1024, 1178, 1266, 6275, 9480
Friday's Child	A Trp 7/1		OH-6A	1971	scout		NO				9895,
Friday's Child II	A Trp 7/1		OH-6A	71-72	scout	69-16061	NO	doghouse			8650,
Friendly Persuasion	336 AHC		UH-1B	68-69	gun		NO	pilot door			668, 9610
Friendship 8	8 TC	117 AHC	CH-21C	1962	lift	56-02075	NO	fuselage		Charles Burns CE	1252,
Frito Bandito	116 AHC		UH-1D	1970	slick	66-01021	NO	nose		L. Pickett AC, R. Salamond CP, Murphy DG, Juan Garcia CE	87, 90, 584, 1020, 9240
Frito Bandito	132 ASHC		CH-47B	70-71	cargo	66-19108	NO	fuselage	Francis Wadginski	Perez FE, Fox	1843, 3850, 7800
Frito Bandito	174 AHC		UH-1H	70-71	slick	69-15767	N+A	nose	Keith Jarrett	Keith Jarett CE	623, 842, 1568, 9430
Frito Bandito	B Co 228 ASHB		CH-47A	70-71	cargo		N+A	fuselage		Pat Glass AC	616,
Frito Bandito (The)	247 Med Det		UH-1H	1969	dustoff		NO			Chet Crump MD, Ray Alvarez CE	376,

Copter Name	Unit	Unit #1	Aircraft	Circa	Function	Serial #	Config	Location	Artist	Crew	Contributors
Frito Bandito II	116 AHC		UH-1H	70-71	slick		NO	nose		Juan Garcia CE	584,
Frito Bandito II	174 AHC		UH-1H	1971	slick	68-16573	N+A	nose		Jarett CE, Boston AC, Oshrio DG	9430,
FTA	92 AHC		UH-1C	1968	gun hog		NO	nose			1811,
FTA	188 AHC		UH-1H	1968	slick	66-16221	NAA	pilot door		Geoff Handel AC, Wolfe CE, Moore DG	115, 686, 1024, 1266, 1849, 6275
Fuck Communism	C Trp 1/9		UH-1B	1969	gun	62-02053	NO	rocket pod			9805,
Fuck It Just Fuck It	176 AHC		UH-1M	1971	gun	66-00618	NO	belly	Garry Roberts	Garry Roberts CE	1486,
Fuck The Cong	68 AHC		UH-1C	68-69	gun		NO	rocket pod			1635, 9200
Fugitive	C-159 ASHB		CH-47C	69-70	cargo	67-18499	NO	fuselage		Brockmeier AC, Sleight AC, Grauff CP, Jones CE, Ranieri DG	2040,
Fugitive Angel (The)	B Co 101 AHB		UH-1C	67-68	gun		NO	pilot door		Tom Wood AC	493, 1953, 5025
Fujimo	61 AHC		UH-1H	1968	slick		NO			Carl Vereen AC	1829,
Full House	117 AHC	Avn Co	UH-1B	63-64	gun		NO	gun pod			1397, 6805
Fulton's Folly	93 TC	121 AHC	CH-21C	1963	lift		N+A	fuselage			1828, 9290
Fur Burger II	173 AHC		UH-1H	68-69	slick		N+A	pilot door		Roger Dubs AC	694, 1455, 1461
Furgs + Beans	15 Med Bn		UH-1H	1971	medevac		NO			Ron Huether	808,
Gail	174 AHC		UH-1H	69-70	slick	68-15223	NO	nose		Hank Dorn CE, John Bailey AC, Sammy Sours CE	67, 9430
Gail Sue	170 AHC		UH-1C	1969	gun		NO	nose			1543, 9400
Gallopin Goose HC	A Co 228 ASHB		CH-47A	67-69	cargo	66-19092	N+A	front fuselage	Jim Rowe	Russ Seelig FE, Mike Killarney CE	475, 1451, 1582, 4050, 8050
Gallopin Guns	11 ACR		AH-1G	68-69	gun	67-15636	NO	bpw		Bruce Eaton CE, Brown AC	462, 1053, 1448, 1708, 4825, 8625
Gang Bang	187 AHC		AH-1G	1971	gun	66-15297	NO	nose			1700, 1954
Gang Green	187 AHC		AH-1G	70-71	gun		NO			Carroll Thompson CE	1769, 9470
Gara Ce Buela	175 AHC		UH-1D	68-69	slick	66-01189	NO	nose		Dan Isenberg AC, Williams CE, Wisneski CE	829,

Copter Name	Unit	Unit #1	Aircraft	Circa	Function	Serial #	Config	Location	Artist	Crew	Contributors
Gator Recovery ^	119 AHC	545 TC	UH-1H	1970	maint	68-16539	N+A	nose		Carl Brader CE	176, 741, 9270, 9910
Genghis	A Trp 7/17		OH-6A	1967	scout	65-12973	NO	doghouse		Bright, Ehrhardt, Young	1972, 6250, 9730
Genocide	F Btry 79 AFA		AH-1G	71-72	gun	68-15147	NO	bpw		Steve Hartnett CE, Bruce Stotler CE, Snow AC	730, 850, 1711
George Of The Jungle	11 ACR		AH-1G	71-72	gun		NO	bpw			1467, 1674, 5400, 5427
George Of The Jungle	114 AHC		UH-1H	69-70	slick		NO	doorpost			2090,
Georgia Boy	114 AHC	Avn Co	UH-1B	64-65	gun		NO	rocket pod			1103, 6650, 6700
Georgia Peach	45 Med Co		UH-1H	1968	dustoff		NO				1040,
Georgia Peach (The)	121 AHC		UH-1D	66-67	slick	64-13664	N+A	nose		Gary Dowler CP, Roy Amerson CE	437, 831, 9290
Geronimo	128 AHC		UH-1B	66-67	gun		NO	pilot door			402, 4825
Get Bent	B Co 228 ASHB		CH-47A	1969	cargo		N+A	front fuselage			475, 903
Ghost (The)	D Co 227 AHB		AH-1G	69-70	gun	69-16442	NO				113,
Ghost (The)	254 Med Det		UH-1H	1969	dustoff	67-17587	NO	pilot door		Robinson CE, Greg Habits CE, Richard Lindekens AC	954,
Ghost Rider	362 ASHC		CH-47A	1972	cargo	66-19038	NO	fuselage		Longman CP, Tarpley AC, Luz DG, Dan Lawrence FE	986, 8125
Ghost Rider	D Trp 3/4		OH-6A	70-71	scout		NO	doghouse		Chuck Poulous	1282,
Ghost Rider (The)	82 Med Det		UH-1D	1965	dustoff		NO	cargo door window panel		Ernie Sylvester AC	812, 1742, 7750
Ghost Rider II	D Trp 3/4		OH-6A	70-71	scout		NO	doghouse		Chuck Poulous	1282,
Ghost Rider III	D Trp 3/4		OH-6A	69-70	scout		NO	doghouse		Chuck Poulous	1282,
Ghost Rider III1/2	D Trp 3/4		OH-6A	70-71	scout		NO	doghouse		Chuck Poulous	1282,
Ghost Rider In The Sky	B Co 25 Avn Bn		AH-1G	68-70	gun		NO	doghouse			134, 5450, 9120
Ghost Ship (The) *	48 AHC		UH-1B	1966	gun	702	v-nn				2045, 5975
Ghost Writer	114 AHC		UH-1H	68-69	slick		NO				1639, 6700

Give Blood: *C Troop 1/9 Cav, OH-6A, (sn 68-17220), 1970-71. Before being lost on 3-17-71, "Give Blood" accumulated 611 in-country hours. Shark teeth on C-1-9 Loaches were unique in-country feature among Army OH-6A's. Photo by Bruce Campbell.*

Copter Name	Unit	Unit #1	Aircraft	Circa	Function	Serial #	Config	Location	Artist	Crew	Contributors
Giddy Up Go	179 ASHC		CH-47A	68-69	cargo	64-13122	N+A	front fuselage	Roy Jacobs, Dave Halder	Roy Jacobs DG/CE/FE, Dave Halder FE	837, 7900
Gidy-Up Go	116 AHC		UH-1D	1967	slick	66-16148	NO	pilot door			852,
Give Blood	C Trp 1/9		OH-6A	70-71	scout	68-17220	NO	fuselage		Bruce Campbell AC	271, 1003
Give Peace A Chance	162 AHC		UH-1H	71-72	slick		NO	nose		M. Weatherly AC, Rampell CE, J. Christenson DG	1426,
Gladiator	175 AHC		UH-1H	69-70	slick		NO				1891, 6805
Gladiator (The)	C Trp 16 Cav		AH-1G	1972	gun	68-17074	NO	bpw		Dan Shaver	134, 1205, 5450
Glamdring The Foe-Hammer	B Trp 1/9		AH-1G	1969	gun	68-15188	NO	bpw		L. J. Babyak AC, Ken Luse CP	259, 1054
Glass Onion	57 AHC		UH-1C	69-70	gun		NO	nose		William Woolley CE	1959,
Glenda	D Trp 1/1		UH-1H	68-69	slick	67-17330	NO	doorpost		Al Brittingham CE	203, 1760, 9835
Gloria	134 AHC		UH-1H	69-70	slick	68-16145	NO	nose		Ray Torres CE	1798,
Gloria	170 AHC		UH-1C	68-69	gun		NO	nose	Bob Snead	Doug MacDougall AC	1066, 1543, 9400
Gloria	B Co 229 AHB		UH-1H	1968	slick	66-16731	NO	nose		Frank Amavisca CE, Charles Harrington AC	492, 994, 8625, 9780
Goat (The)	1 Bde 1 Cav Div		UH-1H	1970	C+C	68-15722	N+A	pilot door			704, 8975
God Is My Co-Pilot	129 AHC		UH-1M	1971	gun		N+A	bulkhead cover-interior			1415,
God Of Hell Fire	48 AHC		UH-1C	70-71	gun		NO	nose		Russ Cowley CP	228, 355, 716, 832, 9150
God Of Hell Fire	134 AHC		UH-1H	1970	slick		NO				1895, 9320
God Of Hell Fire	135 AHC		UH-1C	69-70	gun		NO	pilot door		Mike Guard CE	665,
God Of Hellfire	B Trp 2/17		AH-1G	69-70	gun		NO	bpw			910,
God Of Hell's Fire	A Btry 4/77 ARA		UH-1C	1969	gun		NO	nose			1067,
God Of Hell's Fire (The)	336 AHC		UH-1C	68-69	gun	66-15206	N+A	pilot door		Harold Jones AC, Charlie Bendel CP	867, 9610
Godfather	A Trp 7/1		AH-1G	1970	gun		NO	bpw	downtown Vinh Long artist	Ken Larcher CE, Jim Baker AC	971,

Copter Name	Unit	Unit #1	Aircraft	Circa	Function	Serial #	Config	Location	Artist	Crew	Contributors
God's Will	B Trp 1/9		UH-1H	70-71	slick	69-15106	NO			John Gruber	1208,
God's Will	C Co 229 AHB		UH-1H	71-72	slick		NO				803,
Gold Finger	271 ASHC		CH-47A	1971	cargo	66-19007	NO	nose	Dave Fesmire	Dave Fesmire CE	521, 8100
Gold Knight **	114 AHC		UH-1H	69-70	slick		v-nnp	nose		Joe Papapietro AC, John Smith CP	301, 9230
Golden	176 AHC		UH-1H	68-69	slick	67-17592	NO			Mike Hilton CE, Roger Mothersbaugh AC	751, 9450
Goldfinger	39 Signal Bn		UH-1B	1966	slick	63-08007	NO	pilot door		Lester Heath AC	265,
Goldfinger	180 ASHC		CH-47A	1967	cargo	65-08007	NO			Barr AC, McBeath CP	80,
Goldfinger	B Co 4 Avn Bn		UH-1C	1967	gun	65-09541	NO	doorpost			1614,
Goldfinger **	147 ASHC		CH-47A	67-68	cargo	66-19007	AO	fuselage		J. C. Goodlove AC, S. Taylor CP	264, 1272, 7825
Goliath	A Trp 7/1		AH-1G	71-72	gun		NO			Larry Brown CE	217,
Golieth	498 Med Co		UH-1H	1968	dustoff	66-17025	NO	nose		Charles Gallipeau CE	578, 875
Gonin' Hot	A Trp 3/17		OH-58A	1971	scout	68-16946	NO	doghouse		Tom Knuckey AC, Philip Taylor DG	1206, 4850
Good (The)	371 RRC		UH-1H	68-69	slick		NO	nose			1286,
Good Grief	132 ASHC		CH-47B	69-70	cargo		N+A	front fuselage	Mark Pearlstein	Mark Pearlstein CE	1162, 1362, 1588, 7800
Good Ship Lollipop	D Trp 3-5		UH-1C	1968	gun		NO				509,
Good Ship Lollipop (The)	117 AHC		UH-1H	1971	slick	67-17382	NO	nose			1552,
Good Ship Lollipop (The)	132 ASHC		CH-47B	1969	cargo	67-18451	N+A	front fuselage		Alan Cleaver DG	1275, 7800
Good The Bad And The Ugly (The)	61 AHC		UH-1C	1968	gun	66-15008	NO				1829,
Good The Bad And The Ugly (The)	68 Med Det		UH-1H	70-71	dustoff	68-16335	NO			Dirty Ernie CE, Carlos Solis MD	1661, 7725
Good The Bad And The Ugly (The)	179 ASHC		CH-47C	69-70	cargo		NO				943,
Good The Bad And The Ugly (The)	B Trp 1/9		OH-6A	1969	scout	67-16243	NO	fuselage		Ron Kenerson	898,
Good Times	61 AHC		UH-1C	1971	gun		NO	nose			69,

Good Vibrations*: C Troop 1/9 Cav, UH-1C, Phuoc Vinh, 1970-71.* The smooth, un-riveted surfaces of rocket launchers seemed to beckon painted renderings. Photo by Ben Lipford.

Copter Name	Unit	Unit #1	Aircraft	Circa	Function	Serial #	Config	Location	Artist	Crew	Contributors
Good Vibrations	116 AHC		UH-1C	68-69	gun	66-00661	NO	pilot door		Dave Nancarrow CE	1273,
Good Vibrations	119 AHC		UH-1H	1969	slick	66-16834	NO	nose		M. Bonhuis AC, G. Eggleston DG, Bob Kilpatrick CE	908, 9270
Good Vibrations	132 ASHC		CH-47B	70-71	cargo	67-18438	N+A	front fuselage	SP4 Davis did all '70-'71a/c art		184, 1162, 1266, 7800, 8275, 9430
Good Vibrations	134 AHC		UH-1H	69-70	slick	67-19487	NO	nose			352, 1818
Good Vibrations	170 AHC		UH-1H	1967	slick	66-16219	NO	pilot door		Bob Leopold AC, Merle MacDougal CE	1012,
Good Vibrations	175 AHC		UH-1H	70-71	slick		NO	nose		F. Effenberger AC, Calvin Walls CE, B.Fryant CP, Mike Barter CE '69-'70	94, 467, 1926, 8650
Good Vibrations	179 ASHC		CH-47	69-70	cargo		NO			Mike Rubalcava DG	1522, 7900
Good Vibrations	200 ASHC		CH-47A	67-68	cargo	66-00102	NO	front fuselage	Larry Dumford		995, 1195, 7950, 8275
Good Vibrations	242 ASHC		CH-47A	70-71	cargo	64-13130	NO	nose			1199, 1932
Good Vibrations	B Btry 2/20 ARA		AH-1G	70-71	gun		NO				154, 804
Good Vibrations	B Co 228 ASHB		CH-47A	1968	cargo	66-19064	N+A	fuselage		Gary Stefanini FE	903, 1687, 8275
Good Vibrations	C Co 229 AHB		UH-1H	69-71	slick	66-16816	NO	nose		Edward Dale Griffths CE, Bob McAleer DG	657, 1816
Good Vibrations	C Trp 1/9		UH-1C	70-71	gun		NO	rocket pod			1025, 9805
Good Widow Mrs. Jones (The)	121 AHC		UH-1B	68-69	gun	63-08733	N+A	nose	VN artist	Mike Cusick CE, Rick Thomas AC	306, 768, 1768, 5625
Good Widow Mrs. Jones (The)	121 AHC		UH-1D	67-68	slick	65-09777	N+A	nose	VN artist	Rick Thomas AC, Chris Chrisafully CE, Mike Shakocius CP	395, 439, 477, 1593, 1768, 4825, 5675, 5725
Goodbye Charlie	A Trp 3/17		UH-1C	67-69	gun	66-15028	NO	nose		James Preston CE, John Meadow AC, Tim Wright CP	1421,
Goodship Lollipop (The)	92 AHC		UH-1H	1968	slick	66-16462	NAA	nose	Richard Balsimo	Vinnie Dilworth CE	96, 423, 931, 1339, 9220
Goodship Lollipop II (The)	D Trp 3/5		AH-1G	1968	gun	67-15550	N+A			Tony Ziemeckie AC, James Feltner CE	509, 9860
Goofy **	132 ASHC		CH-47B	70-71	cargo	67-18447	AO	fuselage	SP4 Davis did all '70-'71 a/c art	Bill McRae CP	392, 1162, 2062, 7800
Gook Spook	187 AHC		UH-1D	1967	slick	66-00829	NO			Tom Martin CP, Jorgensen CE, Hudec DG	1100, 4550
Gook Stomper	147 ASHC		CH-47A	67-68	cargo		N+A	front fuselage			189, 396, 563, 7825
Goose (The)	33 TC	118 AHC	CH-21C	1962	lift		N+A	fuselage			1285, 9260

Copter Name	Unit	Unit #1	Aircraft	Circa	Function	Serial #	Config	Location	Artist	Crew	Contributors
Goose (The)	57 TC	120 AHC	CH-21C	1963	lift		N+A	fuselage			1975, 6525
Got Ya	237 Med Det		UH-1H	70-71	dustoff		NO	belly			1094,
Gotterdammerung	57 AHC		UH-1H	71-72	nighthawk	68-15591	N+A	nose			314,
Grace	119 AHC		UH-1H	67-70	slick		NO	nose			741, 9270
Grace Slick	48 AHC		UH-1H	68-69	slick	67-17240	NO	nose		Sheldon Reyher AC	120, 1463, 9150
Grace Slick	135 AHC		UH-1H	1971	slick	69-15374	NO			James Wingrove CE	1936,
Graduate (The)	187 AHC		UH-1H	1970	slick	66-16415	NO	nose			652,
Grand Funk Airways	C Co 229 AHB		UH-1H	70-71	slick	68-15772	NO	nose		Kelly Simonette CE	199, 803, 1616, 1816, 9830
Grampa Chicken	A Co 227 AHB		UH-1H	70-71	slick	68-16479	N+A	nose	Joe Paranal	Dave Fairweather AC, Halliday	1340, 1793, 9700
Granny Goose	132 ASHC		CH-47B	69-70	cargo		N+A	front fuselage			729, 1162, 7800
Granny Twitchett	178 ASHC		CH-47A	66-67	cargo	65-08010	N+A	front fuselage	Bob Telford DG	Joe Hawkins CE '66-'67, Dean Nelson CE '67-'68, Bob Means FE, Bob Telford DG	4050, 8360
Grateful Dead	68 Med Det		UH-1H	69-70	dustoff		NO			Wayne Marshall MD, George Cavin CE	1095,
Grave Digger (The)	281 AHC		UH-1C	67-68	gun		NO			H. Wetmore	946, 1893, 9550
Gray Ghost	175 AHC		UH-1H	69-70	slick		NO			Cliff Gaston CE	594,
Gray Rider	11 ACR		AH-1G	71-72	gun	68-15083	NO	bpw			652, 1417, 1746,4825, 6850
Great Green Vaseline War Machine (The)	45 Med Co		UH-1H	70-71	dustoff		NO	cargo door		Billy Talley CE	1746,
Great Green Vaseline War Machine (The)	498 Med Co		UH-1H	67-68	dustoff		NO	pilot door		Billy Talley CE	1746,
Great Hunter	71 AHC		UH-1C	66-68	gun hog	66-00510	NO			Mike Rogers CE	1502,
Great Pumpkin (The)	A Co 1 Avn Bn		UH-1B	65-66	gun		N+A	M-5 turret			1016,
Great Speckled Bird (The)	68 Med Det		UH-1H	70-71	dustoff	67-17629	NO	nose	Don Wildsmith	Carl Prince CE, Don Wildsmith CE, Carlos Solis MD, Don Wildsmith CE	1425, 1661, 1866, 7725, 8625
Great Spekled Bird (The)	C Trp 16 Cav		AH-1G	70-71	gun	67-15798	NO	bpw		George Hawkins AC, Jack Vick CE	714, 1835

Copter Name	Unit	Unit #1	Aircraft	Circa	Function	Serial #	Config	Location	Artist	Crew	Contributors
Great White Leader	162 AHC		UH-1H	1968	slick		NO	nose		Tom Bryan CE	714, 1835, 9390
Greatful Dead (The)	175 AHC		UH-1C	70-71	gun		N+A	pilot door		Bob Kelly DG	467, 1926, 8650
Green Dragon	147 ASHC		CH-47A	1969	cargo	65-07980	N+A	front fuselage			8275,
Green Eyed Lady	180 ASHC		CH-47C	72-73	cargo	68-15853	NO			Rick Verity FE	1830,
Green Hornet	1 Bde 1 Cav Div		UH-1D	1967	slick		NO	nose		Charles Barone CE	123, 2034, 8975
Green Machine	B Trp 1/9		OH-6A	69-70	scout		NO		Mike Jones		872, 9905
Green Meanie	D Trp 1/4		AH-1G	68-70	gun		N+A	bpw		Bill Church AC, John Loftice, Mike Cassidy	195,
Green Messiah (The)	B Co 158 AHB		UH-1H	1969	slick	67-17653	NO	doorpost		Dave Mussey CE	1265,
Green Monster	200 ASHC		CH-47A	67-68	cargo	66-00099	N+A		Larry Dumford		995, 1195, 1585
Green Speckled Bird (The)	33 TC	118 AHC	CH-21C	62-63	lift	55-04155	NO	fuselage	Paul Beck	Paul Beck CE, Gragido DG	109, 185, 1926
Green Weenie	283 Med Det		UH-1H	67-68	dustoff	66-17005	NO	nose			1638, 9670
Green Weenie (The)	C Trp 1/9		OH-6A	1971	scout	69-15996	N+A	fuselage		Bob Lemaster, Davis Drews, Randy Kekar	1003,
Gremlin (The)	D Co 227 AHB		AH-1G	69-70	gun	67-15803	NO				113, 301, 5275
Gremlin's Castle	242 ASHC		CH-47A	68-71	cargo		NO				1056, 1199
Gremlin's Castle	A Trp 7/1	370 TC	UH-1H	70-71	maint		NO			J. D. Huss AC	818,
Grey Ghost	128 AHC		UH-1H	70-71	slick	68-15724	NO			Dan Bowser AC	165,
Greyhound No Fuckin Slack	176 AHC		UH-1D	1967	C+C	65-10052	N+A	nose		Dale Wiese CE	1905, 9450
Grim Reaper	48 AHC		UH-1C	68-69	gun		NO	nose		Will Stafford, Richard Richards	1676, 9150
Grim Reaper	68 AHC		UH-1C	67-68	gun	65-09487	NO	M-5 turret		John Morgan CE, Sandy Noyes CE, John Frasso CE, Robert King DG	69, 648, 1304, 1683, 1883, 2075, 9200
Grim Reaper	135 AHC		UH-1C	67-68	gun hog	66-15075	N+A	pilot door			3, 322, 9330
Grim Reaper	155 AHC		UH-1C	1968	gun	66-15049	NO	nose		Dennis LaJoie CE	157, 960

Copter Name	Unit	Unit #1	Aircraft	Circa	Function	Serial #	Config	Location	Artist	Crew	Contributors
Grim Reaper	174 AHC		UH-1M	70-71	gun	65-09540	N+A	quarter panel		Stefan, Kauffman, Kline, Thompson	16, 233, 278, 403, 592, 896,1611, 1770, 9210, 9430
Grim Reaper ***	175 AHC		UH-1C	67-69	gun	66-15045	N+A	pilot door		Pappy Martin AC, Ed Timmers CE, Roger Anderson	15, 35, 932, 1493, 1670, 1787, 1926, 6475, 9520
Grim Reaper (The)	176 AHC		UH-1C	67-70	gun	66-00605	NO	nose		Rod Clutter CE, Blom AC, Ococha DG, Appeal DG, Evens DG	312, 1987, 9450
Grim Reaper	187 AHC		UH-1H	70-71	slick	69-15674	NO	nose		Doug Hoselton CE, Mike Mann CE, Mike Babb AC, Gonzales CE	62, 125, 794, 1932, 1908, 1954, 3300, 9470
Grim Reaper	A Trp 1/9		UH-1C	1967	gun		NO	nose		Matthew Lawless	985, 4700
Grim Reaper	C Btry 2/20 ARA		AH-1G	70-71	gun	68-15183	N+A	bpw	McMillan	Jet Jackson AC, Wetsel CE, Bill Baskett AC	833, 1111, 1236, 1627, 1674, 2014, 9880
Grim Reaper	C Trp 16 Cav		AH-1G	72-73	gun	68-17074	NO				1205,
Grim Reaper	F Btry 79 AFA		AH-1G	71-72	gun	68-15183	NO	bpw		Jet Jackson AC, Wetsel CE	833, 1627, 1908, 9710
Grim Reaper (The)	11 ACR		AH-1G	68-69	gun		NO	bpw			1703,
Grim Reaper (The)	68 Med Det		UH-1H	70-71	dustoff	68-16674	NO			Ralph Murray CE	1866, 7725
Grim Reaper (The)	114 AHC		UH-1H	69-70	slick	67-17186	N+A	doorpost		David Barnett AC, Carl Crisp CE, Paul Van Duyne DG	2090,
Grim Reaper (The)	192 AHC		UH-1C	67-69	gun	66-15070	NO			Dan Burns CE, Bill Burns DG, Darell Koenig AC	246, 343, 621, 9510
Grim Reaper (The)	B Trp 7/1		UH-1	1968			NO			Barry Farber DG	498, 9895
Grim Reaper (The) **	C Trp 1/9		UH-1H	1970	slick		AO	nose		Sam Hinch AC	752,
Grim Reaper II ***	175 AHC		UH-1C	1968	gun		N+A	pilot door		Roger Anderson CE	35,
Grunt	135 AHC		UH-1H	1969	slick		N+A	nose		Thomas Staadt CP	1675,
Grunt	155 AHC		UH-1C	1970	gun		NO	doorpost			69, 1685
Grunt Wagon	B Co 227 AHB		UH-1H	1969	slick		NO	nose			1226, 4350
Grunt Wagon (The)	A Co 228 ASHB		CH-47A	67-68	cargo	66-19041	NO	front fuselage		Larry Costley FE, Jerry Pierce CE	813, 1239, 8025, 8275
Grunt's Angel	134 AHC		UH-1H	68-71	slick		NO				352, 1818
Gun Slick (The) *	128 AHC		UH-1D	1967	slick	65-09576	v-nn			Bob Codney AC, Ed Ewing CP, Bill McDonald CE	1138, 9300
Gunfighters ^	B Trp 1/9		UH-1B	1965	gun		N+A	nose		Bobby Zahn AC	535, 770, 1964
Gunky	C Trp 1/9		UH-1H	1968	slick	66-16617	NO			Leo Salazar CE, Don Sargent DG	1536,

Copter Name	Unit	Unit #1	Aircraft	Circa	Function	Serial #	Config	Location	Artist	Crew	Contributors
Gunky	C Trp 2/17		UH-1H	70-71	slick	67-17700	NO			Ricky Miller CE, Glenn Dooley AC	1202, 4950, 8850
Guns + Ammo	114 AHC		UH-1C	1967	gun	66-00661	NO			Adams, D. Carlson, Richardson, C. Claggett	6700, 7095
Guns A-Go-Go *	1 Avn Det		ACH-47A	66-68	gun		NO	fuselage			301, 566, 903, 1266, 1726, 1898, 4600, 5200, 5575, 6100, 6275, 6300, 8025, 8275, 8300
Guns A-Go-Go	11 ACR		AH-1G	68-69	gun		NO	bpw			8625,
Guns A-Go-Go *	53 Avn Det		ACH-47A	66-68	gun		NO	fuselage			301, 566, 903, 1266, 1726, 1898, 4600, 5200, 5575, 6100, 6275, 6300, 8025, 8275, 8300
Guns Are For Bums	C Co 227 AHB		UH-1H	1968	slick		N+A	windshield		Milton Lesemann CP	656, 1013
Gunsmoke	128 AHC		UH-1H	1969	smoke	66-16544	NO	nose		Roly Lavaller AC, Doc Nielsen CE, Bob Reed CE, Glover DG	2081, 8625, 9300
Gutless Wonder (The)	121 AHC		UH-1D	66-67	slick		NO	nose		Rowe CE, G. Dowler CP	437,
Gypsy Moth	119 AHC		UH-1H	69-70	slick		N+A	nose			1325,
Hair	498 Med Co		UH-1H	70-71	dustoff	66-16063	NO	nose		Jerry Paul CE, Dennis Parker MD	1357, 7700
Hammerhead	F Trp 8 Cav		AH-1G	1972	gun	68-15054	NAA	bpw	Neal Thompson	Neal Thompsom AC, Dwayne Shirley CP	1361, 1773, 4825, 6350
Hang On Snoopy	339 TC		CH-37B	1965	lift		N+A	fuselage			395, 1053, 4600, 5675, 6025
Hangar Queen *	114 AHC	Avn Co	UH-1B	1964	slick	62-01961	v-nn			Wes Dunn CE	451,
Hangar Queen *	188 AHC		UH-1H	67-68	slick	66-16127	v-nn				1024,
Hangar Queen *	191 AHC		UH-1H	68-69	slick	725	NO				1570,
Hangar Queen	213 ASHC		CH-47C	71-72	cargo		N+A				998,
Hangar Queen	283 Med Det		UH-1D	1967	dustoff	65-09568	NO	nose		Tom Anglin CE	39,
Hangar Queen	B Co 123 Avn Bn		UH-1H	71-72	slick		NO	tailboom		Johnson CE	1073,
Hangar Queen (The)	D Trp 1/10		UH-1D	1970	slick	66-16614	NO	doorpost			977, 9840
Hangar Queen Abortion (The)	B Co 228 ASHB		CH-47A	68-69	cargo	66-19036	NO	fuselage	Lloyd A. Judd	Cliff Morley FE	1239, 3825
Happiness Is A Warm Gun	192 AHC		UH-1C	1971	gun	66-00597	N+A	doorpost		John Arthur CE, Fred Solis DG, Prince CP, Whitney AC	1901,
Happiness Is A Warm Gun	B Co 9 Avn Bn		AH-1G	1969	gun	67-15815	NO	bpw		Robert Schultz AC, Alewire CE	134, 1451, 4050, 5450

Hawaii Five-O: *B Btry 2/20 ARA, AH-1G, (sn 68-15110), Song Be, 1970-71.* Survived VN after serving in three different units with 2,185 total flight hours. Photo by Paula Huckleberry.

Copter Name	Unit	Unit #1	Aircraft	Circa	Function	Serial #	Config	Location	Artist	Crew	Contributors
Happy Hippie	147 ASHC		CH-47A	1968	cargo	66-00074	N+A	removable panel		Jim Call, John Long	264, 7825, 8275
Happy Ship (The)	unk		UH-1				N+A	nose			1908, 4600
Hard Luck	A Co 227 AHB		UH-1H	70-71	slick	67-19523	NO	nose		Gary Bridges AC	197,
Hardcore	175 AHC		UH-1D	68-69	slick		NO	nose		Dennis Iannazzo AC, Hamilton CE	825,
Harley (The) *	F Trp 9 Cav		OH-6A	1972	scout	69-15999	v-nn			Paul Murtha AC	1264,
Harvy	121 AHC		UH-1D	67-68	slick		N+A	nose			477, 4825, 6975, 9290
Haulin' Ash	11 ACR		UH-1H	71-72	slick		NO				1467,
Have A Nice Day	A Trp 3/17		AH-1G	70-71	gun	68-17044	N+A	turret		Mike Billow AC, Dennis Diamond CE	142,
Have Axes Will Travel	611 TC		CH-21C	1963	maint		NO				1975, 6500, 6525
Have Chicken Will Travel	A Co 227 AHB		UH-1H	70-71	slick	69-15529	N+A	nose	Joe Paranal	Bateman, Keefe	562, 1793, 9700
Have Chicken-Leg Will Travel	A Co 227 AHB		UH-1H	69-70	slick	68-16155	N+A	nose			562,
Have Gun Will Travel	11 ACR		AH-1G	68-69	gun		NO	bpw			134, 1703, 8400
Have Gun Will Travel	134 AHC		UH-1C	68-71	gun		NO				352, 1818
Have Gun Will Travel **	174 AHC		UH-1C	1970	gun	65-09507	AO	nose			184, 278, 1770, 9430
Have Gun Will Travel	192 AHC		UH-1C	67-69	gun	66-15094	NO	nose		Roman Kuchar DG, Joe Revera CE	301, 319, 343, 948, 5150, 9510
Have Gun Will Travel	A Trp 2/17		AH-1G	1971	gun	67-15572	NO	bpw			134, 8400
Have Gun Will Travel	C Btry 2/20 ARA		UH-1B	1966	gun	64-14040	NO	pilot door		Jerry Barnes CP, Gene Matocha AC, T. Ratliff CE, J. Muldrow DG	88, 301, 1181, 1266, 1876, 5175, 6050, 6225
Have Guns Will Travel	128 AHC		UH-1B	65-67	gun	64-14008	NO	pilot door			989, 1823
Have Guns Will Travel	129 AHC		UH-1B	66-68	gun	64-13929	NO			Randy Burnett CE	243, 9310
Hawaii	57 AHC		UH-1H	71-72	slick	67-17352	NO	nose		Milton Caspillo CE	420, 696, 9180
Hawaii	B Co 123 Avn Bn		OH-6A	70-71	scout	69-15997	NO	doghouse			1925, 9750

Copter Name	Unit	Unit #1	Aircraft	Circa	Function	Serial #	Config	Location	Artist	Crew	Contributors
Hawaii Five-O	B Btry 2/20 ARA		AH-1G	70-71	gun	68-15110	NO	bpw		M. F. O'Keefe AC	804, 850
Hawaii Kai	82 Med Det		UH-1D	64-65	dustoff		NO	nose			2071,
Hawaiian (The)	D Co 227 AHB		AH-1G	1969	gun	67-15803	N+A	bpw			34, 555
Hawaiian Eye	15 Med Bn		UH-1H	70-71	medevac	67-17822	N+A	nose + pilot door		Damien Vierra CE, Koisin CE	1837,
Hawaiian Punch	57 AHC		UH-1C	70-71	gun		NO			Calvin Blankenship	147, 9180
Hawaiian Samurai	334 AWC		AH-1G	71-72	gun	67-15494	NO				1674,
Hawk (The)	176 AHC		UH-1C	67-70	gun	66-00605	NO	nose		Rod Clutter CE	312, 1987, 9450
Hawk (The)	D Trp 1/1		AH-1G	68-69	gun		N+A	bpw			1864, 3450
Hawk Eye	117 AHC	Avn Co	UH-1B	65-67	slick		NO	nose			884, 9250
Hawkeye	121 AHC		UH-1D	66-68	slick		N+A	nose			437, 831
Head Hunter	71 AHC		UH-1D	1968	slick	65-10021	NO	nose		Jim Miller AC	1198, 5025
Head Up Your Ass **	178 ASHC		CH-47B	67-68	cargo		AO	front fuselage			841,
Headache *	242 ASHC		CH-47A	1971	cargo	65-07990	v-nn			Larry Witte FE	1942,
Headhunter	175 AHC		UH-1B	1967	gun		N+A	pilot door			301, 8650
Headhunter	B Co 229 AHB		UH-1D	65-66	slick		NO	nose		William Sim DG, Lee Komich AC, Robert Mason CP	1612,
Hearse (The)	605 TC		CH-47A	68-69	cargo		NO	fuselage			1349, 8725
Heather Dawn	C Trp 1/9		AH-1G	70-71	gun	69-16437	NO	bpw		John Craig AC	134, 360, 1674, 5450
Heaven's Devil	271 ASHC		CH-47	68-71	cargo		NO	front fuselage			8100,
Heavy	117 AHC		UH-1H	1970	slick		NO	nose			395, 439, 1266, 5675, 6275
Heavy Metal	176 AHC		UH-1H	1970	slick		NO	cargo door window		Steve Dunn AC	1987, 9450
Hedge Hopper (The)	57 TC	120 AHC	CH-21C	1962	lift	55-04165	NO	fuselage			1975, 6500

Copter Name	Unit	Unit #1	Aircraft	Circa	Function	Serial #	Config	Location	Artist	Crew	Contributors
Hedge Hopper 2	57 TC	120 AHC	CH-21C	1963	lift		NO	fuselage			3600, 8925
Helen Sue	254 Med Det		UH-1D	1966	dustoff	64-13658	NO	jump door		Ron Hannon CE	439, 664, 689, 3925, 5725
Helicopter	C Trp 1/9		UH-1H	70-71	slick	69-15214	NAA	cargo door			1438, 1832
Hell Bound	unk		UH-1B	64-65	gun		NO	cargo door window			1908, 4600
Hell Fire	D Co 227 AHB		AH-1G	68-71	gun		NO				862,
Hell From Above ^^	281 AHC		UH-1H	1970	slick		NO	nose			1545,
Hell From On High	336 AHC		UH-1M	68-69	gun		NO	nose		Dale Wills DG	1924,
Hell On Skids	A Co 227 AHB		UH-1H	1969	slick		NO	belly			1226,
Hell's Angel	45 Med Co		UH-1H	1969	dustoff		NO	nose			7425,
Hell's Angel	48 AHC		UH-1B	66-67	gun		NO	nose			1306, 9150
Hell's Angel	175 AHC	A/502	UH-1D	66-67	slick		NO	nose			1350,
Hell's Angel	243 ASHC		CH-47A	1968	cargo	66-19053	NO	front fuselage		Deitsch AC, Knight CP, Bridges FE, Meldahl CE, Stanton, Lee Perry FE crewed before 10-20-68	236, 8275
Hell's Angel	498 Med Co		UH-1D	65-66	dustoff		NO	nose		Tom McKemey CE	1152,
Hell's Ugly	15 Med Bn		UH-1H	70-71	medevac	69-15183	NAA	nose		R. Huether CE, James Keyes CE, Doug Campbell CE	277, 608, 808, 1139, 8425
Hell's Ugly	215 Composite Svc Bn		UH-1H	71-72	medevac	69-15183	NAA	nose		Pat Cardinal DG	277, 2031, 8425
Helluvacopter	21 Signal Group		UH-1H	70-71	slick	68-15593	NO	nose	Lucas	Lucas CE, Jim Faulk DG, G. Blanton CP, D. Baggott AC	64,
Henchman (The)	D Trp 3/4		AH-1G	69-70	gun	67-15827	N+A	doghouse	Gary Schmidt	Olsen	652, 1282, 1559, 8400
Henchman II (The)	D Trp 3/4		AH-1G	70-71	gun	67-15567	N+A	doghouse	Gary Schmidt	Gary Schmidt CE, Charles Sullivan AC	1559, 8400
Herb's Retrievers	15 Trans Bn	B Co	UH-1D	65-66	slick	63-12982	N+A	nose		Bentley Herbert AC	1053,
Herd	129 AHC		UH-1D	66-67	slick	64-13525	NO	nose		Mike Walker DG, Ed Wells AC, H. D. Sauer CP, W. D. James CE	1947, 6865
Here After 727 ^	4 Trans Command	H+HC	UH-1B	1967	slick	63-08727	NO	pilot door		Bob Chenoweth CE	301, 5225

Here After 727: *4 Trans Command, UH-1B, (sn 63-08727), Tan Son Nhut, 1967.* Previous name was "Wooly Booger"; survived VN with unknown total hours. Photo by Bob Chenoweth.

Copter Name	Unit	Unit #1	Aircraft	Circa	Function	Serial #	Config	Location	Artist	Crew	Contributors
Here Comes Da Judge	132 ASHC		CH-47B	1969	cargo		NO	fuselage			2002, 3175
Here Comes The Judge	116 AHC		UH-1C	68-69	gun frog	66-15005	NO	nose		Jim Boren AC, Joe Capon CE, Ken Plavcan DG, Joe Skarda DG	163, 1273, 1506, 1623, 4825, 6850
Here Comes The Judge	179 ASHC		CH-47B	68-69	cargo		NO	pilot's console			1739,
Here I Come	11 ACR		AH-1G	68-69	gun		NO	bpw			1703,
Here There Everywhere	187 AHC		AH-1G	1971	gun	67-15541	N+A	nose		Bill Sage AC, Woodington AC, White CP	1954,
Here's Mine Where's Yours?	C Co 227 AHB		UH-1H	1969	slick	66-16294	N+A	nose		Varney AC, Beckler CE, Don Nimblett CP	112,
Hermies	498 Med Co		UH-1H	69-70	dustoff		NO	nose			1357, 7700
Heuy's Breakfast Of Champions	147 ASHC		CH-47A	68-69	cargo	66-00123	N+A	fuselage		Larry Smith FE, Paul Michelson CE, Helgason DG	1272, 1640, 7825
Hi Fi	119 AHC		UH-1H	69-70	slick		NO	nose		Al Mixer CE, Fidencio Ramirez	741, 908, 1214, 1440, 9270
High And The Mighty (The)	187 AHC		AH-1G	70-71	gun	67-15868	NO	nose		Rick Renaud AC	1457,
High Freak	120 AHC	Avn Co	UH-1B	64-65	slick	63-08693	NO	doorpost		Larry Arruda CE	48,
Highlander Lead ^	189 AHC	604 TC	UH-1H		maint		NO	pilot door		John Peele	33, 9670
Hillbilly Dilly	187 AHC		UH-1H	1971	slick	66-00886	NO	nose			1700,
Hillbilly Chicken	A Co 227 AHB		UH-1H	1971	slick	66-16064	N+A	nose	Joe Paranal	Calvin Warren CE	750, 1232, 1340, 9700
Hilltopper	187 AHC		UH-1D	1967	slick	66-00928	NO	pilot door		Mike Mullen DG, Steve Eckle AC, Bob Jurries CE	1256, 1700, 9470
Hippie's Bag	B Co 229 AHB		UH-1H	67-68	slick	66-16561	N+A	nose		Chris Mellon CE, Mike Keele CE	886,
Hippo	45 Med Co		UH-1H	1970	dustoff		N+A	nose			7425,
Hit The Slopes	175 AHC		UH-1C	1967	gun		N+A	nose			1316,
Ho Che	134 AHC		UH-1H	68-69	slick	66-16319	NO	nose	two words: E instead of I spelling	Mel Bailey AC, Nat McClain CE, Harold Shonk AC, Carey Boyles AC	352, 1130, 1818
Ho Chi Minh **	539 TC			67-68			v-nnp				481,
Ho Chi Minh Is A Fag	189 AHC		UH-1H	68-69	slick		NO	belly			858,

Copter Name	Unit	Unit #1	Aircraft	Circa	Function	Serial #	Config	Location	Artist	Crew	Contributors
Ho Chi Sucks	68 AHC		UH-1C	1967	gun	66-00654	NO	belly		James T. Poston CE, Woody AC, Dave Henderson DG	257, 1304, 2075, 9200
Hobby Horse	11 GS		UH-1H	69-70	slick	68-16154	NO			Bill Abel CE	2,
Hog (The)	571 Med Det		UH-1H	69-70	dustoff	68-15230	NO				1600,
Hog Of Steel	129 AHC		UH-1B	68-69	gun	64-14010	NO	pilot door		William Courtney AC, D. Wilson CE	9310,
Hog Wash	C Co 227 AHB		UH-1H	1969	gun + night-hawk		NO				120,
Hogan's Goat	7 Airlift Plt		UH-1B	64-65	gun		NO	rocket pod			1975, 6525
Hogan's Goat	A Co 123 Avn Bn		UH-1H	70-71	slick	69-15292	N+A	doorpost		James Repp CE, Del Unsworth DG, S.Hogan AC	772,
Hogan's Heroes	187 AHC		UH-1H	1970	slick	68-15383	NO	nose			1932,
Hoghead	114 AHC		UH-1C	67-68	gun	66-00599	NO	pilot door		R. Miller AC, E. Schwanebeck CE, Bruce Gunn CP, J. Popin, G. Connally, O. Kershaw	634, 666, 696, 870, 1266, 1565, 1569, 1870, 2047, 3100, 5900, 6075, 6700
Hoghead II	114 AHC		UH-1C	1968	gun	66-00635	NO	pilot door		Robin Miller, Eugene Schwanebeck	634, 666, 1266, 1569, 2047, 6075, 6700, 9230
Hogjaws	271 ASHC		CH-47B	69-70	cargo	66-19129	NO			Dan Lampman FE, James Johnson FE '68-'69	964, 8950
Holly	174 AHC		UH-1H	1970	slick	68-15677	NO			Joe Bordeaux CE	162, 9430
Holly Sacra	159 Med Det		UH-1H	70-71	dustoff	69-15352	NO	nose		John Blickenstaff CE	151,
Holy Smokes	B Trp 7/1		UH-1H	1970	slick	66-16248	NO	pilot door		Richard Maxwell AC	1774,
Hombre (The)	192 AHC		UH-1C	68-69	gun	66-15071	NO	nose		Warren Allison CE, Steve Cole CE	25, 319, 343, 1498, 9510
Homeward Bound	335 AHC		UH-1H	69-70	slick		NO				1926,
Honey Bee	A Co 82 Avn Bn		UH-1B	65-66	slick		NO				800,
Honey Bucket (The)	121 AHC		UH-1D	65-66	slick	64-13663	NO	nose		Don Jackson CE, Gary Dowler CP	437, 831, 1135, 9290
Honey Mama	187 AHC		UH-1H	68-69	slick	67-17219	NO	pilot door		Russell Welch AC, Bill Newman CE, Keith Stowell DG	1713,
Honey Wells	121 AHC		UH-1H	1970	slick		N+A	nose			1305, 4825
Honky Tonk Woman	A Trp 1/9		UH-1H	70-71	slick		NO			Chuck Hendron CE, Charlie Adams, G. Schwanke	732, 9690

Copter Name	Unit	Unit #1	Aircraft	Circa	Function	Serial #	Config	Location	Artist	Crew	Contributors
Hoocher	188 AHC		UH-1H	67-68	slick	66-16121	NO	pilot door		Robert Sadouski AC, Beebe AC, Joe Matt CE, Roger Heitzmann CE	1113, 1178
Hooker (The)	200 ASHC		CH-47A	67-68	cargo	66-00095	N+A	front fuselage	Larry Dumford	Joe Boxley FE, M. Kennedy FE, L. Dumford DG, R. Whitney	166, 903, 995, 1195, 1585, 7950, 8275
Hooker (The)	A Trp 3/17		AH-1G	70-71	gun		NO	bpw			8650,
Hop-A-Long	174 AHC		UH-1C	1966	gun	65-09423	NO	doorpost		Tom Miller CE	1204, 9430
Horney Hawk	187 AHC		UH-1H	67-68	slick	66-00925	NO	pilot door		Jesse McLeod CE	1155,
Horny Hooker	180 ASHC		CH-47C	72-73	cargo	68-15853	N+A	fuselage		Curtis Watters CE, Fred Lohr AC	1034, 1299, 1872, 8250, 9842
Horny Hooker (The)	unk		CH-47	1969	cargo		N+A	front fuselage			8275,
Horse	190 AHC		UH-1H	68-69	maint		NO	cargo door		Raymond Roloff MD	1505,
Horse Thief ^	335 AHC	166 TC	UH-1B	65-67	maint	62-01901	N+A	nose + pilot door		Joe Fields DG/CE, Ellis Zack CE, Bob Bowen	301, 405, 523, 1020, 5150, 9590
Horse Thief II ^	335 AHC	166TC/A/82	UH-1D	1967	maint	66-00799	N+A	nose		Van Wert AC, Villerea CP, W. McKey CE, Fields DG	301, 523, 5275, 9590
Hot Stuff	134 AHC		UH-1M	70-71	gun	66-15076	NO			Ed Sutphen CE, Terry McFie CE	352, 1733, 1818
Hot Stuff	213 ASHC		CH-47A	66-67	cargo		N+A	fuselage		Geckler, Coleman	790, 8000
Hot Stuff	C Trp 1/9		AH-1G	68-69	gun	67-15725	N+A	bpw		John Powell AC	1414,
Hotel Juliet	271 ASHC		CH-47B	69-70	cargo	66-19129	NO			Dan Lampman FE	964, 8950
House Of Pain (The)	57 AHC		UH-1C	68-69	gun		NO	nose		Gary Neeley	1278, 1899, 6475
Hover Lover I	45 Med Co		UH-1H	69-70	dustoff	66-16431	NO	nose		Bill Mostek CE, J. Sabanosh CE, J. Baillado MD	1308, 1533, 1831, 7475
Hover Lover II	45 Med Co		UH-1H	69-70	dustoff	66-16431	NO	nose		John Sabanosh CE	1533,
How Do We Look?	68 Avn Co		UH-1B	65-66	gun		N+A	nose		Robert Brown AC	222, 1758, 9200
How Sweet It Is	611 TC		CH-37B	1965	recovery		N+A	fuselage			1266, 6275
Hubschrauberpilot	335 AHC		UH-1H	69-70	slick		NO				1201,
Hud	11 ACR		OH-6A	68-69	scout		NO	clamshell			1703,

Horse: *190 AHC, UH-1H, 1968-69.* Maintenance ship for the Spartans, also part-time ambulance when needed. Photo by Ray Roloff.

Copter Name	Unit	Unit #1	Aircraft	Circa	Function	Serial #	Config	Location	Artist	Crew	Contributors
Huey	117 AHC	Avn Co	UH-1B	63-64	slick		NO	nose			510, 6805
Huey Fury	121 AHC		UH-1D	1966	slick	65-09580	N+A	nose		Gary Dowler CP, Jerry McBee CE	437, 831
Huffer	539 TC		UH-1H	70-71	slick	67-17842	NO	nose		Bud Hinson	754,
Hulk	B Btry 2/20 ARA		AH-1G	70-71	gun	66-15262	NO			John Teetsel AC	2029,
Hulk	D Co 227 AHB		AH-1G	1970	gun	66-15262	NO	bpw		John Henry	113, 134, 301, 5275, 5430
Hulk (The)	200 ASHC		CH-47A	67-68	cargo	66-00107	N+A	front fuselage	Larry Dumford	Bob Langley FE, D. Seals DG, M. Hirsch, J. Morrow	966, 995, 1195, 7950, 8275
Hulk (The)	243 ASHC		CH-47A	1969	cargo		N+A	front fuselage			111, 8075, 8275
Hulk (The)	355 Avn Co		CH-54A	68-69	recovery	67-18425	N+A	avionics door	Jack ? TC mechanic	Jim Sheridan FE	1603,
Hungry	114 AHC	Avn Co	UH-1B	1966	gun	63-08723	NO	pilot door		J. Gosnell, M. Vlcek, L. West, W. Lowie, Moya, Priest, R. Fortenberry	634, 1565, 6700
Hungry Bitch (The)	162 AHC		UH-1C	1968	gun		NO	pilot door			652,
Hungry Bitch (The)	B Trp 3/17		UH-1H	1971	slick	66-16041	NO	nose			1581,
Hungry For Blood	48 AHC		UH-1C	69-70	gun		NO	nose			1053, 1235, 9150
Hungry Hog	161 AHC		UH-1B	1967	gun		N+A	M-3 rocket box		Roger Old AC, Jeff Peecook	710, 1324, 1367, 9370
Hungry II	114 AHC		UH-1C	1967	gun	66-00514	NO	pilot door		James Gosnell, John Little	634, 666, 947, 1569, 6700
Hunter (The)	117 AHC	Avn Co	UH-1B	64-65	gun		NO	nose		Vanzant	1840, 1975, 6525
Hunter (The)	155 AHC		UH-1B	65-66	gun	63-08614	N+A	nose		Jack Kottler AC	617, 939, 9360
Hurdy Gurdy Man	116 AHC		UH-1D	68-69	slick		NO	pilot door		Robert Pearson CE	1363, 9240
Hurry Sundown	unk		UH-1H	67-68	slick		N+A	pilot door		Ken Jump CE	1833, 9160
Hustler	155 AHC		UH-1H	68-70	slick		NO	pilot door			960, 9360
Hustler (The)	17 AHC		UH-1H	67-68	slick		N+A	pilot door		Jim Thompson	1771, 9110
Huzza-Huzza	195 AHC		UH-1H	1970	slick	68-15317	NO	nose		Earl Miller CE	1194,

Copter Name	Unit	Unit #1	Aircraft	Circa	Function	Serial #	Config	Location	Artist	Crew	Contributors
Hydraulics Wonder (The)	176 AHC		UH-1M	69-71	gun	66-15011	NO			Don Wilson CE, Steve Rodriquez DG	186, 9450
I. W. Harper	240 AHC		UH-1H	67-68	slick		NO	pilot door		Robert Eastburn AC, David Sauter CP, Bob Harper CE	1781,
I. W. Harper	A Co 227 AHB		UH-1D	66-67	slick		N+A	nose		Larry Winge CE	1512, 1935
If You Ain't Cav You Ain't Shit! ^^	A Co 229 AHB		UH-1H	71-72	slick	495 ?	NO	nose	Jorgenson painted it himself	Doug Jorgenson AC, Coker CE	652, 874, 1627, 6850, 9710
Igloo (The)	213 ASHC		CH-47A	68-69	cargo	011 or 021	N+A				293,
Igor	128 AHC		UH-1D	67-68	slick	64-13742	NO			Alan Shields CE, Wernli AC	1605, 9300
Igor	128 AHC		UH-1D	67-68	slick	66-01088	NO			Alan Shields CE, Charles Ameigh AC	1605, 9300
Igor's Numba Wun	339 TC		CH-37B	64-65	lift	54-00995	NO	fuselage		Donaldson FE, George Maxwell CE, Joe Pulcini DG	520, 846, 1975, 6525
il Padrone	A Btry 4/77 ARA		UH-1C	1969	gun		N+A	nose		Dennis Mack CP	1067,
Illegal Eagle	176 AHC		UH-1H	69-70	slick	67-17451	NO			David Baker CE, Gary Alstrand DG	72, 9450
Illusive Butterfly	A Trp 7/1		OH-6A	71-72	scout		NO			Larry Brown DG/CE	217,
IMP	128 AHC		UH-1D	68-69	slick	63-13002	NO	pilot door		Ed Ewing AC, Tom Bresnahan CE	494,
Impossible Dream	68 Med Det		UH-1H	70-71	dustoff		NO			Phelps CE, Larry Warner MD	1866, 7725
In A Gadda Da Vida	116 AHC		UH-1C	69-71	gun		NO				90, 820, 1623
In A Gadda Da Vida	116 AHC		UH-1D	70-71	slick		NO	nose			87, 90, 1175, 9010
In A Gadda Da Vida	176 AHC		UH-1H	1970	slick	68-15541	N+A	nose		Ed … CE, Jay….DG, Joe Gross	661, 901, 9450
In Cold Blood	175 AHC		UH-1C	66-67	gun	66-15044	N+A	pilot door		K. Axon CE, T. Daugherty DG, E. Thayer DG, Armijo CE, Chamber AC, Robbie DG, McDowell AC, J. Gammon AC	46, 467, 1764, 1926, 9440
In Crowd (The)	121 AHC		UH-1D	67-68	slick		N+A	nose			477, 1593, 9290
In God's Will	B Co 229 AHB		UH-1H	71-72	slick		NO				803,
In Limbo	129 AHC		UH-1H	70-71	slick		NO			Jim Masencup AC, Matt Casey CE, Pete Nolan DG	1104, 7350
Incredible Hulk (The)	121 AHC		UH-1D	66-67	slick		N+A	nose		William McQuade	437, 477, 831, 1161, 4825, 9290

Copter Name	Unit	Unit #1	Aircraft	Circa	Function	Serial #	Config	Location	Artist	Crew	Contributors
Indefatigable Beaky Buzzard (The)	121 AHC		UH-1D	1968	slick	64-13724	N+A	nose			831, 6975
Insouciance	B Co 123 Avn Bn		UH-1C	68-69	slick		NO	nose			1102,
Iola	174 AHC		UH-1D	1967	slick	65-09621	NO	doorpost		Jim Messinger AC	1184,
Irish Eagle (The)	131 SAC		OH-6A	1967	scout	66-07777	N+A	clamshell			301, 395, 1020, 1041, 1053, 5675, 6025
Irishmen	176 AHC		UH-1C	69-70	gun hog		NO	nose			8925,
Iron Butterfly **	1 Bde 101 ABN	H+HC	UH-1H	1970	slick	68-16326	AO	flight helmet		George Dousis CE	436,
Iron Butterfly	15 Med Bn		UH-1H	70-71	medevac		NO				608,
Iron Butterfly	20 Eng Bde		OH-58A	1970	scout	68-16746	NO	nose			8425,
Iron Butterfly	45 Med Co		UH-1H	68-69	dustoff	66-16432	NO	nose		Steve Huntley CE, Richard Dean CE, David Penfield, Joe Balchitis	288, 378, 817, 916, 1308, 1533, 1831, 7425, 9955
Iron Butterfly	48 AHC		UH-1H	69-70	slick		NO			Glen Morgan CE	1237, 9150
Iron Butterfly	57 AHC		UH-1C	68-69	gun		NO	nose			1899,
Iron Butterfly	92 AHC		UH-1H	68-69	slick		NO		Brian Lee	Steve Lee CE	1968,
Iron Butterfly	116 AHC		UH-1H	1971	slick	69-15769	NO	nose		Jim McDaniel AC	1137,
Iron Butterfly	134 AHC		UH-1H	70-71	slick	68-16263	NO	nose		Lee Gaskill AC, Ray Mangiaracina CE, Dee Sessions DG, Travis Wylie CE	352, 979, 1818
Iron Butterfly	135 AHC		UH-1C	1969	gun		NO	nose		Tom Seward DG	1692, 9330
Iron Butterfly	147 ASHC		CH-47C	69-70	cargo	68-15832	NO	fuselage		Mike Shivley FE	1199, 1606
Iron Butterfly	162 AHC		UH-1H	1969	slick		NO	pilot door		Floyd Stringer	1718, 9390
Iron Butterfly	173 AHC		UH-1H	70-71	slick	68-16352	NO			Larry Lane CE, Pat Sullivan CE	1728, 9300
Iron Butterfly	178 ASHC		CH-47B	68-70	cargo	67-18465	NO	front fuselage		Lionel Caeton	384, 497, 2061
Iron Butterfly	188 AHC		UH-1H	1968	slick		NO				414,
Iron Butterfly	191 AHC		UH-1C	68-69	gun		NO	pilot door			245,

Iron Butterfly II*: 114 AHC, UH-1H, (sn 69-15362), 1970*. UHF antennas suggest this is a C+C bird; note the dual M-60's. Survived VN with 688 total hours, all with the 114th. Photo by Joe Stogner.

Copter Name	Unit	Unit #1	Aircraft	Circa	Function	Serial #	Config	Location	Artist	Crew	Contributors
Iron Butterfly	196 ASHC		CH-47A	1968	cargo	66-00093	NAA	front fuselage	Dan Uhr CE	Joe Riley AC, Doc Livingston CP, Dan Alberts FE, Dan Uhr CE	13, 1477
Iron Butterfly	196 Light Inf Bde		OH-6A	1970	scout		NO				11,
Iron Butterfly	203 ASHC		CH-47A	71-72	cargo		NO				1233,
Iron Butterfly	235 AWC	AHC	AH-1G	1968	gun	67-15617	N+A	bpw			1053,
Iron Butterfly	242 ASHC		CH-47A	1968	cargo	66-19019	NO	fuselage		Gary Roush AC, Roger Olney CP, Al Calderon CE	989, 1199, 1225, 1555, 8350
Iron Butterfly	243 ASHC		CH-47A	68-70	cargo	66-00105	N+A	front fuselage	Gary Crabtree	Gary Crabtree CE, David Behn FE, Bill Bell CE '67-'68	111, 118, 369, 550, 1218, 1555, 1975, 8075
Iron Butterfly	247 Med Det		UH-1H	70-71	dustoff		NO				1780,
Iron Butterfly	254 Med Det		UH-1H	68-70	dustoff		NO	nose		Jorge Ortiz-Santiago CE	424,
Iron Butterfly	271 ASHC		CH-47B	69-70	cargo		NO	front fuselage			964,
Iron Butterfly	281 AHC		UH-1C	1969	gun		NO	nose			9550,
Iron Butterfly	335 AHC		UH-1B	69-70	gun	63-08606	NO	nose		Ralph Luffman CE, John Harmon DG	1049, 1201, 1926
Iron Butterfly	498 Med Co		UH-1H	69-71	dustoff		N+A	nose		H. Modjeski AC, M. Basler CE, J. Morris MD	756, 863, 950, 1217, 1357, 1750, 7700, 9430
Iron Butterfly	A Co 227 AHB		UH-1H	68-71	slick	65-09949	NO	nose	Jim Lietzan	Maury Hearne AC, Jim Lietzan CE, Mike Tartar DG	197, 562, 722, 1022, 1749, 9770
Iron Butterfly	A Trp 1/9		AH-1G	1969	gun		NO	bpw			1053, 1266, 1589, 1724, 1908, 6175
Iron Butterfly	B Co 227 AHB		UH-1H	1969	slick	67-17799	NO	nose			34,
Iron Butterfly	B Trp 1/9		OH-6A	1969	scout	67-16512	NO	doghouse		Robert Hraben	801, 1053, 9740
Iron Butterfly	C Btry 2/20 ARA		AH-1G	69-71	gun	67-15600	NO	bpw	McMillan	Penn CE	154, 1236, 1627, 1908, 2014, 9880
Iron Butterfly	C Co 101 AHB	188 AHC	UH-1H	68-69	slick		NO	pilot door			726,
Iron Butterfly	C Co 229 AHB		UH-1H	68-69	slick	66-16775	NO	nose		Neil Keogh CE	76, 1466, 6805
Iron Butterfly	C Trp 1/9		AH-1G	70-71	gun		NO	doghouse			873, 1266, 1963, 4825, 6275, 6300
Iron Butterfly	D Trp 3/4		OH-6A	69-70	scout	68-17359	NO	doghouse		Tom Fluharty CE, Andrew Elliott AC, John Evans AC	194, 541, 865, 1320, 9920
Iron Butterfly	D Trp 3/5		UH-1C	68-69	gun		NO	pilot door			1710,

Copter Name	Unit	Unit #1	Aircraft	Circa	Function	Serial #	Config	Location	Artist	Crew	Contributors
Iron Butterfly	F Btry 79 AFA		AH-1G	71-72	gun	67-15600	NO	bpw			833, 1627, 9710
Iron Butterfly	unk Cav		AH-1G	1972	gun		NO	nose			3675,
Iron Butterfly (The)	11 ACR		UH-1D	68-69	slick		NO	nose			1703,
Iron Butterfly (The)	114 AHC		UH-1H	1970	slick	69-15122	NO	nose		Frank Akana, T. Franklin, E. Gibson, Tim Meitin	192, 408, 1053, 6700
Iron Butterfly (The)	129 AHC		UH-1H	68-69	slick	67-17431	NO	nose	Richard England	Rick England CE, Roger Austin CE, John Roddick DG, Hammond AC	479, 1248, 4975, 9310
Iron Butterfly (The)	187 AHC		UH-1H	70-71	slick	67-17371	NO	nose			652, 1700, 1932
Iron Butterfly (The)	498 Med Co		UH-1H	1969	dustoff		NO	nose		Mike Basler CE, Howard Modjeski AC, Jeff Morris MD	932, 1266, 6150
Iron Butterfly (The)	498 Med Co		UH-1H	1970	dustoff		NO	doorpost			923,
Iron Butterfly (The)	C Co 229 AHB		UH-1H	69-71	slick	66-16571	N+A	nose		Jordan CE, Dan Tyler, J. Olson, Sharrock, Reg Baldwin	73, 76, 199, 803, 1816, 1767, 6900, 9830
Iron Butterfly (The)	D Trp 1/10		UH-1H	69-70	slick	68-15328	N+A	doorpost	David Barmuchi	David Bramuchi CE, Brad Melvin DG, Ellsworth AC, David Frenz AC, Jim Snyder CP, Doug Maas CP	181, 269, 1064, 1173
Iron Butterfly II	45 Med Co		UH-1H	69-71	dustoff	68-16330	NO	nose		Richard Dean CE	376, 1831, 7425
Iron Butterfly II	114 AHC		UH-1H	1969	slick	66-16838	NO	nose		Chalecki, T. McMahon, S. Huntley, G. Gager	817, 6700
Iron Butterfly II	114 AHC		UH-1H	1970	slick	69-15362	NO	nose		Frank Akana CE, John Palmer AC, Larry Cloer CP, Joe Stogner DG, T. Franklin	192, 1084, 1704, 6700, 9230
Iron Butterfly II	281 AHC		UH-1C	69-70	gun		NO				66,
Iron Butterfly III	114 AHC		UH-1H	1971	slick	67-17289	NO	nose		J. Arends, E. Espinoza, R. Perez, J. Stogner	192, 696, 6700, 9230
Iron Butterfly Too	D Trp 1/10		UH-1H	70-71	slick	68-15339	NO	jump door		Doug Maas CP, David Bramuchi CE, David Frenz AC, Jim Synder CP	181, 1064
Iron Chicken (The)	A Co 227 AHB		UH-1H	68-69	slick	67-17442	N+A			John Gailfoil CE, Price AC, Chip Rumbel AC	572, 9700
Iron Cross **	174 AHC		UH-1C	1970	gun	65-09555	AO	quarter panel		Kenney AC, Gambrell CP, Jack Coffman DG, Fred Carlson CE, Fred Thompson	184, 278, 1770, 6300, 9430
Iron Horse	128 AHC		UH-1D	1971	slick		NO	nose		Mike Waugh	989, 1873
Iron Lung	15 Med Bn		UH-1H	1970	medevac		NO	nose		Godsie Norvell CE	608, 1345, 4300
Iron Spud ^	131 SAC		OH-6A	1967	scout		N+A	clamshell			301, 395, 1041, 1053, 5675, 6025

Copter Name	Unit	Unit #1	Aircraft	Circa	Function	Serial #	Config	Location	Artist	Crew	Contributors
It Takes Two	116 AHC		UH-1C	69-71	gun		NO				820,
It's Clobberin' Time	92 AHC		UH-1H	1968	slick		N+A	nose			931, 1339, 9220
Ivan The Terrible	155 AHC		UH-1C	67-68	gun	66-15212	NO	nose		Phil Lehman AC, Dave Waterous CE	305, 1001, 9360
J. C. + The Boys	D Trp 3/5		UH-1D	68-69	slick		NO				1211,
Jack The Bear	B Trp 3/17		AH-1G	68-69	gun		N+A	bpw		Jack Echols AC	1503, 9380
Jake's Delight (#2)	187 AHC		UH-1H	1970	slick	68-16087	NO	nose			1932,
Janci's Flyin' Lion	121 AHC	Avn Co	UH-1B	1964	slick		N+A	nose	Leone	Mike Beech AC, Leone	116, 1033, 1253, 9290
Jay	334 AWC	AHC	UH-1C	1967	gun		NO	doorpost			301, 696, 5900
Jean	198 Light Inf Bde Americal Div		OH-6A	1971	scout	66-07930	NO			Doug Lackey	1386, 4850
Jeanie	170 AHC		UH-1H	1970	slick		NO	nose			1839, 4150
Jefferson Airplane	11 ACR		UH-1D	68-69	slick		NO	nose			1703,
Jefferson Airplane	45 Med Co		UH-1H	67-68	dustoff	66-16406	NO			Richard Riley CE	1478, 2067, 7425
Jefferson Airplane (The)	92 AHC		UH-1H	67-68	slick	66-16460	NAA	nose	Richard Balsimo	Bob Herndon DG, Rick Walters CE, Rich McClary DG	669, 678, 737, 931, 1858, 9220
Jefferson Airplane (The)	175 AHC		UH-1H	68-70	slick	65-12866	NO			Tim Hostetler CE, Don Hunt AC, Steve Andreoff DG, Tom Stowell AC	38, 796, 1714, 1926, 9440
Jelly Belly	33 TC	118 AHC	CH-21C	1962	lift		NO	fuselage			185, 1285, 1926, 9260
Jet Propelled Martini **	F Trp 9 Cav		OH-6A	1972	scout	69-16071	AO			Paul Murtha AC	1264,
Jezabell	unk		UH-1C	1968	gun		NO	nose			1698, 9660
Jinx	45 Med Co		UH-1H	1970	dustoff	68-16463	NO	nose		Jim Goodman, Rich Ziemba	2065, 2066, 5433
Jinx (The)	117 AHC		UH-1D	67-68	slick	64-13718	NO	nose		Al Bennett CE	253, 753, 1313, 1695, 1732, 9250
Jo Ann	273 Avn Co		CH-54A	70-71	recovery		NO	nose	'465's crew chief	Jack Humphreys FE	815
Jo Ann	D Trp 3/5		OH-6A	68-69	scout	67-16187	NO	doghouse		William Chamberlain, Larry Frady	509, 554, 9860

Copter Name	Unit	Unit #1	Aircraft	Circa	Function	Serial #	Config	Location	Artist	Crew	Contributors
Jo Michele	170 AHC		UH-1C	1968	gun		NO	nose		Bob Snead AC	1877,
Joan I	E Btry 82 Arty Bn		UH-1B	65-66	slick		NO	nose		Robert Stone CE	1020, 4400
Joan Of Arc	D Trp 1/4		AH-1G	1970	gun		NO	bpw			195, 1868, 4825
Joann	A Trp 3/17		OH-6A	69-70	scout	67-16445	NO			Bill Smith AC	1630, 1737
Joann	unk		UH-1H		slick		N+A	pilot door			8925,
Jody	A Trp 3/17		OH-6A	69-70	scout	67-16246	NO	doghouse		Dan Murphy AC, Roger Young CE	503, 1261, 1737, 1976, 3925
Johnnie Reb	339 TC		CH-37B	64-65	recovery	55-00636	NO	fuselage			520, 889
Johnny	D Co 227 AHB		AH-1G	69-70	gun	69-16442	NO				113,
Johnny Reb Jr	339 TC		UH-1B	64-65	gun	63-8648/ 92	NO	doorpost			1975, 6525
Jolly Roger **	174 AHC		UH-1M	1970	gun	65-09540	AO	quarter panel			184, 233, 9430
Jolly Roger **	180 ASHC		CH-47A	68-69	cargo	65-08005	AO	front fuselage			8075,
Jonny Reb	173 AHC		UH-1C	1970	gun		NO	nose			1932,
Joti C	D Co 227 AHB		UH-1C	1968	gun	65-09516	N+A	nose			1760,
Joy	B Btry 82 Arty ?		OH-6A	1969	scout	67-16280	NO	nose			1624, 5025
Joyce	11 ACR		UH-1H	68-69	slick		NO	nose			1448, 1703, 8625
Joyce II	11 ACR		UH-1H	68-69	slick		NO	nose			1703,
Juanita	81 TC	119 AHC	CH-21C	1962	lift	52-8638	NO	fuselage			431,
Judge (The)	45 Med Co		UH-1H	68-69	dustoff		NO				916,
Judge (The)	129 AHC		UH-1H	68-70	slick	66-16265	NO	nose		Lloyd Robinson CE, Larry Jackson CE, Ray Gagner DG	835, 1042, 1248, 1495, 1547, 6865, 9310
Judge (The)	187 AHC		AH-1G	71-72	gun	67-15652	NO			Thomas McKee CE, Steve Wescoat AC	1149, 9470
Judge (The)	334 AWC	AHC	AH-1G	69-70	gun		NO	bpw		Craig Clapper AC	280,

Copter Name	Unit	Unit #1	Aircraft	Circa	Function	Serial #	Config	Location	Artist	Crew	Contributors
Judge (The)	B Co 25 Avn Bn		AH-1G	1970	gun	67-15486	NAA	doghouse		Marek CE, Chuck Gant AC	49, 582, 909, 9120
Judi In D' Skys	335 AHC		UH-1H	69-70	slick		NO	nose			635, 9590
Judy	C Trp 1/9		OH-6A	70-71	scout	66-07916	NO	fuselage		Alton Roberts DG	890, 9805
Judy Ann	1 Bde 1 Cav Div		UH-1H	1970	slick	68-16126	NO	nose	Duke McKinney	Duke McKinney CE, Bernard Villegas DG, C. McAllister, T. Buell	1121, 1153, 2034, 8975
Judy In The Sky	187 AHC		UH-1H	1970	slick	68-16344	NO	nose		Mark Rovere AC, C. Damerow	385, 1688, 1954
Judy In The Sky	C Trp 7/1		AH-1G	68-69	gun	67-15475	NO	bpw		Mike Peterson CE	1382, 7085
Jug Butt **	200 ASHC		CH-47A	67-68	cargo	66-00098	AO	front fuselage	Larry Dumford	Dennis Wilson CE	995, 1195, 1585
Jumbo	117 AHC		UH-1H	69-70	slick / nigthawk	68-15747	NO	nose		Mike Aeilts CE	10,
Jumbo 47	243 ASHC		CH-47A	1970	cargo	64-13143	NO			Carlos Vazquez FE	1826,
June's Ride-Sandy's Pride	187 AHC		UH-1H	1970	slick	66-16792	NO	nose			1932, 1954
Jungle Bunny	247 Med Det		UH-1H	70-71	dustoff		NO				869,
Jungle Cruiser	335 AHC		UH-1B	1970	gun	64-13926	NO	nose		Doug Wilson CE, John Jones, Redd, Roger Hanson, Darrell Findlay	1283, 1926, 9440
Junk Run	B Trp 3/17		UH-1H	1970	slick		NO	pilot door			728,
Jury (The)	129 AHC		UH-1B	69-70	gun		NO				1042,
Just Married	54 Med Det		UH-1H	1968	dustoff		NO	nose		Norman Shanahan	1594, 2002, 5444
Justice (The)	190 AHC		UH-1C	1968	gun	66-00625	NO	nose			69,
Kamaaina	114 AHC	Avn Co	UH-1B	1964	slick		NO				544, 5825
Kansas Bandit	45 Med Co		UH-1H	69-70	dustoff		NO	nose			1412, 7425
Kansas Killer (The)	D Trp 3/4		AH-1G	70-71	gun	68-15135	NO	doghouse	Gary Schmidt / Carl Betsill	Rudy Parris AC, Don Vaughn CE	140, 1559, 8400
Kaptain Klutz	121 AHC		UH-1D	67-68	slick		N+A	nose		Mike Shakocius AC, Jim Noblin CP	477, 1593, 4825, 9290
Karen	45 Med Co		UH-1H	70-71	dustoff	69-15296	NO	nose		Tom Hall CE	683,

Copter Name	Unit	Unit #1	Aircraft	Circa	Function	Serial #	Config	Location	Artist	Crew	Contributors
Karen	D Co 229 AHB		AH-1G	1968	gun		NO	nose		Bob Hunter	1485, 4300
Karen's Carriage	135 AHC		UH-1H	67-68	slick		NO	nose			1249,
Karin	117 AHC	Avn Co	UH-1B	1964	gun	63-08673	NO	nose		Gerald Neiderhammer CE	395, 1840, 1975, 5025, 6525
Karla	114 AHC		UH-1H	1971	slick	69-15433	NO	nose			3100,
Kat (The)	B Co 25 Avn Bn		UH-1D	68-69	slick	65-09657	N+A	nose		Earl Schmuck DG	1562, 9120
Kath II	A Trp 1-9		AH-1G	1969	gun		NO	bpw			1760,
Kathie	A Trp 3/17		OH-6A	69-70	scout	67-16020	NO			Roger Young CE, Reynolds	182, 1093, 1737, 1976, 9720
Kathryn	UTT		UH-1B	1964	gun	62-02065	NO	cargo door window panel			1975, 6500
Kathy	162 AHC		UH-1H	1972	slick		NO	nose			3225,
Kathy	D Trp 3/5		UH-1H	1971	slick		NO	pilot door			182, 1205, 8600, 9935
Kathy Ann	D Trp 3/5		UH-1C	67-68	gun		NO	pilot door		Ron Deciles, Bill Norman, Andy Earle, Roland Florio	1301, 3700
Keep On Truckin'	A Co 229 AHB		UH-1H	71-72	slick		NO	nose			988, 6850
Keep On Truck'n	129 AHC		UH-1D	72-73	slick	65-09910	N+A	nose	VN or Korean artist	Barry Swanson CE, Richard Trumbo AC	1053, 1736, 6865, 9310
Keep The Faith Baby	174 AHC		UH-1	67-69			NO	nose		James Sieben CE	1609, 9430
Keep The Faith Baby	213 ASHC		CH-47A	67-68	cargo		N+A	fuselage			1410, 8000
Keep Your Head	A Co 229 AHB		UH-1H	71-72	slick		N+A	nose			988, 6850
Kelly Sue	114 AHC	Avn Co	UH-1B	1965	slick		NO			G. Jones, J. Boyer	864, 6700
Kennel Keeper ^	240 AHC	619 TC	UH-1H	67-68	maint	66-16187	NO	nose		Frank Bay	106, 439, 1266, 1933, 5725, 9540
Kentucky Woman	D Trp 3/4		AH-1G	70-71	gun	68-17040	NO	doghouse	Gary Schmidt	John Brady CE	1559, 8400
Kick My Ass	242 ASHC		CH-47A	1971	cargo		NO	front pylon			989, 8350
Kid	B Co 123 Avn Bn		OH-6A	1968	scout		NO	nose			1053,

Copter Name	Unit	Unit #1	Aircraft	Circa	Function	Serial #	Config	Location	Artist	Crew	Contributors
Kid (The)	170 AHC		UH-1H	1969	slick		NO	nose			1543, 9400
Kill A Gook For Calley	C Co 229 AHB		UH-1H	1970	slick		NO	below cargo door frame			71, 364, 9870
Kill A Kommie For Christ	57 AHC		UH-1M	70-71	gun		NO			Calvin Blankenship	147, 9180
Kill 'Em All + Let God Sort 'Em Out	B Trp 1/9		UH-1C	67-68	gun		NO	nose			1392,
Kill For Grins	192 AHC		UH-1C	69-70	gun		NO	nose			621,
Kill For Peace	48 AHC		UH-1B	67-68	slick		N+A	nose			81, 226, 9150
Kill For Peace	192 AHC		UH-1C	69-70	gun		NO	rocket pod			621, 343
Kill Mad Dog Kill	240 AHC		UH-1C	1968	gun		NO	nose			1053, 1200
Kill Or Be Killed	F Trp 4 Cav		OH-6A	1972	scout	66-17795	NO	rear crew door			140, 422
Killer Bee **	C Trp 7/1		OH-6A	1971	scout	67-16289	AO	clamshell		Richard O'Connell CE, Mike Rathbone AC	1309,
Killer Hawk	187 AHC		UH-1H	69-70	slick	67-17778	NO	nose			1266, 1700, 1727, 6125
Kimchi Cab	175 AHC		UH-1B	1966	slick		NO	nose		Ken Leiss AC	429, 1926
King Arthur	173 AHC		UH-1D	1967	slick	65-09982	NO	pilot door		Art Kovolesky CE	940, 4725
King Bee ^	116 AHC		UH-1H	1971	slick	70-15719	NO	nose		John Barrera CE, Rodney Tabita DG	90,
King Cobra	11 ACR		AH-1G	1968	gun		NO				1462,
King Cobra	114 AHC		UH-1B	66-67	gun	63-08668	NO	pilot door		G. O'Grady, D. Moorehouse, Miller, L. Ford, L. Willer, Minton, M. Worm	1311, 1565, 6700
King Cobra	114 AHC		UH-1C	66-67	gun	66-00597	NO	pilot door		B. King, P. Evans, D. Cook, Fagan, G. Brooks, J. Williams, H. Swann	301, 491, 666, 696, 912, 1053, 1565, 1569, 3100, 5900, 6700
King Cobra	114 AHC		AH-1G	1971	gun		N+A	nose			250, 1674, 5425, 5427
King Cobra	175 AHC		AH-1G	1971	gun		NO				1370, 9440
King Frog	116 AHC		UH-1C	68-69	gun	66-00722	NO	pilot door		Joe Skarda DG	1623,
King Kuhana	174 AHC		UH-1D	66-67	slick		N+A	nose		Wayne Medeiros CE, John Banke, Ron Newcomer	1168, 1288, 9430

Copter Name	Unit	Unit #1	Aircraft	Circa	Function	Serial #	Config	Location	Artist	Crew	Contributors
King Rat	D Trp 3-4		OH-6A	69-70	scout	68-17175	NO	doghouse			1282, 1989,
King Roach	15 Med Bn		UH-1H	69-70	medevac		NO	nose		Jimmy Odum CE, Hank Tuell AC	548, 608, 1321, 1807, 7375
Kiss Of Death	11 ACR		AH-1G	68-69	gun		NO	bpw			1703,
Kiss Of Death	117 AHC	Avn Co	UH-1B	64-65	gun		N+A	gun pod			1840, 5025
Kiss Of Death	A Trp 7/1		OH-6A	1971	scout		NO	doghouse			1426, 3375
Kiss Of Death (The)	114 AHC		UH-1H	69-70	slick	64-13771	NO	nose		Evan Pinther DG, M. Brown CP, Tom Desimone AC, Steve Walbridge CE	413, 1400, 6700
Kitten	118 AHC	Avn Co	UH-1B	1965	slick	63-08547	NO	pilot door		Jim Tromatter CE	1110, 1803
Kitten	191 AHC		UH-1D	68-69	slick	66-00824	NO	pilot door		Glenn Phenicie CE, Richard Burt AC, Perrin AC	245, 1389
Kitten II	118 AHC		UH-1D	1966	slick	64-13670	NO	pilot door		Tromatter CE	1110, 1779, 1803, 9260
Knight Raider	336 AHC	A/101	UH-1B	66-68	gun		NO	pilot door		Bob Knight	668, 927, 9610
Knight Train	56 TC		UH-1D	1967	recovery		NO	pilot door		Emmett Knight AC	2006, 6475
Knuckle Buster ^	571 TC		UH-1B	64-65	maint		N+A			Joe Sanderlin	1542, 1674
Kommie Killers	48 AHC		UH-1B	67-68	gun		NO	nose			9640,
Kopjlager	A Trp 7/1		AH-1G	71-72	gun		NO	bpw			217, 1426, 3375
Kosher Dill	180 ASHC		CH-47C	72-73	cargo	68-15995	NO	fuselage		Curtis Watters CE	1872, 8250
Kosher Eagle ^	A Co 101 AHB		UH-1D	67-68	slick	66-01115	N+A	pilot door		Howard Klein	921, 9680
Kris	242 ASHC		CH-47A	68-71	cargo		NO	nose			1225, 8350
La Paloma	57 TC	120 AHC	CH-21C	1964	lift		N+A	fuselage			1554,
La Poule De Duerre	539 TC		CH-47A	70-71	recovery	66-19010	NO	fuselage		Bud Hinson	652, 754
La Puta	B Trp 1/9		AH-1G	1969	gun		NO	bpw			69,
Lady	45 Med Co		UH-1H	69-70	dustoff		NO	nose			2068,

Copter Name	Unit	Unit #1	Aircraft	Circa	Function	Serial #	Config	Location	Artist	Crew	Contributors
Lady Ann	C Co 227 AHB		UH-1D	1967	slick	65-09815	NO	nose		Jim Rosser CE	231,
Lady Godiva **	132 ASHC		CH-47B	70-71	cargo	67-18449	AO	fuselage	SP4 Davis did all '70-'71 a/c art		773, 1162, 1588, 7800
Lady Godiva	D Trp 3/4		AH-1G	69-70	gun	68-17107	N+A	doghouse	Gary Schmidt	Jim Kirker CE	917, 1559, 8400, 9855
Lady Jane	116 AHC		UH-1H	70-71	slick	69-15527	NO	nose		John Barrera CE, Rodney Tabita DG	90, 1020, 1532, 1788, 9240
Lady Jane	C Co 101 AHB		UH-1H	1968	slick	67-17437	NO	pilot door	Greg Pepper	Torre AC, Astro CE, Moon DG	1373,
Lady Linda	187 AHC		UH-1H	70-71	slick	68-15279	NO	nose		Skip Davis AC, F. Drinkwine CE, Mike Elliott DG	441, 9470
Lady Linda	A Trp 7/1		AH-1G	1968	gun		NO	nose		John Little AC	1028,
Lady Luck ^	1 Air Cav Div	HHC	UH-1H	68-69	C+C	67-17812	NO	nose		Mike Molish AC, William Dysinger CP	1220,
Lady Luck	178 ASHC		CH-47A	66-67	cargo	64-13162	N+A	front fuselage		George Luster FE, Paul Atkins CE	1294,
Lady Luck	192 AHC		UH-1H	70-71	slick	67-17711	NO	doghouse		Larry Crowder CE	375, 9940
Lady Madona	45 Med Co		UH-1H	68-70	dustoff	66-16515	NO	nose		David Root	1509,
Lady Madonna **	174 AHC		UH-1C	70-71	gun	65-09507	AO	quarter panel			1342,
Lady Of Sin	B Co 4 Avn Bn		UH-1C	1967	gun	66-00539	NO	doorpost		Mike Simmons DG	1614,
Lady Samantha	118 AHC		UH-1H	70-71	slick		NO				228,
Lady Willpower	178 ASHC		CH-47B	68-69	cargo	67-18458	NO	front fuselage			384, 1297, 7875, 9885
Lamont's Lament	121 AHC		UH-1D	66-68	slick		N+A	nose		John Vaille AC, Dave Cunningham AC	379, 437, 831, 770
Lancelot ^	187 AHC	602 TC	UH-1H	69-70	maint	68-16338	NO	nose		Joe Tapko, Douglas Dix, Harold Reed	439, 1688, 1700, 1932, 5725, 9470
Lancelot ^	187 AHC	602 TC	UH-1H	1970	maint	69-15426	NO	nose			1697,
Land Lover	191 AHC		UH-1D	68-69	slick	66-00820	NO	pilot door		L. Arnold AC, T. Jens CP, J. Wilson CE, A. Moniton DG	245,
Laotian Whore	498 Med Co		UH-1H	70-71	dustoff		NAA	nose			709,
Last Chance	282 AHC		UH-1D	67-68	slick	66-00886	NO			Bernie Emswiller DG, Robert Tallent CE	1430, 1745, 9560
Last Hope	68 Med Det		UH-1H	70-71	dustoff	69-15080	NO			Horne CE, Carlos Solis MD	1661, 7725

Copter Name	Unit	Unit #1	Aircraft	Circa	Function	Serial #	Config	Location	Artist	Crew	Contributors
Last Mohican (The)	A Co 227 AHB		UH-1D	66-67	slick	62-12355	N+A	nose		Ben Michels CE	1186,
Laura	189 AHC		UH-1C	69-70	gun		NO	nose			1053, 1689
Le Disiple Du Paix	C Trp 16 Cav		OH-6A	1972	scout	68-17238	NO	doghouse		Tim Brennan, Hugh Mills, Mike King	914, 1053, 1205, 1763, 6025, 8650
Lead Magnet	B Co 123 Avn Bn		OH-6A	1971	scout	67-16518	NO	clamshell		Steve Mangano CE	1080,
Led Sled	180 ASHC		CH-47C	71-72	cargo	68-16008	NO	fuselage		Mike Molish AC	1220,
Led Zeppelin	196 ASHC		CH-47A	1968	cargo		NO				1477,
Led Zeppelin	243 ASHC		CH-47A	70-71	cargo		NO				416, 1555
Led Zeppelin	498 Med Co		UH-1H	69-71	dustoff		NO				863,
Led Zeppelin	A Co 227 AHB		UH-1H	69-70	slick		NO				197,
Led Zeppelin (The)	271 ASHC		CH-47	68-71	cargo		NO	front fuselage			8100,
Leftovers	B Co 228 ASHB		CH-47A	1966	cargo	64-13121	N+A	fuselage		Bill Kee CE	885, 8250
Lemon	B Co 25 Avn Bn		OH-23G	67-68	scout		N+A	nose			9120,
Leper Colony (The)	A Btry 2/20 ARA		UH-1B	66-67	gun		NO	pilot door		Billy Wood CP	1950, 7150
Leprechaun	D Co 227 AHB		AH-1G	69-70	gun	68-15058	NO	bpw		Martin Beckman AC	113, 1181, 1226, 2042, 5475, 6050
Let It Be	498 Med Co		UH-1H	1971	dustoff		NO	nose		Philip Roby	1496,
Life Is A Bitch	174 AHC		UH-1C	67-71	gun		N+A	quarter panel			9430,
Life's A Bitch	196 ASHC		CH-47A	1968	cargo		N+A	front fuselage			1477,
Life's A Bitch	A Co 228 ASHB		CH-47A	1969	cargo		N+A	front fuselage			475,
Light My Fire	134 AHC		UH-1H	67-69	slick	66-16658	NO	nose		Steve Gano CE, Pat Rodriguez CE, Walt Zutter AC	352, 581, 1818, 9320
Lightning Bolt	114 AHC		UH-1C	1968	gun		NO				6700, 7095
Lil' Annie's Fannie	A Co 227 AHB		UH-1H	70-71	slick	69-15715	NO	nose		Jim Jester AC	849,

Copter Name	Unit	Unit #1	Aircraft	Circa	Function	Serial #	Config	Location	Artist	Crew	Contributors
Li'l Brute	11 ACR		OH-6A	71-72	scout		NO				1467,
Lil Feller	C Trp 1/9		UH-1	66-67	gun		NO			Harold Miller CE	1197,
Lil Feller II	C Trp 1/9		UH-1	66-67	gun		NO			Harold Miller CE	1197,
Lil Ivan	155 AHC		UH-1C	69-70	gun	66-15231	NO	nose		McElvey CE, Cliff Allen CE	400, 586, 1257, 9360
Lil Jinx	114 AHC		UH-1D	1969	slick	64-13494	NO			Shelby Mansfield, T. Halpin, F. Strobel, P. Scroggin, Covington	602, 1083, 6700
Lil' Miss Joy	187 AHC		UH-1H	68-69	slick / C+C		NO	pilot door		David A. Brown CE	211, 9470
Lil' Norma Jean	187 AHC		UH-1H	70-71	slick	69-15515	NO	nose		Doug Windsand	125, 1932, 1954, 3300
Lil Pachyderm	200 ASHC		UH-1B	1967	slick	62-04587	N+A	nose		Richard Veach DG	799,
Lil Rita	155 AHC		UH-1D	65-66	slick		NO	nose		Pat Goerig AC	306, 622, 4975
Lil Sister	B Co 228 ASHB		CH-47A	1968	cargo	66-19093	NO				1760,
Lil Sue	117 AHC	Avn Co	UH-1B	63-64	slick		NO	nose			1397, 6805
Linda	134 AHC		UH-1C	1970	gun		NO	nose		Cary Mendelsohn AC, Richard Tipple DG	352, 1818
Linda	334 AWC	AHC	AH-1G	69-70	gun		NO	nose		Graham Stevens AC	1908, 2026, 4600
Linda	498 Med Co		UH-1H	1970	dustoff		NO	nose			923,
Linda 2	1 Sig Bde		OH-58A	1970	scout		NO	nose		Ron Faulkner AC	505,
Linda Ann	A Co 1 Avn Bn		UH-1B	1966	gun		N+A	doorpost			1352, 9460
Linda K (The)	68 AHC		UH-1D	1968	slick / C+C	66-16860	NO	pilot door		Dave Green CE, Paul Hill AC, Allen CP, Mike Strauss DG	69, 648, 4825, 9200
Lindy	114 AHC		UH-1H	1970	slick	67-17321	NO	nose		John Stanis CE	1681,
Lin's Rickshaw	A Co 227 AHB		UH-1D	65-66	slick	63-12964	N+A	nose	Richard Mitchell was unit artist	Mike Schlaudraff CE, J. D. Berry AC, Reggie Nelson DG, Larry Scoggins, Lonetti	1558, 1690, 9700
Liquidator	114 AHC		UH-1C	1968	gun		NO	pilot door		J. Kaltchthaler, R. Brodt, J. Juhrs, J. Kowalczyk	491, 666, 941, 1569, 6700
Liquidator	D Co 227 AHB		UH-1B	66-67	gun hog		NO	nose			84, 3850

Copter Name	Unit	Unit #1	Aircraft	Circa	Function	Serial #	Config	Location	Artist	Crew	Contributors
Litter Bird	498 Med Co		UH-1H	68-69	dustoff	67-17486	NO				380,
Little Angel	173 AHC		UH-1H	67-68	slick		NO	pilot door		Combs AC	330, 8450
Little Annie	243 ASHC		CH-47A	1969	cargo		N+A	front fuselage			111, 1975, 8075
Little Annie	D Trp 3/5		UH-1C	1968	gun	66-00682	N+A	pilot door		Albanese AC, Phipps CP, Minney CE, J. Mason DG	1209, 1301, 9860
Little Annie Fanny	45 Med Co		UH-1H	1969	dustoff		NO	nose			692,
Little Annie Fanny	B Co 25 Avn Bn		UH-1C	66-68	gun	65-09443	N+A	nose		Mark Kimm CE '67-'68, Tom Simons CE '66-'67	242, 909, 1011, 1617, 9120
Little Annie Fanny **	C Co 228 ASHB		CH-47B	68-71	cargo	67-18468	AO	fuselage		Ron Turner FE, Bob Schweitzer CE	1571, 8025
Little Annie Fanny II	B Co 25 Avn Bn		UH-1C	1969	gun		N+A	nose			1011,
Little Annie Fanny III	117 AHC	Avn Co	UH-1D	66-67	slick		NO	nose		Walt Atwood	57, 8650
Little Annie Fanny III	B Co 25 Avn Bn		UH-1C	67-68	gun		N+A	nose			9120,
Little Annie II	D Trp 3/5		UH-1C	68-69	gun		N+A	pilot door			554, 1301, 9860
Little Bear Repair ^	A Co 25 Avn Bn		UH-1D	67-68	maint		NO			Ronnie Thompson CE	1775, 9120
Little Cobra	114 AHC		UH-1C	66-67	gun		NO	pilot door		Donnie Thomas	301, 3100, 6700
Little Egypt	1 Bde 1 Cav Div		OH-6A	68-69	scout	67-16272	NO	tailboom		Sam Estes DG	486,
Little Eileen	187 AHC		UH-1D	67-68	slick		NO	pilot door			1142, 1908
Little Eileen	A Co 82 Avn Bn		UH-1B	65-66	gun		NO	doorpost		Kurt Schultz DG	800, 1567
Little Eve	114 AHC	Avn Co	UH-1B	1964	slick		NO				607, 6700
Little Green Killing Machine	A Trp 1/9		OH-6A	70-71	scout		NO			Lou Rochat	1266, 1497, 4575, 6250
Little Green Killing Machine	E Trp 1/9		OH-6A	70-71	scout		NO			Lou Rochat	1497, 6250
Little Green Taxi Cab ? (The)	162 AHC		UH-1H	71-72	slick		NO	nose		Mitch Wetherley AC	1875, 9390
Little Head Hunter	D Trp 2/1		OH-6A	69-70	scout	67-16349	NO	doghouse			369, 4000

Copter Name	Unit	Unit #1	Aircraft	Circa	Function	Serial #	Config	Location	Artist	Crew	Contributors
Little Hootin Annie	B Co 25 Avn Bn		UH-1C	66-67	gun		N+A				1617,
Little J. C.	117 AHC	Avn Co	UH-1B	64-65	gun		NO	nose			1840,
Little Joe	191 AHC		UH-1C	67-68	gun		NO	nose			1874, 9500
Little John	173 AHC		UH-1H	1970	slick		NO				7200,
Little Leroy	128 AHC		UH-1B	1968	gun	64-13960	NO	gun mount	Roy Graham	Roy Graham CE	69, 913
Little Linda	134 AHC		UH-1C	1968	gun		NO	nose		Don Neiswanger CE	352, 1405, 1818
Little Lu Lu	134 AHC		UH-1H	69-70	slick	68-16447	NO	nose		Stan Heath AC	352, 723, 1818, 9320
Little Mary	unk Signal Gp		UH-1D	1966	slick		NO	nose			265, 6625
Little Miscarriage	173 AHC		UH-1H	1968	slick	67-17222	N+A	pilot door		Richie Wolk CE	1948,
Little Miss Glenda Sue	240 AHC		UH-1H	67-68	slick	66-16601	NO	pilot door		Glenn Hoffman	769, 919, 1781
Little Miss Janet	162 AHC		UH-1D	66-67	slick	64-13856	NO	pilot door		Ed Walsh CE, Tim Murphy DG, Tilly AC, Robertson CP	1854, 9390
Little Miss Jo	173 AHC		UH-1D	66-67	slick	65-09594	NO	pilot door		Gary Mann CE, Tommy Palmertree AC	1078, 1081
Little Orphan Annie	271 ASHC		CH-47B	1968	cargo	66-19113	NO			Jack Reichert	1454,
Little Orphan Annie	B Co 25 Avn Bn		UH-1C	66-67	gun		N+A				1617,
Little Puff	155 AHC		UH-1C	66-67	gun	546 ?	NO	nose		Dan Morton CE, Al Fitzgerald CP	533, 1244, 9360
Little Rudy	UTT		UH-1B	1964		62-02065	NO				1975, 6500
Little Sorrel	11 ACR	H+HC	UH-1H	1968	C+C		NO	pilot door		Charles Watkins AC, COL George S. Patton	2073,
Little Sorrel II	11 ACR	H+HC	UH-1H	1968	C+C		NO	pilot door		Charles Watkins AC, COL George S. Patton	2073,
Little Sorrel III	11 ACR	H+HC	UH-1H	1968	C+C		NO	pilot door		Tom Vogt CE, COL George S. Patton	2073,
Little Sorrel IV	11 ACR	H+HC	UH-1H	1968	C+C		NO	pilot door		Tom Vogt CE, COL George S. Patton	2073,
Little Sorrel V	11 ACR	H+HC	UH-1H	1968	C+C		NO	pilot door		Tom Vogt CE, COL George S. Patton	2073,
Little Surprise	11 ACR		UH-1H	1970	slick		NO	pilot door			1358, 9090

Copter Name	Unit	Unit #1	Aircraft	Circa	Function	Serial #	Config	Location	Artist	Crew	Contributors
Little Texan (The)	C Co 229 AHB		UH-1H	70-71	slick	68-15745	N+A	nose		Robert Peatross CE, James Fleming CE	73, 199, 803, 1364, 1466, 1816, 6900, 9830
Little Toons	121 AHC		UH-1D	66-68	slick	64-13670	NO	nose		Jerry Daly AC	831, 1135
Little Twister	116 AHC		UH-1D	1967	slick	65-09620	NO	pilot door		Alan Horton	852,
Little Vic Dontaria	15 Med Bn		UH-1H	1971	medevac		NO			Ron Huether	808,
Little Windy *	180 ASHC		OH-58A	1970	scout	69-16096	v-nn			Allen Greenawalt CE, Earl AC	650, 1975, 7925
Little Wolf	128 AHC		UH-1H	68-71	slick		NO	nose			1053, 1908, 4600
Littlest Lobo	D Co 227 AHB		OH-6A	1969	scout	67-16326	NO	fuselage			34,
Littlest Maverick (The)	175 AHC		UH-1B	1966	gun	63-08710	NO				1926,
Liz	81 TC	119 AHC	CH-21C	1962	lift		NO	fuselage		Al Doucette DG	431,
Liz	A Trp 1/9		UH-1H	1969	slick		NO	doorpost			439, 1266, 1589, 1727, 5675, 5725, 6125
Liz	D Trp 1/1		OH-6A	1970	scout	68-17348	NO	nose			670,
Load Master ^	118 AHC	573 TC	UH-1B	64-66	maint		N+A	nose		Jim Pirtle CE	395, 655, 6125, 9260
Load Runner	273 Avn Co		CH-54A	69-70	recovery		N+A	nose			10,
Loadmaster ^	118 AHC	573 TC	UH-1B	1966	maint		N+A	nose			9260,
LOH Retriever	7/1	HHT	UH-1H	1968	recovery	66-16919	N+A	pilot door		Ed Walker AC	1848, 7085
Lois	81 TC	119 AHC	CH-21C	1962	lift	52-08621	NO	fuselage		Al Doucette DG	431,
Lola Marie	11 ACR		UH-1C	1968	gun	66-00525	NO	pilot door			855, 5925
Lolly	unk Engineer unit		UH-1H	1967	slick		NO	nose		Kiki, Mike	1035,
Lone Eagle	D Trp 3/5		UH-1D	1967	slick		NO	pilot door			1044, 9860
Lonely Bull (The)	114 AHC		UH-1D	67-68	slick	65-09826	NO	nose			8650,
Loner (The)	336 AHC		UH-1H	69-70	slick		N+A	nose		Turtle DG, Wayne CE, Ron Donakowski AC	1908, 4600
Lonesome Whippoorwill (The)	162 AHC		UH-1C	66-67	gun		NO	pilot door		Dan Baltz CE	1908, 4600

Copter Name	Unit	Unit #1	Aircraft	Circa	Function	Serial #	Config	Location	Artist	Crew	Contributors
Look Out	unknown		UH-1H	1968	slick		NO	nose			1760,
Lookout	11 ACR		UH-1H	1970	slick		NO	pilot door			439, 999, 4825, 5725
Loose Goose	57 TC	120 AHC	CH-21C	1963	lift	56-02047	N+A	fuselage			1975, 6500
Loosey Goosey *	D Trp 1/10		UH-1H	69-70	slick	66-16597	v-nn			Tim LaTour AC, Ed Skaggs CE	977,
Lord Of The Flies	159 Med Det		UH-1H	70-71	dustoff		NO	jump door		Bruce Nelson AC	1266, 6275
Lord's Prayer (The)	A Trp 1/9		AH-1G	1970	gun		NO	bpw			601, 4825
Louise	187 AHC		AH-1G	1970	gun		NO	nose			1932,
Louisiana Man	A Trp 7/1		AH-1G	71-72	gun	66-15330	N+A	bpw		Tom Putnam AC	744, 1431, 4825
Love	92 AHC		UH-1H	67-68	slick	66-16504	NO			Don Amundson CE, Bob Kendrick DG	931, 9220
Love	116 AHC		UH-1D	1967	slick	64-13627	NO	pilot door			852,
Love	188 AHC		UH-1H	1968	slick		N+A	pilot door		Ted Alley CE	24, 414, 9480
Love	B Co 9 Avn Bn		AH-1G	68-69	gun		NO	belly			2072,
Love American Style	C Trp 16 Cav		OH-6A	1972	scout	67-16428	NO	doghouse			1053, 1205, 1266, 6025, 6250
Love Bug	D Trp 3/4		OH-6A	69-70	scout		NO			Eric Brethen AC, Ken Taylor CE, Mathis DG	146, 194
Love Child	192 AHC		UH-1H	69-70	slick	66-16840	NO			Mike Lavenberg CE	981, 9510
Love Child	238 AWC	AHC	UH-1B	69-70	gun		NO	nose		Stratton CE, Luchini AC	1642, 9530
Love Child	281 AHC		UH-1C	1969	gun	036 ? 008 ?	NO	nose	John Gachich	Daryl Evangelho CE, John Gachich DG	66, 488, 570, 9550
Love Craft	242 ASHC		CH-47A	69-70	cargo	65-07999	NO	nose		Larry Spence FE, David Schultz DG, Ross Bedient FE	1199, 1669, 1944, 8050, 8250
Love Generation	B Co 25 Avn Bn		UH-1C	68-69	gun	66-15170	N+A	nose	Farren originated name	Frank Brashor DG, Joe Footer AC '67-'68, Dan Farren CE '68-'69, Tom Linebaugh DG '68-'69	49, 502, 542, 909, 1060, 5025, 9120
Love Portion #9	336 AHC	A/101	UH-1B	66-67	gun	63-12925	NO			Tom Wainscott CE	1846, 9610
Love, Peace, Music	174 AHC		UH-1C	1971	gun	64-14140	N+A	quarter panel		Kevin Crabtree DG, Legault CE	184, 9430
Loved 1 (The)	336 AHC		UH-1C	69-70	gun		NO			John Cronan CE	370, 2089, 9610

Copter Name	Unit	Unit #1	Aircraft	Circa	Function	Serial #	Config	Location	Artist	Crew	Contributors
Lucky 7	173 Abn Bde		UH-1H	68-71	slick		N+A	nose			159,
Lucky 7	C Co 227 AHB		UH-1H	1968	slick		N+A	pilot door			1127, 1376
Lucky 8	unknown		AH-1G	70-71	gun		N+A	nose			2083,
Lucky 13	57 TC	120 AHC	CH-21C	1963	lift		NO	fuselage			1975, 6500
Lucky 13	119 AHC		UH-1H	1967	slick	66-16850	N+A	nose		Rich Olson AC, Dave Calloway CE	1328,
Lucky Eagle ^	2 Bde 101 Abn Div		UH-1H	1968	C+C	67-17554	NO	nose		Zais	926, 4850, 6850
Lucky Joker	62 CAC		UH-1H	69-73	slick		NO	nose			802, 1529, 9190
Lucky Lady	134 AHC		UH-1H	1971	slick	70-15777	NO				352, 1818
Lucky Lady (The)	A Trp 3/17		OH-6A	1968	scout	66-17792	NO	doghouse		Robert Fisher CE	335, 9720
Lucky Leita	175 AHC		UH-1C	1967	gun	66-15045	NO	pilot door		Jack Smith	41, 301, 5275
Lucky Leprechaun	A Co 229 AHB		UH-1D	65-66	slick		NO	nose	Sidney Cowan	Sidney Cowan AC	353,
Lucky Strike	336 AHC		UH-1D	69-70	slick / lightship	65-12885	NO			Dennis Yokum DG, Connelly AC	508, 1809, 1970, 6845, 9610
Lucy In Da Sky	45 Med Co		UH-1H	67-68	dustoff		NO				450,
Lucy In The Sky	A Co 227 AHB		UH-1H	69-70	slick	68-15251	NO	nose		James Cooper CE	342, 9700
Lucy In The Sky With Diamonds	175 AHC		UH-1D	67-68	slick	66-16067	NO	nose		Amburgey, Mike Kenna	15, 9520
Lucy In The Sky With Diamonds	187 AHC		UH-1D	67-68	slick		NO				1882,
Lucy In The Sky With Diamonds	188 AHC		UH-1H	67-68	slick	66-16119	NAA	pilot door	Dick Detra	Charlie Maurer AC, Ron Merlock CE, Jim Trueblood CE, Dick Detra DG	414, 1024, 1115, 1178, 1266, 1849, 6275, 9480
Lucy In The Sky With Diamonds	unk		UH-1C	1968	gun		N+A	nose			739,
Luger Wagon	134 AHC		UH-1H	67-68	slick	66-16321	NO	nose		Yellowhorse CE, Art Yerden DG, Tony Zucco AC	352, 1818, 1969
Luke	155 AHC		UH-1C	1967	gun		NO	XM-156 dust shield			301, 696, 1053, 1187, 5900, 6025, 6225
Lurch	D Trp 1/1		AH-1G	1970	gun		N+A	bpw		Jim Mahoney AC	2060,
Lynda Sue	114 AHC	Avn Co	UH-1B	1964	slick	62-01959	NO	cargo door window panel		J. Danielson, R. Mills, N. Solis, Jackson, R. Davis	397, 1662, 1975, 6525, 6700

Copter Name	Unit	Unit #1	Aircraft	Circa	Function	Serial #	Config	Location	Artist	Crew	Contributors
Lynn	D Trp 1/4		AH-1G	69-70	gun	67-13507	NO	nose			1205,
Mabel	114 AHC	Avn Co	UH-1B	65-66	gun		NO			B. Jones, Anderson, W. Dunnum	860, 6700
Mabel	B Co 159 ASHB		CH-47B	69-70	cargo	67-18434	NO	fuselage		John Hendrickson AC	731,
Macabre	114 AHC		AH-1G	1970	gun	69-16420	NO	bpw		Jeff Carr, Gary Dekay	282, 6700
Macabre	336 AHC		UH-1C	69-70	gun		NO			Raul Segura CE	320, 1212, 1584
Macabre II	336 AHC		UH-1C	69-70	gun		NO			Gary Carter DG, Coleman DG/CE, Raul Segura CE	320, 1584, 2091
Mack	1 Bde 1 Cav Div		OH-6A	1969	scout		NO	nose		Cleveland Grant CE	486, 641, 8975
Mack II	1 Bde 1 Cav Div		OH-6A	1969	scout		NO	nose		Cleveland Grant CE	486, 641, 1337, 8975
Mack III	1 Bde 1 Cav Div		OH-6A	1969	scout	16941	NO	nose		Cleveland Grant CE	486, 641
Mad Bomber	A Co 82 Avn Bn		UH-1D	65-67	MAD		NO	pilot door		Kurt Schultz DG, John Hoza AC	52, 800, 1567
Mad Butcher	F Btry 79 AFA		AH-1G	71-72	gun	67-15637	NO			Axe CE, Tripper CE, Rickenbacker AC	850, 2000
Mad Dog	242 ASHC		CH-47A	68-71	cargo		NO				1199, 1225, 8350
Mad Hatter	62 CAC		UH-1H	1969	slick	662	NO			Mitch Matsuoka DG, Clyde Williams CE	1112, 9190
Mad Irishman (The)	119 AHC		UH-1C	1967	gun		NO	nose			452, 1053, 5750, 6025
Mad Tom	121 AHC		UH-1D	67-68	slick		N+A	nose			477, 1593, 6975, 9290
Madame Num	175 AHC		UH-1D	68-70	slick		NO	nose		Joe Wizneski DG, Tom Stowell AC	429, 904, 1652, 1714, 1926, 9440
Madonna II	A Co 1 Avn Bn		UH-1D	1968	slick	65-12870	NO	cargo door frame top		Pope AC, Milton CP, Butch Weaver CE, E. Alioto DG	20,
Mafia Queen	B Co 25 Avn Bn		UH-1C	1966	gun		N+A	nose + pilot door	Mike Garrity	Pat Shea DG, Tony Adessa CP, Shaw AC	9, 590, 1596, 9120
Maggot Wagon (The) *	71 AHC		UH-1H	70-71	slick		v-nn				614, 1429
Magic	175 AHC		UH-1D	67-68	smoke	65-09794	NO	nose + pilot door		Mike Hersey AC, Mike Kenna DG/CE, Ed Otten, Tony Gaultney	429, 743, 899, 9130, 9440
Magic Bus *	174 AHC		UH-1H	1970	slick	68-15223	v-nn			John Bullen CE, John Bailey AC	233,

Magic Bus: *B Troop 1/9 Cav, UH-1H, (sn 68-16349), 1970-71.* A survivor of VN with 1,911 hours including time with D-229 AHB. Photo by Jerry Hogan via Jeremy Hogan.

Copter Name	Unit	Unit #1	Aircraft	Circa	Function	Serial #	Config	Location	Artist	Crew	Contributors
Magic Bus	178 ASHC		CH-47B	69-70	cargo	67-18464	NO			Joe McLenaghan FE	1154, 7875
Magic Bus	B Trp 1/9		UH-1H	70-71	slick	68-16349	NO	nose		Jerry Hogan DG/CE, George Minda CE	770, 771, 1208, 9905
Magic Carpet Ride	116 AHC		UH-1D	1968	slick		NO	nose			1623,
Magic Carpet Ride	B Co 227 AHB		UH-1H	70-71	slick	68-16171	N+A	nose			1025,
Magic Carpet Ride	C Co 101 AHB		UH-1H	68-69	slick	67-17474	NO	interior floor		Lonnie Heidtke CE, Tom Sweeney AC, P. Pointer DG	726,
Magic Christian (The)	571 Med Det		UH-1H	69-70	dustoff		NO				1600,
Magical Mystery Tour	A Co 227 AHB		UH-1H	1969	slick	66-16825	NO	nose		Dave Ondrey DG, Roger Barnhard CE	562, 1329
Magical Mystery Tour	B Trp 1/9		UH-1H	1970	slick	66-17086	NO	nose			770, 1208
Magical Mystery Tour (The)	D Co 229 AHB		AH-1G	71-72	gun	67-15531	NAA	bpw		Roger Fox AC	134, 1513, 5450
Magnet Ass	45 Med Co		UH-1H	68-69	dustoff		NO	nose		Wayne Davidson CE	391,
Magnet Ass	45 Med Co		UH-1H	70-71	dustoff		NO			John Richardson CE	1746,
Magnet Ass	57 AHC		UH-1C	69-70	gun		NO	nose			409,
Magnet Ass **	178 ASHC		CH-47B	67-68	cargo		AO	front fuselage			842,
Magnet Ass	271 ASHC		CH-47B	68-71	cargo	66-19110	N+A	front fuselage		Phil Miller FE, Redmond, L. Michael Herrin	144, 740, 964, 1087, 1805, 1896, 8100
Magnet Ass	283 Med Det		UH-1H	67-68	dustoff		NO	nose		Tom Anglin CE	39,
Magnet Ass	498 Med Co		UH-1H	1968	dustoff	66-17043	NO	jump door		J. Richardson CE, Ben Knisely CP, Mike Meyer AC	930,
Magnet Ass *	C Trp 1/9		OH-6A	1971	scout		v-nn				1003,
Magnificent Men And Their Flying Machine (The)	175 AHC		UH-1H	71-72	slick	67-17346	NO	nose		E. Hubbard AC, I. Miller CE, J. P. Klink DG	429, 904, 1652, 9440
Magnifico Chicken	A Co 227 AHB		UH-1H	70-71	slick	69-15715	N+A	nose	Joe Paranal	Jim Jester AC	849, 1340, 1789
Magnolia State	121 AHC		UH-1D	1966	slick	64-13673	N+A	nose	Huffman	Will Huffman CE, C. F. Koegel AC, D. H. Angel CP	809,
Magnolia Thunderpussy	361 AWC		AH-1G	1972	gun	67-15825	NO			Stephen Speer CE	1668, 9170

Copter Name	Unit	Unit #1	Aircraft	Circa	Function	Serial #	Config	Location	Artist	Crew	Contributors
Maint Runner	7/1	HHT	UH-1H	1970	maint		NO	nose			173,
Major Malfunction	190 AHC		UH-1D	1970	slick		NO	nose		Tom Harney AC, David Coons CE	699,
Make Love And War	336 AHC	A/101	UH-1B	66-68	gun	64-13905	NO	rocket pod		Bob Knight	668, 927, 9610
Maltese Cross **	174 AHC		UH-1C	1970	gun	65-09555	AO	quarter panel		Fred Thompson	184, 233, 1770, 9430
Maltese Cross **	176 AHC		UH-1C	1969	gun		AO	nose			1595,
Maltese Cross **	191 AHC		UH-1D	67-68	slick	66-00831	AO	pilot door	Richard Weske	Don Williams AC	86, 1913
Mandrake Root	336 AHC		UH-1C	69-70	gun	64-14113	N+A	nose		Raul Segura CE, Coleman DG, David Adams AC	508, 1212, 1584, 9610
Mar	C Trp 7/1		AH-1G	68-69	gun	67-15475	NO	bpw		Mike Peterson CE, Rob Bailey AC	1382,
Marauder	132 ASHC		CH-47B	70-71	cargo	67-18441	N+A	front fuselage	SP4 Davis did all '70-'71 a/c art		729, 1162, 1588, 7800, 8275
Margarita Naomie	119 AHC		UH-1H	69-70	slick		NO	nose			1797,
Marion Spook	81 TC	119 AHC	CH-21C	1962	lift	51-15889	NO	fuselage			431,
Marquis De Sade	48 AHC		UH-1C	70-71	gun		NO	nose		James Jackson CE, Fred Few AC	716, 832, 9150
Marquis De Sade	B Co 227 AHB		UH-1H	69-70	slick	65-09590	N+A	nose		Kevin Mooney CE	1227,
Marrakesh Express	240 AHC		UH-1H	1971	slick		NO	nose			1933, 4825
Marrakesh Express	242 ASHC		CH-47A	70-71	cargo		NO				1056, 1199
Marrakesh Express	B Co 227 AHB		UH-1H	70-71	slick		N+A	nose			965,
Marrakesh Express (The)	D Co 229 AHB		AH-1G	70-71	gun		NO	bpw			1053, 1859, 1908, 4600
Mary Ann	C Co 229 AHB		UH-1H	67-69	slick	66-16734	NO	nose		Stan Wisbith CE	1466, 1939, 9830
Mary Jane	118 AHC		UH-1H	70-71	slick		NO			Ken Simpson DG	1620, 8525
Mary Jane	134 AHC		UH-1H	68-69	slick		NO	nose		Karl Renz DG/CE, Paul Codorniz CE, Frank Synder DG	352, 1459, 1658, 1818, 9320
Mary Jane	336 AHC	A/101	UH-1B	65-67	gun		NO	nose			1428, 9610, 9680

Copter Name	Unit	Unit #1	Aircraft	Circa	Function	Serial #	Config	Location	Artist	Crew	Contributors
Mary Jane	A Co 4 Avn Bn		UH-1H	68-69	slick	66-16598	NO	nose		Gipson AC, Jim Clark CE, Mooney CE, Tom Rowbottom	430, 567, 612, 822, 1242, 9060
Mary Lee	C Trp 7/1		AH-1G	1968	gun	67-15460	NO	bpw	Billy Young	Billy Young AC	1382, 1971
Master Panther	117 AHC		UH-1H	1970	slick		NO	nose		Dick Dutson CP	455,
Maui Girl	114 AHC	Avn Co	UH-1B	1964	slick		NO			Leo Demaso CE, Ted Winowitch DG, Jim Wright AC, Ken DeLozier CP	544, 5825
Max Well	B Trp 1/9		OH-6A	1972	scout		N+A	doghouse		Paul Murtha AC	1264, 1786, 9740
Max Well	F Trp 9 Cav		OH-6A	1972	scout		N+A	doghouse		Paul Murtha AC	1264, 1786, 2007, 4850
Maxine	187 AHC		UH-1D	67-68	slick		NO	pilot door		Ken Scruton CE, E. Mercer AC, Jordan CP, J. Seitz DG	1713,
MBG	11 ACR		UH-1H	1968	recovery		NO				2052,
MBG II	11 ACR		UH-1H	1969	recovery		NO				2052,
MBG III	11 ACR		UH-1H	1970	recovery		NO	pilot door			439, 2052, 5725
Mean Mistreater	117 AHC		UH-1M	71-72	gun	66-00588	NO	nose		Tom Smith CE, Alwinn AC	936, 1654
Mean Motha	C Trp 16 Cav		AH-1G	1972	gun		NO	bpw			1053, 1205
Mean Mother Fucker	120 AHC		UH-1	1968	gun		NO	nose			210,
Mean Mr. Mustard	B Trp 1/9		AH-1G	70-71	gun		NO				1208,
Mean Mr. Mustard	C Btry 2/20 ARA		AH-1G	70-71	gun	67-15670	NO	bpw	C. McMillian	Don Mather CE, Hinch CE, Jerry Martin AC, Bob Cushman AC	850, 1097, 1111, 1169, 1236, 1815, 9880
Mean Mr. Mustard	F Btry 79 AFA		AH-1G	71-72	gun	67-15670	NO	bpw		Shield AC, Northrup CP, Hinch CE	803, 833, 850, 9710
Means To An End	176 AHC		UH-1H	1970	slick	66-16837	NO	nose			1027, 1475, 9450, 9885
Means To An End	176 AHC		UH-1M	70-71	gun	66-00520	NO				901, 1027, 9885
Mela	191 AHC		UH-1H	1969	slick		NO	pilot door			7000,
Mellow Yellow	57 AHC		UH-1	68-69			NO			Dale Warren CE	1867, 9180
Mellow Yellow	178 ASHC		CH-47A	66-67	cargo	65-07999	N+A	front fuselage		Dean Nelson CE, Butch Harvey FE	1280,
Mellow Yellow	B Co 229 AHB		UH-1H	69-70	slick	67-17163	NO			John Martin DG/CE, Peterson AC	1098, 1990, 9710

Copter Name	Unit	Unit #1	Aircraft	Circa	Function	Serial #	Config	Location	Artist	Crew	Contributors
Melvin's Toy	D Trp 1/1		AH-1G	68-70	gun		NO	nose		Mel Walker AC	1850,
Melvin's Toy II	D Trp 1/1		AH-1G	68-70	gun		N+A	nose		Mel Walker AC	670, 1850
Memphis Belle	C Co 229 AHB		UH-1D	65-66	slick		N+A	doorpost			783,
Memphis Belle	C Co 229 AHB		UH-1H	69-71	slick	66-16816	N+A	nose		Danny Brewer CE, Wayne Head AC	36, 720, 9710
Mercenary (The)	170 AHC		UH-1C	1969	gun		NO	nose		John McKee	902, 1543, 9400
Mercenary: You Pay We Slay (The)	17 AHC		UH-1B	1968	gun		NO	nose		Ron Burns CE, Bill Spiller DG	1540,
Merry Christmas	242 ASHC		CH-47		cargo		NO	rear pylon			8925,
Message From Michael	187 AHC		AH-1G	70-71	gun		NO	nose		Mike Hodges AC	1700,
Messanger Service	175 AHC		UH-1H	71-72	slick	68-15482	NO	nose			429,
Metal Rain	unk		UH-1D	1965	slick		NO			Walter Sarratt DG	1546,
Mexican Express	174 AHC		UH-1C	1970	gun	66-00645	N+A	quarter panel	Albert Garza	Albert Garza CE	278, 592, 1053, 1266, 1770, 6025, 6225, 9430
Mexican Express (The)	92 AHC		UH-1C	68-69	gun	66-15144	N+A	nose	Albert Garza	Albert Garza CE	1975
Mi Chata	191 AHC		UH-1D	1968	slick	65-10103	NO	pilot door		Alan Maw CE	1116,
Michele 1	191 AHC		UH-1D	1967	slick	66-00820	NO	pilot door	Richard Weske	Bud Patnode AC, Ron Exley CP, D. Stits CE, C. Wigfall DG	1351,
Michelle 1	240 AHC		UH-1H	67-68	slick	66-16185	NO	pilot door		Martin Klann CE, Tom Carter AC, Franklin Hiner CP	919, 1781
Michigan Menace	A Co 227 AHB		UH-1H	68-69	slick	67-17439	NO	nose		Ron Lazenby CE, Howard Goff DG	990, 9700
Midge	114 AHC	Avn Co	UH-1B	1964	slick	62-01936	NO	cargo door window panel		D. Slauson, P. Wickliffe, R. Garnes, Fogey	615, 1975, 5430, 6525, 6700
Midnite Cowboy	A Trp 1/9		AH-1G	1971	gun	68-17035	NO	bpw		Larry Lilly CP, Schwetzer AC	360, 951, 4300
Mighty Chicken	A Co 227 AHB		UH-1H	70-71	slick	69-15787	N+A	nose	Joe Paranal	Steve Lachiondo CE, Joe Parnell CE, Salizar AC	955, 1232, 1340, 1369, 1789, 9700
Mighty Gun Bird	A Trp 1/9		UH-1B	1969	gun	64-13952	NO	doorpost		Jim Farner CE, Grey, Dyne, Mader, Bridge, Westmore	500, 1069, 1266, 1589, 1724, 6125, 9690
Mighty Mouse (The)	D Trp 1/1		AH-1G	70-71	gun	972 ?	N+A	bpw		Gary Kane CE, Nick Lappos AC	670, 882, 901, 969, 1864, 3450, 5050, 9450, 9835
Mighty Quinn (The)	242 ASHC		CH-47A	70-71	cargo		NO				1056,
Mindbender	B Trp 3/17		UH-1H	1969	slick		NO				undocumented: sequence originator?

007: *240 AHC, UH-1H, (sn 66-16007), 1968.* Visible in the Co-Pilot seat is Bob Cooper. "007" served in four different units and survived VN with 2,317 total hours. Photo courtesy Bob Cooper.

Copter Name	Unit	Unit #1	Aircraft	Circa	Function	Serial #	Config	Location	Artist	Crew	Contributors
Mindbender II	B Trp 3/17		UH-1H	1969	slick		NO	doorpost		Art Duff AC	446, 1395, 9790
Mini Hog *	D Trp 3/4		UH-1C	1968	gun		v-nn			Pat Eastes AC	460,
Mini Mule	242 ASHC		OH-58A	1971	scout	68-16951	NO				1056,
Mini Power	F Trp 4 Cav		OH-6A	1971	scout		NO	minigun housing			140,
Mini Skinner	242 ASHC		UH-1H	1968	slick	66-16333	NO	cargo door frame bottom			1056, 1225, 8350
Miscarriage (The)	271 ASHC		CH-47B	68-70	cargo	66-19127	NO	front fuselage		John Tucker, Joe Clifton	1805, 1896
Misfit (The)	173 AHC		UH-1C	68-69	gun	66-00742	NO	pilot door		Clarence Perkins CE, Lorin Richardson DG/CE	834, 1374, 1472
Miss America	62 CAC		UH-1H	1969	slick		NO	nose		Edward J. Hickey AC	7050,
Miss Arlene	114 AHC	Avn Co	UH-1B	65-66	slick		NO				1290, 6700
Miss Behavin W.E.T.S.U.	175 AHC		UH-1C	67-68	gun	66-15047	N+A	pilot door			932,
Miss Bev	B Co 228 ASHB		CH-47A	67-68	cargo	66-00077	NO	fuselage		Hugh Buzzell FE, Paul Redmon CE, Lynn Thompson DG	251, 8025
Miss Carol	173 AHC		UH-1D	66-67	slick		NO	pilot door		Visel CE	1931,
Miss Carol II	173 AHC		UH-1D	66-67	slick		NO	pilot door		Visel CE	1931,
Miss Carol III	173 AHC		UH-1D	66-67	slick		NO	pilot door		Visel CE	1931,
Miss Carol IV	173 AHC		UH-1H	66-67	slick		NO	pilot door		Visel CE, Mke Wilton AC	1931,
Miss Carriage	116 AHC		UH-1D	68-69	slick		NO	nose		Joe Skarda DG	1623,
Miss Carriage	132 ASHC		CH-47B	68-69	cargo	67-18451	N+A	front fuselage			303, 1162, 1219, 7800
Miss Carriage	187 AHC		UH-1H	1969	slick	68-16795	NO	pilot door		Avery AC, Eddie Lucero CE, Tony Hernandez DG	60,
Miss Carriage	190 AHC		UH-1D	1970	slick		NO	nose	CE + DG	Tom Harney AC, David Coons CE	699,
Miss Carriage	281 AHC		UH-1C	69-70	gun		NO				66,
Miss Carriage	C Co 227 AHB		UH-1D	1967	slick		NO				506,
Miss Chris	178 ASHC		CH-47A	1967	cargo	518895 ?	NO	fuselage		Ron Bearly FE	108, 8525

Copter Name	Unit	Unit #1	Aircraft	Circa	Function	Serial #	Config	Location	Artist	Crew	Contributors
Miss Chris Too	179 ASHC		CH-47A	67-68	cargo	65-07983	NO	fuselage		Ron Bearly FE	108, 8525
Miss Claude	D Trp 1/4		OH-6A	69-70	scout	66-07927	NO	doghouse		Hugh Mills AC	1205,
Miss Claude II	D Trp 1/4		OH-6A	69-70	scout	68-17191	NO	doghouse		Hugh Mills AC	1205,
Miss Claude III	D Trp 1/4		OH-6A	69-70	scout	68-17218	NO	doghouse		Hugh Mills AC	1205,
Miss Clawd IV	C Trp 16 Cav		OH-6A	72-73	scout	68-17340	NO	doghouse		Hugh Mills AC, Jim Christy CE	439, 1053, 1205, 1266, 1763, 4825, 5700, 6025, 6250
Miss Dizzy	B Trp 3/17		AH-1G	71-72	gun		NO	bpw		Bill Simmons AC	1613,
Miss Fit	114 AHC	Avn Co	UH-1B	65-66	slick	62-01968	NO	nose		Howard Chambers CE, McVeigh AC	294, 6700, 6750, 9230
Miss Fortune	336 AHC		UH-1C	68-69	gun		N+A	pilot door		Butch Markley CE	1088,
Miss Fortune II	336 AHC		UH-1C	1969	gun		N+A	pilot door			967, 1442, 1451, 4050
Miss G	A Trp 3/17		OH-6A	1969	scout	67-16261	NO	doghouse		Glasser CE	503, 8625
Miss Jo	129 AHC		UH-1	1971			NO				28, 4925
Miss Judy	135 AHC		UH-1C	70-71	gun	66-15127	NO	nose			69, 187, 8450, 9330
Miss June	335 AHC		UH-1H	70-71	slick	68-16373	NO	nose			69, 695, 1926
Miss Kathy	C Trp 16 Cav		AH-1G	1970	gun		NO	bpw			1205, 1305, 4825
Miss Kathy Ann	D Trp 3/5		OH-6A	68-69	scout	66-14416	NO	doghouse		Tom Fernandez CE	509,
Miss Kristy	117 AHC		UH-1M	1971	gun	65-09554	NO			Tony Cucchiara CE	377, 9250
Miss Lou	114 AHC	Avn Co	UH-1B	65-66	slick	62-01917	NO	nose		Barton, D. Sickler	1266, 1608, 6275, 6700
Miss Lucky 7	119 AHC	Avn Co	UH-1B	65-66	gun	64-13939	N+A	nose		Ed Coombs AC, Jimmy Roberts CE	338, 5725
Miss Mamolani (sp?)	117 AHC	Avn Co	UH-1B	64-65	slick		NO				1840,
Miss Mar-Leen	187 AHC		UH-1H	68-70	slick	67-17767	NO	pilot door		Dave Brown CE	571, 9470
Miss Me	11 ACR		OH-6A	68-69	scout	67-16221	NO	fuselage			1703,
Miss Mini	118 AHC		UH-1C	67-68	gun	65-09510	NO	nose		Fred Eckelmann CE, John Ferrara CE, Carl Creal AC	516, 1185, 1266, 1481, 1975, 2080 6225, 9260

Miss Kathy Ann: *D Troop 3/5 Cav, OH-6A, (sn 66-14416), 1968-69.* Crew Chief Tom Fernandez tends to '416, which accumulated 501 hours before a B-40 rocket abruptly ended her combat mission on 4-6-69. Photo by J. Harold Feltner.

Copter Name	Unit	Unit #1	Aircraft	Circa	Function	Serial #	Config	Location	Artist	Crew	Contributors
Miss Molly Erin Go Braugh	178 ASHC		CH-47A	66-68	cargo	64-13157	N+A	front fuselage			841,
Miss Mynookie	178 ASHC		CH-47B	68-69	cargo	67-18470	NO			Jim Kilgo FE, Earl Evans FE, Gary Grey CE	298, 489, 1946
Miss Mynookie #2	178 ASHC		CH-47B	69-71	cargo	67-18483	NO	front fuselage		Earl Evans FE '69, Gary Grey CE, Dave Reynolds FE '70-'71	489, 1946
Miss Oklahoma	145 Airlift Plt		UH-1B	1965	slick	63-08632	NO	cargo door frame bottom		Jerry Stanfield DG, Darrell Griffin CE	1680, 9550
Miss Patches *	334 AWC	AHC	UH-1C	67-68	gun	64-14167	v-nn			Howie Frith, Jim Aretz CE, John Macedo	45,
Miss Patches II	334 AWC		UH-1C	67-68	gun	66-00506	NO			Jim Aretz CE	45,
Miss Patches III	334 AWC		UH-1C	67-68	gun	66-15185	NO			Jim Aretz CE	45,
Miss Pussy Galore	A Co 227 AHB		UH-1D	66-67	slick	63-08829	NO	nose	Ralph Magliaro	Ralph Magliaro CE	706, 845, 9700
Miss Rita	A Trp 2/17		AH-1G	69-71	gun		NO				8400,
Miss Stony	A Co 228 ASHB		CH-47A	1969	cargo		N+A	front fuselage		Meeks FE	475,
Miss Susan	114 AHC	Avn Co	UH-1B	65-66	slick		NO			C. Scott	1575, 6700
Miss Zoe Ann	8 TC	117 AHC	CH-21C	63-64	lift	135	NO	fuselage		Ron Fimans CE	127, 525, 1397, 6805, 8650, 9250
Missing Link (The)	189 AHC		UH-1H	1970	slick	68-16295	N+A	nose	downtown Pleiku artist	Gordon Rohrs DG, Vergil Rutherford CE, Craig Dobson AC	313, 1530
Mission Impossible	189 AHC		UH-1H	68-69	slick	67-01111	NO	nose		David Munsell CE	760, 1260, 9490
Mission Impossible	B Co 228 ASHB		CH-47B	70-71	cargo	66-19143	NO	fuselage		John Lippert CE	1026, 1239, 8025
Mississippi	B Co 123 Avn Bn		OH-6A	70-71	scout	69-15997	NO	clamshell			1053, 1205,
Mississippi Queen	D Trp 3/4		AH-1G	70-71	gun	67-15546	N+A	doghouse		Randy Jones AC, Jim Hoag CE	759, 1559, 2005, 4300
Mississippi State Flag	121 AHC		UH-1D	1966	slick	64-13673	NAA	nose	Huffman	Will Huffman CE, C. F. Koegel AC, D. H. Angel CP	809,
Missile Muscle	B Btry 2/20 ARA		UH-1B	1967	gun	62-12518	N+A	nose			301,
Missy D	D Co 229 AHB		AH-1G	1969	gun		NO	nose			1727,
Mr. Lonely	114 AHC		UH-1D	1969	slick	64-13831	NO	nose		Leyerly	6700, 6750
Mister Olds **	D Co 227 AHB		AH-1G	1971	gun	69-16442	AO	bpw		Evers AC, Biland CE	280, 1266, 6275, 6300

Miss Mynookie #2: *178 ASHC, CH-47B, (sn 67-18470), 1968-69.* The "#2" is barely visible beside the open door where Door Gunner Steve Wolak is standing. This durable CH-47 survived VN with 1,724 hours, all with the 178th. Photo courtesy Steve Wolak.

Copter Name	Unit	Unit #1	Aircraft	Circa	Function	Serial #	Config	Location	Artist	Crew	Contributors
Misty	187 AHC		UH-1D	1968	slick	66-16845	NO	pilot door		Sanchez DG, Al Duquette AC	1451, 1908, 4050, 4600
Moe's Meatwagon	114 AHC		UH-1D	67-68	slick	66-00902	NO			K. Smith DG, Jack Moe CE, Allan Brown AC, Miller AC	1639, 2015
Molly *	283 Med Det		UH-1H	70-71	dustoff	68-15573	v-nn			Steve Costic CE, Danny Hendren MD	2074,
Mongoloid (The)	C Trp 16 Cav		AH-1G	70-71	gun	68-15055	NO	bpw		George Johnson AC, Jack Vick CE	576, 1835, 9810
Monica Lee	C Trp 7/1		AH-1G	68-69	gun	67-15477	NO	bpw	Joe Dike	Joe Dike CE, Damon Cecil AC	418, 1382
Monster Man	188 AHC		UH-1C	1968	gun		NO			G. Dean Murphy AC	1262, 6475
Montana Mercenary	A Trp 1/9		AH-1G	70-71	gun		NO				1497, 1266, 6250
Montana Mercenary	D Co 227 AHB		AH-1G	68-69	gun		NO	bpw			937, 9700
Montana Mercenary	E Trp 1/9		AH-1G	70-71	gun		NO				1266, 1497, 6259
Moon	175 AHC		UH-1B	66-67	gun	63-08712	NO	pilot door			851, 9130
Moon Equipped	205 ASHC		CH-47A	67-68	cargo		NO	fuselage		George Galo AC	579, 8525
Moonlight Lady	A Trp 3/17		UH-1H	68-69	slick	67-17856	NO	quarter panel		Charles Stutzman AC	719,
Morning After	175 AHC		UH-1C	1967	gun	66-15044	N+A	pilot door		Dwayne Williams AC, Dave Osbourne CE, Tom Greenfield DG, David Savage AC, Bob Elson DG, Mongogna, Smith, Thayer	301, 395, 461, 651, 780, 932, 982, 1330, 1764, 1914, 1926, 5675, 5775, 9440
Mortician (The)	192 AHC		UH-1C	1969	gun		NO	nose		Jose Rivera CE	319,
Mortician (The)	281 AHC		UH-1C	1967	gun	552 ?	N+A	nose		Trubee Krothe DG/CE, Frankie Esquilin CE	946, 9550
Mother Goose	191 AHC		UH-1C	67-68	gun	66-15107	N+A	pilot door		Stan Cherrie AC, Skip Waugh CE	302, 539, 1451, 1701, 4510, 9500
Mother Goose	254 Med Det		UH-1H	68-70	dustoff		NO	pilot door		Ben Trickle CE, Larry Miller CE, Lawrence Turk MD	424, 664, 954
Mother Goose	271 ASHC		CH-47B	1968	cargo	66-19126	NO			Dan Markell FE, Jerry McBee CE	144, 1087, 1122, 8100
Mother Goose II	271 ASHC		CH-47B	1968	cargo	67-18482	N+A	fuselage		Dan Markell FE, Jerry McBee CE, T. C. Smith AC, F. V. Trimeloni CP	144, 964, 1087, 1122, 8100
Mother Hawk	244 Avn Co		UH-1B	67-68	slick		NO	nose		Lord AC, Suttlehan AC	599, 1994
Mother Hawker	175 AHC		AH-1G	1971	gun		NO				1370, 9440
Mother Superior	192 AHC		UH-1C	1971	gun		NO	nose			51, 343, 920, 1298, 1878, 1901

Mother Goose II*: 271 ASHC, CH-47B, (sn 67-18482), Can Tho, 1968*. Flight Engineer Dan Markell, pictured, also crewed 66-19126, the first "Mother Goose." Together with time spent in the B-159 ASHB, '482 accumulated 2,269 hours before returning intact to the U.S. Photo courtesy Dan Markell.

Copter Name	Unit	Unit #1	Aircraft	Circa	Function	Serial #	Config	Location	Artist	Crew	Contributors
Mother Superior's Guns	C Btry 2/20 ARA		AH-1G	70-71	gun		NO				154,
Mother's Grief	134 AHC		UH-1H	69-70	slick	68-15309	NO			Ernie Acosta CE, B.H. Roberts AC, C.E. Taylor CP, M.R. Johnson DG	352, 1818
Mother's Lil' Worry	21 Signal Group		UH-1H	70-71	slick	68-16078	NO	nose		Mattern CP, D. Baggott AC	64,
Mother's Lil' Worry	498 Med Co		UH-1D	66-67	dustoff		NO	nose			1908, 4600
Mother's Worry	134 AHC		UH-1H	68-69	slick		NO			Mike Dzikowski AC	352, 1818
Motown	117 AHC		UH-1H	68-69	slick	65-09679	NO	nose		Keith Alleger AC	21, 395, 439, 5675, 5725
Mr B's Bad Bomber	336 AHC		UH-1B	66-67	gun		NO	nose		Billet AC, Wardwell CE	2038,
Mr B's Bad Bomber II	336 AHC		UH-1B	66-67	gun	977	NO	nose		Billet AC, Wardwell CE	2038,
Mr. Bojangle	B Trp 1/9		UH-1H	1969	slick		NO	nose			193, 9740
Mr. Bojangles	114 AHC		UH-1D	1968	slick	66-16201	NO			Andy Anderson AC, T. McMahon, B. Schulte DG, R. Sciapiti CE	1053, 1566, 1573, 6700
Mr. Bojangles	114 AHC		UH-1H	71-72	slick		NO			Joe Alfano AC	19,
Mr. Bond	283 Med Det		UH-1H	1969	dustoff	66-17007	NO	nose		Mike Rhinehart AC	1465,
Mr. Clean	C Co 229 AHB		UH-1H	70-71	slick	68-16467	N+A	nose			199, 803, 1816, 9830
Mr. Groovy	11 ACR		UH-1H	1970	slick		NAA	pilot door			1358, 9090
Mr. Huey	C Trp 1/9		UH-1B	65-66	gun	62-02063	NO	nose		Mike Kelley CE	893,
Mr. Lonely	173 AHC		UH-1D	66-67	slick		NO	pilot door			1931,
Mr. Lonely	188 AHC		UH-1H	1968	slick		NO	pilot door	Greg Pepper		1373,
Mr. Lucky	114 AHC		UH-1C	1967	gun	66-00563	NO			Bryant, B. Carter, B. Gunn, L. Miller, Caldwell	301, 666, 696, 6700
Mr. Lucky	173 AHC		UH-1C	1967	gun		NO	pilot door			301, 696, 1266, 5275, 5900, 6125
Mr. Lucky	175 AHC		UH-1D	66-67	slick		NO	nose		Dave Eastman AC, Duane Liebe CE, Tom Greenfield DG	461, 1269, 1576, 5775
Mr. Lucky	175 AHC		UH-1D	1967	slick		NO	nose		COL Dempsey	651, 1269
Mr. Lucky	188 AHC		UH-1H	1968	slick	66-16843	NO	pilot door		F. Linster AC, Mike Willie CE, Blankenship DG	148, 414, 1024, 9480

Copter Name	Unit	Unit #1	Aircraft	Circa	Function	Serial #	Config	Location	Artist	Crew	Contributors
Mr. Lucky	C Co 101 AHB		UH-1H	68-69	slick	67-17474	NO	M-60 mount base		Lonnie Heidtke CE, Tom Sweeney AC, P. Pointer DG	726,
Mr. Magoo	D Trp 1/1		OH-6A	70-71	scout	69-16020	N+A	doghouse		Jim McCue AC	670, 703, 1133, 9835
Mrs. Babe Mrs. Edie	B Co 229 AHB		UH-1D	65-66	C+C	65-09583	NO	nose		Kellar AC, Bill Weber CE	1880,
Muff Diver	A Co 1 Avn Bn		UH-1B	67-68	gun	64-13921	NO	nose		Danny McGee DG, Gary Young CE, Jim Lungwitz AC, Galen Licthy AC	1973,
Muff Diver	B Trp 2/17		UH-1H	69-70	slick / C+C	67-17696	N+A	nose	Larry Moore	Larry Moore CE	1230,
Mule Driver	A Trp 1/9		UH-1B	69-70	gun	63-12916	NO	nose		Dan Bennett AC	129,
Murder Inc	48 AHC		UH-1B	1968	gun	64-14083	NO	nose + rocket pod		Terry Rolinger CE, George Kraft DG	1504, 9150
Murder Inc	175 AHC		UH-1B	66-67	gun		NO				1641, 1980, 9440
Murder Inc	C Btry 2/20 ARA		AH-1G	70-71	gun	67-15633	NO	bpw	McMillan	McBride CE	134, 850, 1236, 1338, 2014, 5450, 6300, 9880
Murder Inc	F Btry 79 AFA		AH-1G	71-72	gun	67-15633	NO	bpw			134, 850, 1236, 1338, 9880
Mushroom Molly *	128 AHC		UH-1H	1971	slick	69-15534	v-nn			Johnson Tracey CE, Hoskie Etsitty DG, S. Tillotson AC	1534, 1801
Musk-Shark *	174 AHC		UH-1M	1971	gun	66-15089	v-nn			Fred Thompson AC, Mark Klindt CE	1770, 9430
Mustang	175 AHC	Avn Co	UH-1D	66-67	slick		NO	nose		Ken Stroud CE, Tony Corder AC	1350,
Mustang	D Trp 1/4		AH-1G	68-70	gun		NO	bpw			1205,
Mustang Sally	1 Bde 1 Cav Div		UH-1H	1968	slick		NO	nose		Perry CE, John Herndon DG	781, 2034, 8975
Mustang Sally	161 AHC		UH-1D	1967	slick		NO	nose		Tom Lasser AC, John Congden DG	975,
Mustang Sally	335 AHC		UH-1H	1968	slick		NO				1926,
Muttering Death (The)	119 AHC		UH-1C	68-69	gun		NO	nose			284, 923, 9270
My Brother's Keeper	571 Med Det		UH-1H	71-72	dustoff	69-16651	NO	nose		Ken Warner AC, Ken Bohrman CE, R. Clabby MD	155, 1865
My Diane	C Trp 7/1		AH-1G	67-68	gun	67-15475	NO	bpw		Clyde Strait CE	1382, 2027, 9895
My Girl	unk		UH-1H	1970	dustoff		NO	nose			5025,

Copter Name	Unit	Unit #1	Aircraft	Circa	Function	Serial #	Config	Location	Artist	Crew	Contributors
My Joy	119 AHC	Avn Co	UH-1B	65-66	gun hog	64-13942	NO	nose		Bob Wright AC, Brash CE, Jim Varney DG	338, 1965
My Marie	57 AHC		UH-1C	69-70	gun		NO	nose			409,
My Michelle	134 AHC		UH-1H	69-70	slick		NO	nose			352, 1818
My Yellow Balloon	174 AHC		UH-1H	1968	slick	67-17566	NO	nose		Bob Collins AC, Joe Dundel CE, Ross DG	327, 9430
Mystery Ship	1 Bde 1 Cav Div		UH-1H	69-70	slick	68-16189	NO	nose		William S. Evans DG	1053, 1118, 6025, 8975
Mystery Ship	57 AHC		UH-1H	1971	slick		N+A	nose			395, 1266, 5675, 6275
Mystery Ship	117 AHC		UH-1H	70-71	slick		NO	nose			78, 9250
Mystery Ship	336 AHC		UH-1C	69-70	gun		N+A	nose		Don Benedict AC, Pierce CE, Schultz DG	2089,
Mystery Ship	D Trp 17 Cav		UH-1M	1972	gun		N+A	nose		Bobby Cormack, Hank Eller	1494,
Mystical Wrench	162 AHC	407 TC	UH-1H	71-72	maint	67-17823	NO			George Bell, Dave Moody, Strawberry	122, 9390
Nance	187 AHC		UH-1D	1969	slick		N+A	pilot door		Bob Leith AC	1002,
Nancy	147 ASHC		CH-47A	67-68	cargo	66-19027	N+A	fuselage		Newt Coryell FE	264, 348, 1272, 7825
Nancy	170 AHC		UH-1C	67-69	gun		NO	nose			1451, 1519, 1729, 4050, 9400
Nancy	937 Cbt Eng Gp		UH-1D	65-66	slick		NO	nose		Jerry Borchin AC, John Fluitt CE	161,
Nancy	A Co 1 Avn Bn		UH-1B	1966	gun	64-13921	NO	doorpost			439, 1266, 5725, 6125
Nancy Bare	213 ASHC		CH-47A	66-67	cargo	65-08015	NO	fuselage		Ipalock, Dyre	790, 8000
Nancy Jane	A Co 227 AHB		UH-1D	65-67	slick	63-08847	N+A	nose		Ed Carder AC, Morgan CE	276, 9700
Nancy Lee	54 Med Det		UH-1H	67-68	dustoff	55	NO	nose		Pat Brady AC, Foust CP, Brian Browick CE, Travis Kanida MD	180, 1908
Nancy Lee II	178 ASHC		CH-47B	68-69	cargo	67-18458	N+A	front fuselage		William Eoff	480, 841, 1280, 8275
Nancy's Dream	C Co 227 AHB		UH-1H	1969	slick	66-16642	NO	nose	Howie Belkin	Howie Belkin DG	120,
Nasty	116 AHC		UH-1C	69-71	gun		NO				820,
Nature's Own	334 AWC		AH-1G	71-72	gun	68-15016	NO	bpw			1674, 5400, 5427
Negative Suppression	175 AHC		UH-1D	66-67	slick	65-09991	NO			Stout, Austin, Johnson	461, 1888, 5775
Nevada Gambler	C Co 227 AHB		UH-1H	1969	slick	66-16642	N+A	nose	Howie Belkin	Howie Belkin DG	120,4850, 7125
New Blood, Sweat + Tears (The)	15 Med Bn		UH-1H	1971	medevac		NO			Ron Huether, Bodnar	808,
New Blue Tail	8 TC	117 AHC	CH-21C	63-64	lift	56-02085	NO				127, 525

Copter Name	Unit	Unit #1	Aircraft	Circa	Function	Serial #	Config	Location	Artist	Crew	Contributors
New World Famous Wrecker	121 AHC	80 TC	UH-1D	1968	maint	732	N+A	nose			1135, 1593, 1768, 9290
New Yorker (The)	129 AHC		UH-1H	1970	slick	68-16135	NO			Leo Adams CE	7, 9310
Nickel + Dime	173 AHC		UH-1C	66-67	gun	65-09419	NO	pilot door		Tony Zanfardino CE, Dan Matrisciani, Ron Salmon, Ron Lalli	1931, 1981, 2012
Nicki II	188 AHC		UH-1C	1967	gun	66-00712	NO		Dick Detra	Taylor CE, Dennis Smalley DG	414, 9480
Night Crawler	175 AHC		UH-1H	70-71	slick		NO	nose		Roger Peterson CE	1384,
Night Hawk	A Trp 3/17		UH-1H	70-71	slick		NO	doghouse			1991, 3875
Night Mare	92 AHC		UH-1H	70-71	slick / nigthawk	66-17038	N+A	nose		Morris Lambert CE, Adams DG, S. Hays CE, W. Hadley CE, Stan Edburg AC	931, 961, 9220
Nightmare	240 AHC		UH-1H	1971	slick	67-17522	NO	nose		Wayne Mutza CE	1266,
Ninja	498 Med Co		UH-1H	1968	dustoff		NO	nose		James Van Horn MD	1821,
Nitehawk	238 AWC	AHC	UH-1C	69-70	slick		NO	nose		Mike Russ	1526, 9530
Nitemare	132 ASHC		CH-47B	70-71	cargo	67-18449	NO			Greg Cook AC, Larry Seeger CP, Hancock FE, Padilla CE, Worrell DG	773, 1162, 2062
Nixon's Hired Gun	174 AHC		UH-1C	69-70	gun	65-09507	NO	belly			1342, 1388, 9430
Nixon's Hired Gun	176 AHC		UH-1C	1969	gun		NO	belly			1595,
Nixon's Hired Gun	C Co 101 AHB	188 AHC	UH-1H	68-69	slick		NO	pilot door			726,
Nixon's Hired Gun	F Trp 4 Cav		AH-1G	71-72	gun		NO	nose			3500, 9865
Nixon's Withdrawal	571 Med Det		UH-1H	1971	dustoff		NO	nose			2069,
NJ Devil	179 ASHC		CH-47C	69-70	cargo		NO				943,
No Balls 3	A Co 228 ASHB		CH-47A	69-70	cargo	65-08003	NO	front fuselage		Dewayne Miller FE, Paul Getz AC	996, 1193, 8025, 8250
No Balls At All	196 ASHC		CH-47A	1970	cargo	65-08003	N+A	fuselage		Marcel Massey FE	1107,
No Fare	187 AHC		UH-1H	70-71	slick	68-16305	NO	pilot door			652,
No Quarter	B Trp 2/17		AH-1G	1969	gun	68-15702	NO	bpw		Jimmy Allen	1528, 4825
No Slack	B Trp 2/17		AH-1G	1969	gun	68-15703	NO	bpw		Bill Russell	1528, 4825

The Octopus*: 339 TC, CH-37B, Nha Trang 1964*. The predecessor to the CH-47 Chinook and the CH-54 Flying Crane, this Mojave heavy lifter gets a mission pre-inspection. Photo courtesy U.S Army Aviation Museum.

Copter Name	Unit	Unit #1	Aircraft	Circa	Function	Serial #	Config	Location	Artist	Crew	Contributors
Nobody's Darling	121 AHC	Avn Co	UH-1D	1965	slick		NO			Mike Beech AC	116,
None Better	174 AHC		UH-1D	1967	slick		NO	nose			399, 1020, 3025, 4400, 9430
Norma	B Co 229 AHB		UH-1H	70-71	slick	68-16174	NO	nose		Chuck Emerson AC	476,
Norma Jean	A Co 228 ASHB		CH-47A	65-66	cargo		NO	fuselage			1372,
Not Even	335 AHC		UH-1H	68-69	slick		NO				897,
Not Even II	335 AHC		UH-1H	68-69	slick		NO	nose			897,
Number 10	188 AHC		UH-1H	1968	slick		NAA	pilot door			1024, 1660, 9480
Number Nine *	187 AHC		UH-1H	71-72	slick	69-15135	v-nn			Greg Monroe CE	1222,
Number Thirteen	175 AHC		UH-1D	1969	slick	164 ?	NO	nose		Ken Berowski	135, 429, 1908, 4600
Nuts, Bolts + Safety Wire	134 AHC		UH-1H	69-70	slick		NO	nose			979,
O. D. Green Machine	247 Med Det		UH-1H	69-70	dustoff		NO			William Zinkeler CE	1986, 7725
O. D. Streak (The)	188 AHC		UH-1H	67-68	slick		NO	pilot door		Harold Smith AC	1660, 9480
Octopus (The)	339 TC		CH-37B	1964	recovery		NO	nose			1908, 4600
Odyssey (The)	C Co 228 ASHB		CH-47B	1970	cargo	67-18479	NO	fuselage		Cliff Morley FE	1239, 8370, 8375
Odyssey (The)	D Co 227 AHB		AH-1G	69-70	gun	67-15548	NO				113,
Office (The)	13 CAB		UH-1H	1972	slick		NO	pilot door			121,
Ogre (The)	C Co 229 AHB		UH-1H	70-71	slick	66-17020	N+A	nose		Dan Tyler CE	1816,
Oh God I'm Horny	176 AHC		UH-1M	69-71	gun	66-15011	NO	belly		Don Wilson CE, Steve Rodriquez DG	186, 9450
Ohio Express	D Trp 3/4		AH-1G	69-70	gun	67-15820	NO	doghouse	Gary Schmidt	Jim Kirker CE	917, 1282, 1559, 1989, 8400, 8575, 9855
Ohio Express (The)	187 AHC		UH-1H	68-69	slick	66-16762	NO	pilot door		Bob Leith AC, Herman Scott CE	1002,
OK Babe	478 Avn Co		CH-54A	1966	recovery	64-14202	NO	bpw		J.A. Brown AC, W.T. Lamb CP	1053, 1181, 6050
Okie	D Trp 1/1		AH-1G	71-72	gun		NO	turret		Dean AC, Bickford CE	61, 4825

Copter Name	Unit	Unit #1	Aircraft	Circa	Function	Serial #	Config	Location	Artist	Crew	Contributors
Ol Bullet	B Trp 1/9		UH-1D	67-68	slick	64-13532	NO	pilot door			31, 473, 535, 1418
Ol' Hedge Trimmer	129 AHC		UH-1	1967	slick		NO			Karl Barbee	83, 9310
Old Bastard D *	92 AHC		UH-1D	68-69	slick	64-13853	v-nn			Ty Bynum	254, 9220
Old Bitch (The)	243 ASHC		CH-47A	68-69	cargo	66-19030	NO			James Ferguson CE	512, 1975, 8075
Old Bones	C Trp 1/9		UH-1B	66-67	gun		NO	doorpost		Dennis Rosenthal, Ernest Cairns	260, 866, 9805
Old Dog	48 AHC		UH-1H	70-71	slick	66-16879	NO			Jesse Dize AC, Mike Sathre CE	426, 1548, 6850
Old Friend	F Btry 79 AFA		AH-1G	71-72	gun	66-15331	NO			Squeaky CE, Ehlers AC	850, 2000
Old Glory	A Trp 7/17		OH-6A	1970	scout		NO	nose			855, 5925
Old Magnet Ass	116 AHC	Avn Co	UH-1D	66-67	slick	65-10125	NO			William Burton CE	248, 9240
Old Molly	242 ASHC		CH-47A	68-71	cargo		NO	nose			1671, 4300, 8050
Old Paint	B Co 229 AHB		UH-1D	69-70	slick	64-13617	NO			Mike Rose CE	1510, 9780
Old Patches *	334 AWC	AHC	UH-1C	67-68	gun	64-14151	v-nn			Rick McCurry CE, Don Schweitzer DG	1136,
Old Puta	45 Med Co		UH-1H	67-68	dustoff		NO			Frankie Trujillo CE	5,
Old Reliable	15 Med Bn		UH-1D	66-67	medevac	62-12370	N+A	nose	painted by Larry Hatch	Larry Hatch AC, Ron Trogdon CE	711, 1151, 1802, 7775
Old Reliable	A Trp 3/17		OH-6A	69-70	scout	66-07781	NO	doghouse		Bill Smith AC, Brandenberg CE	503, 1630, 8625
Old Rivers	539 TC		CH-47A	1967	recovery	66-19072	N+A	fuselage		Ted Thompson DG	2030, 6805
Old Rugged Cross	B Co 123 Avn Bn		OH-6A	70-71	scout	69-15997	N+A	nose			1925,
Old Smokey	119 AHC		UH-1D	67-68	slick	527	NO	nose		Doug Drury AC	443, 9270
Old Smokey	B Btry 2/20 ARA		AH-1G	1969	gun	67-15490	NO	bpw			850, 1686, 1853
Old Spot	F Btry 79 AFA		AH-1G	71-72	gun	68-15147	NO			Hartnett CE, Stotler CE, Jetter AC, Snow AC	850, 2000
Old Warrior III ^	145 CAB		UH-1D	1969	maint		NO	nose		Al Breyer CE	196, 299

Copter Name	Unit	Unit #1	Aircraft	Circa	Function	Serial #	Config	Location	Artist	Crew	Contributors
Old Warrior VI ^	145 CAB		UH-1H	69-70	slick	088	NO	nose		Dan Chase CE	196, 299, 9350
Olds	155 AHC		UH-1C	1970	gun	65-09442	NO	nose	Al Meadows was unit artist	Al Meadows DG	1165,
Ole Daddy Rabbit	178 ASHC		CH-47B	68-70	cargo	67-18436	N+A	front fuselage			497, 1946
Ole Hotbox	UTT		UH-1A	1963			NO	doorpost		John Dickerson	301, 5575
Ole Magnet Ass	187 AHC		UH-1D	67-68	slick	66-00854	NO	pilot door		Eric Mercer AC, Forrest Abild CE, John Brahaney DG	1177, 1882, 9470
Ole Magnet Ass *	335 AHC	A/82	UH-1D	65-66	slick	771	v-nn			Don Champlin AC	295,
Ole' Prophet	187 AHC		UH-1D	66-67	slick	66-16488	NO	pilot door		Jerry Wagner AC, Rob Kittleson, Arnold Amorso	918, 1713, 1845, 9470
Ole Reliable	478 Avn Co		CH-54A	67-68	recovery	64-14205	NO	fuselage		Jerry Skinner FE, Ted Jenkins, Dan Rice, Bill Fletcher	846,
Olive Drab Taxicab	114 AHC		UH-1H	69-70	slick		NO	doorpost			2090,
On The Prowl	117 AHC		UH-1H	69-71	slick		NO	nose			78, 685, 1266, 6125, 9259
Only 21 Killin Days Till X-mas	118 AHC		UH-1C	1970	gun		NO	cargo door window panel		Bob Williams CE	1911,
Only You Can Prevent Charlie	128 AHC		UH-1B	1967	smoke		N+A	quarter panel			301, 913, 1480
Oobladi Ooblada Chicken Freak	A Co 227 AHB		UH-1H	1970	slick	67-17389	N+A	nose	Craig Tonjes	C. Tonjes CE, Mark Olmstead DG, John Culhane AC	101, 1793, 9700
Oobladi Ooblada Chicken Freak (#2)	A Co 227 AHB		UH-1H	70-71	slick	69-15051	N+A	nose	Craig Tonjes	C.Tonjes CE, Mark Olmstead DG, John Culhane AC	101, 1789, 1793, 9700
Ooze	173 AHC		UH-1	71-72			NO				593,
Orange Blossom Special	178 ASHC		CH-47B	68-70	cargo	67-18492	NO				497,
Orange Crush	A Trp 1/9		OH-6A	70-71	scout		NO			Onion (pilot nn)	1497,
Orange Crush	E Trp 1/9		OH-6A	70-71	scout		NO			Onion (pilot nn)	1497,
Orange Onion	114 AHC		UH-1D	1968	slick	66-16862	NO	nose		Connor, R. Sciapiti, Smith, J. Cobb, McMullen, M. Roe, K. Smith	1053, 1573, 6700
Orange Sunshine	18 CAC		UH-1	72-73	gun		NO			John Hulbert	814, 4975
Orange Wedge	E Trp 1/9		UH-1H	1970	slick		N+A	nose + pilot door		Limey CE, Russell DG, John Schillerereff	1556, 8875
Oregon Taxi	176 AHC		UH-1D	67-68	slick	66-16230	NO	nose		Dale Wiese DG, David Blatell AC, John Ramsey CE	301, 1760, 1905, 5275, 9450

Pale Horse: *D Troop 1/1, OH-6A, (sn 69-15992), 1970.* Painted in tiny red letters on the nose is "REV 6:8" in reference to the Bible verse, "…and behold a pale horse: and his name that sat on him was Death, and Hell followed with him." *Photo by Russ Elderbaum via Mike Gustin.*

Copter Name	Unit	Unit #1	Aircraft	Circa	Function	Serial #	Config	Location	Artist	Crew	Contributors
Orient Express	192 AHC		UH-1H	70-71	slick	68-15320	NO	nose		Roger "Woody" Mitchell AC, Steve Fensky CE	1005, 1213
Orient Express	283 Med Det		UH-1D	1965	dustoff	64-13645	NO	nose		Roger Tomczak CE, Hunter MD	1791,
Original Mad Bomber (The)	197 Avn Co		UH-1B	1966	gun		NO	nose			69,
Oscar Mayer	D Trp 17 Cav		OH-6A	1972	scout	68-17161	N+A	clamshell	Bill Liberty	Bill Liberty DG, John Robinson AC	1494,
Over Sexed	155 AHC		UH-1B	65-66	gun	64-14003	N+A	nose		F. Cranford CE, Jim Sewell AC, F. Tiner DG, L. Tiner DG	363, 630, 939, 9360
Pabst Blue Flight	240 AHC		UH-1D	69-71	slick		N+A	nose		John Bzdusek AC, Hay CE	439, 770, 1266, 5725
Pabst Blue Ribbon	335 AHC		UH-1B	69-70	gun	62-04592	N+A	rocket pod		Ken Watson CE	1049, 1696, 9590
Pacification	118 AHC		UH-1B	1966	gun		NO	nose	Jack Armstrong	Jack Armstrong AC, Gordy CE	47, 1029, 1037, 9260
Pacifier (The)	D Trp 1/1		OH-6A	1971	scout	69-16047	N+A	doghouse		Russell Johnson AC	6, 670, 857, 922, 1804, 9835
Paddy Runner	121 AHC		UH-1D	1968	slick	782	NO	nose		Franklin Bradley AC	831,
Paddy Wagon	116 AHC		UH-1D	67-68	slick	65-12869	NO	cargo door			1119, 9240
Paddy Wagon	B Co 229 AHB		UH-1D	1967	slick		NO	nose			1335,
Pagan (The)	C Trp 1/9		UH-1	69-70			NO	nose			280,
Paladin **	174 AHC		UH-1C	70-71	gun	65-09507	AO	quarter panel			1568,
Pale Horse	D Trp 1/1		OH-6A	1970	scout	69-15992	NO	nose			670, 922, 9835
Pale Horse (The)	C Trp 7/17		AH-1G	71-72	gun		NO	doghouse		Charles Alexander AC	17, 1602, 7075
Pale Rider	C Trp 16 Cav		AH-1G	1972	gun	68-15035	NO	bpw		Don Hodges AC, Sullivan CE	439, 763, 1361, 1763, 3540, 5700, 6350
Pall Bearer (The)	281 AHC		UH-1C	1967	gun		NO				946, 9550
Pam's Pro Ante's Ace	B Co 227 AHB		UH-1H	1969	slick	68-15740	N+A	nose		Bob Lunde AC	1052,
Pancho Villa	128 AHC		UH-1B	68-70	gun		NO	nose		Dennis Ward CE	1861,
Pancho Villa	D Trp 3/4		UH-1B	1966	gun		NO			Carl Burns AC, Reynald Villereal CE	244,
Pandora	UTT		UH-1B	1964	gun	62-01949	NO	cargo door window panel			1975, 6500
Pandora's Box	187 AHC		UH-1H	68-69	slick	66-16127	N+A	pilot door		Arnie Leak AC, Lux CE, Harrell DG, Gary Drake	991, 1002, 9470
Pandora's Box	238 AWC		AH-1G	71-72	gun	68-15031	NO	bpw		Gene Kennedy AC	134, 1266, 5450, 6200, 6275
Pandora's Box	B Btry 2/20 ARA		AH-1G	70-71	gun	68-15031	NO	bpw		Wayne Richardson AC	154, 439, 1474, 5700, 6475

Copter Name	Unit	Unit #1	Aircraft	Circa	Function	Serial #	Config	Location	Artist	Crew	Contributors
Pandora's Box	B Co 123 Avn Bn		OH-6A	1971	scout	69-15997	N+A	fuselage			89,
Pandora's Box	D Co 227 AHB		AH-1G	70-71	gun	68-15031	NO	bpw			134, 1266, 6200, 6275
Panthan Panther	117 AHC		UH-1H	69-70	slick	68-15441	NO	nose		Oscar Flores CE, Jerry Ellis DG	540, 8650
Papa Gator	119 AHC		UH-1H	68-70	slick		NO	nose		Jimmy A. Conrad	188, 349, 382, 717, 1753, 1797, 9270
Paper Tiger	116 AHC		UH-1D	1967	slick	63-12963	NO	pilot door			852,
Paper Tiger	D Trp 3/4		OH-6A	67-70	scout		NO	doghouse			1855, 4300
Pappy's Killer	243 ASHC		CH-47A	1969	cargo		N+A	front fuselage			111, 8075
Pappy's Pooper	118 AHC		UH-1C	1970	gun	66-00558	NO	nose + rocket pod hardpoint		Darrell Burkhalter AC, J. Rizzo CE, J. Cushing DG	241, 9260
Pappy's Revenooers	243 ASHC		CH-47A	68-69	cargo	66-00092	N+A	front fuselage		Dave Behn CE/FE	118,
Para-Dice	191 AHC		UH-1H	68-69	slick		NO	pilot door			786, 7000
Paranoid	11 ACR		OH-6A	71-72	scout	67-16307	NO	clamshell			1264,
Paranoid	117 AHC		UH-1C	71-72	gun		NO				1654,
Pasa Las Tres	175 AHC		UH-1D	66-67	slick	65-10020	NO	nose		Bill Fry AC, Ray Roth DG, John Perkins CE, Hall	1516, 1641, 9440
Passion	498 Med Co		UH-1H	1972	dustoff		NO	nose		Emory Messersmith MD	1183,
Pat	A Trp 1/9		UH-1H	69-70	slick	67-19535	NO	doorpost		George Anzelmo CE	42,
Patches *	11 CAG		UH-1H	68-69	slick		v-nn			Tucker CE	1348,
Patches	45 Med Co		UH-1H	69-70	dustoff		NO	nose		Pat Farley CE	439, 499, 5725
Patches *	48 AHC		UH-1H	70-71	slick	68-16443	v-nn			Tony Amanzio AC, Ron Thumper CP	29,
Patches *	114 AHC		UH-1H	69-70	slick	69-15126	NO			S. Cagle, C. Trisler, A. Anderson, R. Midgett, J. Addington	1629, 6700, 7095
Patches	118 AHC		UH-1D	1966	slick		NO	pilot door			1053,
Patches	132 ASHC		CH-47B	68-71	cargo	67-18456	N+A	fuselage	SP4 Davis did all '70-'71 a/c art	Herb Kukuk FE, Jeff Rope AC, Bill Cates CP, Terry Lien FE	1021, 1162, 1822, 2002, 3175, 8025, 9885
Patches	134 AHC		UH-1H	68-71	slick		NO				352, 1818
Patches	174 AHC		UH-1C	67-68	gun	66-15165	NO	cargo door frame top		Jim Daniels AC, Ron Conner CE, Rick Dodge CP	1137, 9430
Patches	175 AHC		UH-1D	67-68	slick		NO	nose		Marty Herrell DG (346 Div Avn Support)	738, 9440
Patches	176 AHC		UH-1D	67-68	slick	65-10052	NO	nose		Brain Lambie	962, 3710, 4825

Patience My Ass: *B Troop 3/17 Cav, AH-1G, (sn 67-15646), Phu Loi, 1972.* Crew Chief Larry Witte stands besides a partial quote attributed to a C-2-17 commander whose complete and infamous statement was, "Patience my ass, I want to kill something!" Photo courtesy Larry Witte.

Copter Name	Unit	Unit #1	Aircraft	Circa	Function	Serial #	Config	Location	Artist	Crew	Contributors
Patches	179 ASHC		CH-47A	68-69	cargo	65-08005	NO			Jack Gilmore FE	610, 7900
Patches	205 ASHC		CH-47A	1968	cargo	66-19028	NO	front fuselage		Bill Bray FE	189, 298, 1834, 1836, 7975
Patches	213 ASHC		CH-47A	66-67	cargo	65-08019	N+A	fuselage		Steve Craft DG, Wayne Geckler CE	359, 790, 8000, 8025
Patches	247 Med Det		UH-1H	69-70	dustoff		NO	nose		Pat Farley CE	499,
Patches *	335 AHC		UH-1B	66-67	gun		v-nn				800,
Patches *	498 Med Co		UH-1H	1968	dustoff	66-17007	v-nn			Pappy Richardson CE	1974,
Patches	A Trp 3/17		OH-6A	69-70	scout		NO				1261,
Patches	B Co 227 AHB		UH-1H	68-69	slick		NO			Chris White CE	1897,
Patches	C Co 229 AHB		UH-1H	1968	slick	66-16573	NO	nose		Ken Turner AC	1466, 6805
Patches	D Trp 3/5		OH-6A	1971	scout		NO	fuselage			1581,
Patchwork Cat	117 AHC		UH-1C	71-72	gun	66-00531	NO				1654,
Patience My Ass	B Trp 3/17		AH-1G	1972	gun	67-15646	N+A	bpw		Larry Witte CE	1942,
Patience My Ass I'm Gonna Kill Something	D Trp 17 Cav		UH-1H	1972	night-hawk		N+A	nose			1279, 4825
Patricia	498 Med Co		UH-1H	68-69	dustoff	66-17125	NO	nose		Alan Sibley CE, Gary Jostandt MD	875, 8625
Patricia Ann	C Trp 7/1		AH-1G	1968	gun	67-15474	NO	bpw		Fowler Goodowens AC, Gordon Vandervall CE	301, 306, 390, 418, 627, 1181, 1361, 1674, 5025, 5275, 5425, 5625, 6050, 6325, 6350
Patricia Anne (The)	A Co 4 Avn Bn		AH-1G	1969	gun		NO	nose cone			9270,
Patricia Lynn	C Trp 1/9		AH-1G	70-71	gun		NO			Larry Edeal AC	1003,
Patriot	68 Med Det		UH-1H	70-71	dustoff		NO				1866, 7725
Patriot	498 Med Co		UH-1H	1970	dustoff		NAA	nose		Lyle Condon MD	143, 332, 7725
Patty	114 AHC		UH-1B	1965	gun	63-08667	NO	nose		Ray Rupcic AC, Charles Tucker CP, Clarence Jones CE, Rafael Torres-Rivera DG	1844,
Patty Ann	57 Med Det		UH-1H	1972	dustoff		NO				561,
Patty Ann	236 Med Det		UH-1H	71-72	dustoff		NO	nose		John Braddock MD, Wilbur Wills CE	175,

Copter Name	Unit	Unit #1	Aircraft	Circa	Function	Serial #	Config	Location	Artist	Crew	Contributors
Patty Ann	A Trp 3/17		OH-6A	69-70	scout	65-12962	NO	doghouse		Gary Swartz CE, Roy Benton DG	503, 1737, 8625
Patty Girl Fly	242 ASHC		CH-47A	70-71	cargo		NO				1056, 1199
Patty Wagon	187 AHC		UH-1H	1970	slick	66-16415	NO	nose		Steve Willingham DG	652, 1932
Patty Wagon	B Trp 1/9		UH-1B	66-67	gun		NO	nose		Dick Hale AC	679,
Peace	B Co 9 Avn Bn		AH-1G	68-69	gun		NO	belly			2072,
Peace	B Co 228 ASHB		CH-47A	1969	cargo		N+A	fuselage			903,
Peace Maker	D Co 229 AHB		AH-1G	71-72	gun		NO	bpw			1323, 9890
Peace Maker	D Trp 3/4		UH-1H	70-71	slick		NO	cargo door			439, 1266, 1825, 5725, 6275
Peace On Earth Or Else	71 AHC	A/501	UH-1B	1965	gun		N+A	M-3 rocket box		Paul McPherran CE	1160, 9210
Peace Seekers (The)	237 Med Det		UH-1H	70-71	dustoff	69-15216	N+A	nose		W. Gordon MD, Jerry Graff CE, S. Woods AC, Keith Shafer CP	631, 638, 824
Peacemaker	269 CAB		UH-1H	68-69	slick		N+A				810,
Peacemaker	C Trp 1/9		UH-1C	67-68	gun	66-00658	NO	nose			53, 9805
Peace Maker (The)	UTT		UH-1B	63-64			NO				1908, 4600
Peacemaker ^	A Trp 1/9		OH-6A	70-71	scout		NO				1497,
Peacemaker ^	E Trp 1/9		OH-6A	70-71	scout		NO				1266, 1497, 6250
Peacemaker (The)	B Trp 1/9		AH-1G	1969	gun	66-15325	NO	bpw		Andy Anderson CE, Rick Chesson AC	193, 304, 395, 1053, 1266, 1727, 5675, 6025, 6275, 6300, 9740
Peacemakers ^^^	334 AWC		UH-1H	1971	slick / C+C	69-15410	NO	cargo door		Jim Barnett CE	89,
Peg Of My Heart	121 AHC		UH-1D	67-68	slick		N+A	nose			477, 4825, 9290
Pegasus	B Co 229 AHB		UH-1D	67-68	slick	66-16563	NO	nose		Dennis Osborne CE	1331,
Peggy	170 AHC		UH-1C	68-69	gun		NO	nose			2079,
Penny Lane	128 AHC		UH-1H	68-70	slick		NO	pilot door		Dennis Ward CE	1861,
People Stopper	48 AHC		UH-1B	1969	gun	63-08587	NO	nose		M. Hearne, N. Black, Doug Lott, Clyde Canada	1343, 9150
Persuader (The)	114 AHC		UH-1H	1971	slick	69-15122	NO	nose		John Shoup AC, Pascual Mantanona CE	1723, 3100, 6700
Persuader (The)	176 AHC		UH-1C	67-70	gun	66-00605	N+A	nose	Larry Silva	Larry Silva CE	406, 901, 1610, 1905, 4350, 9450

Copter Name	Unit	Unit #1	Aircraft	Circa	Function	Serial #	Config	Location	Artist	Crew	Contributors
Pete	118 AHC		UH-1B	65-66	gun		NO	rocket pod			1908, 4600
Petunia	155 AHC		UH-1D	66-67	slick		NO	nose			69, 255, 533, 9360
Phantom (The) **	129 AHC		UH-1H	70-71	slick	66-16265	AO	nose	Gary Mount	Gary Mount CE	1248,
Pharaoh (The)	170 AHC		UH-1C	1969	gun	66-15166	NO	nose			1543, 9400
Pharaoh II (The)	170 AHC		UH-1C	1969	gun		NO	nose			1543,
Pheadra Del Immortal	11 ACR		AH-1G	68-69	gun		NO	bpw			1703,
Phenix (The)	D Co 227 AHB		AH-1G	1969	gun	756 or 735	NO	bpw			113, 562, 1226, 1329, 4350
Phigtin' Pig	147 ASHC		CH-47C	69-70	cargo		NO				1199,
Philbert Desenex	200 ASHC		CH-47A	67-68	cargo	66-00094	N+A	front fuselage	Larry Dumford	M. Hirsch CE, J. Sexton, D. Walters, J. Morrow, T. Thomas	995, 1195, 1585, 7950, 8275
Philbert Desenex	C Co 159 ASHB		CH-47A	1968	cargo	66-00094	N+A			Jerry Sexton FE '66-'68, Dan Lawrence FE '71-'72	1591, 1585, 7850
Philly Dog	134 AHC		UH-1H	1969	slick	66-16319	NO	nose		Rick Premerton CE, Harold Shonk AC, John Webb DG, Bill Ogden	352, 1818, 1879
Phoenix	68 Avn Co		UH-1B	65-66	gun		NO	nose		Dan Telfair AC	1758,
Phu Loi Freedom Flight 505 *	213 ASHC		CH-47C	70-71	cargo	67-18505	v-nn			Patrick Corbett CE	344,
Phuquet	187 AHC		UH-1H	1971	slick	67-17625	NO	nose			204, 652, 9470
Piasecki's Practical Joke	57 TC	120 AHC	CH-21C	1963	lift		NO	fuselage			1975, 6500, 6525
Piece Maker	D Trp 1/4		AH-1G	69-70	gun	67-15507	NO	bpw		John Loftice AC	195, 1053, 1205
Piecemaker	134 AHC		UH-1C	68-71	gun		NO				352, 1818
Pied Piper	175 AHC		UH-1B	66-67	gun		NO	pilot door		Russ Prentice CE	1926, 9130
Pig Pen	117 AHC		UH-1H	70-71	slick		NO				78,
Pig Pen	162 AHC		UH-1H	1968	slick		NO	pilot door	Greenhlagh	Bill Greenhalgh AC	652,
Pig Pen	C Trp 7/1		AH-1G	68-69	gun	67-15476	N+A	bpw			1382,
Pig Pen *	D Trp 3/5		OH-6A	70-71	scout	67-16398	v-nn			Don Callison AC, Rene Barneau DG	266, 1221, 3625, 4825, 9860

The Phenix: *D Co 227 AHB, AH-1G, Phuoc Vinh, 1969.* A team of mechanics swarm over this well adorned Huey Cobra readying her for another eventful mission. Photo by Terry Moon.

Copter Name	Unit	Unit #1	Aircraft	Circa	Function	Serial #	Config	Location	Artist	Crew	Contributors
Pig Pen II	117 AHC		UH-1H	70-71	slick		NO	nose		Roy Cawthon CE, Mitsuo Matsaroka CE	78, 9250
Pig Power	242 ASHC		CH-47A	67-69	cargo	66-19012	NO	nose		Ron Peters FE	1225, 1378, 4825, 8050
Pig Slayer	61 AHC		UH-1H	69-71	slick		NO	cargo door		Robert Welsh CE	1887,
Pill (The)	C Co 227 AHB		AH-1G	1968	gun		NO	nose			1518,
Pillow Power	C Trp 16 Cav		AH-1G	72-73	gun	66-15330	NO	bpw		Dan Wright	439, 1205, 1763, 5700
Pinball Wizard	D Trp 3/4		UH-1H	69-70	slick	68-16224	NO	doghouse	Paul Jones	Jack Nemeyer CE, Haggar AC, Keith Williams AC, Paul Jones CE, Ken Rucki AC, Pat O'Brien CP, Floyd Eubanks DG	1282, 1989, 9855
Pineapple Princess	8 TC	117 AHC	CH-21C	1963	lift	309	N+A	fuselage		Fred Gross DG	660, 3550, 4725
Pineapple Princess	68 Avn Co		UH-1B	1964	gun		NO	M-3 rocket box			52, 1975, 6525
Pineapple Princess	114 AHC	Avn Co	UH-1B	1964	slick		NO	cargo door window panel			544, 1451, 4050, 5825
Pineapple Red	175 AHC		UH-1B	1966	gun	63-08701	NO			Steve Hopkins CE, John Reich DG	1926,
Pink Panther **	117 AHC		UH-1D/H	67-71	slick	618, 719	AO	nose		Tom Duvall DG, Dale Phillips CE, Robert Hamilton	456, 685, 9250
Pink Panther **	174 AHC		UH-1C	68-70	gun	66-00590	AO	doorpost	Philip Luft	Alexander CE, Cowling CE, Ratcliffe DG	278, 316, 334, 592, 1441, 1951, 9430
Pink Panther **	B Co 25 Avn Bn		UH-1C	67-68	gun		AO	nose			1562, 9120
Pink Panther **	C Trp 1/9		UH-1B	1966	gun		AO	nose		Frank Hiser AC	757, 893, 9805
Pink Pussy	117 AHC		UH-1D	68-69	slick	64-13718	N+A	nose			127, 526, 972, 4825, 9250
Pink Pussy	147 ASHC		CH-47A	67-68	cargo		N+A	fuselage			307, 7825
Pistol Pete	187 AHC		UH-1H	69-70	slick	67-17778	NO	nose			1266, 1700, 1727, 6125, 9470
Pistol Pete	A Trp 3/17		AH-1G	70-71	gun	68-17075	NO				1757, 9720
Pistol Pete	B Co 25 Avn Bn		UH-1C	67-68	gun		NO				1562,
Pitty Tink	213 ASHC		CH-47A	67-68	cargo	65-08014	N+A	fuselage		Lloyd Blankenship FE, Robert Sexton CE	778, 8000
Play Boy	129 AHC		UH-1H	69-70	slick	66-16322	NO	nose	Korean artist	Lenny Deitz	1495, 1947, 9310
Playboy Bunny **	A Co 227 AHB		UH-1D	66-67	slick	64-13612	AO	nose		George Lenotte CE, Guy Krowl DG	1009, 9700

Pinball Wizard: *D Troop 3/4 Cav, UH-1H, (sn 68-16224), Kontum, 1970.* Passing time between missions during the Cambodian Campaign (*left to right*): Ken Rucki AC, Patrick O'Brien CP, Floyd Eubanks DG, and James Mouser DG (from another ship). Photo by Jack Nemeyer.

Copter Name	Unit	Unit #1	Aircraft	Circa	Function	Serial #	Config	Location	Artist	Crew	Contributors
Playboy Special	173 Abn Bde		UH-1D	1966	slick	64-13570	NO				800, 924, 9350
Pogostick	175 AHC	A/502	UH-1B	1966	slick		NO	nose			485,
Pogy Boat	336 AHC		UH-1B	68-69	gun		NO	pilot door		Morris West CE, J. Ray AC, Lickey DG	1890, 9610
Poison	A Co 1 Avn Bn		UH-1B	65-66	gun		NO	nose			301, 1293
Polack Power	114 AHC		UH-1D	1969	slick	64-13841	NO			McConnell, R. Armstrong, R. McCabe, J. Hilenki	1563, 6700
Polish Power	188 AHC		UH-1H	1967	slick / C+C	66-16113	NO	pilot door		Dluski CE, Gray DG	1024, 1322, 1621
Polish Prize (The)	11 ACR		UH-1H	68-69	slick		NO	nose			1448, 1703, 8625
Pollution IV ^	118 AHC		UH-1H	68-69	smoke		NO	vertical stabilizer		H. Stauber DG, J. Robertson AC, B. Wizard DG, G. Nider AC, Doug Marci DG after Wizard DEROS'd	439, 1228, 1302, 1491, 1945, 1966, 2080, 5725
Polock's Honey Bucket	8 TC	117 AHC	CH-21C	1962	lift	56-151	NO	fuselage		Leon Mruczkowski	1252, 9070
Pony Soldier	C Co 229 AHB		UH-1H	70-72	slick		NO	nose			803, 1601, 1627, 9830
Poppasan	129 AHC		UH-1H	1969	slick		NO	nose		C. P. Bloomfield	1415, 7350, 8875
Porky Revenge	57 AHC		UH-1D	71-72	slick	64-13546	N+A	nose		Kim Dille CE	420,
Porky The Pig	57 AHC		UH-1H	71-72	slick	68-16323	N+A			Kim Dille CE	420,
Portuguese Man O' War	240 AHC		UH-1H	67-68	slick	66-16211	NO	pilot door		Matt Amaral CE, Haron Brown AC, Bill Clauson CP, Ron Kindred DG	953, 1781, 9540
Poseidon	A Trp 7/1		AH-1G	70-71	gun		NO			Will Gibbons	291,
Post Falls Express	C Trp 16 Cav		UH-1H	1972	slick		NO	pilot door			1205, 3425
Post Falls Express	D Trp 1/4		UH-1H	1970	slick		NO	pilot door			1205,
Pray	147 ASHC		CH-47A	1967	cargo		NO	fuselage			563, 7825
Pray For Piece	147 ASHC		CH-47A	67-69	cargo		N+A	front fuselage		Manfred Fernitz AC	515, 563, 7825, 8275
Preparation H	128 AHC		UH-1H	69-70	slick	865	NO	nose			1053, 1908, 4600
Prepared And Loyal ^^	D Trp 1/4		UH-1B	67-68	slick		NO	nose			274, 6805
Prickly Pear	unk		UH-1B	1964			NO			Walter Sarratt DG	1546,

Copter Name	Unit	Unit #1	Aircraft	Circa	Function	Serial #	Config	Location	Artist	Crew	Contributors
Pride Of Carolina	B Co 25 Avn Bn		UH-1C	1967	gun hog		NO	nose			242, 9120
Prince Of Darkness	118 AHC	A/82	UH-1B	65-66	gun		NO			Don Roof CE	1508,
Princess Anne	114 AHC	Avn Co	UH-1D	65-66	slick		NO	nose		Ron Alcott DG	14,
Princess Suzanne	114 AHC	Avn Co	UH-1B	1964	slick	62-01957	NO	cargo door window panel		W. Glasgow, J. Stevens, Hansen	615, 1706, 5436, 6700
Problem Child	116 AHC		UH-1H	70-71	slick	69-15642	NO	nose		Terry Ryan CE, Larry Tindall AC, Ferman Weedon CP	90, 734, 901, 1532, 1788, 4825, 9240
Professionals (The)	175 AHC		UH-1C	67-68	gun		N+A	pilot door			932,
Prophet (The)	A Trp 7/1		AH-1G	71-72	gun	67-15731	NO	bpw		Jim Prine CE	1426, 4825
Pro's (The)	45 Med Co		UH-1H	67-68	dustoff		NO	nose		Gary Poteat CE, Alex Montez MD	1412,
Protected By Batman	336 AHC	A/101	UH-1B	65-67	gun		NO	nose			1428, 9680
Proud Mary	57 AHC		UH-1C	1969	gun		NO	nose		John White AC	1899,
Proud Mary	116 AHC		UH-1H	70-71	slick / C+C	68-15417	NO	nose		Barrera CE, Bob Murphy DG, Erickson AC, Park CP	90, 901, 9450
Proud Mary	132 ASHC		CH-47B	70-71	cargo	67-18451	N+A	front fuselage	SP4 Davis did all '70-'71 a/c art	Monte McDonald FE	1162, 1588, 1843, 2055, 3850, 7800, 8275
Proud Mary	135 AHC		UH-1C	70-71	gun		NO	cargo door frame top		Smith AC	9330,
Proud Mary	176 AHC		UH-1H	1970	slick	67-17239	NO			P. Richards AC, Tom Reynolds CE, Dusty DG	1444, 9450
Proud Mary	192 AHC		UH-1C	69-70	gun	66-15070	N+A	nose		Robert Davis CE, Larry Farmer DG	398,
Proud Mary	242 ASHC		CH-47A	69-71	cargo	65-08008	NO				1199,
Proud Mary	247 Med Det		UH-1H	70-71	dustoff		NO				869,
Proud Mary	254 Med Det		UH-1H	70-71	dustoff	68-16476	N+A	nose	Dale Lacher	Tom Roberts CE, D. Lacher MD, Ray Greiner AC	664, 954, 1489
Proud Mary	498 Med Co		UH-1H	69-71	dustoff		NO	nose	Dennis Bishop	Gordy Burr CE, Gary Krause MD, Foxworthy	143, 553, 863, 942, 7425
Proud Mary	A Co 228 ASHB		CH-47A	70-71	cargo	66-19056	NO			Ronnie Moore FE	1231, 8025, 8250
Proud Mary	B Trp 2/17		AH-1G	70-71	gun	67-15705	NO	bpw right side		Gary Ryan AC	1531,

Copter Name	Unit	Unit #1	Aircraft	Circa	Function	Serial #	Config	Location	Artist	Crew	Contributors
Proud Mary	B Trp 3/17		AH-1G	69-70	gun	68-17033	NO	bpw			270, 754
Proud Mary	D Co 227 AHB		AH-1G	69-70	gun		NO	bpw			562, 862
Proud Mary	D Trp 3/4		OH-6A	1970	scout		NO	doghouse		Jack Cosby	1282, 3475, 4300
Provider (The)	17 AHC		UH-1H	1967	slick	66-16226	NO	pilot door		Mario Meola AC, Tom Konopka CE	1176,
Provider (The)	498 Med Co		UH-1H	69-70	dustoff		NO	nose			1357, 7700
Psychedelic Reaction	C Trp 1/9		AH-1G	70-71	gun		NO	bpw			1164,
Psychedelic Sex	155 AHC		UH-1C	66-67	gun hog		N+A	nose			496, 871, 9360
Psycho	188 AHC		UH-1C	1968	gun		N+A	pilot door	Dick Detra		414, 9480
Psychodelic Death	155 AHC		UH-1C	1968	gun		NAA	nose			157,
P-Turkey	C Co 228 ASHB		CH-47B	1965	cargo		N+A				984,
Puff The Magic Dragon	121 AHC		UH-1D	66-68	slick	64-13590	N+A	nose		Puffenbarger CE	437, 831, 1560, 1889
Pugnacious Porker	147 ASHC		CH-47C	69-70	cargo	68-15816	NO	front fuselage		Melvin Miller	1199, 3775
Pure Hell	117 AHC		UH-1C	1971	gun	65-09531	NO	cargo door		Earl Miller CE	1194,
Pure Hell	134 AHC		UH-1C	67-69	gun	66-15146	NO	nose		Joe Merricks CE	352, 1179, 1818
Pure Hell	C Trp 1-9		AH-1G	1969	gun		NO	rocket pod hardback			1266, 6275
Pure Hell	D Co 227 AHB		UH-1C	68-70	gun		NO	nose		Lightnin CE	687, 1760, 9700
Pure Hell No. 1	A Trp 3/17		OH-58A	1971	scout	68-16855	NO	fuselage		Thomas Richardson AC	1473, 2028, 9720
Pure Sex	117 AHC	Avn Co	UH-1C	66-67	gun	66-00531	NO	M-5 turret			6225, 8650, 9250
Purple Fox	176 AHC		UH-1C	1969	gun	66-15016	N+A			Steve Cundy CE	1595,
Purple Haze	15 Med Bn		UH-1H	69-70	medevac		NO				1345,
Purple Haze	326 Med Bn		UH-1H	70-71	dustoff		NAA	nose			281, 1926
Purple Haze	A Trp 3/17		UH-1H	70-71	slick	69-15468	NO			Al Fleenor AC	1093,

Copter Name	Unit	Unit #1	Aircraft	Circa	Function	Serial #	Config	Location	Artist	Crew	Contributors
Purple Haze Experience (The)	191 AHC		UH-1C	68-69	gun		NAA	pilot door			245, 9500
Pusher (The)	174 AHC		UH-1H	70-71	slick	68-15676	NAA	nose		Dave Rios DG	652, 1479, 8900, 9430
Pusher (The)	178 ASHC		CH-47B	70-71	cargo	67-18467	NO			Rick Novak FE	1303, 1380, 9885
Pusher (The)	179 ASHC		CH-47A	68-69	cargo	66-19020	NO			Stewart Wilson DG/CE	1715, 1929, 7900
Pusher (The)	A Trp 3/17		OH-6A	69-70	scout	67-16055	NO	doghouse			503, 1630, 8625
Pusher (The)	C Co 228 ASHB		CH-47B	1970	cargo	66-19114	NO	fuselage		Larry Mohler AC, John Williams DG, David Petty CE, Cliff Morley FE, Yeager CP, Cliff Morley FE	1239, 3830, 8025, 8365
Pusher (The)	unk		OH-58A	69-71	scout		NO				901, 9450
Pusher Man	170 AHC		UH-1H	1970	slick		NO	nose		Gary Ott CE, Dan McLaughlin DG, J. Hanebrink AC	1839, 4150, 9400
Pusher Man (The)	57 AHC		UH-1C	68-69	gun	66-15233	NO	nose		Jeff Cox AC, Dave Sanchez CE	357, 1899
Pusher Man (The)	134 AHC		UH-1H	69-70	slick	68-16092	NO	nose			352, 1818
Pusherman (The)	187 AHC		UH-1H	1970	slick	66-16659	NO	nose		Kenyon	125,
Pussy Galore	39 Signal Bn		UH-1B	1966	slick	63-08007	NO	pilot door		Lester Heath AC	265,
Pussy Galore	117 AHC		UH-1H	68-69	slick	65-09679	N+A	nose		William Turner CE 1968, Keith Alleger CP	21, 127, 253, 1313, 4825, 9250
Pussy Galore's Flying Circus	121 AHC		UH-1D	66-68	slick	65-09921	NO	nose		Chuck Drone CE	442, 831
Queen	82 Med Det		UH-1D	64-65	dustoff		NO	nose			2071,
Queen	D Trp 3/5		AH-1G	71-72	gun		NO			Tommy Whitfield CE	589, 9080
Queen (The)	A Co 228 ASHB		CH-47A	1969	cargo		NO	front fuselage			475,
Queen Hitmore	C Trp 16 Cav		AH-1G	1972	gun		NO	bpw			1205,
Queenie	147 ASHC		CH-47A	1968	cargo		N+A	fuselage			264,
Queer Frog Named John	A Trp 1/9		OH-6A	68-71	scout	67-16275	N+A	fuselage		William Frazer AC, Jim Thompson CE, Stubbs CP	558, 951, 1004, 1010, 1266, 1497, 1589, 1960, 2051, 3680, 5433, 5560, 6250, 7185
Queer John	361 AWC		AH-1G	70-71	gun		NO	bpw			1559,

Copter Name	Unit	Unit #1	Aircraft	Circa	Function	Serial #	Config	Location	Artist	Crew	Contributors
Queer John	B Trp 3/17		AH-1G	71-72	gun		NO	bpw			728, 1613
Quicksilver	45 Med Co		UH-1D	69-70	dustoff	66-16435	NO	nose		O'Brien CE, Wardell AC, Navone CP	1308, 7425
Quicksilver	118 AHC		UH-1H	1970	slick	68-15672	NO	nose		Tom Morley AC, Mike Cantarini CE, Jim McGeehan DG	1240,
Quicksilver	191 AHC		UH-1D	68-69	slick		NO				539,
Quicksilver 2	45 Med Co		UH-1H	1970	dustoff	68-16463	NO			Mike Nice AC, Bixby CP, O'Brien CE, D. Ross MD	1308, 2068, 7725
Quiet One (The)	114 AHC		UH-1D	1968	slick	65-10069	NO			S. Kinnaman, T. Kron	6700, 6750
Quigley	D Co 227 AHB		UH-1C	68-69	gun		NO			Allan Gates DG/CE	595,
R. L.'s Revenge	A Trp 7/1		OH-6A	71-72	scout		NO		Larry Brown	R. L. Parker AC	217,
Rabbit (The)	117 AHC	Avn Co	UH-1B	64-65	slick		NO	nose			69,
Raccoon Airlines ^	E Co-709 Maint Bn		UH-1H	66-67	maint	67-17821	N+A	fuselage		Kenny Foss AC	545,
Rag (The)	187 AHC		UH-1H	1971	slick	67-17505	NO	nose			652,
Rag I	114 AHC		UH-1D	1970	slick	64-13801	NO			William Mattler	1114, 6700
Rag III	114 AHC		UH-1H	1970	slick		NO			William Mattler	1114, 6700
Raggedy Ann	132 ASHC		CH-47B	70-71	cargo	66-19137	N+A	front fuselage	SP4 Davis did all '70-'71 a/c art	Bailey FE	392, 1162, 1588, 2062, 7800, 8275, 8950
Raggmopp	11 ACR		UH-1D	68-69	slick		NO	pilot door			1703,
Ragin Cajun	188 AHC		UH-1H	67-68	slick	66-16122	NO	pilot door		George Tally AC, Tim Wingerd CE, Bob Matthess DG	414, 1266, 6275, 9480
Ragin Cajun	200 ASHC		CH-47A	67-68	cargo	66-00097	NO	front fuselage	Larry Dumford	Rodger F. Dwyer FE	457, 995, 1195, 1585, 7950, 8250, 8275
Ragin Cajun	336 AHC		UH-1B	1967	gun		NO	nose			301, 2038
Raging Main	62 CAC		UH-1H	68-70	slick		NO	nose		Dave Dickinson CE, John Flake, Mecham, F. Wilson	417, 1927, 2086, 9190
Raid	D Co 227 AHB		AH-1G	69-70	gun	68-15058	NO				113,
Raider	175 AHC		UH-1H	1970	slick		NO	nose			656,
Rajun Cajin	C Co 159 ASHB		CH-47C	1968	cargo	991?	NO			J.C. Brown DG, Rodger Dwyer FE	213, 7850
Ralph II	176 AHC		UH-1D	67-68	slick	65-10062	NO	nose		Bob O'Connell CE, D. Borton CP, H. Connors AC, Rosenbaum DG, Ron Williams took over as CE late '67	1919,

Copter Name	Unit	Unit #1	Aircraft	Circa	Function	Serial #	Config	Location	Artist	Crew	Contributors
Ramblin Rose	A Co 159 ASHB		CH-47C	70-71	cargo	68-15835	NO	fuselage		Joe Seabourn FE	1580,
Rampage	174 AHC		UH-1H	69-71	slick	68-15671	NO	nose			184, 9430
Rape, Pillage, Burn	175 AHC		UH-1C	1967	gun	66-15047	NO	M-3 rocket box			301, 696, 5900
Rapid Transit System	271 ASHC		CH-47B	69-70	cargo	67-18433	NO	fuselage		Jess Cabrera DG, Dwight Gatzemeyer FE	256, 597, 8700
Rare Breed	175 AHC		UH-1H	71-72	slick		NO	nose			429, 1926
Rasputin	A Trp 1/9		UH-1C	67-69	slick / C+C	66-00573	NO	nose		Richard Marks DG, Pete Booth AC	923, 1090, 1287, 2039, 9690
Rat (The)	B Co 159 ASHB		CH-47B	68-70	cargo	66-19101	N+A	front fuselage		Bob Pendergast DG, Bill Mayer	1983,
Rat Fink	121 AHC		UH-1D	66-68	slick		N+A	nose		Jerry McBee CE	437, 831, 1135
Rated PG	15 Med Bn		UH-1H	70-71	dustoff		NO	nose		William Stovall AC	1712,
Raven (The)	92 AHC		UH-1C	1970	gun		NO	nose			931,
Rawhide	B Btry 2/20 ARA		AH-1G	1970	gun	66-15341	NO	bpw			601, 4825
Razorback	D Trp 1/4		OH-13S	1970	scout	181or183	NO				1205,
Reaper	175 AHC		UH-1C	1967	gun	66-15045	N+A	pilot door			35, 395, 1493, 1569, 2087, 5675
Reaper II	175 AHC		UH-1C	1968	gun		N+A	pilot door		Roger Anderson CE	35, 2087
Rebel	92 AHC		UH-1M	1971	gun		NO			John McCarthy AC	1126,
Rebel	114 AHC	Avn Co	UH-1B	64-65	slick	62-01913	N+A	cargo door window panel		Ron Williams CE	1918,
Rebel	222 CAB		UH-1D	1968	slick		NO	nose			1908, 4600
Rebel	B Trp 3/17		AH-1G	70-71	gun		NO	bpw			8650,
Rebel (The)	114 AHC	Avn Co	UH-1B	1964	slick	62-01968	NO	nose + cargo door window panel		Wes Dunn CE, E. Zamora AC, T. Winowitch DG	451,
Rebel (The) **	147 ASHC		CH-47A	1968	cargo	66-00082	AO	fuselage			264, 1053
Rebel (The) **	213 ASHC		CH-47A	66-67	cargo	66-00082	AO	fuselage		George Lake FE, Allco CE	790, 1053, 8000, 8275
Rebel (The)	254 Med Det		UH-1H	68-69	dustoff	66-16634	NO	pilot door		George Roberts CE	424, 1487

Rebel: *114 AHC, UH-1B, (sn 62-01913), 1964-65.* An un-identified 25th Infantry Division door gunner stands beside the cargo door window where an inserted panel displays the art and name for this 1st platoon Red Knight slick. Photo by Ron Williams.

Copter Name	Unit	Unit #1	Aircraft	Circa	Function	Serial #	Config	Location	Artist	Crew	Contributors
Rebel Chicken	A Co 227 AHB		UH-1H	70-71	slick	69-15704	N+A	nose	Joe Paranal	Adams, David Twibault	1340, 1789, 9700
Rebel Devil	11 GS		UH-1B	65-66	slick		N+A			Robert McCrory CE	1132,
Rebel Devil (The)	134 AHC		UH-1C	70-71	gun		NO			Roger Dye DG, Harold Shonk CE	458, 9320
Rebel Rouser	57 TC	120 AHC	CH-21C	1963	lift		N+A	fuselage			3600, 5440, 8925
Rebel Rouser	187 AHC		UH-1D	1968	slick	66-17085	NO	pilot door			1296, 9470
Recovery	11 ACR		UH-1H	1968	maint		NO	nose			1700, 8625
Red Ball Express	48 AHC	390 TC	UH-1D	1968	maint		NO	nose			226, 9640
Red Baron	62 CAC		UH-1H	1970	slick		N+A	nose		Ralph Martin AC, Hixon	987, 1099
Red Baron **	A Co 1 Avn Bn		UH-1B	65-66	gun	64-13914	NO	cargo door frame top			301, 5275
Red Baron	B Co 25 Avn Bn		UH-1C	67-68	gun		NO				1562,
Red Baron (The)	45 Med Co		UH-1H	1969	dustoff	67-17167	NO			O. Poole AC, Will Hix CP, Jim McNish CE, Gary Johnson MD	600, 2013, 7775
Red Devil	336 AHC	167 TC	UH-1D	65-67	maint		N+A	nose	Bob Koonce 1965	Kelley AC	934, 967, 2016, 6275
Red Devil	336 AHC	167 TC	UH-1H	1968	maint		N+A	nose		Scott Woodworth CE	440, 1553, 1957, 9610
Red Leg	62 CAC		UH-1H	69-70	slick		NO	nose		Sullivan	987, 1099
Red Who?	201 CAC		UH-1D	68-69	slick		N+A	nose			1703,
Reeling In A Huey **	539 TC		CH-47	67-68	recovery		v-nnp	fuselage	Cameron Smith	Cameron Smith	1632, 9660
Remember The Alamo	D Trp 3/5		AH-1G	1968	gun		NO	250 lb bomb		Doss Burchfield AC, D.B. Aaronson CP	69,
REMF	128 AHC		UH-1H	69-71	slick	68-16179	NO	nose		David Price CE	644, 9300
Renegade	175 AHC		UH-1B	1967	gun	63-08710	NO	pilot door		Dennis Abella DG, Danny Hudgins CE	1075, 1926, 9130
Renegade	C Trp 1/9		UH-1C	67-68	gun	66-00658	NO	pilot door			53, 9805
Renegade (The)	A Co 4 Avn Bn		UH-1H	1967	slick		NO	pilot door		Steve J. Hyde CE	822, 9060

Copter Name	Unit	Unit #1	Aircraft	Circa	Function	Serial #	Config	Location	Artist	Crew	Contributors
Revasegen	116 AHC		UH-1H	70-71	slick	68-15278	NO	nose		Moses CE, Larry Pickett AC	1393,
Revenge	57 AHC		UH-1H	71-72	night-hawk	68-15591	NO	nose + vertical stablizer		Bob Coe CE	314, 821, 9490
Revenge II	57 AHC		UH-1H	1972	slick / nigthawk		N+A	nose		Robert Terry DG	1762, 4425, 8450, 9180
Reverend Mr. Black	173 AHC		UH-1C	1969	gun		N+A	pilot door			1461, 9420
Revolution Outlaw	175 AHC		UH-1D	1967	slick		NO				1926,
RF Express	D Trp 1/4		UH-1D	1969	slick	66-16509	NO	pilot door			1053, 1205
Rice Paddy Cruiser	175 AHC		UH-1H	1970	slick		NO	nose		Bill Fryant AC	565, 1926
Rice Paddy Daddy	56 TC		UH-1D	1967	recovery		N+A	pilot door			1041, 1053, 1191, 1266, 6025, 6150, 6225, 6275
Rickshaw (The)	1 Bde 1 Cav Div		UH-1H	1967	slick	66-16811	N+A	nose	J. Bell	Stan Childress AC, Jim Zanavich CP, Jim Bell CE	123, 2034, 8975
Ride A Slick To Hell + Back ^^	155 AHC		UH-1D	67-68	slick		NO	nose			4, 400, 1053, 6025
Ride A Slick To Hell + Back	192 AHC		UH-1H	68-69	slick		NO				1192,
Ridge Runner #1	178 ASHC		CH-47B	68-70	cargo	67-18492	NO	front fuselage		David CrockerlI FE	497, 879, 1155, 1266, 1464, 1908, 4600
Right Here Buddy	237 Med Det		UH-1H	71-72	dustoff	70-15805	NO			Dan Halliday	684, 1094
Right On	117 AHC		UH-1H	1971	slick	67-17382	NO	nose + cargo door frame top		Ken Scales CE	1552,
Rigormortis	155 AHC		UH-1C	1968	gun	66-15049	NO	nose			960,
Rita Ann	117 AHC		UH-1H	68-70	slick	67-17725	NO	nose			127, 401, 1996, 9250
Roach Coach (The)	196 ASHC		CH-47A	69-70	cargo	65-08010	NO	front fuselage		Rich Mikesell CE	1188,
Road Runner	33 TC	118 AHC	CH-21C	1963	lift		N+A	fuselage			974, 9260
Road Runner ^	114 AHC	544 TC	UH-1B	1964	maint	62-01953	NO			T. Castle, R. Weathersby, L. Beard, J. Harvey	1938, 6700
Road Runner ^	175 AHC	409 TC	UH-1B	64-65	maint	64-13971	N+A			Bob Koonce CE, Jeff Weber, Jim Kirkley, Jack Moodt, Tim Bisch	301, 934, 1881, 1926, 9130, 9440
Road Runner ^	175 AHC	150 TC	UH-1B	67-69	maint		N+A	nose		Chuck Howard AC, Bob Millward	301, 797, 934, 1881, 9130
Road Runner **	200 ASHC		CH-47A	67-68	cargo	66-00103	AO	front fuselage	Larry Dumford		475, 995, 1195, 8275

Copter Name	Unit	Unit #1	Aircraft	Circa	Function	Serial #	Config	Location	Artist	Crew	Contributors
Road Runner ^	E Co 123 Avn Bn		UH-1H	70-71	maint	68-16317	NO			Mike Hill DG, Gay Atkins CE, Johnson CP	54, 1391, 9885
Road Runner	E Co 723 Mant Bn		UH-1H	69-71	maint	68-16317	N+A	nose		Newton CE, Barricelli	2002, 3050
Road Service ^	114 AHC	544 TC	UH-1D	68-69	maint	8459	NO	nose		Dan Tookmanian, C.Hudson	1413, 1794, 2017, 6700, 9230
Road Service II ^	114 AHC	544 TC	UH-1H	69-70	maint	68-16156	NO	nose		S. McKinnon, J. Akin	289, 333, 1053, 6700, 9230
Road Service III ^	114 AHC	544 TC	UH-1H	70-71	maint	69-15347	NO	nose		Phil Vanderwedge CE, Homer Prevost AC, Mike Clepper DG, Robert Breitner DG	192, 301, 696, 1824, 6700, 9230
Road Service IV ^	114 AHC	544 TC	UH-1H	71-72	maint	69-15422	NO	nose		Ed Hepler CE, George Bradley AC, Bruno Jankowitcz CE, Charles Stufflebeem	735, 1053, 1723
Roadrunner	8 TC	117 AHC	CH-21C	1963	lift	56-02085	N+A	fuselage		Tom Rose CE, Grainger CE	127, 1511
Roadrunner	271 ASHC	361 TC	CH-47B	69-70	maint	66-19129	NO			Dan Lampman FE, Kenny Linsman CE	964, 8100
Roadrunner	B Co 25 Avn Bn		UH-1D	68-69	nighthawk / smoker	65-09961	N+A	nose		Gonzalo Salazar CE, Jack Mosley DG '69	49, 909, 1011, 9120
Roadrunner (The) ^	187 AHC	602 TC	UH-1D	1967	maint	66-00968	NO			J. Stewart AC, Jeff Roy CP, Mike Sun CE, G. Stevenson G	1691, 1908
Roadrunner (The) **	A Co 228 ASHB		CH-47A	1970	cargo	66-19021	AO	front fuselage		John Usry FE	1819,
Roadrunner **	117 AHC	140 TC	UH-1H	71-72	maint		AO			Matt Mano DG, Tom Totzkie CE	1082, 9250
Roadrunner ^	175 AHC	150 TC	UH-1B/D	65-67	maint	64-13971	N+A	nose	Bob Koonce '64-'65 / Kevin Lyles	Lassiter AC, Frenchy Tash CE, Ed Koonce CE, Bob Millward	36, 461, 851, 934, 1207, 1975, 5775, 6525
Roadrunner **	178 ASHC		CH-47A	67-68	cargo	66-19070	AO	front fuselage		Don Bryan CE	841,
Roadrunner **	C Trp 16 Cav		AH-1G	1971	gun		AO	bpw			1053, 1205
Roadrunner II ^	271 ASHC	361 TC	CH-47B	69-70	maint	66-19134	NO			Dan Lampman FE, Madsen AC	964, 8100
Rock and Flint	D Trp 1/4		OH-6A	69-70	scout	68-17308	NO			John Gott AC	195, 1205, 1923
Roho	A Co 227 AHB		UH-1H	69-70	slick	66-16610	NO	nose			562,
Rokin Robin	187 AHC		UH-1D	1968	slick	67-17202	NO	pilot door			1270, 4100
Rookie	B Trp 7/1		OH-6A	68-69	scout	66-17819	N+A	doghouse			639,
Rosalie	A Co 1 Avn Bn		UH-1B	1967	gun	64-13924	NO	doorpost			301,

Copter Name	Unit	Unit #1	Aircraft	Circa	Function	Serial #	Config	Location	Artist	Crew	Contributors
Rosemary's Baby	5 Trans Bn		UH-1H	1968	slick		NO	nose			870,
Rosemary's Baby	48 AHC		UH-1B	68-69	gun		N+A	nose			1000, 9150
Rosemary's Baby	134 AHC		UH-1H	68-69	slick		NO	nose	Frank Synder	Frank Synder DG, Joe Bates CE	352, 1658, 1818, 9320
Rosemary's Baby	176 AHC		UH-1C	69-71	gun hog	66-15089	N+A	nose		Owen Brant CE, Jim Gilroy DG, Larry Silva CE, Tony Commander CE, Frank Donehoo DG	186, 661, 742, 901, 1255, 1595, 9450
Rosemary's Baby	242 ASHC		CH-47A	68-71	cargo		NO				1056, 1199
Rosemary's Baby	A Btry 4/77 ARA		UH-1C	1969	gun		NO	nose			1067,
Rosemary's Baby	C Co 159 ASHB		CH-47C	69-70	cargo	67-18508	NO			Don Stamps FE, C. Stanley, J. Freeman, D. Woodie	179, 776, 826, 1682, 7850
Rosemary's Baby	D Trp 3/4		AH-1G	70-71	gun		NO	doghouse	Gary Schmidt	Bill CE	1559, 8400
Rotor Toter	187 AHC	602 TC	UH-1H	1970	maint	69-15426	NO	nose			1700, 1932
Round Eyes Forever	187 AHC		UH-1H	68-70	slick	67-17767	N+A	hell hole cover		Tom Stino CE	1700, 9470
Round Trip	243 ASHC		CH-47A	1968	cargo	66-19052	N+A	nose		Bill Bell CE	111, 124, 1975
Rubber Duck *	129 AHC		UH-1H	70-71	slick	68-16351	v-nn	scarves for AC, CE, DG		Arthur Foster CE, Larry Brewster CE	546,
Rubber Duck	187 AHC		UH-1H	70-71	slick	68-16193	NO	nose		Danny Clark CE, Terry Smith	1653, 1700, 1932, 1954, 3300
Rubber Ducky	A Trp 7/1		AH-1G	71-72	gun	67-15731	NO	bpw		Jim Prine CE, Robert D. Parker AC	1426, 4825
Ruby Tuesday *	282 AHC		UH-1D	67-68	slick	65-09874	v-nn			Bob Ford AC, Bud Atanian CE	2041,
Rufus II	200 ASHC		CH-47A	67-68	cargo	66-00104	NO		Larry Dumford		995, 1195, 1585, 2057
Rum Rico	162 AHC		UH-1H	1970	slick		NO	nose		Leroy Dike AC, Goins CE, Laboy DG	419, 736, 1908, 4600
Runnin Scared	114 AHC		UH-1D	1967	slick		NO	nose			41, 6700
Runnin Scared	242 ASHC		CH-47A	67-69	cargo	65-08024	N+A	front fuselage	Ron Wetherell	Ron Wetherell FE, Roger Montgomery CE, Butch Smith DG, H. Walden FE	452, 1199, 1225, 1445, 1631, 1892, 1926, 4300, 4825, 5750, 8250, 8275
Running Scared	175 AHC	A/502	UH-1B	1965	slick		NO				1926,
Ruptured Cherry (The)	174 AHC		UH-1H	1969	slick		N+A	nose			1259,

Copter Name	Unit	Unit #1	Aircraft	Circa	Function	Serial #	Config	Location	Artist	Crew	Contributors
Ruptured Duck	243 ASHC		CH-47A	69-70	cargo	65-07993	NO			Carlos Vazquez DG	1826, 2011
Ruthie	A Trp 1/9		UH-1H	69-70	slick	68-15649	NO			Duane Horton	793, 9690
S,A,D, Mrs	187 AHC		UH-1H	68-69	slick	67-17558	N+A	pilot door		Pat Dougan AC, Herman Scott CE	434, 9470
Sadistic Revenge	176 AHC		UH-1C	69-71	gun		N+A	nose			901, 9450
Sally	134 AHC		UH-1C	1970	gun		NO	nose			352, 1818
Sally	A Co 228 ASHB		CH-47A	1968	cargo		N+A	fuselage			510, 6805
Sally J	571 Med Det		UH-1H	70-71	dustoff	68-16368	NO			John Moore CE	1229,
Same Same Spears The Monkey	93 TC	121 AHC	CH-21C	63-64	lift	55-04215	N+A	fuselage		Jon Spears CE	1665,
Sandra	1/9	HHT	UH-1H	1969	slick		NO	nose			1266, 5025, 6275
Sandra	271 ASHC		CH-47B	1968	cargo		N+A	fuselage		Marc Teeter CE, Tony Rios CE	964, 1087, 1707
Sandra Lee	D Trp 3/5		UH-1D	1967	slick		NO	pilot door			1044, 9860
Sandy	11 BDE		UH-1H	69-70	slick		NO				130,
Sandi	D Trp 2/1		OH-6A	68-69	scout	67-16156	NO	doghouse		Jim Norris AD, Patton CE	1034, 4000
Sandy Ghost	unk Cav		UH-1H	1973	slick		NO	nose	Jim Hodgson	Jim Hodgson AC	766,
Sarcophagus	45 Med Co		UH-1H	68-69	dustoff		NO	belly			1040,
Sat Cong	2 Signal Group		UH-1B	1967	slick		NO	cargo door			301,
Sat Cong	57 AHC		UH-1H	71-72	slick		N+A	nose			1841,
Sat Cong	68 AHC		UH-1C	68-69	gun		NO	belly			1304, 1635, 1883, 9200
Sat Cong	118 AHC		UH-1C	68-69	gun		NO	belly			516,
Sat Cong	120 AHC		UH-1B	1966	gun		NO	belly			827,
Sat Cong	175 AHC		UH-1D	1967	slick		NO	nose		John Scott DG, Andy Keeney AC	1576, 1926

Copter Name	Unit	Unit #1	Aircraft	Circa	Function	Serial #	Config	Location	Artist	Crew	Contributors
Sat Cong	190 AHC		UH-1C	1968	gun	66-00624	N+A	nose	Mad Mexican CE	Bob Coveney AC, Mad Mexican CE, Karl DG	350, 8600, 8775
Sat Cong	191 AHC		UH-1C	70-71	gun		NO	belly	Steve Healey	Steve Healey CE	721,
Sat Cong	240 AHC		UH-1C	1967	gun	66-00704	NO	nose		Jim Mitchell AC, Louis Wilson CP, Frank Bay CE, Dennis Jensen DG	106,
Satan	174 AHC		UH-1H	69-71	slick	68-15463	NO	nose		McCabe AC, Toomey CE, Carter, Davison, Hahn, Ben Kennedy, Melvin Heitman	67, 316, 676, 1770, 3250, 9430, 9885
Satan Snake	D Trp 1/4		AH-1G	69-70	gun		N+A	bpw		Dean Sinor AC, John Loftice AC	309, 439, 1053, 1205, 5700
Satan's Image	134 AHC		UH-1H	1969	slick	67-17351	NO	nose			352, 979, 1818
Satan's Playmate	175 AHC		UH-1C	67-69	gun	66-15054	N+A	pilot door		John Mercer AC, Spiers AC, Eddie Adair DG, Tom Kennedy CE, Vance Shearer AC, Dave Osbourne	301, 461, 478, 646, 900, 932, 982, 1330, 1597, 1670, 1926, 5775
Satan's Playpen	57 AHC		UH-1H	1971	slick		N+A	nose			3075,
Satan's Pride	134 AHC		UH-1H	69-70	slick		NO				352, 979, 1818
Satan's Rag	B Trp 3/17		AH-1G	69-70	gun		NO				270,
Satan's Toy	11 ACR		OH-6A	71-72	scout		NO				1467,
Satan's Whore	281 AHC		UH-1C	69-70	gun		NO				66,
Satisfaction	175 AHC		UH-1D	68-69	slick		NO			Tom Kennedy CE, Dennis Smith AC	900, 1926
Satisfaction	188 AHC		UH-1C	67-68	gun	66-15179	N+A	pilot door	Dick Detra	Joe Walker AC, Greg Allen CE, Dick Detra DG, J. Soares AC, Dean Murphy CP, Bill Sondey CE	414, 1024, 1262, 1660, 1849, 6275, 6475, 9480
Scarlet Curse	189 AHC		UH-1H	70-71	slick		NO	nose		Francis Ty Simmons AC	1615, 4350
Scavenger	178 ASHC		CH-47B	68-70	cargo	67-18445	N+A			James Falloway FE	497,
Scavengers ^	D Trp 3/5		UH-1H	1969	maint		N+A	nose		Jim Hyler CE	266, 823, 4825, 9860
Schlitz	335 AHC		UH-1B	69-70	gun	62-04592	N+A	rocket pod			1696, 2050, 9590
Scotch Soda	336 AHC		UH-1D	66-67	slick		NO	nose			2038,
Scotsman (The)	213 ASHC		CH-47A	66-67	cargo	65-08016	N+A	fuselage		Bill MacDougall CE, Hassenbrock	359, 790, 8000
Scout ^	A Trp 1/9		UH-1B	1966	scout		N+A	nose		John Nielson AC, James Croner CP	371, 895, 1964, 4825

Copter Name	Unit	Unit #1	Aircraft	Circa	Function	Serial #	Config	Location	Artist	Crew	Contributors
Scrap Iron	121 AHC		UH-1D	66-68	slick	64-13590	NO	nose			831, 1135, 8925
Screamin Demon	134 AHC		UH-1H	70-71	slick		NO	nose		Joe Rovig	1517, 9320
Screaming Green Zonkers	271 ASHC		CH-47B	69-70	cargo		N+A	front fuselage			964,
Screaming Nighthog	571 Med Det		UH-1H	1973	dustoff		NO	nose	Osgood	Osborne CE	215,
Screaming OD Zonker (The)	F Trp 4 Cav		OH-6A	1971	scout	69-16032	NO	doghouse			140, 1559
Screaming Yellow Zonker	187 AHC		UH-1H	70-71	slick	69-15370	NO	nose		Ross DG, Hunton AC, Bennet CP, Ben Simpson CE	125, 1619, 9470
Screaming Yellow Zonker	A Trp 7/1		OH-6A	1971	scout		NO	doghouse		Mike Skomswold	1426, 1581, 3375
Screw Communism	336 AHC		UH-1H	1970	slick		N+A	nose		Sanowith DG, Wikles DG, Olson AC, Feigel CE	508, 1305, 1327, 4825
Season's Greetings	175 AHC		UH-1D	68-69	slick		N+A	nose		Hans-Peter Naegele CE, Larry Cunningham AC	358, 654
Season's Greetings	A Co 229 AHB		UH-1H	1970	slick		NO	tailboom			548,
Season's Greetings The Cowboys	335 AHC		UH-1H	69-70	slick		N+A	nose	WO Dale Dilts	John Lawler AC	405, 983
Semi-Hemi ^	187 AHC	602 TC	UH-1H	1970	maint	69-15426	v-nn			Ron W. Scott CE	880, 1578, 1932
Semper Mint Julep-Confederate Air Force	A Co 1 Avn Bn		UH-1B	1967	gun	919	N+A	cargo door window			301,
Serendipity	187 AHC		UH-1H	1970	slick	68-16281	NO	nose			1932, 1954
Sexy	57 TC	120 AHC	CH-21C	1963	lift		N+A	fuselage			1975, 6500
Sexy Sadie	116 AHC		UH-1H	69-70	slick		NO				1180,
Sexy Shuffler (The)	242 ASHC		CH-47A	67-69	cargo	66-19016	NO				1199,
Sexy Snake	114 AHC		UH-1C	1967	gun	66-00566	NO	pilot door		L. Boles, G. Brooks, B. Jennings, A. Jensen	634, 848, 1470, 6700, 9230
Sgt Rock	D Trp 1/1		UH-1H	1969	slick		N+A	nose		John Rock CE	929, 4825
Shadow (The)	10 CAB	H+HC	UH-1D	1967	C+C		N+A	nose		Eugene Crooks	373,
Shadow (The)	82 Med Det		UH-1D	1965	dustoff		NO	cargo door window panel			1215, 7750

Short, Don't Shoot Me*: 191 AHC, UH-1D, (sn 66-00818), 1968-69*. Such an earnest request was shared by all in-country short-timers once that "two digit midget" mentality (last 99 days) took over. Apparently, both crew and aircraft—"Old '818"—survived, and were sent home after amassing 1,877 total hours. Photo by Bill Flores.

Copter Name	Unit	Unit #1	Aircraft	Circa	Function	Serial #	Config	Location	Artist	Crew	Contributors
Shadow of Death (The)	228 ASHB		CH-47	69-70	cargo		NO	fuselage			8475,
Shadowfax	E Trp 1/9		AH-1G	70-71	gun	67-15740	N+A	bpw		Vaughn Caine AC	259,
Shaky Eight *	114 AHC	Avn Co	UH-1D	66-68	slick	65-09808	v-nn			T. Borzewski	1794, 6700, 7090
Shaky Lady	179 ASHC		CH-47A	68-69	cargo	66-19020	N+A	fuselage			236, 1057
Sharon	118 AHC		UH-1D	1967	slick	66-01004	NO	vertical stabilizer		Lanny Hansen CE	691, 9260
She Devil	134 AHC		UH-1M	69-70	gun	66-15238	NO	nose			1451, 1738, 4050
Shenandoah	174 AHC		UH-1H	1968	slick	66-16954	NO	nose		Ross Clement AC, Thad Kelly CE	311, 9430
Sheriff's Piecemaker	361 AWC		AH-1G	69-70	gun	68-17032	NO	nose		John Sloan CE	1626,
Sherry Baby	175 AHC		UH-1H	1970	slick		NO	nose			467,
Ship Of Fools	114 AHC		UH-1H	1971	slick	69-15085	NO	nose			1838, 3100, 6700
Ship Of Fools	187 AHC		UH-1H	71-72	slick	69-15705	NO	nose		Pat Strople CE, John Watford DG	427, 853, 1720, 1871, 9470
Ship Of Fools	237 Med Det		UH-1H	70-71	dustoff		NO	nose		Paul Simcoe MD	2069,
Ship Of Fools	D Co 227 AHB		UH-1C	68-69	gun	65-09460	NO	nose		Bobby Buchanan CE	229, 1876, 4825
Shirl Be Good	E Trp 1/9		OH-6A	70-71	scout		NO	fuselage		Dan Prins, Larry Brown	1497, 6475
Shirley Ann	336 AHC	A/101	UH-1D	1966	slick		NO	nose			30, 9680
Shirley Lou	114 AHC		UH-1D	1967	slick	66-00917	NO			D. Duerr, T. Sherman, Akins, D. Owens, D. Dutro, L. Stingeer, L. Whitlow	445, 6700
Short	15 Med Bn		UH-1H	69-70	medevac		NO	nose			548,
Short	174 AHC		UH-1H	69-70	smoke	67-17503		cargo door		Larry Whalen CE, Jim Shedd DG	1894,
Short	203 ASHC		CH-47A	71-72	cargo	64-13112	NO	fuselage	Warren Moore	Larry Sullivan FE, Sheib FE	1233,
Short	D Trp 1/4		OH-6A	68-69	scout		NO	belly			1943,
Short Stomper	C Co 229 AHB		UH-1H	69-70	slick	67-17173	NAA	nose		House AC	1601,
Short, Don't Shoot Me	191 AHC		UH-1D	68-69	slick	66-00818	NO	belly		Bill Flores CE	539,

Copter Name	Unit	Unit #1	Aircraft	Circa	Function	Serial #	Config	Location	Artist	Crew	Contributors
Showboat (The)	200 ASHC		CH-47A	67-68	cargo	66-00107	NO		Larry Dumford	John Schulan CE, Bob Langley FE, Jimmy Morrow DG, David Seals DG	966, 1585
Sic 'Em Puss	173 AHC		UH-1D	66-67	slick	65-09586	NO	pilot door			1908, 4600
Sick-Lo-Girl	134 AHC		UH-1H	1970	slick	68-16064	NO	nose		Ken Blankenship AC	149, 352, 1818, 1895, 9320
Sidney Or The Bush	175 AHC		UH-1D	1967	slick		NO	nose		John Scott DG, Benny Blalock CE, Andy Keeney AC	887, 1576, 1926
Silent Majority	176 AHC		UH-1C	70-71	gun	66-15027	N+A	gun mount		Mark Dekreon CE, Tony Commander DG	504, 9450
Silken Snarl (The)	200 ASHC		CH-47A	67-68	cargo	66-00086	N+A	front fuselage	Larry Dumford	Richard Lee	475, 995, 1195, 1451, 4050, 7950, 8275
Silly Rabbit-Slicks Are For Kids	17 AHC		UH-1C	1968	gun		NO	doorpost		James Post AC	1411,
Silver Lead	189 AHC		UH-1H	68-69	slick		NO	nose			1053, 1686
Sir Lime A Lot	11 ACR		OH-6A	68-69	scout		NO	doghouse			1448, 8625
Sir Reginald Lime-Lime	11 ACR		OH-6A	68-69	scout		N+A	clamshell			1703,
Situation Normal All Fucked Up **	several		various	66-70	slick / scout		NO	various			507, 1406, 1766
Six Pack To Go	339 TC		UH-1B	64-65	gun		NO	rocket pod			1975, 6525
Ski Bum	174 AHC		UH-1H	1969	slick	68-15661	NO	nose		Adam Wilson AC, Richardo Regaldo CP, Forest Hodgkin CE, Ron Ducommun DG	1808,
Sky Hawk	173 Abn Bde		UH-1H	69-70	slick		NO	nose		Don Charlton AC, Don Armstrong DG	1993, 9410
Sky King	178 ASHC		CH-47B	69-70	cargo		NO			Ron Quigley DG, Rick CE, Radcliff FE	497, 1433, 7875
Sky Pig	B Trp 3/17		UH-1H	1971	slick		NO	nose			1581,
Sky Pilot	242 ASHC		CH-47A	68-69	cargo	64-13127	N+A			Jesse Torre, James Count	1199, 8350
Sky Pilot	A Trp 3/17		OH-6A	69-70	scout	65-12962	NO			Gary Swartz CE	1737,
Sky Pilot II	242 ASHC		CH-47A	69-71	cargo	65-08011	NO			Ed Stokley, Richard Byrne	1199,
Sky Queen	243 ASHC		CH-47A	70-71	cargo	64-13112	NO			Curtis Green	647, 8075
Sky Thing	B Trp 1/9		OH-6A	1969	scout		NO	fuselage		Ron Kenerson	898,

Copter Name	Unit	Unit #1	Aircraft	Circa	Function	Serial #	Config	Location	Artist	Crew	Contributors
Skyraider (The)	200 ASHC		CH-47A	67-68	cargo	66-00101	NO		Larry Dumford	Ed Jones	995, 1195, 1585
Slave Driver	611 TC		CH-37B	1965	recovery		N+A	fuselage			1266, 1908, 4600, 6275
Sleasy Rider	236 Med Det		UH-1H	71-72	dustoff		NO	nose		Dale Wills CE	175, 1229, 1924
Sleeping Tigers	8 TC	117 AHC	CH-21C	1964	lift	56-02021	N+A	fuselage		Tom Rose CE	127, 1397, 1511, 6805
Sleepy Slope	114 AHC		UH-1H	69-70	slick	67-17221	NO			Barnes, Diaz, P. Schoenstein	1563, 6700
Sleezee Dee	116 AHC		UH-1D	1970	slick		NO	nose		John Jammer CE	90, 395, 439, 584, 5675, 5725
Slick Chick 1	117 AHC	Avn Co	UH-1D	65-66	slick	64-13672	N+A	nose	Willy Peahy painted female	Tommy Carter CE, William Peahy DG, Roenfranz AC	285,
Slicker Than Shit	162 AHC		UH-1H	71-72	slick	68-15649	NO	nose		George Lauffer AC, Ronnie Teake	978, 1908, 4600, 9390
Slicks Are For Kids - With Balls	282 AHC		UH-1H	71-72	slick		NO	pilot door	Bill Somerfield / Jesus Pagan	Jesus Pagan DG, Jose Cano CE	273, 1663
Sloopy Gal	335 AHC		UH-1D	66-67	slick	65-09679	NO	doorpost		John Poole CE	1409,
Slope Cab	175 AHC		UH-1D	1966	slick		NO				461, 5775
Slope Slayer	336 AHC		UH-1C	1970	gun		N+A	nose		Jim Beddingfield AC	114, 1305, 1996, 4825
Slope Toter	114 AHC		UH-1D	1968	slick	65-12880	NO			Sween	6700, 6775
Slow But Sure	243 ASHC		CH-47A	69-71	maint?		NO			Steve Willert, Jim Wallace, Curt Scheibel	1555, 8075
Smile Or I'll Kill You	unk		UH-1C	1968	gun		NO	belly			2043, 3750, 8650, 9050
Smoke	229 AHB	HHC	UH-1H	71-72	slick		NO	nose		Mike Thornton CE	1778,
Smokey	71 AHC		UH-1H	1970	smoke		NO	nose			614,
Smokey	116 AHC		UH-1H	68-70	smoke	99?	NO	nose	Joe Duvall	Randy Price DG, Tim Templin CP, Joe Duvall CP, Ronan, Isabel, Jack McKnight	1273, 1506, 1623, 4825
Smokey	121 AHC		UH-1D	1968	slick		NO				1889,

Copter Name	Unit	Unit #1	Aircraft	Circa	Function	Serial #	Config	Location	Artist	Crew	Contributors
Smokey	135 AHC		UH-1H	68-69	smoke		NO	nose		Bob Ford DG	543,
Smokey	162 AHC		UH-1H	68-70	smoke	67-17205	NO	nose		Larry Salee DG, Jay Hayden CE, Mario Aguilar DG	1538, 1550, 1908, 8900, 9390
Smokey *	174 AHC		UH-1H	68-71	smoke	67-17503	v-nn	nose		W. Clark AC, Zeberg CE, L. Whalen CE, Jim Shedd, Grogan was AC in 1969, Bill Brown CE '69-'70	223, 1598, 9430
Smokey	176 AHC		UH-1D	1967	slick	66-01186	NO	pilot door		W. Borchart CP, R. Jenks AC, R. Berta CE, J. Whaley DG, Deredron CE '69	93, 1595
Smokey	187 AHC		UH-1C	68-72	gun		NO	nose			1799, 9470
Smokey 500	176 AHC		UH-1H	1968	slick	67-17500	NO	nose			901, 958, 1347, 1595, 1814, 1987, 9450
Smokey III	11 CAB		UH-1D	1967	smoke	65-10126	NO				3975,
Smokey Tail	68 AHC		UH-1D	68-69	smoke	66-06868	NO			Pat Tomkins CE	792, 1792, 9200
Smokey The Baron	269 CAB		UH-1D	1967	smoke		NO	nose			301, 414, 1053, 1908, 4600
Smokey The Baron No 2	269 CAB		UH-1C	1967	smoke		NO	nose		Bill Schwend AC	65, 414, 1572, 9480
Smokey The Baron No 3	269 CAB		UH-1D	1968	smoke		NO	nose			1860, 8650
Smokey The Bear ***	128 AHC		UH-1D	1968	smoke	65-10126	N+A			John Sullivan CE, Jim Wilks CE, Robert Stidd DG, Jim Palmer CE, Al Watkins AC, Jim Leary CP	913, 989, 1480, 1910, 9250
Smokie	188 AHC		UH-1C	67-68	gun / smoker	64-14167	NO			Walker AC, Cabigon CE, Pierpoint DG, Sipes, Staley, McCloud, McMillan	24, 414, 1394
Smokie II	188 AHC		UH-1H	67-68	smoke	66-16155	NO	nose		Kjell Tollefsen AC, Ted Alley CE, Ron Piecuch DG	1024, 1790
Smokie II	C Co 101 AHB		UH-1H	1968	smoke	66-16155	NO	nose		Kjell Tollefsen AC, Ted Alley CE, Ron Piecuch DG	24, 1790
Smokie III	188 AHC		UH-1H	67-68	smoke	66-16176	NO				414,
Smokie III	C Co 101 AHB		UH-1H	68-69	smoke	66-16176	NO	nose		Mains AC, Clements CE, James DG	414,
Smokie IV	C Co 101 AHB		UH-1H	1970	smoke	66-01121	NO	nose		Gary Pease AC, Mike Journeycake DG	876, 9480
SNAFU	173 AHC		UH-1D	66-67	slick	65-09598	NO	pilot door		Mark Brown AC, Vincent Politi CE, Tom Coile DG	1406,
SNAFU	539 TC		UH-1H	69-70	recovery		NO				1766,
SNAFU	D Trp 3/4		OH-6A	68-69	scout	67-16308	NO			Chris Favata CE	507, 8450
SNAFU II	539 TC		UH-1H	70-71	recovery		NO	nose			1766, 9660

Copter Name	Unit	Unit #1	Aircraft	Circa	Function	Serial #	Config	Location	Artist	Crew	Contributors
Snake Bit	C Co 229 AHB		UH-1H	68-70	slick	68-15240	NO	nose		Gary Atkinson CE, Omps AC, Mike Flam CE	56, 534, 1727, 8025
Snake Charmer	COBRA NETT		UH-1H	69-70	maint	68-15331	N+A			Tom McFarland AC	1143,
Snake Charmer	unk		AH-1G	69-70	gun		NO	bpw			1934,
Snake Doctor ^	71 AHC	151 TC	UH-1D	67-68	maint	66-01030	N+A	nose	Pete Repak: pilot door	Tom Bokkes CE '70-'71, Paul Bartlett '67-'68	95, 536, 591, 973, 1109, 1429, 1460, 1525, 1730, 1904, 9210
Snake Doctor ^	71 AHC	151 TC	UH-1H	70-71	maint	69-15376	N+A	nose	Tony Jones	Tom Bokkes CE, Ron Taylor	156, 591, 1429, 1579, 1754, 9210
Snake Eyes	174 AHC		UH-1C	70-71	gun		NO				1611,
Snake Venom	C Trp 7/17		AH-1G	69-71	gun	67-15832	NO	bpw		Clint Haines CE	677,
Sneaky Pete *	281 AHC		UH-1C	1967	gun		v-nn				946,
Snookie's T-Bone	119 AHC		UH-1H	1968	slick	66-17137	N+A	cargo door frame top		Paul Schmitz CE	1561, 6805
Snooper	336 AHC		UH-1B	66-67	gun		NO	nose		CPT Jackson AC	2038,
Snooper II	336 AHC		UH-1B	66-67	gun		NO	nose			2038,
Snoopy **	11 ACR		UH-1C	68-69	gun		AO	quarter panel			1703,
Snoopy ^	48 AHC	390 TC	UH-1D	65-66	maint		AO	nose		Ed Brophy	206, 9640
Snoopy **	116 AHC		UH-1D	1968	slick	66-16337	AO	pilot door		Mike Coleman AC	321, 1270, 4100, 9240
Snoopy	132 ASHC		CH-47B	70-71	cargo	67-18453	N+A	front fuselage	SP4 Davis did all '70-'71 a/c art		392, 1162, 1588, 2062, 7800, 8275
Snoopy	175 AHC		UH-1C	1967	gun	66-15020	N+A			Osborne	906, 1641, 9440
Snoopy	175 AHC		UH-1D	66-67	slick	66-00880	NO			John Myhre AC, James Martinson CP, Mike Kidd CE, Joe Watson DG, David McVay CE, Stonerock DG	1269, 1926
Snoopy **	178 ASHC		CH-47B	68-70	cargo	67-18463	v-nnp	fuselage			1946, 2061
Snoopy	179 ASHC		CH-47A	1968	cargo	66-19067	N+A			David Wilson FE, Alex Mitchell DG, James Luttrell FE	1057,
Snoopy **	188 AHC		UH-1H	67-68	slick		AO				1178, 1660
Snoopy **	213 ASHC		CH-47A	66-67	cargo	65-08022	AO	fuselage		Hassenbrock, Thomsen	359, 636, 790, 1777, 8000
Snoopy **	281 AHC		UH-1C	67-68	gun	449	AO	belly		J. Anderson AC, Dan Digenova CE, Don Creed DG	32,

Copter Name	Unit	Unit #1	Aircraft	Circa	Function	Serial #	Config	Location	Artist	Crew	Contributors
Snoopy	336 AHC	A/101	UH-1B	66-67	gun		NO				undocumented: sequence originator?
Snoopy **	336 AHC		UH-1H	68-69	slick		AO	doorpost		Tom Martin CE, Sweany DG	1101,
Snoopy **	B Co 25 Avn Bn		UH-1C	68-69	gun		AO	nose			306, 5625, 9120
Snoopy **	C Btry 2/20 ARA		UH-1B	1967	gun		AO	pilot door			301, 1451, 4050
Snoopy **	C Co 229 AHB		UH-1H	69-70	slick		AO	nose			1601,
Snoopy **	C Trp 1/9		OH-6A	1971	scout	68-17256	AO	doghouse			1003,
Snoopy	D Trp 3/4		OH-6A	69-70	scout		AO			Richard Reed AC	194,
Snoopy **	F Trp 9 Cav		OH-6A	1972	scout	67-16589	AO	doghouse		Paul Murtha AC	1264,
Snoopy **	unk		UH-1H	1969	slick		AO	nose			336, 9930
Snoopy I	121 AHC	A/502	UH-1B	65-66	gun		NO			Jim Hardbeck AC	932,
Snoopy II	175 AHC		UH-1C	67-68	gun	66-15211	N+A	pilot door		Jim Hardbeck AC	932,
Snoopy II	336 AHC		UH-1B	1967	gun		N+A				calculated assumption
Snoopy III	175 AHC		UH-1C	67-68	gun		N+A	pilot door		Thomas Duff AC, James Hardbeck AC, Vernon Bernard CE	133, 982, 1493, 1926
Snoopy III	175 AHC		UH-1C	70-71	gun		N+A	pilot door			467, 1370, 1493, 8650
Snoopy III	336 AHC		UH-1B	1967	gun	63-13977	N+A				301,
Snoopy IV	175 AHC		UH-1C	67-68	gun		N+A	pilot door			932, 1670, 2087, 6475
Snoopy V	175 AHC		UH-1C	67-68	gun		N+A				982,
Snoopy VI	175 AHC		UH-1C	67-68	gun		N+A				982,
Snoopy VII	175 AHC		UH-1C	67-68	gun		N+A				982,
Snoopy VIII	175 AHC		UH-1C	67-68	gun		N+A				982,
Snoopy's Dream	271 ASHC		CH-47A	70-71	cargo	65-07981	NO	front fuselage		Tom Hope FE, David Stroud CE	791, 1721, 8025, 8250

Copter Name	Unit	Unit #1	Aircraft	Circa	Function	Serial #	Config	Location	Artist	Crew	Contributors
Snoopy's Place	147 ASHC		CH-47A	1967	cargo		N+A	removable panel			396, 7825
Snow Snake	129 AHC	394 TC	UH-1H	1972	maint	65-09910	N+A			Larry Buller CE	234, 9310
Snow Snake ^	129 AHC	394 TC	UH-1H	1970	maint	66-16740	N+A	nose		Hughes AC, Hill CP, Fields CP, Sauer CP, Paige CP, Newell, Johnson, Strong, Campbell, Blue, Ragonese, Blusewicz	1053, 1437, 9310
Snuffy Mad Dog	A Co 1 Avn Bn		UH-1B	65-66	gun		NO	doorpost		J. T. Smith CE, L. McCloud AC, W. Jardine CP, S. Shibata DG	1636, 1973
Snuffy Smith **	205 ASHC		CH-47A	68-69	cargo		AO	front fuselage		Bill Bray FE	1834,
So Cal	61 AHC		UH-1H	69-71	slick		NO	gun mount	Robert Welsh	Robert Welsh CE	1887,
So Other's May Live ^^	247 Med Det		UH-1H	69-71	dustoff		NO	nose		J. Jones CE	499, 707, 774, 869, 954, 1780, 7725
Society's Child	117 AHC		UH-1M	70-72	gun hog	66-15062	NO	nose + rocket pod + cargo door top		Harry Duke DG, Gary Stewart CE, Bill Lance CE	78, 92, 127, 447, 936, 1006, 1383, 1654, 1694, 9250
Sock It To 'Em Snoopy	135 AHC		UH-1H	1969	gun		N+A	cargo door			3200,
Some Times	187 AHC		UH-1D	67-68	slick	65-12774	NO	nose			1713,
Son Of Hell Fire	192 AHC		UH-1H	1971	slick		NO	nose			1005,
Sophia Loren **	242 ASHC		CH-47A	69-70	cargo		AO	nose		Tom Elkins	970, 4300
Sopwith Camel	128 AHC		UH-1D	1967	slick	63-08807	NO	nose		Don Harris AC	1480, 2087, 8625, 9300
Sopwith Camel	175 AHC		UH-1D	67-68	slick	66-16051	NO			Thompson, Perham	1926,
Sopwith Camel	B Co 227 AHB		UH-1H	1970	slick	68-16083	N+A	nose			361,
Sopwith Camel	C Trp 7/1		AH-1G	70-71	gun		N+A	bpw + doghouse		Rick Holder CP, Tom Horn CE	775, 1382
Sorry 'Bout That	B Co 228 ASHB		CH-47A	66-67	cargo	64-13112	N+A			Mike Labriola FE, Richard Sturdivant CE	952,
Soul Bird	240 AHC		UH-1D	1971	slick		NO	nose		Wheaton CE	652,
Soul Inspiration	45 Med Co		UH-1H	1968	dustoff		NO	nose			549, 5025
Soul Of The Demons	134 AHC		UH-1H	1969	slick	65-10055	NO			Arvine Coleman AC, Pat Rodriquez DG, Paul Smith	352, 1735, 1818
Soul Survivor	114 AHC		UH-1D	1968	slick	65-09826	NO	nose		D. Brimage, Kaufman, T. Visentine	1573, 1838, 6700
Sound Of Silence	C Bty 2/20 ARA		AH-1G	70-71	gun	68-17054	NO	bpw	McMillan	Jim Moran, Neil MacMillan, Charlie Gossett	120, 134, 850, 1097, 1236, 5450, 9880

Spirit in the Sky*: 178 ASHC, CH-47B, (sn 67-18465), Chu Lai, 1970-71*. Flight Engineer and artist Dave Reynolds stands besides his handiwork featuring the Cross and Cockade symbols from WWI. A lucky charm it was for '465, which returned home with 2,269 flight hours to her credit. Photo courtesy Dave Reynolds.

Copter Name	Unit	Unit #1	Aircraft	Circa	Function	Serial #	Config	Location	Artist	Crew	Contributors
Southern Belle	B Co 229 AHB		UH-1D	65-66	slick	63-12972	NO	nose		Bill Weber CE, Lee Komich CP, Paul Winkel AC	1880, 2053, 4480
Southern Comfort	68 AHC		UH-1H	1968	slick		NO	pilot door			786,
Southern Comfort	187 AHC		UH-1H	1970	slick	66-16406	NO	nose		Mike Mann CE	1932,
Southern Comfort	F Btry 79 AFA		AH-1G	71-72	gun	68-17077	NO			Riley CE, Stockton AC	850, 2000
Southern General	B Co 227 AHB		UH-1H	1969	slick		NO	nose			1226, 4525
Southern Gentlemen	175 AHC		UH-1D	1968	slick		NO	nose		Glen Klutz AC	761,
Spartan Horse **	190 AHC	605 TC	UH-1H	1970	maint	69-15125	AO	nose		Joe Fisher CE, Jim Petrie AC, Bruce Mitchell DG, Daniel Peterson CP	529, 9350
Spartan Smokey	190 AHC		UH-1D	68-69	smoke	66-00850	NO	nose		Rom Maher CE, Dan Ireland CE, Paul Ouellette	387, 828, 1072, 1333, 8525
Specialist Zig Zag	B Co 228 ASHB		CH-47A	70-71	cargo		N+A	fuselage	Louis De Rouchey	Louis De Rouchey FE	412,
Speckled Pecker	114 AHC		AH-1G	1971	gun	67-15842	N+A	bpw	Oscar from downtown	Jeff Cox AC, B. Butler, Ron Mull CE	250, 357, 6700
Spirit	117 AHC	Avn Co	UH-1D	65-66	slick		NO			Ron Melton DG, James Mimbs AC	1172, 9250
Spirit In The Sky	116 AHC		UH-1H	69-70	slick		NO				1180,
Spirit In The Sky	134 AHC		UH-1H	69-71	slick	67-17211	NO	nose		John Gorsky CE, Lucky Wilson AC, Blankenship CP	149, 352, 632, 1798, 1818, 1928
Spirit In The Sky	174 AHC		UH-1H	70-71	slick		NO				1568,
Spirit In The Sky	175 AHC		UH-1H	71-72	slick		NO			Tony Villarruel DG	1926,
Spirit In The Sky	178 ASHC		CH-47B	70-71	cargo	67-18465	N+A	front fuselage	Dave Reynolds	Dave Reynolds FE	1464, 1541, 1946, 7875
Spirit In The Sky	187 AHC		UH-1H	70-71	slick	66-16534	NO	nose		Leroy Allen AC	652, 1700
Spirit Of Gettysburg (The)	56 TC	56 TC	UH-1B	1967	maint		NO	pilot door		Gerald Royals	1451, 1520, 4050
Spirit Of St. Louis (The)	B Trp 7/17		UH-1H	1969	slick		NO	nose			725, 1458, 9800
Spirit Of The Sky	190 AHC		UH-1H	69-70	slick	68-16432	N+A	doorpost		Jon Logan AC, Street CE, Mike DG	1032,
Spooky	134 AHC		UH-1H	70-71	slick		NO			Dave Czibik AC	352, 1818
Spotted Slick **	174 AHC		UH-1D	67-68	slick	65-09910	AO			W. Nunn CE, Dailey DG, Johnson CP, Wilholm CP, Bill Dunning CE	1307, 9430

Copter Name	Unit	Unit #1	Aircraft	Circa	Function	Serial #	Config	Location	Artist	Crew	Contributors
Squatter Swatter	D Trp 1/4		AH-1G	69-70	gun	68-15139	N+A	bpw		Dean Sinor, Hugh Mills	134, 439, 452, 1053, 1205, 1221, 1371, 5450, 5700, 5750, 6375
Stable Boy ^	D Trp 3/4		UH-1D	1967	maint	65-09662	NO	nose		Hand DG, Crawford CE, Kelly MD, Sholz AC	537, 1282, 9855
Stable Boy ^	D Trp 3/4		UH-1H	66-67	maint		NO	nose		Ron Peabbles DG	537, 1344, 4300
Stable Boy II ^	D Trp 3/4		UH-1H	1969	maint		NO	nose			1282, 1420, 9855
Stache **	192 AHC		UH-1H	1971	slick		AO	nose		Richard Claeys AC	343,
Stache ^	A Co 158 AHB		UH-1H	1969	slick	68-15554	NO	doorpost		Larry Smith AC	1643,
Stagecoach Wrecker ^	155 AHC	165 TC	UH-1D	1965	maint	65-09936	N+A	nose			400, 1655, 9360
Standby Again	117 AHC		UH-1M	70-71	gun	062	NO			Harry Duke DG, Gary Stewart CE	447,
Stepchild (The)	C Trp 1/9		OH-6A	1970	scout	68-17360	NO	clamshell			696, 8575
Stewed Chicken	A Co 227 AHB		UH-1H	1971	slick	69-15482	N+A	nose		David Thibaut CE	750, 1232, 1340, 9700
Stormy	335 AHC		UH-1D	66-67	slick		NO				800,
Stormy Petrel II (The)	162 AHC		UH-1H	1970	slick	68-15257	NO	doorpost		Eric Bray AC, Jim Ewart CP, Walter Hunkler CE	190,
Strange Daze	C Co 229 AHB		UH-1H	69-70	slick	67-17304	N+A	nose		James Townsend CE	73, 657, 1466, 1767, 6900
Strange Vibrations	B Co 159 ASHB		CH-47C	1970	cargo	011 or 012	NO	bottom of front door step			1755,
Strawberry Alarm Clock (The)	92 AHC		UH-1H	68-69	slick	67-17166	N+A	nose	Richard Balsimo	Rich McClary DG, Bob Shipp CE, Hans Herm DG	931, 1339, 9220
Strawberry Babe	121 AHC		UH-1D	1968	slick	822	N+A	nose			9290,
Strawberry Bitch	121 AHC		UH-1D	1968	slick	822	N+A	nose		Robert Fleming AC, Fred Lammers CE, D. Hamilton DG, Mike Shakocius CP	477, 963, 1593, 4825, 9290
Stump Jumper	45 Med Co		UH-1H	67-68	dustoff		NO				5,
Stump Jumper	53 Avn Det		ACH-47A	1966	gun	64-13151	N+A	doorpost			301, 566, 903, 1266, 1726, 1898, 6300, 4600, 4825, 6300, 8025, 8275, 8300
Stump Jumper	117 AHC		UH-1H	1967	slick		NO	nose			395, 404, 439, 1266, 5675, 5725, 6275, 9935
Stump Jumper	A Trp 7/17		UH-1H	68-69	slick		NO			Joe Brinn AC	201,

Copter Name	Unit	Unit #1	Aircraft	Circa	Function	Serial #	Config	Location	Artist	Crew	Contributors
Stump Runner (The)	A Co 228 ASHB		CH-47A	69-70	cargo		N+A	fuselage			475, 1451, 4050
Stumper	128 AHC		UH-1D	1967	slick		NO	pilot door	CE named "Big Shoe	Barry Grimm AC, Bill Means CP, Big Shoe CE	659,
Stupid Stishes	175 AHC		UH-1H	71-72	slick / nigthawk		NO	nose		Fred Rowe, Carl Gustke	429, 1926, 1937, 9440
Sudden Death	114 AHC		UH-1H	1970	slick		NO				1704,
Sudden Death	134 AHC		UH-1C	67-69	gun hog	66-15150	NO	nose		G. A. Murphy AC, J. M. Swickard CP, W. E. Fisher CE, T. R. Lewis DG	352, 979, 1818, 9320
Sudden Death	188 AHC		UH-1C	1968	gun		NAA	pilot door			1660,
Sue	162 AHC		UH-1D	67-68	slick		NO	pilot door		Tom Mockler AC	1216,
Sugar Foot	175 AHC		UH-1B	65-66	slick		NO	nose			429, 485, 1521, 1926
Sugar Pops Pete	155 AHC		UH-1C	1967	gun		NO	nose			496,
Summer Wine	188 AHC		UH-1H	1967	slick	66-16131	N+A	pilot door		George Jones AC, John Moore CE, Piecuch DG, Wesley Gager	1266, 1394, 1790, 6275
Sun King	45 Med Co		UH-1H	69-70	dustoff		NO				1533,
Sun Shine	57 Med Det		UH-1H	69-70	dustoff		N+A	CE jump door		Daryl Franzel CE	557,
Sun Shine Superman	191 AHC		UH-1D	68-69	slick	66-00835	NAA	pilot door		Andy Burney CE, David James AC	245, 839, 9500
Sunkist Special	179 ASHC		CH-47A	67-68	cargo	66-19069	N+A	fuselage		Larry McAdams FE, Bunch FE, Cole CE	877, 1120, 9950
Super Bee ^	116 AHC		UH-1H	1971	slick	70-15719	NO	nose		John Barrera CE, Rodney Tabita DG	90,
Super Dog	175 AHC		UH-1D	1970	slick		NO	nose		Dan Greve AC	654,
Super Egg	D Trp 3/4		OH-6A	68-69	scout	67-16035	NO	doghouse			1855, 4300
Super Egg II	D Trp 3/4		OH-6A	69-70	scout	69-17169	NO	doghouse		Mark Jackson AC, S. Snoddy CE, R. Rhodes DG, Lee Lavoy DG	1559,
Super Frog	188 AHC		UH-1C	1968	gun	66-00713	N+A	pilot door		Cabigon CE	1024, 1660, 1849, 9480
Super Hog	176 AHC		UH-1C	67-68	gun	66-00606	N+A	nose	Larry Silva	Larry Silva CE, John Wheeler AC	901, 1610, 9450
Super Huey	187 AHC		UH-1D	1967	slick	66-00829	N+A	pilot door		Tommy Martin AC, Kurinec CP, Pinner CE, Hudec DG	1100, 4550, 9470
Super Jew (The) **	128 AHC		UH-1H	70-71	slick	69-15443	AO	nose		Dale Onstine AC	1873,

U.S. ARMY HELICOPTER NAMES IN VIETNAM

Copter Name	Unit	Unit #1	Aircraft	Circa	Function	Serial #	Config	Location	Artist	Crew	Contributors
Super King	15 Med Bn		UH-1H	70-71	medevac	68-16571	NAA	nose		Daniel L. Smith CE, Jim Ferguson CE	513, 608, 4300
Super Loach *	128 AHC		UH-1H	1969	C+C		v-nn			Jerry Doud DG	432, 9300
Super Rag	129 AHC		UH-1H	1970	slick	66-16174	NO	belly	maint crew	Matt Casey CE	287, 1248
Super Rag *	175 AHC		UH-1D	1970	slick		v-nn			Sam Hayes CE, Joe Gossum AC	718, 7125
Super Sandpiper	188 AHC		UH-1H	1967	slick		NO	pilot door			1322,
Super Scenic Cruiser	240 AHC		UH-1H	1971	slick	69-16731	NO	nose		Hoffman AC, Malecki CP, Shaefer CE, Badua DG	1266, 6150, 6850, 9540
Super Scouts	A Trp 3/17		OH-58A	1970	scout		NO	fuselage			855,
Super Shark	192 AHC		UH-1C	1971	gun		N+A	nose	Robert Webb		559,
Super Ship **	191 AHC		UH-1D	67-68	slick	66-00817	AO	nose + pilot door	Richard Weske	R. Barkley CE, Gordon Hahn CE, Harold Stitt AC	86, 280, 539, 675, 1570, 1701, 9500
Super Slick	336 AHC		UH-1H	1970	slick / nigthawk	66-16109	N+A	nose + vertical stabilizer		Tom Feigel CE, Charles Flook CP, Olson AC, Sandwith DG, Wilkes DG	372, 508, 1305, 1327, 4825, 9610
Super Slick *	335 AHC		UH-1H	69-70	slick	67-17427	v-nn			P. Miller AC, N. Leonard CP, K. Crabtree DG, Rick Tabor	69, 1201, 1743
Super Slick *	A Co 101 AHB		UH-1H	70-71	night-hawk		v-nn			David Trujillo AC	2032, 6475
Super Slicks **	A Trp 3/17		UH-1H	1970	slick	66-16040	AO	pilot door		Ollie Pate AC, Lenny Roberts CP, Jim Dostal CE	9720,
Super Slope	A Co 1 Avn Bn		UH-1B	65-66	gun	66-00667	NO	cargo door frame top		J. T. Smith CE, L. McCloud AC, W. Jardine CP, S. Shibata DG	1636,
Super Smoker	187 AHC		UH-1C	1969	smoke	66-00667	NO	nose + pilot door		Jim Steiger DG, Claude Sells CE	1688,
Super Snake	235 AWC		AH-1G	1971	gun	67-15656	NO	bpw			1674, 5425, 5427
Super Snake *	114 AHC	Avn Co	UH-1B	1966	gun	63-12938	v-nn			F. Mayer, Shower, Maddox, Anderson	860, 1926, 6700
Super Star	175 AHC		UH-1H	70-71	slick	69-15089	NO	nose		Rick Meana AC, John Davis CE, Fred Fellows AC, Pat Jordan AC	1166,
Supergrunt	unk		UH-1H	1968	slick		NO	nose			2019, 6875
Superstar	A Co 229 AHB		UH-1H	71-72	slick	66-16293	N+A	nose	Chad Richmond		1627, 6850
Surealistic Olive	11 ACR		OH-6A	68-69	scout		NO	clamshell			1703,
Surfer **	174 AHC		UH-1C	70-71	gun hog	66-15161	AO	quarter panel	Budd Vann	Bruce Marshall CP, James Souder AC	184, 233, 1568, 1770, 9430

Copter Name	Unit	Unit #1	Aircraft	Circa	Function	Serial #	Config	Location	Artist	Crew	Contributors
Surrealistic Pillow (The)	92 AHC		UH-1H	67-68	slick	66-16499	NAA	nose	Richard Balsimo	Bobby Stewart CE, Jerry Eastburg DG	931, 1693
Susan	189 AHC		UH-1H	70-71	slick		NO	nose		Francis Ty Simmons AC	1615, 4350
Susie	117 AHC	Avn Co	UH-1B	64-65	slick	62-04573	NO	nose		John Gallegos CE	510, 577
Susie	117 AHC	Avn Co	UH-1D	1965	slick	64-13674	NO	nose		John Gallegos CE	577, 6805
Susie	C Trp 1/9		OH-13S	1967	scout	67-15877	NO	doorpost			69,
Susie Q	188 AHC		UH-1H	67-68	slick		NO				414,
Susie Q	C Trp 3/17		OH-6A	69-70	scout	66-07786	NO	doghouse			158, 4825
Susie Q	D Trp 3/5		OH-6A	69-70	scout	786?	NO			George Branigan	158, 9860
Suzi Q	C Trp 16 Cav		AH-1G	1972	gun		NO	bpw		Chuck Chadwell AC	1205,
Suzi Q II	C Trp 16 Cav		AH-1G	1972	gun	66-15330	NO	bpw		Chuck Chadwell AC	1205,
Suzi Q III	C Trp 16 Cav		AH-1G	1972	gun	70-16030	NAA	bpw		Chuck Chadwell AC	1053, 1205, 1266, 6200, 6250
Suzie	174 AHC		UH-1H	68-70	slick	67-17445	NO	nose		Sterrit AC, Kennedy AC, Zimmerman CE, Hicks DG	9430,
Suzie Creamcheese	57 AHC		UH-1C	1970	gun		NO				1050,
Suzie Creamcheese	116 AHC		UH-1H	1971	slick	66-16982	NO	nose		Jay Bowman AC, John Pepe CP, R. L. Tabita CE, Jim Highsmith DG	2082, 8625, 9240
Suzie Creamcheese	A Trp 1/9		UH-1C	69-70	gun	66-00648	NO	nose		Chris Gray CE, Mike Gifford CE	500, 609, 1727, 9690
Suzie Q	114 AHC		UH-1H	1969	slick	67-17221	NO			F. Medvitz	1158, 1563, 6700
Suzy Q	118 AHC	Avn Co	UH-1B	1965	slick	63-08587	NO	pilot door		Pat Matheny CE, McGlone AC, McBee DG	1110,
Suzy Q II	118 AHC	A/82	UH-1D	65-66	slick	64-13726	NO	pilot door		Pat Matheny CE, Fischer AC, Brogle DG, Mac Hooper DG	1110, 9260
Swamp Fox 2	8 TC	117 AHC	CH-21C	62-63	lift	52-08648	NO	fuselage			1975, 6500
Swamp Fox IV	118 AHC		UH-1H	1970	slick		NO	nose			69, 1061, 8650
Swamp Rat	178 ASHC		CH-47C	71-72	cargo	68-15818	NO			Raul Sanchez FE	1541,
Swamp Rat - Gator Recovery	119 AHC	545 TC	UH-1H	1970	maint	68-16539	N+A	nose		Carl Brader CE	176, 741, 1325, 9270, 9910

Copter Name	Unit	Unit #1	Aircraft	Circa	Function	Serial #	Config	Location	Artist	Crew	Contributors
Swamprat (The)	175 AHC	Avn Co	UH-1D	66-67	slick	65-09792	NO	nose		Larry Parsley DG, Will Hazelton CE, Ray Leuty AC, Neff	1350, 9440
Sweat Hog	D Co 229 AHB		AH-1G	1970	gun		NO	bpw		Bill Walton	1859,
Sweet Barbara	117 AHC	Avn Co	UH-1B	64-65	slick		NO				1840,
Sweet Bee	335 AHC		UH-1B	66-67	gun		NO	doorpost		Kurt Schultz DG	800, 1567
Sweet Cream Lady	187 AHC		UH-1H	1971	slick	69-15785	NO	nose		Larry Packett CE	652,
Sweet Irene	119 AHC		UH-1H	69-70	slick		NO	nose		Al Mixer CE, Fidencio Ramirez	741, 908, 1214, 9270
Sweet Jean	155 AHC		UH-1D	1966	slick		NO	pilot door			630, 9360
Sweet Pea	C Trp 16 Cav		OH-6A	1972	scout	66-17782	NO				1205,
Sweet Reba	162 AHC		UH-1D	1968	slick		NO	pilot door		Gary Drotar AC	652,
Sweet Revenge	176 AHC		UH-1H	1969	slick		NO				1595,
Sweet Sally	176 AHC		UH-1H	1969	slick		NO				1595,
Sweet Sandy	B Trp 1/9		UH-1H	67-68	slick	66-16545	NO	pilot door		Jim Pratt AC	535, 1418
Sweet Sandy II	B Trp 1/9		UH-1H	67-68	slick	66-16924	NO	pilot door		Jim Pratt AC	535, 1418
Sweet Sue	173 AHC		UH-1D	1967	slick	65-09597	NO			Clarence Perkins CE	834, 1374
Sweet Sue	B Trp 1/9		AH-1G	1969	gun		NO	bpw		Fran Stewart AC	898,
Sweet Thang	188 AHC		UH-1H	67-68	slick		NO				414,
Sweet Thing	147 ASHC		CH-54A	1967	recovery		NO	fuselage			6925,
Swill Barrel (The)	335 AHC		UH-1B	1969	gun		NO	nose			1908, 1926, 4600
Sympathetic Journey	15 Med Bn		UH-1H	70-71	medevac		NO			Bill Stovall AC, Steve Turkowske CP	608, 1709
Sympathetic Journey	215 Composite Svc Bn		UH-1H	71-72	medevac		NO	nose		Eric Traub	2031,
T.N.T.	187 AHC		UH-1H	70-71	slick	68-16305	NO	nose		R. Daniels CP, E. Guynn CE, R. Bellerue CE, Kirkpatrick DG	652,
T.W.A	119 AHC	Avn Co	UH-1D	65-66	slick	64-13707	NO	doorpost		Bill Walter DG	1856,

Copter Name	Unit	Unit #1	Aircraft	Circa	Function	Serial #	Config	Location	Artist	Crew	Contributors
Taco Wagon	335 AHC		UH-1D	66-67	slick	65-09910	NO	doorpost		Don Snyder CE, Tom Sanchez DG	1657, 9590
Tail Wind ^	15 Trans Bn	HHC	UH-1H	1968	maint	66-16984	N+A	nose		Al Schlim, John Deperro	411, 487, 861, 1053, 1247, 1376, 2056, 5800, 6300
Tailwing	243 ASHC		CH-47A	69-70	cargo	64-13117	NO			Lloyd Lewis FE	1019, 8075
Taking Care Of Business *	135 AHC		UH-1M	1970	gun	66-00609	NO	pilot door		Rick Idol AC, Russell Andreasen CE	37, 8525
Tally Ho	14 Trans Bn		UH-1B	1965	slick	63-08647	N+A	nose			69,
Tangellary Smoth	114 AHC		UH-1H	1971	slick		NO	nose		Don Coe, Tom Nesbitt	315, 2090, 6700, 7175
Tarr Baby	242 ASHC		CH-47A	69-70	cargo	66-00106	NO			Larry Spence CE, Tom Elkins FE, Vorlaufer FE, Fugman CE	1199, 1669, 8250
Tarheel Rebel	A Co 228 ASHB		CH-47A	69-70	cargo	66-19078	N+A	fuselage		Elton Chappel FE	903, 996
Tater ^	17 AHC	613 TC	UH-1H	67-68	maint		N+A	nose	Eugene McGinnis, 613 TC Det	Bryce Whitson	1648, 1902, 9110
Tatter's Pad	B Co 228 ASHB		CH-47A	1970	cargo	64-13134	NO	fuselage		John Griswold FE	1239,
Taxpayer's Regret	57 TC	120 AHC	CH-21C	1964	lift		NO	fuselage			1975, 6525
Tay-Ninh Taxi Co	187 AHC		UH-1H	70-71	slick	68-16305	NO	nose		Rik Bellerue CE, Rich Kirkpatrick DG	125, 652
TCB	135 AHC		UH-1M	1970	gun	66-00609	NO	pilot door		Rick Idol AC, Russell Andreasen CE	37, 8525
Teacher (The)	116 AHC		UH-1H	1971	slick	69-15760	NO	doorpost		Jim McDaniel AC	1137,
Tears Of Fire	128 AHC		UH-1M	71-72	gun	65-09560	NO	nose		Adams CE, Mike Honara AC	785,
Teddi Bare	57 TC	120 AHC	CH-21C	1963	lift		NO	fuselage			3600, 8925
Tee Tom Twenty ^	281 AHC		UH-1H	1970	slick		NO	nose			1545,
Teenie Weenie Airlines	119 AHC	Avn Co	UH-1D	65-66	slick	64-13707	NO	doorpost		Bill Walter DG	1856,
Ten Toes Up Ten Toes Down **	243 ASHC		CH-47A	1969	cargo		AO	fuselage			111, 8050
Terry	1/9	HHT	UH-1H	1968	slick	66-16945	NO	nose		Ray Chamberland CE	7125,
Tessie	C Co 159 ASHB		CH-47C	68-69	cargo	333?	NO			Dave Peterson CE, Jim Reynolds	1353, 7850

Copter Name	Unit	Unit #1	Aircraft	Circa	Function	Serial #	Config	Location	Artist	Crew	Contributors
Texas **	F Trp 9 Cav		OH-6A	1972	scout	67-16138	AO	doghouse		Paul Murtha AC	1264,
Texas Flag **	135 AHC		UH-1H	68-69	slick	66-16269	AO	nose		John Rogers AC, Jay Harris CE	1501, 9330
Texas Flag **	174 AHC		UH-1C	68-70	gun	66-00646	AO	nose		Zimmerman CE, Radcliffe CE, Riggs DG	278, 592, 9430
Texas Flag **	A Trp 3/17		UH-1H	1970	slick	67-17195	AO	nose		Mike Platner AC	1403,
Theo	191 AHC		UH-1H	67-71	slick		NO	pilot door			1699, 9500
Think I Care	61 AHC		UH-1H	68-69	slick	66-01120	N+A	nose			202,
Think Snow	C Trp 7/1		AH-1G	71-72	gun		NO	pilot's window		Dayne Smith	1634,
Thinker (The)	355 Avn Co		CH-54A	1969	recovery		N+A	front fuselage			1408, 9945
Third Revolution (The)	175 AHC		UH-1H	1969	slick		NO	nose			1908, 4600
This Fish Swims In Booze	174 AHC		UH-1H	1968	slick	67-17543	N+A	nose	Ben Kennedy	Harry Cooper CE	341, 9430
Thor	129 AHC		UH-1H	71-72	slick	68-15451	NO	nose		August Bailey CP, Wayne Hagg CE	1955, 9310
Thor	155 AHC		UH-1C	68-69	gun	66-15232	NO	nose		Llyod Wussow CE, Terry, Pratt, Goodness, Arney	586, 1246, 1564, 1967, 9360
Thor's Hammer	11 ACR		AH-1G	68-69	gun		NO	bpw			645, 1703
Thor's Hammer	A Trp 7/1		AH-1G	1971	gun	67-15536	NO	bpw		Mel Hinton AC, John Cattilini AC, Bruce Boettger CP, Lunquist CE	291, 755, 4825
Three A's (The)	145 Airlift Plt		UH-1B	1965		63-08633	NO	cargo door frame bottom			1840, 1975, 6525
Three Massketeers (The)	175 AHC		UH-1B	1966	gun		NO			Wayne Hawthorne DG, Sabins CE, Rosbeck AC	1926,
Three Quarter Whore	132 ASHC		CH-47B	70-71	cargo	67-18444	NO	front pylon	SP4 Davis did all '70-'71 a/c art		184, 729, 7800, 9430
Thumper	117 AHC	Avn Co	UH-1D	65-66	slick	64-13583	NO	nose		Dennis Wood CE	127, 1952
Thumper	121 AHC		UH-1B	67-70	gun		N+A	M-5 turret			395, 439, 1809, 5675, 5725
Thumper	235 AWC		UH-1C	69-70	gun	007 ?	NO	nose			4350,
Thumper *	D Co 227 AHB		UH-1B	66-67	gun		v-nn	turret		Jim Bridges CE	198,

Copter Name	Unit	Unit #1	Aircraft	Circa	Function	Serial #	Config	Location	Artist	Crew	Contributors
Thumpy 1	C Co 229 AHB		UH-1H	69-70	slick	68-16123	N+A	nose		White CE	73, 1466, 9830
Thunder Bug	3 Bde 101 AB	HHC	OH-6A	1969	scout	67-16550	NO	doghouse			672, 1266, 6259
Thunder Chicken	254 Med Det		UH-1H	70-71	dustoff		NO	nose			1489,
Thunder Chicken ^^^	195 AHC		UH-1C	68-69	gun		NO	nose		Paul Keil CP	346, 386, 1996, 9700
Thunder Olive	B Trp 3/17		OH-6A	1969	scout		NO	doghouse		Steve Brownell CE	224, 9790
Thunder Road	178 ASHC		CH-47A	66-67	cargo	64-13153	N+A	front fuselage		Steve Niedbala FE, Grady Tolbird FE, Joe Brest CE, Art Smith DG, Al Musselman FE, Joe Delistrico FE	1294,
Tiajuana Taxi	128 AHC		UH-1D	68-69	slick	65-09612	NO			Herbert Gladwill Jr CE	613, 8950, 9300
Tiger Lady	121 AHC		UH-1D	67-68	slick		N+A	nose			477, 4825, 9290
Tiger Surprise ^	121 AHC		UH-1D	69-70	lightship	66-16991	NAA	nose	Don Jackson	Jim Hencin DG, Bob Hofmann AC, Don Jackson CE, Wayne McGregor DG	306, 831, 1146, 1809, 5625, 9290
Tiger Wagon **	129 AHC		UH-1H	1971	slick	68-15351	AO				546, 1053, 1248, 1547, 1827, 7350, 9310
Tiger Wagon **	129 AHC		UH-1H	70-72	slick	67-17600	AO			Larry Brewster	545, 844, 956, 1415, 1547, 1649, 7350
Tijuana Taxi	15 Med Bn		UH-1H	1971	medevac		NO			Ron Huether	808,
Tijuana Taxi	176 AHC	411 TC	UH-1D	1967	maint		NO			Mike Reed	1449,
Tijuana Taxi	191 AHC		UH-1C	1967	gun	66-00717	NO	pilot door			301,
Tiki	57 TC	120 AHC	CH-21C	1964	lift	56-02050	N+A	fuselage		Felipe Lariosa CE	1554,
Tiki #2	57 TC	120 AHC	CH-21C	1964	lift		N+A	fuselage			395, 1266, 1554, 5675, 6275
Tiki Fly Hawaiian Little Jet	114 AHC	Avn Co	UH-1B	1964	slick	62-01956	NO			H. Baruz, J. Gayler, M. Burke, Dawson, H. Preusz, A. Jarrell, O. Kobashigawa	97, 634
Timujin Ship	D Co 227 AHB		AH-1G	70-71	gun	67-15768	NO	bpw			113, 301, 562, 1497, 5275, 6250
Tin Bin (The)	121 AHC		UH-1D	67-68	slick		N+A	nose			477, 1593, 4825, 9290
Tink	A Trp 7/1		OH-6A	69-70	scout	67-17793	NO	fuselage		Randy Willis AC	1922,
Tinker Toy	118 AHC	Avn Co	UH-1D	1965	slick		NO	pilot door			603, 9260

Copter Name	Unit	Unit #1	Aircraft	Circa	Function	Serial #	Config	Location	Artist	Crew	Contributors
Tiny	D Trp 17 Cav		AH-1G	72-73	gun	68-15027	NO	turret			1075, 4825, 9130
Tired Angel	54 Med Det		UH-1H	70-71	dustoff		NO	nose			1175, 1946
To Charlie With Love	192 AHC		UH-1C	69-70	gun		N+A	M-5 turret			343, 398, 9510
Tombstone Shadow	114 AHC		UH-1H	1971	slick	68-16591	NO	nose		G. Dickenson, H. Hodges, L. Lentz, A. Mirati, W. Barnes	764, 1210, 6700
Tonka	11 ACR		UH-1H	68-69	slick		NO	nose			712, 1703
Tootsie Roll	92 AHC		UH-1C	1969	gun	66-15003	NO	nose			1053, 1187
Tootsie Roll	118 AHC	Avn Co	UH-1D	1965	slick		NO	pilot door			603, 9260
Top Cat	116 AHC		UH-1B	1967	gun	64-13952	NO	pilot door			301,
Top Cat	117 AHC		UH-1H	68-69	slick		NO	nose			21,
Top Guns Will Travel	173 AHC		UH-1C	66-68	gun	65-09417	NO	pilot door		Tony Zanfardino CE	1931, 1981
Top Tiger Tail ^	68 AHC	391 TC	UH-1D	67-70	maint		N+A	pilot door	unk unit member	Sweet AC, C. Lindstrom CP, G. Robinson DG, Dave Green CE, Bill Seifert AC	648, 1366, 1490, 1586, 2008, 9200, 9650
Toy Tiger	11 ACR		OH-6A	68-69	scout	67-16221	NO	clamshell			1703,
Tracy II *	2 Signal Group		UH-1D	1966	slick	64-13694	v-nn			Bob Callaghan CE	265, 6625
Trail Boss	335 AHC		UH-1H	68-69	slick	66-16654	N+A	nose	Terry Buchanon	Larry Kendrick DG, Terry Buchanon CE	69, 897, 1926
Traumatic Experience	119 AHC		UH-1D	1968	slick	66-16297	NO	nose		Given AC, Storey CP, Ontis CE, Sumpter DG	1561, 6805
Traveling Excutioner (The)	57 AHC		UH-1H	1972	slick		NO	nose			980, 5025
Traveling Executioner (The)	117 AHC		UH-1H	71-72	slick		NO	cargo door frame top			936,
Trick Or Treat	11 ACR		AH-1G	1969	gun	68-15122	NO	bpw			712, 1417, 1674, 8000, 8875
Trip Ate	A Trp 3/17		OH-58A	1971	scout	68-16888	N+A	fuselage		Ratso AC, Ed Kictarek CE	2004, 8525, 9720
Trip Eight *	174 AHC		UH-1D	67-68	slick	66-00888	v-nn			J.C. Pennington	9430,
Triple Deuce *	134 AHC		UH-1H	69-70	slick	68-16222	v-nn			Ronnie Poarch CE	1404, 1583, 9320

Copter Name	Unit	Unit #1	Aircraft	Circa	Function	Serial #	Config	Location	Artist	Crew	Contributors
Triple Nickel *	48 AHC		UH-1H	71-72	slick	67-17555	v-nn			Mike Topping CE, Pete Gerstenberger CE	605, 1795, 4825, 9150
Triple Nickel *	134 AHC		UH-1H	70-71	slick	555	v-nn			Dan Swank CE, James Smith DG, Craig Britton CE	352, 1637, 1818, 9320
Triple Nickel *	147 ASHC		UH-1C	66-67	C+C	65-09555	v-nn			David Kilborn CE	907,
Triple Nickel *	174 AHC		UH-1C	1970	gun	65-09555	AO	quarter panel		Kenney AC, Gambrell CP, Jack Coffman DG, Fred Carlson CE, Fred Thompson	184, 278, 1770, 9430
Triple Nickel *	A Co 229 AHB		UH-1H	68-69	slick	555	v-nn			Sandy Collier CE, Ashmore CE	326,
Triple Nickel *	A Trp 1/9		UH-1H	70-71	slick	67-17555	v-nn			Roger Snow DG	1266, 1497, 6250
Triple Nickel *	B Trp 1/9		UH-1H	1970	slick	67-17555	v-nn			R. Maanao CE, Ed Gallant DG, Steve Jackson DG	898, 1063, 4725
Triple Nickel *	B Trp 3/17		AH-1G	68-71	gun	67-15555	v-nn				652, 1613
Triple Nickel *	E Trp 1/9		UH-1H	70-71	slick	67-17555	v-nn			Roger Snow DG	1497, 1656, 4825
Triple Nickel **	C Trp 7/1		OH-6A	69-71	scout	67-16555	AO	doghouse		James Groth CE	662, 1308, 9895
Triple Nickel	unk		UH-1B	1965	gun	555	NO			Walter Sarratt DG, Mike O'Connell DG	1546,
Triple Nickel Deuce *	192 AHC		UH-1H	1969	slick	66-16352	v-nn				621,
Triple Nickle	187 AHC		UH-1H	68-69	slick	67-17555	NO	pilot door			1002,
Triple Niner	162 AHC		UH-1D	66-67	slick	65-09999	NO	pilot door			1490,
Triple One *	189 AHC		UH-1H	68-69	slick	66-01111	NO			David Munsell CE	760, 1260, 9490
Triple Penny	A Trp 7/17		OH-58A	1971	scout	69-16111	NO	doghouse			1369,
Triple Penny	D Trp 1/10		OH-58A	1971	scout	69-16111	NO	doghouse		Don Pender AC	463, 1369
Triple Trey *	176 AHC		UH-1H	1969	slick	68-15333	v-nn			Dick Sear CE	1595,
Triple Trouble	C Co 228 ASHB		CH-47A	1967	cargo	64-13111	NO			Robert Hadgkiss FE	673, 8025, 8250
Triple Whiskey *	15 Med Bn		UH-1D	67-68	medevac	63-12999	v-nn				263, 7375
Triple Zip *	B Trp 3/17		OH-6A	1971	scout	69-16000	v-nn			Roger Searcy	1581,
Tripship	335 AHC		UH-1H	1970	slick		NO				695, 1926

Copter Name	Unit	Unit #1	Aircraft	Circa	Function	Serial #	Config	Location	Artist	Crew	Contributors
Trojan Hoss	187 AHC		UH-1H	70-71	slick	66-16415	NO	nose		Steve Willingham DG	1716, 9470
Troll	188 AHC		UH-1H	67-68	slick	66-16155	NAA	pilot door		Kjell Tollefsen AC	309, 2790
Troll (The) **	498 Med Co		UH-1H	68-70	dustoff		AO	nose			553,
Trouble Shooter	187 AHC		UH-1	1967			NO				1908, 4600
Troy New York Home Of Uncle Sam	222 CSAB		CH-47	1967	cargo		N+A	fuselage			1776, 1908, 4600
True Grit	116 AHC		UH-1H	70-71	slick	69-15698	NO	nose			90,
Tubber's Tiger	C Trp 16 Cav		AH-1G	1971	gun	67-15758	N+A	bpw		Wayne Burk AC	239, 763, 1053, 1205, 1674, 6025, 9810
Tuff Enuff	B Trp 2/17		UH-1H	69-70	slick		NO	doorpost			23,
Tumbleweed	D Trp 3/5		UH-1H	70-71	slick		N+A	nose			2020, 4825
Tupelo Mississippi Flash	135 AHC		UH-1H	67-68	slick		NO				1249,
Tweety Bird	B Co 25 Avn Bn		OH-23G	67-68	scout		NO				1562,
Twin Mini	C Trp 7/1		AH-1G	68-69	gun	67-15468	NO	turret	Owen Hamiel		1382,
Two Bits Minus Five	71 AHC		UH-1H	1970	slick	67-17520	NO	nose		Chuck Martin DG, Dave Friske CE, Pat Boyington AC	1096, 9210
Two Stepper	C Btry 2/20 ARA		AH-1G	1971	gun	67-15836	NO	bpw		Dean Doudna CE	433, 730
Two Stepper	F Btry 79 AFA		AH-1G	1972	gun	67-15836	NO	bpw		Henn AC, Hosaka CP, Doudna CE, Hendrickson CE	433, 730, 833
UC VC No C	81 TC	119 AHC	CH-21C	62-63	lift	56-02037	N+A	fuselage		Reagan CE	528,
UFO	B Trp 1/9		OH-13S	1967	scout		NO			Jerry Anderson CP	218, 4825
UFO	C Btry 2/20 ARA		AH-1G	70-71	gun		NO	bpw			1236, 1627
Ugly (The)	371 RRC		UH-1H	68-69	slick		NO	nose			1286,
Ugly American (The)	192 AHC		UH-1C	1969	gun		NO	nose			301, 932, 5575
Ugly Duckling (The)	254 Med Det		UH-1H	69-70	dustoff		NAA	nose		Eric Procter CE	664, 816, 954

Copter Name	Unit	Unit #1	Aircraft	Circa	Function	Serial #	Config	Location	Artist	Crew	Contributors
Ulysses	155 AHC		UH-1C	67-68	gun hog	65-09484	NO	nose		Tom Hunt CE, Dave Nachtigall CE	305, 586, 640, 1257, 9360
Un Cobra (The)	D Co 229 AHB		AH-1G	1970	gun		NO				1859,
Unclaimed Light Ship	117 AHC		UH-1H	69-70	slick	66-16599	NO			Gordon Berthould CE	127,
Under Dog ^	A Co 158 AHB		UH-1H	1969	slick	67-17632	NO	doorpost		Frank Simonson CE, Paul Edgar AC	1618,
Undertaker	187 AHC		UH-1H	70-71	slick	67-17787	NO	nose			441, 652
Undertaker (The)	132 ASHC		CH-47B	70-71	cargo	67-18454	NO	front fuselage	SP4 Davis did all '70-'71 a/c art		729, 7800, 8275
Undertaker (The) *	195 AHC		UH-1C	1970	gun		v-nn			Chuck Croley CE	368,
Undertaker (The)	281 AHC		UH-1C	67-68	gun		NO			H. Wetmore	1893,
Undertaker (The)	D Trp 3/4		AH-1G	70-71	gun	68-15126	N+A	doghouse	Gary Schmidt		1559, 8400
Undertaker II	187 AHC		UH-1D	1971	slick	64-13626	NO	nose		Mike Elliott DG, Frank Drinkwine CE	441, 471, 642, 652, 9470
Unlimited Hell	192 AHC		UH-1H	1972	slick		NO	nose		Dennis Javens AC	843,
Unlucky Lady (The)	175 AHC		UH-1H	69-70	slick	108 or 894	NO			Tom Pratt CE	1419, 1995
Untouchable Chickenman	A Co 227 AHB		UH-1H	70-71	slick	69-15553	N+A	nose	Joe Paranal	Head AC, Darrell Boothe CP, Braxton Cox CE	356, 1340, 1793, 9700
Up, Up and Away ? **	200 ASHC		CH-47A	67-68	cargo	66-00104	AO	front fuselage	Larry Dumford	Phil Roscoe FE	995, 1195, 8275
USA1	F Btry 79 AFA		AH-1G	71-72	gun	68-15147	NAA	bpw		Art Jetter AC, Steve Hartnett CE	850, 1111, 9880
V. D.	162 AHC		UH-1D	1968	slick		NO	pilot door		Larry Salee DG	652, 1538, 1702, 8925, 9390
V. D.	173 AHC		UH-1H	68-69	slick		NO	pilot door			593, 1455
Vagabond (The)	175 AHC		UH-1H	70-71	slick		NO	nose			1210,
Vagabond Virgin	A Trp 1/9		AH-1G	70-71	gun		NO	bpw			1266, 1497, 6250
Vagabond Virgin	E Trp 1/9		AH-1G	70-71	gun		NO	bpw			1266, 1497, 6250
Vagabonds Of The Sky	155 AHC		UH-1H	69-70	slick	67-17669	NO			John Harris CE	702, 9910

Copter Name	Unit	Unit #1	Aircraft	Circa	Function	Serial #	Config	Location	Artist	Crew	Contributors
Valerie	335 AHC		UH-1H	1970	slick	66-16572	NO				695, 1926
Valhalla	92 AHC		UH-1C	69-70	gun		NO	nose			4350,
Valhalla Messenger	121 AHC		UH-1B	69-70	gun		NO	doorpost		Rodger Tunnell AC	1809,
VC Birth Control	114 AHC		AH-1G	70-71	gun	68-15209	NO	bpw		Robert Baker AC, Riley CE	70, 134, 2085, 5450, 6700
VC Elephant	A Co 123 Avn Bn		UH-1H	70-71	slick	69-15292	N+A	doorpost		James Repp CE, Del Unsworth DG, S. Hogan AC	772
VC For Lunch Bunch	176 AHC		UH-1C	67-69	gun	66-00606	N+A	cargo door window		Larry Silva CE	395, 901, 1610, 5675, 9450
VC Widow Maker	192 AHC		UH-1C	70-71	gun		NO			Don Sellers AC	1587, 9510
VC Widow Maker	308 CAB		UH-1C	1969	gun		NO				859,
VC Widow Maker	A Co 82 Avn Bn		UH-1B	65-66	gun		NO	doorpost		Kurt Schultz DG	1567,
Vengeance	134 AHC		UH-1H	1970	slick	68-16263	NO	nose		Corky Lauritsen DG, Ricky Denton CE, Lee Gaskill AC, Duane Dillingham CP	352, 979, 1818
Veni Vidi Vici	175 AHC		UH-1D	67-68	slick	64-13493	NO	nose		Roland Ferland AC	514,
Veni Vidi Vici	B Co 9 Avn Bn		AH-1G	68-69	gun		NO	bpw			1710,
Veto	15 Med Bn		UH-1H	1970	medevac		NO			Godsie Norvell CE	608,
Vi Vicious	121 AHC		UH-1B	69-70	gun		NO	doorpost			1809,
Vicious Circle	243 ASHC		CH-47A	68-70	cargo		N+A				550,
Vicki	B Co 229 AHB		UH-1H	67-68	slick		NO	nose		Dennis Osborne CE	1331,
Vietnam Sucks	191 AHC		UH-1	68-69	slick		NO	belly		Gordon Hahn CE	539, 675
Vigilante (The)	170 AHC		UH-1C	68-70	gun	66-15036	NO	nose		David Hooper CE	789, 4825
Vigilante II (The)	170 AHC		UH-1C	1971	gun		NO			David Hooper CE, Willie AC	789, 9400
Viking Delight	121 AHC		UH-1B	69-70	gun		NO	doorpost			1809,
Viking Queen (The)	121 AHC		UH-1B	68-69	gun		N+A				undocumented: sequence originator?

Copter Name	Unit	Unit #1	Aircraft	Circa	Function	Serial #	Config	Location	Artist	Crew	Contributors
Viking Queen II (The)	121 AHC		UH-1B	68-69	gun		N+A	hell hole cover			1432, 9290
Viking Surprise	121 AHC		UH-1D	67-70	smoke / lightship	64-13670	NO	pilot door		Jerry Daly AC, McDonald CP	461, 1809
Villa Flyies Again (sp?)	173 Abn Bde		OH-6A	1969	scout	67-16076	NO	fuselage		Jaime Longoria CE, Jesse Saldivar CE	915, 9410
Village Stomper (The)	281 AHC		UH-1C	69-70	gun		NO				66,
Village Stompers	114 AHC		UH-1C	1967	gun	66-15177	NO	pilot door		Brighur, E. Hunt, W. Nelson	301, 1053, 6700
Vilmita	A Trp 1/9		UH-1D	66-67	slick		NO	nose		Robert Swain AC	1734,
Vinh Long MTA You Call We Haul	114 AHC		UH-1H	1971	slick	69-15777	NO	nose		S. Hovis, R. Mollencamp, M. Gilpen, A. MacKenzie, Cordle, Rodriquez	6700, 9230,
Virgin Eater	1 Bde 101 Abn	HHC	UH-1H	1969	slick		NO	nose		Richard Vonhatten, Bruce Sutton	2059, 4825
Virgin Hunter (The)	132 ASHC		CH-47B	69-70	cargo	67-18440	N+A	front fuselage	SP4 Davis did all '70-'71 a/c art	Ben Gatliff CE	174, 301, 392, 395, 729, 1162, 1266, 2062, 5675, 6100, 7800, 8275
Virginia Rose 1	COBRA NETT		AH-1G	1967	gun		NO	bpw			98, 301, 1181, 1266, 6050, 6100, 6175
Virginia Rose II	COBRA NETT		AH-1G	1967	gun	66-15259	NO	bpw		Paul Anderson, Nick Stein	134, 5450
Von Bryan's Express **	178 ASHC		CH-47A	67-68	cargo	66-19070	AO	front fuselage	Joe Boylan	Don Bryan CE	841,
Von Zipper's Express	119 AHC		UH-1H	67-68	slick		NO	nose		Richard Leirer DG	2078,
Voodoo Lady	11 ACR		AH-1G	1969	gun	67-15687	NO	bpw			134, 1266, 5450, 6200, 6300
Voodoo Child	116 AHC		UH-1C	69-71	gun		NO			Nasty Joe CE, Darrell Hutson DG	820,
Voyager	C Co 229 AHB		UH-1D	66-67	slick	65-09582	NO	nose		Rittman AC, G. Bortolus CP, D.Verville CE, D. Cameron DG	1482, 6475
Voyager (The)	191 AHC		UH-1C	67-68	gun		N+A	cargo door frame bottom		Skip Waugh CE	1874, 9500
Vulture (The) ^	155 AHC	165 TC	UH-1D	65-66	maint	65-09936	N+A	nose		Ed Gliet CE	574, 617
Vulture Dog	162 AHC		UH-1D	1968	slick	64-13862	NO	pilot door		Larry Salee DG, Bruce Stoehr AC, Mike Fitzpatrick CE	652, 1538, 1702
Vung Tau Express	135 AHC	614 TC	UH-1H	67-68	maint	66-16266	NO			Robert Mounts CE	1249,
Wabash Cannonball	187 AHC		AH-1G	1971	gun	67-15652	N+A	bpw		Rodney Woods AC, Dan Clark CE	1954,
Waleare Cadillac	114 AHC		UH-1H	1970	slick	67-17506	NO	nose		William Mattler	1053, 1527, 6700, 9230

Copter Name	Unit	Unit #1	Aircraft	Circa	Function	Serial #	Config	Location	Artist	Crew	Contributors
Walking Finger **	2 Bde 1 Cav		OH-6A	1969	scout		AO	nose			1724, 6250
Wanderer (The)	11 ACR		AH-1G	68-69	gun	67-15669	NO	bpw		Paul Madsen AC, Rick Bono CE	160, 462, 1070, 1703, 4825
Wanted: Uncle Ho Dead Or Alive	335 AHC		UH-1H	68-69	slick		N+A	nose			897,
War Bird	A Co 228 ASHB		CH-47A	1968	cargo	66-19036	NO	fuselage		Dick Synder AC	388, 903, 1898, 8300
War Child	A Trp 7/1		OH-6A	71-72	scout		NO				217,
War Eagle	114 AHC		UH-1D	1967	slick	65-09806	NO	nose		H. Lawley, J. MacDonald, R. Tolbert, W. Rogers, Whitter	301, 696, 1181, 3100, 6050, 6700
War Hoop	336 AHC	A/101	UH-1B	66-67	gun	62-02008	NO			Tom Wainscott CE, David Lape AC	1846, 9610
War Lord (The)	187 AHC		UH-1D	67-68	slick	66-00925	NO	pilot door		J. McLeod CE, David Smith AC, Matt Worner DG	1155, 1700, 1962
War Paint	175 AHC		UH-1D	1966	slick	66-00880	NO	nose		Jon Myhre AC	1269,
War Pig	129 AHC		UH-1H	69-70	slick	66-16322	NO	nose		Bill Wolf CE	1437, 1947, 6865
War Wagon	129 AHC		UH-1H	1970	slick		NO	nose			18, 1908, 4600
War Wagon	155 AHC		UH-1B	1967	gun	63-08601	NO	nose		Steve Austin CE	59, 235, 496, 533, 1484, 9360
War Wagon (The)	196 ASHC		CH-47A	68-69	cargo	66-19083	N+A	fuselage		Joe Oswald FE, Wheeler CE, Raswick DG, Roger Vestal FE	1332,
War Wagon	235 AWC		UH-1H	1970	C+C		NO			Lou Bouault	1513, 6400
War Wagon	A Trp 3/17		OH-6A	67-70	scout		NO	doghouse		Bill Reynolds AC	1224, 1630
War Wagon	B Co 227 AHB		UH-1H	70-71	slick		N+A	nose			1025,
War Wagon	B Co 228 ASHB		CH-47A	67-68	cargo	66-00069	NO	fuselage		William McClain FE, Lee Dorsey FE	395, 1129, 1266, 1447, 5675, 8025
War Wagon	B Co 228 ASHB		CH-47A	1971	cargo	66-19092	N+A	fuselage			1266, 6100
War Wagon	D Trp 3/5		OH-6A	68-69	scout		NO				1710,
War Wagon (The)	68 AHC		UH-1D	67-68	slick		NO			Smith CE	648,
War Wagon (The)	121 AHC		UH-1B	69-70	gun		NO	doorpost			1809,

Copter Name	Unit	Unit #1	Aircraft	Circa	Function	Serial #	Config	Location	Artist	Crew	Contributors
War Wagon (The)	242 ASHC		CH-47A	67-68	cargo	66-19014	N+A	front fuselage		Galen Wallum FE	1199, 8050
War Witch	129 AHC		UH-1H	1969	slick		NO	nose			1725, 9915
Wargasm	11 ACR		OH-6A	71-72	scout	66-17795	NO	clamshell		Dave Ripley AC	1467, 1627
Wargasm	F Trp 4 Cav		OH-6A	1972	scout	66-17795	NO	clamshell			140, 422
Warlock	11 ACR		OH-6A	68-69	scout		NO	clamshell			1703,
Warlock	134 AHC		UH-1H	1971	slick	68-16593	NO	nose		Phil Fusilier AC	352, 568
Warlord	C Trp 2/17		OH-6A	69-70	scout	67-16391	NO	clamshell			1908, 4600
Warlord (The)	92 AHC		UH-1C	1970	gun	65-09418	NO	nose		John Boyd AC, Ward CE	169,
Warlord (The)	92 AHC		UH-1M	1971	gun	65-09472	NO	nose		J. Boyd AC, Chuck McDonough CE, M. Morrissey DG	169,
Warlord	D Trp 3/4		AH-1G	70-71	gun	67-15825	NO	doghouse	Paul LaClaire	Paul LaClaire CE	1559, 8400, 8575
Warlord Aero Scout	B Co 123 Avn Bn		UH-1H	70-71	slick		N+A	nose			69,
Warrior (The)	117 AHC	Avn Co	UH-1B	1964	slick		NO	nose			394,
Wart Hog	242 ASHC		CH-47A	68-71	cargo		NO				1199, 1225, 8350
Warwagon	117 AHC		UH-1M	70-71	gun	65-09554	NO	cargo door frame top		C. Putnam AC, Vance Cowart CE, Jim Barrie DG	92, 127, 177, 1006
Watch Out Gooks	B Trp 1/9		AH-1G	1970	gun		NO	turret			8925,
Wayne's Work Horse	339 TC		CH-37B	64-65	recovery	54-00998	NO	fuselage		Frank Ferry DG, Don Kaye FE, Armand Litch CE, Buckley FE, Willie Harper FE	520, 846, 889, 1975, 6525, 9620
We Buy US Bonds	121 AHC		UH-1D	67-68	slick		N+A	nose			477, 1593, 4825, 9290
We Eat This Shit Up **	several		UH-1B/D	64-68	slick / gun		NO	various			932, 1703, 1931, 1961
We Help The Hurt	unk		CH-47		cargo		N+A	fuselage			1053, 1908, 4600
We Live To Kill VC For Lunch Bunch	114 AHC		UH-1H	69-70	slick		NO	flare box			289, 1400, 1563, 6700
We Make The Most Out Of War	A Co 228 ASHB		CH-47A	1968	cargo		N+A	fuselage			903,
We The People	11 ACR		AH-1G	69-72	gun	68-15067	NO	bpw			422, 747, 868, 1065, 1092, 1674, 5400, 5427
Weasel	176 AHC		UH-1C	1969	gun	66-15024	NO			David Matwiju DG	1079, 9450

Copter Name	Unit	Unit #1	Aircraft	Circa	Function	Serial #	Config	Location	Artist	Crew	Contributors
Wee Luck	2 Signal Group		UH-1B	66-67	slick	63-08711	N+A	cargo door	Bob Callaghan	Lee Cannon AC, Callaghan CE, Huey Nelson AC, Oliver Ridgway DG, Lester Heath AC	265, 1041, 4775, 6625
Wee Willie's War Wagon	539 TC		CH-47A	1967	recovery	071 ?	NO	fuselage			2030, 6805
Wendy	189 AHC		UH-1H	1968	slick	66-16153	NO	nose		Mike Ytsen DG	1977,
Wendy	37 Sig Bn		UH-1H	71-72	slick	68-15526	NO	nose		Bill Case CE	286, 9140
We're Slick ^^	155 AHC		UH-1H	67-68	slick		NO	nose		Jerry Bourquin	4, 400, 1053, 9360
West By God Virginia	176 AHC		UH-1H	1971	slick		NO	nose			1254, 8650
Wetback	271 ASHC		CH-47B	1968	cargo		N+A	fuselage		Marc Teeter CE, Tony Rios CE	1087,
WETSU	11 ACR		UH-1D	68-69	slick		NO	nose			1703,
WETSU ^^	62 Avn Co	150 TC	UH-1B	64-65	maint		N+A			James Workman DG	1961,
WETSU #1	173 AHC		UH-1D	66-67	slick		NO	pilot door			1931,
What ! Me Worry? **	20 TC		UH-1D	1967	recovery	66-01008	AO	nose		William McGowan AC	1145,
What ! Me Worry? **	57 AHC		UH-1C	67-68	gun		AO	doorpost			696, 5900
What ! Me Worry?	121 AHC		UH-1D	67-68	slick	66-16098	N+A	nose		Beaver AC	1593, 6975
What ! Me Worry?	283 Med Det		UH-1H	67-68	dustoff	66-17005	N+A	jump door			1638, 9670
What ! Me Worry?	C Co 228 ASHB		CH-47B	68-70	cargo	67-18480	N+A	front fuselage	Mel Chappell	Mel Chappell FE, Steve Keller CE, Steve Bolton CE	297, 347, 1571
Wheel Standing Willie	B Co 228 ASHB		CH-47A	1968	cargo	66-19039	NO	fuselage		Bill Scott FE, Richard Lewis CE, Alfred Lott FE	1239, 1574, 8025
When You Care Enough To Send The Very Best	71 AHC	151 TC	UH-1D	66-67	maint		N+A	nose		Glen Summers	1730,
When You're Out Of Schlitz You're Out Of Beer	174 AHC		UH-1H	69-70	slick	67-17543	N+A	nose	Ben Kennedy	Harry Cooper CE, Tom Roddery DG	341, 530, 9430
Whiskey 1	114 AHC		UH-1D	66-67	slick	65-09826	NO	nose		Larry Flis CE, C. Cauley AC, Jack Payne CP, Don Brimage CP	1998, 7175
Whispering Death *	12 CAG		UH-1B	1972			NO	nose		Hill, Gannon	439, 1266, 5725
White Rabbit **	254 Med Det		UH-1H	69-70	dustoff		AO	nose		Zollar CE	954,

Copter Name	Unit	Unit #1	Aircraft	Circa	Function	Serial #	Config	Location	Artist	Crew	Contributors
White Tiger Lead ^	121 AHC		UH-1D	67-68	slick		N+A	nose			477, 4825, 9290
Whomp Bird (The)	254 Med Det		UH-1H	69-70	dustoff	68-15404	NO	pilot door		White CE, Salmon AC, Englehardt CP, Zollar CE	954,
Why	498 Med Co		UH-1H	70-71	dustoff		NO	nose			109, 709, 997, 1045, 5448, 7325, 9950
Wicked Wahine	188 AHC		UH-1H	67-68	C+C	66-16089	NAA			James Merrymen (Black Baron 6)	414, 1678, 1790
Wicked Wahine	269 CAB		UH-1D	1967	C+C	66-16089	NAA	pilot door		LTC James Merryman	1675, 1790
Widow Maker	11 ACR		AH-1G	71-72	gun	68-15095	NO	bpw			138, 905, 1092, 1266, 1448, 1467, 1524, 1674, 4825, 5400, 6175, 6850, 8625
Widow Maker	53 Avn Det		ACH-47A	1966	gun	unk	NO				1898, 8300
Widow Maker	114 AHC		UH-1H	1968	slick	005	NO	nose		Tom Visentine CE	1838,
Widow Maker	118 AHC		UH-1C	69-70	gun		NO	nose			529, 1920, 9260
Widow Maker ^	119 AHC		UH-1C	1969	gun		NO				301, 908
Widow Maker	134 AHC		UH-1C	68-69	gun	66-15062	NO	nose	Pointer	Danny Pettit CE, Randy Pointer DG, D. Jones AC, J.T. Donnelly AC, Chuck Bernis CP	352, 1387, 1405, 1818, 1908, 4600, 9320
Widow Maker	170 AHC		UH-1C	1969	gun		NO	nose			928, 1543, 2079, 9400
Widow Maker	175 AHC		UH-1B	66-67	gun	63-08712	NO	pilot door			107, 1599, 1926, 1980, 7175, 9130
Widow Maker	176 AHC		UH-1C	1969	gun	66-00605	NO			Larry Shatto CE '67, Larry Silva CE '68	1595,
Widow Maker	238 AWC	AHC	UH-1B	1969	gun		NO			Davis Stiefel DG	1697, 9530
Widow Maker	539 TC		CH-47A	69-70	cargo		NO	fuselage			1305, 4825
Widow Maker	B Trp 1/9		UH-1B	66-67	gun		NO	M-5 turret		Dick Hale AC	679,
Widow Maker	B Trp 7/17		AH-1G	1969	gun		N+A	nose			1076,
Widow Maker	D Trp 1/4		UH-1B	66-67	gun	63-08597	NO	doorpost		Kelly Hudson AC, Jim Sharper CE, Irtus Miller DG, Dean Babcock DG	806, 1759
Widow Maker (The)	68 AHC		UH-1B	66-67	gun		NO	M-5 turret		John Frasso CE, Robert King DG	2075,
Widow Maker (The)	68 AHC		UH-1C	67-68	gun	66-00688	NO	M-5 turret		Sandy Noyes CE	69, 415, 648, 811, 1304, 1883, 2075, 9200
Widow Maker (The)	192 AHC		UH-1C	1971	gun		NO	nose		Klein AC, Dick Synder CP	51, 343, 1298, 1878, 1901

Copter Name	Unit	Unit #1	Aircraft	Circa	Function	Serial #	Config	Location	Artist	Crew	Contributors
Widow Maker (The)	281 AHC		UH-1C	1967	gun		NO	nose		Art Slater CE, Harry Wetmore	946, 1893, 9550
Widow Maker (The)	B Co 25 Avn Bn		AH-1G	1970	gun	68-15084	NO	turret + doghouse		Chuck Gant AC, Larry Carpenter CE	466, 519, 582, 9120
Widow Maker (The)	D Trp 1/4		AH-1G	1970	gun		NO	bpw			134, 5450
Widow Maker II	D Trp 1/4		UH-1B	67-68	gun	64-14059	NO	nose + doorpost		Bob Tenney AC, Doug Thomas CP	1759,
Widow Maker RIP	D Trp 1/4		AH-1G	69-70	gun		NO	bpw			1053, 1205
Widowmaker	B Trp 2/17		AH-1G	70-71	gun	67-15705	NO	bpw left side		Gary Ryan AC	1531,
Wild Aces	611 TC		CH-21C	63-64	lift		N+A	fuselage		Chuck Edson AC	465, 6775
Wild Bill	188 AHC		UH-1H	67-68	slick		NO	pilot door			1113,
Wild Child	45 Med Co		UH-1H	67-68	dustoff		NO	nose			378, 7450
Wild Child	187 AHC		UH-1H	1970	slick	68-16087	NO	nose			1932,
Wild Child	A Trp 1/9		UH-1H	69-70	slick		NO	doorpost		Hoke AC, Gene Ficker CE	522,
Wild Child	B Co 25 Avn Bn		UH-1C	1968	gun		NO	nose			909,
Wild Child (The)	335 AHC		UH-1B	69-70	gun		NO			Andy Hooker CE	788, 1926
Wild Child II	45 Med Co		UH-1H	68-69	dustoff		NO	nose		Dennis Telischak, R. Cunnare, Drexel Johnson	288, 378, 7425
Wild Child III	45 Med Co		UH-1H	1969	dustoff		NO				1308,
Wild Child IV	45 Med Co		UH-1H	1970	dustoff		NO				1308,
Wild Mary Jane	A Trp 7/1		OH-6A	1969	scout	66-07885	NO	clamshell			1810, 8625
Wild Thang	178 ASHC		CH-47B	1970	cargo	67-18488	N+A	front fuselage			1053, 1181, 6050
Wild Thang	D Trp 3/5		UH-1C	67-68	gun	66-00678	NO	pilot door		Billy Brooks DG	1301,
Wild Thing	11 Light Inf Bde		OH-6A	70-71	scout	69-16037	NO	clamshell		Danny Aiken CE	11,
Wild Thing	68 AHC		UH-1D	67-68	slick / smoker	66-01097	NO	pilot door	E. Packard	John Post AC, Bodwen CP, Ernie Packard CE, Robert Horning DG	648, 792, 1334, 9200

Copter Name	Unit	Unit #1	Aircraft	Circa	Function	Serial #	Config	Location	Artist	Crew	Contributors
Wild Thing	116 AHC		UH-1D	1968	slick	66-00987	N+A	pilot door		Dan Johnson CE	852, 9240
Wild Thing	D Trp 3/5		UH-1H	1971	slick		NO	pilot door			1453, 9860
Wild Willie's Taxi	117 AHC	140 TC	UH-1D	1967	maint	64-13535	N+A	nose		Williams AC, B. Knox AC, M. O'Leary AC, K. Condict CP, D. Bascom CE, J. McGovern, J. Mason, W. Atwood, C. B. Grimmet	57, 99, 127, 1266, 6125, 9250
Wildest Deuce	48 AHC		UH-1H	71-72	slick	67-17388	NO	nose		Mike Topping CE	1795, 9150
Wiley Coyote **	B Co 123 Avn Bn		OH-6A	69-71	scout	68-17226	AO	doghouse			69,
Willowdean	187 AHC		UH-1D	67-68	slick	66-00925	NO	pilot door			1713,
Wimps	57 TC	120 AHC	CH-21C	1964	lift		N+A	fuselage			395, 1554, 5675
Wind Watcher ^	118 AHC		UH-1D	1967	slick		NO	nose			1020, 4400
Winged Warrior	45 Med Co		UH-1H	69-70	dustoff		NO				1533,
Wingless Warrior	187 AHC		UH-1H	1971	slick	67-17757	NO	nose		Richard Doke CE	427,
Witch Bitch **	174 AHC	409 TC	UH-1H	1971	maint	69-16650	AO			Mel Lutgring CE	1055, 1071, 9430
Witch Doctor ^	57 AHC	615 TC	UH-1H	69-70	maint	66-16006	N+A	nose		Charles Deming CE, Larry Maddox AC	316, 409, 564
Witch Doctor ^	128 AHC	393 TC	UH-1B/D	1967	maint	64-13960	N+A	nose		Jim Wilks	444, 840, 944, 989, 1434, 1817, 1910, 1916, 2033, 9250, 9300
Witch Doctor ^	174 AHC	409 TC	UH-1H	68-71	maint	67-17410	N+A	nose			316, 472, 1055, 1071, 1456, 1568, 9430
Witch Doctor II ^	128 AHC	393 TC	UH-1D	1967	maint	65-09917	N+A				696,
Witch Doctor II ^	174 AHC	409 TC	UH-1H	69-71	maint	68-16340	N+A	nose	Dave Smalley	Elliott AC, Gabauer CP, Smalley CE, Brasket DG	472, 9430
Witch Doctor III ^	174 AHC	409 TC	UH-1H	1971	maint	69-16650	N+A	nose	Mel Lutgring	Mel Lutgring CE, Butch Elliott AC	472, 9430
Witch Doctor Recovery ^	57 AHC	615 TC	UH-1H	69-73	maint	66-16006	N+A	nose		Ron Frigstad AC, Maxwell, Duke, Hicks, Magnan, Sandner, Contz, Hrubiec, Ward, Hayduk, Zuber	395, 564, 1997, 3075, 5675, 9180
Witchdoctor III ^	128 AHC	393 TC	UH-1D	67-68	maint	65-09781	N+A	nose		John Sullivan CE	
Witchdoctor IV ^	128 AHC	393 TC	UH-1H	67-68	maint		N+A				

Copter Name	Unit	Unit #1	Aircraft	Circa	Function	Serial #	Config	Location	Artist	Crew	Contributors
Witchdoctor V ^	128 AHC	393 TC	UH-1H	68-69	maint		N+A				undocumented: calculated assumption
Witchdoctor VI ^	128 AHC	393 TC	UH-1D	69-70	maint	67-17282	N+A	nose		Tom Ferrigan AC	444, 517, 1138, 4825
Witchdoctor VII ^	128 AHC	393 TC	UH-1H	70-71	maint		N+A	nose		Tom Ferrigan AC	517,
Witchdoctor VIII ^	128 AHC	393 TC	UH-1H	1971	maint		N+A			Wes Coffman CE	317,
Wolf **	B Co 25 Avn Bn		UH-1C	1969	gun		AO	pilot door		Jim Parham CP	1341,
Wolf Man	B Co 25 Avn Bn		UH-1C	67-68	gun		NO				1562,
Wolly Bully	A Co 227 AHB		UH-1D	66-67	slick	65-12865	N+A	nose		Krowlczyk CE	706, 9700
Wonder Wart-Hog	200 ASHC		CH-47A	67-68	cargo	66-00094	N+A	front fuselage	Larry Dumford	Terry Thomas DG, David Walters FE	995, 1195, 1591
Wonder Wart-Hog	A Co 159 ASHB		CH-47A	1968	cargo	66-00094	N+A	front fuselage		David Walters CE	1857, 7850, 8275
Wonder Wart-Hog	B Trp 1/9		UH-1B	67-68	gun		NO	nose		Tom Maherline AC	1392,
Woodstock **	174 AHC		UH-1M	70-71	gun	64-14140	AO	quarter panel	Bob Legault	Allan Harris AC, Bob Legault CE, Blake CP, Yates DG	696, 5900, 9430
Woodstock	571 Med Det		UH-1H	70-71	dustoff	68-15230	NO	nose		John Moore CE	1229,
Woodstock	D Co 229 AHB		AH-1G	71-72	gun		NO			Eagle, Clark, Armelin	620, 9850
Woodstock I	F Btry 79 AFA		AH-1G	1972	gun		NO	bpw			220, 518
Woodstock II	F Btry 79 AFA		AH-1G	1972	gun		NO	bpw			220, 518
Woody	117 AHC	Avn Co	UH-1B	1965	gun		NO	pilot door			4575,
Wooly Booger	4 Trans Command		UH-1B	65-67	slick	63-08727	N+A	pilot door		James H. Haddox CE '66, Bob Chenoweth CE '67, Rodger Williamson, Coxwell, Souders	301, 1852, 1921, 2058, 8525
Wooly Booger	478 Avn Co		CH-54A	65-66	recovery	64-14204	NO	nose		A. Gajan, R. Lane, J. Hetzer, L. Bryan, C. English	877, 892, 1975, 4850
Wooly Bully	56 TC		CH-37B	1965	recovery	57-01658	N+A	nose			1266, 1975, 6275, 6525
Wooly Bully	B Co 25 Avn Bn		UH-1C	68-69	gun		N+A	nose		Eugene Whitey	242, 1060, 1900, 3950, 9120
Woolyberger	339 TC		CH-37B	63-64	lift	55-00636	NO	fuselage			395, 1053, 5675, 6025
Wop Wagon	189 AHC		UH-1H	1968	slick	67-17272	NO	nose		Jim Lomonaco AC	1036,

Wretched Mildred: *D Troop 3/4 Cav, AH-1G, (sn 68-15189), Cu Chi, 1969-71.* Chinese script adorned this gunship after Crew Chief Gary Schmidt's Tai Pai R&R provided creative inspiration. The "ye ole battle-ax" term of endearment apparently warded off any fatal enemy blows, as after 1,885 in-country flight hours she safely made it home. Photo and art by Gary Schmidt.

Copter Name	Unit	Unit #1	Aircraft	Circa	Function	Serial #	Config	Location	Artist	Crew	Contributors
Wrecker	121 AHC	80 TC	UH-1B	64-66	maint		N+A	nose			1908, 4600
Wrecker ^	121 AHC	80 TC/ 93 TC	UH-1D	66-68	maint	65-09969	N+A	nose			477, 4825, 9290
Wrecker ^	155 AHC	165 TC	UH-1D	67-68	maint	66-16440	N+A	nose		Burris McRee DG, Joe DeLaTorre CE	1163, 1379, 1765
Wrench Bender ^	235 AWC	608 TC +571 TC	UH-1H	1971	maint	68-16289	NO				1150, 1674
Wretched Mildred	D Trp 3/4		AH-1G	69-71	gun	68-15189	N+A	doghouse	Gary Schmidt	Keith Nichols CE, Gary Schmidt CE	1282, 1559, 1674, 8400
Xavius	A Trp 3/17		OH-6A	69-70	scout	66-07790	NO	doghouse		George Carter AC	503, 1630, 8625
Xin Loi	173 AHC		UH-1C	66-67	gun	64-14189	NO	pilot door		T. Zanfardino CE, Haase CE '67, Bud Harton CE '68	708, 1981
Yankee Peddler	121 AHC		UH-1D	66-67	slick		N+A	nose		Gary Dowler CP	437, 831
Yellow Cab	175 AHC		UH-1D	66-67	slick		NO	nose		Bob Tidd DG	461, 1266, 1784, 5675, 5775, 6275
Yellow Rose Of Texas (The)	121 AHC		UH-1D	1966	slick	65-09580	N+A	nose		Gary Dowler CP, Jerry McBee CE, John Smith DG, Dennis Yost CP, R. L. Buxton AC	395, 437, 439, 831, 1135, 1266, 2024, 4600, 5675, 5725, 6275
Yosemite Sam **	92 AHC		UH-1C	67-69	gun	66-15116	AO	nose		J.Zaletskis CE, Brian Mahoney DG, Steve Sawicki DG	1979, 9220
Yosemite Sam **	196 ASHC		CH-47A	1968	cargo		AO				1477,
Yosemite Sam **	335 AHC		UH-1H	69-70	slick	68-16090	AO	nose		Louis Souza CE	1664, 9590
Yosemite Sam **	B Co 25 Avn Bn		UH-1C	67-70	gun		AO	nose			242, 909, 1060, 3950, 9120
You Bet Your Life	243 ASHC		CH-47A	1968	cargo		NO	front fuselage		Bill Bunger FE	236, 819
You Burp We Hurt	117 AHC	Avn Co	UH-1C	66-67	gun		NO	cargo door frame top			884, 9250
You Call We Haul	187 AHC		UH-1D	68-69	slick	66-00929	NO	pilot door		Tom Tesmar	1002,
You Call We Maul	192 AHC		UH-1C	70-71	gun	212,676, 444	NO			Mike Zimmerman CE	1985, 9510
You Crash + Call We Dash + Haul ^/^^	56 TC	56 TC	UH-1D	1967	maint		N+A	nose		Emmett Knight AC	727, 1053, 1451, 2006, 2021, 4050, 9450
You Hoot We Shoot	117 AHC	Avn Co	UH-1B	66-67	gun		NO	M-3 rocket box			323, 9250
You Maul Em We Haul Em	45 Med Co		UH-1H	67-68	dustoff		NO				8475,

Copter Name	Unit	Unit #1	Aircraft	Circa	Function	Serial #	Config	Location	Artist	Crew	Contributors
You Maul Em We Haul Em	571 Med Det		UH-1H	69-70	dustoff		NO				1600,
Yvonne	179 ASHC		CH-47C	70-71	cargo	67-18528	NO	fuselage		Tom Messenger FE, Foley CE, Byron Raney DG	1182,
Zap You're Sterile	48 AHC		UH-1B	68-69	gun		NO	nose			1000, 9150
Zapata's Rights	187 AHC		UH-1H	70-71	slick	68-16305	NO	nose		Joe Caha AC, Don Smalley DG, Luis Campos CE	652,
Zeppelin	132 ASHC		CH-47B	1970	cargo	67-18442	N+A				1162,
Zeppelin II	132 ASHC		CH-47B	70-71	cargo	67-18448	N+A	front fuselage	SP4 Davis did all '70-'71 a/c art		184, 1162, 1588, 7800, 8275, 9430
Zig Zag	178 ASHC		CH-47B	70-71	cargo		N+A	front fuselage			1541, 1946
Zig Zag **	unk Cav		OH-6A	69-70	scout		AO	fuselage			2022, 4275
Zig Zag Man **	C Co 227 AHB		UH-1H	1971	slick	69-15368	AO	nose	Ben Lipford	Tom Fifield CE	524, 1025, 1171
Zip Zapper	117 AHC		UH-1C	67-68	gun		NO	belly			474,
Zit	C Trp 1/9		OH-6A	70-71	scout	69-15990	NO	fuselage		Nate Shaffer DG, Bruce Campbell AC	271, 360, 873, 1266, 1592, 6250, 9805
Zorba	173 AHC		UH-1H	1968	slick	66-16091	NO			C.G. Zagkos AC, George Pedroza DG	1336, 6805

Little Miss Janet: *162 AHC, UH-1D, (sn 64-13856), 1966-67.* Crew Chief Ed Walsh calms his nerves with a cigarette after an apparent hard landing on 1-2-67. All 2,066 VN flight hours were with the 162nd. Photo by Ed Walsh.

ARMY HELICOPTER NAMES

UNIT/NUMERICAL

Unit	Copter Name	Origin / Definition	Notes / Call Signs ( ) < >	Fate Aircraft / Crew
1 Air Cav Div	Lady Luck ^		COL Dysinger was 1st Cav DISCOM C.O. / '812 was Dysinger's command ship	
1 Avn Det	Birth Control		attached to 228 ASHB / better known as GUNS-A-GO-GO	DD 2-2-68
1 Avn Det	Cost Of Living	forward crown insignia preserved at Ft. Rucker Army Avn Museum / replacement for "STUMP JUMPER"	aka "CRAZY 8" / attached to 228 ASHB / also known as GUNS-A-GO-GO / skull logo saved from forward crown	DD 5-5-67
1 Avn Det	Easy Money		attached to 228 ASHB as GUNS-A-GO-GO / restored 5-1-00 / on display: Redstone Arsenal, Huntsville, AL	
1 Avn Det	Guns A-Go-Go *	"Birth Control," "Cost of Living," "Easy Money"	world's largest military gunship: serial #'s: 64-13145, 64-13149, 64-13154	
1 Bde 1 Cav Div	Chuck You Farlie	spoonerism = transposition of the letters C and F		
1 Bde 1 Cav Div	Goat (The)		Brigade C.O.'s ship	
1 Bde 1 Cav Div	Green Hornet	comic book character		
1 Bde 1 Cav Div	Judy Ann	name of Duke McKinney's wife		
1 Bde 1 Cav Div	Little Egypt	song lyrics in Elvis "Roustabout" movie		
1 Bde 1 Cav Div	Mack	fire engine manufacturer's name		
1 Bde 1 Cav Div	Mack II	fire engine manufacturer's name		
1 Bde 1 Cav Div	Mack III	fire engine manufacturer's name		
1 Bde 1 Cav Div	Mustang Sally	Wilson Pickett song title		
1 Bde 1 Cav Div	Mystery Ship	The Blues Image song title	C+C ship	
1 Bde 1 Cav Div	Rickshaw (The)	C+C for 1st Bde C.O. (Rick Shaw?)	unit's first UH-1H	
1 Bde 101 Abn	Iron Butterfly **	steam powered butterfly painted on the helmet of George Dousis	not allowed personal markings because the Bde C.O. flew in this ship	
1 Bde 101 Abn	Cherry Popper	mythical Griffin (callsign) only ate virgins		
1 Bde 101 Abn	Virgin Eater	mythical Griffin (callsign) only ate virgins		
1 Bn 50 Inf	Bad News		LTC Bertholf's personal C+C ship: 1st Field Force	
1 Sig Bde	CBS Special	three different CE's: 3 last names = CBS		

Unit	Copter Name	Origin / Definition	Notes / Call Signs ( ) < >	Fate Aircraft / Crew
1 Sig Bde	Linda 2			
2 Bde 1 Cav	Walking Finger **	middle finger salute	graphic only, no lettering	
2 Bde 101 Abn Div	Lucky Eagle ^		Division C.O.'s ship / HQ's "callsign" also	
2 Signal Group	Chug A Lug	Roger Miller song title	Oliver Ridgway was former DG on "WEE LUCK" / on display: Kenosha Military Museum, WI ?	
2 Signal Group	Sat Cong	"kill VC"		
2 Signal Group	Tracy II *	no TRACY 1:name reserved for future baby girl		
2 Signal Group	Wee Luck		Leprechaun painted on left cargo door	
3 Bde 1 Cav Div	Chuck You Farlie	spoonerism = transposition of the letters C and F / hourglass with '3' painted on pilot door	painted Snoopy on nose also	
3 Bde 101 AB	Thunder Bug			
4 Trans Command	Here After 727 ^	"HERE AFTER" was unit call sign	was named WOOLY BOOGER before Chenoweth changed it	
4 Trans Command	Wooly Booger	Bigfoot type creature / hairy female anatomy	Chenoweth changed nn to "HERE AFTER 727" in '67 / "WOOLY BOOGER" nn by Haddox / voodoo doll ?	
5 Trans Bn	Donna			
5 Trans Bn	Rosemary's Baby	Hollywood horror film title		
7 Airlift Plt	Hogan's Goat			
8 TC	Blue Angel	H. Oakes originated name, Nov-Dec '62	transitioned to the 117 Avn Co	
8 TC	Dragon Ass	dragon painted along length of ship		
8 TC	Dragon Wagon		'087 "BLUE ANGEL" was renamed "DRAGON WAGON" by Bogges after Oakes DEROS'd	
8 TC	Friendship 8	NASA spacecraft of same name		
8 TC	Miss Zoe Ann	UH-1B + CH-21 carried this name?		
8 TC	New Blue Tail			
8 TC	Pineapple Princess	two pineapples painted on fuselage for kills	Shotgun 8 program	
8 TC	Polock's Honey Bucket	Leon Mruczkowski was Polish / Korean waste container		
8 TC	Roadrunner			
8 TC	Sleeping Tigers	small tiger head painted with nn	was carried on a CH-21 or UH-1B in '64	

Unit	Copter Name	Origin / Definition	Notes / Call Signs ( ) < >	Fate Aircraft / Crew
8 TC	Swamp Fox 2			
10 CAB	Shadow (The)	MAJ Ken Stickler originated name		
11 ACR	11th ARM. CAV. Recovery			
11 ACR	Angel Of Death			
11 ACR	Angel Of Death II			
11 ACR	Angel Of The Mourning			
11 ACR	Birth Control			
11 ACR	Blackhorse Recovery			
11 ACR	Blacksmith ^	adopted name of the maintenance platoon's aircraft that imitated the 11th's BLACKHORSE callsign		
11 ACR	Born Free	1966 song + movie title		
11 ACR	Cheap Thrills	Janis Joplin album title		
11 ACR	Crazy Horse			
11 ACR	Crystal Ship (The)	Doors song title		
11 ACR	El Gato			
11 ACR	Electrical Egg		pic featured in "American Warrior" book by Doc Bahnsen	DD 3-4-69
11 ACR	Everyday People	Sly + The Family Stone 1968 song title		
11 ACR	Gallopin Guns			
11 ACR	George Of The Jungle	1967 animated TV series that spoofed the Tarzan character		
11 ACR	Gray Rider	pilot's last name reference	VHPA webpic mis-named: should be Gray, not Grey	
11 ACR	Grim Reaper (The)			
11 ACR	Guns A-Go-Go			
11 ACR	Haulin' Ash			

Unit	Copter Name	Origin / Definition	Notes / Call Signs ( ) < >	Fate Aircraft / Crew
11 ACR	Have Gun Will Travel			
11 ACR	Here I Come			
11 ACR	Hud	Hollywood film title starring Paul Newman		
11 ACR	Iron Butterfly (The)	60's rock band by the same name		
11 ACR	Jefferson Airplane	1960's rock band name		
11 ACR	Joyce			autorotation crash
11 ACR	Joyce II			
11 ACR	King Cobra			
11 ACR	Kiss Of Death			
11 ACR	Li'l Brute			
11 ACR	Little Sorrel	named after Civil War GEN Stonewall Jackson's horse	GEN George Patton of WWII fame was COL Patton's father / COL Patton was Regimental C. O. of the 11 ACR	copter sustained combat damage
11 ACR	Little Sorrel II	named after Civil War GEN Stonewall Jackson's horse	GEN George Patton of WWII fame was COL Patton's father / COL Patton was Regimental C. O. of the 11 ACR	copter sustained combat damage
11 ACR	Little Sorrel III	named after Civil War GEN Stonewall Jackson's horse	GEN George Patton of WWII fame was COL Patton's father / COL Patton was Regimental C. O. of the 11 ACR	copter sustained combat damage
11 ACR	Little Sorrel IV	named after Civil War GEN Stonewall Jackson's horse	GEN George Patton of WWII fame was COL Patton's father / COL Patton was Regimental C. O. of the 11 ACR	copter sustained combat damage
11 ACR	Little Sorrel V	named after Civil War GEN Stonewall Jackson's horse	GEN George Patton of WWII fame was COL Patton's father / COL Patton was Regimental C. O. of the 11 ACR	
11 ACR	Little Surprise		psych-ops speakers in cargo bay	
11 ACR	Lola Marie	name of pilot's wife		
11 ACR	Lookout			
11 ACR	MBG	MBG = "money back guarantee" ?	OH-6 recovery ship for 11 ACR	
11 ACR	MBG II	MBG = "money back guarantee" ?	OH-6 recovery ship for 11 ACR / was original "MBG" destroyed ? /	
11 ACR	MBG III	MBG = "money back guarantee" ?	OH-6 recovery ship for either 11 ACR / "MBG II" destroyed ?	

Unit	Copter Name	Origin / Definition	Notes / Call Signs ( ) < >	Fate Aircraft / Crew
11 ACR	Miss Me		aka "TOY TIGER"	
11 ACR	Mr. Groovy			
11 ACR	Paranoid	Black Sabbath song title		
11 ACR	Pheadra Del Immortal	"Phaedra The Immortal"		
11 ACR	Polish Prize			
11 ACR	Raggmopp	Ames Brothers song title		
11 ACR	Recovery			
11 ACR	Satan's Toy			
11 ACR	Sir Lime A Lot			
11 ACR	Sir Reginald Lime-Lime	painted British pilot with leather flight hat+goggles: replicated 1960's Pillsbury powdered drink mix graphic		
11 ACR	Snoopy **			
11 ACR	Surealistic Olive	mis-spelling of Surrealistic / parody of Jefferson Airplane's '67 album title "Surrealistic Pillow"		
11 ACR	Thor's Hammer			
11 ACR	Tonka			
11 ACR	Toy Tiger		aka "MISS ME"	
11 ACR	Trick Or Treat	2 versions of painted words: possible 2 sn's		
11 ACR	Voodo Lady	Jimmy Hendrix song title		
11 ACR	Wanderer (The)			
11 ACR	Wargasm		AAHF flyable a/c, Hampton, GA / Curt Knapp piloted same a/c in-country with 2 Bde, 101 Abn in '68 + today	
11 ACR	Warlock			
11 ACR	We The People		2 versions: words painted in arc + words perfectly aligned	
11 ACR	WETSU	"we eat this shit up"		
11 ACR	Widow Maker		Summer '74, page 158, AAHS issue / on display: VHPA facility, Hillsborough, NC	

Unit	Copter Name	Origin / Definition	Notes / Call Signs ( ) < >	Fate Aircraft / Crew
11 CAB	Smokey III	smoke ship	shares serial # with "SMOKEY" of 128 AHC / on display: Smithsonian NASM Udvar-Hazy Ctr, Chantilly,VA	2500 hrs, 4 VN tours
11 CAG	First Hoss	Brig General's personal Huey	parent unit of crew was the 229 AHB, General Services (GS) unit	
11 CAG	Patches *	over 100 bullet holes covered by patches		
11 GS	Baby Huey	powerful but self destructive cartoon character	baby helo compared to previous D model / traded in old D for B model	
11 GS	Hobby Horse		aka "PENNY-NICKEL-FOUR" / formerly GEN Elvy B. Robert's ship, Cav Commander	
11 GS	Rebel Devil			
11 Light Inf Bde	Sandy			crashed with Benton as passenger
11 Light Inf Bde	Wild Thing		small air recon company called Primo Avn was an attachment	
12 CAG	Whispering Death *		TOW missile Huey	
13 CAB	Office (The)		C.O.'s ship	
14 Trans Bn	Tally Ho		attached to 117 AHC as maintenance company	DD Oct, 1965 while assisgned to Co A, 1 Avn Bn
15 Med Bn	Angel Of Mercy			
15 Med Bn	Blood, Sweat + Tears	1960's rock band name		
15 Med Bn	Bucket Of Blood *		D model with new engine	
15 Med Bn	California Dreamer	crew all from California		reportedly was shot down, destroyed ?
15 Med Bn	Cheap Thrills	Janis Joplin album title		
15 Med Bn	Easy Rider	Hollywood movie title		
15 Med Bn	Furgs + Beans	C-Rations reference		
15 Med Bn	Hawaiian Eye	Hawaii was D.Vierra's home of record / also 1960's TV detective show	painted eye on door + nose = "EYE"	
15 Med Bn	Hell's Ugly	Keyes's father's comment about WW II prompted "Hells Ugly" name		
15 Med Bn	Iron Butterfly	60's rock band by the same name		

For God, Country, & Body Count*: F Troop 4 Cav, OH-6A, (sn 69-16003), 1971-72*. The flat surface of the OH-6A rotor cowling, aka "doghouse," was a favorite location for art and names. Before the fateful mission on 5-1-72, she accumulated 1,617 flight hours. Photo by Carl Betsill.

Unit	Copter Name	Origin / Definition	Notes / Call Signs ( ) < >	Fate Aircraft / Crew
15 Med Bn	Iron Lung		aka "VETO": replaced "IRON LUNG"	
15 Med Bn	King Roach	chewed big plug of tobacco that resembled a "roach", small marijuana cigarette, according to Hank Tuell	"SHORT" painted on right cheek of Medevac nose also	
15 Med Bn	Little Vic Dontaria			
15 Med Bn	New Blood, Sweat + Tears (The)			
15 Med Bn	Old Reliable	duck with crossed crutches painted by Hatch	copter name found on the Dustoff Memorial Registry guest book	6-19-67: Ron Trogdon CE, KIA
15 Med Bn	Purple Haze	ref: purple smoke at LZ / Jimmy Hendrix song title		
15 Med Bn	Rated PG			
15 Med Bn	Short		aka "KING ROACH"	
15 Med Bn	Super King	Dan Smith originated name	Ferguson inherited name when Smith DEROS'd	
15 Med Bn	Sympathetic Journey			
15 Med Bn	Tijuana Taxi	Herb Albert + The Tijuana Brass 1965 song title / flashy, highly decorated automobile		
15 Med Bn	Triple Whiskey *	refers to .999 pure whiskey + serial # sequence		
15 Med Bn	Veto		aka "IRON LUNG"	
15 Trans Bn	Boom Boom #6	probable call-sign of Battalion C.O. who utilized this ship	nose panel survives, Al Schlim was gifted this item upon DEROS / Battalion C.O.'s ship	
15 Trans Bn	Herb's Retrievers	painted helo getting hoisted by mechanical hand		
15 Trans Bn	Tail Wind ^	painting of Little Annie Fanny of Playboy origin	nose cover survives, Al Schlim shipped it home	
17 AHC	Elusive Butterfly	Bob Lind's 1966 song title		
17 AHC	Hustler (The)	1961 Hollywood movie: Paul Newman+Jackie Gleason / dice + cards painted on door also		
17 AHC	Mercenary: You Pay We Slay (The)			
17 AHC	Provider (The)			
17 AHC	Silly Rabbit-Slicks Are For Kids	friendly in-unit rivalry		
17 AHC	Tater ^	C.O. of the 613 TC was a Fearless Fosdick lookalike and Tater was Fosdick's son's name		
18 CAC	Elizabeth Ann		CAC, "Green Delta" IV Corps, Can Tho, Command a/c	

Unit	Copter Name	Origin / Definition	Notes / Call Signs ( ) < >	Fate Aircraft / Crew
18 CAC	Orange Sunshine	slang for "LSD, acid"		
20 Eng Bde	Iron Butterfly	60's rock band by the same name	(Snoopy 25)	
20 TC	Alfred E. Neuman **	Alfred E. Neuman wearing red baseball cap sideways on head / Pipesmoke recovery slick	MAD magazine icon + slogan "What, Me Worry?" was counterpart to WWII's "Kilroy Was Here"	
20 TC	What ! Me Worry? **	painting of Alfred E. Neuman wearing red baseball cap sideways on head	Pipesmoke recovery slick	
21 Signal Group	California Dream'n	Mamas + Papas 1965 song title		
21 Signal Group	Easy Rider	COL Mattern's copter / Hollywood movie title	on display: Valiant Air Command Warbird Museum, Titusville, FL	
21 Signal Group	Flying Circus (The)		"RINGLEADER" on AC door, "CLOWN" on P door, "SIDESHOW" on gun mounts	
21 Signal Group	Helluvacopter			3-18-71: autorotated on beach, hooked out
21 Signal Group	Mothers Lil Worry	based on Ed Roth's "Mother's Worry" monster car		
33 TC	Goose (The)			
33 TC	Green Speckled Bird (The)	overall in-country touch-up paint job of 2 shades resembled a spotty skin	"TGSB" featured on the book cover of "Thunderbird Lounge" by author Bob Brandt / possible sn '150	
33 TC	Jelly Belly		"Thunderbird Lounge" book citation	
33 TC	Road Runner			
37 Sig Bn	Wendy		on display: Am Legion Post 957, New Berlin, PA	
39 Signal Bn	Goldfinger	James Bond movie reference	aka "PUSSY GALORE" on left pilot door	
39 Signal Bn	Pussy Galore	James Bond female adversary	aka "GOLDFINGER" painted on right pilot door	
45 Med Co	Alive + Kickin'		aka "KAREN"	
45 Med Co	Alive N' Kickin'		apparently the "N" replaced a previously documented "+" sometime during the life of this helicopter in this unit	
45 Med Co	Angel Of Mercy			DD 5-27-68: after Tibbetts transferred to another unit: Ken Rucker among KIA
45 Med Co	Auggie	CE SP4 Jackson originated name		DD 4-8-69
45 Med Co	Bac Si	Vietnamese for "doctor"		
45 Med Co	Band-Aid Special			
45 Med Co	Blood, Sweat + Tears	60's rock band by the same name		
45 Med Co	Body Snatcher (The)	Hollywood horror film		

Unit	Copter Name	Origin / Definition	Notes / Call Signs ( ) < >	Fate Aircraft / Crew
45 Med Co	Body Snatcher II (The)	Hollywood horror film		DD 4-30-70
45 Med Co	C. C. Rider	old blues song title		
45 Med Co	California Dreamin'	Mamas + Papas song title		
45 Med Co	Daisy Mae	cartoon character		
45 Med Co	Docter Copter	intentionally mis-spelled / Alan Matte suggested name	Clif Adams' father's WW II B-26 "SCRUMPTIOUS" pic in Gary Valant's book	
45 Med Co	Flower Power	Mark Kimm CE, Apr-Dec '68, originated name		May, 1969: hard landing, shipped to USA for repairs
45 Med Co	Foxy Lady	Jimmy Hendrix song title		
45 Med Co	Georgia Peach			
45 Med Co	Great Green Vaseline War Machine (The)	referred to sliding in + out of hot LZ's		
45 Med Co	Hell's Angel	notorious American motorcycle club		
45 Med Co	Hippo			
45 Med Co	Hover Lover I	Bill Mostek CE named it in 1968-69		
45 Med Co	Hover Lover II		nose section had combat damaged+replaced with "II" added	
45 Med Co	Iron Butterfly	60's rock band by the same name		
45 Med Co	Iron Butterfly II			
45 Med Co	Jefferson Airplane	1960's rock band name	2nd platoon	
45 Med Co	Jinx	named after Jinx Dawson, lead singer in the 60's rock band, The Coven	red painted kangaroo on stinger cover denoted Aussie support at Nui Dat / Army Reporter, 8-31-70, page 3 pic	
45 Med Co	Judge (The)			
45 Med Co	Kansas Bandit			
45 Med Co	Karen	name of Hall's girlfriend	aka "ALIVE + KICKIN'"	
45 Med Co	Lady			
45 Med Co	Lady Madona	artist mis-spelled Madonna / Bealtes song title		

U.S. ARMY HELICOPTER NAMES IN VIETNAM

Unit	Copter Name	Origin / Definition	Notes / Call Signs ( ) < >	Fate Aircraft / Crew
45 Med Co	Little Annie Fanny			
45 Med Co	Lucy In Da Sky	Beatles song title		
45 Med Co	Magnet Ass	reputation for drawing enemy fire		
45 Med Co	Magnet Ass	reputation for drawing enemy fire		
45 Med Co	Old Puta	Spanish for "old whore"		
45 Med Co	Patches			
45 Med Co	Pro's (The)			
45 Med Co	Quicksilver	Quicksilver Messenger rock band name		DD 1-14-70
45 Med Co	Quicksilver 2	Quicksilver Messenger rock band name		DD 2-5-69: all KIA: O. Poole AC, Will Hix CP, Jim McNish CE, Gary Johnson MD
45 Med Co	Red Baron (The)	Snoopy's WWI arch rival in the skies over France	(DO 13)	
45 Med Co	Sarcophagus		ordered removed because not PC	
45 Med Co	Soul Inspiration	Righteous Brothers 1966 song title	area of operation was War Zone C	
45 Med Co	Stump Jumper	sexual term		
45 Med Co	Sun King	Beatles song title		
45 Med Co	Wild Child	Doors song title / Ed Roth's custom monster car		DD 2-1-68
45 Med Co	Wild Child II	Doors song title / Ed Roth's custom monster car		
45 Med Co	Wild Child III	Doors song title / Ed Roth's custom monster car	4th platoon	
45 Med Co	Wild Child IV	Doors song title / Ed Roth's custom monster car	4th platoon	
45 Med Co	Winged Warrior			
45 Med Co	You Maul Em We Haul Em			
48 AHC	Advengers (The)	VN artist mis-spelling of Avengers		
48 AHC	American Woman	Guess Who song title		

Unit	Copter Name	Origin / Definition	Notes / Call Signs ( ) < >	Fate Aircraft / Crew
48 AHC	Assassins (The)			
48 AHC	Banshee			
48 AHC	Battlin Bitch			
48 AHC	Blood, Sweat + Tears	1960's rock band name		
48 AHC	Brother Love's Travelin' Salvation Show	Neil Diamond song title / named by Jerry Winchester CE	shares serial # with 176 AHC's "MEANS TO AN END" / nose cover survived, reunited with Lester in '71 USA	
48 AHC	Brotherhood (The)	name adopted from 1968 Kirk Douglas movie title?		
48 AHC	Charlie Chaser			
48 AHC	Death Dealer			
48 AHC	Devil's Delight			
48 AHC	Easy Rider	Hollywood movie title		
48 AHC	Eliminator			
48 AHC	Elvira	blue spider on nose + black spade on back		
48 AHC	Fate Is The Hunter	Ernest K. Gann's 1961 aviation book title + Hollywood film title	Al Meadows became the unit artist during his stint with the 48th	
48 AHC	Flower Power	60's counterculture slogan for non-violence		
48 AHC	Flyin' Coffin			
48 AHC	Ghost Ship (The) *	gunship landed back at base with all crew WIA and unable to exit aircraft		
48 AHC	God Of Hell Fire	Arthur Brown 1967 rock song lyrics		
48 AHC	Grace Slick	double entendre / female singer on the Jefferson Airplane rock band		
48 AHC	Grim Reaper			
48 AHC	Hell's Angel	notorious American motorcycle club		
48 AHC	Hungry For Blood			
48 AHC	Iron Butterfly	60's rock band by the same name		

Unit	Copter Name	Origin / Definition	Notes / Call Signs ( ) < >	Fate Aircraft / Crew
48 AHC	Kill For Peace			
48 AHC	Kommie Killers			
48 AHC	Marquis De Sade			
48 AHC	Murder Inc			
48 AHC	Old Dog	bad paint job	currently: N879AH, Abbatare Inc, Arlington, WA	
48 AHC	Patches *			
48 AHC	People Stopper		shares serial # with 118th's "SUZY Q"	DD 10-30-69: all KIA
48 AHC	Red Ball Express			
48 AHC	Rosemary's Baby	Hollywood horror film title		
48 AHC	Snoopy ^			
48 AHC	Triple Nickel *	refers to 5-5-5 sequence in serial #		
48 AHC	Wildest Deuce		brought home avionics nose panel from 67-17388	
48 AHC	Zap You're Sterile			
50 Med Det	Di-Di	"hurry up" in Vietnamese		
53 Avn Det	Birth Control		better known as GUNS-A-GO-GO	DD 2-22-68
53 Avn Det	Cost Of Living	better known as "Guns A-Go-Go"	forward crown insignia preserved at Ft. Rucker Army Avn Museum	DD 5-5-67
53 Avn Det	Crazy 8		later became "COST OF LIVING"	
53 Avn Det	Easy Money		better known as GUNS-A-GO-GO / restored 5-1-00	
53 Avn Det	Guns A-Go-Go *	"Birth Control," "Cost of Living," "Crazy 8," "Easy Money," "Stump Jumper," "Widow Maker"	world's largest military gunship: serial #'s: 64-13145, 64-13149, 64-13151, 64-13154	
53 Avn Det	Stump Jumper	sexual term	better known as GUNS-A-GO-GO	DD 8-5-66
53 Avn Det	Widow Maker		early name reportedly attached to one of the GUNS-A-GO-GO gunships	
54 Med Det	Armageddon's Child			

Unit	Copter Name	Origin / Definition	Notes / Call Signs ( ) < >	Fate Aircraft / Crew
54 Med Det	Blood, Sweat + Tears	1960's rock band name		
54 Med Det	Just Married	groom + bride flying limo	CW2 Don Sewell + CPT Patricia Mann wedding limo / MAJ Pat Brady was Best Man	
54 Med Det	Nancy Lee	first + middle name of Brady's wife	Congressional Medal of Honor for 1-6-68 mission	
54 Med Det	Tired Angel		Wolak's 178th hook slinged it out / Mendez was 1/6 Inf grunt	
56 TC	Bad News!	painting of pregnant female in bikini		
56 TC	Knight Train	named after Emmett Knight		
56 TC	Rice Paddy Daddy		aka "GOOD NATURE" on nose / assigned to the 120 Avn Co ?? according to Miller	
56 TC	Spirit Of Gettysburg (The)		attached to 120 AHC ?	
56 TC	Wooly Bully	Sam The Sham + The Pharaohs song title		
56 TC	You Crash + Call We Dash + Haul ^/^^		"Good Nature" is callsign / aka "RICE PADDY DADDY" / re: VHPA book Emmett Knight bio pg 259	
57 AHC	Alfred E. Neuman **	painted MAD magazine iconic facial expression	MAD magazine icon + slogan "What, Me Worry?" was counterpart to WWII's "Kilroy Was Here"	DD 1-10-68: by sapper
57 AHC	American Flag **			
57 AHC	Bunny Bird **	heads of 2 bunnies + Playboy female	Playboy bunny logo on vertical stabilizer / also American flag on tail cap	
57 AHC	Captain America	comic book character		
57 AHC	Cherry Buster	no longer a virgin		
57 AHC	Cougar's Revenge ^		nighthawk gunship	
57 AHC	Glass Onion	Beatles song title	huge 214th Cougar painted on nose also	
57 AHC	Gotterdammerung	"twilight of the gods"	aka "REVENGE" aka "COUGAR'S REVENGE"	
57 AHC	Hawaii			
57 AHC	Hawaiian Punch	popular flavored drink		
57 AHC	House Of Pain (The)		Mercury automobile cougar logo on nose: red, gray + black	
57 AHC	Iron Butterfly		Mercury automobile cougar logo on nose: red, gray + black	

Unit	Copter Name	Origin / Definition	Notes / Call Signs ( ) < >	Fate Aircraft / Crew
57 AHC	Kill A Kommie For Christ			
57 AHC	Magnet Ass	reputation for drawing enemy fire		
57 AHC	Mellow Yellow	Donovan song title		
57 AHC	My Marie			
57 AHC	Mystery Ship	part of the 1970 "Ride Captain Ride" lyrics by The Blues Image / sailing galleon painted on nose	"ARE YOU WONDERING" also on nose	
57 AHC	Porky Revenge			
57 AHC	Porky The Pig			
57 AHC	Proud Mary	Creedence Clearwater Revival song title	Mercury automobile cougar logo on nose: red, gray + black	
57 AHC	Pusher Man (The)	Steppenwolf song title	Mercury automobile cougar logo on nose: red, gray + black	
57 AHC	Revenge	"GOTTERDAMMERUNG" (twilight of the gods) painted on nose also	"TEAM COUGAR" nose graphic also	
57 AHC	Revenge II		nighthawk ship	
57 AHC	Sat Cong	"kill VC"	large ace of spades painted on nose also	
57 AHC	Satan's Playpen			
57 AHC	Suzie Creamcheese	Frank Zappa's fictional female musical character on music albums		
57 AHC	Traveling Excutioner (The)			
57 AHC	What! Me Worry? **	painted Alfred E. Neuman face on doorpost	MAD magazine icon + slogan "What, Me Worry?" was counterpart to WWII's "Kilroy Was Here"	victim of sapper attack at Kontum 1-10-68
57 AHC	Witch Doctor ^	native with bone-in-the-nose depicted	on display: Willow Run Airport, Detroit, MI	
57 AHC	Witch Doctor Recovery ^		Frigstad was Service Platoon Leader	
57 Med Det	Alive N' Kickin'			
57 Med Det	Alive N' Kickin' II			
57 Med Det	Patty Ann		"white elephant" paint job	
57 Med Det	Sun Shine	sunburst painting with nn enclosed		

Unit	Copter Name	Origin / Definition	Notes / Call Signs ( ) < >	Fate Aircraft / Crew
57 TC	Born To Raise Hell		aka "THE GOOSE"	
57 TC	Chattanooga Choo-Choo	popular song title		
57 TC	Cherry Boy	slang meaning "virgin"		
57 TC	Cherry Girl	slang meaning "virgin"		
57 TC	Chicken Runner			
57 TC	Combattre Chien	"dog fighter"		
57 TC	Goose (The)		aka "BORN TO RAISE HELL"	
57 TC	Hedge Hopper (The)			
57 TC	Hedge Hopper 2			
57 TC	La Paloma	"the dove"		
57 TC	Loose Goose		on display: Mid Atlantic Air Museum, Reading, PA	
57 TC	Lucky 13		aka "PIASECKI'S PRACTICAL JOKE"	
57 TC	Piasecki's Practical Joke	Piasecki was helicopter aviation pioneer	aka "LUCKY 13"	
57 TC	Rebel Rouser	1958 Duane Eddy song title		
57 TC	Sexy			
57 TC	Taxpayer's Regret			
57 TC	Teddi Bare			
57 TC	Tiki	good luck symbol		
57 TC	Tiki #2	CE was Hawaiian / good luck symbol	bright yellow-orange painting of tiki	
57 TC	Wimps			
60 AHC	Bull Frog			
61 AHC	Fujimo	"fuck you jack, i'm moving on"		

Unit	Copter Name	Origin / Definition	Notes / Call Signs ( ) < >	Fate Aircraft / Crew
61 AHC	Good The Bad And The Ugly (The)	Clint Eastwood Western movie title		
61 AHC	Good Times		artwork on nose? or unit insignia	
61 AHC	Pig Slayer	bar-b-q of killed wild pig prompted nn on door by anonymous artist	lasted 3 days: ordered removed by MP's	
61 AHC	So Cal	Welsh was a USC alumni, Southern California		
61 AHC	Think I Care	Snoopy laying atop his doghouse		
62 Avn Co	WETSU ^^	"we eat this shit up" / painted gator carrying a toolbox also	alternate definition: "we endeavor to strive utmost" provided by Workman	
62 CAC	Lucky Joker		heart painted on nose re: they supported 24 Corps	
62 CAC	Mad Hatter			
62 CAC	Miss America	commemorate May, 1969 visit by Miss America	"MISS AMERICA" painted on nose of chosen Huey	
62 CAC	Raging Main	reference to King Neptune and his domain	large painted heart on copter nose = they supported 24 Corps / GEN Wheeler was frequent passenger	
62 CAC	Red Baron	nn is c-sign of COL Hixon of 24 Corps Arty		
62 CAC	Red Leg		white heart on nose also	
68 AHC	Assassin (The)			
68 AHC	Birth Control			
68 AHC	Bitch (The)	named after ex-wife		DD 9-13-66
68 AHC	Black Widow (The)	spider + web painted on nose	"THE GREEK" painted on Kanakaris crew door	DD 4-13-66: all KIA
68 AHC	Broken Bull	named after maintenance officer's breeding bull who could not perform		
68 AHC	Canuck			
68 AHC	Colt 45	name referred to 45 caliber Army issue handgun		shot down December 1966
68 AHC	Devil's Disciple (The)	American motorcycle club / 1959 Burt Lancaster film of same name		
68 AHC	Every Man A Tiger ^^	tiger head painted on copter nose also	currently: Army Transportation Museum, Ft. Eustis, VA or Fireland's Museum of Military History, Norwalk, OH	
68 AHC	Fuck The Cong			

Unit	Copter Name	Origin / Definition	Notes / Call Signs ( ) < >	Fate Aircraft / Crew
68 AHC	Grim Reaper	two sets of serial #'s (65-09487+66-00653) may reflect two UH-1C "GRIM REAPER(s)" during '67	aka "SAT CONG" painted on belly / equipped with 40mm "pooper" grenade launcher on gunship nose	
68 AHC	Ho Chi Sucks		suffered same fate as "SAT CONG" and was ordered to remove politically incorrect graffiti	shot down July 1967
68 AHC	Linda K (The)	name of WO Paul Hill's wife		DD 8-18-68: by RPG, 20 days after D. Green DEROS'd / Hill KIA in different ship
68 AHC	Sat Cong	"kill VC" / aka "GRIM REAPER"	ordered to remove "SAT CONG" after over-flying the "cardboard Pentagon" - Long Binh Army hdqs	
68 AHC	Smokey Tail	smoke ship		
68 AHC	Southern Comfort	American bourbon whiskey		
68 AHC	Top Tiger Tail ^	nude female figure painted on nose	special permission granted to unit by top brass to carry this artwork on one particular ship	
68 AHC	War Wagon (The)	John Wayne 1967 movie		
68 AHC	Widow Maker (The)	UH-1B: this was the original "WIDOW MAKER" in the 68 AHC, serial # unkown	equipped with 40mm "pooper" grenade launcher on gunship nose	
68 AHC	Widow Maker (The)	UH-1C: this was the unit's 2nd "WIDOW MAKER"	equipped with 40mm "pooper" grenade launcher on gunship nose / DeVerennes was 118 AHC member	
68 AHC	Wild Thing	1966 song title of same name by The Troggs		
68 Avn Co	How Do We Look?	painting of human figure with it's head up his ass		
68 Avn Co	Phoenix	"immortal bird" / Jimmy Stewart 1965 Hollywood film		DD 1966: loss in Mekong River
68 Avn Co	Pineapple Princess		UTT = 68 Avn Co 8-15-64 / then 197 AHC 3-1-65	
68 Med Det	Good The Bad And The Ugly (The)	Clint Eastwood Western movie title		
68 Med Det	Grateful Dead	San Francisco rock group		
68 Med Det	Great Speckled Bird (The)	Don Wildsmith originated name		
68 Med Det	Grim Reaper (The)			
68 Med Det	Impossible Dream			
68 Med Det	Last Hope			
68 Med Det	Patriot			
71 AHC	4 More Shooting Days Til Xmas			

Unit	Copter Name	Origin / Definition	Notes / Call Signs ( ) < >	Fate Aircraft / Crew
71 AHC	Anka	Greek word for "peace"	<19>	
71 AHC	Aquarius	wife's astrological sign / 5th Dimension song title		
71 AHC	Boot (The)	boot wearing snake crushing VC combatant		
71 AHC	Chicken Heart			
71 AHC	Great Hunter			
71 AHC	Head Hunter		May '68, '021 became H model	
71 AHC	Maggot Wagon (The) *	mission memory of ARVN KIA's recovery		
71 AHC	Peace On Earth Or Else	Christmas season greeting	"MERRY CHRISTMAS" painted on cargo door window / late 1966 A-501 was re-designated the 71 AHC	
71 AHC	Smokey	unit Smoke ship		
71 AHC	Snake Doctor ^	adopted name of the maintenance platoon's aircraft that imitated the 71st's RATTLERS callsign	Ken Shiner provided serial #	
71 AHC	Snake Doctor ^	adopted name of the maintenance platoon's aircraft that imitated the 71st's RATTLERS callsign	Tom Bokkes donated saved nose panel to 71st Assn	
71 AHC	Two Bits Minus Five	refers to serial #		
71 AHC	When You Care Enough To Send The Very Best	Hallmark cards motto	"attached to A-501, later 71 AHC, as SNAKE DOCTOR"	
81 TC	? (question mark)	question mark on fuselage referred to absence of female name due to unmarried status		
81 TC	Baby Hewey	mis-spelling of Huey / CE was cartoon HUEY lookalike	CE painted "BABY HEWEY" on fuselage / C.O. subsequently ordered removal of all unofficial markings	
81 TC	Carol		originally 81 TC, became the 119 Avn Co in 1963	
81 TC	Juanita	wife's name reportedly		
81 TC	Liz	wife's name reportedly		
81 TC	Lois	wife's name reportedly		
81 TC	Marion Spook	wife's name reportedly		
82 Med Det	Blood, Sweat + Tears	1960's rock band name		
82 Med Det	Day Tripper	Beatles song title		

Unit	Copter Name	Origin / Definition	Notes / Call Signs ( ) < >	Fate Aircraft / Crew
82 Med Det	Day Tripper II	Beatles song title		
82 Med Det	Dr. Know	name is parody of "Dr. No", a James Bond film		
82 Med Det	Dr. Strangelove	Peter Seller's 1964 Hollywood film of same name	observed on TV's Military Channel featuring this very helicopter	
82 Med Det	Exterminator	lettering styled after Gahan Wilson's cartoon as featured in Playboy magazine		
82 Med Det	Ghost Rider (The)			
82 Med Det	Hawaii Kai	"beautiful Hawaii"		
82 Med Det	Queen			
82 Med Det	Shadow (The)			
92 AHC	Ali Baba	"AMF" painted on copter belly: "adios mother fucker"		
92 AHC	AMF	AMF = "adios mother fucker"	aka "ALI BABA"	
92 AHC	Bad Moon		Nighthawk ship: Zeon light + mini-gun	DD 1970: by sapper
92 AHC	Balls Three *	refers to 0-0-3 sequence in serial #		
92 AHC	Born Free	song + movie title	map of the USA painted on nose also	
92 AHC	Born Free II	song + movie title		
92 AHC	Born Free III	song + movie title		DD 2-24-68: Devore, Brooks, Ross, Ozbun: KIA on '460
92 AHC	Budweiser	"BUDWEISER" beer can label replicated on rocket pods	Chinnery book: CE Pete Peterson painted Bud rocket pod	
92 AHC	Cheap Thrills	Janis Joplin album title	(SK 8)	
92 AHC	Coors	"COORS" beer can label replicated on rocket pod		DD 9-7-69
92 AHC	Dragnet	TV detective show		
92 AHC	Evil Ways	Santana song title	(SK 8)	
92 AHC	FTA	"Fu*k The Army" or "Fun, Travel, Adventure"		
92 AHC	Goodship Lollipop (The)	also Shirley Temple song title		
92 AHC	Iron Butterfly	60's rock band by the same name		

Unit	Copter Name	Origin / Definition	Notes / Call Signs ( ) < >	Fate Aircraft / Crew
92 AHC	It's Clobberin' Time	comic book character's battle cry		
92 AHC	Jefferson Airplane (The)	1960's rock band	was "WHIRLAWAY" in the states prior to VN	
92 AHC	Love			10-27-68: KIA's on '504: Ackerman, Mullins, Head, Bray: "LOVE" still on nose late '68?
92 AHC	Mexican Express (The)	large sombrero on nose would later be replicated on a 174 AHC UH-1C in '70 painted + crewed by Albert Garza, who originated both names	scoreboard on left doorpost with 17 stenciled VC stick figures	
92 AHC	Night Mare	painting of a red Pegasus with lightning shooting out of its nose	painted all black, flew night missions only	
92 AHC	Old Bastard D *	last D model in 92nd + lethargic	worn-out + under-powered / Stallion Lead ship	
92 AHC	Raven (The)		(SK 7)	
92 AHC	Rebel		(SK 4)	
92 AHC	Strawberry Alarm Clock (The)	rock band name		
92 AHC	Surrealistic Pillow (The)	1967 Jefferson Airplane album title		Tet 1968: sapper attack victim
92 AHC	Tootsie Roll			
92 AHC	Valhalla	"Viking warrior heaven"	in-country commemorative plaque sold on EBAY / (SK 6)	
92 AHC	Warlord (The)	1965 Charlton Heston movie of same name	possibly 66-15106 / (SK 10)	
92 AHC	Warlord (The)	1965 Charlton Heston movie of same name		
92 AHC	Yosemite Sam **	animated cartoon character		
93 TC	Boneyard Special (The)			
93 TC	Droopy			
93 TC	Fred's Flying Fool			
93 TC	Fulton's Folly	paddle-wheeler painted near name		
93 TC	Same Same Spears The Monkey	gorilla painted on fuselage lampooned Spears hairy body		
114 AHC	Ace Of Spades			
114 AHC	Alice In Wonderland		currently: N807SB, Phoenix, AZ / (WK 8)	
114 AHC	Ancient Age	popular Bourbon brand		

Unit	Copter Name	Origin / Definition	Notes / Call Signs ( ) < >	Fate Aircraft / Crew
114 AHC	Anna Marie		(RK 8)	
114 AHC	Avenger		(CB 8)	
114 AHC	Beach Boy			
114 AHC	Beats Walkin			
114 AHC	Blue Ass Buzzard	title of 1967 Playboy magazine article / gunship tail painted blue		
114 AHC	Blue Max (The)	foreign military award		
114 AHC	Blue Max (The)	foreign military award		
114 AHC	Brat (The)		currently: N62767, Richland, WA / (RK 7)	
114 AHC	Bug	painting of lightning bug holding .50 cal machine gun	flare-bug ship	
114 AHC	Cheap Charlie	referred to a downtown Vinh Long shop keeper		
114 AHC	Checkmate			
114 AHC	Chicago Transit		aka "KARLA"	
114 AHC	Chuck Crusher		shares serial # with "HUNGRY II" / (CB 4)	
114 AHC	Chuck Crusher II		aka "COBRAS KILL" on M-3 rocket box / (CB 2, 4)	
114 AHC	Cobra Lead ^		aka "HOGHEAD" / (CB 5)	
114 AHC	Cobra Surprise		borrowed ship from A-7-1 + had it outfitted with flares	
114 AHC	Cobra's Kill		aka "CHUCK CRUSHER II" on pilot door / (CB 2, 4)	
114 AHC	Color Me Death	parody of "Color Me Barbara" (Streisand) '66 album title		
114 AHC	Comanche			
114 AHC	Cosa Nostra	"mafia"	aka "THE KISS OF DEATHS"	
114 AHC	Death American Style	name is parody of TV's "Love American Style " show	shares serial # with "THE FLYING JACKASS"	
114 AHC	Death Rides A White Horse			

U.S. ARMY HELICOPTER NAMES IN VIETNAM

Unit	Copter Name	Origin / Definition	Notes / Call Signs ( ) < >	Fate Aircraft / Crew
114 AHC	Death's Little Angel			
114 AHC	Delta Sweetheart			
114 AHC	Delta Yank	114th's C.O.'s ship / named in response to 175th's C.O.'s ship the "THE DELTA REBEL"		
114 AHC	Devil's Disciple	American motorcycle club / 1959 Burt Lancaster film of same name	shares serial # with "SHIP OF FOOLS"	
114 AHC	Dial L	aka "DIAL LIQUIDATOR" / parody of "Dial M For Murder" Hitchcock movie	aka "LIQUIDATOR" / (CB 7)	
114 AHC	Eve Of Destruction (The)	Barry McGuire song title	(CB 1)	
114 AHC	Fat Albert *	20mm weapon / fictional character created by Bill Cosby		
114 AHC	Flying Coffin (The)		aka "MISTER LONELY"	
114 AHC	Flying Fool			
114 AHC	Flying Jackass (The)		shares serial # with "DEATH AMERICAN STYLE"	
114 AHC	For A Few Dollars More	Clint Eastwood movie title	aka "IRON BUTTERFLY III" / smoke ship also at one time	
114 AHC	George Of The Jungle	1967 animated TV series spoofing the Tarzan character		
114 AHC	Georgia Boy			
114 AHC	Ghost Writer			
114 AHC	Gold Knight **	C. O.'s ship / unit emblem emblazoned in gold paint		
114 AHC	Grim Reaper (The)	flying skull painted on doorpost also		
114 AHC	Guns + Ammo	firearms magazine of same name		
114 AHC	Hangar Queen *	propensity for needing excessive repairs / wore crown in hangar until repaired		
114 AHC	Hoghead	OJ + Vodka drink: "had to be in trim to drink it" (Maurice Worm CE)	aka "COBRA LEAD" / (CB 5)	
114 AHC	Hoghead II		aka "COBRA LEAD" / (CB 5 Lead)	
114 AHC	Hungry	Gosnell originated name	(CB 4)	
114 AHC	Hungry II		shares serial # with "CHUCK CRUSHER" / (CB 4)	
114 AHC	Iron Butterfly (The)	60's rock band by the same name	shares serial # with "THE PERSUADER"	
114 AHC	Iron Butterfly II	60's rock band by the same name	nose panel ended up at London auction house in 1996 / purchaser was John Conway, VHPA museum curator	

Unit	Copter Name	Origin / Definition	Notes / Call Signs ( ) < >	Fate Aircraft / Crew
114 AHC	Iron Butterfly II	60's rock band by the same name		
114 AHC	Iron Butterfly III	60's rock band by the same name	aka "FOR A FEW DOLLARS MORE" / smoke ship also at one time	
114 AHC	Kamaaina	"old timer" in Hawaiian / Hawaiian CE named it		
114 AHC	Karla		aka "CHICAGO TRANSIT"	
114 AHC	Kelly Sue			
114 AHC	King Cobra		currently: N400SD / (CB 5)	
114 AHC	King Cobra	Schrumpf CE named it late '66	(CB 5)	
114 AHC	King Cobra		Confederate flag painted on tail cone / (CB 32)	
114 AHC	Kiss Of Death (The)	mafia term	aka "COSA NOSTRA"	
114 AHC	Lightning Bolt			
114 AHC	Lil Jinx			
114 AHC	Lindy	name of Stanis' girlfriend	currently: N366SD, State Dept, Patrick AFB, FL	
114 AHC	Liquidator		aka "DIAL L" / (CB 7)	
114 AHC	Little Cobra	Jan + Dean song title		
114 AHC	Little Eve			
114 AHC	Lonely Bull (The)	Tijuana Brass song title		
114 AHC	Lynda Sue		aka "WHITE ON WHITE"	
114 AHC	Mabel	name of Bailey Jones' wife		
114 AHC	Macabre			
114 AHC	Maui Girl	Hawaiian CE named it		
114 AHC	Midge		currently: N1564F, Skyline Exploration, SLC, UT / (WK 4)	
114 AHC	Miss Arlene			

Unit	Copter Name	Origin / Definition	Notes / Call Signs ( ) < >	Fate Aircraft / Crew
114 AHC	Miss Fit	1st Red Knight to have "name" painted on copter, '65-'66	currently: N98F, Logan Co Fire Dept, WV/ Hollywood movie appearances: Under Siege, The Rock, Die Hard, China Beach, Outbreak / (RK 3)	Night Hawk missions also with .50 cal + Xeon lite
114 AHC	Miss Lou	VN secretary's name ?	(WK 3)	
114 AHC	Miss Susan	name of Scott's daughter	(WK 7)	
114 AHC	Mister Lonely	Bobby Vinton's 1964 hit song of same title	shares serial # with "THE FLYING COFFIN"	
114 AHC	Moe's Meatwagon			
114 AHC	Mr. Bojangles	Nitty Gritty Dirt Band song title		
114 AHC	Mr. Bojangles	Nitty Gritty Dirt Band song title		
114 AHC	Mr. Lucky	TV detective show	(LC 1)	
114 AHC	Olive Drab Taxicab			
114 AHC	Orange Onion			
114 AHC	Patches *	numerous bullet holes		
114 AHC	Patty	name of Rupcic's wife		4-6-65: all crew KIA
114 AHC	Persuader (The)		shares serial # with "IRON BUTTERFLY"	
114 AHC	Pineapple Princess	Hawaiian CE named it	(WK 7)	
114 AHC	Polack Power			
114 AHC	Princess Anne			
114 AHC	Princess Suzanne			
114 AHC	Quiet One (The)	famous American documentary film title		
114 AHC	Rag I	derogatory term for excessive need for repairs		
114 AHC	Rag III	derogatory term for excessive need for repairs		
114 AHC	Rebel	Rebel flag on nose panel + cargo door panel / CE from South Carolina	crossed swords also on cargo door panel / (RK 3)	DD 1-21-65
114 AHC	Rebel (The)		(RK 7)	12-30-64: Winowitch KIA with UTT / 68 Avn Co
114 AHC	Road Runner ^		currently: N50023, Americas, GA	

Unit	Copter Name	Origin / Definition	Notes / Call Signs ( ) < >	Fate Aircraft / Crew
114 AHC	Road Service ^			
114 AHC	Road Service II ^			
114 AHC	Road Service III ^			
114 AHC	Road Service IV ^		the last Road Service ship for 114 AHC / "IV" not included on copter nose	
114 AHC	Runnin Scared			
114 AHC	Sexy Snake		(CB 2)	
114 AHC	Shaky Eight *	couldn't eliminate bad one-to-one vibration		
114 AHC	Ship Of Fools	Doors song title	shares serial # with "DEVILS DISCIPLE"	
114 AHC	Shirley Lou	name of Duerr's wife		
114 AHC	Sleepy Slope		aka "SUZIE Q"	
114 AHC	Slope Toter	derogatory term for VC	a/c restoration project, Floyd Bennett Field, NY in 2003	
114 AHC	Soul Survivor	1967 rock group by same name		
114 AHC	Speckled Pecker	double entendre		
114 AHC	Sudden Death			
114 AHC	Super Snake *			
114 AHC	Suzie Q	classic rock-n-roll standard	aka "SLEEPY SLOPE"	
114 AHC	Tangellary Smoth	was a made-up name		
114 AHC	Tiki Fly Hawaiian Little Jet		currently: N841M, Hendrickson Flying Service, Rochelle, IL	
114 AHC	Tombstone Shadow	Creedence Clearwater Revival 1969 song title		
114 AHC	VC Birth Control			
114 AHC	Village Stompers		(CB 2)	
114 AHC	Vinh Long MTA You Call We Haul			

Unit	Copter Name	Origin / Definition	Notes / Call Signs ( ) < >	Fate Aircraft / Crew
114 AHC	Waleare Cadillac			
114 AHC	Walrus (The)	refers to Beatles song title "I Am The Walrus"		
114 AHC	War Eagle			
114 AHC	We Live To Kill VC For Lunch Bunch		flare-bug ship	
114 AHC	Whiskey 1			
114 AHC	Widow Maker			
116 AHC	Adkinson's Reb Raiders	Mike Adkinson was AC / rebel flag painted on door also		
116 AHC	Bee Keeper ^	adopted name of the maintenance platoon's aircraft that imitated the 116th's HORNETS callsign	"HORNET 8" pilot door	
116 AHC	Bee Keeper ^	adopted name of the maintenance platoon's aircraft that imitated the 116th's HORNETS callsign		
116 AHC	Big Daddy	famous funny car artist Ed Roth's nickname	20mm cannon slung under belly	
116 AHC	Big Leroy		hog gunship	
116 AHC	Blind Faith	1960's rock group name		
116 AHC	California Flash			
116 AHC	Carolina Kid			
116 AHC	Cathy's Clown	Everly Brothers song title		
116 AHC	Earth Wind + Fire	1960's rock band name		
116 AHC	Electric Ladyland	Jimmy Hendrix 1968 album title		
116 AHC	Elvira			
116 AHC	Elvira II			
116 AHC	Exhibit A			
116 AHC	Flaming Mime		"Hornet C + C" painted on pilot door also	
116 AHC	Foxy Lady	Jimmy Hendrix song title		
116 AHC	Foxy Lady II	Jimmy Hendrix song title		
116 AHC	Free Huey	tie-in with Huey Newton (60's activist) in jail?		
116 AHC	Frito Bandito	cartoon mascot for Fritos Corn Chips	story in VETERANS magazine Sept '07, pgs 62-63	DD 8-7-70
116 AHC	Frito Bandito II	Garcia is of Mexican descent		DD 8-7-70: original "FRITO BANDITO"

Unit	Copter Name	Origin / Definition	Notes / Call Signs ( ) < >	Fate Aircraft / Crew
116 AHC	Gidy-Up Go			
116 AHC	Good Vibrations	"rode like a short-legged pony at a trot"		
116 AHC	Here Comes The Judge	TV's Laugh-In refrain	Dave Nancarrow: possible sn was 66-00729 / currently: Patriots Point Naval Maritime Museum, Mt. Pleasant, SC	10-1-68: Ken Plavcan KIA as DG on "THE JUDGE"
116 AHC	Hurdy Gurdy Man	Donovan song title	painted yellow flower also on pilot door	
116 AHC	In A Gadda Da Vida	1960's rock band Iron Butterfly song title		
116 AHC	In A Gadda Da Vida	1960's rock band Iron Butterfly song title	Mendez was a B/1/6 grunt that rode on nn slick / can't read the nn in pic but caption says it was there	
116 AHC	Iron Butterfly	1960's rock band name		
116 AHC	It Takes Two			
116 AHC	King Bee ^		VIP ship / aka "SUPER BEE"	
116 AHC	King Frog			
116 AHC	Lady Jane	Rolling Stone's 1966 song title of same name		
116 AHC	Little Twister		photo depicts ship in damaged condition	
116 AHC	Love			
116 AHC	Magic Carpet Ride	Steppenwolf song title		
116 AHC	Miss Carriage	double entendre		
116 AHC	Nasty			
116 AHC	Old Magnet Ass		currently: N9214X, U.S. Border Patrol, El Paso, TX	
116 AHC	Paddy Wagon	"Irish conveyance"	pic caption reads "PADDY WAGON" / partial view of nickname "…GON" on cargo door	
116 AHC	Paper Tiger			
116 AHC	Problem Child	electrical system problems prompted name		
116 AHC	Proud Mary	Creedence Clearwater Revival song title		
116 AHC	Revasegen	tornado that Pecos Bill rode according to folklore		

Unit	Copter Name	Origin / Definition	Notes / Call Signs ( ) < >	Fate Aircraft / Crew
116 AHC	Sexy Sadie	Beatles song title		
116 AHC	Sleezee Dee	"DEE" meant 'D' model Huey		
116 AHC	Smokey	smoke ship		
116 AHC	Snoopy **	painting of Snoopy without lettering		
116 AHC	Spirit In The Sky	Norman Greenbaum 1969 song title		
116 AHC	Super Bee ^	VIP ship	aka "KING BEE"	
116 AHC	Suzie Creamcheese	Frank Zappa's fictional female musical character on musical albums		DD 4-1-71: KIA, Jim Highsmith
116 AHC	Teacher (The)			
116 AHC	Top Cat			
116 AHC	True Grit	John Wayne movie title		
116 AHC	Voodoo Child	1968 Jimmy Hendrix song title of same name		
116 AHC	Wild Thing	fire breathing dragon painted on pilot door		
117 AHC	Aimless Lady	Grand Funk Railroad song title	engine change May '71 became UH-1M / yellow lemon painted on chicken plate / (SW 1)	
117 AHC	American Woman	Guess Who song title	Behm had dream night before that turned out true / T. Stansbury played bit part in" Midnite Cowboy" film	9-30-71: all crew KIA
117 AHC	Aquarian Effort	"collaborative effort for important change"		
117 AHC	Bad Lady			
117 AHC	Barking Dog *	pilot tagged this name onto ship because "it was old and tired"		
117 AHC	Beantown Bandit (The) *	Vogel was Boston native		
117 AHC	California Dreamin'	Mamas + Papas 1965 song title		
117 AHC	Cassie	named for Scales' girlfriend	aka "RIGHT ON"	
117 AHC	Cat Ballou	1965 Hollywood movie title		
117 AHC	Chicago II	rock band Chicago album title / Goodwin was from Chicago suburb	currently: N30111, Indianapolis, IN	
117 AHC	Chi-Town Hustler	named after funny car of the era / Goodwin was from Chicago suburb		
117 AHC	Coffin (The)			

Unit	Copter Name	Origin / Definition	Notes / Call Signs ( ) < >	Fate Aircraft / Crew
117 AHC	Comin' On Strong			
117 AHC	Country Boy			
117 AHC	Death's Orgasm		(SW 4)	DD 9-30-71: I KIA
117 AHC	Devil Or Angel	CE painted name on nose / 1963 Bobby Vee song	<9>	
117 AHC	Diana			
117 AHC	Dirty D			
117 AHC	El Toro			
117 AHC	Evil Woman	Black Sabbath song title		
117 AHC	Fighting Fifth	booze bottle graphic		
117 AHC	Flying Scotsman (The)	London to Edinburgh train name		
117 AHC	Foreign Aid	visiting General ordered name be removed		
117 AHC	Friday's Child	Nancy Sinatra 1966 song title		
117 AHC	Full House		painted on .50 caliber external covering	
117 AHC	Good Ship Lollipop (The)	previous CE painted this name		
117 AHC	Hawk Eye			
117 AHC	Heavy		aka "STUMP JUMPER"	
117 AHC	Huey			
117 AHC	Hunter (The)		became 155 AHC gunship wearing same nose art nn	
117 AHC	Jinx (The)			
117 AHC	Jumbo	named after 747 jumbo jet	survived VN: unknown to Aeilts was stationed 2 miles from his home for over 15 yrs	
117 AHC	Karin	name of CE's wife	aka "STOGIE 6" on pilot door	
117 AHC	Kiss Of Death			

Unit	Copter Name	Origin / Definition	Notes / Call Signs ( ) < >	Fate Aircraft / Crew
117 AHC	Lil Sue			
117 AHC	Little Annie Fanny III	1st artwork of the "LITTLE ANNIE FANNY"		
117 AHC	Little J.C.			
117 AHC	Master Panther	was possible AC callsign on nose		
117 AHC	Mean Mistreater	Grand Funk Railroad song title		
117 AHC	Miss Kristy			DD 12-21-71
117 AHC	Miss Mamolani (sp?)			
117 AHC	Motown	Alleger was Detroit native	rebuilt D model into H model / aka "PUSSY GALORE"	
117 AHC	Mystery Ship	part of the 1970 "Ride Captain Ride" lyrics by The Blues Image / sailing galleon painted on nose		
117 AHC	On The Prowl			
117 AHC	Panthan Panther	Panthan: meant "path" in Sanskrit	lead helo in 2nd platoon	
117 AHC	Paranoid	Black Sabbath song title		
117 AHC	Patchwork Cat			
117 AHC	Pig Pen	Peanut's cartoon character		
117 AHC	Pig Pen II		was original "PIG PEN" destroyed?	
117 AHC	Pink Panther **	painted Pink Panther of Hollywood movie fame		
117 AHC	Pink Pussy			
117 AHC	Pure Hell	funny car artist Ed Roth's VN War decal quotation		
117 AHC	Pure Sex		aka "VILLAGE……"	
117 AHC	Pussy Galore	James Bond female adversary	aka "MOTOWN" / rebuilt D model into H model / shares serial # with 335 AHC's "SLOOPY GAL"	
117 AHC	Rabbit (The)			
117 AHC	Right On	Ken Scales replaced "GOODSHIP LOLLIPOP" name when he became CE	aka "CASSIE" painted on cargo door: Scales girlfriend's name	

Unit	Copter Name	Origin / Definition	Notes / Call Signs ( ) < >	Fate Aircraft / Crew
117 AHC	Rita Ann		currently: N408KC, USDA Forest Service, Bakersfield, CA	
117 AHC	Roadrunner **		Mano was DG on "ROADRUNNER" till stand-down, March '72	
117 AHC	Slick Chick 1	painted blond female on nose also	(SW 3)	
117 AHC	Society's Child	1966 Janis Ian song title	aka "STANDBY AGAIN"	
117 AHC	Spirit			
117 AHC	Standby Again		aka "SOCIETY'S CHILD"	
117 AHC	Stump Jumper	Little Annie Fanny graphic on nose / sexual term	aka "HEAVY"	
117 AHC	Susie	named after girlfriend, now wife of 44 yrs		
117 AHC	Susie	name of Gallegos' girlfriend		DD 3-21-66
117 AHC	Sweet Barbara			
117 AHC	Thumper	named after girlfriend, now wife of 43 years		
117 AHC	Top Cat		animated TV series in 1960's	
117 AHC	Traveling Executioner (The)			
117 AHC	Unclaimed Light Ship			
117 AHC	Warrior (The)			
117 AHC	Warwagon	John Wayne 1967 movie of same name		
117 AHC	Wild Willie's Taxi	"WILLIE" referred to CPT Charles E. Williams AC		DD 10-31-67
117 AHC	Woody		<6>	
117 AHC	You Burp We Hurt			
117 AHC	You Hoot We Shoot			
117 AHC	Zip Zapper	"zip" was a derogatory term to describe the enemy		
118 AHC	Archangel (The)		(Blue 8)	
118 AHC	Arleen's Clown	name of Alley's girlfriend	(Blue 4)	

Unit	Copter Name	Origin / Definition	Notes / Call Signs ( ) < >	Fate Aircraft / Crew
118 AHC	Assassin (The)			
118 AHC	Avenger			
118 AHC	Avenger II		was original "AVENGER" destroyed?	
118 AHC	Avenger III		was "AVENGER II" destroyed? / (Bandit 6)	
118 AHC	Bird Watcher ^	adopted name of the maintenance platoon's aircraft that imitated the 118th's THUNDERBIRDS callsign		
118 AHC	Bird Watcher	adopted name of the maintenance platoon's aircraft that imitated the 118th's THUNDERBIRDS callsign		
118 AHC	Bird Watcher ^	adopted name of the maintenance platoon's aircraft that imitated the 118th's THUNDERBIRDS callsign		
118 AHC	Birth Control		(Bandit 5)	
118 AHC	Cathy's Clown	named for CE's girlfriend / Everly Brothers tune		
118 AHC	Cheap Thrills	Janis Joplin album title	<9>	
118 AHC	Color Me Death	parody of "Color Me Barbara" (Streisand) 1966 album title	(Bandit 8)	
118 AHC	Death Trap		Chip Austin was assigned to the 25th Div Shotgunner program, Apr-Sept 1965	
118 AHC	El Devastator		aka "BIG DEUCE" / (Bandit 2)	
118 AHC	Executioner		<4>	
118 AHC	Fabulous Blue 7 (The) *	2nd platoon slick, #7, blue signifier		
118 AHC	Kitten	pet name for Tromatter's wife	(Blue 2)	
118 AHC	Kitten II		on display: VN Vets Nat'l Memorial, Angel Fire, NM / (Blue 3)	
118 AHC	Lady Samantha			
118 AHC	Load Master ^			
118 AHC	Loadmaster ^			
118 AHC	Mary Jane	slang for marijuana		
118 AHC	Miss Mini	operated two mini guns on board	"KILL" painted on belly of gunship / (Bandit 3)	4-20-69: Creal KIA on "MISS MINI"

Unit	Copter Name	Origin / Definition	Notes / Call Signs ( ) < >	Fate Aircraft / Crew
118 AHC	Only 21 Killin Days Till X-mas	Christmas of 1970		
118 AHC	Pacification		540 rotor system + C model tail boom / (Bandit 6)	
118 AHC	Pappy's Pooper	referred to former M-5 turret which was no longer attached to copter nose	(Bandit 6)	
118 AHC	Patches		(Blue 4)	
118 AHC	Pete			
118 AHC	Pollution IV ^	smoke ship callsign	"PIV" had 2nd platoon assignment / (Blue 4)	
118 AHC	Prince Of Darkness			
118 AHC	Quicksilver	AC was fan of Quicksilver Messenger Service rock group	"RED FOX" painted on nose refers to AC callsign + being redheaded / (Red Tail 11)	
118 AHC	Sat Cong	"kill VC"		
118 AHC	Sharon	name of Hansen's girlfriend	(Red 8)	
118 AHC	Suzy Q	name for Matheny's girlfriend + future wife / popular rock tune	shares serial # with 48th's "PEOPLE STOPPER" / still married 40+ yrs	
118 AHC	Suzy Q II	name for Matheny's girlfriend + future wife / popular rock tune	still married 40+ years / (Blue 7)	DD 1-17-67
118 AHC	Swamp Fox IV		<4>	
118 AHC	Tinker Toy			
118 AHC	Tootsie Roll			
118 AHC	Widow Maker			
118 AHC	Wind Watcher ^			
119 AHC	UC VC No C	iconic "Kilroy Was Here" figure with eyes peering over a fence		
119 AHC	Baby Huey	powerful but self destructive cartoon character		
119 AHC	Bad News			
119 AHC	Birth Control			
119 AHC	Bloody Mary			

Unit	Copter Name	Origin / Definition	Notes / Call Signs ( ) < >	Fate Aircraft / Crew
119 AHC	Boo-Boo-A-Go-Go			
119 AHC	Boo-Boo-A-Go-Go II		Pilat inherited ship from Scalf	
119 AHC	Boxcars *	twelve in serial # prompted name		
119 AHC	California Dreamer	Corbin was from California	Corbin temporarily crewed a different helo on 9-2-67	DD 9-2-6: KIA's: Jim Bosley AC + Jim Daniels CP / CE + DG survived crash
119 AHC	Double Nothing *	two zeroes in serial # prompted name	no personal markings policy enforced during tour	
119 AHC	Dutch			
119 AHC	Gator Recovery ^			
119 AHC	Good Vibrations	Beach Boys song title		
119 AHC	Grace			
119 AHC	Gypsy Moth	"destructive pest"	(GT 13)	
119 AHC	Hi Fi	Fidencio Ramirez aka Hi-Fi	aka "SWEET IRENE" painted below "HI FI" also	
119 AHC	Lucky 13	copter last 3 serial #'s add up to = 13 / also 13 letters in AC + CE names	black cat image painted on copter nose also / 2nd "LUCKY 13" was 66-16751	
119 AHC	Mad Irishman (The)			
119 AHC	Margarita Naomie			
119 AHC	Miss Lucky 7	pair of dice showing 3 + 4 on nose also	shot down 4 times previously so figured new call # of Croc 7 might just help survive VN / (Croc 7)	
119 AHC	Muttering Death (The)			
119 AHC	My Joy	Joy was Wright's wife's name	Wright was platoon leader / (Lead)	
119 AHC	Old Smokey	referred to the puffs of smoke after engine was shut-down		
119 AHC	Papa Gator	C.O.'s ship	C + C also ?	
119 AHC	Snookie's T-Bone	"SNOOKIE" was girlfriend's nn + "T-BONE" was CE's nn	painted above CE's seat	
119 AHC	Swamp Rat - Gator Recovery			
119 AHC	Sweet Irene	Fidencio Ramirez aka Hi-Fi	aka "HI FI" painted above "SWEET IRENE" also	

Unit	Copter Name	Origin / Definition	Notes / Call Signs ( ) < >	Fate Aircraft / Crew
119 AHC	T.W.A	"T.W.A" = "TEENIE WEENIE AIRLINES" / goofy looking baby duck wearing diaper / '707 in serial # reference		
119 AHC	Teenie Weenie Airlines	"TEENIE WEENIE AIRLINES" = "T.W.A" / goofy looking baby duck wearing diaper / serial # '707 reference		
119 AHC	Traumatic Experience		the day after crew was ordered to remove nn "cherry" ship was shot down	DD 11-21-68
119 AHC	Von Zipper's Express	name reportedly is reference to pilot's nickname		
119 AHC	Widow Maker ^	"Widow Makers" was callsign		
120 AHC	Charlie's Chow	painted boar-hog riding a rocket and from its mouth "SAY AH"	Avn News, Nov 20-Dec 3, 1981, pgs 4-7	
120 AHC	Dean Fixer ^	adopted name of the maintenance platoon's aircraft that imitated the 120th's DEANS callsign		
120 AHC	Eliminator			
120 AHC	High Freak	refers to high frequency vibration in the tail rotor pedals but could never solve it		
120 AHC	Mean Mother Fucker			
120 AHC	Sat Cong	"kill VC"		
121 AHC	Alfred E. Neuman **	painted MAD magazine iconic face + slogan	MAD magazine icon + slogan "What, Me Worry?" was counterpart to WWII's "Kilroy Was Here"	
121 AHC	Andy Capp	British comic strip character	aka "BUZZ OFF"	
121 AHC	Arfunt Annie II	Hawaiian CE pronunciation of "orphan"	was there a previous 121st gunship named "ARFUNT ANNIE"?	
121 AHC	Beer Bullets + Blood		White Agent sprayer / "BEER, BULLETS + BLOOD" = "bia vien dan huyet" in Vietnamese	
121 AHC	Blitz Krieg			
121 AHC	Born Free	1966 song + movie title		
121 AHC	Buzz Off	British comic strip Andy Capp retort	aka "ANDY CAPP"	
121 AHC	Cannibal (The)			
121 AHC	Charriot (The)	mis-spelling of Chariot / Snoopy in armed chariot pulled by 2 tigers	avionics cover saved and shipped home by Ray Burke / (Tiger 22)	
121 AHC	Cherry Buster	no longer a virgin	aka "THUMPER" / WW II plane of CE's father's had "CHERRY BUSTER" also / <36>	
121 AHC	Cutlass Mandir (The)	religious sword		

Unit	Copter Name	Origin / Definition	Notes / Call Signs ( ) < >	Fate Aircraft / Crew
121 AHC	Devastator			
121 AHC	Dike Runner Beep Beep	Roadrunner graphic painted on nose		
121 AHC	Double Trouble	2 blonde women holding weapons	ordered to remove painted image from copter nose	
121 AHC	Georgia Peach (The)	Roy Amerson was a Georgia boy		
121 AHC	Good Widow Mrs. Jones (The)	art copied from June '64 Vargas Playboy issue	transferred avionics door to '733 on 7-2-68 / former DELTA 6 bird	DD 7-2-68
121 AHC	Good Widow Mrs. Jones (The)	art copied from June '64 Vargas Playboy issue	after April '69 crash nose art panel was retired ; upon DEROS Rick Thomas states that item was stolen from luggage during processing at Long Binh	
121 AHC	Gutless Wonder (The)			
121 AHC	Harvy			
121 AHC	Hawkeye	caricature painting of a hawk wearing sneakers		
121 AHC	Honey Bucket (The)	little yellow house on nose / porta potty		
121 AHC	Honey Wells	female pop singer		
121 AHC	Huey Fury	yellow rose painted on nose	aka "THE YELLOW ROSE OF TX" painted on nose also	
121 AHC	In Crowd (The)			
121 AHC	Incredible Hulk (The)	painting of green "HULK" character on nose		
121 AHC	Indefatigable Beaky Buzzard (The)	animated cartoon character	nose art panel transferred to another ship on 7-11-68	DD 7-11-66
121 AHC	Janci's Flyin' Lion	painting of lion with M-60 wearing rotors in-flight	C.O.'s ship? / "BAY SU TU" ("fly + shoot") painted below lion	
121 AHC	Kaptain Klutz	superhero comic book character		
121 AHC	Lamont's Lament	name of Vaille's wife	Cunningham inherited ship + name from Vaille / aka "SUPER SLICK"	
121 AHC	Little Toons	shares serial # with "VIKING SURPRISE" and "KITTEN II" of the 118th	on display: VN Vets Nat'l Memorial, Angel Fire, NM	
121 AHC	Mad Tom		aka "WHITE TIGER LEAD"	
121 AHC	Magnolia State	Huffman was Mississippi native	Mississippi State flag painted on nose / aka "MISSISSIPPI STATE FLAG" / (Blue Tiger 4)	7-23-66: crashed, sent back to USA for repairs
121 AHC	Mississippi State Flag	Huffman was Mississippi native	aka "MAGNOLIA STATE" / (Blue 4)	7-23-66: crashed, sent back to USA for repair

Unit	Copter Name	Origin / Definition	Notes / Call Signs ( ) < >	Fate Aircraft / Crew
121 AHC	New World Famous Wrecker			
121 AHC	Nobody's Darling			
121 AHC	Paddy Runner	rice paddy		2-9-68: crashed, all aboard KIA
121 AHC	Peg Of My Heart		aka "WHITE TIGER LEAD"	
121 AHC	Puff The Magic Dragon	Peter, Paul + Mary song title / origin of nn is the spelling of CE's last name Puffenbarger	painting of a dragon on nose / previously was "SCRAP IRON"	
121 AHC	Pussy Galore's Flying Circus	James Bond's female adversary		
121 AHC	Rat Fink	mouse figure also on nose 'RF' / famous funny car artist Ed Roth's creation logo		
121 AHC	Scrap Iron	name painted on copter nose after an accident	aka "PUFF'S MAGIC DRAGON"	
121 AHC	Smokey			
121 AHC	Snoopy I			
121 AHC	Strawberry Babe	was originally named "STRAWBERRY BITCH"	Elke Sommer image on 2nd similar nose panel ?	
121 AHC	Strawberry Bitch	infamous WW II bomber name / Shakocius suggested name / Elke Sommers Dec '67 image Playboy mag	Lammers tasked with del + p/u panel from downtown artist / nose panel accompanied Fleming back to USA	later changed to "STRAWBERRY BABE" ?
121 AHC	Thumper	40mm canon + two 19 shot rocket pods	aka "CHERRY BUSTER" / <36>	
121 AHC	Tiger Lady		2nd "T.S." was 67-10129	
121 AHC	Tiger Surprise ^	large "TS" painted on nose	1st was '980 / 2nd 67-10129 / Stars + Stripes article 8-19-70	4-2-70: 4 KIA: Coffman, Silva, Skuza, Vaspory
121 AHC	Tin Bin (The)			
121 AHC	Valhalla Messenger		heavy hog	
121 AHC	Vi Vicious		aka "V V"	
121 AHC	Viking Delight		aka "VD"	
121 AHC	Viking Queen (The)			
121 AHC	Viking Queen II (The)	painting on hell hole plate of Viking female holding large size ammo	was original "VIKING QUEEN" destroyed?	
121 AHC	Viking Surprise	firefly-lightship for off-base missions / "VS" painted on pilot's door	Jerry Daly was highly decorated pilot in Delta / on display: VN Vets Nat'l Memorial, Angel Fire, NM	smoke ship on Easter Sunday, 1968

Unit	Copter Name	Origin / Definition	Notes / Call Signs ( ) < >	Fate Aircraft / Crew
121 AHC	War Wagon (The)	John Wayne 1967 movie		
121 AHC	We Buy US Bonds			
121 AHC	What ! Me Worry?	painted Alfred E. Neuman face on nose panel	MAD magazine icon + slogan "What, Me Worry?" was counterpart to WWII's "Kilroy Was Here"	
121 AHC	White Tiger Lead ^		aka "PEG OF MY HEART"	
121 AHC	Wrecker		also painted on pilot door: "80 Trans Det-Wrecker Service-Open 24 Hours-Phone 415-Don't Cuss-Call Us"	
121 AHC	Wrecker ^			
121 AHC	Yankee Peddler			
121 AHC	Yellow Rose Of Texas (The)	yellow rose painted on nose / popular folk song	aka "HUEY FURY" painted on nose also / 1,000th Huey produced: naming contest = "YELLOW ROSE OF TX" was appropo since the Bell plant was located in TX	
128 AHC	Alfi	Dionne Warwick song title		
128 AHC	All American Frog **	red-white-blue painted turret	chunker + door mounted minigun	
128 AHC	Billy The Kid	Old West outlaw	crossed revolvers on rear access doors	
128 AHC	Bits + Pieces	Dave Clark Five 1964 song title by same name / parts cannibalized for other ships while sitting in hangar for 2 months		
128 AHC	Bonita			
128 AHC	California Dreamin'	Mamas + Papas 1965 song title	shares serial # with "TIAJUANA TAXI"	
128 AHC	Cherry Boy	slang for virgin	2 cherries, stems + leaves painted also	
128 AHC	Cisco Kid	painted crossed revolvers also		
128 AHC	Double Ought Duce *	"IMP": Ewing's pet name (little devil) for girl friend	aka "IMP"	
128 AHC	Elusive Butterfly (The)	1966 Bob Lind song lyrics to "Butterfly of Love"		
128 AHC	Feelin' Groovy	The Rascals rock group song title		
128 AHC	First American (The) *	DG+CE both Navajo Indians+Tomahawks platoon	aka "MUSHROOM MOLLY" after 4-3-71	
128 AHC	Geronimo			
128 AHC	Grey Ghost	referred to COL John Mosby, American Civil War hero / CE named it as he was from the South / copter painted all gray		

Unit	Copter Name	Origin / Definition	Notes / Call Signs ( ) < >	Fate Aircraft / Crew
128 AHC	Gun Slick (The) *	McDonald originated name	slick's firing power included forward pointing M-60's / setup never used against combat targets	
128 AHC	Gunsmoke	unit smoke ship		
128 AHC	Have Guns Will Travel			
128 AHC	Igor		'088 + '742 both carried this name	
128 AHC	Igor		'088 + '742 both carried this name	
128 AHC	IMP	Ewing's pet name (little devil) for girl friend	aka "DOUBLE OUGHT DUCE"	
128 AHC	Iron Horse			
128 AHC	Little Leroy		painted nn on minigun gun-mount	
128 AHC	Little Wolf		Tomahawk on nose	
128 AHC	Mushroom Molly *	Cu Chi area known as "mushroom"	aka "THE FIRST AMERICAN" / "MOLLY" didn't refer to any particular female, merely generic	
128 AHC	Only You Can Prevent Charlie	Smokey the Bear trademark profile painted on quarter access panel	iconic Smokey the Bear face graphic painted on quarter panel / aka "Smokey" verbal nickname	
128 AHC	Pancho Villa			
128 AHC	Penny Lane	Beatles song title		
128 AHC	Preparation H	hemorrhoid cream		
128 AHC	REMF	"rear echelon mother fucker"		
128 AHC	Smokey The Bear ***	painted partial full name / In-flight pic doesn't show it	shares serial # with "SMOKEY III" 11 Avn Bn / on display: Smithsonian NASM Udvar-Hazy Ctr, Chantilly, VA	
128 AHC	Sopwith Camel	Snoopy's chosen fighter plane in his many duels with the Red Baron over WW I France	blurb in unit newsletter "Smoke Sticker", dated 7-19-67, page 2, written by Jim Mann, Editor	
128 AHC	Stumper	former slick red-x'd from landing on a tree stump in LZ / replacement had nn	painted on pilot door by CE	
128 AHC	Super Jew (The) **			
128 AHC	Super Loach *			
128 AHC	Tears Of Fire		on display: VFW Post 545, Beverly, MA	
128 AHC	Tiajuana Taxi	mis-spelling of Tijuana / Herb Albert + The Tijuana Brass 1965 song title / flashy, highly decorated automobile	shares serial # with "CALIFORNIA DREAMIN'"	
128 AHC	Witch Doctor ^		utilized as a C+C ship also	
128 AHC	Witch Doctor II ^			

Unit	Copter Name	Origin / Definition	Notes / Call Signs ( ) < >	Fate Aircraft / Crew
128 AHC	Witchdoctor III ^			
128 AHC	Witchdoctor IV ^			
128 AHC	Witchdoctor V ^			
128 AHC	Witchdoctor VI ^			
128 AHC	Witchdoctor VII ^			
128 AHC	Witchdoctor VIII ^			
129 AHC	#1	"#1" meant that it was the best (VN lingo)		DD 6-13-69
129 AHC	Big Gun			
129 AHC	Bite + Strike ^^			
129 AHC	Captain America	comic book character		
129 AHC	Carol	wife's name		
129 AHC	Carol Ann		on display: VFW Post 7166, South Hill, VA	
129 AHC	Chicken Wagon			
129 AHC	Crater Creator	arced lettering across nose / unit #'s on pilot door	heavy hog gunship / Reeves was a 335 TC helo mechanic	
129 AHC	Death Destruction			
129 AHC	Executioner (The)			
129 AHC	Free And Easy	referred to 1969's Crosby, Stills + Nash song lyrics in "WOODEN SHIPS"		
129 AHC	God Is My Co-Pilot	referred to 1944's Robert Scott aviation biography	big brother-Zig Zag man graphic also	
129 AHC	Have Guns Will Travel	TV Western referrence		
129 AHC	Herd		<3>	DD 4-23-67: KIA's: Walker, Wells
129 AHC	Hog Of Steel	underground comic reference to WONDER WARTHOG?	currently: N5448, Lee CO Mosquito Control, Ft. Meyers, FL	
129 AHC	In Limbo			
129 AHC	Iron Butterfly (The)	1960's rock band by the same name	currently: N3013R, Robinson Air Crane, Opalocka, FL	

Unit	Copter Name	Origin / Definition	Notes / Call Signs ( ) < >	Fate Aircraft / Crew
129 AHC	Judge (The)		Korean artist painted "THE FUDGE" by mistake	
129 AHC	Jury (The)			
129 AHC	Keep On Truck'n	Granny Twitchett character painted on nose	shares serial # with "SNOW SNAKE"+335's "TACO WAGON"	UH-1H 69-15559 had same nose art cover during '72-'73
129 AHC	Miss Jo			
129 AHC	New Yorker (The)			
129 AHC	Ol' Hedge Trimmer			
129 AHC	Phantom (The) **	painting of skull + crossbones with fangs dripping blood	was also his personal callsign / nn	
129 AHC	Play Boy	"BITE N STRIKE" above the Bulldog	renamed "WAR PIG" by Wolf	
129 AHC	Poppasan			
129 AHC	Rubber Duck *	not allowed to paint name on ship, so had scarves imprinted with a duck	Foster was CE on "TIGER WAGON" also, Jun-Jul-Aug '71	
129 AHC	Snow Snake ^	adopted name of the maintenance platoon's aircraft that imitated the 129th's KING COBRAS callsign		'740 shot down north of Pleiku / transferred nose art cover to '910
129 AHC	Snow Snake	adopted name of the maintenance platoon's aircraft that imitated the 129th's KING COBRAS callsign	shares serial # with "KEEP ON TRUCKIN"+335's "TACO WAGON"	'740 shot down north of Pleiku / transferred nose art cover to '910
129 AHC	Super Rag	repeated visits to maintenance for parts earned nn		
129 AHC	Thor	"THOR" was callsign of unidentified pilot	"MICKEY MOUSE" painted on cargo door: CE nickname	
129 AHC	Tiger Wagon **	ROK flying duties	Assigned to fly Commanding Gen of the Korean Tiger Div	
129 AHC	Tiger Wagon **	ROK flying duties	Assigned to fly Commanding Gen of the Korean Tiger Div	
129 AHC	War Pig		aka "PLAY BOY"	
129 AHC	War Wagon	John Wayne 1967 movie		
129 AHC	War Witch			
131 SAC	Irish Eagle (The)		aka "IRON SPUD": call sign name for 131 SAC (Surveillance Airplane Co)	
131 SAC	Iron Spud ^	"IRON SPUD" is 131 SAC's (Surveillance Airplane Co) call-sign	aka "THE IRISH EAGLE"	
132 ASHC	Banshee		shares serial # with "THE UNDERTAKER" / converted to CH-47D, 88-00082	

Unit	Copter Name	Origin / Definition	Notes / Call Signs ( ) < >	Fate Aircraft / Crew
132 ASHC	Big Mac			
132 ASHC	Boony Bus	fanciful painted yellow bus with tandem rotors	Taglauer A-4-77 observed this colorful ship land / converted to CH-47D, 87-00114	Wadginski was shot down in this ship
132 ASHC	Cherry Picker	sexual term	converted to CH-47D, 87-00073	
132 ASHC	Easy Rider	painting of Peter Fonda riding a souped-up Stingray bicycle / Hollywood movie title	shares serial # with "FOXY LADY" / converted to CH-47D, 83-24115	
132 ASHC	Filthy Few	American motorcycle club self designation	converted to CH-47D, 86-01637	
132 ASHC	Foxy Lady	Jimmy Hendrix song title	aka "EASY RIDER", "PATCHES" / converted to CH-47D, 83-24115	
132 ASHC	Frito Bandito	cartoon mascot for Fritos Corn Chips	converted to CH-47D, 88-00080	
132 ASHC	Good Grief	painted Charlie Brown cartoon character		
132 ASHC	Good Ship Lollipop (The)	three colorful balloons painted below nn		
132 ASHC	Good Vibrations	Beach Boys song title	converted to CH-47D, 86-01637	
132 ASHC	Goofy **	Disney character painted on fuselage	converted to CH-47D, 88-00064	
132 ASHC	Granny Goose	painting of an old lady	converted to CH-47D, 87-00077	
132 ASHC	Here Comes Da Judge	TV's Laugh-In refrain		
132 ASHC	Lady Godiva **	nude female with flowing hair riding a white horse	shares serial # with "NITEMARE"	
132 ASHC	Marauder	painted knight welding a lance	converted to CH-47D, 88-00071	
132 ASHC	Miss Carriage	painting of a young female / double entendre	converted to CH-47D, 86-01652	
132 ASHC	Nitemare	original artist sketching of a flying horse (NITEMARE) + later painted on '449 still survives	shares serial # with "LADY GODIVA"	DD 2-27-71: shot down in Laos
132 ASHC	Patches	mission story + name origin news article in THE FALCON, 16 CAG newsletter, 11-15-68, pg 6	aka "FOXY LADY", "EASY RIDER" / converted to CH-47D, 88-00079	
132 ASHC	Proud Mary	Creedence Clearwater Revival song title	converted to CH-47D, 86-01652	
132 ASHC	Raggedy Ann	painted female monstrosity	converted to CH-47D, 83-24102	
132 ASHC	Snoopy	Snoopy riding his doghouse firing mounted machine guns	converted to CH-47D, 87-00085	
132 ASHC	Three Quarter Whore	referred to serial #	converted to CH-47D, 86-01669	
132 ASHC	Undertaker (The)		shares serial # with "BANSHEE" / converted to CH-47D, 88-00082	
132 ASHC	Virgin Hunter (The)	2 versions: devil only and Indian removing stuck arrow from female figure		collided with a Chinook during Lam Sam 719 at Phu Bai, no KIA's

Unit	Copter Name	Origin / Definition	Notes / Call Signs ( ) < >	Fate Aircraft / Crew
132 ASHC	Zeppelin			DD 3-17-70: all KIA
132 ASHC	Zeppelin II		converted to CH-47D, 86-01672	
134 AHC	11th Commandment (The)			
134 AHC	AlJan			
134 AHC	Birth Control		"PILLS" transcribed on M-5 turret / on display: Army Avn Museum, Ft. Rucker, AL	DD 1-1-70: CE KIA (not Berg)
134 AHC	Bits N Pieces	Dave Clark Five song title	currently: N2417U, David Abreu Vineyard Mgt, Rutherford, CA	
134 AHC	Blood, Sweat And Lead			
134 AHC	Bubbles		"HAVE GUN WILL TRAVEL" painted on brass catcher bags on both door guns	
134 AHC	Color Me Peace	Color Me Barbara (Streisand) 1966 album parody		
134 AHC	D. J.	"da judge" ?		
134 AHC	Daddy Rabbit			
134 AHC	Devil's Disciple	American motorcycle club / 1959 Burt Lancaster film of same name		
134 AHC	Fat Albert	obese character created by comedian Bill Cosby	aka "SOUL OF THE DEMONS"	
134 AHC	Foxey Lady	Jimmy Hendrix song title	aka "TRIPLE DEUCE"	
134 AHC	Gloria	name of Torres' girlfriend / now married 40 yrs		
134 AHC	God Of Hell Fire	Arthur Brown 1967 rock song lyrics		
134 AHC	Good Vibrations	Beach Boys song title		
134 AHC	Grunt's Angel			
134 AHC	Have Gun Will Travel	TV Western		
134 AHC	Ho Che	VN workers nn'd Nat because his eyes made him look like Ho Chi Minh	shares serial # with "PHILLY DOG" / aka "THE REBEL" by Harold Shonk, CE, '67 (verbal nn)	
134 AHC	Hot Stuff		shares serial # with 191 AHC's "MOTHER GOOSE" / on display: USS Intrepid, Sea-Air-Space Museum, NY	
134 AHC	Iron Butterfly	1960's rock band name	aka "VENGEANCE"	

Unit	Copter Name	Origin / Definition	Notes / Call Signs ( ) < >	Fate Aircraft / Crew
134 AHC	Light My Fire	Doors song title		
134 AHC	Linda			
134 AHC	Little Linda	comic book character		
134 AHC	Little Lu Lu	comic book character		
134 AHC	Lucky Lady			
134 AHC	Luger Wagon			
134 AHC	Mary Jane	slang for marijuana		
134 AHC	Mother's Grief			
134 AHC	Mother's Worry	based on Ed Roth's "Mother's Worry" monster car		
134 AHC	My Michelle	Beatles song title		
134 AHC	Nuts, Bolts + Safety Wire			
134 AHC	Patches			
134 AHC	Philly Dog		shares serial # with "HO CHE"	
134 AHC	Piecemaker			
134 AHC	Pure Hell	funny car artist Ed Roth's VN War decal quotation		
134 AHC	Pusher Man (The)	Steppenwolf song title	currently: N385SD, US Dept of State, Patrick AFB, FL	
134 AHC	Rebel Devil (The)			
134 AHC	Rosemary's Baby	Hollywood horror film title		
134 AHC	Sally			
134 AHC	Satan's Image			
134 AHC	Satan's Pride			
134 AHC	Screamin Demon		'6' painted on nose also	

Unit	Copter Name	Origin / Definition	Notes / Call Signs ( ) < >	Fate Aircraft / Crew
134 AHC	She Devil		frog configuration / chunker / on display: VVA Chapter 451, Baltimore, MD	
134 AHC	Sick-Lo-Girl	"bicycle driven taxi"		
134 AHC	Soul Of The Demons		aka "FAT ALBERT"	
134 AHC	Spirit In The Sky	Norman Greenbaum 1969 song title	currently: N7247L, FBI, Wash DC	
134 AHC	Spooky	Classics IV song title		
134 AHC	Sudden Death			
134 AHC	Triple Deuce *	refers to 2-2-2 sequence in serial #	aka "FOXY LADY"	
134 AHC	Triple Nickel *	refers to 5-5-5 sequence in serial #	C.O.'s ship	
134 AHC	Vengeance		aka "IRON BUTTERFLY"	
134 AHC	Warlock			
134 AHC	Widow Maker	Pointer named her		
135 AHC	American Woman	Guess Who song title	rocket pods+tailboom tip painted in stars + stripes aka US flag	
135 AHC	Angel Baby			
135 AHC	Bismarck (The)			
135 AHC	Bonnie	name of Joe Ralph's wife		
135 AHC	Boss's Hoss (The)		VHCMA newsletter #61 cover pic / caption	
135 AHC	Boss's Hoss II (The)			
135 AHC	California Dreamin'	Mamas + Papas 1965 song title		
135 AHC	Death From Above		aka "GRACE SLICK"	DD 11-14-71
135 AHC	Freedom Bird *	tail # '747 = commercial airliner / any passenger plane headed for USA		
135 AHC	God Of Hell Fire	Arthur Brown 1967 rock song lyrics	Mike Guard is the 2008 author of "In The Sanctity of the Snake Pit"	
135 AHC	Grace Slick	slick = UH-1 troop carrier + Jefferson Airplane's female singer's name Grace Slick	aka "DEATH FROM ABOVE"	DD 11-14-71

Unit	Copter Name	Origin / Definition	Notes / Call Signs ( ) < >	Fate Aircraft / Crew
135 AHC	Grim Reaper			
135 AHC	Grunt	"infantryman, foot soldier"	painted flowers on nose also	
135 AHC	Iron Butterfly	1960's rock band by the same name	(Taipan 19)	
135 AHC	Karen's Carriage			
135 AHC	Miss Judy		on display: Wheeler AAF, Wahiawa, HI	
135 AHC	Proud Mary	Creedence Clearwater Revival song title	"TAIPAN 31" painted on pilot door / (Taipan 31)	
135 AHC	Smokey	smoke ship		
135 AHC	Sock It To 'Em Snoopy	Snoopy riding his doghouse firing mounted machine guns		
135 AHC	Taking Care Of Business *	refers to The Supremes song title: "Taking Care of Business" / aka "TCB"	on display: Battleship Cove, Fall River, MA	
135 AHC	TCB	refers to The Supremes song title: "Taking Care of Business" / aka "TAKING CARE OF BUSINESS"	on display: Battleship Cove, Fall River, MA	
135 AHC	Texas Flag **	Texas flag painted on nose		
135 AHC	Tupelo Mississippi Flash			
135 AHC	Vung Tau Express			
145 Airlift Plt	Miss Oklahoma	Griffin was from Oklahoma	at time of pic was 145 Airlift Plt / later became 281st / on display: Frontiers of Flight Museum, Love Field, Dallas, TX	
145 Airlift Plt	Three A's (The)			
145 CAB	Old Warrior III ^	unit name / Battalion Operations' ship		
145 CAB	Old Warrior VI ^	unit name / Battalion C.O.'s ship		
147 ASHC	Biere 33 Export	VN beer		
147 ASHC	Big Zilch		photographed aboard naval tender USS Corpus Christi Bay	
147 ASHC	Buzzards	painted buzzard sitting on branch		
147 ASHC	C Ration Sall			
147 ASHC	Calif		aka "THE CALIFORNIA GENERAL" / hippie general painting also	

Unit	Copter Name	Origin / Definition	Notes / Call Signs ( ) < >	Fate Aircraft / Crew
147 ASHC	California General (The) **	aka "CALIF" / hippie general painting also		
147 ASHC	Dry Place Dry Time			
147 ASHC	Flying Conex (The)	conex = large metal military storage container		
147 ASHC	Flying Leak *	"propensity for excessive leaks"	same enlisted crew for "HEUY'S BREAKFAST OF CHAMPIONS"	
147 ASHC	Goldfinger **	'007 sn + James Bond movie reference		captured by NVA 1975
147 ASHC	Gook Stomper		busted cherry graphic referred to first recorded bullet hole / "13 Nov 1966" date painted above cherry	
147 ASHC	Green Dragon		converted to CH-47D, 86-01656	
147 ASHC	Happy Hippie	nice artwork of happy Chinook reacting to LSD	converted to CH-47D, 86-01647	
147 ASHC	Heuy's Breakfast Of Champions	parody of Wheaties cereal		
147 ASHC	Iron Butterfly			DD 6-15-87
147 ASHC	Nancy			DD 3-23-75
147 ASHC	Phigtin' Pig			
147 ASHC	Pink Pussy	painting of Pink Panther-like character also		
147 ASHC	Pray		Operation Junction City participant	
147 ASHC	Pray For Piece			
147 ASHC	Pugnacious Porker	Mel Miller originated name	converted to CH-47D, 90-00183	
147 ASHC	Queenie	painting of female in bikini		
147 ASHC	Rebel (The) **	painting of Confederate soldier running with Rebel flag	previously assigned to 213 ASHC from '66-early '68	DD 11-9-73
147 ASHC	Snoopy's Place			
147 ASHC	Sweet Thing			
147 ASHC	Triple Nickel *	refers to 5-5-5 sequence in serial #	became 174 AHC's "IRON CROSS" in 1970	survived the war thru Dec, 1975
155 AHC	Ares		aka" LUKE" / 2nd gunship named "ARES"	

U.S. ARMY HELICOPTER NAMES IN VIETNAM

Unit	Copter Name	Origin / Definition	Notes / Call Signs ( ) < >	Fate Aircraft / Crew
155 AHC	Baby Jo	came from B/229 with name "BABY JO" on nose		
155 AHC	California Beachboy (The)			
155 AHC	California Beachboy II (The)		was original "CALIFORNIA BEACHBOY" destroyed?	
155 AHC	California Dreamer			
155 AHC	Devil Or Angel			
155 AHC	Devil Or Angel II			
155 AHC	El Bandit-O			
155 AHC	Exterminator (The)			DD 1-30-68: 1st day of Tet
155 AHC	Grim Reaper		aka "RIGORMORTIS"	
155 AHC	Grunt	slang for "infantryman, foot soldier"		
155 AHC	Hunter (The)		previously 117 AHC gunship wearing same nose art nn	
155 AHC	Hustler			
155 AHC	Ivan The Terrible		on display: Camp Robinson, Little Rock, AR	
155 AHC	Lil Ivan			
155 AHC	Lil Rita			
155 AHC	Little Puff		64-13546 UH-1D, 10/66-2/67 possible?	
155 AHC	Luke		aka "ARES"	
155 AHC	Olds	Oldsmobile car	Meadows painted name on nose / Meadows was unit artist: helmets, signs, etc	
155 AHC	Over Sexed		F. Tiner + L. Tiner were twin brothers	
155 AHC	Petunia			
155 AHC	Psychedelic Sex			
155 AHC	Psychodelic Death	intentional mis-spelling of "Psychedelic"	very colorful nose art !!	

Unit	Copter Name	Origin / Definition	Notes / Call Signs ( ) < >	Fate Aircraft / Crew
155 AHC	Ride A Slick To Hell + Back ^^		1st platoon motto painted on all 1st platoon slicks	
155 AHC	Rigormortis		aka "GRIM REAPER"	
155 AHC	Stagecoach Wrecker ^			
155 AHC	Sugar Pops Pete	breakfast cereal mascot		
155 AHC	Sweet Jean			
155 AHC	Thor		possibly 66-00731	crashed at Duc Lap
155 AHC	Ulysses			
155 AHC	Vagabonds Of The Sky		currently: N378SD, US Dept of State, Patrick AFB, FL	
155 AHC	Vulture (The) ^	adopted name of the maintenance platoon's aircraft that imitated the 155th's FALCONS callsign		
155 AHC	War Wagon	John Wayne 1967 movie		Nov, 1967: mortar damaged
155 AHC	We're Slick ^^		2nd platoon motto painted on all 2nd platoon slicks	
155 AHC	Wrecker ^		late '66: 65-09733 and early '67: 66-16385 / also 66-16441 was "WRECKER"	
159 Med Det	Ethyl's Ambulance	name of Jim Seal's wife		
159 Med Det	Holly Sacra	named after Blickenstaff's sister who was named after Holloman AFB and Sacramento Mountains		
159 Med Det	Lord Of The Flies	literary novel on human nature		
161 AHC	10 Thou *	serial # reference		
161 AHC	Hungry Hog			
161 AHC	Mustang Sally	Wilson Pickett song title		
162 AHC	Ace Of Spades			
162 AHC	American Woman	Guess Who song title / old lady in rocking chair artwork	"EASY RIDERS" on nose + artwork / (V-23)	
162 AHC	Autumn Mist *	referred to Agent Orange sprayer missions		
162 AHC	Baby Huey	powerful but self destructive cartoon character		destroyed in mortar attack

Unit	Copter Name	Origin / Definition	Notes / Call Signs ( ) < >	Fate Aircraft / Crew
162 AHC	Beautiful Balloon	Montgolfier balloon painted on door also / song lyrics to popular 1967 5th Dimension hit "Up, Up + Away"		DD 6-28-68: only two weeks after door painted
162 AHC	Big Bright Green Pleasure Machine	Simon + Garfunkel song title	Larry Tiebay also painted "BEAUTIFUL BALLOON"	
162 AHC	BIOYA	"blow it out your ass"	(V-28)	
162 AHC	Blow It Out Your Ass **	definition of "BIOYA"		
162 AHC	Bonnie G		currently: N9114M, Nash Creek Companies, Fayetteville, GA / (V-18)	
162 AHC	Bonny's Baby		(V-18)	
162 AHC	Charlie Chaser	painted image of a running VC		
162 AHC	Cheap Thrills	Janis Joplin album title		
162 AHC	Die Goldene Rose	"the golden rose"		
162 AHC	Elmira			
162 AHC	Fly The Friendly Skys	starting in '65 United Airlines motto		
162 AHC	Foxy Lady	Jimmy Hendrix song title		
162 AHC	Give Peace A Chance	John Lennon song title		
162 AHC	Great White Leader	2nd flight platoon Lead ship		
162 AHC	Hungry Bitch (The)			
162 AHC	Iron Butterfly			
162 AHC	Kathy		(V-21)	
162 AHC	Little Green Taxi Cab ? (The)			
162 AHC	Little Miss Janet	name of Walsh's girlfriend	broken skids in pic / on display: Ft. Hood AAF, TX	
162 AHC	Lonesome Whippoorwill (The)	Hank Williams song title		
162 AHC	Mystical Wrench			
162 AHC	Pig Pen	"dirty job"	short lived: CE painted over it because it constituted insult to his reputation + craft / (V-28)	

Unit	Copter Name	Origin / Definition	Notes / Call Signs ( ) < >	Fate Aircraft / Crew
162 AHC	Rum Rico	nn of Dike: favorite drink+PR ancestry= RUM RICO	brother of Joe Dike named his C-1-9 Cobra the "MONICA LEE": daughter+brother names combo	
162 AHC	Slicker Than Shit		"VULTURES EXECUTIONERS" on nose also / (V-16)	
162 AHC	Smokey	smoke ship	(V 29)	
162 AHC	Stormy Petrel II (The)	"bird of doom" / mascot name of Oglethorpe Univ, Atlanta, GA / Eric Bray credited with copter name	"Stormy Petrel I" was B-17 flown by Oglethorpe Univ alum in WW II	
162 AHC	Sue			
162 AHC	Sweet Reba	pilot named it	(V-27)	
162 AHC	Triple Niner	refers to 9-9-9 sequence in serial #	chase ship	
162 AHC	V.D.	(vulture) dog = poor lift power from copter engine	aka "VULTURE DOG"	
162 AHC	Vulture Dog	weak engine = dog	aka "VD"	
165 TC	Family Car (The)	Ma+Pa+Cousin were mechanic nn's: FAMILY CAR became logical choice for helo name		
170 AHC	Ann			
170 AHC	Barbara		(Bik 24)	
170 AHC	Bitch (The) **	flawed artwork generated pejorative name		
170 AHC	Bounty Hunter			
170 AHC	Bounty Hunter II		was original "BOUNTY HUNTER" destroyed? / (Buc 7)	
170 AHC	Chuck You Farlie	spoonerism = transposition of the letters C and F		
170 AHC	Coffin Dodgers (The)		aka "THE PUSHERMAN" / (Bik 26)	
170 AHC	Death From Above			
170 AHC	Drydock ^	adopted name of the maintenance platoon's aircraft that imitated the 170th's BUCCANEERS callsign	maintenance "callsign" also	
170 AHC	Easy Flyer			
170 AHC	Gail Sue		(Buc 2)	
170 AHC	Gloria	name of MacDougall's girlfriend	MacDougall was Gun platoon Leader / (Buc 6)	

U.S. ARMY HELICOPTER NAMES IN VIETNAM

Unit	Copter Name	Origin / Definition	Notes / Call Signs ( ) < >	Fate Aircraft / Crew
170 AHC	Good Vibrations	shaky copter / Beach Boys song title	C.O. ordered it removed immediately	
170 AHC	Jeanie		(Bik 6)	
170 AHC	Jo Michele	Bob Snead's wife-daughter names	Bob Snead was also ARMY TIMES cartoonist / (Buc 4)	
170 AHC	Kid (The)		aka "BIKINI 27"	
170 AHC	Mercenary (The)		(Buc 9)	
170 AHC	Nancy		(Buc 2)	
170 AHC	Peggy			
170 AHC	Pharaoh (The)		(Buc 8)	
170 AHC	Pharaoh II (The)		(Buc 8)	
170 AHC	Pusher Man	Steppenwolf song title	aka "THE COFFIN DODGERS" / nose panel now displayed at Ft. Rucker, 1 Avn Bde conference room / (Bik 26)	
170 AHC	Vigilante (The)		(Buc 4)	
170 AHC	Vigilante II (The)		(Buc 4)	
170 AHC	Widow Maker		(Buc 3)	
173 Abn Bde	Caspar Night Hawk	cartoon character Caspar, The Friendly Ghost, dressed as the Grim Reaper		
173 Abn Bde	Lucky 7	on nose: painted pair of dice equaling seven	Bono was grunt who remembers dice + name	
173 Abn Bde	Playboy Special	Playmate of the Year visited unit	was shuttled around in specially painted slick: story in May '66 issue of Playboy magazine	
173 Abn Bde	Sky Hawk		C+C ship	
173 Abn Bde	Villa Flyies Again (sp?)	mis-spelling of Flies		
173 AHC	Balls Niner *	refers to 0-0-9 sequence in serial #	currently: N774AR, Houston, TX	
173 AHC	Blood, Sweat 'N Tears	1960's rock band name		
173 AHC	Born Free	1966 movie + Matt Monroe song of same name		
173 AHC	Day Tripper	Tom Sutton named copter / Beatles song title	on display: VFW Post 374, Arcade, NY	

Unit	Copter Name	Origin / Definition	Notes / Call Signs ( ) < >	Fate Aircraft / Crew
173 AHC	Destroyer (The)			
173 AHC	Double O Soul			
173 AHC	Easy Rider	Hollywood movie title		
173 AHC	Flower Power	painting of a flowerpot minigun shooting flowers		
173 AHC	Friar Tuck ^	named because only non-combat aircraft in unit		
173 AHC	Friar Tuck ^	adopted name of the maintenance platoon's aircraft that imitated the 173rd's ROBIN HOODS callsign		
173 AHC	Fur Burger II	painting of 2 legs protruding from hamburger	visiting Donut Dollies protested to C. O. and was subsequently removed from helicopter door	
173 AHC	Iron Butterfly	1960's rock band of same name	C.O. ordered nn removed	
173 AHC	Jonny Reb			
173 AHC	King Arthur	named after Arthur Kovolesky CE		
173 AHC	Little Angel	Combs' daughter born while he was in VN	obtained info from Fine Scale Modeling post by WO Combs	
173 AHC	Little John			
173 AHC	Little Miscarriage	Lucy of Peanuts cartoon depicted		
173 AHC	Little Miss Jo	name of Palmertree's wife		
173 AHC	Misfit (The)	Hollywood movie title	wore camo paint scheme	
173 AHC	Miss Carol			
173 AHC	Miss Carol II			
173 AHC	Miss Carol III			
173 AHC	Miss Carol IV			
173 AHC	Mr. Lonely	1964 Bobby Vinton song title of same name		
173 AHC	Mr. Lucky	TV detective show		
173 AHC	Nickel + Dime	1 + 4 = nickel 1 + 9 = dime		

Unit	Copter Name	Origin / Definition	Notes / Call Signs ( ) < >	Fate Aircraft / Crew
173 AHC	Ooze			
173 AHC	Reverend Mr. Black	Kingston Trio song title		
173 AHC	Sic 'Em Puss			
173 AHC	SNAFU	"situation normal all fucked up"		
173 AHC	Sweet Sue			DD 12-28-67: while Perkins on 30 day leave
173 AHC	Top Guns Will Travel			
173 AHC	V.D.			
173 AHC	WETSU #1	"we eat this shit up"		
173 AHC	Xin Loi	Vietnamese for "sorry bout that"		
173 AHC	Zorba	AC was Greek		
174 AHC	Ace Of Spades **		during '70-'71 all unit gunships utilized the rear access panels to exhibit their extensive individualized artwork	DD 3-31-71: Lam Son
174 AHC	Ace Of Spades II **	see "Notes" citation for "ACE OF SPADES"	shares serial # with "CHARLIE TUNA"	2-24-71: Fred Thompson WIA
174 AHC	American Woman	Guess Who song title		
174 AHC	Battlin Bitch **	painted Madona figure / see "Notes" citation for "ACE OF SPADES"	aka "HAVE GUN WILL TRAVEL" in 1970 / aka "LADY MADONNA", "NIXON'S HIRED GUN"	
174 AHC	Black Jack **	ace of spades+jack of diamonds on nose	currently: N658HA, Forestry Services Inc, Frederick, MD	
174 AHC	Black Knight **	painted chess piece akin to TV's Paladin logo / see "Notes" citation for "ACE OF SPADES"	aka "BATTLIN BITCH", "MADONNA", "PALADIN", "HAVE GUN WILL TRAVEL" in 1971	
174 AHC	Buddha	door gunner's nickname		
174 AHC	Carolyn		"2nd Flt Plt" on copter nose, also painted Grim Reaper riding a dolphin on copter nose	loss to inventory 11-20-70
174 AHC	Charlie Tuna	weak engine / "sorry charlie" tuna commercial / see "Notes" citation for "ACE OF SPADES"	shares serial # with "ACE OF SPADES II"	2-24-71: Thompson WIA
174 AHC	Christine	CPT Peterson's daughter's name + portrait	copter nose painting of "CHRISTINE" is stunning !	
174 AHC	Cobra **	see "Notes" citation for "ACE OF SPADES"	aka "WOODSTOCK"	
174 AHC	Connie		3,368 hours, most Dolphin hours in unit	

Unit	Copter Name	Origin / Definition	Notes / Call Signs ( ) < >	Fate Aircraft / Crew
174 AHC	De Judge	TV's "Laugh-In" expression		
174 AHC	Debbie	name of Gauby's wife	aka "GAIL" / yellow skid caps + Dolphin tail stripe	
174 AHC	Easy Rider	Hollywood movie title / see "Notes" citation for "ACE OF SPADES"	VHPA calendar pic	DD 11-23-70
174 AHC	Easy Rider II	Hollywood movie title / see "Notes" citation for "ACE OF SPADES"		
174 AHC	Flying Coffin (The)	painted coffin on doorpost with lettering	aka "IOLA" / currently: N32741 N. Michigan Univ, Marquette, MI	
174 AHC	Flying Pig **	sluggish take off = verbal nn	graphic of flying pig posted on cargo door window	
174 AHC	Frito Bandito	cartoon mascot for Fritos Corn Chips	avionics panel moved to '573 upon crash of '767	
174 AHC	Frito Bandito II	cartoon mascot for Fritos Corn Chips	avionics nose panel originally from '767	
174 AHC	Gail	name of John Bailey's girlfriend	aka "DEBBIE"	
174 AHC	Grim Reaper	see "Notes" citation for "ACE OF SPADES"	shares serial # with "JOLLY ROGER"	
174 AHC	Have Gun Will Travel **	TV Western's Paladin chess piece / see "Notes" citation for "ACE OF SPADES"	aka "BATTLIN BITCH", "MADONNA", " PALADIN"	
174 AHC	Holly			
174 AHC	Hop-A-Long	under powered	on display: Am Society of Mil History, El Monte, CA	
174 AHC	Iola	name of Messinger's wife	currently: N32741, N. Michigan Univ, Marquette, MI / aka "THE FLYING COFFIN"	
174 AHC	Iron Cross **	see "Notes" citation for "ACE OF SPADES"	aka "TRIPLE NICKEL" and "MALTESE CROSS"	
174 AHC	Jolly Roger **	painting of skull + cross bones / see "Notes" citation for "ACE OF SPADES"	aka "GRIM REAPER" late '70	
174 AHC	Keep The Faith Baby			
174 AHC	King Kuhana	Medeiros was Hawaiian		
174 AHC	Lady Madonna **	see "Notes" citation for "ACE OF SPADES"	aka "NIXON'S HIRED GUN", "BATTLIN BITCH", "HAVE GUN WILL TRAVEL"	
174 AHC	Life Is A Bitch	Snoopy character also in painting		
174 AHC	Love, Peace, Music	Woodstock concert logo emblem / see "Notes" citation for "ACE OF SPADES"	aka "WOODSTOCK" / Cobra image painted on quarter access door	
174 AHC	Magic Bus *	The Who song title	aka "DOUBLE DEUCE TRIP" by pilot	

U.S. ARMY HELICOPTER NAMES IN VIETNAM

Unit	Copter Name	Origin / Definition	Notes / Call Signs ( ) < >	Fate Aircraft / Crew
174 AHC	Maltese Cross **	see "Notes" citation for "ACE OF SPADES"	aka "TRIPLE NICKEL" v-nn	
174 AHC	Mexican Express	large sombrero on access panel is a '68 replica of UH-1C art from 92 AHC painted + crewed by Albert Garza, who originated both names / see "Notes" citation for "ACE OF SPADES"	Latino crew chief named it	
174 AHC	Musk-Shark *		former Musket 176th gunship	
174 AHC	My Yellow Balloon			
174 AHC	Nixon's Hired Gun		aka ""HAVE GUN WILL TRAVEL", "BATTLIN BITCH", "LADY MADONNA"	
174 AHC	None Better		pic also found in 14 CAB '67 yearbook	
174 AHC	Paladin **	TV Western / paladin means "knight, or the champion of a cause"	aka "HAVE GUN WILL TRAVEL" / see "Notes" citation for "ACE OF SPADES"	
174 AHC	Patches			
174 AHC	Pink Panther **	Hollywood movie title		
174 AHC	Pusher (The)	Steppenwolf song title		
174 AHC	Rampage			Lam Son 719 survivor
174 AHC	Ruptured Cherry (The)			1969: shot down
174 AHC	Satan		spray ship also / currently: N334SD U.S. State Dept, Patrick AFB, FL	
174 AHC	Shenandoah			
174 AHC	Short	"few in-country days remaining"	utilized as the unit Smoke ship	
174 AHC	Ski Bum	painting of skier	side view pic taken before crash day by Tuerk	11-15-69: entire crew KIA
174 AHC	Smokey *	smoke ship	"SHORT" painted on cargo door by Larry Whalen CE	
174 AHC	Snake Eyes			
174 AHC	Spirit In The Sky	Norman Greenbaum 1969 song title		
174 AHC	Spotted Slick **	only camouflaged bird ever in unit		
174 AHC	Surfer **	aka "SILVER SURFER" / "Endless Summer" movie poster image replicated	see "Notes" citation for "ACE OF SPADES"	2-21-7: loss in Laos / Dustoff named "IRON BUTTERFLY" from the 498 MD rescued crew
174 AHC	Suzie			

Unit	Copter Name	Origin / Definition	Notes / Call Signs ( ) < >	Fate Aircraft / Crew
174 AHC	Texas Flag **		painted TX flag ?	
174 AHC	This Fish Swims In Booze	"WHEN YOU'RE OUT OF SCHLITZ YOU'RE OUT OF BEER" painted above	aka "WHEN YOU'RE OUT OF SCHLITZ YOU'RE OUT OF BEER"	
174 AHC	Trip Eight *	refers to 8-8-8 sequence in serial #		
174 AHC	Triple Nickel *	refers to 5-5-5 sequence in serial #	aka "TRIPLE NICKEL" and "IRON CROSS"	
174 AHC	When You're Out Of Schlitz You're Out Of Beer	"THIS FISH SWIMS IN BEER" painted below	aka "THIS FISH SWIMS IN BOOZE"	
174 AHC	Witch Bitch **		aka "WITCHDOCTOR III"	
174 AHC	Witch Doctor ^			
174 AHC	Witch Doctor II ^	"II" not included on nose		Elliott flew into trees Lam Son 719, rescued 2 days later
174 AHC	Witch Doctor III ^	"III" not included on nose / aka "WITCH BITCH"		
174 AHC	Woodstock **	infamous 1969 rock concert / see "Notes" citation for "ACE OF SPADES"	aka "COBRA" prior to" WOODSTOCK" / "LOVE, PEACE, MUSIC" painted also	8-29-71: Harris KIA
175 AHC	Ace Of Spades	playing card painted on pilot's door	(Mav 34)	
175 AHC	Ain't It A Bitch		aka "DADDY RABBIT", "COLOR ME BAD" / (OL 13)	
175 AHC	Apocalypse		Maverick Lead / (Mav 35)	
175 AHC	Avenger (The)		(OL 10)	
175 AHC	Ba Moui Ba	translation means "33 Beer"	aka "BIERE 33 EXPORT" Vietnamese beer / (Mav 33)	
175 AHC	Bad News		(Mav 33)	
175 AHC	Bandit		(OL 27)	
175 AHC	Bat Masterson	1960's TV Western / old West lawman	(OL 28)	
175 AHC	Belle Star	Old West female outlaw	(OL 26)	
175 AHC	Biere 33 Export	VN brew	aka "BA MOUI BA" / Dale Roland's pic has downtown artist Oscar painting pilot door / (Mav 33)	
175 AHC	Billy The Kid	Western outlaw	(OL 17)	1967: Easter Sunday casualty
175 AHC	Black Bicth	mis-spelling of Bitch by VN artist	aka "BLACK BITCH" on left side / (OL 11)	

Unit	Copter Name	Origin / Definition	Notes / Call Signs ( ) < >	Fate Aircraft / Crew
175 AHC	Black Bitch		aka "BLACK BICTH" (mis-spelled) on right side / (OL 11)	
175 AHC	Blackjack Dealer		(OL 21)	
175 AHC	Blood, Sweat + Tears	1960's rock band name	(Mav 36)	
175 AHC	Blood, Sweat + Tears	1960's rock band name	(OL 21)	
175 AHC	Bret And Bart	TV Western series	(Mav 34)	
175 AHC	Buckaroo		(OL 11)	
175 AHC	Cajun Queen		(Mav 31)	
175 AHC	Cat Ballou	1965 Hollywood movie title	(OL 23)	
175 AHC	Cheap Thrills	Janis Joplin album title	aka "EASY RIDER" ? / Hunter Killer missions mostly / (OL 24)	DD 1969
175 AHC	Checker Cab			
175 AHC	Cherry		(OL 29)	
175 AHC	Chicken Coop	named after pilot Cooper	(OL 18)	
175 AHC	Chicken Little		(OL 18)	
175 AHC	Chief Smoke	C.O.'s ship	(OL 1)	
175 AHC	Color Me Bad	parody of "Color Me Barbara" (Streisand) 1966 album title	aka "DADDY RABBIT", "AIN'T IT A BITCH" / (OL 13)	
175 AHC	Curse You Red Baron	Snoopy refrain	aka "SNOOPY III" / (Mav 35)	
175 AHC	Daddy Rabbit		aka "COLOR ME BAD", "AIN'T IT A BITCH" / went thru entire war without taking single hit / (OL 13)	
175 AHC	Déjà Vu	Crosby, Stills + Nash song title	(OL 11)	
175 AHC	Delta Rebel (The)	C.O.'s ship	(OL 6)	
175 AHC	Deuces Wild			
175 AHC	Devil's Anger		(Mav 33)	
175 AHC	Dirty Dozen		(OL 12)	5-17-68: all crew KIA

Unit	Copter Name	Origin / Definition	Notes / Call Signs ( ) < >	Fate Aircraft / Crew
175 AHC	Easy Rider	Hollywood movie title	aka "CHEAP THRILLS" ? / (OL 24)	
175 AHC	Easy To Be Hard	Three Dog Night song title	(OL 12)	
175 AHC	Eve Of Destruction	red painted Grim Reaper on door / Barry McGuire song title	(Mav 34)	
175 AHC	Gara Ce Buela	Spanish for "the flying rag"		
175 AHC	Gladiator			
175 AHC	Good Vibrations	Beach Boys song title	(OL 10)	
175 AHC	Gray Ghost	copter name refers to flying at dusk	C+C and Night Hunter Killer missions	
175 AHC	Greatful Dead (The)	parody of the Grateful Dead's name, 1960's rock band	(Mav 39)	
175 AHC	Grim Reaper ***	aka "GRIM"	all 175th UH-1C's DD in 8/4/70 ammo dump explosion / (Mav 32)	
175 AHC	Grim Reaper II ***	partial full name painted	Bob was a civilian stationed at Vinh Long	
175 AHC	Hardcore	CE named it	(OL 25)	
175 AHC	Headhunter		cannibal ? painted on door also	
175 AHC	Hell's Angel	notorious American motorcycle club	(OL 14)	
175 AHC	Hit The Slopes			
175 AHC	In Cold Blood	Truman Capote book+movie / ordered to re-name ship because name was too violent	aka "MORNING AFTER" / (Mav 31)	
175 AHC	Jefferson Airplane (The)	1960's rock band name	UH-1H 67-17192 carried this name also / (OL 26)	
175 AHC	Kimchi Cab	"Korean taxi cab"	(OL 25)	
175 AHC	King Cobra			
175 AHC	Littlest Maverick (The)		(Mav 38)	
175 AHC	Lucky Leita		(Mav 32)	
175 AHC	Lucy In The Sky With Diamonds	Beatles song title	(OL 17)	
175 AHC	Madame Num	Vinh Long whore house	(OL 16)	

U.S. ARMY HELICOPTER NAMES IN VIETNAM

Unit	Copter Name	Origin / Definition	Notes / Call Signs ( ) < >	Fate Aircraft / Crew
175 AHC	Magic		(OL 16)	ship was an Easter Day battle vet
175 AHC	Magnificent Men And Their Flying Machine (The)	British film comedy	avionics panel was saved, returned to USA: Harry Khachadourian brought nose panel home / (OL 13)	
175 AHC	Messanger Service		(OL 18)	
175 AHC	Miss Behavin W.E.T.S.U.	WETSU: "We Eat This Shit Up"	aka "RAPE PILLAGE BURN" / (Mav 39)	
175 AHC	Moon		cargo bay .50 cal / shares serial # with "WIDOW MAKER" / (Mav 34)	
175 AHC	Morning After	hangover blues depicted graphically	formerly "IN COLD BLOOD", which had been banned by C.O. orders / (Mav 31)	DD 9-12-68
175 AHC	Mother Hawker			
175 AHC	Mr. Lucky	TV detective show	(OL 24)	
175 AHC	Mr. Lucky	TV detective show	(OL 10)	DD Easter Sunday, 3-27-67
175 AHC	Murder Inc			
175 AHC	Mustang		(OL 6)	
175 AHC	Negative Suppression		(OL 19)	
175 AHC	Night Crawler	Fire Fly at night patrolling Mekong Delta canals at slow speed		
175 AHC	Number Thirteen		(OL 13)	
175 AHC	Pasa Las Tres	"it passes the three" translation	(OL 12)	
175 AHC	Patches		Herrell assigned to 346 Div Avn Support, Vinh Long	
175 AHC	Pied Piper		(Mav 39)	
175 AHC	Pineapple Red		(Mav 32)	
175 AHC	Pogostick			
175 AHC	Professionals (The)	1966 Burt Lancaster film by same name	(Mav 34)	
175 AHC	Raider		(OL 25)	
175 AHC	Rape, Pillage, Burn		aka "MISS BEHAVIN W.E.T.S.U." / (Mav 39)	
175 AHC	Rare Breed		(OL 27)	

Unit	Copter Name	Origin / Definition	Notes / Call Signs ( ) < >	Fate Aircraft / Crew
175 AHC	Reaper		painting of iconic Grim Reaper on pilot's door	
175 AHC	Reaper II		"GRIM" not included in inscription	
175 AHC	Renegade		(Mav 38)	
175 AHC	Revolution Outlaw		(OL 15)	
175 AHC	Rice Paddy Cruiser		CE was Hispanic / (OL 26)	
175 AHC	Road Runner ^		Bob Koonce designed unit emblem / insignia	
175 AHC	Road Runner ^		aka "BEEP BEEP"	
175 AHC	Roadrunner ^			
175 AHC	Running Scared		(OL 13)	
175 AHC	Sat Cong	"kill VC"	painted "IIIII IIII" (9 KBA) on nose also / (OL 27)	
175 AHC	Satan's Playmate	door art painted Spring 1967	(Mav 36)	
175 AHC	Satisfaction	Rolling Stones song title	(OL 21)	
175 AHC	Season's Greetings	Christmas 1970	bows + bells painted below Outlaw emblem also	
175 AHC	Sherry Baby	Four Seasons song title	(OL 26)	
175 AHC	Sidney Or The Bush	Peanuts cartoon parody by Keeney / California or Bust / unintentional mis-spelling of SYDNEY, the city in Australia, gave definition a whole different twist	the Aussie equivalent to "California or Bust" / (OL 27)	
175 AHC	Slope Cab	slope = Vietnamese civilian		
175 AHC	Snoopy		(OL 17)	
175 AHC	Snoopy		aka "WAR PAINT" / (Mav 35, 38)	3-26-67: shot down
175 AHC	Snoopy II		on display: Heartland Museum of Mil Vehicles, Lexington, NE / (Mav 35, 38)	
175 AHC	Snoopy III		aka "CURSE YOU RED BARON" on M-3 rocket box / frog configuration / (Mav 35)	
175 AHC	Snoopy III		(Mav 32)	
175 AHC	Snoopy IV	Snoopy's dog house painted on pilot's door / "Curse You Red Baron" painted on XM-159 rocket pod	"pooper" M-5 grenade launcher on nose + XM-159 rocket pod = Heavy Hog weapons system (Mav 38)	

Unit	Copter Name	Origin / Definition	Notes / Call Signs ( ) < >	Fate Aircraft / Crew
175 AHC	Snoopy V			
175 AHC	Snoopy VI			
175 AHC	Snoopy VII			
175 AHC	Snoopy VIII			
175 AHC	Sopwith Camel	WW I British fighter plane	(OL 10)	
175 AHC	Southern Gentlemen			
175 AHC	Spirit In The Sky	Norman Greenbaum 1969 song title	(OL 26)	
175 AHC	Stupid Stishes		Nighthawk missions with Bushwacker platoon	
175 AHC	Sugar Foot	TV Western character	(OL 11)	
175 AHC	Super Dog		(OL 28)	
175 AHC	Super Rag *	oldest helo in unit	(OL 11)	
175 AHC	Super Star		(OL 10)	
175 AHC	Swamprat (The)		(OL 14)	
175 AHC	Third Revolution (The)		(OL 15)	
175 AHC	Three Massketeers (The)		(Mav 36)	
175 AHC	Unlucky Lady (The)		(OL 29)	
175 AHC	Vagabond (The)		(OL 13)	
175 AHC	Veni Vidi Vici	"I Came, I Saw, I Conquered"	(OL 22)	
175 AHC	War Paint		renamed "SNOOPY" July 1966 / (OL 17)	DD 3-26-67
175 AHC	Widow Maker		shares serial # with "MOON" / (Mav 34)	
175 AHC	Yellow Cab		(OL 26)	
176 AHC	1%	99% of population stay safe on ground	"FUCK IT, JUST FUCK IT" painted on belly also / miniguns were chrome plated	

Unit	Copter Name	Origin / Definition	Notes / Call Signs ( ) < >	Fate Aircraft / Crew
176 AHC	2%er	98% of population stay safe on ground	companion of fellow 176th ship named "1%"	
176 AHC	744's Revenge	Varnum's second assigned helo after 66-00744 was shot down 5-13-69 and destroyed		
176 AHC	Birth Control			
176 AHC	Blacksmith ^	adopted name of the maintenance platoon's aircraft that imitated the 176th's MINUTEMEN callsign	<6>	DD 8-13-71
176 AHC	Boston Patriot	both the AC + CP were brothers from Boston		
176 AHC	Bush Rat	painting of a Speedy Gonzales gone bad		
176 AHC	Canadian Club	Ralph Bigelow was Canadian citizen / maple leaf painted on copter nose also		
176 AHC	Cheap Thrills	Janis Joplin album title		
176 AHC	Exterminator			
176 AHC	Flower Power	counterculture slogan meaning non-violence		
176 AHC	Fuck It Just Fuck It		aka "1%"	
176 AHC	Golden			
176 AHC	Greyhound No Fuckin Slack	Greyhound 6 was C.O. of 2/327 Infantry, 101Airborne	LTC Edmund Abood "Black Panther" / switched nose art panels when LTC Abood was to fly C+C	
176 AHC	Grim Reaper		"aka THE HAWK", "THE PERSUADER", "WIDOW MAKER" / sounded siren during gun runs	
176 AHC	Hawk (The)		aka "GRIM REAPER", "THE PERSUADER"," WIDOW MAKER"	
176 AHC	Heavy Metal	highly amplified guitars in rock music		
176 AHC	Hydraulics Wonder (The)		"OH GOD I'M HORNY" painted on belly	
176 AHC	Illegal Eagle			
176 AHC	In A Gadda Da Vida	1960's rock band Iron Butterfly song title		
176 AHC	Irishmen			
176 AHC	Maltese Cross **		artwork ordered removed so CE painted entire avionics door red	
176 AHC	Means To An End			

Unit	Copter Name	Origin / Definition	Notes / Call Signs ( ) < >	Fate Aircraft / Crew
176 AHC	Means To An End		shares serial # with 48 AHC's "BROTHER LOVE'S TRAVELIN' SALVATION SHOW"	
176 AHC	Nixon's Hired Gun			
176 AHC	Oh God I'm Horny		aka "THE HYDRAULICS WONDER"	
176 AHC	Oregon Taxi	Dale Wiese was Oregon native		
176 AHC	Patches	old helo, many hours, many patches	cannibalized for parts later on	
176 AHC	Persuader (The)		aka "GRIM REAPER", "THE HAWK", "WIDOW MAKER"	
176 AHC	Proud Mary	Creedence Clearwater Revival song title		
176 AHC	Purple Fox	painting of a purple fox on tail boom		
176 AHC	Ralph II	Bob O'Connell '67 CE named it	was original "RALPH" destroyed?	DD 1-18-68: in Laos
176 AHC	Rosemary's Baby	Hollywood horror film title		
176 AHC	Sadistic Revenge			
176 AHC	Silent Majority			
176 AHC	Smokey			12-13-67: all crew KIA
176 AHC	Smokey 500		on display: Am Legion Post 30, New Rockford, ND	
176 AHC	Super Hog		aka "VC FOR LUNCH BUNCH" / M-3 rockets + M-5 grenade launcher	
176 AHC	Sweet Revenge			
176 AHC	Sweet Sally			
176 AHC	Tijuana Taxi	Herb Albert + The Tijuana Brass 1965 song title / flashy, highly decorated automobile	maintenance recovery ship	
176 AHC	Triple Trey *	refers to 3-3-3 sequence in serial #		
176 AHC	VC For Lunch Bunch		aka "SUPER HOG"	
176 AHC	Weasel			
176 AHC	West By God Virginia			

Unit	Copter Name	Origin / Definition	Notes / Call Signs ( ) < >	Fate Aircraft / Crew
176 AHC	Widow Maker		aka "GRIM REAPER" ," PERSUADER" , "THE HAWK"	
178 ASHC	Alfred E. Wall **	painted reference to pilot's name + parody of MAD magazine's Alfred E. Neuman	MAD magazine icon + slogan "What, Me Worry?" was counterpart to WWII's "Kilroy Was Here"	
178 ASHC	Balls One *	refers to 0-0-1 sequence in serial #	converted to CH-47D, 84-24170	
178 ASHC	Balls Two *	refers to 0-0-2 sequence in serial #	shares serial # with 243 ASHC's "BALLS TWO" and "ALFRED E. WALLS"	DD 3-23-75
178 ASHC	Big Mack	painting of a Chinook peeling out	converted to CH-47D, 87-00072	
178 ASHC	Cathy's Clown	Everly Brothers song title		
178 ASHC	Charlie Lima Express	Charlie Lima = Chu Lai	aka "CHU LAI EXPRESS" / converted to CH-47D, 87-00115	
178 ASHC	Cherry	rendition of a Vargas Playboy pic	converted to CH-47D, 86-01670	
178 ASHC	Chu Lai Express *		aka "CHARLIE LIMA EXPRESS" / converted to CH-47D, 87-00115	
178 ASHC	Crimson King (The)	sunburst painting with nn inside		
178 ASHC	Cupid's Quiver		converted to CH-47D, 86-01658	
178 ASHC	Da Judge	painting of Snoopy also on fuselage	aka "SNOOPY" / converted to CH-47D, 87-00110	
178 ASHC	Day Tripper	Beatles song title		
178 ASHC	Eve Of Destruction	painting of mushroom cloud also	converted to CH-47D, 84-24166	DD 1985: test flight
178 ASHC	Far Far Eastern Airways		converted to CH-47D, 88-00102	
178 ASHC	Granny Twitchett	Playboy magazine cartoon character / Savannah Morning News, Aug 10, 2001 article	shares serial # with 196 ASHC's "THE ROACH COACH" / converted to MH-47D, 85-24367	still flying as of 2001
178 ASHC	Head Up Your Ass **			
178 ASHC	Iron Butterfly		shares sn with "SPIRIT IN THE SKY" / converted to CH-47D, 88-00090	
178 ASHC	Lady Luck	painted red heart		DD 6-27-66
178 ASHC	Lady Willpower	Gary Puckett + The Union Gap song title		DD 5-15-69
178 ASHC	Magic Bus	The Who song title	lasted 3 years in VN / converted to CH-47D, 83-24108	
178 ASHC	Magnet Ass **			

U.S. ARMY HELICOPTER NAMES IN VIETNAM

Unit	Copter Name	Origin / Definition	Notes / Call Signs ( ) < >	Fate Aircraft / Crew
178 ASHC	Mellow Yellow	Donovan song title / yellow lemon painted on nose with tandem Chinook rotors	shares serial # with 242 ASHC's "LOVE CRAFT"	DD 7-10-70
178 ASHC	Miss Chris	"CHRIS" was Bearly's fiancé	they didn't marry	
178 ASHC	Miss Molly Erin Go Braugh	"Ireland forever" / painted shamrock		DD-5-10-72
178 ASHC	Miss Mynookie	Jim Kilgo named it / double entendre		DD 2-23-69
178 ASHC	Miss Mynookie #2	double entendre	#2 repainted but numeral #2 left off / converted to CH-47D, 83-24105	
178 ASHC	Nancy Lee II		original "NANCY LEE" destroyed?	DD 5-15-69: no KIA's
178 ASHC	Ole Daddy Rabbit	painting of a rabbit also	converted to CH-47D, 87-00078	
178 ASHC	Orange Blossom Special	old Country-Western tune	shares serial # with "RIDGE RUNNER" / converted to CH-47D, 88-00076	
178 ASHC	Pusher (The)	Steppenwolf song title	converted to CH-47D, 87-00091	
178 ASHC	Ridge Runner #1		shares serial # with "ORANGE BLOSSOM SPECIAL" / Kaminski was a LRRP / converted to CH-47D, 88-00076	
178 ASHC	Roadrunner **		aka "VON BRYAN'S EXPRESS"	DD 3-23-75
178 ASHC	Scavenger			DD 8-26-70: AC was lone survivor
178 ASHC	Sky King	rancher + aircraft pilot series on TV		
178 ASHC	Snoopy **	no lettering, just painted likeness of popular comic strip character	aka "DA JUDGE"	
178 ASHC	Spirit In The Sky	Norman Greenbaum 1969 song title	German+British WW 1 insignias painted / shares sn with "IRON BUTTERFLY" / converted to CH-47D, 88-00090	
178 ASHC	Swamp Rat	fuselage painting of a rat attired in swamp clothing		
178 ASHC	Thunder Road	painting of an old man with hat fishing / bluegrass song about moonshine / Hiway 13 nickname		DD 6-25-67
178 ASHC	Von Bryan's Express **	parody of "Von Ryan's Express" movie title	aka "ROADRUNNER", no lettering, figure only	DD 3-23-75
178 ASHC	Wild Thang	The Troggs 1965 song title	converted to CH-47D, 88-00086	
178 ASHC	Zig Zag	artwork painting of the Zig Zag cigarette paper logo		
179 ASHC	Big Brother			
179 ASHC	Blood, Sweat + Tears	1960's rock band name		
179 ASHC	Chicago Transit		aka "YVONNE" painted on side door / converted to CH-47D, 89-00173	

Unit	Copter Name	Origin / Definition	Notes / Call Signs ( ) < >	Fate Aircraft / Crew
179 ASHC	Chubby Cheeks	physical attributes of CH-47 as seen straight-on	C.O. made crew paint over it later	
179 ASHC	Cloud 9	1968 Temptations song title / slang expression	Rubalcava originated + painted name in Aug '69 / converted to CH-47D, 89-00171	
179 ASHC	Crystal Ship (The)	Doors song title		
179 ASHC	For Sale	graphic: tired looking CH-47 + "FOR SALE" sign	converted to CH-47D, 82-23769	
179 ASHC	Giddy Up Go	song "Giddy Up Go" by Red Sovine	civilian license plate has same "name" / converted to CH-47D, 83-24120	
179 ASHC	Good The Bad And The Ugly (The)	Clint Eastwood western movie title		
179 ASHC	Good Vibrations	Beach Boys song title		
179 ASHC	Here Comes The Judge	TV's Laugh-In refrain		
179 ASHC	Miss Chris Too	"TOO" : clever word play that means 'also' and '2nd' combined	converted to CH-47D, 85-24322	
179 ASHC	NJ Devil	professional ice hockey team of same name		
179 ASHC	Patches		shares serial # with 242 ASHC's "BALLS FIVE" / converted to CH-47D, 82-23769	
179 ASHC	Pusher (The)	Steppenwolf song title	converted to MH-47G, 05-13762	
179 ASHC	Shaky Lady	painting of champagne, dice, and a blond in pink dress	Bunger observed hook + name at LBJ or Saigon TCN / converted to MH-47G, 05-13762	
179 ASHC	Snoopy		painted Snoopy holding a Huey	DD 10-5-68: Mitchell + Wilson KIA
179 ASHC	Sunkist Special	excess mechanical problems / painting of lemon		DD 4-26-68: all KIA
179 ASHC	Yvonne	name of Foley's girlfriend	aka "CHICAGO TRANSIT" / converted to CH-47D, 89-00173	
180 ASHC	Baby Huey	powerful but self destructive cartoon character		
180 ASHC	Balls Eight *	refers to 0-0-8 sequence in serial #	aka "LED SLED" / converted to CH-47D, 89-00144	
180 ASHC	Big Brother			
180 ASHC	Blood, Sweat + Tears	1960's rock band name	converted to CH-47D, 88-00095	
180 ASHC	Boeing's Blunder	Chinook manufacturer	aka "HANGAR QUEEN"	
180 ASHC	Charlie Chopper			

U.S. ARMY HELICOPTER NAMES IN VIETNAM

Unit	Copter Name	Origin / Definition	Notes / Call Signs ( ) < >	Fate Aircraft / Crew
180 ASHC	Goldfinger	movie title of 1964 James Bond movie		DD 2-1-67: total loss, crashed in ravine, rolled over
180 ASHC	Green Eyed Lady	Sugarloaf 1970 song title	converted to CH-47D, 90-00210	
180 ASHC	Horny Hooker	2 versions: with + without female figure	converted to CH-47D, 90-00210	
180 ASHC	Kosher Dill		converted to CH-47D, 88-00105	
180 ASHC	Led Sled	reference to Led Zeppelin rock band	aka "BALLS 8" / converted to CH-47D, 89-00144	
180 ASHC	Little Windy *	as opposed to Big Windy's CH-47's	two of the unit 's OH-58's were named "LITTLE WINDY": sn's 69-16096 + 69-16097	
187 AHC	15 Cents	'555 in serial # adds up to "15 CENTS"	aka "TRIPLE NICKLE" painted on pilot door also	
187 AHC	Alabama		shares serial # with "SOUTHERN COMFORT"	
187 AHC	Alerquin	named after Duquette's grandfather		
187 AHC	Avenging Angel			
187 AHC	Bad News		renamed "TAY NINH TAXI" by Bellerue / aka "T.N.T", "NO FARE", "ZAPATA'S RIGHT" / (Crus 28)	
187 AHC	Batmobile	Batman's vehicle	no pic or text but "II" best evidence that original "BATMOBILE" existed	
187 AHC	Batmobile II	Batman's vehicle	pic has them parked in a strawberry patch at Kontum / Crus 24)	
187 AHC	C. C. Rider	old blues song title		
187 AHC	Captain America **	painted stars + stripes on tailcone		
187 AHC	Clark Bar	replicated image of the Clark Candy Bar	aka "WABASH CANNONBALL"	
187 AHC	Color Me Gone	parody of "Color Me Barbara" (Streisand) '66 album title		
187 AHC	Crystal Ship (The)	Doors song title		
187 AHC	Debbie II			
187 AHC	Dee's Delight		aka "LUCKY LINDA"	
187 AHC	Devil's Disciple's	American motorcycle club / painted trident on pilot door	"LT Shann" painted on pilot door window / "Havemann" painted on gun mount	
187 AHC	Dove Of Peace		replaced "KILLER HAWK" + "PISTOL PETE" / .50 cal and minigun weapons / (Crus 22, 20, 29)	

Unit	Copter Name	Origin / Definition	Notes / Call Signs ( ) < >	Fate Aircraft / Crew
187 AHC	Eighter From Decatur	2 rolling dice painted on fuselage	aka "GANG BANG" / upgraded to a AH-1S at the Aberdeen Proving Grounds, MD	DD 2-12-71
187 AHC	Erinaala I		(Crus 6)	
187 AHC	Executioner (The)		currently: N62619, CA Dept of Justice, Mather, CA	
187 AHC	Gang Bang		aka "EIGHTER FROM DECATUR" / upgraded to a AH-1S at the Aberdeen Proving Grounds, MD	2-12-71: shot down in Cambodia
187 AHC	Gang Green	gangrene medical term parody		
187 AHC	Gook Spook		aka "SUPER HUEY"	DD 9-26-67
187 AHC	Graduate (The)	Dustin Hoffman 1967 Hollywood film title	aka "PATTY WAGON"	
187 AHC	Grim Reaper	C.O.'s private Huey	VHPA book pic + caption pg 119 / Gonzales was CE when Mike Babb was AC in '71	
187 AHC	Here There Everywhere	Beatles song title		March, 1971: shot down in Cambodia
187 AHC	High And Mighty (The)		(RP 33)	
187 AHC	Hill Billy Dilly		shares serial # with 282 AHC's "LAST CHANCE"	
187 AHC	Hilltopper			
187 AHC	Hogan's Heroes	TV's WW II comedy		
187 AHC	Honey Mama	co-pilot was Southern native who named copter	on display: VFW Post 9122, Magee, MS near Vets bldg, 10 mi from Camp Shelby, MS	
187 AHC	Horney Hawk		aka "THE WAR LORD"	
187 AHC	Iron Butterfly (The)			
187 AHC	Jake's Delight		shares serial # with "WILD CHILD"	
187 AHC	Judge (The)		shares serial # with "WABASH CANNONBALL"	
187 AHC	Judy In The Sky	parody of the 1967 hit "Judy In Disguise" (With Glasses) by John Fred + His Playboy Band	CE saved avionics door according to Windsand	DD Sept, 1970: nose door survives?
187 AHC	June's Ride-Sandy's Pride			
187 AHC	Killer Hawk		ordered removed + replaced with "DOVE OF PEACE" / aka "PISTOL PETE" / (Crus 22, 29)	
187 AHC	Lady Linda	name of pilot's wife	aka "DEE'S DELIGHT"	

Unit	Copter Name	Origin / Definition	Notes / Call Signs ( ) < >	Fate Aircraft / Crew
187 AHC	Lancelot ^	adopted name of the maintenance platoon's aircraft that imitated the 187th's CRUSADERS callsign	<11>	
187 AHC	Lancelot ^	adopted name of the maintenance platoon's aircraft that imitated the 187th's CRUSADERS callsign	aka "ROTOR TOOTER", "SEMI-HEMI"	
187 AHC	Lil' Miss Joy			
187 AHC	Lil' Norma Jean		(Crus 6)	
187 AHC	Little Eileen			
187 AHC	Louise			
187 AHC	Lucy In The Sky With Diamonds	Beatle's song title		
187 AHC	Maxine			1-5-68: Ken Scruton KIA in this helo
187 AHC	Message From Michael	Dionne Warwick song title		
187 AHC	Miss Carriage	double entendre		
187 AHC	Miss Mar-Leen	combo of Gaffney's wife+daughter names	aka "ROUND EYES FOREVER"	
187 AHC	Misty			
187 AHC	Nance	name of Leith's fiance who he later married in September 1969		
187 AHC	No Fare		aka "TAY NINH TAXI CO", "TNT", "ZAPATA'S RIGHT", "BAD NEWS"	
187 AHC	Number Nine *	add 1+3+5 = 9 / also Beatles song title	name never painted on copter	
187 AHC	Ohio Express (The)	Herman Scott was from Ohio		
187 AHC	Ole Magnet Ass	was Mercer's nickname also		
187 AHC	Ole' Prophet	named by Jerry Wagner		
187 AHC	Pandora's Box	"create evil that cannot be undone"	Ray Wilhite stated that the serial # may not be correct / (Crus 27)	
187 AHC	Patty Wagon		aka "THE GRADUATE" / shares serial # with "TROJAN HOSS"	
187 AHC	Phuquet	island off of Thailand		
187 AHC	Pistol Pete		aka "KILLER HAWK" and "DOVE OF PEACE"	

Unit	Copter Name	Origin / Definition	Notes / Call Signs ( ) < >	Fate Aircraft / Crew
187 AHC	Pusherman (The)	Steppenwolf song title		
187 AHC	Rag (The)	derogatory term for excessive need for repairs		
187 AHC	Rebel Rouser	1958 Duane Eddy song title		
187 AHC	Roadrunner (The) ^			
187 AHC	Rokin Robin	Bobby Day song title		
187 AHC	Rotor Toter		aka "LANCELOT", "SEMI-HEMI"	
187 AHC	Round Eyes Forever		aka "MISS MAR-LEEN"	
187 AHC	Rubber Duck	funny car artist Ed Roth's custom car name		
187 AHC	S,A,D, Mrs	Dougan's wife's initials	punctuation commas in-between S,A,D, resembled painted teardrops / (Crus 16)	
187 AHC	Screaming Yellow Zonker	American tracer rounds / American snack food	(Crus 25)	
187 AHC	Semi-Hemi ^		aka "LANCELOT", "ROTOR TOOTER"	
187 AHC	Serendipity		(Crus 17)	
187 AHC	Ship Of Fools	Doors song title		
187 AHC	Smokey			
187 AHC	Some Times			
187 AHC	Southern Comfort	American bourbon whiskey	shares serial # with "ALABAMA"	
187 AHC	Spirit In The Sky	Norman Greenbaum 1969 song title	(Crus 11)	
187 AHC	Super Huey		aka "GOOK SPOOK"	DD 9-26-67
187 AHC	Super Smoker	smoke ship		
187 AHC	Sweet Cream Lady	The Box Tops 1968 song title by the same name	aka "TAY-NINH TAXI CO" on nose also	
187 AHC	T.N.T.	"T.N.T" = "TAY NINH TAXI" / aka "TAY NINH TAXI"	aka "BAD NEWS", "NO FARE", "ZAPATA'S RIGHT"	
187 AHC	Tay-Ninh Taxi Co		aka "BAD NEWS", "NO FARE", "TNT", "ZAPATA'S RIGHT"	

Unit	Copter Name	Origin / Definition	Notes / Call Signs ( ) < >	Fate Aircraft / Crew
187 AHC	Triple Nickle	refers to 5-5-5 sequence in serial #	aka "15 CENTS" on pilot door also	
187 AHC	Trojan Hoss		shares serial # with "PATTYWAGON"	
187 AHC	Trouble Shooter			
187 AHC	Undertaker			shot down in Cambodia
187 AHC	Undertaker II		rebuilt D model	
187 AHC	Wabash Cannonball	two painted 2.75 rockets with fire coming from nozzles	shares serial # with "THE JUDGE" / Clark candy bar painted on gunship nose (re: Dan Clark CE)	
187 AHC	War Lord (The)	1965 Charlton Heston movie by same name	aka "YOU CALL WE HAUL" atop pilot door frame / aka "HORNEY HAWK" / 1965 Hollywood movie title / (Crus 19)	
187 AHC	Wild Child	Doors song title / Ed Roth's custom monster car	shares serial # with "JAKE'S DELIGHT"	
187 AHC	Willowdean	American female first name		
187 AHC	Wingless Warrior	helo has no wings, also, Chickenman was aka Winged Warrior		
187 AHC	You Call We Haul		aka "TET": Tesmar's initials on doorpost	
187 AHC	Zapata's Rights		aka "TAY NINH TAXI CO", "TNT", "BAD NEWS", "NO FARE"	
188 AHC	Anna B			
188 AHC	Asassins Inc	mis-spelling of Assassins		
188 AHC	Balls Seven *	refers to 0-0-7 sequence in serial #		
188 AHC	Black Sheep			
188 AHC	Boom Boom A-Go-Go	"boom-boom" was VN slang for sexual intercourse	currently: N205KM, Rice Aircraft Services, Marysville, CA / might possibly have been 66-16119	
188 AHC	Boots			
188 AHC	Climax		(SP 65)	
188 AHC	Cold Sweat	James Brown song title		
188 AHC	Cowboy Joe			
188 AHC	Crap Shooter			

Unit	Copter Name	Origin / Definition	Notes / Call Signs ( ) < >	Fate Aircraft / Crew
188 AHC	Crimson And Clover	Tommy James + The Shondells song title		
188 AHC	Eradicator			
188 AHC	Flight To America	PC version of "fuck The Army" / aka "FTA"	senior Officer was so incensed that he ordered it removed but it was later painted back on / (BW 26)	
188 AHC	Flower Power	counterculture slogan meaning non-violence		
188 AHC	Fornicator 44	mentioned in King James Bible 44 times		
188 AHC	Frenchy's Folly			
188 AHC	Friday's Child	Nancy Sinatra 1966 song title		
188 AHC	FTA	PC version of "fuck The Army" ? aka "FLIGHT TO AMERICA"	senior Officer was so incensed that he ordered it removed but it was later painted back on / (BW 26)	
188 AHC	Hangar Queen *	derogatory term for excessive need for repairs	(BW 44)	
188 AHC	Hoocher	"female anatomy"		
188 AHC	Iron Butterfly	1960's rock band of same name		
188 AHC	Love			
188 AHC	Lucy In The Sky With Diamonds	Beatles song title	(BW 42)	
188 AHC	Monster Man			
188 AHC	Mr. Lonely	1964 Bobby Vinton song title of same name		
188 AHC	Mr. Lucky	TV detective show	(BW 4)	
188 AHC	Nicki II		currently: N3126U / was original "NICKI" destroyed?	
188 AHC	Number 10	Vietnamese expression meaning "bad, the worst"		
188 AHC	O. D. Streak (The)			
188 AHC	Polish Power		(BW 13)	
188 AHC	Psycho			
188 AHC	Ragin Cajun		currently: N205KM, Rice Aircraft Services, Marysville, CA / might possibly have been 66-16119 / (BW 35)	George Jones AC, Jerry Doht CP, WIA during OPERATION RAPID FIRE

Unit	Copter Name	Origin / Definition	Notes / Call Signs ( ) < >	Fate Aircraft / Crew
188 AHC	Satisfaction	Rolling Stone song title	Academy plastic model kit + decals 2008 / (SP 68)	
188 AHC	Smokie	smoke ship	(SP 68)	
188 AHC	Smokie II	smoke ship	on display: VFW Post 374, Arcade, NY/ aka "TROLL" / "II" not included on copter nose / (BW 45)	
188 AHC	Smokie III	smoke ship	"III" not included on copter nose / (BW 25)	
188 AHC	Snoopy **			
188 AHC	Sudden Death			
188 AHC	Summer Wine	Nancy Sinatra song title	(BW 43)	
188 AHC	Super Frog	XM-159 rockets + M-5 grenade launcher	painted frog with cape + mini-gun	
188 AHC	Super Sandpiper		(BW 12)	
188 AHC	Susie Q	popular rock tune		
188 AHC	Sweet Thang			
188 AHC	Troll	Tollefsen's nickname	aka "SMOKIE I" / troll doll painted on pilot door / on display: VFW Post 374, Arcade, NY	
188 AHC	Wicked Wahine	nickname given to Merryman's wife while on Hawaii R+R	temporary loaner to 269 CAB as C+C / (BB 6)	
188 AHC	Wild Bill			
189 AHC	Ann			
189 AHC	Barbie	name of Steinbrunn's girlfriend	shares serial # with "WOP WAGON"	
189 AHC	Black Label	BLACK LABEL beer can label replicated on rocket pod		
189 AHC	Caroline	name of pilot's girlfriend	aka "MISSION IMPOSSIBLE"	
189 AHC	Crystal Ship	Doors song title	C.O. ordered name removal: drug related / (Aveng 9)	
189 AHC	Denise			
189 AHC	Four Balls *	last 3 serial #'s: '400	MacDonald was Pleiku Tower Operator who volunteered as DG on off days	
189 AHC	Highlander Lead ^		maintenance platoon attached to 189 AHC	

Unit	Copter Name	Origin / Definition	Notes / Call Signs ( ) < >	Fate Aircraft / Crew
189 AHC	Ho Chi Minh Is A Fag	written in Vietnamese		
189 AHC	Laura			
189 AHC	Missing Link (The)	Lincoln (Link) was Dobson's middle name	currently: N7247C, U.S. Border Patrol, El Paso, TX	
189 AHC	Mission Impossible	TV's Mission Impossible series	aka "CAROLINE"	
189 AHC	Scarlet Curse		aka "SUSAN" painted on nose	
189 AHC	Silver Lead			
189 AHC	Susan	aka "SCARLET CURSE" painted on nose		
189 AHC	Triple One *	refers to 1-1-1 sequence in serial #	aka "MISSION IMPOSSIBLE", "CAROLINE"	
189 AHC	Wendy	CE overruled the DG that The Association song was WENDY instead of the correct title WINDY		
189 AHC	Wop Wagon	named after Lomonaco aka The Wop	shares serial # with "BARBIE"	
190 AHC	Foxy Lady	Jimmy Hendrix song title		
190 AHC	Horse			
190 AHC	Justice (The)			
190 AHC	Major Malfunction		shares serial # with "MISS CARRIAGE" / name was removed by order of the C.O.	
190 AHC	Miss Carriage	double entendre	shares serial # with "MAJOR MALFUNCTION" / name was removed by order of the C.O.	
190 AHC	Sat Cong	"kill VC"	painted severed head of VC / reportedly artist was former Disney employee	
190 AHC	Spartan Horse **	adopted name of the maintenance platoon's aircraft that imitated the 190th's GLADIATORS callsign	painted horse head with "HORSE" below	DD 8-11-70 : 2 WIA
190 AHC	Spartan Smokey	smokeship	"SS" painted on nose also	
190 AHC	Spirit Of The Sky		DG's nickname "STREET" painted on doorpost plaque also	
191 AHC	Ace Of Spades **	ace of spades graphic on both pilot doors		
191 AHC	Baby Huey **	powerful but self destructive cartoon character	painted on right pilot door only, no lettering, just figure	5-21-68: Richard Weske KIA
191 AHC	Bad Ass		<39>	

Unit	Copter Name	Origin / Definition	Notes / Call Signs ( ) < >	Fate Aircraft / Crew
191 AHC	Batship **	Batman logo on copter nose	<19>	5-21-68: Richard Weske KIA
191 AHC	Be Nice Or I Will Kill You		aka "MOTHER GOOSE" / shares serial # with 134 AHC's "HOT STUFF"/ on display: Sea-Air-Space Museum, NY	
191 AHC	Big Brother	"God Is My Co-Pilot" painted on interior wall	66-00818, UH-1D, '67-'68 possible? / on display: Granite City, IL	
191 AHC	Captain America	comic book character	aka "CONG STOMPER"	
191 AHC	Cathy's Clown	Everly Brothers song title	aka "LAND LOVER" / shares serial # with "MICHELE 1"	8-12-68: entire crew KIA
191 AHC	Cong Stomper		aka "CAPTAIN AMERICA"	6-5-68: crashed, all aboard KIA
191 AHC	Faye's Love			
191 AHC	Hangar Queen *	disreputable term for excessive need for repairs		
191 AHC	Iron Butterfly			
191 AHC	Kitten			
191 AHC	Land Lover		aka "CATHY'S CLOWN"	8-12-68: entire crew KIA
191 AHC	Little Joe	name of Welch's son		
191 AHC	Maltese Cross **	painting origin due to AC's German wife: aka "THE GERMAN MEDEVAC" / painting of Maltese cross	on display: Am Legion Post 79, Massena, NY	
191 AHC	Mela			
191 AHC	Mia Cha Cha	named by Latino pilot		
191 AHC	Michele 1	named after Patnode's daughter	Boomerang 6 was unit C.O.'s ship / shares serial # with "CATHY'S CLOWN" / (Boom 6)	
191 AHC	Mother Goose		shares serial # with 134 AHC's "HOT STUFF" / on display: USS *Intrepid*, Sea-Air-Space Museum, NY	
191 AHC	Para-Dice	rhymes with paradise and pair of dice?		
191 AHC	Purple Haze Experience (The)	Jimmy Hendrix song title	heavy hog	
191 AHC	Quicksilver			
191 AHC	Sat Cong	"kill VC"	reportedly the ARVN's loved it	
191 AHC	Short, Don't Shoot Me	term used to signify near end of 12 month tour	shot down 3 days later after "SHORT, DON'T SHOOT ME" was painted on copter belly	
191 AHC	Sun Shine Superman	Donovan song title	currently: N83CF, Robinson Air Crane Inc, Opalocka, FL	

Unit	Copter Name	Origin / Definition	Notes / Call Signs ( ) < >	Fate Aircraft / Crew
191 AHC	Super Ship **	Superman logo painted on copter nose		
191 AHC	Theo			
191 AHC	Tijuana Taxi	Herb Albert + The Tijuana Brass 1965 song title / flashy, highly decorated automobile		
191 AHC	Vietnam Sucks		aka "SUPER SLICK", Superman logo on pilot doors	
191 AHC	Voyager (The)		"OOH WAUGH" painted above glass on cargo door (re: CE's last name)	
192 AHC	Avenger (The)			
192 AHC	Balls Five *	refers to 0-0-5 sequence in serial #		
192 AHC	Bean Bandit (The)			
192 AHC	Day Tripper	Beatles song title / Jon Creel named ship		2-18-70: crashed at Dalat
192 AHC	Executioner (The)	Zig Zag man figure painted on nose also	"HAPPINESS IS A WARM GUN" painted on doorpost / aka "THE EXECUTIONER"	
192 AHC	Grim Reaper (The)		aka "PROUD MARY"	
192 AHC	Happiness Is A Warm Gun	Beatles song title / baby cuddling an M-60 drawn on doorpost	aka "THE EXECUTIONER"	
192 AHC	Have Gun Will Travel	TV Western show		
192 AHC	Hombre (The)	Allison named ship		
192 AHC	Kill For Grins	words painted within Tigershark nose art		
192 AHC	Kill For Peace			
192 AHC	Lady Luck	'711 = lucky #		
192 AHC	Love Child	1968 Supremes song title		
192 AHC	Mortician (The)		hog frog	
192 AHC	Mother Superior	Beatles song title	Tigershark painted on nose also / Ashley was unit test pilot	
192 AHC	Orient Express	Fensky named ship		
192 AHC	Proud Mary	painted flowers also on copter nose / Creedence Clearwater Revival song title	aka "GRIM REAPER"	

U.S. ARMY HELICOPTER NAMES IN VIETNAM

Unit	Copter Name	Origin / Definition	Notes / Call Signs ( ) < >	Fate Aircraft / Crew
192 AHC	Ride A Slick To Hell + Back			
192 AHC	Son Of Hell Fire			
192 AHC	Stache **	Richard Claeys was known as "STACHE" / large mustache painted on copter nose		
192 AHC	Super Shark		hog gunship	
192 AHC	To Charlie With Love		M-5 chunker artwork + lettering	
192 AHC	Triple Nickel Deuce *	refers to 3-5-2 sequence in serial #		
192 AHC	Ugly American (The)	epithet meaning "arrogance + ignorance of local culture" / also '58 novel + '63 movie of same name		
192 AHC	Unlimited Hell			
192 AHC	VC Widow Maker		(TS 36)	
192 AHC	Widow Maker (The)		Tigershark painted on nose also / Ashley was unit test pilot	
192 AHC	You Call We Maul			
195 AHC	Deuce + A Dime *	named for last three serial #'s 2+10		
195 AHC	Executioner (The) *			
195 AHC	Huzza-Huzza	a notable expression found in a popular comic book	greased penciled on copter nose	
195 AHC	Thunder Chicken ^^^		positive ID by Curt Cornell, 195th webmaster / this copter helped in 12-11-68 Medevac mission	March, 1969: crashed ?
195 AHC	Undertaker (The) *			
196 ASHC	Borrowed Time			DD 11-9-73
196 ASHC	Crystal Ship (The)	Doors song title	converted to CH-47D, 82-23762	
196 ASHC	Iron Butterfly		converted to CH-47D, 85-24357	rolled down hill LZ English
196 ASHC	Led Zeppelin	British rock band name		
196 ASHC	Life's A Bitch			
196 ASHC	No Balls At All	painted pair of dice + 003 serial # reference	converted to CH-47D, 86-01680	

Unit	Copter Name	Origin / Definition	Notes / Call Signs ( ) < >	Fate Aircraft / Crew
196 ASHC	Roach Coach (The)	slang for marijuana	shares serial # with 178 ASHC's "GRANNY TWITCHETT" / converted to MH-47D, 85-24367	
196 ASHC	War Wagon	John Wayne 1967 movie		
196 ASHC	Yosemite Sam **	animated cartoon character		
196 Light Inf Bde	Iron Butterfly	1960's rock band of same name		entire crew KIA blowing NVA bunkers
197 AHC	Duff And Dilly's		Heavy Hog: M-5 on nose, M-3 rocket pods	
197 AHC	Original Mad Bomber (The)	MAD = "mortar aerial delivery"	"ORIGINAL" is in parenthesis above nn	
198 Light Inf Bde Americal Div	Jean			
200 ASHC	"A" Modified	car culture term	converted to CH-47D, 82-23770	
200 ASHC	Beep Beep Yurass	Wiley Coyote throttling Roadrunner at last	greeting card found by Boxley + Ledbetter during Japan R+R was inspiration for coyote + roadrunner painting	captured by NVA 1975
200 ASHC	Born Free	1966 song + movie title		captured by NVA 1975
200 ASHC	Condemned		shares serial # with "GREEN MONSTER"	DD 4-26-72
200 ASHC	Desert Rat (The)		listed on PACHYDERM PARK outdoor sign post / converted to CH-47D, 86-01650	
200 ASHC	Double Trouble			DD 1-19-75
200 ASHC	Exodus		converted to CH-47D, 82-23768	
200 ASHC	Good Vibrations	Beach Boys song title	converted to CH-47D, 86-01659	
200 ASHC	Green Monster		shares serial # with "CONDEMNED"	DD 4-26-72
200 ASHC	Hooker (The)		2 versions: modified (covered) + unmodified (topless)	captured by NVA 1975
200 ASHC	Hulk (The)	comic book character	converted to CH-47D, 85-24344	
200 ASHC	Jug Butt **	"fat, over-weight"		DD 3-23-75
200 ASHC	Lil Pachyderm			
200 ASHC	Philbert Desenex	comic book character: when he isn't fighting crime as "WW," he poses as reporter Philbert Desenex	aka "WONDER WARTHOG"	DD 3-23-75
200 ASHC	Ragin Cajun		unit later became 159 ASHC / converted to CH-47D, 87-00069	

Unit	Copter Name	Origin / Definition	Notes / Call Signs ( ) < >	Fate Aircraft / Crew
200 ASHC	Road Runner **		converted to CH-47D, 86-01650	
200 ASHC	Rufus II	dog mascot was original RUFUS	listed on PACHYDERM PARK outdoor sign post / converted to CH-47D, 86-01674	
200 ASHC	Showboat (The)		listed on PACHYDERM PARK outdoor sign post / converted to CH-47D, 85-24344	
200 ASHC	Silken Snarl (The)	1968 Dodge Coronet, muscle car	on display: War Remnants Museum, HCMC, VN	
200 ASHC	Skyraider (The)		converted to CH-47D, 85-24348	
200 ASHC	Up, Up and Away ? **	Fifth Dimension tune	converted to CH-47D, 86-01674	
200 ASHC	Wonder Wart-Hog	underground comic book character, parody of Superman	aka "PHILBERT DESENEX"	DD 3-23-75
201 CAC	Red Who?	painted Snoopy inquiry / painted red iron cross		
203 ASHC	Autobus	motor coach		
203 ASHC	Blood, Sweat + Tears	1960's rock band name		
203 ASHC	Iron Butterfly			
203 ASHC	Short	huge shortimer calendar painted on fuselage	converted to CH-47D, 83-24114	
205 ASHC	Ace Of Spades **	playing card painted near doorway	no lettering visible	
205 ASHC	Captain Klutz	comic strip character	still-frame from movie film	
205 ASHC	Moon Equipped	quality car cylinder rings / FE's idea		
205 ASHC	Patches	dozens of bullet hole patches	painting of cartoon figure Snuffy Smith also / aka "SNUFFY SMITH"	finally retired because of structural damage
205 ASHC	Snuffy Smith **	painting of cartoon figure Snuffy Smith	aka "PATCHES"	
213 ASHC	Bonzai Boss **	no lettering, just artwork		DD 3-23-75
213 ASHC	Bouncy **	head picture of Bugs Bunny also		DD 2-22-72: in Korea
213 ASHC	Cat In The Hat **	no lettering, just artwork	cat wearing top hat painting	DD 3-23-75
213 ASHC	Hangar Queen	had golden yellow queen crowns on the cowling / derogatory term excess need for repairs		
213 ASHC	Hot Stuff			

Unit	Copter Name	Origin / Definition	Notes / Call Signs ( ) < >	Fate Aircraft / Crew
213 ASHC	Igloo (The)	FE was from Alaska / painting of an igloo also	not Cayze's hook: another hook had this name+artwork	
213 ASHC	Keep The Faith Baby		white stallion rearing up painting also	
213 ASHC	Nancy Bare		converted to CH-47D, 86-01651	
213 ASHC	Patches	painting of a magnet on fuselage	converted to CH-47D, 85-24339	
213 ASHC	Phu Loi Freedom Flight 505 *		converted to CH-47D, 89-00134	
213 ASHC	Pitty Tink	famous flat track motorcycle	converted to CH-47D, 85-24335	
213 ASHC	Rebel (The) **	no lettering, just artwork		DD 11-9-73
213 ASHC	Scotsman (The)	Scotsman painting is a copy of WW II nose art from MacDougall's Dad's aircraft		captured by NVA 1975
213 ASHC	Snoopy **	no lettering, just artwork	shares serial # with A-228 ASHB's "DOUBLE DEUCE"	10-25-70: bad crash, returned USA, stricken: July '71
215 Composite Svc Bn	Blood, Sweat + Tears	1960's rock band name	215th inherited "BLOOD SWEAT + TEARS" after 15 Med Bn stood down in April of 1971	
215 Composite Svc Bn	Hell's Ugly		215th inherited "HELL'S UGLY" after 15 Med Bn stood down in April of 1971	
215 Composite Svc Bn	Sympathetic Journey		215th inherited "SYMPATHETIC JOURNEY" after 15 Med Bn stood down in April of 1971	
222 CAB	Rebel			
222 CSAB	Troy New York Home Of Uncle Sam	Uncle Sam's red-white-blue hat		
235 AWC	Delta To DMZ		aka "SUPER SNAKE"	
235 AWC	Devil's Advocate (The)		2nd platoon Flare Ship	
235 AWC	Iron Butterfly	painted flowers around name		
235 AWC	Super Snake		aka "DELTA TO THE DMZ"	
235 AWC	Thumper	M-5 chunker on nose		
235 AWC	War Wagon	John Wayne 1967 movie		
235 AWC	Wrench Bender ^			
236 Med Det	Foxey Lady	based on a Jimmy Hendrix song title, "Foxy Lady"		

Unit	Copter Name	Origin / Definition	Notes / Call Signs ( ) < >	Fate Aircraft / Crew
236 Med Det	Patty Ann	named by crew chief		
236 Med Det	Sleasy Rider	parody of Easy Rider	"SLEASY GAL" was original guess by Moore-Braddock	
237 Med Det	Angel Of Mercy *			
237 Med Det	Black Bitch	unpopular ship, 1st Cav castoff, dog of an aircraft	shares serial # + name with 571 Med Det / currently: N357SD, U.S. State Dept, Patrick AFB, FL	Bradley + Hill later KIA, September, 1970
237 Med Det	Curious Yellow	X-rated film title	deserted at Khe Sanh airfield for several weeks, used for target practice during that time	DD 6-4-71
237 Med Det	Got Ya			
237 Med Det	Peace Seekers	"Gordon" painted on cargo door		
237 Med Det	Right Here Buddy			
237 Med Det	Ship Of Fools	1970 Doors song by same name		
238 AWC	Chunky			
238 AWC	Love Child	1968 Supremes song title		
238 AWC	Nitehawk			
238 AWC	Pandora's Box	"create evil that cannot be undone"	shares serial # with B-2-20 ARA + D-227 AHB	
238 AWC	Widow Maker		Stiefel was also DG on the Thumper gunship	
240 AHC	007	James Bond type missions / painted "7" on copter nose in the shape of a handgun	Special Opns with the 5th Special Forces / .50 cal machine gun in cargo bay	
240 AHC	Avenger	Frank Reed renamed it to avenge Klann's KIA	former nn "MICHELLE I" before Klann KIA / Frank Reed was CE for 1 month after Klann KIA	1-10-68: Klann KIA on "MICHELLE 1"
240 AHC	Bad Moon Risin'	based on a Creedence Clearwater Revival song title, "Bad Moon Rising"		
240 AHC	Bitches Brew	Miles Davis 1970 album title	aka "SOUL BIRD"	
240 AHC	Chartwriter (The)			5-2-68: MOH mission involving Ray Benavidez
240 AHC	Death On Call ^^		unit gunships during this time period sported this slogan below the painted dog graphic on copter nose	
240 AHC	Deer Slayer	title of James Fenimore Cooper's book by the same name; subtitle was "The First Warpath"		
240 AHC	Foxy Lady	Jimmy Hendrix song title		
240 AHC	I. W. Harper	named for famous whiskey + CE (Harper)		1-10-68: both Eastburn + Harper WIA

Unit	Copter Name	Origin / Definition	Notes / Call Signs ( ) < >	Fate Aircraft / Crew
240 AHC	Kennel Keeper ^	adopted name of the maintenance platoon's aircraft that imitated the 240th's MAD DOGS callsign	69-15552 was also "KENNEL KEEPER"	
240 AHC	Kill Mad Dog Kill		"FRENCHY" on nose also	
240 AHC	Little Miss Glenda Sue	name of MAJ Hoffman's daughter	MAJ Hoffman's C+C ship carried this nn	
240 AHC	Marrakesh Express	Crosby, Stills + Nash song title		
240 AHC	Michelle 1	named after the CE's niece Michelle Klann	renamed "AVENGER" after Klann was KIA	1-10-68: Martin Klann KIA
240 AHC	Nightmare			
240 AHC	Pabst Blue Flight	PABST beer can label replicated on copter nose / PABST Blue flight = 2nd slick platoon		
240 AHC	Portuguese Man O' War	Amaral was of Portuguese descent		12-14-67: all crew KIA
240 AHC	Sat Cong	"kill VC"	ordered to remove nn but crashed before it could be carried out / (MD 88)	DD 12-22-67: all four crew survived, 2 serious injuries
240 AHC	Soul Bird	Cal Tjader 1965 album title	aka "BITCHES BREW"	
240 AHC	Super Scenic Cruiser			DD 9-13-71: in accident
242 ASHC	Balls Five *	refers to 0-0-5 sequence in serial #	shares serial # with 179 ASHC's "PATCHES" / converted to CH-47D, 82-23769	
242 ASHC	Beep Beep Yuass		converted to CH-47D, 85-24362	
242 ASHC	Big Brother		painted Zig Zig label graphic also	DD 8-18-71: W. Germany
242 ASHC	Big Tuffy			DD 5-30-70
242 ASHC	Cheap Thrills	Janis Joplin album title		
242 ASHC	Debbie		aka "IRON BUTTERFLY" on fuselage / aka" KISS MY ASS" on mast	
242 ASHC	Debbie Jo			
242 ASHC	Dragon Fly			
242 ASHC	Dud (The)		converted to CH-47D, 84-24163	
242 ASHC	Easy Rider	Hollywood movie title		
242 ASHC	Eight Ball		aka "PROUD MARY" / converted to CH-47D, 92-0304	

Unit	Copter Name	Origin / Definition	Notes / Call Signs ( ) < >	Fate Aircraft / Crew
242 ASHC	Good Vibrations	Beach Boys song title	converted to CH-47D, 84-24180	
242 ASHC	Gremlin's Castle	citation in Ernest Gann's "Island in the Sky" book		
242 ASHC	Headache *	hydraulics problem unable to solve	converted to CH-47D, 84-24169	
242 ASHC	Iron Butterfly		"KICK MY (ASS)" on front pylon above mule graphic	DD 11-21-66
242 ASHC	Kick My Ass		painting of kicking mule also	
242 ASHC	Kris			
242 ASHC	Love Craft	American author H.P. Lovecraft was master of weird fiction + horror	shares serial # with 178 ASHC's "MELLOW YELLOW"	DD 7-10-70: 2 KIA's: D. Schultz DG + Ross Bedient FE
242 ASHC	Mad Dog			
242 ASHC	Marrakesh Express	Crosby, Stills + Nash song title		
242 ASHC	Merry Christmas		unit emblem was white circle with dark center	
242 ASHC	Mighty Quinn (The)			
242 ASHC	Mini Mule	"Muleskinner" was unit's formal name consisting mainly of Chinooks	currently: San Juan Co Sheriff Dept, Aztec, NM	
242 ASHC	Mini Skinner			
242 ASHC	Old Molly			
242 ASHC	Patty Girl Fly			
242 ASHC	Pig Power			DD 2-26-69: by sappers
242 ASHC	Proud Mary	Creedence Clearwater Revival song title	aka "EIGHT BALL" / converted to CH-47D, 92-0304	
242 ASHC	Rosemary's Baby	Hollywood horror film title		
242 ASHC	Runnin Scared		0 enemy hits until satchel charge destroyed it	DD 2-26-69: by sappers
242 ASHC	Sexy Shuffler			DD 2-26-69: by sappers
242 ASHC	Sky Pilot	traditional slang term for a military chaplain / James Count named copter / Animals song title	converted to CH-47D, 83-24123	
242 ASHC	Sky Pilot II	military chaplain / Animals song title	converted to CH-47D, 82-23764	
242 ASHC	Sophia Loren **	voluptuous Italian actress		

Unit	Copter Name	Origin / Definition	Notes / Call Signs ( ) < >	Fate Aircraft / Crew
242 ASHC	Tar Baby		converted to CH-47D, 82-23768	
242 ASHC	War Wagon (The)	painting of oxcart carrying large rocket / John Wayne 1967 movie		DD 2-26-69: by sappers
242 ASHC	Wart Hog			
243 ASHC	Balls Two *	refers to 0-0-2 sequence in serial #	shares serial # with 178 ASHC's "ALFRED E. NEUMAN"	DD 3-23-75
243 ASHC	Blood, Sweat + Tears	1960's rock band name		
243 ASHC	Body By Fisher	Detroit automobile coachbuilder	Moser in-country Oct '67-Oct '68 / converted to CH-47D, 82-23766	
243 ASHC	Damn You Charlie	Snoopy with goggles exclaiming "..."		
243 ASHC	Flying Doily *	had so many patches she was dubbed this name		
243 ASHC	Hell's Angel	notorious American motorcycle club		10-20-68: entire crew KIA
243 ASHC	Hulk (The)	comic book character		
243 ASHC	Iron Butterfly	1960's rock group with same name	possible serial#66-19052 or two different unit Chinooks at different times carried this name / converted to CH-47D, 82-23382	DD 1-19-75
243 ASHC	Jolly Roger **	painted skull + cross bones	possible lettering above skull, not sure	
243 ASHC	Jumbo 47			
243 ASHC	Led Zeppelin	British rock band name		
243 ASHC	Little Annie			
243 ASHC	Old Bitch (The)		converted to CH-47D	
243 ASHC	Pappy's Killer			
243 ASHC	Pappy's Revenooers			captured by NVA 1975
243 ASHC	Round Trip	also had a white "?" painted on nose	Cross of Lorraine (two horizontal arms + one vertical) painted on nose also / converted to CH-47D, 82-23382	
243 ASHC	Ruptured Duck	infamous name of B-25 bomber of WW II's Doolittle Raid over Tokyo	converted to CH-47D, 86-01653	
243 ASHC	Sky Queen		shares serial # with B-228 ASHB's "SORRY 'BOUT THAT" / converted to CH-47D, 83-24114	
243 ASHC	Slow But Sure			

Unit	Copter Name	Origin / Definition	Notes / Call Signs ( ) < >	Fate Aircraft / Crew
243 ASHC	Tailwing		converted to CH-47D, 84-24171	
243 ASHC	Ten Toes Up Ten Toes Down **	no lettering, just painted image / sexual reference		
243 ASHC	Vicious Circle	painted red circle with teeth		
243 ASHC	You Bet Your Life	Grouch Marx quiz show		
244 Avn Co	Mother Hawk		2 different nose panel designs noted on 2 pics / only 2 Huey's in OV-1 Mohawk unit	
247 Med Det	Angel Of Mercy			
247 Med Det	Blood, Sweat + Tears	1960's rock band name		
247 Med Det	Frito Bandito (The)	cartoon mascot for Fritos Corn Chips		
247 Med Det	Iron Butterfly	1960's rock group with same name		
247 Med Det	Jungle Bunny			
247 Med Det	O. D. Green Machine			
247 Med Det	Patches			
247 Med Det	Proud Mary	Creedence Clearwater Revival song title		
247 Med Det	So Other's May Live ^^			
254 Med Det	Blood, Sweat + Tears	1960's rock band name		6-27-70: Jack Wolfe KIA
254 Med Det	Crystal Ship	Doors song title		
254 Med Det	Donna Sue	after Jan '67 crash DONNA SUE jump door was mounted on new Dustoff with "II" added	aka "TWA 1" painted on copter nose	loss to inventory January '67
254 Med Det	Donna Sue II	after Jan '67 crash DONNA SUE jump door was mounted on new Dustoff with "II" added		
254 Med Det	Ghost (The)			
254 Med Det	Helen Sue	"Houston, Tex" painted below name / Helen Sue finally married Hannon in '02 / didn't fly day of fatal crash	name transferred to new UH-1H, 8-13-66, after crash / Karl Danckwerth was medic on this ship	8-13-66: KIA's: MAJ H.Phillips AC +MAJ Kent Gandy CP/Gerry Posumka DG+unk CE both WIA
254 Med Det	Iron Butterfly	1960's rock group with same name		
254 Med Det	Mother Goose			

Unit	Copter Name	Origin / Definition	Notes / Call Signs ( ) < >	Fate Aircraft / Crew
254 Med Det	Proud Mary	female face painted on nose also / Creedence Clearwater Revival song title	currently: N857M, Lee Co Mosquito Control Dist, Lehigh Acres, FL	
254 Med Det	Rebel (The)			
254 Med Det	Thunder Chicken			
254 Med Det	Ugly Duckling			
254 Med Det	White Rabbit **	Jefferson Airplane song title	painting of a white rabbit on dustoff nose	
254 Med Det	Whomp Bird (The)	"lethal"	sunk in ocean on tactical approach to beach 4-1-70	
269 CAB	Peacemaker	peace sign on crew doors	269 CAB C.O.'s ship	
269 CAB	Smokey The Baron	smoke ship		
269 CAB	Smokey The Baron No 2	smoke ship		
269 CAB	Smokey The Baron No 3	smoke ship		
269 CAB	Wicked Wahine	LTC Merryma+D612n's pet name for wife while on Hawaii R+R	Black Baron 6 C+C ship was a 188 ship on loan	
271 ASHC	Beep Beep Ya Ass		aka "HOTEL JULIET", "ROADRUNNER", "HOGJAWS" / converted to CH-47D, 88-00070	
271 ASHC	Big Kahuna			
271 ASHC	Blood, Sweat + Tears	1960's rock band name	converted to CH-47D, 87-00105	
271 ASHC	Boss Hoss			
271 ASHC	Buffy			
271 ASHC	Bull Of The Woods			
271 ASHC	Cambodian Clearwater Revival	parody of Creedence Clearwater Revival name		
271 ASHC	Captain America	American flag painted between 2 words		Feb-March '71: crashed / stricken, July 1972
271 ASHC	City Of Eufaula	Alabama hometown of 1st Sgt Willie Williams / named at FT. Benning / multiple hits, re-named "MAGNET ASS"	flagship CH-47 of unit	8-19-80: crashed
271 ASHC	Cyclops	giant eyeball painted on forward pylon	converted to CH-47D, 86-01675	
271 ASHC	Delta Rat	painted black rat swinging a spiked club	2 different versions of artwork depicted in photos	DD 1-13-69

Unit	Copter Name	Origin / Definition	Notes / Call Signs ( ) < >	Fate Aircraft / Crew
271 ASHC	Delta Rat II	painting of cigar chomping rat with M-60 + band-aid on tail		
271 ASHC	Easy Rider	Hollywood movie title	John Brennan of 114 AHC should be credited for "EASY RIDER" pic instead of Pete Harlem in Mutza's CH-47 book	
271 ASHC	El Bandito			
271 ASHC	Gold Finger	middle finger salute		captured by NVA 1975
271 ASHC	Heaven's Devil			
271 ASHC	Hogjaws		aka "HOTEL JULIET", "ROADRUNNER", "BEEP YA ASS" / converted to CH-47D, 88-00070	
271 ASHC	Hotel Juliet	phonetic words for "Hog Jaws"	aka "HOGJAWS", "ROADRUNNER", "BEEP BEEP YA ASS" / converted to CH-47D, 88-00070	
271 ASHC	Iron Butterfly	1960's rock group with same name		
271 ASHC	Led Zeppelin (The)	British rock band name		
271 ASHC	Little Orphan Annie	comic book character		DD 7-16-68: 1 KIA, John Simpson CP
271 ASHC	Magnet Ass	reputation for drawing enemy fire	"MAGNET ASS" + "CITY OF EUFAULA" both on '110 / human figure + large peach paintings also	8-19-80: crashed
271 ASHC	Miscarriage (The)		converted to CH-47D, 87-00105	
271 ASHC	Mother Goose			DD 5-8-68: 1st CH-47B shot down, destroyed in Mekong Delta
271 ASHC	Mother Goose II	painted broken egg with black spots denoting bullet holes on original "MOTHER GOOSE	presently flying in Panama / converted to CH-47D, 88-00077	
271 ASHC	Rapid Transit System	Gatzemeyer originated name		DD 12-21-70: accident, C/228 / Fred Wilken AC + Art Cordry CP: both injured
271 ASHC	Roadrunner		aka "HOTEL JULIET", BEEP BEEP YA ASS", HOGJAWS"	
271 ASHC	Roadrunner II ^		shares serial # with B-159 ASHB's "ASHAU EXPRESS"	
271 ASHC	Sandra	name of Teeter's girlfriend	aka "WETBACK"	
271 ASHC	Screaming Green Zonkers	NVA-VC tracer rounds / slang for marijuana		
271 ASHC	Snoopy's Dream		only 'A' model in unit according to Stroud / converted to CH-47D, 85-24323	
271 ASHC	Wetback	derogatory term for people of Mexican descent	aka "SANDRA"	
273 Avn Co	Jo Ann	both FE + CE wife's name	yellow paint	

Unit	Copter Name	Origin / Definition	Notes / Call Signs ( ) < >	Fate Aircraft / Crew
273 Avn Co	Load Runner	picture of a Roadrunner on nose		
281 AHC	Chuck Crusher			
281 AHC	Deacon (The)	funeral motif		
281 AHC	Death Dealer			
281 AHC	Death Express			
281 AHC	Death Merchant			Thanksgiving, 1969: shot down
281 AHC	Death On Call ^^			
281 AHC	Delta Air ^^^	refers to Project Delta missions, 5th Special Forces, Detachment B-52	aka "DOUBLE DEUCE"	
281 AHC	Double Deuce		aka "DELTA AIR"	
281 AHC	Executioner (The)	unit gunship names reflected funeral motif		
281 AHC	Grave Digger (The)	funeral motif		
281 AHC	Hell From Above ^^			
281 AHC	Iron Butterfly			
281 AHC	Iron Butterfly II			
281 AHC	Love Child	nn ordered removed, too hippie lingo: CE refused, another ordered to do it / Supremes song title		
281 AHC	Miss Carriage			
281 AHC	Mortician (The)	funeral motif		
281 AHC	Pall Bearer (The)	funeral motif		
281 AHC	Satan's Whore			
281 AHC	Sneaky Pete *	top secret MAC-SOG missions	wolf figure painted on doorpost	
281 AHC	Snoopy **	painted Snoopy "flipping the bird' at VC		DD 3-16-68: Ashau Valley
281 AHC	Tee Tom Twenty ^	combination callsign + nickname	painted "DELTA AIR" on nose also	

Unit	Copter Name	Origin / Definition	Notes / Call Signs ( ) < >	Fate Aircraft / Crew
281 AHC	Undertaker (The)	funeral motif		
281 AHC	Village Stomper (The)			
281 AHC	Widow Maker (The)	funeral motif		
282 AHC	Bell's Lemon	painted lemon for each maintenance problem	(BC 11)	
282 AHC	Blivet	named after rubber fuel bladder	Gabriel+Bush flew with 2 different crews / currently: N81499, US State Dept, Patrick AFB, FL	
282 AHC	Bones 11 ^	pair of dice painted on door: five + six = 11 / pilot call sign also		
282 AHC	Cat Doctor ^	adopted name of the maintenance platoon's aircraft that imitated the 282nd's BLACK CATS callsign	484 TC/ Ray Boyle CE	
282 AHC	Cherry			
282 AHC	Doris			
282 AHC	Last Chance		shares serial # with 187 AHC's "HILL BILLY DILLY"	
282 AHC	Ruby Tuesday *	Rolling Stones song title		
282 AHC	Slicks Are For Kids - With Balls	rebuff to gunship braggadocio	Somerfield painted helmets and 1st platoon doors / Jesus Pagan also painted pilot doors	
283 Med Det	Alfred E. Neuman	painted Alfred E. Neuman on cargo door / aka "GREEN WEENIE"	MAD magazine icon + slogan "What, Me Worry?" was counterpart to WWII's "Kilroy Was Here"	
283 Med Det	Bell's Misfit	BELL = UH-1 manufacturer	photo shows it wrecked + on flatbed truck	
283 Med Det	Green Weenie	getting screwed over	aka "WHAT! ME WORRY"	
283 Med Det	Hangar Queen	derogatory term for excessive need for repairs		
283 Med Det	Magnet Ass	reputation for drawing enemy fire		
283 Med Det	Mr. Bond	James Bond 007 reference + tail # 007	'488 + '283 interchanged ships cause high attrition rate	
283 Med Det	Molly *			
283 Med Det	Orient Express			shot down by RPG round
283 Med Det	What ! Me Worry?	painted Alfred E. Neuman on cargo door / aka "GREEN WEENIE"	MAD magazine icon + slogan "What, Me Worry?" was counterpart to WWII's "Kilroy Was Here"	
308 CAB	VC Widow Maker			

Unit	Copter Name	Origin / Definition	Notes / Call Signs ( ) < >	Fate Aircraft / Crew
326 Med Bn	Band-Aid Machine (The)			
326 Med Bn	Foxy Lady	Jimmy Hendrix song title		
326 Med Bn	Purple Haze	Jimmy Hendrix song title		
334 AWC	Double Trouble *	copied WW II vet father's B-24 "Double Trouble" name	aka "WHISKEY + WOMEN" verbal name	
334 AWC	Miss Patches II			
334 AWC	Miss Patches III			
334 AWC	FireFly		"RAIDERS" also painted on nose	DD 2-16-67: 4 KIA
334 AWC	Hawaiian Samurai			
334 AWC	Jay			
334 AWC	Judge (The)			
334 AWC	Linda			
334 AWC	Miss Patches *		.50 caliber machine gun	
334 AWC	Nature's Own			
334 AWC	Old Patches *	numerous battle damage patches		
334 AWC	Peacemakers ^^^	flare ship and C+C with .50 caliber machine gun	"callsign" also	DD 11-10-71
335 AHC	2nd Try	1st assigned slick was destroyed	currently: N362SD, U.S. State Dept, Patrick AFB, FL	
335 AHC	Ace High			
335 AHC	Aeroplane		aka "MISS JUNE"	
335 AHC	Ava's Darlin	letter sign-off "Larry, you are a darlin" / resident of Ava, Missouri		
335 AHC	Bad News			
335 AHC	Bad News II	painting of VC combatant in crosshairs	was original "BAD NEWS" destroyed?	
335 AHC	Beer Wagon (The)	Schlitz beer can label replicated on rocket pods		

Unit	Copter Name	Origin / Definition	Notes / Call Signs ( ) < >	Fate Aircraft / Crew
335 AHC	Bitch (The)	Hoza renamed "BIG TRAIN" to "BITCH" when he was assigned this gunship		
335 AHC	Blenda's Rage			
335 AHC	Buckeye			
335 AHC	Buschwacker	BUSCH beer can label replicated on copter nose		
335 AHC	Cajun Queen		<31>	
335 AHC	Calif. Dreamer	CE + DG both from CA	Pabst Blue Ribbon beer can label replicated on rocket pods	
335 AHC	California Republic	CA State flag	CA state flag painted on nose	DD 1970
335 AHC	Crystal Ship	Doors song title		
335 AHC	Double O Pig *	refers to serial #, also UH-1B ?		
335 AHC	Fantastic Plastic Machine	1969 surfing movie title		
335 AHC	Forget Hell		confederate flag painted on nose also	
335 AHC	Freedom Bird	bird flashing Peace sign / G.I. term for any U.S. bound commercial airliner		
335 AHC	Homeward Bound	1966 Simon + Garfunkel song by same name		
335 AHC	Horse Thief ^	adopted name of the maintenance platoon's aircraft that imitated the 335th's COWBOYS callsign	named by CPT McConnell / wore a camo paint job / reportedly, oldest, continuous duty B model in VN	
335 AHC	Horse Thief II ^	adopted name of the maintenance platoon's aircraft that imitated the 335th's COWBOYS callsign	wore a camo paint job	DD 2-22-67
335 AHC	Hubschrauberpilot	German word for "helicopter pilot"		
335 AHC	Iron Butterfly	1960's rock group by same name	"HARMON" + "LUFFMAN" painted on sync elevators	
335 AHC	Judi In D' Skys	John Fred + His Playboy Band song title	<10>	
335 AHC	Jungle Cruiser			
335 AHC	Miss June		aka "AEROPLANE"	
335 AHC	Mustang Sally	Wilson Pickett song title		
335 AHC	Not Even			

Unit	Copter Name	Origin / Definition	Notes / Call Signs ( ) < >	Fate Aircraft / Crew
335 AHC	Not Even II		was original "NOT EVEN" destroyed?	
335 AHC	Ole Magnet Ass *	propensity for drawing enemy fire	Champlin was C.O. of A-82/335 in 1965-66	
335 AHC	Pabst Blue Ribbon	PABST beer can label replicated on rocket pod	possible 64-14049 also	
335 AHC	Patches *	over 100 shrapnel holes		
335 AHC	Schlitz	SCHLITZ beer can label replicated on rocket pod		
335 AHC	Season's Greetings The Cowboys	bows+bells+Western dude painted on nose also		
335 AHC	Sloopy Gal	The McCoys song title	shares serial # with 117 AHC's "PUSSY GALORE"	
335 AHC	Stormy	Classics IV song title		
335 AHC	Super Slick *	ref: the last 3 #'s in sn (427) mimicked the Chevy Impala 427 Super Sport car of the time	'427 + Rick Tabor CE down for maint on 3-31-70	3-31-70: entire crew minus Tabor WIA on 68-16076 / K.Sheldon CE of '076 KIA 3-31-70
335 AHC	Sweet Bee	tear gas aircraft		
335 AHC	Swill Barrel (The)	"unpleasant odor"		
335 AHC	Taco Wagon	door gunner named it	shares serial # with 129 AHC's "KEEP TRUCKIN", "SNOW SNAKE"	
335 AHC	Trail Boss	flattened beer can covers .51 nose bullet hole	2 nn versions painted on nose / 335 AHC C.O.'s ship / on display: Humboldt Co, Winnemucca, NV	
335 AHC	Tripship			
335 AHC	Valerie			
335 AHC	Wanted: Uncle Ho Dead Or Alive	facsimile of HCM's face depicted on a poster		
335 AHC	Wild Child (The)	Doors song title / Ed Roth's custom monster car		
335 AHC	Yosemite Sam **	animated cartoon character	no lettering, just painted image	
336 AHC	Angel Of Death		"CHIEF" painted above T-Bird logo on nose	
336 AHC	Baroness	semi-nude female painted on nose	accident photo, copter lying on its side	
336 AHC	Bird Of Pray	intentionally mis-spelled	(TB 38)	
336 AHC	Birth Control			

Unit	Copter Name	Origin / Definition	Notes / Call Signs ( ) < >	Fate Aircraft / Crew
336 AHC	Blue Max (The)	foreign military award		
336 AHC	California			
336 AHC	Chief		aka "KNIGHT RAIDER" and "MAKE LOVE + WAR"	
336 AHC	Color Me Bad News	parody of "Color Me Barbara" (Streisand) '66 album title		
336 AHC	Colorado		(War 26)	
336 AHC	Crystal Blue Persuasion	Tommy James + The Shondells song title	(TB 37)	12-20-69: Beddingfield WIA
336 AHC	Dreadnaught			
336 AHC	Fly Delta's Big Jets	referred to Delta Bn-Mekong Delta-Delta Huey model	promotional stickers by Delta Airlines / (War 25)	
336 AHC	Friendly Persuasion	Hollywood Civil War film of same name		
336 AHC	God Of Hell's Fire (The)	Arthur Brown 1967 rock song lyrics	(TB 4)	
336 AHC	Hell From On High			
336 AHC	Knight Raider	CPT Knight's last name / TB Lead	"MAKE LOVE AND WAR" on rocket pods / "CHIEF" on vertical stabilizer	
336 AHC	Loner (The)	Indian riding 4 eyed green monster	(War 19)	
336 AHC	Love Portion #9	VN artist mis-spelled Potion / David Lape named it / Lape later KIA'd / The Searcher's song title	(TB 9)	
336 AHC	Loved One (The)	1965 Hollywood cult movie	(TB 31)	
336 AHC	Lucky Strike	airfield security lightship	Night Hawk ship with .50 caliber machine gun + Xeon light	DD 2-27-70: 6 KIA: Connelly, McCormick, Pace, Proctor, Stafford, Swartz
336 AHC	Macabre		(TB 38)	
336 AHC	Macabre II		either 66-00564 or 66-0069: Oct-Dec '70 incident / avionics panel taken back to USA / (TB 38)	
336 AHC	Make Love And War	CPT Knight's last name / TB Lead	aka "KNIGHT RAIDER" and "CHIEF"	
336 AHC	Mandrake Root	Deep Purple song title	"according to the legend, when the root is dug up it screams and kills all who hear it" / (TB 38)	
336 AHC	Mary Jane	slang for marijuana		
336 AHC	Miss Fortune	double entendre	girl in martini glass graphic on door / (TB 37)	

Unit	Copter Name	Origin / Definition	Notes / Call Signs ( ) < >	Fate Aircraft / Crew
336 AHC	Miss Fortune II	double entendre	was original "MISS FORTUNE" destroyed?	
336 AHC	Mr B's Bad Bomber			
336 AHC	Mr B's Bad Bomber II			
336 AHC	Mystery Ship	part of the 1970 "Ride Captain Ride" lyrics by The Blues Image / sailing galleon painted on nose		
336 AHC	Pogy Boat	to be used as bait + 2nd rate foodstuff		
336 AHC	Protected By Batman			
336 AHC	Ragin Cajun			
336 AHC	Red Devil			
336 AHC	Red Devil	scantily dressed female with wrench	nose panel was shipped home to former unit member	
336 AHC	Scotch Soda	1958 Kingston Trio hit song by same title		
336 AHC	Screw Communism		aka "SUPER SLICK"	
336 AHC	Shirley Ann			
336 AHC	Slope Slayer	slope =Vietnamese	(TB 32)	
336 AHC	Snooper			
336 AHC	Snooper II			
336 AHC	Snoopy			
336 AHC	Snoopy **	snoopy+doghouse with mounted machine guns	aka "LUCKY 13" / (War 13)	
336 AHC	Snoopy II		was original SNOOPY destroyed?	
336 AHC	Snoopy III		was SNOOPY II destroyed? / (TB 3)	
336 AHC	Super Slick		aka "SCREW COMMUNISM" / also "SUPER SLICK" on vertical stabilizer / (War 21)	
336 AHC	War Hoop	David Lape originated name	(TB 8)	
339 TC	Always In Good Hands ^^			
339 TC	Baby Huey	painting of large baby on nose / powerful but self destructive cartoon character		DD 2-20-68: all aboard KIA

U.S. ARMY HELICOPTER NAMES IN VIETNAM

Unit	Copter Name	Origin / Definition	Notes / Call Signs ( ) < >	Fate Aircraft / Crew
339 TC	City Of Nha Trang		"FLAGSHIP" painted above "CITY OF NHA TRANG"	
339 TC	Hang On Snoopy	Snoopy carrying fire hydrant		
339 TC	Igor's Numba Wun	named after Igor Sikorsky, designer of CH-37	possible serial # was '995, according to Frank Ferry	
339 TC	Johnnie Reb			
339 TC	Johnny Reb Jr		"JOHNNIE REB" was on a CH-37 in unit	
339 TC	Octopus (The)			
339 TC	Six Pack To Go	"armed rockets ready for deployment"		
339 TC	Wayne's Work Horse	C.O. was MAJ Wayne Barker / "Work Horse" was official CH-37 military designation		
339 TC	Woolyberger	Bigfoot type creature		
355 Avn Co	Hulk (The)	name of comic book character	aka "F*CK YOU CHARLIE" walking finger art / currently: N245AC, Erickson Air-Crane Inc, Central Point, OR	
355 Avn Co	Thinker (The)	parody of Roden's famous marble statue which shows head in ass image instead		
361 AWC	Magnolia Thunderpussy	hippie ice cream and desert parlor, known for its late-night delivery service	famed 1960's San Francisco hippie restaurant / cited in Aug '09 issue of S.F. Mag / Wikipedia also	
361 AWC	Queer John	pilot nickname / Cajun slang		
361 AWC	Sheriff's Piecemaker	Sheriff was CE's nickname: from Beach Boys song reference ?		
362 ASHC	Fly Me			DD 5-10-72: all 32 KIA
362 ASHC	Ghost Rider			captured by NVA 1975
371 RRC	Bad (The)	unit had three slicks, each displaying parts of the phrase, "the good, the bad and the ugly"	Army Security Agency: Radio Research Company (RRC) / specially equipped copters for eavesdropping	
371 RRC	Good (The)	unit had three slicks, each displaying parts of the phrase, "the good, the bad and the ugly"	Army Security Agency: Radio Research Company / (RRC) special equipped copters for eavesdropping	
371 RRC	Ugly (The)	unit had three slicks, each displaying parts of the phrase, "the good, the bad and the ugly"	Army Security Agency: Radio Research Company / (RRC) special equipped copters for eavesdropping	
478 Avn Co	Big Bad John	Jimmy Dean song title		
478 Avn Co	Big Mother	first + only helo bomber in the Army inventory: dropped 4-10,000 lbs bombs Sep-Oct '68	currently: Reno Nat'l Guard, Stead Airport, NV	
478 Avn Co	OK Babe		1st CH-54 built by Sikorsky	DD 8-9-66: no KIA's

Unit	Copter Name	Origin / Definition	Notes / Call Signs ( ) < >	Fate Aircraft / Crew
478 Avn Co	Ole Reliable			DD 4-19-69: Ashau Valley
478 Avn Co	Wooly Booger	Bigfoot type creature / hairy female anatomy		DD 1-5-66: 1st CH-54 loss in VN with fatalities
498 Med Co	007 *	secret agent James Bond's moniker	aka "BOND", "PATCHES"	
498 Med Co	Blood, Sweat + Tears	1960's rock band name		
498 Med Co	Blood, Sweat + Tears No 2	1960's rock band name		
498 Med Co	Bond	serial # '007 matched secret agent James Bond's moniker	aka "007" +" PATCHES" / "MR.BOND" possible nn also	
498 Med Co	Buzzard			
498 Med Co	Color Me Gone	parody of "Color Me Barbara" (Streisand) '66 album title		
498 Med Co	Deadbone **	lizard from Vaughn Bode comic strip		
498 Med Co	Double Eagle	two eagles painted on nose replicate the double eagles depicted on American $20 gold coin piece		
498 Med Co	Easy Rider	Hollywood movie title	stars + stripes on nose also	
498 Med Co	Electric Banana	tailboom covered in yellow primer / "e-lec-tri-cal banana" Donovan lyrics in song "Mellow Yellow"		
498 Med Co	Fixer (The)			
498 Med Co	Golieth	intentionally mis-spelled		
498 Med Co	Great Green Vaseline War Machine (The)	sliding in + out of hot LZ's	same name used on 498 MC + 45 MC Dustoff ships	
498 Med Co	Hair			
498 Med Co	Hell's Angel	notorious American motorcycle club of same name		
498 Med Co	Hermies	"messenger, guide" in Greek mythology, spelled Hermes		
498 Med Co	Iron Butterfly	painting of a butterfly of iron	rescued 174 AHC's "SURFER" crew in Laos	
498 Med Co	Iron Butterfly (The)	1960's rock group by same name		
498 Med Co	Iron Butterfly (The)	1960's rock group by same name		
498 Med Co	Laotian Whore			

U.S. ARMY HELICOPTER NAMES IN VIETNAM

Unit	Copter Name	Origin / Definition	Notes / Call Signs ( ) < >	Fate Aircraft / Crew
498 Med Co	Led Zeppelin	British rock band name		
498 Med Co	Let It Be	Beatle's song title		
498 Med Co	Linda			
498 Med Co	Litter Bird			
498 Med Co	Magnet Ass	reputation for drawing enemy fire	last mission written up in Cook's book	DD 4-6-68: Richardson KIA / Bruce Knipe MD, was thrown into trees + rescued
498 Med Co	Mother's Lil' Worry	based on Ed Roth's "Mother's Worry" monster car	'55' painted on nose	
498 Med Co	Ninja		old Chinese type lettering	
498 Med Co	Passion			
498 Med Co	Patches *	over 25+ bullet holes	aka "007" and "BOND" because of serial # reference to James Bond's moniker	
498 Med Co	Patricia	was name of Sibley's girlfriend		DD 6-30-69: near DMZ
498 Med Co	Patriot			
498 Med Co	Proud Mary	Creedence Clearwater Revival song title		
498 Med Co	Provider (The)			
498 Med Co	Troll (The) **	painting only, no lettering	image copied from Hustler magazine	
498 Med Co	Why		July '09 VVA's "Arts of War On The Web" features in-country pic of 498th Med Det ship named "WHY"	
539 TC	Body Snatcher	Hollywood horror film	aka "PIPESMOKE" painted on fuselage	
539 TC	Ho Chi Minh **		poster of HCM would adorn a particular helo that was in for repairs and had over-stayed its welcome	
539 TC	Huffer	"a fit of anger or annoyance"	aka "PIPESMOKE" painted on pilot door	
539 TC	La Poule De Duerre	"chicken of war"	aka "PIPESMOKE" painted on fuselage / over 100 recovery stencils painted on fuselage	
539 TC	Old Rivers	painting of hillbilly also	Pipesmoke Recovery	
539 TC	Reeling In A Huey **	painting: old man fishing with a hooked Huey on the line		
539 TC	SNAFU	"situation normal, all fucked up"		

ARMY HELICOPTER NAMES: UNIT/NUMERICAL

Unit	Copter Name	Origin / Definition	Notes / Call Signs ( ) < >	Fate Aircraft / Crew
539 TC	SNAFU II	"situation normal, all fucked up"	original SNAFU destroyed?	
539 TC	Wee Willie's War Wagon		Pipesmoke Recovery	
539 TC	Widow Maker		Pipesmoke Recovery	
571 Med Det	Black Bitch	painted black	shares serial # + name with 237 Med Det / currently: N357SD, U.S. State Dept, Patrick AFB,	
571 Med Det	California Dreamin'	Bohrman was Fresno, CA native	aka "MY BROTHER'S KEEPER" on nose	
571 Med Det	Dynamic Duo (The)	borrowed Batman + Robin's cartoon character's nickname	Zig Zag man painting also; currently: N4228V, Patrick AFB, FL	
571 Med Det	Hog (The)		shares serial # with "WOODSTOCK"	
571 Med Det	Magic Christian (The)	1969 Peter Seller's movie by same name		
571 Med Det	My Brother's Keeper		aka "CALIFORNIA DREAMIN" on CE jump door	
571 Med Det	Nixon's Withdrawal	refers to the troop reduction order by President Nixon in the later years of the war		
571 Med Det	Sally J			
571 Med Det	Screaming Nighthog			
571 Med Det	Woodstock	infamous 1969 rock concert	shares serial # with "THE HOG"	
571 Med Det	You Maul Em We Haul Em			
571 TC	Knuckle Buster ^	clinched hand with crossed wrenches painted on copter nose	during 1971 the 571st operated a UH-1H serial # 68-16289 with "KNUCKLE BUSTER" painted on the copter nose	
605 TC	Hearse (The)			
611 TC	Big Daddy ^	famous artist Ed Roth's nickname		
611 TC	Big Ed			
611 TC	Big Nick ^			
611 TC	Bird Shippers (The)		re: pg 249, VHPA's "Helicopter History of IV Corps"	
611 TC	Don Juan			
611 TC	Have Axes Will Travel			
611 TC	How Sweet It Is	painting of horned steer resting on its back		

U.S. ARMY HELICOPTER NAMES IN VIETNAM

Unit	Copter Name	Origin / Definition	Notes / Call Signs ( ) < >	Fate Aircraft / Crew
611 TC	Slave Driver	painted skull + cross bones also		
611 TC	Wild Aces	five playing cards painted		
937 Cbt Eng Gp	Nancy	name of CE's wife		
A Btry 2/20 ARA	Leper Colony (The)	"12 O'Clock High" movie reference to a B-17 bomber manned by less than admirable crew		
A Btry 4/77 ARA	God Of Hell's Fire	Arthur Brown 1967 rock song lyrics		
A Btry 4/77 ARA	il Padrone	Italian for "the boss"	Mafia black hand painted on nose	
A Btry 4/77 ARA	Rosemary's Baby	Hollywood horror film title		
A Co 1 Avn Bn	Baby Huey	painted cartoon character Baby Huey: powerful but self destructive reputation	aka "LINDA ANN" / Patrick was 184 RAC pilot / camouflage paint scheme / 40 mm in nose-Hog	
A Co 1 Avn Bn	Big Iron	Marty Robbins song title	aka "RED BARON" / on display: Miracle of America Museum + Pioneer Village, Polson, MT	
A Co 1 Avn Bn	Black Power	social cause of the 1960's		
A Co 1 Avn Bn	Cassy	daughter's nickname		
A Co 1 Avn Bn	El Cid		aka "ROSALIE"	
A Co 1 Avn Bn	Great Pumpkin (The)	Charlie Brown + Peanuts reference / turret painted orange with lettering		
A Co 1 Avn Bn	Linda Ann	painted Baby Huey cartoon character	aka "BABY HUEY"/ Patrick was 184 RAC pilot / camouflage paint scheme / 40 mm in nose-Hog	
A Co 1 Avn Bn	Madonna II	mis-spelling of Madonna / named after CE's wife:1st Madonna was mother of Jesus	there was no MADONNA # I because the mother of Jesus was the original Madonna says Alioto the crew chief	7-26-68: shot down, crew member WIA
A Co 1 Avn Bn	Muff Diver	sexual occupation		
A Co 1 Avn Bn	Nancy		(Rebel 21)	
A Co 1 Avn Bn	Poison			
A Co 1 Avn Bn	Red Baron **		aka "BIG IRON"	
A Co 1 Avn Bn	Rosalie		aka "EL CID"	
A Co 1 Avn Bn	Semper Mint Julep-Confederate Air Force	CAF blood chit		

Unit	Copter Name	Origin / Definition	Notes / Call Signs ( ) < >	Fate Aircraft / Crew
A Co 1 Avn Bn	Snuffy Mad Dog	Rebel flag decals compliments of Confederate Air Force of TX	aka "SUPER SLOPE" opposite doorpost / (Rebel 26)	
A Co 1 Avn Bn	Super Slope		aka "SNUFFY MAD DOG" / Rebel flag decals compliments of the Confederate Air Force, TX / (Rebel 26)	
A Co 4 Avn Bn	Electric Banana (The)	British rock band		
A Co 4 Avn Bn	Mary Jane	slang for marijuana / named by Frank Morrison CE		
A Co 4 Avn Bn	Renegade (The)			
A Co 9 Avn Bn	Flower Power *	callsign to tower		
A Co 25 Avn Bn	Birth Control			
A Co 25 Avn Bn	Little Bear Repair ^			
A Co 82 Avn Bn	Big Train		68 Avn Co became 197 Avn Co on 3-1-65	
A Co 82 Avn Bn	Honey Bee			
A Co 82 Avn Bn	Little Eileen			
A Co 82 Avn Bn	Mad Bomber	Mortar Air Delivery (MAD) system	attached to 173 Abn Bde as of 10-18-65	
A Co 82 Avn Bn	VC Widow Maker			
A Co 101 AHB	Anheuser-Busch **	Anheuser-Busch icon of an American bald eagle and a fancy letter 'A'	A-2-17, A-2-20 and A-101 replicated the beer company 'A' on their copter noses	
A Co 101 AHB	For Sale	unit stood down, Huey prepared for transit		
A Co 101 AHB	Kosher Eagle ^	Jewish pilot		
A Co 101 AHB	Super Slick *	night vision and minigun		
A Co 123 Avn Bn	Hogan's Goat	AC's last name was Hogan	painted "VC ELEPHANT" (KBA, Killed By Air) on doorpost also	
A Co 123 Avn Bn	VC Elephant	enemy elephant bagged by DG	"HOGAN'S GOAT" on doorpost also	
A Co 158 AHB	Amazing Spiderman (The) ^	colorful "callsign" nameplate depicts action figure / "SPIDERMAN" was Franck's callsign also		
A Co 158 AHB	Cheap Thrills	Janis Joplin album title		
A Co 158 AHB	Stache ^	"STACHE" was Smith's callsign because of signature moustache	colorful "callsign" nameplate depicts mustached gentleman	

Unit	Copter Name	Origin / Definition	Notes / Call Signs ( ) < >	Fate Aircraft / Crew
A Co 158 AHB	Under Dog ^	American animated television series / nameplate on doorpost		DD 7-26-70
A Co 159 ASHB	Balls Deuce *	refers to 0-0-2 sequence in serial #	converted to CH-47D, 89-00149	
A Co 159 ASHB	Beep Beep Yur Butt	101st C.O. ordered name changed from "YURASS" to "YUR BUTT"		captured by NVA 1975
A Co 159 ASHB	Ramblin' Rose	Nat King Cole 1962 song title		DD 2-15-71: all KIA when Seabourn was on R+R
A Co 159 ASHB	Wonder Wart-Hog	underground comic book character, parody of Superman	aka "PHILBERT DESENEX"	DD 3-23-75
227 AHB	Baja Bush Bandit			
227 AHB	Flying Hemorrhoid (The)		currently: N456SD, Maricopa Co Sheriff's Office, Phoenix, AZ	
A Co 227 AHB	#1 Boom Boom	good sex / playboy bunny on nose above nickname		
A Co 227 AHB	Bare Chicken		During '70-'71 the CHICKENMAN call-sign was incorporated into individualized nose art with a customized name to boot on every Huey in the unit's rotor fleet: feat unequaled in VN	
A Co 227 AHB	Brother Bird	see "Notes" citation for "BARE CHICKEN"	'471 + '936 both carried this name	
A Co 227 AHB	Brother Bird	see "Notes" citation for "BARE CHICKEN"	'471 + '936 both carried this name	
A Co 227 AHB	Buck Shot		painting of ace of spades on nose also	
A Co 227 AHB	Can Do		aka "ROHO"	
A Co 227 AHB	Captain Zig Zag	parody of Zig Zag of cigarette brand paper		
A Co 227 AHB	Cheap Thrills	Janis Joplin album title		
A Co 227 AHB	Chicken Coupe	see "Notes" citation for "BARE CHICKEN"		Sept, 1970: crashed
A Co 227 AHB	Chicken Little	see "Notes" citation for "BARE CHICKEN"		
A Co 227 AHB	Chicken Ship	see "Notes" citation for "BARE CHICKEN"		
A Co 227 AHB	Chicken Slick	see "Notes" citation for "BARE CHICKEN"		
A Co 227 AHB	Chickenest Chicken	see "Notes" citation for "BARE CHICKEN"		
A Co 227 AHB	Chickenman America	see "Notes" citation for "BARE CHICKEN"		
A Co 227 AHB	Chickenman Chicken	see "Notes" citation for "BARE CHICKEN"		

Unit	Copter Name	Origin / Definition	Notes / Call Signs ( ) < >	Fate Aircraft / Crew
A Co 227 AHB	Chickenman's Magnet Ass	painted wild chicken with magnet around its ass	see "Notes" citation for "BARE CHICKEN"	
A Co 227 AHB	Chickenman's Rotary Connection	see "Notes" citation for "BARE CHICKEN"		3-31-71: WO Roger Reid KIA in this ship
A Co 227 AHB	Cloud 9	1968 Temptations song title / slang expression	Batey identified pic frame captured from Ed Friday's video	
A Co 227 AHB	Colleene	"COLLEENE" was Burden's sweetheart, later married	Grunt leaves pic of daughter Collenne who was same name as Burden's wife!! / aka "THE LAST MOHICAN"	
A Co 227 AHB	Comely Cock (The)	see "Notes" citation for "BARE CHICKEN"		
A Co 227 AHB	Crash's Mistake	Wheatley crashed in flight school	aka "HARD LUCK"	
A Co 227 AHB	Death From Above			
A Co 227 AHB	Devil's Advocate			
A Co 227 AHB	Dr. Chicken Chickenman	see "Notes" citation for "BARE CHICKEN"		
A Co 227 AHB	Flying Dutchman	according to legend, a ghost ship can never go home, doomed to sail the oceans forever		
A Co 227 AHB	Flying Dutchman II			
A Co 227 AHB	Grampa Chicken	see "Notes" citation for "BARE CHICKEN"		
A Co 227 AHB	Hard Luck		aka "CRASH'S MISTAKE"	
A Co 227 AHB	Have Chicken Will Travel	see "Notes" citation for "BARE CHICKEN"		
A Co 227 AHB	Have Chicken-Leg Will Travel	see "Notes" citation for "BARE CHICKEN"		
A Co 227 AHB	Hell On Skids			
A Co 227 AHB	Hillbilly Chicken	see "Notes" citation for "BARE CHICKEN"	Warren was known as "Country"	
A Co 227 AHB	I. W. Harper	whiskey brand name / painted whiskey bottle with slogan, "It's Always A Pleasure"		
A Co 227 AHB	Iron Butterfly		pic found at Texas Tech Archive, HEARNE collection	
A Co 227 AHB	Iron Chicken (The)	see "Notes" citation for "BARE CHICKEN"		
A Co 227 AHB	Last Mohican (The)		aka "COLLEENE"	
A Co 227 AHB	Led Zeppelin	British rock band name		

U.S. ARMY HELICOPTER NAMES IN VIETNAM

Unit	Copter Name	Origin / Definition	Notes / Call Signs ( ) < >	Fate Aircraft / Crew
A Co 227 AHB	Lil' Annie's Fannie	"ANNIE" was Jester's wife's name		
A Co 227 AHB	Lin's Rickshaw	"LIN" short for Linda, CE's wife's name		
A Co 227 AHB	Lucy In The Sky	Beatles song title	possible artwork also	DD 2-18-70: all crew KIA
A Co 227 AHB	Magical Mystery Tour	Beatles tune	"PIPE DREAMS" was not allowed to accompany "M.M.T." on copter nose; negative outlook was not PC according to C.O.	
A Co 227 AHB	Magnifico Chicken	see "Notes" citation for "BARE CHICKEN"	Jester was White Flight Lead	
A Co 227 AHB	Michigan Menace	Lazenby was native of Pontiac, MI		
A Co 227 AHB	Mighty Chicken	see "Notes" citation for "BARE CHICKEN"		
A Co 227 AHB	Miss Pussy Galore	James Bond female adversary		
A Co 227 AHB	Nancy Jane			
A Co 227 AHB	Oobladi Ooblada Chicken Freak	'389 was grounded after 2nd PE / see "Notes" citation for "BARE CHICKEN"	1st incarnation of "CHICKEN FREAK: / Tonjes was assigned '051 after '389: re-painted it "CHICKEN FREAK"	
A Co 227 AHB	Oobladi Ooblada Chicken Freak	Beatles song title / see "Notes" citation for "BARE CHICKEN"	2nd incarnation of CHICKEN FREAK / on display: American Legion Post 639, Springfield, MO	
A Co 227 AHB	Playboy Bunny **	painted icon bunny ears of Playboy magazine fame		
A Co 227 AHB	Rebel Chicken	see "Notes" citation for "BARE CHICKEN"	aircraft utilized during Medal of Honor mission	DD 5-25-71: MAJ Adams shot down in this a/c, all crew KIA
A Co 227 AHB	Roho		aka "CAN DO"	
A Co 227 AHB	Stewed Chicken	see "Notes" citation for "BARE CHICKEN"	gstbk entry mis-identified this bird as "SCREWED "CHICKEN	
A Co 227 AHB	Untouchable Chickenman	see "Notes" citation for "BARE CHICKEN"		
A Co 227 AHB	Wolly Bully	Sam The Sham + The Pharaohs song title		
228 ASHB	Shadow of Death (The)			
A Co 228 ASHB	Big Boob (The)			
A Co 228 ASHB	Boss (The)			
A Co 228 ASHB	Chuck You Farlie	spoonerism = transposition of the letters C and F		
A Co 228 ASHB	Crap Shooter	painting of two large dice also		

Unit	Copter Name	Origin / Definition	Notes / Call Signs ( ) < >	Fate Aircraft / Crew
A Co 228 ASHB	Double Deuce	pair of dice showing 2 pip spots on both	shares serial # with 213 ASHC's "SNOOPY"	10-25-70: bad crash
A Co 228 ASHB	Flower Power	counterculture slogan meaning non-violence	converted to CH-47D, 85-24359	4-24-68: David Caballero DG, KIA
A Co 228 ASHB	Flying Coffin (The)			
A Co 228 ASHB	Gallopin Goose HC	named after New Orleans motorcycle club	Killarney borrowed name, colors and graphics / HC = helicopter club, mimics MC = motorcycle club	DD '71-'72
A Co 228 ASHB	Grunt Wagon (The)			10-3-68: mid-air collison with C-7A Caribou, Camp Evans, all KIA
A Co 228 ASHB	Life's A Bitch			
A Co 228 ASHB	Miss Stony			
A Co 228 ASHB	No Balls 3	serial # reference	converted to CH-47D, 86-01680	
A Co 228 ASHB	Norma Jean	Marilyn Monroe's original first name		
A Co 228 ASHB	Proud Mary	Creedence Clearwater Revival song title		DD 12-5-74
A Co 228 ASHB	Queen (The)			
A Co 228 ASHB	Roadrunner (The) **	painting only, no lettering	roadrunner painted on fuselage / converted to CH-47D, 85-24324	
A Co 228 ASHB	Sally		shamrock outline beside name	
A Co 228 ASHB	Stump Runner (The)			
A Co 228 ASHB	Tarheel Rebel	Chappell was North Carolina native		DD 3-23-75
A Co 228 ASHB	War Bird		converted to CH-47D, 85-24329	
A Co 228 ASHB	We Make The Most Out Of War	"51 Trans" included in artwork	artwork: Hamm's beer can with rotors	
229 AHB	Smoke	mark LZ with smoke	artillery spotter mostly	
A Co 229 AHB	Diane		either 66-16641 (D) or 66-15641(H)	
A Co 229 AHB	Donna	"DONNA" was Noonan's wife	still married to "DONNA"	
A Co 229 AHB	Fang			
A Co 229 AHB	If You Ain't Cav You Ain't Shit! ^^	unofficial unit slogan		

Unit	Copter Name	Origin / Definition	Notes / Call Signs ( ) < >	Fate Aircraft / Crew
A Co 229 AHB	Keep On Truckin'			
A Co 229 AHB	Keep Your Head			
A Co 229 AHB	Lucky Leprechaun			
A Co 229 AHB	Season's Greetings	Christmas holidays of 1970		
A Co 229 AHB	Superstar	raccoon in triangle, Walt Disney commissioned image	Black Bandit = unit callsign	
A Co 229 AHB	Triple Nickel *	refers to 5-5-5 sequence in serial # / named by Ashmore		
1/9	Sandra		large X on pilot doors denotes Hdqs Troop	
1/9	Terry			
A Trp 1/9	Apache Flash	Apache was 1st platoon name		
A Trp 1/9	Charla II	name of Senkowsksi's girlfriend		
A Trp 1/9	Deho	"Hi-De-Ho" tune by Blood, Sweat + Tears or maybe Carole King song title ?	reference to lyrics "gonna get me a piece of the sky" ?	
A Trp 1/9	Diane			
A Trp 1/9	Doctor Death			
A Trp 1/9	Double Ace *	refers to last 3 numerals in serial #: '011	(Apache 32)	
A Trp 1/9	Flower Power	counterculture slogan meaning peace + non-violence / painted flowers on copter nose also	(Apache 23)	
A Trp 1/9	Grim Reaper		pic furnished by his son Brigham Lawless	
A Trp 1/9	Honky Tonk Woman	Rolling Stones 1969 song title	(Apache 9)	
A Trp 1/9	Iron Butterfly	1960's rock group by same name		
A Trp 1/9	Little Green Killing Machine		Rochat's OH-6 Loach had painted bulls eye on belly	
A Trp 1/9	Liz			
A Trp 1/9	Lord's Prayer (The)		(Apache 21)	
A Trp 1/9	Midnite Cowboy	Hollywood film title		DD 3-17-71: Lilly KIA, Cambodia, LamSon 719

Unit	Copter Name	Origin / Definition	Notes / Call Signs ( ) < >	Fate Aircraft / Crew
A Trp 1/9	Mighty Gun Bird	Jim Farner	George Sullivan slide	
A Trp 1/9	Montana Mercenary			
A Trp 1/9	Mule Driver	unit mascot was "Maggie the Mule"	photo rec'd doesn't show "name"	
A Trp 1/9	Orange Crush	soft drink or Agent Orange reference ?		
A Trp 1/9	Pat	name of Anzelmo's wife		
A Trp 1/9	Peacemaker ^			
A Trp 1/9	Queer Frog Named John	Cajun slang / painted sleepy eyed frog resting on a Purple Heart ribbon	infamous OH-6 for surviving several shoot downs / news article late '70, S+S / Army Reporter, May, '69	DD 6-11-72: possible SA-7 strike, while assigned to F/8 Cav
A Trp 1/9	Rasputin		Chaplain Claude Newby authored "It Took Heroes" which speaks of his time with 1-9 Cav air units circa '69-'70	
A Trp 1/9	Ruthie			
A Trp 1/9	Scout ^		Croner was unit CO	
A Trp 1/9	Suzie Creamcheese	Frank Zappa's fictional female musical character on albums		
A Trp 1/9	Triple Nickel *	refers to 5-5-5 sequence in serial #		
A Trp 1/9	Vagabond Virgin			
A Trp 1/9	Vilmita	name of Continental Flight Attendant, Vilma, who Swain married in Bangkok while on leave		
A Trp 1/9	Wild Child	Doors song title / Ed Roth's custom monster car		
A Trp 1-9	Kath II			
A Trp 2/17	Have Gun Will Travel	TV Western series	previously in 2/20 ARA ?	
A Trp 2/17	Miss Rita	CE named it after his wife	lasted only one week	
A Trp 3/17	AA/G	double-A gas	current owner: Sunrise Helicopters, TX	
A Trp 3/17	Anacronistic	mis-spelling of Anachronistic		
A Trp 3/17	Ball Buster			
A Trp 3/17	Beast (The)			

U.S. ARMY HELICOPTER NAMES IN VIETNAM

Unit	Copter Name	Origin / Definition	Notes / Call Signs ( ) < >	Fate Aircraft / Crew
A Trp 3/17	Bounty Hunter		Aero Scout Platoon Commander (SS 16)	
A Trp 3/17	Connie			
A Trp 3/17	Coors Special	"once almighty and exotic beer" (Dave Nickel)	(SS 16)	
A Trp 3/17	El Diablo			
A Trp 3/17	Fancy's Boy	"FANCY" was name of CE's girlfriend		
A Trp 3/17	Foxy Lady	Jimmy Hendrix song title	firefly missions 1969-70	
A Trp 3/17	Gonin' Hot			
A Trp 3/17	Goodbye Charlie	Hollywood film title / VC kiss off	on display: Vet Memorial Park, Long Beach	
A Trp 3/17	Have A Nice Day	orange, smiling happy face, radiating sun with lettering around the circumference of the sticker	(SS 38)	
A Trp 3/17	Hooker (The)		"SPUR 31" painted above "name"	
A Trp 3/17	Joann			
A Trp 3/17	Jody			
A Trp 3/17	Kathie	named by Roger Young	currently: N488UH	DD April, 1970: CPT Richardsilon WIA, Cu Chi
A Trp 3/17	Lucky Lady (The)	#1 favorite American bomber name in WWII	currently: Gainesville, FL Police Dept	
A Trp 3/17	Miss G			
A Trp 3/17	Moonlight Lady			
A Trp 3/17	Night Hawk		stenciled name on rotor housing (doghouse)	
A Trp 3/17	Old Reliable			
A Trp 3/17	Patches			
A Trp 3/17	Patty Ann		temporary name by pilot, reverted back to "SKY PILOT" / on display: Army Avn Museum, Ft. Rucker, AL	
A Trp 3/17	Pistol Pete	nickname of basketball phenom Pete Maravich of Louisiana State Univ in late 1960's		
A Trp 3/17	Pure Hell No. 1	funny car artist Ed Roth's VN War decal quotation		

Unit	Copter Name	Origin / Definition	Notes / Call Signs ( ) < >	Fate Aircraft / Crew
A Trp 3/17	Purple Haze	Jimmy Hendrix song title		
A Trp 3/17	Pusher (The)	Steppenwolf song title		
A Trp 3/17	Sky Pilot	military chaplain / rock group The Animals song title by same name	aka "PATSY ANN" / on display: Army Avn Museum, Ft. Rucker, AL	
A Trp 3/17	Super Scouts	cowboy riding a copter depicted on fuselage		
A Trp 3/17	Super Slicks **	Superman emblem 'S' on door	currently: N6132N, USDA Forest Service, Clayton, NC	
A Trp 3/17	Texas Flag **	CE was from Texas		
A Trp 3/17	Trip Ate	refers to 8-8-8 sequence in serial #	Zig Zag man painted between "TRIP" + "ATE"	
A Trp 3/17	War Wagon	John Wayne 1967 movie		
A Trp 3/17	Xavius			
7/1	LOH Retriever	LOH (OH-6) stencils coded to each Troop colors: red, white or yellow	37 OH-6's recovered during '68 / profiled in 10-23-68 Army Times article	
7/1	Maint Runner			
A Trp 7/1	96 Tears	1960's rock group Question Mark and The Mysterians song title	on display: Evergreen Avn Museum, McMinnville, OR	
A Trp 7/1	Aloha		litter carrier	
A Trp 7/1	Apocalypse (The)			
A Trp 7/1	Big Bertha			
A Trp 7/1	Big Brother	middle finger painted on copter belly, then 2-finger peace sign to appease C.O.	ordered to remove painted middle finger= revision / currently: Warrensburg, MO	
A Trp 7/1	Cloud Dancer			
A Trp 7/1	Cuddles	named by Matthews		
A Trp 7/1	Electric Butterfly			
A Trp 7/1	Electric Olive		currently: being restored at Nat'l VN War Museum, Mineral Wells, TX	
A Trp 7/1	Flying Miss Gail			
A Trp 7/1	Friday's Child	Nancy Sinatra 1966 song title		

Unit	Copter Name	Origin / Definition	Notes / Call Signs ( ) < >	Fate Aircraft / Crew
A Trp 7/1	Friday's Child II	Nancy Sinatra 1966 song title	was original "BOUNTY HUNTER" destroyed?	
A Trp 7/1	Godfather			reportedly shot down, destroyed
A Trp 7/1	Goliath			
A Trp 7/1	Gremlin's Castle	Gremlin was his call-sign so added "CASTLE": he was 370 TC C.O.	reference to Ernest Gann's "Island In the Sky" book	
A Trp 7/1	Illusive Butterfly			
A Trp 7/1	Kiss Of Death			
A Trp 7/1	Kopjlager	German for "headhunter"		
A Trp 7/1	Lady Linda			
A Trp 7/1	Louisiana Man	Tom Putnam was Louisiana native		
A Trp 7/1	Poseidon	Gibbons		
A Trp 7/1	Prophet (The)		formerly "RUBBER DUCKY" in 1971	
A Trp 7/1	R.L.'s Revenge	named for R.L. Parker who had gotten thru one tour up north then got shot with A-7-1 in '71		
A Trp 7/1	Rubber Ducky	AC liked the Rubber Ducky song	aka "THE PROPHET"; J. Prine changed name in '72	
A Trp 7/1	Screaming Yellow Zonker	American tracer rounds / American snack food		
A Trp 7/1	Thor's Hammer	named by John Cattilini	(Apache 32)	
A Trp 7/1	Tink	"TINK" = Tinkerbell, nickname that Willis gave wife		
A Trp 7/1	War Child			
A Trp 7/1	Wild Mary Jane			
A Trp 7/17	76			
A Trp 7/17	Anachronistic Bummer			
A Trp 7/17	Blue Lu		aka "GENGHIS"	
A Trp 7/17	Cong Stalkers			

Unit	Copter Name	Origin / Definition	Notes / Call Signs ( ) < >	Fate Aircraft / Crew
A Trp 7/17	Genghis	two names on '973: "BLUE LU" also	one different name on each side of '973	
A Trp 7/17	Old Glory			
A Trp 7/17	Stump Jumper	loss 3 tailbooms to tree stumps / sexual term		
A Trp 7/17	Triple Penny	refers to 1-1-1 sequence in serial #	same aircraft + name with D-1-10	
B Btry 2/20 ARA	Bad News		on display: VVA Chapter 42 facility, Zanesville, OH	
B Btry 2/20 ARA	Blood, Sweat + Tears	named by Mike Cole / 1960's rock band name	(BM 63)	
B Btry 2/20 ARA	Canned Heat	1960's rock band name	(BM 28)	
B Btry 2/20 ARA	Chi Town Hustler	funny car of 1960's / Chicago reference	on display: VVA Chapter42, Zanesville, OH; the "K2" in the painted call sign (49k2) refers to an algebraic equation = 0	
B Btry 2/20 ARA	Firebird	1967 Pontiac brand car	on display: City of Ligerwood, ND / (BM 69)	
B Btry 2/20 ARA	Good Vibrations	Beach Boys song title		
B Btry 2/20 ARA	Hawaii Five-O	TV detective show	on display: Am legion Post 1376, New Hartford, NY / (BM 10)	
B Btry 2/20 ARA	Hulk	comic book character	(BM 44)	
B Btry 2/20 ARA	Missle Muscle	mis-spelling of Missile	great artwork	
B Btry 2/20 ARA	Old Smokey	named by Walowicz	Stedman belonged to 595 Sig Co, 36 Bn, 1 Sig Bde; the "K2" in the painted call sign (49k2) refers to an algebraic equation = 0	
B Btry 2/20 ARA	Pandora's Box	"a prolific source of troubles"	shares serial # w/ 238 AWC / (BM 31)	
B Btry 2/20 ARA	Rawhide	TV Western series	(BM 41)	
B Btry 82 Arty	Joy			
B Co 1 Avn Bn	Executioner	Rebel Flag = B/1/1, not 235 AWC as Bernstein portrays it	unofficial "active" wing of the Confederate Air Force, TX	
B Co 4 Avn Bn	7-11	painted pair of dice		
B Co 4 Avn Bn	Goldfinger	James Bond movie title		
B Co 4 Avn Bn	Lady Of Sin			
B Co 4 Avn Bn	Patricia Anne (The)		no shark mouth or other markings / photo found on 119 AHC website	
B Co 9 Avn Bn	Caution: This Box Contain FOD	FOD = Foreign Object Debris	tool box sticker on aircraft	

Unit	Copter Name	Origin / Definition	Notes / Call Signs ( ) < >	Fate Aircraft / Crew
B Co 9 Avn Bn	Happiness Is A Warm Gun	Beatles song title		
B Co 9 Avn Bn	Love	name was painted in big white letters on the underside of the gunship		
B Co 9 Avn Bn	Peace	name was painted in big white letters on the underside of the gunship		
B Co 9 Avn Bn	Veni Vidi Vici	"I Came, I Saw, I Conquered"		
B Co 25 Avn Bn	Ain't War Hell			
B Co 25 Avn Bn	Aluminum Butterfly (The)			
B Co 25 Avn Bn	American Dream			
B Co 25 Avn Bn	Batship	Batman logo		
B Co 25 Avn Bn	Batship II **	Bat symbol with "II"		
B Co 25 Avn Bn	Betty Lee (The)	name of Moorhead's wife		
B Co 25 Avn Bn	Dennis The Menace **			
B Co 25 Avn Bn	Flintstone Flyer	named after flying machine seen on Flintstones early 1960's animated TV series		
B Co 25 Avn Bn	Ghost Rider In The Sky	Son of the Pioneers song title or Vaughn Monroe song title		
B Co 25 Avn Bn	Judge (The)			
B Co 25 Avn Bn	Kat (The)		aka "PINK PANTHER"	
B Co 25 Avn Bn	Lemon			
B Co 25 Avn Bn	Little Annie Fanny	comic strip character from Playboy magazine		reportedly shot down, destroyed
B Co 25 Avn Bn	Little Annie Fanny II	comic strip character from Playboy magazine		reportedly shot down, destroyed
B Co 25 Avn Bn	Little Annie Fanny III	comic strip character from Playboy magazine		
B Co 25 Avn Bn	Little Hootin Annie			
B Co 25 Avn Bn	Little Orphan Annie	comic book character		
B Co 25 Avn Bn	Love Generation	baby boomers		

Unit	Copter Name	Origin / Definition	Notes / Call Signs ( ) < >	Fate Aircraft / Crew
B Co 25 Avn Bn	Mafia Queen	female figure with gun		
B Co 25 Avn Bn	Pink Panther **	painted Pink Panther of Hollywood movie fame		
B Co 25 Avn Bn	Pistol Pete	nickname of basketball phenom Pete Maravich of Louisiana State Univ in late 1960's		
B Co 25 Avn Bn	Pride Of Carolina			
B Co 25 Avn Bn	Red Baron	Snoopy's arch rival in skies over France in WWI		
B Co 25 Avn Bn	Roadrunner	animated cartoon character	currently: N503TW, 25 Inf Div Huey, Bend, OR / reportedly 1st ship in VN with door mounted mini-gun	
B Co 25 Avn Bn	Snoopy **		metal detector setup extended both sides of ship	
B Co 25 Avn Bn	Tweety Bird	animated cartoon character		
B Co 25 Avn Bn	Widow Maker (The)		aka "BIRTH CONTROL" painted on turret	
B Co 25 Avn Bn	Wild Child	Door's song title		
B Co 25 Avn Bn	Wolf **	named after Husky dog of same name		
B Co 25 Avn Bn	Wolf Man			
B Co 25 Avn Bn	Wooly Bully	Sam The Sham + The Pharaohs 1964 song title		
B Co 25 Avn Bn	Yosemite Sam **	animated cartoon character		
B Co 101 AHB	Fugitive Angel (The)		call-sign "BLACK ANGELS" on nose	
B Co 123 Avn Bn	Beelzebub	"lord of the flies, Satan" / painting of a magic wand also	only Vulcan canon among unit's AH-1G's / "once in sights they were dead meat" (Walt Lynn)	
B Co 123 Avn Bn	Blind Faith	1960's rock group name		
B Co 123 Avn Bn	Captain America	comic book character	skids painted red-white-blue also	
B Co 123 Avn Bn	Challenger		skids painted also	
B Co 123 Avn Bn	Hangar Queen	derogatory term for excessive need for repairs		
B Co 123 Avn Bn	Hawaii		currently: N59HC, Hernando Co Sheriff's Office, New Port Richey, FL / aka "OLD RUGGED CROSS"	
B Co 123 Avn Bn	Insouciance	"calm, carefree, unbothered, indifferent"	"beat up old slick" according to Martin / painted black below Pelican logo	

Unit	Copter Name	Origin / Definition	Notes / Call Signs ( ) < >	Fate Aircraft / Crew
B Co 123 Avn Bn	Kid			
B Co 123 Avn Bn	Lead Magnet	always took hits, yet always brought crew home		April 1971: Red-X'd
B Co 123 Avn Bn	Mississippi		currently: N59HC, Hernando Co Sheriff's Office, Brooksville, FL	
B Co 123 Avn Bn	Old Rugged Cross	old gospel hymn title	currently: N59HC, Hernando Co Sheriff Office, Brooksville, FL	
B Co 123 Avn Bn	Pandora's Box	"a prolific source of troubles" / jolly roger flag painted near rotor	currently: N59HC, New Port Richey, FL 34654	
B Co 123 Avn Bn	Warlord Aero Scout		very elaborate artwork	
B Co 123 Avn Bn	Wiley Coyote **	painting of Wiley Coyote, nn not visible / arch nemesis of the Roadrunner, a cartoon character		
B Co 158 AHB	For Sale		rec'd major mortar damage 2-18-71, loss to inventory	
B Co 158 AHB	Green Messiah (The)			
B Co 159 ASHB	A Shau Express		shares serial # with 271 ASHC's "ROADRUNNER II" / converted to CH-47D, 87-00091	
B Co 159 ASHB	Ball's Deuce	refers to 0-0-2 sequence in serial # / "Deuce" not spelled out, painted playing card depicted	Norman Bass was DG, CE, FE on "BALLS DEUCE" / converted to CH-47D, 82-23773	In flyable serice as of May 2006
B Co 159 ASHB	Blood, Sweat + Tears	1960's rock band name		
B Co 159 ASHB	Fly The Friendly Skies	United Airlines slogan of same title		
B Co 159 ASHB	Mabel		converted to CH-47D, 87-00095	
B Co 159 ASHB	Rat (The)	painted rat also		DD 4-13-70: 1 KIA, Bob Pendergast
B Co 159 ASHB	Strange Vibrations	based on Beach Boys song title "Good Vibrations"	only seen from inside when steps were raised / 101st didn't allow personal markings	
B Co 227 AHB	A Slight Touch Of Death		night hawk ship / aka "MAGIC CARPET RIDE"	
B Co 227 AHB	American Woman	Guess Who song title / clenched fist painted on nose also		
B Co 227 AHB	Grunt Wagon		Terry Moon was 1st Cav PIO official photog 1969	
B Co 227 AHB	Iron Butterfly	1960's rock group by same name	"VI" on doghouse	
B Co 227 AHB	Magic Carpet Ride	Steppenwolf song title	aka "A SLIGHT TOUCH OF DEATH"	
B Co 227 AHB	Marquis De Sade	painting of devil + flames in red + yellow also		
B Co 227 AHB	Marrakesh Express	Crosby, Stills + Nash song title	human fist painted in middle of nn	

Unit	Copter Name	Origin / Definition	Notes / Call Signs ( ) < >	Fate Aircraft / Crew
B Co 227 AHB	Pam's Pro Antes Ace	"PAM" was Lunde's wife / "ANTE" was CE's wife	ace of hearts painted on nose	
B Co 227 AHB	Patches			
B Co 227 AHB	Sopwith Camel	British WW I fighter plane painted on nose with lettering		
B Co 227 AHB	Southern General			
B Co 227 AHB	War Wagon	John Wayne 1967 movie		
B Co 228 ASHB	Behemoth			
B Co 228 ASHB	Big Bertha		converted to MH-47D	
B Co 228 ASHB	Bitch (The) *	small painting of Mad magazine's Spy vs Spy character on front fuselage	no large personalized markings policy implemented '67	DD 2-7-68
B Co 228 ASHB	California Dremin'	all California crew / Mamas + Papas 1965 song title	converted to CH-47D, 84-24176	
B Co 228 ASHB	Cav Heart **	red heart + Cav horse head pierced by arrow		
B Co 228 ASHB	Chi Town	Chicago	converted to CH-47D, 85-24336	
B Co 228 ASHB	Frenchie		shares serial # with "WAR WAGON"	captured by NVA 1975
B Co 228 ASHB	Frito Bandito	cartoon mascot for Fritos painted on fuselage		
B Co 228 ASHB	Get Bent			
B Co 228 ASHB	Good Vibrations	Beach Boys song title		DD 9-12-70: all KIA
B Co 228 ASHB	Hangar Queen Abortion (The)	replaced painted lemon	Lloyd A. Judd was known as the B/228 artist / converted to CH-47D, 85-24329	initial hangar queen reputation, but then became more reliable afterwards
B Co 228 ASHB	Leftovers	buzzard with cane under its wing	converted to CH-47D, 84-24174	
B Co 228 ASHB	Lil Sister		color pic doesn't show nn	DD 8-14-72
B Co 228 ASHB	Miss Bev		aka "BALLS 77" / converted to CH-47D, 85-24341	
B Co 228 ASHB	Mission Impossible	TV drama series		DD 10-26-71: all KIA, assigned to 68 AVN CO
B Co 228 ASHB	Peace			
B Co 228 ASHB	Sorry 'Bout That	2 versions: scantily clad woman in nylons blowing down LZ tents + hook blowing down LZ tents	shares serial # with 243 ASHC's "SKY QUEEN" / ordered to paint over original art / converted to CH-47D, 83-24114	

Unit	Copter Name	Origin / Definition	Notes / Call Signs ( ) < >	Fate Aircraft / Crew
B Co 228 ASHB	Specialist Zig Zag	Zig Zag man painted black over yellow field / cigarette paper logo		
B Co 228 ASHB	Tatter's Pad			
B Co 228 ASHB	War Wagon	John Wayne 1967 movie	shares serial # with "FRENCHIE"	4-17-68: rocket hit / captured by NVA 1975
B Co 228 ASHB	War Wagon	John Wayne 1967 movie	regular 2 wheel requirement on many a mission + "WILLIE" referred to Bill Scott	
B Co 228 ASHB	Wheel Standing Willie	two wheel missions, 2 on ground, 2 in air, were very common		DD 10-30-68: shot down, destroyed in rice paddy
B Co 228 ASHB	Zip Zapper	"zip" was a derogatory term to describe the enemy / FE confirmed enemy KBA	only a/c that responded to ground unit's call for suppressive fire	
B Co 229 AHB	Baby Jo		sent to 155 AHC with name intact	
B Co 229 AHB	Beaver's Abortion			
B Co 229 AHB	Blue Womb			
B Co 229 AHB	California Girl	Beach Boys song title		
B Co 229 AHB	Dale	named after the AC ?		
B Co 229 AHB	Devil's Disciple	American motorcycle club / 1959 Burt Lancaster movie of same name	also "VICKI" painted on nose / UPI-AP pic in major newspaper, April 1968	
B Co 229 AHB	Foxie Lady (The)	based on Jimmy Hendrix song title, "Foxy Lady""	currently: N341SD, US Dept of State, Patrick AFB, FL	
B Co 229 AHB	Gloria		Leathers helped rig copter + took photo	
B Co 229 AHB	Headhunter			
B Co 229 AHB	Hippie's Bag	Mellon originated name, he was known as Hippie / Pisces fish painted on copter nose also	Silent Preacher was callsign / inside blue square was monk holding mallet behind back + a squashed VC	
B Co 229 AHB	In God's Will			
B Co 229 AHB	Mellow Yellow	Donovan song title		
B Co 229 AHB	Mrs. Babe Mrs. Edie	"MRS. BABE" was COL Kellar's wife, "MRS. EDIE" was MAJ Panzetti's wife	was COL Kellar's C+C ship	
B Co 229 AHB	Norma	name of Emerson's wife	currently: N386SD, US Dept of State, Patrick AFB, FL	
B Co 229 AHB	Old Paint	traditional name for a horse	currently: N205PJ, PJ Helicopters, Red Bluff, CA	
B Co 229 AHB	Paddy Wagon	"Irish conveyance"		

Unit	Copter Name	Origin / Definition	Notes / Call Signs ( ) < >	Fate Aircraft / Crew
B Co 229 AHB	Pegasus		also "VICKI" painted on nose	
B Co 229 AHB	Southern Belle	SOUTH = 11 Air Assault, Ft. Benning + BELLE = Bell Helicopter Co	on display: VVA Chapter 649, Batavia, OH	
B Co 229 AHB	Vicki	name of Osborne's girlfriend	also "DEVIL'S DISCIPLE" on nose / UPI-AP pic in major newspaper, April 1968	
B Trp 1/9	An Khe Annie		aka "WIDOW MAKER" on turret	
B Trp 1/9	Avenger			shot down, used for parts
B Trp 1/9	Baby Snooks	Flanagan's girlfriend at the time / mischievous child of 1930's radio fame	girlfriend became future wife, going on 40+ years now / <37>	DD 11-13-67
B Trp 1/9	Baby Snooks II	Flanagan's girlfriend at the time / mischievous child of 1930's radio fame	girlfriend became future wife, going on 40+ years now	
B Trp 1/9	Born Free	1966 song + movie title		
B Trp 1/9	Brain Bucket (The)	term used for military helmet	troop commander's ship also	
B Trp 1/9	Business Has Been Good	painting of several prone bodies near rotor housing	<19>	4-4-69: 3 KIA's: James, Lofton, Weigle
B Trp 1/9	Canned Heat	1960's rock band name	aka "TRIPLE NICKEL"	
B Trp 1/9	Cherry Picker	painted cherries / sexual term	<11>	
B Trp 1/9	Crum Snatcher	named after Burgess's girlfriend Nancy Crum	<39>	DD 10-10-69
B Trp 1/9	Darlin Jenny			
B Trp 1/9	Darlin Jenny II		famous pic disembarking troopers from a B-1-9 Huey, also featured on USPS stamp	
B Trp 1/9	Death On Call		<24>	
B Trp 1/9	Dixie Bell	Confederate flag painted on nose also		
B Trp 1/9	Donna			DD 3-18-70: WIA's: Jones, Scott, Marc Abel
B Trp 1/9	Easy Rider	Hollywood movie title		
B Trp 1/9	Easy Rider	Hollywood movie title	painted wheel spokes graphic / Gold Book has this belonging to A Troop / <18>	
B Trp 1/9	Exterminator (The)		name and skid caps painted yellow / image seen in YOUTUBE video: "90 Days In Vietnam"	
B Trp 1/9	Glamdring The Foe-Hammer	gunship named by Babyak / name of sword owned by Gandalf in Lord of the Rings		DD 11-29-69: both pilots KIA
B Trp 1/9	God's Will			

Unit	Copter Name	Origin / Definition	Notes / Call Signs ( ) < >	Fate	Aircraft / Crew
B Trp 1/9	Good The Bad And The Ugly (The)	Clint Eastwood Western movie title			
B Trp 1/9	Green Machine				
B Trp 1/9	Gunfighters	Yosemite Sam image on nose also	hog gunship		
B Trp 1/9	Iron Butterfly	1960's rock group by same name	<12>		
B Trp 1/9	Kill 'Em All + Let God Sort 'Em Out				
B Trp 1/9	La Puta	"the whore"			
B Trp 1/9	Magic Bus	The Who song title	on display: VFW Post 5850, Eufaula, AL as a UH-1V / <38>		
B Trp 1/9	Magical Mystery Tour	Beatles song title			
B Trp 1/9	Max Well	iconic "Kilroy was here" looking over fence painted on copter doghouse			
B Trp 1/9	Mean Mr. Mustard	Beatles song title	20mm cannon on left pylon		
B Trp 1/9	Mr. Bojangle	Nitty Gritty Dirt Band song title	<38>		
B Trp 1/9	Ol Bullet		aka "VIGILANTES" on nose		
B Trp 1/9	Patty Wagon				
B Trp 1/9	Peacemaker (The)		other "PEACEMAKER" photos are without "THE" / on display: VFW Post 5095, East Hampton, CT / <21>		
B Trp 1/9	Sky Thing				
B Trp 1/9	Sweet Sandy	name of Pratt's girlfriend	<39>		
B Trp 1/9	Sweet Sandy II	name of Pratt's girlfriend	<39>		
B Trp 1/9	Sweet Sue	name of Stewart's wife	<6>		
B Trp 1/9	Triple Nickel *	refers to 5-5-5 sequence in serial #			
B Trp 1/9	UFO				
B Trp 1/9	Watch Out Gooks		image seen in YOUTUBE video: "90 Days In Vietnam"		
B Trp 1/9	Widow Maker		aka "AN KHE ANNIE" on pilot door		
B Trp 1/9	Wonder Wart-Hog	underground comic book character, parody of Superman			

Unit	Copter Name	Origin / Definition	Notes / Call Signs ( ) < >	Fate Aircraft / Crew
B Trp 2/17	Eve Of Destruction	Barry McGuire song title / Scott Kerr name credit		
B Trp 2/17	God Of Hellfire	Arthur Brown 1967 rock song lyrics		
B Trp 2/17	Muff Diver	sexual occupation / painted crossed spoon+fork, salt+pepper shakers	C+C ship	
B Trp 2/17	No Quarter	named by Jimmy Allen		
B Trp 2/17	No Slack	named by Bill Russell		
B Trp 2/17	Proud Mary	former girlfriend's name, later married / Creedence Clearwater Revival song title	aka "WIDOWMAKER" on left side / marriage is 35+ years now	
B Trp 2/17	Tuff Enuff			
B Trp 2/17	Widowmaker		aka "PROUD MARY"	
B Trp 3/17	Avenger			
B Trp 3/17	Avenger II		was original "AVENGER" destroyed?	
B Trp 3/17	Birdie Num Num	Peter Seller's mantra in the movie "The Party"		
B Trp 3/17	Birdie Num Num Jr	Peter Seller's mantra in the movie "The Party"		
B Trp 3/17	Capt Zig Zag **	reference to Zig Zag tobacco paper logo	C.O.'s favorite ship to fly	
B Trp 3/17	Chi-Town Hustler	famous Chicago drag racer		
B Trp 3/17	Courier Of Death			
B Trp 3/17	Creature Of Death			
B Trp 3/17	Cry Of The Banshee			shot down in Cambodia
B Trp 3/17	Devil's Sister (The)		Witte notes serial # as 67-15717/ on display: Am Legion Post 250, Arlington, MN	
B Trp 3/17	Double O Pig *	flew very poorly thus the name		
B Trp 3/17	Double O Soul		converted D model	
B Trp 3/17	Eight Balls *			

U.S. ARMY HELICOPTER NAMES IN VIETNAM

Unit	Copter Name	Origin / Definition	Notes / Call Signs ( ) < >	Fate Aircraft / Crew
B Trp 3/17	Flying Circus			
B Trp 3/17	Hungry Bitch (The)			
B Trp 3/17	Jack The Bear	refers to AC's first name / painted bear's head	gun platoon leader	
B Trp 3/17	Junk Run			
B Trp 3/17	Mindbender	The Mindbenders were a 1960's rock band		
B Trp 3/17	Mindbender II	The Mindbenders were a 1960's rock band	was original "MINDBENDER" destroyed?	
B Trp 3/17	Miss Dizzy	Tommy Roe song from 1969		
B Trp 3/17	Patience My Ass	painted vulture sitting on tree limb		
B Trp 3/17	Proud Mary	Creedence Clearwater Revival song title		
B Trp 3/17	Queer John	Cajun slang		
B Trp 3/17	Rebel			
B Trp 3/17	Satan's Rag			
B Trp 3/17	Sky Pig			
B Trp 3/17	Thunder Olive			
B Trp 3/17	Triple Nickel *	refers to 5-5-5 sequence in serial #		
B Trp 3/17	Triple Zip *	refers to 0-0-0 sequence in serial #	also called "BALLS"	
B Trp 7/1	Boot Hill	Old West graveyard in Tombstone, Arizona		
B Trp 7/1	Grim Reaper (The)		C.O.'s ship at Dian	
B Trp 7/1	Holy Smokes	refers to Richard Maxwell's nn "Smokey"		
B Trp 7/1	Rookie	painted Linus character from Peanuts		
B Trp 7/17	Death Angel			
B Trp 7/17	Flying Alone (The)			
B Trp 7/17	Spirit Of St. Louis (The)	homage to aviation pioneer Charles Lindberg and hometown of individual copter crew		

ARMY HELICOPTER NAMES: UNIT/NUMERICAL

Unit	Copter Name	Origin / Definition	Notes / Call Signs ( ) < >	Fate Aircraft / Crew
B Trp 7/17	Widow Maker	peace symbol painted on nose also	pic shows gunship in damaged state	
C Btry 2/20 ARA	Avenger			
C Btry 2/20 ARA	Baby Huey	powerful but self destructive cartoon character		
C Btry 2/20 ARA	Cannabis Sativa	scientific name for marijuana / nose art was leaf	ordered by C.O. to remove marijuana leaf graphic	
C Btry 2/20 ARA	Challenger		(BM 45)	
C Btry 2/20 ARA	Flying Circus **	refers to CPT Eddie Rickenbacker's WW1's unit	aka "GRIM REAPER", "HAT IN THE RING" / (BM 83)	
C Btry 2/20 ARA	Flying Nunn	parody of TV comedy series, "The Flying Nun"		
C Btry 2/20 ARA	Free Huey	tie-in with Huey Newton (1960's activist) in jail?		
C Btry 2/20 ARA	Grim Reaper	iconic Hat In The Ring graphic from WW 1, CPT Eddie Rickenbacker's American fighter a/c unit	possibly F/79 assignment also / (BM 83)	
C Btry 2/20 ARA	Have Gun Will Travel	TV Western series	(BM 40)	
C Btry 2/20 ARA	Iron Butterfly	1960's rock group by same name	8-69 to 5-71, C/2/20 + 6-71 to 7-72, F/79 / (BM 00)	
C Btry 2/20 ARA	Mean Mr. Mustard	Beatles song title	(BM 70)	DD 6-20-72: KIA's: LT Shields + CPT Northrup, in this F/79 gunship
C Btry 2/20 ARA	Mother Superior's Guns	Beatles song title	from Beatles song, "Happiness Is A Warm Gun"	
C Btry 2/20 ARA	Murder Inc	"mafia hit men"	on display: NAS, Wildwood Avn Museum, Rio Grande, NJ (Cape May County) / (BM 33)	
C Btry 2/20 ARA	Snoopy **	painted Snoopy flying a rocket	Maxwell rocket on outer pod	
C Btry 2/20 ARA	Sound Of Silence	Simon + Garfunkel song title	(BM 54)	
C Btry 2/20 ARA	Two Stepper	VN snake venom bite so lethal that victim usually walked two steps + died	(BM 36)	DD 5-24-72: KIA's: Hosaka + Henn in this F/79 gunship
C Btry 2/20 ARA	UFO			
C Btry 4/77 ARA	Circus Wagon			
C Co 101 AHB	Bloody Mary			
C Co 101 AHB	Bloody Mary		formerly a 188 AHC ship	
C Co 101 AHB	Iron Butterfly	1960's rock group by same name	formerly a 188 AHC ship	

Unit	Copter Name	Origin / Definition	Notes / Call Signs ( ) < >	Fate Aircraft / Crew
C Co 101 AHB	Lady Jane	Rolling Stones song title	(BW 20)	
C Co 101 AHB	Magic Carpet Ride	Steppenwolf song title	aka "MR. LUCKY" / 101st didn't allow nose art or nn's/ formerly a 188 AHC ship	
C Co 101 AHB	Mr. Lucky	TV detective show	aka "MAGIC CARPET RIDE" / 101st didn't allow nose art or nn's / formerly a 188 AHC ship	
C Co 101 AHB	Nixon's Hired Gun		formerly a 188 AHC ship	
C Co 101 AHB	Smokie II	smoke ship	on display: VFW Post 374, Arcade, NY	
C Co 101 AHB	Smokie III	smoke ship 8/68-9/69	(BW 25)	
C Co 101 AHB	Smokie IV	smoke ship 3/70-10/70		
C Co 159 ASHB	Airhorne	intentional mis-spelling of "Airborne"		
C Co 159 ASHB	Balls Nine *	refers to 0-0-9 sequence in serial #	converted to CH-47D, 82-23779	
C Co 159 ASHB	Fugitive		unit marking was a large blue triangle / pic found on Wuthrich's personal website at "vietnam68-69.com"	bad crash 7-3-70, returned to USA but stricken May '71
C Co 159 ASHB	Philbert Desenex	comic book character: when he isn't fighting crime as "WW", he poses as reporter Philbert Desenex	aka "WONDER WARTHOG"	DD 3-23-75
C Co 159 ASHB	Rajun Cajin			
C Co 159 ASHB	Rosemary's Baby	named after Stamp's girlfriend / Hollywood horror film title		DD 5-11-70
C Co 159 ASHB	Tessie			
C Co 227 AHB	Big Fanny			
C Co 227 AHB	Cajun Queen	Louisiana CE named it	aka "GUNS ARE FOR BUMS" on windshield	
C Co 227 AHB	Capt. Crude	named after obnoxious Officer in unit		
C Co 227 AHB	Death Trap (The)			
C Co 227 AHB	Death Trap II			
C Co 227 AHB	Dixie J			
C Co 227 AHB	El Taco	named by Frank Parra	subsequently ordered to remove name	
C Co 227 AHB	Eli Is Coming	based on 3 Dog Night song title, "Eli's Coming"		

Unit	Copter Name	Origin / Definition	Notes / Call Signs ( ) < >	Fate Aircraft / Crew
C Co 227 AHB	Flying Souls			
C Co 227 AHB	Guns Are For Bums		aka "CAJUN QUEEN"	
C Co 227 AHB	Here's Mine Where's Yours?	red cherry painted on nose also		
C Co 227 AHB	Hog Wash		nighthawk gunship	
C Co 227 AHB	Lady Ann	name of Rosser's girlfriend		
C Co 227 AHB	Lucky 7	one dice showing seven pips (dots)		
C Co 227 AHB	Miss Carriage	double entendre	Chaplain complaint resulted in name removal	
C Co 227 AHB	Nancy's Dream	name of CE's girlfriend	aka "NEVADA GAMBLER"	
C Co 227 AHB	Nevada Gambler	inspired by "ARIZONA GAMBLER" gunship	aka "NANCY'S DREAM"	
C Co 227 AHB	Pill (The)			
C Co 227 AHB	Zig Zag Man **	artwork painting of the Zig Zag cigarette paper logo		
C Co 228 ASHB	Alfred E. Neuman	MAD magazine icon + slogan "What, Me Worry?" was counterpart to WWII's "Kilroy Was Here"	aka "THE WONDERFUL WHITE WINGED WARRIOR" (parody of Chickenman's title) painted on DG window cover	DD 5-4-70
C Co 228 ASHB	Coon's Ass	reference to a person of Cajun ethnicity		
C Co 228 ASHB	Double Duce	pair of dice painted on fuselage	converted to CH-47D, 88-00073	
C Co 228 ASHB	Easy Rider	Hollywood movie title	converted to CH-47D, 87-00113	
C Co 228 ASHB	Little Annie Fanny **	Playboy magazine comic strip character		DD 2-15-71
C Co 228 ASHB	Odyssey (The)	Homer's long, dangerous journey / C. Morley adopted name	converted to YCH-47D	
C Co 228 ASHB	P-Turkey	"you don't know the first thing about something"	painting of long legged turkey in black with flat red wattle and flat yellow legs	
C Co 228 ASHB	Pusher (The)	Steppenwolf song title	converted to CH-47D, 86-01655	crashed in Cambodia
C Co 228 ASHB	Triple Trouble	refers to 1-1-1 sequence in serial #	converted to MH-47D, 83-24110	
C Co 228 ASHB	What ! Me Worry?	MAD magazine icon + slogan "What, Me Worry?" was counterpart to WWII's "Kilroy Was Here"	aka "THE WONDERFUL WHITE WINGED WARRIOR" (parody of Chickenman's title) painted on DG window cover	DD 5-4-70
C Co 229 AHB	Alice's Restaurant	folk singer Arlo Guthrie song title		

Unit	Copter Name	Origin / Definition	Notes / Call Signs ( ) < >	Fate Aircraft / Crew
C Co 229 AHB	Bad Man Jose	re: to lyrics in '65 song "Come A Little Bit Closer" by Jay +The Americans / Mexican bandito painting	"THE CAVALAIR" unit newspaper, 4-22-70, page 7: "Graffiti Gives Birds Colorful Personality" (5 pics)	
C Co 229 AHB	Cav Jester	painting of "King" playing card		
C Co 229 AHB	Checkmate ^			
C Co 229 AHB	Cherry Buster	no longer a virgin		
C Co 229 AHB	Crystal Ship	Doors song title	ordered to remove after only one week / Buchheister recalls nn when being transported on this ship	
C Co 229 AHB	Da Judge		initially used as BN C.O.'s bird, then as Dayhawk duties	
C CO 229 AHB	Day Tripper	Beatles song title		
C Co 229 AHB	God's Will			
C Co 229 AHB	Good Vibrations	Beach Boys song title		
C Co 229 AHB	Grand Funk Airways	Grand Funk Railroad was a rock band		
C Co 229 AHB	Iron Butterfly	1960's rock group by same name		
C Co 229 AHB	Iron Butterfly (The)	painting of a strange looking butterfly / 1960's rock group by same name	"THE CAVALAIR" in-country newspaper, 4-22-70, pg 7: "Graffiti Gives Birds Colorful Personality" (5 pics)	Nov, 1972: Laningham later KIA in Chinook
C Co 229 AHB	Kill A Gook For Calley	refers to LT CALLEY of '69 My Lai incident	Crawford was infantryman in Mekong Delta area	
C Co 229 AHB	Little Texan (The)	painted Yosemite Sam type character on copter nose / also utilized as a smokeship	THE CAVALAIR, 4-22-70, pg 7, "Graffiti Gives Birds Colorful Personality", 5 pics	
C Co 229 AHB	Mary Ann	AC's wife name		
C Co 229 AHB	Memphis Belle	pin-up girl painted on doorpost / WW II B-17 name		
C Co 229 AHB	Memphis Belle	Brewer was from Memphis / infamous WW II bomber name		
C Co 229 AHB	Mr. Clean	maintenance officer 1LT Vern Ashbrook was look-a-like to TV's Mr. Clean, advertisement product symbol		
C Co 229 AHB	Ogre (The)			
C Co 229 AHB	Patches			
C Co 229 AHB	Pony Soldier		<6>	
C Co 229 AHB	Short Stomper			

Unit	Copter Name	Origin / Definition	Notes / Call Signs ( ) < >	Fate Aircraft / Crew
C Co 229 AHB	Snake Bit	open snake mouth baring fangs painted on nose	aka "THE MAGNET" / currently: N4391A	
C Co 229 AHB	Snoopy **	painted Snoopy from Peanuts cartoon		
C Co 229 AHB	Strange Daze	Doors song title / painting of giant eye ball on copter nose	currently: N816SC, Almont, MI 48003 / in-country newspaper, THE CAVALAIR, 4-22-70, pg 7, 5 pics	
C Co 229 AHB	Thumpy 1	reference to short + stocky 1LT Don Thompson / his nn was Stumpy + Thumper	THE CAVALAIR" in-country newspaper, 4-22-70, pg 7: "Graffiti Gives Birds Colorful Personality" (5 pics)	
C Co 229 AHB	Voyager			
C Trp 1/9	5th Dimension	American pop singing group	on display: March Field Air Museum, Riverside, CA	
C Trp 1/9	Alaskan (The)	Wright's home State was Alaska	Wright was first to paint shark teeth on unit AH-1G Cobra / (Cav 24)	
C Trp 1/9	Bad Breath	nn painted next to gunship's shark mouth	Stedman assigned to 595 Sig Co, 36 Bn, 1 Sig Bde	
C Trp 1/9	Betty K		aka "HEATHER DAWN"/ on display: Avn Hall of Fame, Teterboro, NJ	
C Trp 1/9	Blind Faith	1960's rock group name		
C Trp 1/9	Cara Mia	Jay + The Americans song title		12-1-66: George Gavaria KIA
C Trp 1/9	Cindy Ann	Zahn's girlfriend + future wife	(Cav 24)	
C Trp 1/9	Crystal Ship (The)	Doors song title		3-12-71: crashed in Cambodia: KIA's Van Joyce + Joel Hageman
C Trp 1/9	Death Before Dishonor	motto of the Airborne also	also an E Troop slick later on	
C Trp 1/9	Donna		(Cav 25)	
C Trp 1/9	Family Car (The)	wording arranged to form the outline of an automobile	maintenance or headquarters ship?	
C Trp 1/9	Fuck Communism	originally written in Vietnamese on rocket pod		
C Trp 1/9	Give Blood		shark teeth under copter nose chin	DD 3-17-71
C Trp 1/9	Good Vibrations	Beach Boys song title		
C Trp 1/9	Green Weenie (The)	painted Snoopy character also / "getting screwed over"		
C Trp 1/9	Grim Reaper (The) **	iconic Grim Reaper graphic, no lettering	(Cav 41)	
C Trp 1/9	Gunky		"JUNKY" was 1st choice but was KO'd by C.O. orders	

Unit	Copter Name	Origin / Definition	Notes / Call Signs ( ) < >	Fate Aircraft / Crew
C Trp 1/9	Heather Dawn	daughter's name	aka "BETTY K" / on display: Avn Hall of Fame, Teterboro, NJ	
C Trp 1/9	Helicopter	wording arranged to form the outline of a Huey copter		
C Trp 1/9	Hot Stuff	painted little red devil		
C Trp 1/9	Iron Butterfly	1960's rock group by same name	"PURE HELL" painted on rocket launcher hardpoint	
C Trp 1/9	Judy			4-13-71: Alton Roberts, KIA
C Trp 1/9	Lil Feller			
C Trp 1/9	Lil Feller II			
C Trp 1/9	Magnet Ass *	no matter what mission the crew were on it always drew fire		
C Trp 1/9	Mr. Huey		'603 was veteran of the Ia Drang campaign / Mike Kelley arrived in-country Dec 1965	
C Trp 1/9	Old Bones			
C Trp 1/9	Pagan (The)			
C Trp 1/9	Patricia Lynn			
C Trp 1/9	Peacemaker		aka "RENEGADE"	
C Trp 1/9	Pink Panther **	Pink Panther idea was from LT Joe Waters / Hollywood movie title		
C Trp 1/9	Psychedelic Reaction	parody of song, "Psychotic Reaction" by rock band, The Count Five		
C Trp 1/9	Pure Hell		aka "IRON BUTTERFLY"	
C Trp 1/9	Renegade		aka "PEACEMAKER"	
C Trp 1/9	Snoopy **	Charlie Brown's dog in Peanuts comic strip		
C Trp 1/9	Stepchild (The)			
C Trp 1/9	Susie			
C Trp 1/9	Zit	name of Shaffer's girlfriend spelled backwards	currently: N6186Y, US Border Patrol Air Operations, El Paso, TX	
C Trp 2/17	Beverly			DD 5-18-70

Unit	Copter Name	Origin / Definition	Notes / Call Signs ( ) < >	Fate Aircraft / Crew
C Trp 2/17	Eve Of Destruction	Barry McGuire song title		
C Trp 2/17	Gunky	copter painted black		
C Trp 2/17	Warlord			
C Trp 3/17	America Love It Or Leave It	conservative political slogan of 1960's+1970's		
C Trp 3/17	Bear's Pig	Bear refers to Bear Bryant, famous college football coach and AC's last name		
C Trp 3/17	Duit Tuit		Night Hawk duties: protected airfield at night	
C Trp 3/17	Susie Q	classic rock-n-roll standard	currently: N28JK, U.S. Border Patrol, El Paso, TX	
C Trp 7/1	America Love It Or Leave It	conservative political slogan of 1960's+1970's		
C Trp 7/1	American Sportsmen	hunting magazine title	this gunship was flown by platoon Leader, James Drury	
C Trp 7/1	Judy In The Sky	parody of the 1967 song hit "Judy In Disguise" (With Glasses) by John Fred + His Playboy Band	aka "MAR", "MY DIANE" / on display: Vets Memorial Park, Dixon, IL	
C Trp 7/1	Killer Bee **	bee with minigun painted on copter clamshell		
C Trp 7/1	Mar	name of Rob Bailey's wife	aka "JUDY IN THE SKY", "MY DIANE" / on display: Vets Memorial Park, Dixon, IL	
C Trp 7/1	Mary Lee	name of Bill Young's wife	currently: outdoor museum display, Ft. Bliss, TX	
C Trp 7/1	Monica Lee	"MONICA" = J. Dike's daughter's name + "LEE" = J. Dike's older brother's name	presently used as a training aid in NV desert / Joe Dike's older brother served in Can Tho	
C Trp 7/1	My Diane	name of Clyde Strait's wife	aka "MAR", "JUDY IN THE SKY" / on display: Vets Memorial Park, Dixon, Ill	
C Trp 7/1	Patricia Ann	name of Goodowens' daughter	J. Sprinkle's article, AAHS, Fall '75, pg 163 / on display: Vets Park, Village of Mark, IL	
C Trp 7/1	Pig Pen	bad repaint job inspired derogatory name	Peanuts character painted above words / used as a range target today ?	
C Trp 7/1	Sopwith Camel	Snoopy's personal choice aircraft for pursuing the Red Baron / Snoopy figure painted on gunship's doghouse		
C Trp 7/1	Think Snow	mind over matter in hot climate		
C Trp 7/1	Triple Nickel **	refers to 5-5-5 sequence in serial # / also 3 Indian head nickels painted on doghouse		
C Trp 7/1	Twin Mini			
C Trp 7/17	Pale Horse (The)	quoted name from unit slogan: "and behold, a pale horse! And its rider's name was Death": Revelations 6:8	stenciled "kill" markings from Lam Son 719	

Unit	Copter Name	Origin / Definition	Notes / Call Signs ( ) < >	Fate Aircraft / Crew
C Trp 7/17	Snake Venom			
C Trp 16 Cav	Arbitrator (The)			
C Trp 16 Cav	Barbara		(DH 32)	
C Trp 16 Cav	Barbara II		(DH 32)	
C Trp 16 Cav	Dark Death	painted all black, April '72, Willis renamed OH-6 and flew till unit stood down	aka "THE ENFORCER", "ELECTRIC OLIVE II" / June-Sept '72 when active	
C Trp 16 Cav	Electric Olive		Rod Willis succeeded Bob Todd as platoon leader	DD 1-5-72: Bob Todd was WIA while flying '310
C Trp 16 Cav	Electric Olive II	name was on ship when Bob Todd's "ELECTRIC OLIVE" was destroyed 1-5-72	aka "ENFORCER" + "DARK DEATH" / Dec 71-Feb 72 when active	
C Trp 16 Cav	Enforcer (The)		aka "DARK DEATH", "ELECTRIC OLIVE II" / 3 name incarnations with same serial #	
C Trp 16 Cav	Gladiator (The)		66-15328 was 1st "GLADIATOR" / on display: MCL Detachment #754, Lowville, NY	
C Trp 16 Cav	Great Spekled Bird (The)	mis-spelling of Speckled	(DH 36)	
C Trp 16 Cav	Grim Reaper		second scheme / on display MCL Detachment #754, Lowville, NY / (DH 35)	
C Trp 16 Cav	Le Disiple Du Paix	"the disciple of peace"	disiple in wrong spelling: disciple is correct / Mar-June, '72 was active	
C Trp 16 Cav	Love American Style	1960's TV comedy series		
C Trp 16 Cav	Mean Motha			
C Trp 16 Cav	Miss Clawd IV	Claudia Cox was name of Mill's girlfriend / mis-spelled by unit artist on Loach #4	"MISS CLAUDE/CLAWD" series of names began in '69 + ended in '72 / on display: Army Avn Museum, Ft. Rucker, AL	
C Trp 16 Cav	Miss Kathy			
C Trp 16 Cav	Mongoloid (The)		Mustang platoon	
C Trp 16 Cav	Pale Rider	quoted name from unit slogan: "and behold, a pale horse! And its rider's name was Death": Revelations 6:8		
C Trp 16 Cav	Pillow Power	extra cockpit cushion accessory	(DH 35)	
C Trp 16 Cav	Post Falls Express	Idaho town		

Unit	Copter Name	Origin / Definition	Notes / Call Signs ( ) < >	Fate Aircraft / Crew
C Trp 16 Cav	Queen Hitmore			
C Trp 16 Cav	Roadrunner **	painted Roadrunner holding minigun		
C Trp 16 Cav	Suzi Q	classic rock-n-roll standard		
C Trp 16 Cav	Suzi Q II	popular rock tune		
C Trp 16 Cav	Suzi Q III	old rock-n-roll standard	(DH 36)	
C Trp 16 Cav	Sweet Pea	Popeye's adopted baby	currently: N13SD, Snohomish Co Sheriff's Office, Everett, WA	
C Trp 16 Cav	Tubber's Tiger	TUBS was nickname for wife (diet conscious)	two Burk AH-1G's carried this name;1st was destroyed / on display: VFW Post, Cedar Falls, IA / (DH 30)	
D Co 227 AHB	Arizona Gambler		two gunships, UH-1B + UH-1C, had this name	
D Co 227 AHB	Arizona Gambler	coiled cobra superimposed over green diamond with yellow lightning bolt	Muncey painted both Mike Obrecht CE Cobra's too / Aamot assigned to A-5-7 Cav ? / (Lobo 6)	
D Co 227 AHB	Avenger		frog ship / was B model 64-14176 earlier: combo B+C	
D Co 227 AHB	Bed Of Roses	Statler Brothers song title		
D Co 227 AHB	Big Daddy	famous artist Ed Roth's nickname	yellow lettering	
D Co 227 AHB	Corsair	"privateer"	skull + cross bones flag painted below "CORSAIR" / (Lobo 5)	
D Co 227 AHB	El Loch-O		(Lobo 13)	
D Co 227 AHB	Experience (The)		Terry Moon was 1st Cav PIO, official photog, 1969	
D Co 227 AHB	Ghost		(Lobo 8)	
D Co 227 AHB	Gremlin (The)		aka "TIMUJIN SHIP" / VHPA magazine, vol 23, #1, pic / on display: City of Greer, SC / (Lobo 10)	
D Co 227 AHB	Hawaiian (The)		on display: Am Legion Post 11, Florence, AL / (Lobo 10)	
D Co 227 AHB	Hell Fire			
D Co 227 AHB	Hulk	comic book character	shares serial # with B/2/20's "HULK" / (Lobo 9)	
D Co 227 AHB	Johnny		(Lobo 8)	
D Co 227 AHB	Joti C		painted Playboy bunny on doorpost / pinup girl on nose in similar style as WW II "Memphis Belle" bomber art	Jul-Aug 1968: crashed

Unit	Copter Name	Origin / Definition	Notes / Call Signs ( ) < >	Fate Aircraft / Crew
D Co 227 AHB	Leprechaun	four leaf clover superimposed over name	shares serial # with "RAID" / "Huey Cobra Gunships": Osprey Publication, pg 23, color / (Lobo 3)	
D Co 227 AHB	Liquidator			
D Co 227 AHB	Littlest Lobo		currently: N369MV, Wilmington, DE	
D Co 227 AHB	Mister Olds **	442 was muscle car built by Oldsmobile	aka "DOCTER OLDSMOBILE": checkered flag+hippie flashing peace sign / on display: South Plainfield, NJ	
D Co 227 AHB	Montana Mercenary			
D Co 227 AHB	Odyssey (The)	"Homer's long, dangerous journey"	(Lobo 7)	
D Co 227 AHB	Pandora's Box	"a prolific source of troubles"	possible in-country unit assignments: 57 AHC, 147 ASHC, 238 AWC, 361 AWC	
D Co 227 AHB	Phenix (The)	intentionally mis-spelled	Terry Moon was 1st Cav PIO, official photog, 1969	
D Co 227 AHB	Proud Mary	Creedence Clearwater Revival song title		
D Co 227 AHB	Pure Hell	funny car artist Ed Roth's VN War decal quotation		
D Co 227 AHB	Quigley	cowboy gunslinger		
D Co 227 AHB	Raid		shares serial # with "LEPRECHAUN" / (Lobo 3)	
D Co 227 AHB	Ship Of Fools	Doors song title		
D Co 227 AHB	Thumper *			
D Co 227 AHB	Timujin Ship	Genghis Khan's original name before he was named G.K.	aka "THE GREMLIN" / on display: City of Greer, SC / (Lobo 11)	
D Co 229 AHB	Cajun Lady			
D Co 229 AHB	Cheap Thrills	Janis Joplin album title		
D Co 229 AHB	Das Leichte Katzchen	"the frivolous kitten"	citation found in Heinrich Heine's poetry, CE girlfriend's favorite	
D Co 229 AHB	Easy Rider	Hollywood movie title		
D Co 229 AHB	El Culo Malo	"half hog configuration (bad mix)"	donkey painted on doorpost also	
D Co 229 AHB	Karen			
D Co 229 AHB	Magical Mystery Tour (The)	Beatles song title		

Unit	Copter Name	Origin / Definition	Notes / Call Signs ( ) < >	Fate Aircraft / Crew
D Co 229 AHB	Marrakesh Express (The)	Crosby, Stills + Nash song title		
D Co 229 AHB	Missy D			
D Co 229 AHB	Peace Maker			
D Co 229 AHB	Sweat Hog			
D Co 229 AHB	Un Cobra (The)	parody of the Un Cola 7 UP drink advertisement		
D Co 229 AHB	Woodstock	infamous 1969 rock concert	Eagle, Clark, Armelin all piloted this gunship	
D Trp 1/1	Aloha		unit webpic	serious accident 6-30-70
D Trp 1/1	Bear (The)	painted snarling grizzly bear head	(Saber 77)	
D Trp 1/1	DDAP ^^	DDAP = "dead dinks are pacified"	(Saber 77)	
D Trp 1/1	DDAP ^^	DDAP = "dead dinks are pacified"		
D Trp 1/1	Dead Dinks Are Pacified **	definition of "DDAP"	featured on the OH-6A and AH-1G	
D Trp 1/1	Dixie	generic name, no one in particular	aka "GLENDA" on doorpost: Britt's girlfriend's name / (Sword 23)	DD 1-27-69: Walt Ferrell KIA / Brittingham didn't fly the day '330 was destroyed
D Trp 1/1	Dog (The)			
D Trp 1/1	Glenda	name of Brittingham's girlfriend	aka "DIXIE" on nose / Tepper pic shows it as a wreck / (Sword 23)	DD 1-27-69: Walt Ferrell KIA / Brittingham didn't fly the day '330 was destroyed
D Trp 1/1	Hawk (The)	bald eagle painted below nn		
D Trp 1/1	Liz		currently: N5186J, U.S. Border Patrol, El Paso, TX	
D Trp 1/1	Lurch	Lurch from the Adams Family TV show painted on fuselage throwing rockets with his hands	Adams Family TV show character of same name / also Mahoney's nickname	
D Trp 1/1	Melvin's Toy	named after Mel Walker AC		DD July, 1970
D Trp 1/1	Melvin's Toy II	referred to Mel Walker, the AC		
D Trp 1/1	Mighty Mouse (The)	animated cartoon character		
D Trp 1/1	Mr. Magoo	McCue became MAGOO / cartoon character	(Saber 18)	

Unit	Copter Name	Origin / Definition	Notes / Call Signs ( ) < >	Fate Aircraft / Crew
D Trp 1/1	Okie			
D Trp 1/1	Pacifier (The)			5-22-71: Russell loses leg in combat flying this ship
D Trp 1/1	Pale Horse	REV 6:8 bible quote: "…and behold a pale horse: and his name that sat on him was Death, and Hell followed with him."	"REV 6:8" also painted on nose	
D Trp 1/1	Sgt Rock	named after CE John Rock, SGT / comic book SGT ROCK was popular at the time also	only 2 months life-span: 101 Abn ordered it removed	
D Trp 1/4	Baron Von Lemon	cartoon character created by the Pillsbury Company in 1967, to promote a powdered drink of the same name		
D Trp 1/4	Black Stallion	painting of a black stallion on fuselage		
D Trp 1/4	Charlie Chopper	painted gunship chopping up Charlie; "COBRA" in red letters streaming out of snake's mouth		
D Trp 1/4	Darkhorse Air Maintenance			
D Trp 1/4	Dee Dee Mow M.F.	"do it now mother fucker"		
D Trp 1/4	Devil's Disciple	devil riding a rocket with weapon in hand / notorious motorcycle club by same name	American motorcycle club / 1959 Burt Lancaster movie of same name	
D Trp 1/4	Down In The Boondocks	1965 Billy Joe Royal song title		
D Trp 1/4	Green Meanie	"Yellow Submarine" (Beatles) film reference to the evil Blue Meanies / also enemy tracer rounds	aka "LYNN" painted on extreme nose	
D Trp 1/4	Joan Of Arc			
D Trp 1/4	Lynn		aka "PIECE MAKER"	
D Trp 1/4	Miss Claude	girlfriend name of pilot Hugh Mills		
D Trp 1/4	Miss Claude II	girlfriend name of pilot Hugh Mills		
D Trp 1/4	Miss Claude III	girlfriend name of pilot Hugh Mills		
D Trp 1/4	Mustang			
D Trp 1/4	Piece Maker		aka "LYNN" on gunship nose	
D Trp 1/4	Post Falls Express	Idaho town		
D Trp 1/4	Prepared And Loyal ^^	unit motto		

Unit	Copter Name	Origin / Definition	Notes / Call Signs ( ) < >	Fate Aircraft / Crew
D Trp 1/4	Razorback			
D Trp 1/4	RF Express	Regional Force, SVN local militia		
D Trp 1/4	Rock and Flint	nicknames of crew members	currently: N46TP, Tampa Police Dept, Tampa, FL	
D Trp 1/4	Satan Snake		Hunter-Killer duo partner with Mills OH-6A	
D Trp 1/4	Short	term used to signify near end of 12 month tour	pic shows destroyed Loach upside down	
D Trp 1/4	Squatter Swatter			
D Trp 1/4	Widow Maker		twin 60's for each gunner, rockets + chunker	
D Trp 1/4	Widow Maker (The)			
D Trp 1/4	Widow Maker II			
D Trp 1/4	Widow Maker RIP			
D Trp 1/10	Calico Cat *	camouflage paint scheme inspired verbal nickname	same paint scheme applied to a OH-6A + UH-1H in unit / on display: VFW Post 8259, Stittville, NY	
D Trp 1/10	Hangar Queen (The)	derogatory term for excess need for repairs		sapper attack victim
D Trp 1/10	Iron Butterfly (The)	large butterfly painted on jump door also / 1960's rock group by same name		4-5-70: victim of sapper attack in revetment
D Trp 1/10	Iron Butterfly Too			
D Trp 1/10	Loosey Goosey *	pilot named it, loose feel of the cyclic		
D Trp 1/10	Triple Penny	refers to 1-1-1 sequence in serial #	same aircraft + name with A-7-17	
D Trp 2/1	Blood, Sweat N Tears	1960's rock band name		
D Trp 2/1	Little Head Hunter		currently: N1156X	
D Trp 2/1	Sandy			
D Trp 3/4	Beloved		very rare doghouse location of painted "name": only three known: 2-D/3/4 + 1-A/3/17 Nighthawk	
D Trp 3/4	Betty's Boobs		on display: Ft. Irwin, CA	

Unit	Copter Name	Origin / Definition	Notes / Call Signs ( ) < >	Fate Aircraft / Crew
D Trp 3/4	Borrowed Time		currently: N8880X	
D Trp 3/4	California Dreamin'	Mamas + Papas 1965 song title	name was painted on right side of doghouse / aka "KANSAS KILLER" on left side / transitioned to F/4 Cav summer '71	
D Trp 3/4	For God, Country + Body Count		F/4 Cav Loach carried on this name into '71-'72	'359, DD 6-9-70: KIA's: S. Dobry, J. McGlothien, Andrew Elliott
D Trp 3/4	For God, Country + Body Count		carried on this name from previous OH-6, D/3/4 Cav	'359 DD 6-9-70
D Trp 3/4	Ghost Rider			
D Trp 3/4	Ghost Rider II			
D Trp 3/4	Ghost Rider III		1971-72 yearbook pic	
D Trp 3/4	Ghost Rider III1/2			
D Trp 3/4	Henchman (The)			
D Trp 3/4	Henchman II (The)	executioner mask painted near name	transitioned to F/4 Cav summer '71	
D Trp 3/4	Iron Butterfly	painted butterflies also	Fluharty DEROS'd May 1970	DD 6-9-70: Elliott POW
D Trp 3/4	Kansas Killer (The)	Parris was from Kansas / name on left side	aka "CALIFORNIA DREAMING" on right side / transitioned to F/4 Cav summer '71	
D Trp 3/4	Kentucky Woman	Brady was from Kentucky / Neil Diamond tune	transitioned to F/4 Cav summer '71 / on display: Am Legion Post 65, Statesville, NC	
D Trp 3-4	King Rat	1965 Hollywood movie title		
D Trp 3/4	Lady Godiva	20mm on wing stub	transitioned to F/4 Cav summer '71	
D Trp 3/4	Love Bug	Disney film title / painted flowers also		
D Trp 3/4	Mini Hog *	19 rocket pods+minigun	strong engine allowed extra load of munitions	
D Trp 3/4	Mississippi Queen	ship's wheel painted near name	rock band Mountain song title / on display: Ozark Military Museum, Fayetteville, AR	
D Trp 3/4	Ohio Express	Kirker was from Ohio	transitioned to F/4 Cav summer '71	
D Trp 3/4	Pancho Villa	CE of Mexican descent+CE's last name forms part of outlaw's name		DD July, 1966
D Trp 3/4	Paper Tiger			
D Trp 3/4	Peace Maker		chase ship / retrieved down crews	

Unit	Copter Name	Origin / Definition	Notes / Call Signs ( ) < >	Fate Aircraft / Crew
D Trp 3/4	Pinball Wizard	The Who song title / named by Adrian Williams	very rare doghouse location of painted UH-1 "name": only two others known: D/3/4 "LOVE" + A/3/17 "NIGHTHAWK"	DD 3-26-02, Argentina
D Trp 3/4	Proud Mary	Creedence Clearwater Revival song title		
D Trp 3/4	Rosemary's Baby	Hollywood horror film title	transitioned to F/4 Cav summer '71/ on display: Army Avn Heritage Foundation, Hampton, GA	
D Trp 3/4	SNAFU	"situation normal all fucked up"	1st OH-6A with door mounted mini-gun	
D Trp 3/4	Snoopy	Charlie Brown's dog in Peanuts comic strip		
D Trp 3/4	Stable Boy ^	adopted name of the maintenance platoon's aircraft that imitated the D/3/4's CENTAURS callsign		
D Trp 3/4	Stable Boy ^	adopted name of the maintenance platoon's aircraft that imitated the D/3/4's CENTAURS callsign		
D Trp 3/4	Stable Boy II ^	adopted name of the maintenance platoon's aircraft that imitated the D/3/4's CENTAURS callsign		
D Trp 3/4	Super Egg			
D Trp 3/4	Super Egg II	OH-6 resembled egg shape		10-28-69: Mark Jackson KIA, Snoddy WIA, Rhodes WIA
D Trp 3/4	Undertaker (The)	coffin painted near name	transitioned to F/4 Cav summer '71	
D Trp 3/4	Warlord (The)		transitioned to F/4 Cav summer '71	
D Trp 3/4	Wretched Mildred	pilot's name for his grandmother; Chinese script spelling out serial # on vertical stabilizer + "snake" on fuselage	transitioned to F/4 Cav summer '71 / painted female centaur holding spear + sword	
D Trp 3/5	America Love It Or Leave It	conservative political slogan of 1960's+1970's		
D Trp 3/5	Angel Babe			
D Trp 3/5	Arkansas Highway Patrol	Mills was from Arkansas	Mills rec'd Highway Patrol door decals from AR / flew '802, Oct '71-Feb '72	DD 1-30-72: near Laos border
D Trp 3/5	Bastard Cav	unit was cut loose from 1st Cav	(LK 24)	
D Trp 3/5	Boo		on display: Naval Post Grad School, Monterey, CA	
D Trp 3/5	Cyclops			
D Trp 3/5	Death Committee	"LONGKNIFE BASTARD CAV" on nose also		
D Trp 3/5	Goodship Lollipop II (The)	eyeballs painted on front turret / ShirleyTemple song title	2,612 flying hours, the most in unit / 1st AH-1G in unit	

U.S. ARMY HELICOPTER NAMES IN VIETNAM

Unit	Copter Name	Origin / Definition	Notes / Call Signs ( ) < >	Fate Aircraft / Crew
D Trp 3/5	Iron Butterfly	1960's rock group by same name		
D Trp 3/5	J. C. + The Boys	J. C. = Jesus Christ		
D Trp 3/5	Jo Ann			
D Trp 3/5	Kathy			
D Trp 3/5	Little Annie			
D Trp 3/5	Little Annie II			
D Trp 3/5	Lone Eagle			
D Trp 3/5	Miss Kathy Ann	name of Ron Decile's girlfriend		DD 4-6-69
D Trp 3/5	Patches	multiple patches covering bullet damage	shot down 11 times, over 2,000 flying hours	
D Trp 3/5	Pig Pen *	comic strip Peanuts character's name	most powerful Loach in unit / (WW 14)	
D Trp 3/5	Queen			
D Trp 3/5	Remember The Alamo		1st bomb dropped in combat by an AH-1G, 10-2-68 / aka "GOOD LUCK CHARLIE" written on bomb	
D Trp 3/5	Sandra Lee			
D Trp 3/5	Scavengers ^	unit maintenance platoon		
D Trp 3/5	Susie Q	classic rock-n-roll standard		
D Trp 3/5	Tumbleweed		(LK 26)	
D Trp 3/5	War Wagon	John Wayne 1967 movie		
D Trp 3/5	Wild Thang	The Troggs 1965 song title		
D Trp 3/5	Wild Thing	The Troggs 1965 song title		

Unit	Copter Name	Origin / Definition	Notes / Call Signs ( ) < >	Fate Aircraft / Crew
D Trp 17 Cav	Mystery Ship	part of the 1970 "Ride Captain Ride" lyrics by the Blues Image	SS-11 wire guided missiles	
D Trp 17 Cav	Oscar Mayer	hot dog suspended on a string, symbolized dog bait teaser that OH-6 missions entailed		DD 11-5-72: KIA's: Deano Denardo AC, Steve Taylor DG
D Trp 17 Cav	Patience My Ass I'm Gonna Kill Something	political cartoon quote		
D Trp 17 Cav	Tiny			
E Btry 82 Arty Bn	D.B. (The) *	DB = Dumb Bunny, Douche Bag		DD 11-12-65
E Btry 82 Arty Bn	D.B. II (The) *	DB = Dumb Bunny, Douche Bag		DD 12-14-65
E Btry 82 Arty Bn	D.B. III (The)	DB = Dumb Bunny, Douche Bag / two assigned OH-13's destroyed, thus origin of "DB III" name	two previous aircraft were OH-13's	
E Btry 82 Arty Bn	Douche Bag (The) *	DB = Dumb Bunny, Douche Bag		
E Btry 82 Arty Bn	Douche Bag II (The) *	DB = Dumb Bunny, Douche Bag		
E Btry 82 Arty Bn	Douche Bag III (The) **	DB = Dumb Bunny, Douche Bag		
E Btry 82 Arty Bn	Dumb Bunny III (The) **	polite company (PC) definition of "DB"	DB = Dumb Bunny, Douche Bag	
E Btry 82 Arty Bn	Joan I			
E Co 123 Avn Bn	Road Runner ^	Wiley Coyote nemesis		
E Co 704 Maint Bn	Buzzards ^	painted cigar smoking buzzard wearing a flight helmet		
E Co 709 Maint Bn	Raccoon Airlines ^	Raccoon was callsign	artwork: raccoon holding a wrench + firing pistol / Foss was C.O. of E-709	
E Co 723 Maint Bn	Road Runner	painting of a roadrunner also		
E Trp 1/9	As Ye Sow So Shall Ye Reap	Job 4:8 bible verse	Grim Reaper graphic above verse	
E Trp 1/9	Doctor Death			
E Trp 1/9	Doctor Oldsmobile	product advertisement character for 442 car		
E Trp 1/9	Little Green Killing Machine	Rochat's OH-6 had bulls eye painted on belly		
E Trp 1/9	Montana Mercenary			
E Trp 1/9	Orange Crush	soft drink or Agent Orange ref		

Unit	Copter Name	Origin / Definition	Notes / Call Signs ( ) < >	Fate Aircraft / Crew
E Trp 1/9	Orange Wedge	psychedelic Baltimore rock band 1968		
E Trp 1/9	Peacemaker ^			
E Trp 1/9	Shadowfax	Lord of the Rings horse	pic no longer exists: only rendering is on cadet class wall; artist discarded only surviving pic after mural was painted	
E Trp 1/9	Shirl Be Good		Scout platoon leader's bird	VHPA book pic shows it destroyed
E Trp 1/9	Triple Nickel *	refers to 5-5-5 sequence in serial #		
E Trp 1/9	Vagabond Virgin			
F Trp 4 Cav	#1 Du Me Mi	"#1 Bad Mother Fucker" in Vietnamese	Frank Dillon worked on ship, says it was worn out, over worked aircraft	
F Trp 4 Cav	3-5 Pig	"weak engine" / also, "3-5" = serial # sequence, plus "PIG" which refers to the shape of the number "8"		
F Trp 4 Cav	Creeping Jesus	"hypocritically pious"	1971-72 F/4 yearbook pics on unit website	
F Trp 4 Cav	For God, Country + Body Count		carried on this name from OH-6, D/3/4 Cav	DD 6-9-70
F Trp 4 Cav	For The Love Of Freedom			
F Trp 4 Cav	Kill Or Be Killed	painted "WARGASM" on Loach clamshell also	Army Avn Heritage Foundation, Hampton, GA, flyable a/c	
F Trp 4 Cav	Mini Power			
F Trp 4 Cav	Nixon's Hired Gun			
F Trp 4 Cav	Screaming OD Zonker (The)	possible reference to tracer rounds		DD 11-17-71
F Trp 4 Cav	Wargasm	painted "KILL OR BE KILLED" on left rear door	owned+operated by Army Avn Heritage Foundation, Hampton, GA	
F Trp 8 Cav	Doctor 570	maintenance ship of the 570 TC		
F Trp 8 Cav	Dog (The)			damaged aircraft, loss to inventory
F Trp 8 Cav	Hammerhead		colorful history / on display: VN Memorial Committee, Big Springs, TX	
F Trp 9 Cav	Boeing 707 *	in honor of KIA WO Ron Boeing	on display: Nat'l VN War Museum, Mineral Wells, TX / formerly N75707	
F Trp 9 Cav	Harley *	CE was hardcore biker	currently: N53BN, Addison Air LLC, Wilmington, DE	

Unit	Copter Name	Origin / Definition	Notes / Call Signs ( ) < >	Fate Aircraft / Crew
F Trp 9 Cav	Jet Propelled Martini **	green olive color paint job		
F Trp 9 Cav	Max Well	iconic "Kilroy was here" looking over fence painting	E-43 on rear stabilizer / half of Cav hunter-killer team	
F Trp 9 Cav	Snoopy **	Snoopy as Sopwith Camel pilot, WW 1 flying ace		
F Trp 9 Cav	Texas **	Texas star on doghouse		
F Btry 79 AFA	9,000 Lbs Of Romp + Stomp	possible parody of funny car artist Ed Roth's VN War decal: "52 Tons of Rolling Death"		
F Btry 79 AFA	Avenger			
F Btry 79 AFA	Challenger			
F Btry 79 AFA	Fireball			
F Btry 79 AFA	Flying Circus **	Eddie Rickenbacker's WWI fighter a/c unit		
F Btry 79 AFA	Genocide		shares serial # with "USA1"	
F Btry 79 AFA	Grim Reaper			
F Btry 79 AFA	Iron Butterfly	1960's rock group by same name	unit assignments: 8/69-5/71, C/2/20 + 6/71-7/72, F/79	
F Btry 79 AFA	Mad Butcher			
F Btry 79 AFA	Mean Mr. Mustard	Beatles song title		DD 6-20-72: KIA's: Shield AC Northrup CP
F Btry 79 AFA	Murder Inc	"mafia hit men"		
F Btry 79 AFA	Old Friend			
F Btry 79 AFA	Old Spot			
F Btry 79 AFA	Southern Comfort	American bourbon whiskey		
F Btry 79 AFA	Two Stepper	VN snake venom bite so lethal that victim usually walked two steps + died		DD 5-24-72: KIA's: Henn AC, Hosaka CP in this F/79 gunship
F Btry 79 AFA	USA1	Chevy promotional license plate / Hartnett was Chevy aficionado, mimicked Chevy ad slogan	shares serial # with "GENOCIDE" / on turret "TO CHARLIE WITH LOVE FROM USA1"	
F Btry 79 AFA	Woodstock I	infamous 1969 rock concert		

U.S. ARMY HELICOPTER NAMES IN VIETNAM

Unit	Copter Name	Origin / Definition	Notes / Call Signs ( ) < >	Fate Aircraft / Crew
F Btry 79 AFA	Woodstock II	infamous 1969 rock concert		
COBRA NETT	Snake Charmer	adopted name of the maintenance platoon's aircraft that imitated the COBRA NETT callsign	maintenance ship	
COBRA NETT	Virginia Rose 1	"highly adaptive flower"	camouflage color scheme	
COBRA NETT	Virginia Rose II	"highly adaptive flower"	camouflage color scheme	
UTT	Big Bertha			
UTT	Kathryn		aka "LITTLE RUDY"	
UTT	Little Rudy		aka "KATHRYN"	
UTT	Ole Hotbox			
UTT	Pandora			
UTT	Peacemaker			
unknown	Bah Humbug	slick from unk unit delivered '67 Xmas mail to LZ Ross	Doc McBride was medic in D Co, 5/7 Cav	
unknown	Bennie's Bomb		cat with halo above its head depicted on copter nose	
unknown	Bits And Pieces	Dave Clark Five song title		
unknown	Boxcar			
unknown	Busy Boy			
unknown Cav	Cheap Thrills	Janis Joplin album title	Reid was sniper with 5/12, 199 LIB enroute to Cambodia	
unknown	Chicago Police Dept	CPD badge emblem painted below pilot's window	"CHICAGO POLICE DEPT" painted on belly	
unknown	Choo Choo's Train	painting of train spouting smoke		
unknown	Creeping Ginnie	"rampant invader"	graphic of cartoonish character	
unknown	Cross Ways Breezer	Hue prostitute name + oral sex term	belonged to Hue, Phu Bai helo unit	
unknown	Cucaracha	"cockroach"		

Unit	Copter Name	Origin / Definition	Notes / Call Signs ( ) < >	Fate Aircraft / Crew
unknown	Death N Destruction			
unknown	Drinking Problem	painting of glass of beer	aka "GUINNESS, KILLER G's"	
unknown	Family Car (The)			
unknown	Fannie C (The)	Fannie C = fantasy	photo depicts C+C slick dropping off advisor in dried rice paddy	
unknown	Flower Power	counterculture slogan meaning non-violence	painted flowers on turret	
unknown	Flying Tank (The)	profile of a military tank painted on pilot's door		
unknown	Happy Ship (The)	smiling male face		
unknown	Hell Bound			
unknown	Horny Hooker (The)			
unknown	Hurry Sundown	painted sunrise on nose / folk song + movie title	former slick of Jump's friend who had infused into unit in late '68	
unknown Cav	Iron Butterfly	crossed sabers on gunship nose / 1960's rock group by same name	Gluck was renown VN War photographer	
unknown	Jezabell	mis-spelling of Jezebel		
unknown	Joann		yellow crest on nose with black chess piece?	
unk Signal Gp	Little Mary			
unk Engineer unit	Lolly		one of the two crew was Hawaiian / unk Engineer or Arty unit	
unknown	Look Out			
unknown	Lucky 8	painted "8 ball" on copter nose also	photographed in Tan Son Nhut hangar	
unknown	Lucy In The Sky With Diamonds	psychedelically painted lettering with female Lucy depicted / Beatles song title by same name		
unknown	Metal Rain		Cu Chi unit, SHOTGUN 8 DG	
unknown	My Girl	1964 song title by The Temptations by same name		
unknown	Prickly Pear		Sarratt was Shotgun 8 DG, Soc Trang unit	
unknown	Pusher (The)	Steppenwolf tune		
unknown Cav	Sandy Ghost	sand + weeds + partially gutted but flyable	reportedly last Army chopper flown in VN before final truce	handed over to the SVN Air Force

U.S. ARMY HELICOPTER NAMES IN VIETNAM

Unit	Copter Name	Origin / Definition	Notes / Call Signs ( ) < >	Fate Aircraft / Crew
several	Situation Normal All Fucked Up **	definition of "SNAFU"	copters in these three units carried this name:173 AHC, 539 TC, D-3-4	
unknown	Smile Or I'll Kill You		nn is not visible in pic	
unknown	Snake Charmer		Wayne was assigned to 142 TC when he viewed this gunship land at Camp Viking	
unknown	Snoopy **			
unknown	Supergrunt		enroute to Khe Sanh pic	
unknown	Triple Nickel	refers to 5-5-5 sequence in serial #	BN based out of Da Nang / Sarratt was Shotgun 8 member, 25 Inf Div	
several	We Eat This Shit Up **	definition of "WETSU"	copters in these four units carried this name: 11 ACR, 62 Avn Co, 173 AHC, 175 AHC	
unknown	We Help The Hurt	doctor in white frock coat		

INDIVIDUAL CONTRIBUTORS

A - Z

Numbers correspond to Contributor notations in the Helicopter Names A-Z section.

1. Aamot, Leif A-5-7, 1968-69
2. Abel, Bill 11Gen Supp, CE, 1969-70
3. Abels, Jerry 135 AHC, CE, 1967-68
4. Acker, Ken 155 AHC, P, 1966-67
5. Adams, Clif 45 MC, CE, 1967-68
6. Adams, David D-1-1, P, 1969-70
7. Adams, Leo 129 AHC, CE, 1970
8. Adams, Tom 282 AHC, CE, 1965-66
9. Adessa, Tony B-25 Avn Bn, P, 1966
10. Aeilts, Mike 117 AHC, CE, 1969-70
11. Aiken, Dan HHC 11 Bde 23 Div, CE, 1970-71
12. Akin, Joe 114 AHC, CE, 1970-71
13. Alberts, Dan 196 ASHC, FE, 1967-68
14. Alcott, Ron 28 Sig Det, DG, 1965-66
15. Aldridge, Dan 199 RAC, P, 1967-68
16. Alejandro, John F-8 Cav, DG, 1971
17. Alexander, Charles, C-7-17, P, 1969-71
18. Alexander, Jack 129 AHC, P, 1970
19. Alfano, Joe 114 AHC, P, 1971-72
20. Alioto, Ernie A Co 1 Avn Bn, DG, 1968
21. Alleger, Keith 117 AHC, P, 1968-69
22. Allen, Bill 498 MC, CE, 1968-69
23. Allen, Larry B-2-17, 1969-70
24. Alley, Ted 188 AHC, CE, 1968
25. Allison, Warren 192 AHC, CE, 1967-68
26. Allman, Darrell B-1-9, P, 1970-71
27. Almaraz, Art 191 AHC, CE, 1967-68
28. Alvis, Fred 129 AHC, DG, 1971
29. Amanzio, Tony 48 AHC, P, 1970-71
30. Amato, Art A-101 AHB, CE, 1966-67
31. Anderson, Jere B-1-9, P, 1967-68
32. Anderson, Joe 281 AHC, P, 1967-68
33. Anderson, Larry 604 TC/189 AHC, 1968-69
34. Anderson, Paul 2 Bde 1 Cav, P, 1969-70
35. Anderson, Roger 175 AHC, CE, 1967-69
36. Anderson, Tom C-229, 1969-70
37. Andreasen, Russell 135 AHC, CE, 1969-70
38. Andreoff, Steven 175 AHC, DG, 1970-71
39. Anglin, Tom 283 MD, CE, 1967-68
40. Anthony, Jeff A-7-17, P, 1970-71
41. Anzalone, Tony 114 AHC, CE, 1967-68

42. Anzelmo, George A-1-9, CE, 1969-70
43. Appel, Dirk A-227, 1969-70
44. Arcouette, Ron 162 AHC, 1968-69
45. Aretz, James 334 AHC, CE, 1967-68
46. Armijo, Ross 175 AHC, CE, 1970-71
47. Armstrong, Jack 118 AHC, P, 1966
48. Arruda, Larry 120 AHC, CE, 1964-65
49. Asberry, Andy B-25 Avn Bn, CE, 1968-69
50. Ash, Larry 15 MB, DG, 1970-71
51. Ashley, Art 192 AHC, P, 1970-71
52. Ashton, Larry A-82 Avn Bn, CE, 1965
53. Askew, Mike C-1-9, CE, 1967-68
54. Atkins, Gaylord E-123 Avn Bn, CE, 1970-71
55. Atkinson, Dave D-3-4, DG, 1970
56. Atkinson, Gary C-229, CE, 1969-70
57. Atwood, Walt 117 AHC, P, 1966-67
58. Austin, Harold 118 Avn Co, DG, 1965
59. Austin, Steve 155 AHC, CE, 1966-67
60. Avery, Dennis 187 AHC, P, 1969
61. Ayers, Dave, D-1-1, P, 1972
62. Babb, Mike 187 AHC, P, 1971
63. Badgley, James 118 AHC, P, 1970
64. Baggott, Dave 21 Sig Gp, P, 1970-71
65. Bagnaschi, Chuck 4th Avionics Co, P, 1967-68
66. Bailey, Jim 281 AHC, CE, 1969-70
67. Bailey, John 174 AHC, P, 1969-70
68. Baird, Mark 178 ASHC, FE, 1971
69. Bajc, Marko, VN War researcher
70. Baker, Bob 114 AHC, P, 1970-71
71. Baker, Dale F-8, CE, 1969-70
72. Baker, David 176 AHC, CE, 1969-70
73. Baker, Roger C-229, P, 1969-70
74. Baker, Wade, 242 ASHC, 1970-71
75. Baldwin, Earl 165 TC/155 AHC, DG, 1967-68
76. Baldwin, Reg, C-229, P, 1968-69
77. Balentine, John 539 TC, 1968
78. Balfrey, Roger 117 AHC, CE, 1970-71
79. Ballinger, Phil, 48 AHC, 1966-67
80. Balmer, Jerry 178 ASHC, FE, 1967
81. Balog, Jim 48 AHC, DG, 1969-70
82. Banicki, John C-2-8 Cav, 1972

83. Barbee, Karl 129 AHC, P, 1967
84. Barber, Lou C-227, P, 1966-67
85. Bargala, Sonny C-229, CE, 1970
86. Barkley, Roger 191 AHC, CE, 1967-68
87. Barlow, Mike 116 AHC, 1970-71
88. Barnes, Jerry C-2-20 ARA, P, 1966-67
89. Barnett, Jim 334 AHC, CE, 1971
90. Barrera, John 116 AHC, CE, 1970-71
91. Barrett, James D-1-1, 1969
92. Barrie, Jim 117 AHC, CE, 1970-71
93. Barron, David 176 AHC, CE, 1967
94. Barter, William 175 AHC, CE, 1969-70
95. Bartlett, Paul 71 AHC, P, 1967-68
96. Bartlett, Robert A-228 ASHB, FE, 1967
97. Baruz, Howard 114 AHC, CE, 1964-65
98. Bary, Victor 11 CAB, 1967
99. Bascom, Don 117 AHC, CE, 1967
100. Bass, Norm B-159 ASHB, DG, 1970-72
101. Bateman, Bobby A-227, P, 1970-71
102. Batey, Bill A-227, P, 1969-71
103. Bauer, Scott 571 MD, Medic, 1972
104. Bauman, Mike D-1-1, P, 1967-68
105. Baumgartner, Ken 339 TC, CE, 1967-68
106. Bay, Frank 240 AHC, CE, 1967-68
107. Bean, Jerry 28 Sig Det, 1966
108. Bearley, Ron 178/179 ASHC, FE, 1967-68
109. Beck, Paul 33 TC, CE, 1962-63
110. Beckenhauer, John 180 ASHC, P, 1968
111. Beckenhauer, Jon 243 ASHC, CE, 1968-71
112. Beckler, Dennis C-227, CE, 1968-69
113. Beckman, Martin D-227, P, 1969-70
114. Beddingfield, Jim 336 AHC, P, 1969-70
115. Beebe, Max 188 AHC, P, 1967-68
116. Beech, Mike 121 AHC, P, 1965
117. Behm, Chris 117 AHC, CE, 1971
118. Behn, Dave 243 ASHC, CE/FE, 1968-69
119. Belis, Mike D-1-10, 1969-70
120. Belkin, Howie C-227, DG, 1969-70
121. Bell, Carl C-3-17, P, 1972
122. Bell, George 162 AHC, CE, 1971-72
123. Bell, Jim 1 Bde 1 Cav, 1967

124. Bell, William 243 ASHC, CE, 1968
125. Bellerue, Rik 187 AHC, CE, 1970-72
126. Benka, Jim 189 AHC, CE, 1967-70
127. Bennett, Allen 117 AHC, DG/CE, 1967-68
128. Bennett, Bob 117 AHC, 1969-70
129. Bennett, Dan A-1-9, P, 1969-70
130. Benton, Robin 11 Bde, 1969-70
131. Berg, Jerry 134 AHC, CE, 1968-69
132. Bergeron, Richard A-227, 1970
133. Bernard, Vernon 175 AHC, CE, 1967-68
134. Bernstein, Jonathan author
135. Berowski, Ken 175 AHC, 1970-71
136. Berthel, George B-3-17, CE, 1969-70
137. Bertholf, Cheney 1 Bn 50 Inf, 1968
138. Bertolini, Frank 37 Med Co, 1970-71
139. Beson, Jim 159 MD, P, 1969-7
140. Betsill, Carl F-4, 1971
141. Bigelow, Ken, brother of Ralph, (KIA), 176 AHC,
     1969-70
142. Billow, Mike A-3-17, P, 1970-71
143. Bishop, Dennis 498 MC, 1970-71
144. Bjurstrom, Mark 271 ASHC, CE, 1968-69
145. Black, Ron A-1-9, P, 1969-70
146. Blackmon, Billy D-3-4, DG, 1969-70
147. Blankenship, Calvin 57 AHC, 1970-71
148. Blankenship, Dennis 188 AHC, DG, 1968-69
149. Blankenship, Ken 134 AHC, P, 1970-71
150. Blazina, Tom 271 ASHC, CE, 1968-69
151. Blickenstaff, Jon 159 MD, CE, 1970-71
152. Bodnar, Mike C-2-7, 1970
153. Boettger, Tim 176 AHC, CE, 1971
154. Bogue, Jeff B-2-20 ARA, P, 1970-71
155. Bohrman, Ken 571 MD, CE, 1971-72
156. Bokkes, Tom 71 AHC, CE, 1970-71
157. Bollens, Al 155 AHC, P, 1968-69
158. Bonevich, Art C-3-17, DG, 1969-70
159. Bono, Lou, 173 Abn Bde, 1968-71
160. Bono, Rick 11 ACR, CE, 1968-69
161. Borchin, George 937 Cbt Eng Gp, P, 1965-66
162. Bordeaux, Joe 174 AHC, CE, 1970
163. Boren, Jim 116 AHC, P, 1967-68
164. Bowling, Richard D-227 AHB, 1967-68
165. Bowser, Dan 128 AHC, P, 1970-71
166. Boxley, Joe 200 ASHC, FE, 1967-68

167. Boyce, John 118 Avn Co, DG, 1965
168. Boyd, Barc 8 TC, P, 1962-63
169. Boyd, John 92 AHC, P, 1971
170. Boyd, Roger 179 ASHC, FE, 1969
171. Boyd, Tim 237 MD, CE, 1970-71
172. Boyle, Ray 282 AHC, CE, 1969-70
173. Bracewell, Jim B-229AHB/HHT 7-1, P,
     1966-67/1970
174. Blank *************************
175. Braddock, John 236 MD, Medic, 1971-72
176. Brader, Carl 119 AHC, CE, 1970
177. Bradley, Lee 117 AHC, CE, 1970-71
178. Brady, Dan 15 MB, Medic, 1970
179. Brady, Jim C-159 ASHB, FE, 1971
180. Brady, Pat 54 MD, P, 1967-68
181. Bramuchi, David D-1-10, CE, 1969-70
182. Branigan, George D-3-5, CE, 1971-72
183. Brainard, Charles 57 AHC, P, 1970-71
184. Brackenhoff, Robert 409 TC/174 AHC, 1968-71
185. Brandt, Bob, author, 33 TC, P, 1962-63
186. Brant, Owen 176 AHC, CE, 1970-71
187. Bratkovic, Robert 135 AHC, P, 1970-71
188. Braum, David 81 TC, CE, 1963-64
189. Bray, Bill 147/205 ASHC, FE, 1967-68
190. Bray, Eric 162 AHC, P, 1970-71
191. Breaux, Michael 118 AHC, 1971
192. Brennan, John 114 AHC, Flt Opns, 1970-71
193. Breski, Joe B-1-9, P, 1969
194. Brethen, Eric D-3-4, P, 1969-70
195. Brewer, Gary D-1-4/C-16, CE, 1969-70
196. Breyer, Alex 145 CAB, CE, 1969-70
197. Bridges, Gary A-227, P, 1970-71
198. Bridges, Jim D-227, CE, 1966-67
199. Bridges, Roy C-229, DG, 1970-71
200. Brimmer, Vic 128 AHC, P, 1969-70
201. Brinn, Joe A-7-17, P, 1968-69
202. Brisker, Frank 61 AHC, P, 1968-69
203. Brittingham, Al D-1-1, CE, 1968-69
204. Brooker, Dan 187 AHC, DG, 1971
205. Brooks, Bill, C-1-9, 1970
206. Brophy, Ed 48 AHC/390 TC, 1965-66
207. Broussard, Harry 92 AHC, P, 1967-68
208. Brouwers, Dan C-229, DG, 1970-71
209. Brown, Danny E-704 Mnt Bn, CE, 1969-70

210. Brown, Dave 120 AHC, CE, 1967-68
211. Brown, David 187 AHC, CE, 1968-69
212. Brown, Gary 25 Avn Bn, 1968-69
213. Brown, J. C. C-159 ASHB, DG, 1968
214. Brown, Jerry 173 Abn Bde, CE, 1970
215. Brown, John 571 MD, Medic, 1972-73
216. Brown, Ken 155 AHC, CE, 1968-69
217. Brown, Larry A-7-1, CE, 1971-72
218. Brown, Larry B-1-9, P, 1967-68
219. Brown, Mike 213 ASHC, FE, 1966-67
220. Brown, Mike F-79 AFA, P, 1972
221. Brown N.G. C-2-20 ARA, P, 1968-69
222. Brown, Robert 68 AHC, P, 1965-66
223. Brown, William 174 AHC, CE, 1969-70
224. Brownell, Steve B-3-17, CE 1969
225. Bruce, Bobby 11 CAG, P, 1972
226. Bruss, Al 390 TC/48 AHC, 1965-68
227. Bryan, Tom 162 AHC, CE, 1968
228. Bryant, William 118 AHC, 1970-71
229. Buchanan, Bobby 174 AHC, P, 1969
230. Buchheister, Bill B-2-5, 1968-69
231. Buehler, Dick C-227, CE, 1967
232. Buffington, John 173 AHC
233. Bullen, John 174 AHC, CE, 1970
234. Buller, Larry 129 AHC, CE, 1972
235. Bundage, Herb 155 AHC/165 TC, 1966-67
236. Bunger, Bill 243 ASHC, FE, 1968
237. Burden, Dennis A-227, CE, 1966-67
238. Burgess, Chris B-1-9, P, 1968-69
239. Burk, Wayne C-16, P, 1970-71
240. Burke, Ray 121 AHC, CE, 1970
241. Burkhalter, Darrell 118 AHC, P, 1970
242. Burnett, Chuck B-25 Avn Bn, DG, 1966-67
243. Burnett, Randy 129 AHC, CE, 1966-68
244. Burns, Carl D-3-4, P, 1966-67
245. Burney, Andy 191 AHC, CE, 1967-68
246. Burns, Danny 192 AHC, DG, 1967-68
247. Burrow, Roy, 243 ASHC, 1969
248. Burton, William 116 AHC, CE, 1966-67
249. Bush, Jim 282 AHC, CE, 1970-71
250. Butler, Bruce 114 AHC, P, 1971-72
251. Buzzell, Hugh B-228 ASHB, FE, 1968
252. Byars, Harold 116 AHC, P, 1967-68
253. Bynum, Tom 117 AHC, DG, 1967-68

254. Bynum, Ty 92 AHC, P, 1968-69
255. Byrnes, Ken 155 AHC, CE, 1966-67
256. Cabrera, Jess 271 ASHC, DG, 1969-70
257. Cady, Ray 68 AHC, CE, 1966-67
258. Cahill, David 82 MD, Medic, 1969-70
259. Caine, Vaughn E-1-9, P, 1970-71
260. Cairns, Ernest C-1-9, CE, 1966-67
261. Calaway, Joe 92 AHC, CE, 1968-69
262. Calderon, Gary 162 AHC, DG, 1968-69
263. Calibro, Jim 15 MB, DG, 1967-68
264. Call, Jim 147 ASHC, CE, 1967-68
265. Callaghan, Bob 2nd Sig Gp, CE, 1966-67
266. Callison, Don D-3-5, P, 1970-71
267. Calloway, James 178 ASHC, 1968-70
268. Calton, Dick 191 AHC, DG, 1967-68
269. Cambo, Pablo C-7-17, 1969-70
270. Camp, Ken B-3-17, P, 1969-70
271. Campbell, Bruce C-1-9, P, 1970-71
272. Cannizzaro, Sal A-25 Avn Bn, DG, 1968-69
273. Cano, Jose 282 AHC, CE, 1971
274. Caraker, Robert D-1-4, P, 1967-68
275. Carden, Harold 162 AHC, 1968-69
276. Carder, Ed A-227, P, 1966-67
277. Cardinal, Patrick 215 Composite Svc Bn, CE, 1971-72
278. Carlson, Fred 174 AHC, CE, 1969-70
279. Carlson, Kent 282 AHC, DG, 1966-67
280. Carlton, Ken 191 AHC, P, 1969-70
281. Carnes, Ed, 326 MB, 1970-71
282. Carr, Jeff 114 AHC, P, 1969-70
283. Carr, Ron B-229, CE, 1969-70
284. Carroll, Eugene 119 AHC, 1968-69
285. Carter, Tommy 117 AHC, CE, 1965-66
286. Case, Bill 37 Sig Bn, CE, 1971-72
287. Casey, Matt 129 AHC, CE, 1970
288. Casper, John 45 MC, CE, 1968-69
289. Cataldo, Nick 114 AHC, Svc Plt, 1969-70
290. Cathey, George 116 AHC, DG, 1967-70
291. Cattilini, Jack A-7-1, P, 1970-71
292. Cauley, Bud 242 ASHC, DG, 1968-69
293. Cayze, Bob 213 ASHC, FE, 1968-69
294. Chambers, Howard 114 AHC, CE, 1965-66
295. Champlin, Don A-82 Avn Bn, P, 1965-66

296. Chapman, Ralph C-3-17/D-3-5, CE, 1971-72
297. Chappell, Mel C-228 ASHB, FE, 1968-69
298. Chappell, Ralph 178/205 ASHC, P, 1968-69
299. Chase, Dan 145 CAB, CE, 1969-70
300. Chavez, Bill 116 AHC, CE, 1970-71
301. Chenoweth, Bob, author, 4 TC/120 AHC/58 Avn Det, CE, 1967-68
302. Cherrie, Stan 191 AHC, P, 1967-68
303. Chesser, Ben 132 ASHC, 1968
304. Chesson, Rick B-1-9, P, 1968-69
305. Chido, Bruce 155 AHC, P, 1967-68
306. Chinnery, Philip, author
307. Choate, James 147 ASHC, FE, 1967-68
308. Clapper, Craig 68 AHC, P, 1970-71
309. Clark, Larry 188 AHC, P, 1968
310. Clarke, Wayne B-159 ASHB, DG, 1969
311. Clement, Ross 174 AHC, P, 1968-69
312. Clutter, Ron 176 AHC, CE, 1967-68
313. Cockrell, Gordon 189 AHC, P, 1970-71
314. Coe, Bob 57 AHC, CE, 1971-72
315. Coe, Don 114 AHC, P, 1970-71
316. Coffman, Wayne 174 AHC, 1969-70
317. Coffman, Wes 128 AHC, P, 1970-71
318. Cole, Mike B-2-20 ARA, CE, 1969-70
319. Cole, Steve 192 AHC, CE, 1968-69
320. Coleman, Bill 336 AHC, CE, 1969-71
321. Coleman, Mike 116 AHC, P, 1968
322. Coleman, Rick 135 AHC, DG, 1967-68
323. Coleman, Ron 117 AHC, P, 1966-67
324. Coles, Dan D-3-4, 1970-71
325. Coletta, Mark 162 AHC, P, 1971-72
326. Collier, Sandy A-229, CE, 1968-69
327. Collins, Bob 174 AHC, P, 1968
328. Collins, Dan 45 MC, Medic, 1969
329. Collins, George 117 AHC, P, 1964-65
330. Combs, Jerry 173 AHC, P, 1967-68
331. Comrey, Bill 21 Sig Gp, 1969
332. Condon, Lyle 498 MC, Medic, 1968-70
333. Conley, Carl 114 AHC, P, 1970
334. Conner, Ron 174 AHC, CE, 1967-69
335. Connor, John A-3-17, 1968
336. Constantine, Ralph 6 Bn 27 Arty, 1969
337. Coogan, Tim 498 MC, Medic, 1969-70

338. Coombs, Ed 119 AHC, P, 1965-66
339. Cooper, Bill F-4 Cav, P, 1971-72
340. Cooper, Bob 240 AHC, P, 1969-70
341. Cooper, Harry 174 AHC, CE, 1968
342. Cooper, James A-227, CE, 1969
343. Cope, Bill 192 AHC, P, 1971
344. Corbett, Patrick 213 ASHC, CE, 1970-71
345. Corbin, Ron 119 AHC, P, 1967
346. Cornell, Curt 195 AHC, P, 1968-69
347. Cornwell, Jim A-2-7 Cav, 1968-69
348. Coryhell, Newt 147 ASHC, FE, 1966-68
349. Cosgriff, Joe 119 AHC, P, 1969-70
350. Coveney, Bob 190 AHC, P, 1968
351. Covert, Charles D-229, CE, 1970-71
352. Cowan, Jean 134 AHC Assn Associate
353. Cowan, Sidney A-229, P, 1965-66
354. Cowart, Jim 175 AHC, P, 1971
355. Cowley, Russ 48 AHC, P, 1970-71
356. Cox, Braxton A-227, CE, 1970-71
357. Cox, Jeff 57/114 AHC, P, 1968-69/ 70-71
358. Cox, Tim 175 AHC, CE, 1969-70
359. Craft, Steve 213 ASHC, DG, 1966-67
360. Craig, John A-1-9/C-1-9, P, 1967-68/1970-71
361. Cramer, Gary C-5-7, Medic, 1970
362. Crance, Dan 48 AHC, DG, 1967
363. Cranford, Floyd 155 AHC, CE, 1965-66
364. Crawford, Bernie F-8, 1970
365. Creamer, Ron 271 ASHC, CE, 1969-70
366. Crews, Tom 21 Sig Gp, 1969
367. Cribbs, Larry 178 ASHC, P, 1968-70
368. Croley, Chuck 195 AHC, CE, 1970
369. Cron, Mike D-2-1, 1969-70
370. Cronan, John 336 AHC, CE, 1969-70
371. Cronen, James, A-1-9, P, 1966
372. Cronin, Earl 336 AHC, P, 1970
373. Crooks, Eugene 10 CAB, P, 1967
374. Crow, Dick 173 AHC, P, 1970
375. Crowder, Larry 192 AHC, CE, 1970-71
376. Crump, Chet 247 MD/45 MC, Medic, 1969-71
377. Cucchiara, Tony 117 AHC, CE, 1971
378. Cunnare, Richard 45 MC, CE, 1967-68
379. Cunningham, Dave 121 AHC, P, 1966-67
380. Cunningham, Kerry 498 MC, 1968-69

381. Cupp, Paul A-7-1, CE, 1969-70
382. Curran, Mike 119 AHC, 1968-69
383. Dalton, Daily 117 AHC, CE, 1963-64
384. Dameron, Les 178 ASHC, Opns, 1968-70
385. Damerow, Chuck 187 AHC, P, 1970-71
386. Dan, Tweek Van, 1969
387. Dancsecs, Frank 190 AHC, P, 1969
388. Daniel, Garry A-228 ASHB, P, 1968
389. Daniel, Richard, 187 AHC, P, 1969-70
390. Davidson, Van M, 1968
391. Davidson, Wayne 45 MC, CE, 1968-69
392. Davis, Clarke 132 ASHC, 1970-71
393. Davis, Conrad 178 ASHC, P, 1967-68
394. Davis, Jim 117 AHC, DG, 1964
395. Davis, Larry, author
396. Davis, Richard 147 ASHC, FE, 1967-68
397. Davis, Robert 114 AHC, CE, 1964-65
398. Davis, Robert 192 AHC, CE, 1969-70
399. Davis, Sam 174 AHC, CE, 1967-68
400. Davison, Les 155 AHC, CE, 1969-70
401. Deady, Michael 117 AHC, P, 1968-70
402. Decker, Charles 128 AHC, P, 1966-67
403. Decker, Doug 174 AHC, P, 1971
404. DeCook, Phil A-3-5, 1967
405. DeCurtis, Dan 335 AHC, P, 1967-68
406. Deland, George, EBAY
407. Delarosa, Lionel C-1-9, 1969-70
408. Dell, Terry 114 AHC, CE, 1969-70
409. Deming, Charles 57 AHC, CE, 1970
410. Blank ************************
411. Deperro, John 15 TB, P, 1968-69
412. DeRouchey, Louis B-228 ASHB, FE, 1970-71
413. DeSimone, Tom 114 AHC, P, 1969-70
414. Detra, Dick 188 AHC, DG, 1967-68
415. DeVarennes, Ed 118 AHC, 1968
416. Dickerson, Walt 243 ASHC, 1970-71
417. Dickinson, Dave 62 CAC, CE, 1969-71
418. Dike, Joe C-7-1, CE, 1968-69
419. Dike, Leroy 162 AHC, P, 1970
420. Dille, Kim 57 AHC, CE, 1971-72
421. Dillman, John 54 MD, 1971
422. Dillon, Frank F-4, 1971-72
423. Dilworth, Vinnie 92 AHC, CE, 1968-69
424. Dinsmore, Richard 254 MD, Medic, 1968-70

425. Dirnberger, Jay A-227, P, 1967-68
426. Dize, Jesse 48 AHC, P, 1970-71
427. Doke, Richard 187 AHC, CE, 1971
428. Donahue, John 162 AHC, P, 1968-69
429. Donnelly, Jim 175 AHC, DG, 1971-72
430. Donoghue, Jay A-4 Avn Bn, P, 1967-68
431. Doucette, Al, 81 TC, DG, 1962
432. Doud, Jerry 128 AHC, DG, 1969
433. Doudna, Dean C-2-20 ARA/F-79 AFA, CE, 1971-72
434. Dougan, Pat 187 AHC, P, 1968-69
435. Douglas, Mike 117 AHC, P, 1968-69
436. Dousis, George HHC 1 Bde 101 Abn, CE, 1969-70
437. Dowler, Gary 121 AHC, P, 1966-67
438. Draper, Gary, 20 Eng Bn, 1970-71
439. Drendel, Lou, author
440. Drennon, Lloyd 336 AHC, P, 1969-70
441. Drinkwine, Frank 187 AHC, CE, 1970-71
442. Drone, Chuck 121 AHC, CE, 1967-68
443. Drury, Doug 119 AHC, P, 1967-68
444. Dubaj, Paul 128 AHC, CE, 1970
445. Duerr, Dick 114 AHC, P, 1966-67
446. Duff, Art B-3-17, 1969
447. Duke, Harry 117 AHC, DG, 1970-71
448. Duke, Philip C-228 ASHB, FE, 1970
449. Dunlap, Bud 48 AHC, CE, 1970-71
450. Dunn, Billy 45 MC, 1967-68
451. Dunn, Wes 114 AHC, CE, 1964
452. Dunstan, Simon, author, 1968
453. Dupuis, Dennis 335 AHC, P, 1969-70
454. Duquette, Al 187 AHC, P, 1967-68
455. Dutson, Dick 117 AHC, P, 1970
456. Duvall, Tom 117 AHC, DG, 1967
457. Dwyer, Rodger 200 ASHC, FE, 1967-68
458. Dye, Roger 134 AHC, DG, 1970-71
459. Earhart, Donivan, B-3-17, 1972
460. Eastes, Pat D-3-4, P, 1967-68
461. Eastman, Dave, author, 175 AHC, P, 1966-67
462. Eaton, Bruce 11 ACR, CE, 1968
463. Eaton, Chuck D-1-10, 1970-71
464. Eckelson, Marty 178 ASHC, FE, 1970-71
465. Edson, Chuck 611 TC, P, 1963-64
466. Edwards, J.P. B-25 Avn Bn, P, 1970
467. Effenberger, Frank 175 AHC, P, 1970-71
468. Eggert, Wayne B-229, DG, 1969-70

469. Elam, Danny 11 LIB, 1969-71
470. Elderbaum, Russ D-1-1, 1969
471. Elliot, Mike 187 AHC, CE, 1970-71
472. Elliott, Butch 174 AHC, P, 1970-71
473. Elliott, Richard B-1-9, P, 1966-67
474. Elliott, Robert 117 AHC, 1967-68
475. Ellis, Tom A-228 ASHB, P, 1968-70
476. Emerson, Chuck B-229, P, 1970-71
477. Eneix, Lowell 121 AHC, P, 1967-68
478. England, Norm 175 AHC, P, 1971-72
479. England, Rick 129 AHC, CE, 1968-69
480. Eoff, William 178 ASHC, P, 1968
481. Erickson, Jim 539 TC, 1967-68
482. Erickson, Robert A-1-9, P, 1968-69
483. Escher, Doug 21 Sig Gp, CE, 1969-70
484. Espinoza, Eddie 114 AHC, CE, 1971-72
485. Estes, Frank A-502 Avn Bn, 1966
486. Estes, Sam 1 Bde 1 Cav, DG, 1968-69
487. Ethel, Jeff, author
488. Evangelho, Daryl 281 AHC, CE, 1969
489. Evans, Earl 178 ASHC, CE/FE, 1968-69
490. Evans, James 91 Evac, 1970
491. Evans, Parker 114 AHC, DG, 1967-68
492. Evans, Robert B-229, P, 1968-69
493. Everhart, Tom B-101 Avn Bn, P, 1968-69
494. Ewing, Ed 128 AHC, P, 1968-69
495. Faddis, Rodger 180 ASHC, FE, 1969
496. Fadz, Paul 155 AHC, CE, 1966-68
497. Falloway, Jim 178 ASHC, FE, 1968-70
498. Farber, Barry B-7-1, CE, 1968
499. Farley, Pat 45 MC/247 MD, CE, 1969/1970
500. Farner, Jim A-1-9, CE, 1968-69
501. Farrell, Kirk 116 AHC, P, 1969-71
502. Farren, Dan B-25 Avn Bn, CE, 1967-70
503. Farrier, Craig A-3-17, 1969-70
504. Fatheree, Chuck 176 AHC, P, 1970-71
505. Faulkner, Ron 21 Sig Gp, P, 1970
506. Faux, Tom C-227 AHB, 1967
507. Favata, Chris D-3-4, CE, 1968-69
508. Feigel, Tom 336 AHC, CE, 1969-70
509. Feltner, James D-3-5, CE, 1968-69
510. Fenton, Bryan, 117 AHC, 1964-65
511. Ferg, John 498 MC, Medic, 1967-68
512. Ferguson, James 243 ASHC, CE, 1968-69

513. Ferguson, Jim 15 MB, CE, 1970-71
514. Ferland, Roland 175 AHC, P, 67-68
515. Fernitz, Manfred 147 ASHC, P, 1967-69
516. Ferrara, John 118 AHC, CE, 1968-69
517. Ferrigan, Tom 128 AHC, P, 1969-70
518. Ferris, Bob C-2-8, 1972
519. Ferris, Norm B-25 Avn Bn, Maint, 1969-70
520. Ferry, Frank 339 TC, DG, 1963-64
521. Fesmire, Dave 271 ASHC, CE, 1971
522. Ficker, Gene A-1-9, CE, 1969-70
523. Fields, Joe 335 AHC, DG, 1966-67
524. Fifield, Tom C-227, CE, 1971
525. Fiman, Ron 8 TC, CE, 1963-64
526. Fink, Al, 195 AHC, P, 1968-69
527. Finke, Edward 179/180 ASHC, FE, 1968-70
528. Fisher, Harry 81 TC, 1962-63
529. Fisher, Joe 190 AHC, CE, 1969-70
530. Fisher, Mark 174 AHC, P, 1968-69
531. Fitcher, Thomas unk unit, 1967
532. Fitzgerald, Al 147 ASHC, P, 1969-70
533. Fitzgerald, Al 155 AHC, P, 1966-67
534. Flam, Mike C-229, CE, 1968-69
535. Flanagan, John B-1-9, P, 1967-68
536. Flecke, Ned 71 AHC, DG, 1966-67
537. Fleming, Tom D-3-4, P, 1967
538. Fletcher, Ray 92 AHC, CE, 1968-70
539. Flores, Bill 191 AHC, CE, 1968-69
540. Flores, Oscar 117 AHC, CE, 1969-70
541. Fluharty, Tom D-3-4, CE, 1969-70
542. Footer, Joe B-25 Avn Bn, P, 1968
543. Ford, Bob 135 AHC, DG, 1968-69
544. Ford, Dan, author
545. Foss, Ken E-709 Mnt Bn, P, 1966-67
546. Foster, Arthur 129 AHC, CE, 1970-71
547. Foster, Bill A-227, CE, 1967-68
548. Foster, Hugh B-1-5 Cav, 1970-71
549. Foulke, William 1968
550. Foutz, Daryl 243 ASHC, FE, 1968-70
551. Fowler, Larry 92 AHC, CE, 1970-71
552. Fox, Dave 240 AHC, CE, 1968-69
553. Foxworthy, Dennis 498 MC, Medic, 1968-70
554. Frady, Larry D-3-5, CE, 1968
555. Francis, Jim A-227, 1969

556. Franck, Eugene A-158 AHB, P, 1969-70
557. Franzel, Daryl 57 MD, CE, 1969-70
558. Frazer, Bill A-1-9, P, 1970-71
559. Frazier, Don 192 AHC, CE, 1971-72
560. Freel, Jon 192 AHC, CE, 1969-70
561. Freeman, Dave 57 MD, P, 1971-72
562. Friday, Ed A-227, CE, 1969
563. Friend, Ross 147 ASHC, DG/CE, 1966-67
564. Frigstad, Ron 57 AHC, P, 1969-70
565. Fryant, Bill 175/191 AHC, P, 1970-71
566. Frye, Jim 1 Avn Det, P, 1967-68
567. Fuller, Henry A-4 Avn Bn, CE, 1968-69
568. Fusilier, Phil 134 AHC, P, 1971
569. Gabriel, Kent 282 AHC, DG, 1969-70
570. Gachich, John 281 AHC, DG, 1968-69
571. Gaffney, Jim 187 AHC, P, 1968-69
572. Gailfoil, John A-227, CE, 1969
573. Gale, David 147 ASHC, FE, 1967-68
574. Gale, Gary 155 AHC, 1965-66
575. Gallagher, Mike 162 AHC, DG, 1968
576. Gallardo, Orlando C-16, 1970-71
577. Gallegos, John 117 AHC, CE, 1964-66
578. Gallipeau, Charles 498 MC, CE, 1968
579. Galo, George 205 ASHC, P, 1967-68
580. Gamache, Ray 48 AHC, 1967
581. Gano, Steve 134 AHC, CE, 1967-68
582. Gant, Chuck B-25 Avn Bn, P, 1970
583. Garcia, Frank 611 TC, 1964-65
584. Garcia, Juan 116 AHC, CE, 1970-71
585. Garcia, Santos 116 AHC, CE, 1966-67
586. Gardner, Bob 155 AHC, P, 1968-69
587. Garrett, Bob C-2-17, P, 1969-70
588. Garrett, Don B-2-17, 1969-70
589. Garrison, Bill D-3-5, CE, 1971-72
590. Garrity, Mike B-25 Avn Bn, 1965-66
591. Gary, Roger 71 AHC, CE, 1970
592. Garza, Albert 174 AHC, CE, 1970
593. Gaston, Cliff 173 AHC, P, 1971-72
594. Gaston, Cliff 175 AHC, CE, 1970-71
595. Gates, Alan D-227, CE, 1968-69
596. Gatliff, Ben 132 ASHC, CE, 1970-71
597. Gatzemeyer, Dwight 271 ASHC, FE, 1969-70
598. Gauby, Tom 174 AHC, CE, 1969

599. Gaylord, Bruce 244 Avn Co, 1968
600. Geer, Bucky 1969
601. Geiger, Robert, 1970
602. Gendron, Roger 114 AHC, CE, 1969-70
603. George, Warren 118 Avn Co, P, 1965
604. Georger, Tom, A-229, 71-72
605. Gerstenberger, Pete, 48 AHC, CE, 71-72
606. Gibbons, Will A-7-1, P, 1970-71
607. Gibbs, Charles 114 AHC, Chaplain, 1966
608. Gibbs, Murray 15 MB, DG, 1967-68
609. Gifford, Mike A-1-9, CE, 1969-70
610. Gilmore, Jack 179 ASHC, FE, 1968-69
611. Gilpin, Mike 114 AHC, P, 71-72
612. Gipson, Beck A-4 Avn Bn, P, 1968-69
613. Gladwell, Herbert 128 AHC, CE, 1968-69
614. Glasco, John 71AHC, CE, 1970
615. Glasgow, Bill 114 AHC, CE, 1964
616. Glass, Pat B-228 ASHB, P, 1970-71
617. Gliet, Ed 165 TC/155 AHC, CE, 1965-66
618. Gluck, Barbara VN War Photographer, 1972
619. Godbold, Randy 174 AHC, CE, 1971
620. Godden, Glen D-229, DG, 1971-72
621. Godfrey, Jim 192 AHC, P, 1969-70
622. Goerig, Pat 155 AHC, P, 1965-66
623. Gomes, Abe 174 AHC, CE, 1971
624. Gomez, Joe 48 AHC, DG, 1966-67
625. Gooch, Rex C-3-17, P, 1971-72
626. Goodknight, Mike C-228 ASHB, FE, 1969-71
627. Goodowens, Fowler C-7-1, P, 1968
628. Goodwin, Paul 117 AHC, CE, 1971-72
629. Goosman, John B-227, DG, 1970-71
630. Gordon, Jack 155 AHC, 1966
631. Gordon, Wayne 237 MD, Medic, 1970-71
632. Gorsky, John 134 AHC, CE, 1969-71
633. Gosch, Gordon 191 AHC, DG, 1970-71
634. Gosnell, Jim 114 AHC, DG, 1966-67
635. Gould, Tom 335 AHC, P, 1969-70
636. Goyea, Rich 213 ASHC, 1967-68
637. Gozier, Juan B-228 ASHB, CE, 1969-70
638. Graff, Jerry 237 MD, CE, 1970-71
639. Granby, Jon 611 TC, 1968-69
640. Grant, Carl 155 AHC, 1967-68
641. Grant, Cleveland 1 Bde 1 Cav, CE, 1969

642. Gray, Bob 187 AHC, P, 1971-72
643. Gray, Carl B-3-17, P, 1968-69
644. Gray, Charles 128 AHC, 1969-71
645. Gray, Randy 11 ACR, P, 1968-69
646. Gray, Steve 175 AHC, Svc Plt, 1967-68
647. Green, Curtis 243 ASHC, 1970-71
648. Green, Dave 68 AHC, CE, 1968
649. Green, John A-227, CE, 1971
650. Greenawalt, Allen 180 ASHC, CE, 1970
651. Greenfield, Tom 175 AHC, DG, 1967
652. Greenhalgh, Bill 162 AHC, P, 1968-69
653. Greenleaf, Frank, 1966
654. Greve, Dan 175 AHC, P, 1970-71
655. Griffin, Jim 118 AHC, P, 1966
656. Griffin, Robert 13 Sig Corps, Army Photographer, 1967-68
657. Griffiths, Ed C-229, CE, 1969-70
658. Griffo, Frank 611 TC, 1966
659. Grimm, Barry 128 AHC, P, 1967
660. Gross, Fred 8TC/117 AHC, DG, 1963
661. Gross, Joe 176 AHC, P, 1970
662. Groth, Jim C-7-1, CE, 1970-71
663. Grow, John 155 AHC, P, 1966-67
664. Grubbs, Barry 254 MD, Medic, 1967-68
665. Guard, Mike 135 AHC, 1969-70
666. Gunn, Bruce 114 AHC, P, 1967-68
667. Gunter, James A-227, DG, 1966-67
668. Gustafson, Allan 336 AHC, Flt Opns, 1967-69
669. Gustafson, John 92 AHC, DG, 1968
670. Gustin, Mike D-1-1, CE, 1970-71
671. Guynn, Edward 187 AHC, CE, 1969-70
672. Gwizdak, Joe, HHC 3 Bde 101 Abn, 1969
673. Hadgkiss, Robert C-228 ASHB, FE, 1967
674. Hadley, Harry 114 AHC, P, 1963-64
675. Hahn, Gordon 191 AHC, CE, 1968-69
676. Hahn, Roy 174 AHC, DG, 1971
677. Haines, Clint C-7-17, CE, 1969-70
678. Hair, Ed 173 Abn, 1968
679. Hale, Dick B-1-9, P, 1966-67
680. Hale, Oscar 48 AC, CE, 1966-67
681. Haler, Ron B-7-17, 1970
682. Haley, Mike 175 AHC, P, 1968-69
683. Hall, Thom 45 MC, CE, 1970-71
684. Halliday, Dan 237 MD, Medic, 1971-72

685. Hamilton, Robert 117 AHC, P, 1970-71
686. Handel, Geoff 188 AHC, P, 1967-68
687. Hankins, Randy A-227, CE, 1968-70
688. Hanley, Dan A-1-1, DG, 1966
689. Hannon, Ron 254 MD, CE, 1966-67
690. Hansen, Dave 237 MD, P, 1970-71
691. Hansen, Lanny 118 AHC, CE, 1967
692. Hanson, Norm 551 TC, 1969
693. Hanson, Scott 571 MD, Medic, 1972
694. Harbison, Joe 173 AHC, P, 1968-69
695. Harelson, Dave 335 AHC, DG, 1970-71
696. Harlem, Pete, author, D-227 AHB, CE, 1970
697. Harmon, Dave 92 AHC, DG, 1967-68
698. Harms, Fred 92 AHC, P, 1967-68
699. Harney, Tom 190 AHC, P, 1970
700. Harrell, William 7th Surg Hosp, 1966-67
701. Harris, Edwin 68 AHC, P, 1965-66
702. Harris, John 155 AHC, CE, 1969-70
703. Harris, John D-1-1, 1970-71
704. Harris, Jon 1 Bde 1 Cav, P, 1969-70
705. Harrison, Richard 119 AHC, CE, 1967-68
706. Harrison, Tom A-227, P, 1966-67
707. Hartman, Malcomb 247 MD, P, 1970
708. Harton, Bud 173 AHC, CE, 1968
709. Hastie, Mike 1-10 Cav, Medic, 1970-71
710. Hastings, John 161 AHC, CE, 1967-68
711. Hatch, Larry 15 MB, P, 1966-67
712. Hathaway, Allen 11 ACR, 1964-67
713. Haviland, Peter 1 Sqd 4 Cav, 1968-69
714. Hawkins, George C-16, P, 1970-71
715. Hawkins, Joe 178 ASHC, CE, 1966-67
716. Haws, Curtis 48 AHC, DG, 1970-71
717. Hayes, Larry 119 AHC, 1968-69
718. Hayes, Sam 175 AHC, CE, 1970
719. Hays, John A-3-17, CE, 1968-69
720. Head, Wayne C-229, P, 1970-71
721. Healy, Steve 191 AHC, CE, 1970-71
722. Hearne, Maury A-227, P, 1969
723. Heath, Stan 134 AHC, P, 1969-70
724. Hedrick, Herman 155 AHC, CE, 1969-70
725. Hefferman, Richard, B-7-17, CE, 1968
726. Heidtke, Lonnie C-101, CE, 1968-69
727. Heikkila, Dave 56 TC, 1971-72
728. Heinlein, Greg B-3-17, DG, 1970

729. Heminger, Dave 132 ASHC, P, 1969-70
730. Hendrickson, Bruce C-2-20 ARA/F-79 AFA, CE, 1971-72
731. Hendrickson, John B-159 ASHB, P, 1969-70
732. Hendron, Chuck A-1-9, CE, 1970-71
733. Henry, 388 TC/A-227 AHB, 1967-68
734. Hensley, Wes 116 AHC, P, 1971
735. Hepler, Ed 114 AHC, CE, 1971-72
736. Herdon, Dan 162 AHC, P, 1970
737. Herndon, Bob 92 AHC, CE, 1967-68
738. Herrell, Marty 346 Div Avn Supp, DG, 1967-68
739. Herrera, Mike 45 Med Co, Medic, 1968-69
740. Herrin, Mike 271 ASHC, CE, 1968-69
741. Herring, Mark 119 AHC, CE, 1969-70
742. Herrington, Tom 176 AHC, P, 1969-70
743. Hersey, Mike 175 AHC, P, 1966-67
744. Hesselbein, Bob A-7-1, P, 1972
745. Heyn, Jim 92 AHC, CE, 1967-68
746. Hickerson, Larry 282 AHC, P, 1970-71
747. Hien, John, 11 ACR, 1967-68
748. Higgerson, Tom, 21 Sig Gp, DG, 1969-70
749. Hill, Robert 237 MD, P, 1970
750. Hill, Stephen A-227, CE, 1971-72
751. Hilton, Mike 176 AHC, CE, 1968-69
752. Hinch, Sam C-1-9, P, 1970-71
753. Hines, Joe 117 AHC, P, 1968-69
754. Hinson, Bud 539 TC, 1970-72
755. Hinton, Mel A-7-1, P, 1971-72
756. Hise, Richard 498 MC, Medic, 1969-70
757. Hiservia, Frank C-1-9, 1966
758. Hnizdil, James B-1-9, 1969-70
759. Hoag, Jim D-3-4, CE, 1970-71
760. Hoagland, Ray 604 TC/ 189 AHC, 1968
761. Hoder, Andy 175 AHC, DG, 1968
762. Hodges, Chris 174 AHC, CE, 1970
763. Hodges, Don C-16, P, 1971-72
764. Hodges, Harry 114 AHC, P, 1971-72
765. Hodges, Mike 187 AHC, P, 1970-71
766. Hodgson, Jim 120 AHC, P, 1972-73
767. Hoff, Terry 335 AHC, P, 1969-70
768. Hoffman, Bob 114 AHC, P, 1971-72
769. Hoffman, Glenn 240 AHC, P, 1967-68
770. Hogan, Jeremy, son of Jerry Hogan B-1-9, DG, 1969-71

771. Hogan, Jerry B-1-9, DG/CE, 1969-71
772. Hogan, Steve A-123 Avn Bn, P, 1970-71
773. Holbert, Craig 132 ASHC, 1970-71
774. Holcomb, Ron 247 MD, 1969-70
775. Holder, Rick C-7-1, P, 1970-71
776. Holdings, David C-159 ASHB, FE, 1971
777. Holiday, Mark 15 MB, CE, 1970-71
778. Hollan, Jesse 213 ASHC, 1967-68
779. Holland, Howard B-1-9, DG, 1968-69
780. Holmes, Alan 175 AHC, CE, 1966-67
781. Holmes, Ed 1 Bde 1 Cav, P, 1968-69
782. Holmes, Gordon 114 AHC, DG, 1970-71
783. Holt, John D-229, CE, 1965-66
784. Holte, Dave C-229, CE, 1969-70
785. Honara, Mike 128 AHC, P, 1971-72
786. Honl, Jim S-1 Advisor, III Corps, 1968
787. Hood, Dewey 271 ASHC, FE, 1969
788. Hooker, Andy 335 AHC, CE, 1968-70
789. Hooper, David 170 AHC, CE, 1970-71
790. Hoopes, Tom 213 ASHC, 1966-67
791. Hope, Tom 271 ASHC, CE, 1970-71
792. Horning, Bob 68 AHC, DG, 1968
793. Horton, Duane A-1-9, 1969-70
794. Hoselton, Douglas 187 AHC, CE, 1970-71
795. Hostetler, Mark F-9 Cav, CE, 1972
796. Hostetler, Tim 175 AHC, CE, 1968-69
797. Howard, Chuck 150 TC/175 AHC, 1968-69
798. Howell, Dennis A-227, CE, 1971-72
799. Howlett, David 200 ASHC, FE, 1967
800. Hoza, John A-82 Avn Bn/335 AHC, P, 1966
801. Hraben, Robert B-1-9, 1969
802. Hubbard, Rollie 62 CAC, 1970
803. Hubbs, John C-229, DG, 1971-72
804. Huckleberry, Paula B-2-20 ARA, P, 1970-71
805. Hudak, Ron 117 AHC, P, 1965-66
806. Hudson, Kelly D-1-4, AC, 1967-68
807. Hudspeth, Lew 114 AHC, P, 1967-68
808. Huether, Ron 15 MB, P, 1971
809. Huffman, Bill 121 AHC, CE, 1966
810. Huffman, Steve 269 CAB, Courier, 1968-69
811. Hufford, Kent 68 AHC, P, 1967-68
812. Hughes, Bill 57 MD, Medic, 1965
813. Hughes, Bill A-228 ASHB, CE, 1968-69

814. Hulbert, John 18 CAC, 1972-73
815. Humphreys, Jack 273 Avn Co, FE, 1970-71
816. Hunt, Tom 155 AHC, CE, 1968-69
817. Huntley, Steve 114 AHC, CE, 1968-69
818. Huss, J.D. 370 TC, P, 1970-71
819. Hutson, Bill 243/271 ASHC, FE, 1968
820. Hutson, Darrell 116 AHC, DG, 1969-71
821. Hutson, Greg 189 AHC, 1971-72
822. Hyde, Steven A-4 Avn Bn, CE, 1966-67
823. Hyler, Jim D-3-5, 1968-69
824. Iacobacci, Ed 237 MD, Medic, 1971-72
825. Iannazzo, Dennis 175 AHC, P, 1968-69
826. Ianniello, Bill C-159 ASHB, CE, 1969-70
827. Iglesias, Pete 120 AHC, CE, 1968
828. Ireland, Danny 190 AHC, CE, 1968
829. Isenberg, Don 175 AHC, P, 1968-69
830. Jackson, Dave 48 AHC, P, 1967-68
831. Jackson, Don 121 AHC, CE, 1966-68
832. Jackson, James 48 AHC, 1970-71
833. Jackson, James F-79 AFA, P, 1972
834. Jackson, John 173 AHC, CE, 1967-69
835. Jackson, Larry 129 AHC, CE, 1968-69
836. Jackson, Wayne A-227, CE, 1969-70
837. Jacobs, Roy 179 ASHC, CE, 1968-69
838. Jacobsen, Gary C-1-9, P, 1969-70
839. James, David 191 AHC, P, 1968-69
840. Janiec, Jerry 128 AHC, CE 1969-70
841. Janousek, Richard 178 ASHC, FE, 1967-68
842. Jarett, Keith 174 AHC, CE, 1971-72
843. Javens, Dennis 192 AHC, P, 1971
844. Jeanes, Bill 129 AHC, P, 1972-73
845. Jefferson, Thom A-227, CE, 1966-67
846. Jenkins, Ted 478 Avn Co, P, 1967-68
847. Jennings, George 335 AHC, CE, 1968
848. Jensen, Allen 114 AHC, DG, 1966-67
849. Jester, Jim. A-227, P, 1970-71
850. Jetter, Art C-2-20 ARA/F-79 AFA, P, 1970-71
851. Johnson, Alan 28/96 Sig Det, 1966-67
852. Johnson, Dan 116 AHC, CE, 1967-68
853. Johnson, Johnny 187 AHC, P, 1971
854. Johnson, Larry 173 AHC, P, 1969
855. Johnson, Lawrence, author
856. Johnson, Loren 282 AHC, CE, 1968-69

857. Johnson, Russell D-1-1, P, 1971
858. Johnston, Bruce 189 AHC, 1968-69
859. Jolet, Joe 308 CAB, 1969
860. Jones, Bailey, author, 114 AHC, P, 1965-66
861. Jones, Dan 15 TB, P, 1968
862. Jones, Dave D-227, 1968-71
863. Jones, Don 498 MC, CE, 1969-71
864. Jones, Gary 114 AHC, P, 1965-66
865. Jones, Gary D-3-4, P, 1969
866. Jones, Gordon C-1-9, DG, 1966-67
867. Jones, Harold 336 AHC, DG, 1967-69
868. Jones, Jack 15 MB, 1969
869. Jones, Jerry 247 MD, CE, 1970-71
870. Jones, John, VN War researcher
871. Jones, Lacy 155 AHC, 1966-67
872. Jones, Mike B-1-9, CE, 1969-70
873. Jones, Walker C-1-9, P, 1970-71
874. Jorgenson, Doug A-229, P, 1971
875. Jostandt, Gary 498 MC, Medic, 1968-69
876. Journeycake, Mike C-101, CE, 1969-70
877. Joyce, Don 1 Avn Co, P, 1962-63
878. Kahler, Doug 155 AHC, 1969-70
879. Kaminski, William, LRRP, 1971
880. Kammers, Tom 187 AHC, CE, 1970-71
881. Kanakaris, George 98 TC/120 AHC, DG, 1965-66
882. Kane, Gary D-1-1, CE, 1971
883. Kastens, Charles 196 ASHC, 1968-69
884. Kayfus, Bill 117 AHC, 1965-67
885. Kee, Bill B-228 ASHB, FE, 1966-67
886. Keele, Mike B-229, CE, 1967-68
887. Keeney, Andrew 175 AHC, P, 1967
888. Keirsey, Dan F-4 Cav, P, 1972-73
889. Keith, Cecil 339 TC, DG, 1963-64
890. Kekar, Randy C-1-9, DG, 1970-71
891. Keller, John A-159 ASHB, P, 1971
892. Keller, Robert A-227 AHB, 1965-66
893. Kelley, Mike C-1-9, CE, 1965-66
894. Kelly, Colin D-1-4, DG, 1965-66
895. Blank ************************
896. Kelly, Thad 174 AHC, 1968-70
897. Kendrick, Larry 335 AHC, DG, 1968-69
898. Kenerson, Ron B-1-9, CE, 1969-70
899. Kenna, Mike 175 AHC, DG, 1967-68

900. Kennedy, Tom 175 AHC, CE, 1968-69
901. Kerchenfaut, Steve 176 AHC, P, 1969-71
902. Kernodle, Charles 170 AHC, P, 1969-70
903. Ketcham, Jim C-228 ASHB, FE, 1967-68
904. Khachadourian, Harry 175 AHC, TI, 1971-72
905. Kibbey, Doug 11 ACR, 1971-72
906. Kidd, Mike 175 AHC, CE, 1967-68
907. Kilborn, David 147 ASHC, CE, 1966-67
908. Kilpatrick, Bob 119 AHC, CE, 1969
909. Kimm, Mark B-25 Avn Bn, CE, 1968
910. Kincaid, John B-2-17, P, 1969-70
911. Kinder, Joe 155 AHC, 1966-69
912. King, Boyd 114 AHC, P, 1966-69
913. King, Larry 128 AHC, CE, 1967-69
914. King, Mike C-16, P, 1971-72
915. Kinney 173 Abn Bde, 1969
916. Kipp, Larry 45 MC, Medic, 1968-69
917. Kirker, Jim D-3-4, CE, 1969-70
918. Kittleson, Rob 187 AHC, P, 1966-68
919. Klann, Martin 240 AHC, CE, 1967-68
920. Klein, Dennis 192 AHC, P, 1971
921. Klein, Howard A-101 AHB, P, 1967-68
922. Klein, Jay D-1-1, 1970
923. Kline, Joe B-101, CE, 1970-71
924. Klinefelter, Lowell, 1966
925. Kluge, Stan 196 ASHC, FE, 1969-70
926. Knapp, Curt 2 Bde 101 Abn, P, 1967-68
927. Knight, Bob 336 AHC, P, 1965-68
928. Knight, Gary 170 AHC, P, 1969-70
929. Knight, Ray B-2-17, P, 1969
930. Knisely, Ben 498 MC, P, 1968
931. Koch, Jim 92 AHC, P, 1967-68
932. Koenig, Dick 175 AHC, P, 1967-68
933. Komich, Lee B-228 ASHB, P, 1968-69
934. Koonce, Bob 150 TC/A-502, CE, 1964-65
935. Koone, Mike 121 AHC, P, 1968-69
936. Kopperude, Mike 117AHC, CE, 1971-72
937. Korbel, Rick, A-227 AHB, CE, 1968-69
938. Koss, John 45 MC, Medic, 1971
939. Kottler, Jack 155 AHC, P, 1965-66
940. Kovolesky, Arthur, 173 AHC, CE, 1967-68
941. Kowalczyk, Joe 114 AHC, DG, 1968-69
942. Krause, Gary 498 MD, Medic, 1969
943. Kremp, Ralph 179 ASHC, DG, 1969-70

944. Kriegsmann, Karl 128 AHC, P, 1969-70
945. Krol, Joe 142 TC/11 CAG, 1970-71
946. Krothe, Trubee, 281 AHC, CE, 1967-68
947. Krumbiegel, Ed 114 AHC, CE, 1967-68
948. Kuchar, Roman 192 AHC, DG/CE, 1968-70
949. Kudel, Leo F-8 Cav, 1971
950. Kulik, Gary 61 MB, 1969-70
951. Kurtz, Jim A-1-9, 1970-71
952. Labriola, Mike B-228 ASHB, FE, 1966-67
953. LaChance, Frenchy 240 AHC, CE, 1967-68
954. Lacher, Dale 254 MD, Medic, 1969-70
955. Lachiondo, Steve A-227, CE, 1970-71
956. Lackey, Larry 129 AHC, P, 1971-72
957. Blank **************************
958. Ladd, Roger 176 AHC, P, 1970-71
959. Ladue, John B/D-227 AHB, P, 1966-67
960. Lajoie, Dennis 155 AHC, CE, 1968-70
961. Lambert, Morris 92 AHC, CE, 1970-71
962. Lambie, Brian 176 AHC, P, 1968-69
963. Lammers, Fred 121 AHC, CE, 1968
964. Lampman, Dan 271 ASHC, FE, 1969-70
965. Lander, Jack D-1-9, 1970-71
966. Langley, Bob 200 ASHC, FE, 1967-68
967. Langlois, Lucien 167 TC/336 AHC, 1965-66
968. LaPointe, Ray B-123 Avn Bn, P, 1971
969. Lappos, Nick D-1-1, P, 1969-70
970. Larce 242 ASHC, 1969-70
971. Larcher, Ken A-7-1, CE, 1970-71
972. Laroue, Butch 117 AHC, P, 1967-68
973. Larson, Gary 71 AHC, CE, 1967
974. Larson, Jim 33 TC, 1963
975. Lasser, Tom 161AHC, P, 1967
976. Last, Daniel 175 AHC, P, 1967-68
977. LaTour, Tim D-1-10, P, 1969-70
978. Lauffer, George 162 AHC, P, 1971-72
979. Lauritsen Corky 134 AHC, DG, 1969-70
980. Lavelle, Allan unk unit, 1971-72
981. Lavenberg, Mike 192 AHC, CE, 1969-70
982. Law, Tony 175 AHC, Armorer, 1967-68
983. Lawler, John 335 AHC, P, 1969-70
984. Lawless, Bill B-228 ASHB, 1965-66
985. Lawless. Matthew A-1-9, P, 1967
986. Lawrence, Dan 362 ASHC, FE, 1971-72
987. Lawrence, John 62 CAC, 1969-70

988. Layman, Joe A-229, P, 1971-72
989. Layton, Russ 128 AHC, CE, 1968-69
990. Lazenby, Ron A-227, CE, 1968-69
991. Leak, Arnie 187 AHC, P, 1968-69
992. Leandro, John 336 AHC, P, 1969-70
993. Leary, Pat 189 AHC, P, 1967-68
994. Leathers, Jack B-229, CE, 1968
995. Ledbetter, Garry 200 ASHC, FE, 1967-68
996. Lee, Neil A-228 ASHB, P, 1969-70
997. Leepson, Mark VVA Arts editor, 1 Log Comd,
     1967-68
998. LeFavor, George 213 ASHC, 1971-72
999. LeGrand, Harold, 11 ACR, P, 1971-72
1000. Lehman, Hal 48 AHC, 1967-69
1001. Lehman, Phil 155 AHC, P, 1967-68
1002. Leith, Bob 187 AHC, P, 1968-69
1003. Lemaster, Bob C-1-9, P, 1970-71
1004. Lemay, Bruce A-1-9, DG, 1968-69
1005. Lemke, Don 192 AHC, P, 1971
1006. Lemons, Dennis 117 AHC, P, 1970-71
1007. Lemp, Ed E-82 Arty, CE, 1965-66
1008. Lenning, Don 114 AHC, DG, 1966-67
1009. Lenotte, George A-227, CE, 1966-67
1010. Lentino, Mike A-1-9, DG, 1969-70
1011. Leonard, Ron B-25 Avn Bn, CE, 1968-69
1012. Leopold, Bob 170 AHC, P, 1967
1013. Lesemann, Milton C-227, P, 1968-69
1014. Lester, Rick 48 AHC, P, 1970-71
1015. Levengood, Joe D-227 AHB, CE, 1967-68
1016. Lewis, Carl A-1 Avn Bn, 1965-66
1017. Lewis, Fred 281 AHC, 1967-68
1018. Lewis, James 162 AHC, CE, 1971-72
1019. Lewis, Lloyd 243 ASHC, FE, 1969-70
1020. Liebrandt, Geoff digital artist
1021. Lien, Terry 132 ASHC, FE, 1968-69
1022. Lietzan, Jim A-227, CE, 1968-69
1023. Linder, Laurie 116 AHC, DG/CE,
1024. Linster, Frank 188 AHC, P, 1967-68
1025. Lipford, Ben C-227, 1970-71
1026. Lippert, John B-228 ASHB, CE, 1970-71
1027. Lipscomb, Henry 176 AHC, DG, 1971
1028. Little, John A-7-1, P, 1968-69
1029. Little, Richard 118 AHC, CE, 1966-67
1030. Livingston, Del 82 MD, P, 1968-69

1031. Lockhart, Ken A-1-9, CE, 1970-71
1032. Logan, Jon 190 AHC, P, 1969-70
1033. Lohman, Jim 121 AHC, 1964-65
1034. Lohr, Fred D-2-1 Cav/180 ASHC, P, 1968-69/1972-73
1035. Lokey, George 15 TC,1967-68
1036. Lomonaco, Jim 189 AHC, P, 1967-68
1037. Long, Willis 118 AHC, 1966-68
1038. Louche, Bill 15 MB, DG, 1966-67
1039. Loughlin, Tom A-227, CE, 1966-67
1040. Louie, Ron 45 MC, Medic, 1968
1041. Love, Terry 1 Sig Bde, CE, 1966-68
1042. Loveday, Frank 129 AHC, CE,1969-70
1043. Lovelace, H.C A-227, CE, 1969-71
1044. Lovell, Wayne D-3-5, P, 1967
1045. Lovely, Mike, 1970
1046. Lowden, Milton 121 AHC, 1964
1047. Lucas, Jim, author
1048. Lucky, James, unk unit, P, 1967
1049. Luffman, Ralph 335 AHC, CE, 1969-70
1050. Lumpkin, Tom 119 AHC, Avionics, 1970
1051. Lund, Pat 165 TC, CE, 1971
1052. Lunde, Bob B-227, P, 1969-70
1053. Lundh, Lennart, author, USS *Tripoli,* 1968-69
1054. Luse, Glen bro of Ken Luse (KIA), B-1-9, P, 1969
1055. Lutgring, Melvyn 174 AHC, CE, 1971
1056. Luttenberger, Ed 242 ASHC, P, 1970-71
1057. Luttrell, James 179 ASHC, CE, 1968
1058. Lynch, John 179 ASHC, DG, 1966-67
1059. Lynn, Walter B-123 Avn Bn, CE, 1969-71
1060. Lyons, Ed B-25 Avn Bn, DG, 1968-69
1061. Lyons, Rocklin 118 AHC, P, 1971
1062. Lyons, Walter A-7-17, DG, 1968-69
1063. Maanao, Robert B-1-9, CE, 1969-71
1064. Maas, Doug D-1-10, P, 1970-71
1065. MacDonald, Harold, 125 ATC, 1970
1066. MacDougall, Doug 170 AHC, P, 1968
1067. Mack, Dennis A-4-77 ARA, P, 1968-69
1068. Maddock, John B-159 ASHB, FE, 1969
1069. Mader, John A-1-9, DG, 1969
1070. Madsen, Paul 11 ACR, P, 1968-69
1071. Magee, Art 174 AHC, P, 1970-71
1072. Maher, Rom 190 AHC, CE, 1967-69

1073. Mahler, Cloudy B-123 Avn Bn, DG, 1971-72
1074. Mahoney, George 242 ASHC, 1967-68
1075. Mahoney, Ray, 28/96 Sig Det, 1966-67
1076. Maker, Don B-7-17, 1968-69
1077. Malick, Len 162 AHC, CE, 1971-72
1078. Malone, Howard 173 AHC, P, 1966-67
1079. Malwiju, David 176 AHC, DG, 1969
1080. Mangano, Steve B-123 Avn Bn, CE, 1971
1081. Mann, Gary 173 AHC, CE, 1966-67
1082. Mano, Matt 117 AHC, DG, 1971-72
1083. Mansfield, Shelby 114 AHC, P, 1969-70
1084. Mantanona, Pascual 114 AHC, CE, 1969-70
1085. Marcieski, Stan 326 MB, P, 1971
1086. Maring, Marshall C-1-9, CE, 1970-71
1087. Markell, Dan 271 ASHC, FE, 1968
1088. Markley, Butch 336 AHC, CE, 1968-69
1089. Markovich, Craig 271 ASHC, FE, 1969-70
1090. Marks, Richard A-1-9, DG, 1967-68
1091. Marsden, Russ D-3-5, CE, 1970-71
1092. Marshall, Jake 11 ACR, 1969-70
1093. Marshall, John A-3-17, CE, 1970-71
1094. Marshall, Phil 237 MD, P, 1969
1095. Marshall, Wayne 68 MD, Medic, 1969-70
1096. Martin, Chuck 71 AHC, DG, 1970
1097. Martin, Jerry C-2-20 ARA, P, 1970-71
1098. Martin, John B-229, CE, 1969-70
1099. Martin, Ralph 62 CAC, P, 1969-70
1100. Martin, Tom 187 AHC, P, 1967-68
1101. Martin, Tom 336 AHC, CE, 1968-69
1102. Martin, Wes 161 AHC, 1966-67
1103. Marzen, Claus 114 AHC, Armorer, 1964-65
1104. Masencup, Jim 129 AHC, P, 1970-71
1105. Mason, Mike 11 CAG, DG, 1971-72
1106. Massard, Gus 271 ASHC, 1970-71
1107. Massey, Marcel 196 ASHC, FE, 1969-70
1108. Materene, Tom 336 AHC, DG, 1968-69
1109. Mateyko, John A-501 Avn Bn/71 AHC, P, 1965-66
1110. Matheny, Pat 118 AHC, CE, 1965-66
1111. Mather, Don C-2-20 ARA/F-79 AFA, CE, 1970-72
1112. Matsuoka, Mitch 62 CAC, DG, 1969
1113. Matt, Joe 188 AHC, CE, 1967
1114. Mattler, Bill 114 AHC, CE, 1970
1115. Maurer, Charlie 188 AHC, P, 1966-68

1116. Maw, Alan 191 AHC, CE, 1968-69
1117. Maxey, Robert D-3-4, 1971-72
1118. Maycen, Ed 1 Bde 1 Cav, CE, 1970
1119. McAdams, Dave 116 AHC, P, 1967-68
1120. McAdams, Larry 179 ASHC, FE, 1967-68
1121. McAllister, Charlie 1 Bde 1 Cav, 1970
1122. McBee, Jerry 271 ASHC, FE, 1967-68
1123. McBride Doc D-5-7, 1967-68
1124. McCalister, Bill A-3-17, P, 1969
1125. McCamish, John 162 AHC, P, 1967-68
1126. McCarthy, John 92 AHC, P, 1971
1127. McCarty, Chuck 15 MB, 1968
1128. McChesney, Frank 114 AHC, P, 1965-66
1129. McClain, Bill B-228 ASHB, FE 1967-68
1130. McClain, Nat 134 AHC, CE, 1968-69
1131. McCort, Don 129 AHC, CE, 1971-72
1132. McCrory, Bob 11 GS , CE, 1965-66
1133. McCue, Jim D-1-1, P, 1970-71
1134. McCullough, Dennis A-9 Avn Bn, CE, 1967-68
1135. McCullough, Tim 121 AHC, 1966-68
1136. McCurry, Rick 334 AHC, CE, 1967-68
1137. McDaniel, Jim 174/116 AHC, P, 1967-68/1971
1138. McDonald, Bill 128 AHC, CE, 1966-67
1139. McDonald, James 15 MB, Medic, 1971-72
1140. McDougal, John 120 AHC, CE, 1965-66
1141. McDowell, Terry 175 AHC, P, 1966-67
1142. McEntyre, Don 539 TC, 1967-68
1143. McFarland, Tom COBRA NETT, P, 1970
1144. McGarrett, Buddy 81 TC, CE, 1962-63
1145. McGowan, Bill 20 TC, P, 1967
1146. McGregor, Wayne 121 AHC, DG, 1969-70
1147. McGuire, Ed 175 AHC, DG, 1969-70
1148. McGuire, John 60 AHC, DG, 1972
1149. McKee, Thomas 187 AHC, CE, 1970-71
1150. McKeever, Denny 608 TC/235 AWC, 1967
1151. McKellar, Fred 15 MB, P, 1966-67
1152. McKemey, Tom 498 MC, Medic, 1965-66
1153. McKinney, Duke 1 Bde 1 Cav, CE, 1970
1154. McLenaghan, Joe 178 ASHC, FE, 1969-70
1155. McLeod, Jesse 187 AHC, CE, 1967-68
1156. McMahan, Guy D-227, CE, 1968-69
1157. McMillin, Larry B-229, CE, 1968-69
1158. McMullen, Richard 114 AHC, CE, 1969

1159. McNees, Richard 17 AHC, DG, 1967-68
1160. McPherran, Paul A-501 Avn Bn/71 AHC, CE, 1965-66
1161. McQuade, William G. 121 AHC, P, 1967
1162. McRae, Bill 132 ASHC, P, 1970-71
1163. McRee, Burris 155 AHC/165 TC, DG, 1967-68
1164. McWaters, John C-1-9, P, 1970-71
1165. Meadows, Al 48/155 AHC, 1970/1970-71
1166. Meana, Richard 175 AHC, P, 1970-71
1167. Means, Bob 178 ASHC, FE, 1967-68
1168. Medeiros, Wayne 174 AHC, CE, 1966-67
1169. Medlock, Rick 15 MB, 1970-71
1170. Meeker, George 189 AHC, 1968-69
1171. Mellquist, John B-227, DG, 1969-71
1172. Melton, Ron 117 AHC, DG, 1965-66
1173. Melvin, Brad D-1-10, DG, 1969-70
1174. Mendenhall, Reid 199 LIB, 1970
1175. Mendez, Ray 1-6-198 LIB, 1970-71
1176. Meola, Mario 17 AHC, P, 1967
1177. Mercer, Eric 187 AHC, P, 1967-68
1178. Merlock, Ron 188 AHC, CE, 1967-68
1179. Merricks, Joe 134 AHC, CE, 1968-69
1180. Merrill, Dan 116 AHC, 1969-70
1181. Mesko, Jim, author
1182. Messenger, Tom 179 ASHC, FE, 1970-71
1183. Messersmith, Emory 498 MC, Medic, 1972
1184. Messinger, Jim 174 AHC, P, 1967-68
1185. Michalkiewicz, Joe 118 AHC, P, 1967-68
1186. Michels, Ben A-227, CE, 1966-67
1187. Mignard, Rob 92 AHC, P, 1969-70
1188. Mikesell, Rich 196 ASHC, CE, 1971
1189. Milan, Charlie 118 AHC, P, 1966-67
1190. Milavic, Jack, A-101 AHB, P, 1965-66
1191. Miller, Bob 120 AHC, 1967-68
1192. Miller, Bob 192 AHC, P, 1968-69
1193. Miller, DeWayne A-228 ASHB, FE, 1969-70
1194. Miller, Earl 195/117 AHC, CE, 1970/1971
1195. Miller, George 200 ASHC, P, 1967
1196. Miller, Harlan 116 AHC, CE, 1970
1197. Miller, Harold C-1-9, CE, 1966-67
1198. Miller, Jim 71 AHC, P, 1968
1199. Miller, Mel 147 ASHC, FE, 1969-70
1200. Miller, Morris 240 AHC, CE, 1968
1201. Miller, Phil 335 AHC, P, 1969-70

1202. Miller, Ricky C-2-17, CE, 1971
1203. Miller, Terrry 179 ASHC, FE, 1969-71
1204. Miller, Tom 174 AHC, CE, 1966
1205. Mills, Hugh D-1-4/D-3-5/C-16, P, 1969/1971-72/1972
1206. Mills, Robert A-3-17, P, 1970-71
1207. Millward, Bob 175 AHC, P, 1967
1208. Minda, George B-1-9, CE, 1970-71
1209. Minney, Mel D-3-5, CE, 1967-68
1210. Mirati, Al 114 AHC, P, 1970-71
1211. Mitchell, Bruce D-3-5, CE, 1968-69
1212. Mitchell, Frank 336 AHC, DG, 1969-70
1213. Mitchell, Roger 192 AHC, P, 1969-71
1214. Mixer, Al 119 AHC, CE, 1969-70
1215. Mock, Robert, 57 MD, P, 1964-65
1216. Mockler, Tom 162 AHC, P, 1967-68
1217. Modjeski, Howard 498 MC, P, 1970-71
1218. Moenich, Thomas 243 ASHC, 1969-70
1219. Moist, Gary 132 ASHC, FE, 1968
1220. Molish, Mike 15 MD/HHC-1 ACD/180 ASHC, P, 1968/1968-69/1971-72
1221. Mong, Don commercial artist
1222. Monroe, Greg 187 AHC, DG, 1971-72
1223. Montana, Jim B-25 Avn Bn, CE, 1966-68
1224. Montana, Paul A-3-17, 1967-68
1225. Montgomery, Roger 242 ASHC, CE, 1967-68
1226. Moon, Terry 1st Cav Division PIO Photographer, 1969
1227. Mooney, Kevin B-227, CE, 1969-70
1228. Moore, Dale 118 AHC, P, 1968-70
1229. Moore, John 571 MD, CE, 1970-71
1230. Moore, Larry B-2-17, CE, 1969-70
1231. Moore, Ron A-228 ASHB, FE, 1970-71
1232. Moore, Terry A-227, CE, 1970-71
1233. Moore, Warren 203 ASHC, DG/CE/FE, 1971-72
1234. Moorhead, Bob B-25 Avn Bn, CE, 1967
1235. Moorman, Gary 48 AHC, CE, 1968-69
1236. Moran, Jim C-2-20 ARA, P, 1970-71
1237. Morgan, Glen 48 AHC, CE, 1969-70
1238. Morhland, Rick 116 AHC, CE, 1967-68
1239. Morley, Clifford B-228 ASHB, FE, 1968-69
1240. Morley, Thomas 118 AHC, P, 1969-70
1241. Morris, Arnold 71 AHC, P, 1966-67
1242. Morrison, Frank A-4 Avn Bn, CE, 1968-69
1243. Morrison, Larry 335 AHC, P, 1968-69

1244. Morton, Dan 155 AHC, CE, 1966-67
1245. Moser, Tom 243 ASHC, FE, 1967-68
1246. Mosher, Craig 155 AHC, CE, 1965-69
1247. Mosley, Ken 15 TB, P, 1968
1248. Mount, Gary 129 AHC, CE, 1970-71
1249. Mounts, Bob 135 AHC, CE, 1967-68
1250. Mowery, Scott 135 AHC, DG, 1969-71
1251. Moy, Innis 159 MD, Medic, 1970-71
1252. Mruczkowski, Leon 8 TC, CE, 1962
1253. Muccianti, George 121 AHC, 1964
1254. Mulcahy, Jim 198 LIB, 1971
1255. Mull, Don 176 AHC, CE, 1969-70
1256. Mullen, Mike 187 AHC, DG, 1967
1257. Mullen, Tom 155 AHC, DG, 1968-69
1258. Mullinax, Bobby B-227, DG, 1970-71
1259. Mumaw, Carl F-8/570 TC, 1968-70
1260. Munsell, David 189 AHC, CE, 1968-69
1261. Murphy, Dan A-3-17, P, 1969-70
1262. Murphy, Gilbert 188 AHC, P, 1968-69
1263. Murray, Norbert 117 AHC, DG, 1965-66
1264. Murtha, Paul B-1-9/F-9, P, 1971/1972
1265. Mussey, Dave B-158 Avn Bn, CE, 1968-69
1266. Mutza, Wayne, author, 240 AHC, CE, 1971
1267. Blank ************************
1268. Myers, Harry A-1 Avn Bn, CE, 1966-67
1269. Myhre, Jon 175 AHC, P, 1966-67
1270. Nadal, Hector 25 Div Combat Photographer, 1968
1271. Nadeau, Thomas 195 AHC, P, 1970
1272. Nagel, Sam 147 ASHC, P, 1967-68
1273. Nancarrow, Dave 116 AHC, CE, 1968-69
1274. Nash, Stan B-1-9, P, 1966-67
1275. Nawrot, Bill 132 ASHC, 1969-70
1276. Neally, Michael 180 ASHC, 1971
1277. Neckerman, Stan 179 ASHC, FE, 1969-70
1278. Neeley, Gary 57 AHC, P, 1969-70
1279. Neely, Rich, D-17, P, 1972-73
1280. Nelson, Dean 178 ASHC, CE, 1966-67
1281. Nelson, Rob A-7-1, P, 1969-70
1282. Nemeyer, Jack D-3-4, CE, 1969-70
1283. Nesbitt, Tom 335 AHC, P, 1970
1284. Nesbitt, Woody 50 MD, P, 1968
1285. Ness, John 33 TC, P, 1962-63
1286. Newby, Carl 371 RRC, 1968-69
1287. Newby, Claude A-1-9, Chaplain, 1969-70
1288. Newcomer, Ron 174 AHC, P, 1966-67

1289. Nichols, Dave 610 TC, DG, 1969
1290. Nichols, John 114 AHC/544 TC, 1965-66
1291. Nicholson, Don 162 AHC, P, 1970-71
1292. Nickel, Dave A-3-17, P, 1970-71
1293. Nicolich, Joe 129 AHC, CE, 1965-66
1294. Niedbala, Stephen 178 ASHC, FE, 1965-67
1295. Nieto, Dan 162 AHC, CE, 1969
1296. Nivens, Kirk 187 AHC, P, 1968
1297. Nix, Don 178 ASHC, 1969-70
1298. Noble, Dave 192 AHC, CE, 1970-71
1299. Nolan, Jim 180 ASHC, P, 1972
1300. Noonan, Dan A-229, CE, 1968-69
1301. Norman, Billy D-3-5, DG, 1967-68
1302. Norton, Dave 118 AHC, CE, 1969-70
1303. Novak, Rick 178 ASHC, FE, 1970-71
1304. Noyes, Ralph 68 AHC, CE, 1967-68
1305. Null, Jan C-16/520 TC, 1969-70
1306. Nunn, Dave, 48 AHC, DG, 1966-67
1307. Nunn, Wally 174 AHC, DG, 1967-68
1308. O'Brien, Mike 45 MC, CE, 1969-70
1309. O'Connell, Richard C-7-1, CE, 1970-71
1310. O'Connor, Tim A-227, CE, 1969-70
1311. O'Grady, George 114 AHC, P, 1965-66
1312. O'Grady, Steve B-1-9, CE, 1968-69
1313. O'Malley, Jack 117 AHC, 1967-68
1314. O'Neil, Joe 93 TC, P, 1962-63
1315. O'Neil, Mike D-227, P, 1970
1316. O'Neill, Joe 175 AHC, P, 1967-68
1317. Oakes, Hiawatha 8 TC, CE, 1962-63
1318. Obrecht, Mike D-227, CE, 1968-69
1319. Oden, Jim 478 Avn Co, P, 1968-69
1320. Odom, Jerry D-3-4, P, 1968-69
1321. Odum, Jim 15 MB, CE, 1969-70
1322. Ogle, Jim 188 AHC, P, 1967-68
1323. Okken, Wayne H-75 Inf, 1971-72
1324. Old, Roger 161 AHC, P, 1967
1325. Olive, Merv 119 AHC, P, 1969-70
1326. Oliver, Tom 13 CAB, 1965-66
1327. Olson, Randy 336 AHC, P, 1969-70
1328. Olson, Rich 119 AHC, P, 1967
1329. Ondrey, Dave A-227, DG, 1968-69
1330. Osborne, David 175 AHC, DG, 1966-67
1331. Osborne, Dennis B-229, CE, 1967-68

1332. Oswald, Joe 196 ASHC, FE, 1967-68
1333. Ouellette, Paul 190 AHC, CE, 1967-68
1334. Packard, Ernie 68 AHC, CE, 1967-68
1335. Packham, Bob B-229, CE, 1966-67
1336. Padroza, George 173 AHC, DG, 1968
1337. Paitz, Mike 1 Bde 1 Cav, 1969
1338. Palkow, John C-2-20 ARA, 1970-71
1339. Palmer, Mike 92 AHC, P, 1968-69
1340. Paranal, Joe A-227, CE, 1970-71
1341. Parham, Jim B-25 Avn Bn, P, 1969
1342. Parker, Dale 174 AHC, CE, 1970-71
1343. Parker, Steve 48 AHC, P, 1969
1344. Parks D-3-4, CE, 1968-69
1345. Parks, Dave 15 MB, DG, 1969-70
1346. Parra, Frank C-227, CE, 1968-69
1347. Parris, Mike 176 AHC, DG, 1968-69
1348. Parrish, Dan 11 CAG, 1968-69
1349. Parsley, David 605 TC, 1968-69
1350. Parsley, Larry 175 AHC, DG, 1966-67
1351. Patnode, Bud 191 AHC, P, 1967
1352. Patrick, Rod 184 RAC, P, 1966
1353. Patterson, Dave C-159 ASHB, CE, 1968-69
1354. Patterson, Lynn A-101 AHB, 1965-66
1355. Patterson, Tom, 1971
1356. Patton, Rex 114 AHC, P, 1964-65
1357. Paul, Jerry 498 MC, CE, 1970-71
1358. Paul, Sean 11 ACR, 1970
1359. Paull, John 92 AHC, P, 1968-70
1360. Payne, Tom 118 AHC, P, 1966-67
1361. Peacock, Lindsay, author
1362. Pearlstein, Mark 132 ASHC, DG, 1969-70
1363. Pearson, Robert 116 AHC, CE, 1968-69
1364. Peatross, Rob C-229, CE, 1970-71
1365. Pederson, Mike 192 AHC, CE, 1970-71
1366. Pedigo, Bob 68 AHC, P, 1970-71
1367. Peecook, Jeff 161 AHC, P, 1967
1368. Pelliccia, Dennis 174 AHC, CE, 1967-68
1369. Pender, Don D-1-10, P, 1971
1370. Pengov, James 175 AHC, 1970-71
1371. Peoples, Ken, author
1372. Pepe, Matt A-228 ASHB, DG, 1965-66
1373. Pepper, Greg 188 AHC, 1968-69
1374. Perkins, Clarence 173 AHC, CE, 1967-68

1375. Perrin, Wayne 173 AHC, 1969-70
1376. Perry, Jim 15 MB, Avionics, 1968
1377. Peters, Greg 117 AHC, 1971-72
1378. Peters, Ron 242 ASHC, FE, 1967-69
1379. Petersen, Bradley 165 TC/155 AHC, P, 1967-68
1380. Peterson, Larry 178 ASHC, 1970-71
1381. Peterson, Mike 135 AHC, CE, 1971-72
1382. Peterson, Mike C-7-1, CE, 1968-69
1383. Peterson, Pat 117 AHC, 1971
1384. Peterson, Roger 175 AHC, CE, 1970-71
1385. Petra, Eugene 190 AHC, DG, 1968-70
1386. Petrovich, Ron 198 LIB, P, 1971
1387. Pettit, Danny 134 AHC, CE, 1968-69
1388. Petty, Tom B-3-1, 1969
1389. Phenicie, Glenn 191 AHC, CE, 1968-69
1390. Phillips, Rick 176 AHC, CE, 1970-71
1391. Phillipson, Charles E-123 Avn Bn, 1970-71
1392. Phipps, Wayne B-1-9, CE, 1967-68
1393. Pickett, Larry 116 AHC, P, 1970-71
1394. Piecuch, Ron 188 AHC, DG, 1967
1395. Pierce, Robert B-3-17, 1969
1396. Pierce, Roger 134 AHC, CE, 1969-70
1397. Pike, Bob 117 AHC, 1963-64
1398. Pike, Douglas, Historian, VN Center & Archive,
     TX Tech Univ
1399. Pilat, George 119 AHC, P, 1967-68
1400. Pinther, Evan 114 AHC, DG, 1969-70
1401. Piper, Dennis 116 AHC, P, 1969-70
1402. Platacis, Andrew 68 AHC, 1965-66
1403. Platner, Mike A-3-17, P, 1970
1404. Poarch, Ron 134 AHC, CE, 1969-70
1405. Pointer, Randy 134 AHC, DG, 1968
1406. Politi, Vincent 173 AHC, CE, 1966-67
1407. Polman, Gerald B-4 Avn Bn, DG, 1967
1408. Poole, David 1969
1409. Poole, John 335 AHC, CE, 1966-67
1410. Posey, Ward 213 ASHC, CE, 1967-68
1411. Post, James 17 AHC, P, 1968
1412. Poteat, Gary 45 MC, CE, 1967-68
1413. Potter, Bill 114 AHC, CE, 1968-69
1414. Powell, John C-1-9, P, 1968-69
1415. Powers, Dave 129 AHC, CE, 1971
1416. Powers, Dave 191 AHC, 1969

1417. Powis, William, 11 ACR, 1969-71
1418. Pratt, Jim B-1-9, P, 1967
1419. Pratt, Tom 175 AHC, CE, 1969-70
1420. Preqent, Tom D-3-4, 1969
1421. Preston, James A-3-17, CE, 1967-68
1422. Prevost, Frank 173 AHC, CE, 1968-69
1423. Price, Walter 174 AHC, DG, 1968-69
1424. Priddy, Don 71 AHC, P, 1969-70
1425. Prince, Carl 68 MD, CE, 1970-71
1426. Prine, Jim A-7-1, CE, 1971-72
1427. Pritchett, Ron C-229, CE, 1967
1428. Proff, Mike A-101 AHB/336AHC, CE, 1965-67
1429. Pruett, Norm 71 AHC, CE, 1970-71
1430. Pullen, Tom 282 AHC, P, 1967-68
1431. Putnam, Tom A-7-1, P, 1971-72
1432. Quackenbush, George 121 AHC, P, 1968-69
1433. Quigley, Ron 178 ASHC, DG, 1969-70
1434. Rackley, Lawrence 128 AHC, CE, 1967-71
1435. Radabaugh, Dana 121 AHC, CE, 1967-68
1436. Rago, A.J., B-1-9, DG, 1968-69
1437. Ragonese, Lou 129 AHC, Svc Plt, 1970
1438. Rainwater, Ross C-1-9, P, 1970-71
1439. Ralph, Joe 135 AHC, CE, 1969-70
1440. Ramirez, Fidencio 119 AHC, P, 1969-70
1441. Ratcliffe, Steve 174 AHC, CE, 1969-70
1442. Ray, John 336 AHC, P, 1968-69
1443. Reasoner, John A-158, P, 1969-70
1444. Reavill, Rick 176 AHC, CE, 1969-70
1445. Redburn, J.D. 242 ASHC, 1967-69
1446. Redmon, John 129 AHC, P, 1966-67
1447. Redmon, Paul B-228 ASHB, 1967-69
1448. Reed, Don 11 ACR/398 TC, 1968-69
1449. Reed, Mike 176 AHC, CE, 1966-68
1450. Reese, Bob C-16, CE, 1970-71
1451. Reese, George 25 Avn Bn, 1967-68
1452. Reeves, George, 335 TC, 1966-67
1453. Reeves, Kinsey D-3-5, 1971
1454. Reichert, Jack 271 ASHC, CE, 1968
1455. Reigel, Jay 173 AHC, DG, 1968-69
1456. Reinshagen, Tom 174 AHC, P, 1968-69
1457. Renaud, Rick 187 AHC, P, 1970-71
1458. Renfro, Doug B-7-17, 1970
1459. Renz, Karl 134 AHC, CE, 1968-69
1460. Repak, Pete A-501/71 AHC, 1965

1461. Revels, Jack 173 AHC, P, 1968-69
1462. Rex, Robert B-228 ASHB, FE, 1966-67
1463. Reyher, Sheldon 48 AHC, P, 1968-69
1464. Reynolds, Dave 178 ASHC, FE, 1970-71
1465. Rhinehart, Mike 283 MD, P, 1969
1466. Rhoades, Alan C-229, CE, 1968-69
1467. Rhoades, Ron 11 ACR, P, 1971-72
1468. Rhodes, Allen 237 MD, P, 1970-71
1469. Richardson, Charles 11 GS, P, 1968
1470. Richardson, Curtis Lee 114 AHC, Svc Plt, 1966
1471. Richardson, Don 174 AHC, CE, 1968
1472. Richardson, Rich 173 AHC, CE, 1967-68
1473. Richardson, Tom A-3-17, P, 1970-71
1474. Richardson, Wayne B-2-20 ARA, P, 1970-71
1475. Richmond, Murlen 176 AHC, CE, 1970-71
1476. Rickenbacker, Ernest C-2-20 ARA/F-79 AFA, P,
    1971
1477. Riley, Joe 196 ASHC, P, 1968-69
1478. Riley, Richard 45 MC, CE, 1967-68
1479. Rios, Dave 174 AHC, DG, 1970-71
1480. Riseden, Jay 128 AHC, P, 1967-68
1481. Rissman, Dick 118 AHC, 1968-69
1482. Rittman, David C-229, P, 1966-67
1483. Rivera, Juan 243 ASHC, 1968-69
1484. Roalofs, Ray 155 AHC, P, 1967
1485. Roberge, Norm 15 MB, 1968
1486. Roberts, Garry 176 AHC, CE, 1970-71
1487. Roberts, George 254 MD, CE, 1968-69
1488. Roberts, Jerry 48 AHC, 1966-67
1489. Roberts, Tom 254 MD, Medic, 1970-71
1490. Robertson, Gary 162/68 AHC, 1966-67/1967-68
1491. Robertson, John 118 AHC, P, 1968-69
1492. Robie, Bill 92 AHC, P, 1968-69
1493. Robinson, Cindy, sister of Tommy Ivey (KIA) 175
    AHC, CE, 1970-71
1494. Robinson, John D-17, P, 1972-73
1495. Robinson, Lloyd 129 AHC, CE, 1969-70
1496. Roby, Phillip 498 MC, P, 1971-72
1497. Rochat, Lou A/E-1-9, P, 1970/1970-71
1498. Rockenstire, Walt 192 AHC, DG, 1970
1499. Rodgers, Jim 68 AHC, P, 1965-66
1500. Rogers, Bill A-227, 1969-70
1501. Rogers, John 135 AHC, P, 1968-69
1502. Rogers, Mike 71 AHC, CE, 1967

1503. Rogers, Peter B-3-17, P, 1969
1504. Rolinger, Terry 48 AHC, CE, 1968
1505. Roloff, Raymond 190 AHC, 1968-69
1506. Ronan, Pat 116 AHC, 1968-69
1507. Ronning, Garrett 118 AHC, P, 1969
1508. Roof, Don 118 AHC, CE, 1965-66
1509. Root, David 45 MC, CE, 1968-70
1510. Rose, Mike B-229, CE, 1969-70
1511. Rose, Tom 8 TC, CE, 1963-64
1512. Rose, Tom A-227, CE, 1966-67
1513. Rosenberg, Bob, author
1514. Rosenthal, David 174 AHC, P, 1970
1515. Ross, Don 242 ASHC, 1968
1516. Roth, Ray 175 AHC, DG 1966-67
1517. Rovig, Joe 134 AHC, P, 1970-71
1518. Roy, Andy C-227, DG, 1968
1519. Roy, Tom 170 AHC, P, 1967-68
1520. Royals, Gerald 56 TC, P, 1967
1521. Rozanski, Walter 175 AHC, 1966
1522. Rubalcava, Mike 179 ASHC, DG, 1969-70
1523. Ruckhaber, Fred 82 MD, Medic, 1968-70
1524. Rundle, (first name unk), P, 11 ACR, 1971-72
1525. Runnells, Everett A-501/71 AHC, DG, 1965-66
1526. Russ, Mike 238 AWC, P, 1969-70
1527. Russell, Bill 114 AHC, P, 1969-70
1528. Russell, Bill B-2-17, P, 1969
1529. Russell, Larry B-227 AHB/1 Avn Bde, P,
    1968-69/1971-72
1530. Rutherford, Claude 189 AHC, CE, 1969-70
1531. Ryan, Gary B-2-17, P, 1970-71
1532. Ryan, Terry 116 AHC, CE, 1970-71
1533. Sabanosh, John 45 MC, CE, 1969-70
1534. Sabatini, Joe 128 AHC, CE, 1971
1535. Sala, Ron 1968, unk personal data
1536. Salazar, Rolando bro of Leo Salazar, C-1-9, CE,
    1968-69
1537. Sale, David 128 AHC, P, 1966-67
1538. Salee, Larry 162 AHC, CE, 1968-69
1539. Salger, Glenn 116 AHC, P, 1970
1540. Sams, Johnny 17 AHC, CE, 1967-68
1541. Sanchez, Raul 178 ASHC, FE, 1971-72
1542. Sanderlin, Joe 571 TC, 1964-65
1543. Sanders, Ron 170 AHC, CE, 1969-70
1544. Sandrock, Don 191 AHC, P, 1967-69

1545. Sangl, Rudy 281 AHC, P, 1970
1546. Sarrat, Walter 25 Inf Div, DG, 1965-66
1547. Sartor, John 129 AHC, CE, 1969-70
1548. Sathre, Mike 48 AHC CE, 1970-71
1549. Saufley, Jim 119 AHC, P, 1969-70
1550. Saunders, David 162 AHC, P, 1968-69
1551. Sauter, Al 282 AHC, 1969-70
1552. Scales, Ken 117 AHC, CE, 1970-71
1553. Scates, Lester 167 TC/336 AHC, P, 1968-69
1554. Schaefer, Wil 145 CAB Medic, 1964
1555. Scheibel, Curt 243 ASHC, CE/FE, 1970-71
1556. Schillereff, John C-1-9, P, 1970-71
1557. Schimpf, Mark 335 AHC, P, 1969-70
1558. Schlaudraff, Mike A-227, CE, 1965-66
1559. Schmidt, Gary D-3-4, CE, 1970-71
1560. Schmied, John 121 AHC, 1966-67
1561. Schmitz, Paul 119 AHC, CE, 1968
1562. Schmuck, Earl B-25 Avn Bn, DG, 1967-68
1563. Schoenstein, Paul 114 AHC, CE, 1969-70
1564. Schrader, Jeff 155 AHC, P, 1968-69
1565. Schrumpf, Mike 114 AHC, CE, 1966-67
1566. Schulte, Brian 114 AHC, DG, 1968-69
1567. Schultz, Kurt A-82 Avn Bn, DG, 1965-66
1568. Schumacher, Rex 174 AHC, CE, 1970-71
1569. Schwanebeck, Gene 114 AHC, CE, 1967-68
1570. Schwartz, Dave 191 AHC, P, 1968-69
1571. Schweitzer, Bob C-228 ASHB, CE, 1968
1572. Schwend, Bill 269 CAB, P, 1967
1573. Sciapiti, Rich 114 AHC, CE, 1968-69
1574. Scott, Bill B-228 ASHB, FE, 1967-69
1575. Scott, Clyde 114 AHC, P, 1965-66
1576. Scott, John 175 AHC, DG, 1966-67
1577. Scott, Richard 114 AHC, DG, 1967-68
1578. Scott, Ron 187 AHC, CE, 1970
1579. Seabolt, Ron 71 AHC, CE, 1966-67
1580. Seabourn, Joe A-159 ASHB, FE, 1969-71
1581. Searcy, Roger B-3-17, P, 1971-72
1582. Seelig, Russ A-228 ASHB, FE, 1967-68
1583. Seesions, Dee 134 AHC, CE, 1969-70
1584. Segura, Raul 336 AHC, CE, 1968-70
1585. Seibert, David A-159 ASHB, 1968
1586. Seifert, Bill, 68 AHC, P, 1970
1587. Sellers, Don 192 AHC, P, 1970-71

1588. Semanek, Jim 132 ASHC, P, 1970
1589. Senkowski, Glen A-1-9, P, 1969-70
1590. Seward, William 162 AHC, CE, 1969-70
1591. Sexton Jerry C-159 ASHB, FE, 1967-68
1592. Shaffer, Nate C-1-9, DG, 1970-71
1593. Shakocius, Mike 121 AHC, P, 1967-68
1594. Shanahan, Norman 54 MD, P, 1968
1595. Shatto, Larry 176 AHC, CE, 1969
1596. Shea, Pat B-25 Avn Bn, DG, 1966
1597. Shearer, Vance 175 AHC, P, 1967-68
1598. Shedd, Jim 174 AHC, CE, 1969-70
1599. Sheldon, Stephen, Army Photographer
1600. Shelly, Jay 571 MD, 1969-70
1601. Shemley, Larry C-229, P, 1969-70
1602. Shepard, Steve A/C-7-17, P, 1971-72/1972
1603. Sheridan, Jim 355 Avn Co, FE, 1968-69
1604. Sheridan, Scott B-228 ASHB, CE, 1969-70
1605. Shields, Alan 128 AHC, CE, 1967-68
1606. Shivley, Mike 147 ASHC, FE, 1969-70
1607. Shows, Jimmy 15 TB, CE, 1966-68
1608. Sickler, David 114 AHC, P, 1965-66
1609. Sieben, James 174 AHC, CE, 1967-69
1610. Silva, Larry 176 AHC, CE, 1967-69
1611. Silva, Mike F-8 Cav, P, 1970-71
1612. Sim, William B-229, DG, 1965-66
1613. Simmons, Bill B-3-17, P, 1971-72
1614. Simmons, Mike B-4 Avn Bn, DG, 1967
1615. Simmons, Ty 189 AHC, P, 1970-71
1616. Simonett, Kelly C-229, CE, 1969-70
1617. Simons, Tom B-25 Avn Bn, CE, 1966-67
1618. Simonson, Frank A-158 AHB, CE, 1969-70
1619. Simpson, Benjamin 187 AHC, CE, 1970-71
1620. Simpson, Ken 118 AHC, DG, 1970-71
1621. Sites, Joe 188 AHC, P, 1967
1622. Sites, Ron C-229 AHB, DG, 1970
1623. Skarda, Joe 116 AHC, DG, 1968-69
1624. Skinner, William, B Btry 82 Arty, 1969
1625. Slate, Dennis 116 AHC, DG, 1967-68
1626. Sloan, John 361 AHC, CE, 1969-70
1627. Sloniker, Mike A-229 AHB, P, 1971-72
1628. Smalley, Joe 114 AHC, TI, 1967-68
1629. Smith, Al 114 AHC, CE, 1970-71
1630. Smith, Bill A-3-17, P, 1969-70

1631. Smith, Butch 242 ASHC, DG, 1967-68
1632. Smith, Cameron 539 TC, 1967-68
1633. Smith, Dan 326 MB, P, 1969-70
1634. Smith, Dayne C-7-1, P, 1971-72
1635. Smith, Howard 68 AHC, P, 1969-70
1636. Smith, J.T. A-1 Avn Bn, CE, 1965-66
1637. Smith, James 134 AHC, DG, 1970-71
1638. Smith, Joe 604 TC, 1967-68
1639. Smith, Ken 114 AHC, CE, 1968-69
1640. Smith, Larry 147 ASHC, FE, 1967-68
1641. Smith, Larry 175 AHC, DG, 1966-67
1642. Smith, Larry 238 AWC, P, 1968-69
1643. Smith, Larry A-158 AHB, P, 1969-70
1644. Smith, Lee 114 AHC, CE, 1970-71
1645. Smith, Mike C-1-9, P, 1970-71
1646. Smith, Robert 335 AHC, DG, 1969-70
1647. Smith, Robert C-4-77 ARA, P, 1969
1648. Smith, Roger 17 AHC, 1967-68
1649. Smith, Ron 129 AHC, P, 1969-70
1650. Smith, Russell B-1-9, P, 1968-69
1651. Smith, Sam 179 ASHC, FE, 1968-69
1652. Smith, Steven 175 AHC, DG, 1969-70
1653. Smith, Terry 187 AHC, CE, 1970-71
1654. Smith, Tom 117 AHC, CE, 1971-72
1655. Smith, Warren 155 AHC/165 TC, 1965
1656. Snow, Roger B/E-1-9, DG, 1969-70/1970-71
1657. Snyder, Don 335 AHC, CE, 1966-67
1658. Snyder, Frank 134 AHC, DG, 1968-69
1659. Snyder, Jim D-1-10, P, 1969-70
1660. Soares, John 188 AHC, P, 1968
1661. Solis, Carlos 68 MD, Medic, 1970-71
1662. Solis, Noel 114 AHC, CE, 1963-64
1663. Somerfield, Bill 282 AHC, P, 1971-72
1664. Souza, Louis 335 AHC, CE, 1969-70
1665. Spears, Jon 93 TC, CE, 1963-64
1666. Spears, Steve 162 AHC, 1968-69
1667. Blank ************************
1668. Speer, Steve 361 AWC, CE, 1971-72
1669. Spence, Larry 242 ASHC, CE/FE, 1969-70
1670. Spiers, Jim 175 AHC, P, 1968-69
1671. Spillane, John 242 ASHC
1672. Spratt, Greg, 334 AHC, CE, 1967-68
1673. Springer, Robert 118 AHC, 1969-70

1674. Sprinkle, James author, 235/334 AWC, CE, 1971-72
1675. Staadt, Tom 135 AHC, P, 1969-70
1676. Stafford, Will 48 AHC, P, 1968-69
1677. Stagman, Gary 281 AHC, CE, 1966-70
1678. Stahlkuppe, Joe 269 CAB, 1967-68
1679. Stamps, Don C-159 ASHB, CE, 1969
1680. Stanfield, Jerry 145 Airlift Plt/281 AHC, DG, 1965-67
1681. Stanis, John 114 AHC, CE, 1970-71
1682. Stanley, Cleve C-159 ASHB, CE, 1970
1683. Stanley, Dave 68 AHC, DG, 1967-68
1684. Stanley, James 213 ASHC, CE, 1967-68
1685. Stark, Jim 155 AHC, P, 1970-71
1686. Stedman, Craig 595 Sig Co, 1969
1687. Stefanini, Gary B-228 ASHB, FE, 1968-69
1688. Steiger, Jim 187 AHC, CE, 1967-68
1689. Steinback, Joe 189 AHC, CE, 1968-69
1690. Stevens, Chuck A-227 AHB, CE, 1965-66
1691. Stevenson, Glenn 187 AHC, DG, 1967-68
1692. Steward, Tom 135 AHC, DG, 1969
1693. Stewart, Bob 92 AHC, CE, 1967-68
1694. Stewart, Gary 117 AHC, CE, 1971
1695. Stewart, Tim 117 AHC, 1966-67
1696. Stibbe, Russ 335 AHC, CE, 1967-71
1697. Stiefel, David 238 AWC, DG, 1969
1698. Stillwell, Dexter 539 TC, 1968
1699. Stinnett, Roger 191 AHC, 1967-68
1700. Stino, Tom 187 AHC, CE, 1969-70
1701. Stitt, Harold 191 AHC, P, 1967-68
1702. Stoehr, Bruce 162 AHC, P, 1967-68
1703. Stogner, Grady, 11 ACR, 1968-69
1704. Stogner, Joe 114 AHC, DG, 1970-71
1705. Stokes, Larry 129 AHC, CE, 1972-73
1706. Stone, Charlie 114 AHC, P, 1965
1707. Stone, Eric 271 ASHC, CE, 1968
1708. Stone, Joe unk personal data, 1968-69
1709. Stonecipher, Charles 54 MD, P, 1971
1710. Stonner, Dean A-9 Avn Bn, P, 1968-69
1711. Stotler, Bruce F-79 AFA, CE, 1971-72
1712. Stovall, William 15 MB, P, 1971-72
1713. Stowell, Kieth 187 AHC, DG, 1967-68
1714. Stowell, Tom 175 AHC, P, 1969-70
1715. Strand, Phil 179 ASHC, 1968-69

1716. Stratton, Mike 187 AHC, P, 1969-70
1717. Strew, Jerrell, 1 Cav (Air), 1965-66
1718. Stringer, Floyd, 162 AHC, CE, 1969
1719. Strobel, Frank 114 AHC, P, 1969-70
1720. Strople, Pat 187 AHC, CE, 1971-72
1721. Stroud, David 271 ASHC, CE, 1970-71
1722. Studer, Mike 243 ASHC, 1968-69
1723. Stufflebeem, Charles 114 AHC, Svc Plt, 1971-72
1724. Sturgill, Enoc 175 AHC, CE, 1965-66
1725. Stymerski, John 483 CAMS, USAF, 1968-69
1726. Suggs, Pat, son of Guns A-Go-Go vet, 1966-67
1727. Sullivan, George 15 TC, 1968
1728. Sullivan, Pat 173 AHC, CE, 1970-71
1729. Summers, Don 170 AHC, CE, 1969
1730. Summers, Glenn A-501/71 AHC, 1965-66
1731. Summey, Paul B-123 Avn Bn, P, 1970-71
1732. Sura, Richard 117 AHC, DG, 1967-68
1733. Sutphen, Ed 134 AHC, CE, 1970-71
1734. Swain, Robert A-1-9, P, 1966-67
1735. Swank, Dan 134 AHC, CE, 1970-71
1736. Swanson, Barry 129 AHC, CE, 1972-73
1737. Swartz, Gary A-3-17, CE, 1969-70
1738. Swickard, Jack 134 AHC, P, 1967-68
1739. Swift, Ron 179 ASHC, CE, 1968-69
1740. Swinford, Marvin A-3-17, P, 1971
1741. Swol, Paul 281 AHC, CE, 1969-70
1742. Sylvester, Ernie 57 MD, P, 1964-65
1743. Tabor, Rick 335 AHC, CE, 1969-70
1744. Taglauer, Richard A-4-77 ARA, 1970-71
1745. Tallent, Robert 282 AHC, CE, 1967-68
1746. Talley, Bill 45 MC, CE, 1970-71
1747. Talmich, Ben A-3-17, 1969-70
1748. Tarnovsky, Joe 240 AHC, CE, 1969-70
1749. Tartar, Mike A-227, DG, 1969
1750. Taylor, Alan, 498 MC, 1969-71
1751. Taylor, Don B-25 Avn Bn, DG, 1966-67
1752. Taylor, Max 173 AHC, 1968-69
1753. Taylor, Rob 119 AHC, P, 1966-67
1754. Taylor, Ron 71 AHC, CE, 1970-71
1755. Taylor, Tom B-159 ASHB, FE, 1970
1756. Taylor, Tommy B-158 Avn Bn, CE, 1969
1757. Tela, Dave A-3-17, P, 1969-70
1758. Telfair, Dan 68 Avn Co, P, 1965-66
1759. Tenney, Bob D-1-4, P, 1967-68

1760. Tepper, Art 610 TC, TI, 1968-70
1761. Terry, Don 57 AHC, CE, 1971
1762. Terry, Robert 57 AHC, DG, 1972
1763. Thacker, Greg C-16, DG, 1972
1764. Thayer, Ed 175 AHC, DG, 1966-67
1765. Thibodeau, Charles 165 TC/155 AHC, P, 1965-66
1766. Thies, Mike 20 TC, 1970-71
1767. Thomas, Craig 229 AHB Surgeon, 1969-70
1768. Thomas, Rick 121 AHC, P, 1968-70
1769. Thompson, Carroll 187 AHC, CE, 1970-71
1770. Thompson, Fred 174 AHC, P, 1970-71
1771. Thompson, Jim 17 AHC, 1967-68
1772. Thompson, Ken 92 AHC, CE, 1969-70
1773. Thompson, Neal F -8 Cav, P, 1972
1774. Thompson, Rich B-7-1, P, 1969-70
1775. Thompson, Ronnie A-25 Avn Bn, CE, 1967-68
1776. Thompson, Thomas 222 CSAB, 1967
1777. Thomsen, Craig 213 ASHC, 1967
1778. Thornton, Mike HHC 229 AHB, CE, 1971-72
1779. Thornton, Tom 118 AHC, P, 1965-66
1780. Thorson, Richard 247 MD, Flight Opns, 1970-71
1781. Thrift, John 240 AHC, CE, 1967-68
1782. Tibbers, Jackie 162 AHC, CE, 1971-72
1783. Tibbetts, Greg 45 MC, CE, 1967-68
1784. Tidd, Bob 175 AHC, DG, 1965-67
1785. Tiller, Art A-101 AHB, 1971
1786. Timberlake, Ron B-1-9, 1971
1787. Timmers, Ed 175 AHC, CE, 1969-70
1788. Tindall, Larry 116 AHC, P, 1970
1789. Tobias, P.J. A-227, 1970-71
1790. Tollefsen, Kjell 188 AHC, P, 1968
1791. Tomczak, Roger 283 MD, CE, 1965-66
1792. Tompkins, Pat 68 AHC, CE, 1968-69
1793. Tonjes, Craig A-227, CE, 1970-71
1794. Tookmanian, Dan 114 AHC, TI, 1968-69
1795. Topping, Mike 48 AHC, CE, 1971-72
1796. Torres, Don 189 AHC, CE, 1968-69
1797. Torres, Jose 119 AHC, P, 1969-70
1798. Torres, Ray 134 AHC, CE, 1969-70
1799. Tortolano, Vincent 187 AHC, P, 1967-68
1800. Touchstone, Gene 119 AHC, 1969
1801. Tracey, Johnson 128 AHC, CE, 1971
1802. Trogdon, Ron 15 MB, CE, 1967
1803. Trommatter, Jim 118 AHC, CE, 1965-66

1804. Tucker, Bill D-1-1, DG, 1970-71
1805. Tucker, John 271 ASHC, CE/FE, 1968-70
1806. Tucker, Tom 92 AHC, CE, 1967-68
1807. Tuell, Hank 15 MB, P, 1969-70
1808. Tuerk, Jerry 174 AHC, DG, 1969-70
1809. Tunnell, Rodger 121 AHC, P, 1969-70
1810. Turnbull, Jack A-7-1, P, 1967-69
1811. Turner, Denny 92 AHC, P, 1968-69
1812. Turner, Jerry A-101 AHB, P, 1965-66
1813. Turner, Ron 48 AHC, P, 1970-71
1814. Tuttle, Scott son of Jerry Tuttle, 176 AHC, P, 1969
1815. Tyler, Dan C-2-20 ARA, P, 1970
1816. Tyler, Dan C-229, P, 1970-71
1817. Ulrich, Don 128 AHC, P, 1971-72
1818. Underwood, Hans 134 AHC, CE, 1970-71
1819. Usry, John A-228 ASHB, FE, 1970
1820. Valentine, Jerry 92 AHC, DG, 1969-70
1821. Van Horn, James 498 MC, Medic, 1968
1822. Van Rope, Jeff 132 ASHC, P, 1968
1823. Vanbenthusen, Eric 128 AHC, 1965-67
1824. Vanderwedge, Phil 114 AHC, CE, 1970
1825. VanZilen, Art 336 AHC/A-7-1, CE,
       1969-70/1971-72
1826. Vasquez, Carlos 243 ASHC, DG/FE, 1969-70
1827. Vega, Tony 129 AHC, CE, 1971
1828. Verebely, Bill 93 TC, 1963-64
1829. Vereen, Carl 61 AHC, P, 1968
1830. Verity, Rick 180 ASHC, FE, 1972-73
1831. Vermillion, Steve 45 MC, P, 1969-70
1832. Verner, Larry C-1-9, CE, 1970-71
1833. Versteeg, Bruce A-101 AHB, 1967-68
1834. Veteto, Ricci 205 ASHC, 1968-69
1835. Vick, Jack C-16, CE, 1970-71
1836. Viol, Adolf 205 ASHC, CE, 1968-69
1837. Vierra, Damien 15 MB, CE, 1970-71
1838. Visentine, Tom 114 AHC, CE, 1967-68
1839. Vitale, Vincent 101 Abn, 1970
1840. Vogel, Carl 117 AHC, P, 1964-65
1841. Vogel, Rick A-227 AHB/57 AHC, 1971/1971-72
1842. Voss, James B-159 ASHB, 1968
1843. Wadginski, Francis 132 ASHC, P, 1971
1844. Wagner, Dawn daughter of Ray Rupcic (KIA), 114
       AHC, P, 1964-65

1845. Wagner, Jerry 187 AHC, P, 1967-68
1846. Wainscott, Tom 336 AHC, CE, 1966-67
1847. Walker, Bob 191 AHC, CE, 1967-68
1848. Walker, Ed HHT 7-1, P, 1968-69
1849. Walker, Joe 188 AHC, P, 1967-68
1850. Walker, Mel D-1-1, P, 1968-70
1851. Wall, Tim F-4 Cav, 1972
1852. Wallace, Kim daughter of Rodger Williamson, 4
       Trans Command, P, 1966
1853. Walowicz, Les 128 AHC, 1969-70
1854. Walsh, Ed 162 AHC, CE, 1966-67
1855. Walt, Jim D-3-4, 1968-69
1856. Walter, Bill 119 AHC, DG, 1965-66
1857. Walters, David A-159 ASHB, FE, 1967-68
1858. Walters, Rick 92 AHC, CE, 1967-68
1859. Walton, Bill D-229, CE, 1970-71
1860. Walton, Scott 269 CAB, 1968
1861. Ward, Dennis 128 AHC, CE, 1968-70
1862. Ward, Doug 173 AHC, CE, 1967
1863. Ward, Jay B-3-17, P, 1971-72
1864. Wargi, Don D-1-1, P, 1969-70
1865. Warner, Ken 571 MD, P, 1971-72
1866. Warner, Larry 68 MD, Medic, 1970-71
1867. Warren, Dale 57 AHC, CE, 1968-69
1868. Washburn, Woody, 1970
1869. Waskom, Joe C-2-27 Wolfhounds, 1969
1870. Waters, Dudley, Caribou Assn, 1968
1871. Watford, John 187 AHC, DG, 1971-72
1872. Watters, Curtis 180 ASHC, CE, 1972-73
1873. Waugh, Mike 128 AHC, P, 1971-72
1874. Waugh, Skip 191 AHC, CE, 1967-68
1875. Weatherly, Mitch 162 AHC, P, 1971-72
1876. Weaver, Randolph D-227, 1967-68
1877. Weaver, Roger 170 AHC, P, 1967-68
1878. Webb, Rob 192 AHC, CE, 1971
1879. Webb, John 134 AHC, CE, 1968-69
1880. Weber, Bill B-229 AHB, CE, 1965-66
1881. Weber, Jeff 175 AHC, CE, 1968-69
1882. Webster, David 187 AHC, P, 1967-68
1883. Webster, Geoff 68 AHC, P, 1968-69
1884. Weddle, Carl 162 AHC, CE, 1967-68
1885. Weiler, Logan 48 AHC, P, 1968-69
1886. Wells, Bill A-4 Avn Bn, CE, 1969-70

1887. Welsh, Robert 61 AHC, CE, 1969-71
1888. Wesselman, Gary 175 AHC, P, 1966-67
1889. West, Gary 121 AHC, 1968
1890. West, Morris 336 AHC, CE, 1968-69
1891. Westburg, Rick 175 AHC, DG, 1969-70
1892. Wetherell, Ron 242 ASHC, FE, 1967-68
1893. Wetmore, Harry 281 AHC, P, 1967-68
1894. Whalen, Larry 174 AHC, CE, 1969-70
1895. Whitaker, George 134 AHC, P, 1969-70
1896. Whitaker, Woody 271 ASHC, 1968-69
1897. White, Chris B-227, CE, 1968-69
1898. White, Frank webmaster, Guns A-Go-Go
1899. White, John 57 AHC, P, 1968-69
1900. Whitey, Eugene B-25 Avn Bn, 1968-69
1901. Whitney, Bruce 192 AHC, P, 1970-71
1902. Whitson, Bryce 17 AHC, 1967-68
1903. Whitt, Eugene 117 AHC, P, 1968-69
1904. Wiederhold, Gerry 71 AHC, 1969
1905. Wiese, Dale 176 AHC, CE, 1967-68
1906. Wikoff, Al C-7-1, CE, 1971-72
1907. Wilder, Billy 174 AHC, CE, 1971
1908. Wilhite, Ray U. S. Army Avn Museum, USAAM
1909. Wilkerson, Richard B-1-9, 1967
1910. Wilks, Jim 128 AHC, CE, 1967-68
1911. Williams, Bob 118 AHC, CE, 1970
1912. Williams, Delmus 45 MC, CE, 1969-70
1913. Williams, Don 191 AHC, P, 1967-68
1914. Williams, Dwayne 175 AHC, P, 1966-67
1915. Williams, Earl unk unit, 1964
1916. Williams, James 128 AHC, 1965-67
1917. Williams, Phil C-227, CE, 1971-72
1918. Williams, Ron 114 AHC, CE, 1964-65
1919. Williams, Ron 176 AHC, CE, 1967-68
1920. Williams, Tony 118 AHC, CE, 1969-70
1921. Williamson, Rodger 4 Trans Command, P, 1966
1922. Willis, Randy A-7-1, P, 1969-70
1923. Willis, Rod D-1-4/C-16, P, 1969-70/1970-73
1924. Wills, Dale 336 AHC/236 MD, CE,
       1968-69/1971-72
1925. Wilson, Chuck, B-123 Avn Bn, 1970-71
1926. Wilson, Doug A-502/114 /335 /326, 1965-71
1927. Wilson, Frank 62 CAC, P, 1968-70
1928. Wilson, Lucky 134 AHC, P, 1970-71

1929. Wilson, Stewart 179 ASHC, CE, 1967-68
1930. Wilson, William 176 AHC, CE, 1970-71
1931. Wilton, Mike 173 AHC, P, 1966-67
1932. Windsand, Doug 187 AHC/602 TC, 1970
1933. Windsor, Greg 240 AHC, 1971-72
1934. Winegard, Wayne 142 TC, 1968
1935. Winge, Larry A-227 AHB, CE, 1966-67
1936. Wingrove, James 135 AHC, CE, 1971
1937. Wininger, Roger 175 AHC, Armorer, 1971-72
1938. Winslow, Roger 114 AHC, P, 1964-65
1939. Wisbith, Stan C-229, CE, 1967-68
1940. Wise, Alan 187 AHC, DG, 1968-69
1941. Wisell, George 335 AHC, P, 1968-69
1942. Witte, Larry 242 ASHC/A-3-17, FE/CE,
    1971/1971-72
1943. Witter, Tom D-1-4, 1968-69
1944. Wittner, Rickey 242 ASHC, CE, 1970
1945. Wizard, Brian 118 AHC, DG, 1968-69
1946. Wolak, Steve 178 ASHC, FE, 1970-71
1947. Wolf, Bill author, 129 AHC, CE, 1969-70
1948. Wolk, Richie 173 AHC, CE, 1968-69
1949. Blank ***********************
1950. Wood, Billy A-2-20 ARA, P, 1966-67
1951. Wood, Charlie FSB 4-11, D Btry, 1970
1952. Wood, Dennis 117 AHC, CE, 1965-66
1953. Wood, Thomas B-101 Abn, P, 1967-68
1954. Woods, Rodney 187 AHC, P, 1970-71
1955. Woodward, Gary 129 AHC, CE, 1971-72
1956. Woodward, James 339 TC, CE, 1962-63
1957. Woodworth, Scott 167 TC/336 AHC, CE, 1968-69
1958. Woody, Harold A Co 82 Avn Bn, DG, 1965
1959. Woolley, Bill 57 AHC, CE, 1969-70
1960. Woolwine, Don A-1-9, 1968-70
1961. Workman, James, 62 Avn Co/A-502 Avn Bn/150
    TC, 1964-65
1962. Worner, Matt 187 AHC, DG, 1968
1963. Wright, Grover C-1-9, P, 1969-70
1964. Wright, Larry A-1-9, CE, 1965-66
1965. Wright, Robert 119 AHC, P, 1965-66
1966. Wrinkle, Bob 118 AHC, P, 1968-69
1967. Wussow, Lloyd 155 AHC, CE, 1968
1968. Yee, Brian 92 AHC, CE, 1968-69
1969. Yerden, Art 134 AHC, DG, 1967-68
1970. Yokum, Dennis 336 AHC, DG, 1968-69

1971. Young, Billy C-7-1, P, 1968-69
1972. Young, Bob A-7-17, P, 1967-68
1973. Young, Gary A Co 1 Avn Bn, CE, 1967-68
1974. Young, Jerry 498 MC, CE, 1968-69
1975. Young, Ralph, author, 54 Gen Spt Gp, 1968-69
1976. Young, Roger A-3-17, CE, 1970
1977. Ytsen, Mike 189 AHC, DG, 1968
1978. Zahn, Randy, author, C-1-9, P, 1970-71
1979. Zaletskis, John 92 AHC, CE, 1968-69
1980. Zanetti, Al 175 AHC, DG, 1966-67
1981. Zanfardino, Tony 173 AHC, CE, 1966-67
1982. Zavis, Joe D-3-5, CE, 1970-71
1983. Zednick, George B-159 ASHB, FE, 1968-69
1984. Zehr, Roger 114 AHC, P, 1965-66
1985. Zimmerman, Mike 192 AHC, CE, 1970-71
1986. Zinkeler, William 247 MD, CE, 1969-70
1987. Zipperer, Carl 176 AHC, P, 1970-71
1988. Zubrinic, Ed 128 AHC, CE, 1968-70
1989. Allen, Stan D-3-4, 1969-70
1990. Breyer, Harry B-229 AHB, 1970
1991. Cannon, Dan A-3-17, 1971
1992. Caughlin, Sonny C-2-17, CE, 1969-70
1993. Charlton, Don 173 Abn Bde, P, 1969-70
1994. Charlton, Rod 244 Avn Co, P, 1967-68
1995. Claymore, Clay 175 AHC, CE, 1969-70
1996. Curtis, Grant B-1-9, P, 1969-70
1997. Demumbreum, Jim 57 AHC, CE, 1971-72
1998. Flis, Larry 114 AHC, CE, 1966-67
1999. Franks, Gary 191 AHC, CE, 1969-70
2000. Hartnett, Steve C-2-20 ARA/F-79 AFA, CE,
    1971-72
2001. Hathaway, Kevin 173 AHC, CE, 1967
2002. Hines, Les A-123 Avn Bn, CE, 1968-70
2003. Kerr, Mike 21 Sig Gp, DG, 1969-70
2004. Kictarek, Ed A-3-17, CE, 1971
2005. Kloppel, Ken D-3-4, 1970-71
2006. Knight, Emmett 56 TC, P, 1967
2007. Kurtz, Jack B-1-9, P, 1970-71
2008. Lemner, Dennis 68 AHC, DG, 1969
2009. Marchetti, Bill 24O AHC, CE, 1969-70
2010. Marling, Pat D-1-12 Cav, Medic, 1971
2011. Marriott, Eric 179 ASHC, 1970
2012. Matriscians, Dan 173 AHC, CE, 1966-67
2013. McCain, Dwight 45 MB, P, 1968-69

2014. McMillan, Mac C-2-20 ARA, P, 1970-71
2015. Moe, Jack 114 AHC, CE, 1967-68
2016. Morris, Crayton 336 AHC, P, 1967
2017. O'Hara, Bill 544 TC/114 AHC, P, 1968-69
2018. Papapietro, Joe 114 AHC, P, 1969-70
2019. Robinson, Steve 2-7 Cav Photographer, 1968
2020. Rokey, Mike D-3-5, P, 1970-71
2021. Scheck, Roland 176 AHC, DG, 1967
2022. Sherrer, Larry A-3-17, P, 1970-71
2023. Smith, Dan 326 MB, P, 1969-70
2024. Smith, John 121 AHC, DG, 1967-69
2025. Sot, Wayne 13 Sig Bn, 1969-70
2026. Stevens, Graham 334 AHC, P, 1969-70
2027. Strait, Clyde C-7-1, CE, 1967-68
2028. Strickland, Larry A-3-17, 1971
2029. Teetsel, John B-2-20 ARA, P, 1970-71
2030. Thompson, Ted 539 TC, DG, 1967-68
2031. Traub, Eric 215 Composite Svc Bn, Medic,
    1971-72
2032. Trujillo, Davis A-101 Abn Bn, P, 1970-71
2033. Trumper, Gerry 128 AHC, CE, 1966-67
2034. Vanatta, Frank 1 Bde 1 Cav, P, 1967-68
2035. Vollmar, Davis 661 TC, 1967-68
2036. Wade, Jim 117 AHC, P, 1971-72
2037. Walsh, Bill 15 MB, Medic, 1970-71
2038. Wardwell, Robert 336 AHC, CE, 1966-67
2039. Washburn, Jack A-1-9, 1967-69
2040. Wuthrich, Val 3-187-101 Abn, 1968-69
2041. Atanian, Bud 282 AHC, CE, 1967-68
2042. Bishop, Chris, author
2043. Dodd, Dennis, 2 Bn 60 Inf, 1968
2044. Kearney, Michael, VN War researcher
2045. Kelley, Mike, author, D-1-502 Inf, 101 Abn,
    1969-70
2046. Mikulan, Mik 116 AHC/269 CAB, P, 1969-70
2047. Miller, Robin 114 AHC, P, 1967-68
2048. Schuckman, Thomas 240 AHC, DG, 1969-70
2049. Steinbrunn, Robert, author, P, A-7-17 Cav/189 AHC,
    1967-68
2050. Stiles, Howard 335 AHC, P, 1969
2051. Brennan, Matthew, author, 1-9 Cav, 1965-69
2052. Horton, Glenn 199 LIB, Medic, 1969-70
2053. Mason, Robert B-229 AHB, P, 1965
2054. Aleshire, Gordon, 132 ASHC, FE, 1970

2055. McDonald, Monte 132 ASHC, FE, 1970
2056. Schlim, Albert 15 TB, P, 1968
2057. Roscoe, Phil 200 ASHC, FE, 1967-68
2058. Williamson II, Rodger, son of Rodger Williamson,
      4 Trans Command, P, 1966
2059. Rzeminski, Pete H+HC 1 Bde 101 Abn, P, 1968-69
2060. Mahoney, Jim D-1-1, P, 1969-70
2061. Caeton, Lionel 178 ASHC, 1969-70
2062. Seeger, Larry 132 ASHC, P, 1970-71
2063. Bynum, Jim 254 MD, P, 1966-67
2064. Stidd, Robert 11 CAG, DG, 1969
2065. Ziemba, Rich 45 MC, P, 1970
2066. Goodman, Jim 254 MD, P, 1969-70
2067. McCollum, Jim 498 MC/45 MC, P, 1968-69
2068. McCartney, Bruce 45 MC, Medic, 1969-70
2069. Simcoe, Paul 237 MD, Medic, 1970-71
2070. Parmenter, Richard 45 MC, Medic, 1970
2071. Mueller, Richard 45 MC, Medic, 1964-65
2072. Jones, Dale 9 Inf Div, Medic, 1968-69
2073. Vogt, Tom 11 ACR, CE, 1968
2074. Hendren, Danny 283 MD, Medic, 1970-71
2075. Poston, Jamie 68 AHC, CE, 1966-67
2076. Livings, Jim 68 AHC, DG, 1966-68
2077. McMahan, Waul 254 MD, Medic, 1967-68
2078. Leirer, Richard 170 AHC, Avionics/DG, 1967-68
2079. Jaimes, Jose 170 AHC, CE, 1967-69
2080. Evans, Dave 118 AHC, DG, 1968-69
2081. Angeles, Dan 128 AHC, DG, 1969-70
2082. Thomas, Tyler 116 AHC, P, 1970-71
2083. Lintl, Steve D-1-20, 11 LIB, 1970-71
2084. Berry, Russell A-1-20, 11 LIB, 1970-71
2085. Codney, Bob 114 AHC, P, 1969-71
2086. Russell, Storm 62 CAC, DG, 1970
2087. Anderson, Roger 175 AHC, DG, 1967-68
2088. Mann, Jim 128 AHC, P, 1966-67
2089. Benedict, Dan 336 AHC, P, 1969-70
2090. Crisp, Carl 114 AHC, CE, 1969-70
2091. Carter, Gary 336 AHC, DG, 1970
2092. Tooke, Pat 117 AHC, CE, 1969-70
2093. Bogges, Bill 8 TC, DG/CE, 1963-64

INDIVIDUAL CONTRIBUTORS

UNIT/NUMERICAL

U.S. ARMY HELICOPTER NAMES IN VIETNAM

The word AUTHOR in the Unit-Numerical section refers to the BOOK AUTHORS listed in the Bibliography section, numbered 5450 thru 6550. Photographs or text citations contained in these BOOKS give reference to a particular copter NAME.

Unit	Reference
Hdqs + Hdqs Co -1 Air Cav Div	Molish, Mike H+HC-1 ACD, P, 1968-69
1 Avn Detachment	Army Avn Mus USAAM
1 Avn Detachment	Chenoweth, Bob author: BIRTH CONTROL, COST OF LIVING, EASY MONEY
1 Avn Detachment	Davis, Larry author: BIRTH CONTROL
1 Avn Detachment	Frye, Jim 1 Avn Det, P, 1967-68
1 Avn Detachment	Greenhalgh, Bill 162 AHC, P, 1968-69
1 Avn Detachment	Ladue, John D-227 AHB, P, 1966-67
1 Avn Detachment	Mutza, Wayne author: EASY MONEY
1 Avn Detachment	Suggs, Pat son of a Guns A-Go-Go vet, 1966-67
1 Avn Detachment	White, Frank webmaster, Guns A-Go-Go
1 Bn 50 Inf	Bertholf, Cheney 1 Bn 50 Inf, 1968
1 Bde 1 Air Cav	Bell, Jim 1-1, 1967
1 Bde 1 Air Cav	Estes, Sam 1-1, DG, 1968-69
1 Bde 1 Air Cav	Grant, Cleveland 1-1, CE, 1969
1 Bde 1 Air Cav	Harris, Jon 1-1, P, 1969-70
1 Bde 1 Air Cav	Holmes, Ed 1-1, P, 1968-69
1 Bde 1 Air Cav	Lundh, Lennart author: MYSTERY SHIP
1 Bde 1 Air Cav	Maycen, Ed 1-1, CE, 1970
1 Bde 1 Air Cav	McAllister, Charlie 1-1, 1970
1 Bde 1 Air Cav	McKinney, Duke 1-1, CE, 1970
1 Bde 1 Air Cav	Paitz, Mike 1-1, 1969
1 Bde 1 Air Cav	Vanatta, Frank 1-1, P, 1967-68
Hdqs + Hdqs Co-1 Bde 101 Abn	Dousis, George 1 Bde, 101 Abn, CE, 1969-70
Hdqs + Hdqs Co-1 Bde 101 Abn	Rzeminski, Pete H+HC 1 Bde 101 Abn, P, 1968-69
1 Signal Bde	Comrey, Bill 21 Sig Gp, 1969
1 Signal Bde	Crews, Tom 21 Sig Gp, 1969
1 Signal Bde	Faulkner, Ron 21 Sig Gp, P, 1970
2 Bde-1 Cav	Sullivan, George 15 TC, 1968
2 Bde-101 Airborne	Knapp, Curt 2 Bde 101 Abn, P, 1967-68
2 Signal Group	Callaghan, Bob 2nd Sig Gp, CE, 1966-67
2 Signal Group	Love, Terry 1 Sig Bde, CE, 1966-68
2 Signal Group	Mutza, Wayne author: CHUG-A-LUG
3 Bde -1 Cav	Moon, Terry 1 Cav Div PIO Photographer, 1969
Hdqs + Hdqs Co-3 Bde 101 Abn	Gwizdak, Joe H+HC-3 Bde, 101 Abn, 1969
4 Trans Command	Chenoweth, Bob 4 Trans Comm, CE, 1967
4 Trans Command	Wallace, Kim, daughter of Rodger Williamson, 4 TC, P, 1966
4 Trans Command	Williamson, Rodger 4 Trans Comm, P, 1966
4 Trans Command	Williamson II, Rodger, son of Rodger Williamson, 4 TC, P, 1966
5 Trans Bn	Jones, John VN War researcher:
7 Airlift Platoon	Young, Ralph author: HOGAN'S GOAT
8 Trans Co	Bennett, Allen 117 AHC, CE, 1967-68
8 Trans Co	Boyd, Barc 8 TC, P, 1962-63
8 Trans Co	Fiman, Ron 8 TC, CE, 1963-64
8 Trans Co	Gross, Fred 8 TC, DG, 1963
8 Trans Co	Bogges, Bill 8 TC, DG/CE, 1963-64
8 Trans Co	Mruczkowski, Leon 8 TC, CE, 1962
8 Trans Co	Oakes, Hiawatha 8 TC, CE, 1962-63
8 Trans Co	Pike, Bob, 1963-64
8 Trans Co	Rose, Tom 8 TC/117 AHC, CE, 1963-64
8 Trans Co	Woodward, Jim 339 TC, 1962-63
8 Trans Co	Young, Ralph author: SWAMP FOX 2
10 Combat Avn Bn	Crooks, Eugene 10 CAB, P, 1967
11 Armored Cav Reg	Bernstein, Jonathan author: VOODO LADY
11 Armored Cav Reg	Bertolini, Frank 37 MC, 1970-71
11 Armored Cav Reg	Bono, Rick 11 ACR, CE, 1968-69
11 Armored Cav Reg	Davis, Larry author: BANDITS

Unit	Contributor
11 Armored Cav Reg	Dillon, Frank F-4, 1971-72
11 Armored Cav Reg	Drendel, Lou author: BANDITS, LOOKOUT
11 Armored Cav Reg	Eaton, Bruce 11 ACR, CE, 1968
11 Armored Cav Reg	Gray, Randy 11 ACR, P, 1968-69
11 Armored Cav Reg	Greenhalgh, Bill 162 AHC, P, 1968-69
11 Armored Cav Reg	Hathaway, Allen 11 ACR, 1964-67
11 Armored Cav Reg	Haviland, Peter 1-4, 1968-69
11 Armored Cav Reg	Hien, John, 11 ACR, 1967-68
11 Armored Cav Reg	Horton, Glenn 199 LIB, Medic, 1969-70
11 Armored Cav Reg	Johnson, Lawrence author: LOLA MARIE
11 Armored Cav Reg	Jones, Jack 15 Med Bn, 1969
11 Armored Cav Reg	Kibbey, Doug 11 ACR, 19 71-72
11 Armored Cav Reg	LeGrand, Harold 11 ACR, P, 1971-72
11 Armored Cav Reg	Lundh, Lennart USS *Tripoli* 1968-69
11 Armored Cav Reg	Madsen, Paul 11 ACR, P, 1968-69
11 Armored Cav Reg	Marshall, Jake 11 ACR, 1969-70
11 Armored Cav Reg	Mesko, Jim author: EL GATO
11 Armored Cav Reg	Murtha, Paul B-1-9, P, 1971
11 Armored Cav Reg	Mutza, Wayne author: VOODO LADY, WIDOW MAKER
11 Armored Cav Reg	Nunn, Lowen 11 ACR, CE, 1969-70
11 Armored Cav Reg	Paul, Sean 11 ACR, 1970
11 Armored Cav Reg	Powis, William, 11 ACR, 1969-71
11 Armored Cav Reg	Reed, Don 11 ACR/398 TC, 1968-69
11 Armored Cav Reg	Rhoades, Ron 11 ACR, P, 1971-72
11 Armored Cav Reg	Rundle, first name unk, P, 1971-72
11 Armored Cav Reg	Sloniker, Mike A-229 AHB, P, 1971-72
11 Armored Cav Reg	Sprinkle, James 235/334 AWC, CE, 1971-72
11 Armored Cav Reg	Sprinkle, James author: GEORGE OF THE JUNGLE, WE THE PEOPLE, WIDOW MAKER
11 Armored Cav Reg	Stogner, Grady, 11 ACR, 1968-69
11 Armored Cav Reg	Stone, Joe 1968-69
11 Armored Cav Reg	Vogt, Tom 11 ACR, CE, 1968
11 Combat Avn Bn	Smithsonian Institution: SMOKEY III
11 Combat Avn Group	Bruce, Bobby 11 CAG, P, 1972
11 Combat Avn Group	Mason, Mike 11 CAG, DG, 1971-72
11 Combat Avn Group	Parrish, Dan 11 CAG, 1968-69
11 Combat Avn Group	Stidd, Robert 11 CAG, DG, 1969
11 Gen Support 1 Cav	Abel, Bill 11 GS, CE, 1969-70
11 Gen Support 1 Cav	McCrory, Bob 11 GS, CE, 1965-66
11 Gen Support 1 Cav	Richardson, Charles 11 GS, P, 1968
11 Light Inf Brigade	Aiken, Dan HHC 11 LIB 23 Div, CE, 1970-71
11 Light Inf Brigade	Benton, Robin 11 LIB, 1969-70
14 Transportation Bn	Bajc, Marko VN War researcher
15 Medical Bn	Ash, Larry 15 Med Bn, DG, 1970-71
15 Medical Bn	Bodnar, Mike C-2-7, 1970
15 Medical Bn	Brady, Dan 15 Med Bn, Medic, 1970
15 Medical Bn	Cardinal, Patrick 15 Med Bn, DG, 1972
15 Medical Bn	Calibro, Jim 15 Med Bn, DG, 1967-68
15 Medical Bn	Ferguson, Jim 15 Med Bn, CE, 1970-71
15 Medical Bn	Foster, Hugh B-1-5 Cav, 1970-71
15 Medical Bn	Gibbs, Murray 15 Med Bn, DG, 1967-68
15 Medical Bn	Hatch, Larry 15 Med Bn, P, 1966-67
15 Medical Bn	Holiday, Mark 15 Med Bn, CE, 1970-71
15 Medical Bn	Huether, Ron 15 Med Bn, P, 1971
15 Medical Bn	Louche, Bill 15 Med Bn, DG, 1966-67
15 Medical Bn	McDonald, James 15 Med Bn, Medic, 1971-72
15 Medical Bn	McKellar, Fred 15 Med Bn, P, 1966-67
15 Medical Bn	Medlock, Rick 15 Med Bn, 1970-71
15 Medical Bn	Odum, Jim 15 Med Bn, CE, 1969-70
15 Medical Bn	Parks, Dave 15 Med Bn, Svc Plt, DG, 1969-70
15 Medical Bn	Perry, Jim 15 Med Bn, Avionics, 1967-68
15 Medical Bn	Stovall, William 15 Med Bn, P, 1971-72
15 Medical Bn	Trogdon, Ron 15 Med Bn, CE, 1967
15 Medical Bn	Tuell, Hank 15 Med Bn, P, 1969-70
15 Medical Bn	Vierra, Damien 15 Med Bn, CE, 1970-71
15 Medical Bn	Walsh, Bill 15 Med Bn, Medic, 1970-71
Hdqs + Hdqs Co-15 Trans Bn	Deperro, John 15 TB, P, 1968-69
Hdqs + Hdqs Co-15 Trans Bn	Ethel, Jeff author: TAIL WIND
Hdqs + Hdqs Co-15 Trans Bn	Jones, Dan, 15 TB, P, 1968
Hdqs + Hdqs Co-15 Trans Bn	Mosley, Ken 15 TB, P, 1968
Hdqs + Hdqs Co-15 Trans Bn	Perry, Jim, 15 Med Bn, Avionics, 1967-68
Hdqs + Hdqs Co-15 Trans Bn	Schlim, Albert, 15 TB, P, 1968
Hdqs + Hdqs Co-15 Trans Bn	Shows, Jimmy, 15 TB, CE, 1966-68
17 Assault Hel Co	McNees, Richard 17 AHC, DG, 1967-68
17 Assault Hel Co	Meola, Mario 17 AHC, P, 1967
17 Assault Hel Co	Post, James 17 AHC, P, 1968

17 Assault Hel Co	Sams, Johnny 17 AHC, CE, 1967-68	45 Medical Co	Goodman, Jim 45 MC, P, 1969-70
17 Assault Hel Co	Smith, Roger 17 AHC, 1967-68	45 Medical Co	Hall, Thom 45 MC, CE, 1970-71
17 Assault Hel Co	Thompson, Jim 17 AHC, 1967-68	45 Medical Co	Hanson, Norm 551 TC, 1969
17 Assault Hel Co	Whitson, Bryce 17 AHC, 1967-68	45 Medical Co	Harrell, William 7th Surg Hosp, 1966-67
		45 Medical Co	Hendren, Danny 283 MD, Medic, 1970-71
18 Corps Avn Co	Hulbert, John 18 CAC, 1972-73	45 Medical Co	Huntley, Steve 45 MC, CE, 1968
18 Corps Avn Co	Jones, John VN War researcher	45 Medical Co	Kipp, Larry 45 MC, Medic, 1968-69
		45 Medical Co	Koss, John 45 MC, Medic, 1971
20 Engineer Bde	Armchair General Forum	45 Medical Co	Louie, Ron 45 MC, Medic, 1968
		45 Medical Co	O'Brien, Mike 45 MC, CE, 1969-70
20 Trans Co	McGowan, Bill 20 TC, P, 1967	45 Medical Co	McCain, Dwight 45 MC, P, 1968-69
		45 Medical Co	McCartney, Bruce 45 MC, Medic, 1969-70
21 Signal Group	Baggott, Dave 21 Sig Gp, P, 1970-71	45 Medical Co	McCollum, Jim 498/45 MC, P, 1968-69
21 Signal Group	Comrey, Bill 21 Sig Gp, 1969	45 Medical Co	Parmenter, Richard 45 MC, Medic, 1970
21 Signal Group	Escher, Doug 21 Sig Gp, CE, 1969-70	45 Medical Co	Poteat, Gary 45 MC, CE, 1967-68
21 Signal Group	Higgerson, Tom, 21 Sig Gp, DG, 1969-70	45 Medical Co	Riley, Richard 45 MC, CE, 1967-68
21 Signal Group	Kerr, Mike 21 Sig Gp, DG, 1969-70	45 Medical Co	Root, David 45 MC, CE, 1968-70
		45 Medical Co	Sabanosh, John 45 MC, CE, 1969-70
33 Trans Co	Beck, Paul 33 TC, CE, 1962-63	45 Medical Co	Talley, Bill 45 MC, CE, 1970-71
33 Trans Co	Brandt, Bob author: THE GREEN SPECKLED BIRD, JELLY BELLY	45 Medical Co	Tibbetts, Greg 45 MC, CE, 1967-68
		45 Medical Co	Vermillion, Steve 45 MC, P, 1969-70
33 Trans Co	Larson, Jim 33 TC, 1963	45 Medical Co	Williams, Delmus 45 MC, CE, 1969-70
33 Trans Co	Ness, John 33 TC, P, 1962 -63	45 Medical Co	Ziemba, Rich 45 MC, P, 1970
33 Trans Co	Wilson, Doug A-501 Avn Bn, 1965-66		
		48 Assault Hel Co	Amanzio, Tony 48 AHC, P, 1970-71
37 Signal Bn	Case, Bill 37 Sig Bn, CE, 1971-72	48 Assault Hel Co	Baldwin, Earl 155 AHC, 1969
		48 Assault Hel Co	Ballinger, Phil, 48 AHC, 1966-67
39 Signal Bn	Callaghan, Bob 2nd Sig Gp, CE, 1966-67	48 Assault Hel Co	Balog, Jim 48 AHC, DG, 1969-70
		48 Assault Hel Co	Belkin, Howie C-227 AHB, DG, 1969-70
45 Medical Co	Adams, Clif 45 MC, CE, 1967-68	48 Assault Hel Co	Brophy, Ed 48 AHC/390 TC, 1965-66
45 Medical Co	Caspar, John 45 MC, CE, 1968-69	48 Assault Hel Co	Bruss, Al 48 AHC/390 TC, 1965-68
45 Medical Co	Collins, Dan 45 MC, Medic, 1969	48 Assault Hel Co	Bryant, William 118 AHC, 1970-71
45 Medical Co	Crump, Chet 45 MC, Medic, 1969-71	48 Assault Hel Co	Cowley, Russ 48 AHC, P, 1970-71
45 Medical Co	Cunnare, Richard 45 MC, CE, 1967-68	48 Assault Hel Co	Crance, Dan 48 AHC, DG, 1967
45 Medical Co	Davidson, Wayne 45 MC, CE, 1968-69	48 Assault Hel Co	Dize, Jesse 48 AHC, P, 1970-71
45 Medical Co	Drendel, Lou author: PATCHES	48 Assault Hel Co	Dunlap, Bud 48 AHC, CE, 1970-71
45 Medical Co	Dunn, Billy 45 MC, 1967-68	48 Assault Hel Co	Fitcher, Thomas unk unit, 1967
45 Medical Co	Farley, Pat 45 MC, CE, 1969	48 Assault Hel Co	Gamache, Ray 48 AHC, 1967
45 Medical Co	Foulke, William unk unit, 1968	48 Assault Hel Co	Gerstenberger, Pete, 48 AHC, CE, 1971-72
45 Medical Co	Geer, Bucky unk unit, 1969	48 Assault Hel Co	Gomez, Joe 48 AHC, DG, 1966-67

Unit	Contributor
48 Assault Hel Co	Hale, Oscar 48 AC, CE, 1966-67
48 Assault Hel Co	Haws, Curtis 48 AHC, DG, 1970-71
48 Assault Hel Co	Jackson, Dave 48 AHC, P, 1967-68
48 Assault Hel Co	Jackson, James 48 AHC, 1970-71
48 Assault Hel Co	Kelley, Mike author: THE GHOST SHIP
48 Assault Hel Co	Lehman, Hal 48 AHC, 1967-69
48 Assault Hel Co	Lester, Rick 48 AHC, P, 1970-71
48 Assault Hel Co	Lundh, Lennart author: BATTLIN BITCH, BLOOD SWEAT + TEARS
48 Assault Hel Co	Meadows, Al 48 AHC, 1970
48 Assault Hel Co	Moorman, Gary 48 AHC, CE, 1968-69
48 Assault Hel Co	Morgan, Glen 48 AHC, CE, 1969-70
48 Assault Hel Co	Mutza, Wayne author: BATTLIN BITCH
48 Assault Hel Co	Nunn, Dave, 48 AHC, DG, 1966-67
48 Assault Hel Co	Parker, Steve 48 AHC, P, 1969
48 Assault Hel Co	Reese, George personal website
48 Assault Hel Co	Reyher, Sheldon 48 AHC, P, 1968-69
48 Assault Hel Co	Roberts, Jerry 48 AHC, 1966-67
48 Assault Hel Co	Rolinger, Terry 48 AHC, CE, 1968
48 Assault Hel Co	Sathre, Mike 48 AHC CE, 1970-71
48 Assault Hel Co	Stafford, Will 48 AHC, P, 1968-69
48 Assault Hel Co	Topping, Mike 48 AHC, CE, 1971-72
48 Assault Hel Co	Turner, Ron 48 AHC, P, 1970-71
48 Assault Hel Co	Weiler, Logan 48 AHC, P, 1968-69
50 Medical Det	Nesbitt, Woody 50 MD, P, 1968
53 Avn Det	Chenoweth, Bob author: BIRTH CONTROL, COST OF LIVING, EASY MONEY, STUMP JUMPER
53 Avn Det	Greenhalgh, Bill 162 AHC, P, 1968-69
53 Avn Det	Greenleaf, Frank, 1966
53 Avn Det	Lundh, Lennart USS *Tripoli*, 1968-69
53 Avn Det	Suggs, Pat son of a Guns A-Go-Go vet, 1966-67
53 Avn Det	Mutza, Wayne author: CRAZY 8, EASY MONEY
53 Avn Det	White, Frank, webmaster, Guns-A-Go-Go
54 Medical Det	Brady, Pat 54 MD, P, 1967-68
54 Medical Det	Dillman, John 54 MD, 1971
54 Medical Det	Hines, Les A-123 Avn Bn, CE, 1968-70
54 Medical Det	Mendez, Ray 1/6 198 Bde, 1970-71
54 Medical Det	Shanahan, Norman 54 MD, P, 1968
54 Medical Det	Stonecipher, Charles 54 MD, P, 1971
54 Medical Det	Wilhite, Ray USAAM
54 Medical Det	Winegard, Wayne 142 TC, 1968
54 Medical Det	Wolak, Steve 178 ASHC, 1970-71
56 Trans Co	Hanley, Dan A-1-1, DG, 1966
56 Trans Co	Heikkila, Dave 56 TC, 1971-72
56 Trans Co	Knight, Emmett 56 TC, P, 1967
56 Trans Co	Lundh, Lennart author: GOOD NATURE, RICE PADDY DADDY
56 Trans Co	Mutza, Wayne historian: RICE PADDY DADDY, WOOLY BULLY
56 Trans Co	Reese, George personal website
56 Trans Co	Royals, Gerald 56 TC, P, 1967
56 Trans Co	Williamson, Rodger 4 Trans Comm, 1966
56 Trans Co	Young, Ralph author: WOOLLY BULLY
57 Assault Hel Co	Blankenship, Calvin 57 AHC, 1970-71
57 Assault Hel Co	Brainard, Charles 57 AHC, P, 70-71
57 Assault Hel Co	Coe, Bob 57 AHC, CE, 1971-72
57 Assault Hel Co	Cox, Jeff 57/114 AHC, P, 1968-69/70-71
57 Assault Hel Co	Davis, Larry author: BUNNY BIRD, MYSTERY SHIP, WITCH DOCTOR RECOVERY
57 Assault Hel Co	Deming, Charles 57 AHC, CE, 1970
57 Assault Hel Co	Demumbreum, Jim 57 AHC, CE, 1971-72
57 Assault Hel Co	Dille, Kim 57 AHC, CE, 1971-72
57 Assault Hel Co	Frigstad, Ron 57 AHC, P, 1969-70
57 Assault Hel Co	Harlem, Pete author: ALFRED E. NEWMAN
57 Assault Hel Co	Hutson, Greg 189 AHC, 1971-72
57 Assault Hel Co	Lavelle, Allan unk unit, 1971-72
57 Assault Hel Co	Lumpkin, Tom 119 AHC, 1970
57 Assault Hel Co	Mutza, Wayne author: MYSTERY SHIP, TWO BUNNIES
57 Assault Hel Co	Neeley, Gary 57 AHC, P, 1969-70
57 Assault Hel Co	Terry, Don 57 AHC, CE, 1971
57 Assault Hel Co	Terry, Robert 57 AHC, DG, 1972
57 Assault Hel Co	Vogel, Rick 57 AHC, 1971-72
57 Assault Hel Co	Warren, Dale 57 AHC, CE, 1968-69

Name / Entry	Unit
White, John 57 AHC, P, 1968-69	57 Assault Hel Co
Woolley, Bill 57 AHC, CE, 1969-70	57 Assault Hel Co
Franzel, Daryl 57 MD, CE, 1969-70	57 Medical Det
Freeman, Dave 57 MD, P, 1971-72	57 Medical Det
Hughes, Bill 57 MD, Medic, 1965	57 Medical Det
Chenoweth, Bob author: CHICKEN RUNNER	57 Trans Co
Davis, Larry author: TIKI #2, WIMPS	57 Trans Co
Lundh, Lennart author: CHERRY BOY, CHICKEN RUNNER	57 Trans Co
Mutza, Wayne author: TIKI #2	57 Trans Co
Schaefer, Wil 145 CAB medic: 57 TC, 1964	57 Trans Co
Young, Ralph author: BORN TO RAISE HELL, CHATTANOOGA CHOO-CHOO, CHICKEN RUNNER, COMBATTRE CHIEN, THE GOOSE, THE HEDGE HOPPER, LOOSE GOOSE, PIASECKI'S PRACTICAL JOKE, SEXY, TAXPAYER'S REGRET	57 Trans Co
McGuire, John 60 AHC, DG, 1972	60 Assault Hel Co
Bajc, Marko VN War researcher	61 Assault Hel Co
Brisker, Frank 61 AHC, P, 1968-69	61 Assault Hel Co
Vereen, Carl 61 AHC, P, 1968	61 Assault Hel Co
Welsh, Robert 61 AHC, CE, 1969-71	61 Assault Hel Co
Workman, James 150 TC, 1964-65	62 Aviation Co
Dickinson, Dave 62 CAC, CE, 1969-71	62 Corps Avn Co
Hubbard, Rollie 62 CAC, 1970	62 Corps Avn Co
Lawrence, John 62 CAC, 1969-70	62 Corps Avn Co
Martin, Ralph 62 CAC, P, 1969-70	62 Corps Avn Co
Matsuoka, Mitch 62 CAC, DG, 1969	62 Corps Avn Co
Roberts, Jack 62 CAC, P, 1970	62 Corps Avn Co
Russell, Larry B-227 AHB/1 Avn Bde, P, 68-69/71-72	62 Corps Avn Co
Russell, Storm, 62 CAC, DG, 1970	62 Corps Avn Co
Wilson, Frank 62 CAC, P, 1968-70	62 Corps Avn Co
Bajc, Marko VN War researcher	68 Assault Hel Co
Brown, Robert 68 AHC, P, 1965-66	68 Assault Hel Co
Cady, Ray 68 AHC, CE, 1966-67	68 Assault Hel Co
DeVarennes, Ed 118 AHC, 1968	68 Assault Hel Co
Green, Dave 68 AHC, CE, 1968	68 Assault Hel Co
Harris, Edwin 68 AHC, P, 1965-66	68 Assault Hel Co
Honl, Jim III Corps Advisor, 1968	68 Assault Hel Co
Horning, Bob 68 AHC, DG, 1968	68 Assault Hel Co
Hufford, Kent 68 AHC, P, 1967-68	68 Assault Hel Co
Kanakaris, George 68 AHC, DG, 1965-66	68 Assault Hel Co
Lemner, Dennis 68 AHC, DG, 1969	68 Assault Hel Co
Livings, Jim 68 AHC, Armorer/DG, 1966-68	68 Assault Hel Co
Noyes, Ralph 68 AHC, CE, 1967-68	68 Assault Hel Co
Packard, Ernie 68 AHC, CE, 1967-68	68 Assault Hel Co
Pedigo, Bob 68 AHC, P, 1970-71	68 Assault Hel Co
Platacis, Andrew 68 AHC, 1965-66	68 Assault Hel Co
Poston, Jamie 68 AHC, CE, 1966-67	68 Assault Hel Co
Robertson, Gary 68 AHC, CE, 1967-68	68 Assault Hel Co
Rodgers, Jim 68 AHC, P, 1965-66	68 Assault Hel Co
Seifert, Bill, 68 AHC, P, 1970	68 Assault Hel Co
Smith, Howard 68 AHC, P, 1969-70	68 Assault Hel Co
Stanley, Dave 68 AHC, DG, 1967-68	68 Assault Hel Co
Tompkins, Pat 68 AHC, CE, 1968-69	68 Assault Hel Co
Webster, Geoff 68 AHC, P, 1968-69	68 Assault Hel Co
Telfair, Dan 68 Avn Co, P, 1965-66	68 Avn Co
Young, Ralph author: PINEAPPLE PRINCESS	68 Avn Co
Marshall, Wayne 68 MD, Medic, 1969-70	68 Medical Det
Prince, Carl 68 MD, CE, 1970-71	68 Medical Det
Solis, Carlos 68 MD, Medic, 1970-71	68 Medical Det
Warner, Larry 68 MD, Medic, 1970-71	68 Medical Det
Bartlett, Paul 71 AHC, P, 1967-68	71 Assault Hel Co
Bokkes, Tom 71 AHC, CE, 1970-71	71 Assault Hel Co
Decker, Doug 71 AHC, CE, 1970	71 Assault Hel Co
Flecke, Ned 71 AHC, DG, 1966-67	71 Assault Hel Co
Gary, Roger 71 AHC, CE, 1970	71 Assault Hel Co
Glasco, John 71 AHC, CE, 1970	71 Assault Hel Co

Unit	Contributor
71 Assault Hel Co	Larson, Gary 71 AHC, CE, 1967
71 Assault Hel Co	Martin, Chuck 71AHC, DG, 1970
71 Assault Hel Co	Mateyko, John 71 AHC/A-501 Avn Co, P, 1965-66
71 Assault Hel Co	McPherran, Paul 71 AHC/A-501 Avn Co, CE, 1965-66
71 Assault Hel Co	Miller, Jim 71 AHC, P, 1968
71 Assault Hel Co	Morris, Arnold 71 AHC, P, 1966-67
71 Assault Hel Co	Priddy, Don 71 AHC, P, 1969-70
71 Assault Hel Co	Pruett, Norm 71 AHC, CE, 1970-71
71 Assault Hel Co	Repak, Pete 71 AHC/A-501 Avn Co, 1965
71 Assault Hel Co	Rogers, Mike 71 AHC, CE, 1967
71 Assault Hel Co	Runnells, Everett 71 AHC/A-501 Avn Co, DG, 1965-66
71 Assault Hel Co	Seabolt, Ron 71 AHC, CE, 1966-67
71 Assault Hel Co	Summers, Glenn 71 AHC/A-501 Avn Co, 1965-66
71 Assault Hel Co	Taylor, Ron 71 AHC, CE, 1970-71
71 Assault Hel Co	Wiederhold, Gerry 71 AHC, 1969
81 Trans Co	Braum, David 81 TC, CE, 1963-64
81 Trans Co	Doucette, Al, 81 TC, DG, 1962
81 Trans Co	Fisher, Harry 81 TC, 1962-63
81 Trans Co	McGarrett, Buddy 81 TC, CE, 1962-63
82 Medical Det	Cahill, David 82 MD, Medic, 1969-70
82 Medical Det	Hughes, Bill 57 MD, Medic, 1964-65
82 Medical Det	Livingston, Del 82 MD, P, 1968-69
82 Medical Det	Mock, Robert, 57 MD, P, 1964-65
82 Medical Det	Mueller, Richard 82 MD, Medic, 1964-65
82 Medical Det	Ruckhaber, Fred 82 MD, Medic, 1968-70
82 Medical Det	Sylvester, Ernie 57 MD, P, 1964-65
92 Assault Hel Co	Boyd, John 92 AHC, P, 1971
92 Assault Hel Co	Broussard, Harry 92 AHC, P, 1967-68
92 Assault Hel Co	Bynum, Ty 92 AHC, P, 1968-69
92 Assault Hel Co	Calaway, Joe 92 AHC, CE, 1968-69
92 Assault Hel Co	Dilworth, Vinnie 92 AHC, CE, 1968-69
92 Assault Hel Co	Fletcher, Ray 92 AHC, CE 1968-70
92 Assault Hel Co	Fowler, Larry 92 AHC, CE, 1970-71
92 Assault Hel Co	Gustafson, John 92 AHC, DG, 1968
92 Assault Hel Co	Hair, Ed 173 Abn, 1968
92 Assault Hel Co	Harmon, Dave 92 AHC, DG, 1967-68
92 Assault Hel Co	Harms, Fred 92 AHC, P, 1967-68
92 Assault Hel Co	Herndon, Bob 92 AHC, CE, 1967-68
92 Assault Hel Co	Heyn, Jim 92 AHC, CE, 1967-68
92 Assault Hel Co	Koch, Jim 92 AHC, P, 1967-68
92 Assault Hel Co	Lambert, Morris 92 AHC, CE, 1970-71
92 Assault Hel Co	Lundh, Lennart USS *Tripoli*, 1968-69
92 Assault Hel Co	McCarthy, John 92 AHC, P, 1971
92 Assault Hel Co	Mignard, Rob 92 AHC, P, 1969-70
92 Assault Hel Co	Palmer, Mike 92 AHC, P, 1968-69
92 Assault Hel Co	Paull, John 92 AHC, P, 1968-70
92 Assault Hel Co	Robie, Bill 92 AHC, P, 1968-69
92 Assault Hel Co	Stewart, Bob 92 AHC, CE, 1967-68
92 Assault Hel Co	Thompson, Ken 92 AHC, CE, 1969-70
92 Assault Hel Co	Tucker, Tom 92 AHC, CE, 1967-68
92 Assault Hel Co	Turner, Denny 92 AHC, P, 1968-69
92 Assault Hel Co	Valentine, Jerry 92 AHC, DG, 1969-70
92 Assault Hel Co	Walters, Rick 92 AHC, CE, 1967-68
92 Assault Hel Co	Yee, Brian 92 AHC, CE, 1968-69
92 Assault Hel Co	Young, Ralph 54 Gen Suppt Gp, 1968-69
92 Assault Hel Co	Zaletskis, John 92 AHC, CE, 1968-69
93 Trans Co	O'Neil, Joe 93 TC, P, 1962-63
93 Trans Co	Spears, Jon 93 TC, CE, 1963-64
93 Trans Co	Verebely, Bill 93 TC, 1963-64
93 Trans Co	Young, Ralph author: DROOPY
114 Assault Hel Co	Akin, Joe 114 AHC, CE, 1970-71
114 Assault Hel Co	Alcott, Ron 28 Sig Det, DG, 1965-66
114 Assault Hel Co	Alfano, Joe 114 AHC, P, 1971-72
114 Assault Hel Co	Anzalone, Tony 114 AHC, CE, 1967-68
114 Assault Hel Co	Baker, Bob 114 AHC, P, 1970-71
114 Assault Hel Co	Baruz, Howard 114 AHC, CE, 1964-65
114 Assault Hel Co	Bernstein, Jonathan author: VC BIRTH CONTROL
114 Assault Hel Co	Brennan, John 114 AHC, Flt Opns, 1970-71
114 Assault Hel Co	Butler, Bruce 114 AHC, P, 1971-72
114 Assault Hel Co	Carr, Jeff 114 AHC, P, 1969-70
114 Assault Hel Co	Cataldo, Nick 114 AHC, Svc Plt, 1969-70
114 Assault Hel Co	Chambers, Howard 114 AHC, CE, 1965-66
114 Assault Hel Co	Chenoweth, Bob author: ROAD SERVICE III
114 Assault Hel Co	Chenoweth, Bob 4 TC/120 AHC/58 Avn Det, CE, 1967-68
114 Assault Hel Co	Codney, Bob 114 AHC, P, 1969-71

114 Assault Hel Co	Coe, Don 114 AHC, P, 1970-71
114 Assault Hel Co	Conley, Carl 114 AHC, P, 1970
114 Assault Hel Co	Cox, Jeff 57/114 AHC, P, 1968-69/70-71
114 Assault Hel Co	Crisp, Carl 114 AHC, CE, 1969-70
114 Assault Hel Co	Davis, Robert 114 AHC, CE, 1964-65
114 Assault Hel Co	Dell, Terry 114 AHC, CE, 1969-70
114 Assault Hel Co	DeSimone, Tom 114 AHC, P, 1969-70
114 Assault Hel Co	Duerr, Dick 114 AHC, P, 1966-67
114 Assault Hel Co	Dunn, Wes 114 AHC, CE, 1964
114 Assault Hel Co	Espinoza, Eddie 114 AHC, CE, 1971-72
114 Assault Hel Co	Evans, Parker 114 AHC, DG, 1967-68
114 Assault Hel Co	Flis, Larry 114 AHC, CE, 19 66-67
114 Assault Hel Co	Ford, Dan author: KAMAAINA, MAUI GIRL, PINEAPPLE PRINCESS
114 Assault Hel Co	Gendron, Roger 114 AHC, CE, 1969-70
114 Assault Hel Co	Gibbs, Charles 114 AHC, Chaplain, 1966
114 Assault Hel Co	Gilpin, Mike 114 AHC, P, 1971-72
114 Assault Hel Co	Glasgow, Bill 114 AHC, CE, 1964
114 Assault Hel Co	Gosnell, Jim 114 AHC, DG, 1966-67
114 Assault Hel Co	Gunn, Bruce 114 AHC, P, 1967-68
114 Assault Hel Co	Hadley, Harry 114 AHC, P, 1963-64
114 Assault Hel Co	Hepler, Ed 114 AHC, CE, 1971-72
114 Assault Hel Co	Harlem, Pete author: BEATS WALKIN, COBRA LEAD,, IRON BUTTERFLY III, KING COBRA, MR. LUCKY, ROAD SERVICE III, WAR EAGLE
114 Assault Hel Co	Hepler, Ed 114 AHC, CE, 1971-72
114 Assault Hel Co	Hodges, Harry 114 AHC, P, 19 71-72
114 Assault Hel Co	Hoffman, Bob 114 AHC, P, 19 71-72
114 Assault Hel Co	Holmes, Gordon 114 AHC, DG, 1970-71
114 Assault Hel Co	Hudspeth, Lew 114 AHC, P, 1967-68
114 Assault Hel Co	Huntley, Steve 114 AHC, CE, 1968-69
114 Assault Hel Co	Jensen, Allen 114 AHC, DG, 1966-67
114 Assault Hel Co	Jones, Bailey 114 AHC, P, 1965-66
114 Assault Hel Co	Jones, Gary 114 AHC, P, 1965-66
114 Assault Hel Co	Jones, John VN War researcher
114 Assault Hel Co	King, Boyd 114 AHC, P, 1966-69
114 Assault Hel Co	Kowalczyk, Joe 114 AHC, DG, 1968-69
114 Assault Hel Co	Krumbiegel, Ed 114 AHC, CE, 1967-68
114 Assault Hel Co	Lenning, Don 114 AHC, DG, 1966-67
114 Assault Hel Co	Lucas, Jim author: THE BRAT
114 Assault Hel Co	Lundh, Lennart, USS *Tripoli*, 1968-69
114 Assault Hel Co	Mansfield, Shelby 114 AHC, P, 1969-70
114 Assault Hel Co	Mantanona, Pascual 114 AHC, CE, 1969-70
114 Assault Hel Co	Marzen, Claus 114 AHC, Armorer, 1964-65
114 Assault Hel Co	Mattler, Bill 114 AHC, CE, 1970
114 Assault Hel Co	McChesney, Frank 114 AHC, P, 19 65-66
114 Assault Hel Co	McMullen, Richard 114 AHC, CE, 1969
114 Assault Hel Co	Mesko, Jim author: WAR EAGLE
114 Assault Hel Co	Miller, Robin 114 AHC, P, 1967-68
114 Assault Hel Co	Mirati, Al 114 AHC, P, 1970-71
114 Assault Hel Co	Moe, Jack 114 AHC, CE, 1967-68
114 Assault Hel Co	Mutza, Wayne author: CHUCK CRUSHER II, COBRA'S KILL, EVE OF DESTRUCTION, HOGHEAD I+II, MISS LOU
114 Assault Hel Co	Nichols, John 544 TC/114 AHC, 1965-66
114 Assault Hel Co	O'Grady, George 114 AHC, P, 1965-66
114 Assault Hel Co	O'Hara, Bill 114 AHC/544 TC, P, 1968-69
114 Assault Hel Co	Oliver, Tom 13 CAB, 1965-66
114 Assault Hel Co	Papapietro, Joe 114 AHC, P, 1969-70
114 Assault Hel Co	Patton, Rex 114 AHC, P, 19 64-65
114 Assault Hel Co	Pinther, Evan 114 AHC, DG, 1969-70
114 Assault Hel Co	Potter, Bill 114 AHC, CE, 1968-69
114 Assault Hel Co	Reese, George personal website
114 Assault Hel Co	Richardson, Curtis Lee 114 AHC, Svc Plt, 1966
114 Assault Hel Co	Russell, Bill 114 AHC, P, 1969-70
114 Assault Hel Co	Schoenstein, Paul 114 AHC, CE, 1969-70
114 Assault Hel Co	Schrumpf, Mike 114 AHC, CE, 1966-67
114 Assault Hel Co	Schulte, Brian 114 AHC, DG, 19 68-69
114 Assault Hel Co	Schwanebeck, Gene 114 AHC, CE, 1967-68
114 Assault Hel Co	Sciapiti, Rich 114 AHC, CE, 1968-69
114 Assault Hel Co	Scott, Clyde 114 AHC, P, 1965-66
114 Assault Hel Co	Scott, Richard 114 AHC, DG, 1967-68
114 Assault Hel Co	Sickler, David 114 AHC, P, 1965-66
114 Assault Hel Co	Smalley, Joe 114 AHC, TI, 1967-68
114 Assault Hel Co	Smith, Al 114 AHC, CE, 1970-71
114 Assault Hel Co	Smith, Ken 114 AHC, CE, 1968-69
114 Assault Hel Co	Smith, Lee 114 AHC, CE, 1970-71
114 Assault Hel Co	Smith, Steve 175 AHC, DG, 1969-60

114 Assault Hel Co	Solis, Noel 114 AHC, CE, 1963-64
114 Assault Hel Co	Sprinkle, Jim author: KING COBRA
114 Assault Hel Co	Stanis, John 114 AHC, CE, 1970-71
114 Assault Hel Co	Stogner, Joe 114 AHC, DG, 1970-71
114 Assault Hel Co	Stone, Charlie 114 AHC, P, 1965
114 Assault Hel Co	Strobel, Frank 114 AHC, P, 1969-70
114 Assault Hel Co	Stufflebeem, Charles 114 AHC, Svc Plt, 1971-72
114 Assault Hel Co	Tookmanian, Dan I 114 AHC, TI, 1968-69
114 Assault Hel Co	Vanderwedge, Phil 114 AHC, CE, 1970
114 Assault Hel Co	Visentine, Tom 114 AHC, CE, 1967-68
114 Assault Hel Co	Wagner, Dawn daughter of Ray Rupcic (KIA), P, 1964-65
114 Assault Hel Co	Waters, Dudley, Caribou Assn, 1968
114 Assault Hel Co	Williams, Ron 114 AHC, CE, 1964-65
114 Assault Hel Co	Wilson, Doug 114 AHC, CE, 1969
114 Assault Hel Co	Winslow, Roger 114 AHC, P, 1964-65
114 Assault Hel Co	Young, Ralph author: LYNDA SUE, MIDGE
114 Assault Hel Co	Zehr, Roger 114 AHC, P, 1965-66
116 Assault Hel Co	Bajc, Marko VN War researcher
116 Assault Hel Co	Barlow, Mike 116 AHC, 1970-71
116 Assault Hel Co	Barrera, John 116 AHC, CE, 1970-71
116 Assault Hel Co	Boren, Jim 116 AHC, P, 1967-68
116 Assault Hel Co	Burton, William 116 AHC, CE, 1966-67
116 Assault Hel Co	Byars, Harold 116 AHC/392 TC, P, 1967-68
116 Assault Hel Co	Cathey, George 116 AHC, DG, 1967-70
116 Assault Hel Co	Chavez, Bill 116 AHC, CE, 19 70-71
116 Assault Hel Co	Chenoweth, Bob author: ELVIRA
116 Assault Hel Co	Chenoweth, Bob 4 TC/120 AHC/58 Avn Det, CE, 1967-68
116 Assault Hel Co	Coleman, Mike 116 AHC, P, 1968
116 Assault Hel Co	Curtis, Grant B-1-9, P, 1969-70
116 Assault Hel Co	Davis, Larry author: SLEEZEE DEE
116 Assault Hel Co	Drendel, Lou author: SLEEZEE DEE
116 Assault Hel Co	Farrell, Kirk 116 AHC, P, 1969-71
116 Assault Hel Co	Garcia, Juan 116 AHC, CE, 1970-71
116 Assault Hel Co	Garcia, Santos 116 AHC, CE, 1966-67
116 Assault Hel Co	Hensley, Wes 116 AHC, P, 1971
116 Assault Hel Co	Hutson, Darrell 116 AHC, DG, 1969-71
116 Assault Hel Co	Johnson, Dan 116 AHC, CE, 1967-68
116 Assault Hel Co	Kerchenfaut, Steve 176 AHCP, 1969-71
116 Assault Hel Co	Linder, Laurie 116 AHC, DG/CE, 1967-68
116 Assault Hel Co	Lucky, James, unk unit, P, 1967
116 Assault Hel Co	McAdams, Dave 116 AHC, P, 1967-68
116 Assault Hel Co	McDaniel, Jim 116 AHC, P, 1971
116 Assault Hel Co	Mendez, Ray 1/6 198 Bde, 1970-71
116 Assault Hel Co	Merrill, Dan 116 AHC, 1969-70
116 Assault Hel Co	Mikulan, Mik 116 AHC, P, 1969
116 Assault Hel Co	Miller, Harlan 116 AHC, CE, 1970
116 Assault Hel Co	Morhland, Rick 116 AHC, CE, 1967-68
116 Assault Hel Co	Nadal, Hector, Army photog, 1968
116 Assault Hel Co	Nancarrow, Dave 116 AHC, CE, 1968-69
116 Assault Hel Co	Pearson, Robert 116 AHC, CE, 1968-69
116 Assault Hel Co	Pickett, Larry 116 AHC, P, 1970-71
116 Assault Hel Co	Piper, Dennis 116 AHC, P, 1969-70
116 Assault Hel Co	Reese, George personal website
116 Assault Hel Co	Ronan, Pat 116 AHC, P, 1968-69
116 Assault Hel Co	Ryan, Terry 116 AHC, CE, 1970-71
116 Assault Hel Co	Salger, Glenn 116 AHC, P, 1970
116 Assault Hel Co	Skarda, Joe 116 AHC, DG, 1968-69
116 Assault Hel Co	Slate, Dennis 116 AHC, DG, 1967-68
116 Assault Hel Co	Tindall, Larry 116 AHC, P, 1970
116 Assault Hel Co	Tyler, Thomas 116 AHC, P, 1970-71
116 Assault Hel Co	Waskom, Joe C-2-27 Wolfhounds, 1969
117 Assault Hel Co	Aeilts, Mike 117 AHC, CE, 1969-70
117 Assault Hel Co	Alleger, Keith 117 AHC, P, 1968-69
117 Assault Hel Co	Atwood, Walt 117 AHC, P, 1966-67
117 Assault Hel Co	Bajc, Marko VN War researcher
117 Assault Hel Co	Balfrey, Roger 117 AHC, CE, 1970-71
117 Assault Hel Co	Barrie, Jim 117 AHC, CE, 1970-71
117 Assault Hel Co	Bascom, Don 117 AHC, CE, 1967
117 Assault Hel Co	Behm, Chris 117 AHC, CE, 1971
117 Assault Hel Co	Bennett, Allen 117 AHC, DG/CE, 1967-68
117 Assault Hel Co	Bennett, Bob 117 AHC, 1969-70
117 Assault Hel Co	Boothe, Riley 117 AHC, P, 1968-69
117 Assault Hel Co	Boyd, Barc 8TC/117 AHC, P, 1962-63
117 Assault Hel Co	Bradley, Lee 117 AHC, CE, 1970-71
117 Assault Hel Co	Bynum, Tom 117 AHC, DG, 1967-68
117 Assault Hel Co	Carter, Tommy 117 AHC, CE, 1965-66
117 Assault Hel Co	Coleman, Ron 117 AHC, P, 1966-67
117 Assault Hel Co	Collins, George 117 AHC, P, 1964-65

117 Assault Hel Co	Cucchiara, Tony 117 AHC, CE, 1971	117 Assault Hel Co	Peterson, Pat 117 AHC, 1971
117 Assault Hel Co	Curtis, Grant B-1-9, P, 1969-70	117 Assault Hel Co	Pike, Bob 117 AHC, 1963-64
117 Assault Hel Co	Dalton, Daily 117 AHC, CE, 1963-64	117 Assault Hel Co	Roberts, Jack 117 AHC, P, 1967
117 Assault Hel Co	Davis, Jim 117 AHC, DG, 1964	117 Assault Hel Co	Rose, Tom 117 AHC, CE, 1963
117 Assault Hel Co	Davis, Larry author: HEAVY, MOTOWN, STUMP JUMPER	117 Assault Hel Co	Scales, Ken 117 AHC, CE 1970-71
		117 Assault Hel Co	Smith, Tom 117 AHC, CE, 1971-72
117 Assault Hel Co	Deady, Michael 117 AHC, P, 1968-70	117 Assault Hel Co	Stewart, Gary 117 AHC, CE, 1971
117 Assault Hel Co	DeCook, Phil A-3-5, 1967	117 Assault Hel Co	Stewart, Tim 117 AHC, 1966-67
117 Assault Hel Co	Douglas, Mike 117 AHC, P, 1968-69	117 Assault Hel Co	Sura, Richard 117 AHC, DG, 1967-68
117 Assault Hel Co	Drendel, Lou author: MOTOWN, STUMP JUMPER	117 Assault Hel Co	Tooke, Pat 117 AHC, CE, 169-70
		117 Assault Hel Co	Vogel, Carl 117 AHC, P, 1964-65
117 Assault Hel Co	Duke, Harry 117 AHC, DG, 1970-71	117 Assault Hel Co	Wade, Jim 117 AHC, P, 1971-72
117 Assault Hel Co	Dutson, Dick 117 AHC, P, 1970	117 Assault Hel Co	Whitt, Eugene 117 AHC, P, 1968-69
117 Assault Hel Co	Duvall, Tom 117 AHC, DG, 1967	117 Assault Hel Co	Wood, Dennis 117 AHC, CE, 1965-66
117 Assault Hel Co	Elliott, Robert 117 AHC, P, 1967-68	117 Assault Hel Co	Young, Ralph author: THE HUNTER, KARIN, SWAMP FOX 2
117 Assault Hel Co	Fenton, Bryan 117 AHC, 1964-65		
117 Assault Hel Co	Fink, Al, 195 AHC, P, 1968-69		
117 Assault Hel Co	Flores, Oscar 117 AHC, CE, 1969-70	118 Assault Hel Co	Armstrong, Jack 118 AHC, P, 1966
117 Assault Hel Co	Gallegos, John 117 AHC, CE, 1964-66	118 Assault Hel Co	Austin, Harold 118 AHC, DG, 1965
117 Assault Hel Co	Goodwin, Paul 117 AHC, CE, 1971-72	118 Assault Hel Co	Badgley, James 118 AHC, P, 1970
117 Assault Hel Co	Gross, Fred 8 TC/117 AHC/8 TC, DG, 1963	118 Assault Hel Co	Bajc, Marko VN War researcher
117 Assault Hel Co	Hamilton, Robert 117 AHC, P, 1970-71	118 Assault Hel Co	Beck, Paul 33 TC/118 AHC, CE, 1962-63
117 Assault Hel Co	Hines, Joe 117 AHC, P, 1968-69	118 Assault Hel Co	Boyce, John 118 AHC, DG, 1965
117 Assault Hel Co	Hudak, Ron 117 AHC, P, 1965-66	118 Assault Hel Co	Brandt, Bob author: THE GREAT GREEN SPECKLED BIRD, JELLY BELLY
117 Assault Hel Co	Kayfus, Bill 117 AHC, 1965-67		
117 Assault Hel Co	Kopperude, Mike 117 AHC, CE, 1971-72	118 Assault Hel Co	Breaux, Michael 118 AHC, 1969-71
117 Assault Hel Co	Laroue, Butch 117 AHC, P, 1967-68	118 Assault Hel Co	Bryant, William 118 AHC, P, 1970-71
117 Assault Hel Co	Lemons, Dennis 117 AHC, P, 1970-71	118 Assault Hel Co	Burkhalter, Darrell 118 AHC, P, 1970
117 Assault Hel Co	Mano, Matt 117 AHC, DG, 1971-72	118 Assault Hel Co	Davis, Larry author: LOAD MASTER
117 Assault Hel Co	Marling, Pat D-1-12 Cav, Medic, 1971	118 Assault Hel Co	Drendel, Lou author: LOAD MASTER, POLLUTION IV
117 Assault Hel Co	Melton, Ron 117 AHC, DG, 1965-66		
117 Assault Hel Co	Miller, Earl 117 AHC, CE, 1971	118 Assault Hel Co	Evans, Dave 118 AHC, DG, 1968-69
117 Assault Hel Co	Mruczkowski, Leon 8 TC/117 AHC, CE, 1962	118 Assault Hel Co	Ferrara, John 118 AHC, CE, 1968-69
117 Assault Hel Co	Murray, Norbert 117 AHC, DG, 1965-66	118 Assault Hel Co	Fisher, Joe, 190 AHC, CE, 1969-70
117 Assault Hel Co	Mutza, Wayne author: FIGHTING FIFTH, HEAVY, ON THE PROWL, PURE SEX, STUMP JUMPER, WILD WILLIE'S TAXI	118 Assault Hel Co	George, Warren 118 AHC, P, 1965-66
		118 Assault Hel Co	Griffin, Jim 118 AHC, P, 19 65-66
		118 Assault Hel Co	Hansen, Lanny 118 AHC, CE, 1967
117 Assault Hel Co	O'Malley, Jack 117 AHC, DG, 1967-68	118 Assault Hel Co	Larson, Walter 33 TC, P, 1962-63
117 Assault Hel Co	Peters, Greg 117 AHC, 1971-72	118 Assault Hel Co	Little, Richard 118 AHC, CE, 1966-67

Unit	Contributor
118 Assault Hel Co	Long, Willis 118 AHC, 1966-68
118 Assault Hel Co	Lundh, Lennart USS *Tripoli*, 1968-69
118 Assault Hel Co	Lyons, Rocklin 118 AHC, P, 1971
118 Assault Hel Co	Matheny, Pat 118 AHC, CE, 1965-66
118 Assault Hel Co	Michalkiewicz, Joe 118 AHC, P, 1967-68
118 Assault Hel Co	Milan, Charlie 118 AHC, P, 1966-67
118 Assault Hel Co	Moore, Dale 118 AHC, P, 1968-70
118 Assault Hel Co	Morley, Thomas 118 AHC, P, 1969-70
118 Assault Hel Co	Mutza, Wayne author: LOAD MASTER, MISS MINI
118 Assault Hel Co	Ness, John 33 TC, P, 1962-63
118 Assault Hel Co	Norton, Dave 118 AHC, CE, 1969-70
118 Assault Hel Co	Payne, Tom 118 AHC, P, 1966-67
118 Assault Hel Co	Rissman, Dick 118 AHC, 1968-69
118 Assault Hel Co	Robertson, John 118 AHC, P, 1968-69
118 Assault Hel Co	Roof, Don 118 AHC, CE, 1965-66
118 Assault Hel Co	Ronning, Garrett 118 AHC, P, 1969
118 Assault Hel Co	Simpson, Ken 118 AHC, DG, 1970-71
118 Assault Hel Co	Springer, Robert 118 AHC, 1969-70
118 Assault Hel Co	Thornton, Tom 118 AHC, P, 1965-66
118 Assault Hel Co	Trommatter, Jim 118 AHC, CE, 1965-66
118 Assault Hel Co	Williams, Bob 118 AHC, CE, 1970
118 Assault Hel Co	Williams, Tony 118 AHC, CE, 1969-70
118 Assault Hel Co	Wilson, Doug 114 AHC, CE, 1969
118 Assault Hel Co	Wilhite, Ray USAAM
118 Assault Hel Co	Wizard, Brian 118 AHC, DG, 1968-69
118 Assault Hel Co	Wrinkle, Bob 118 AHC, P, 1968-69
118 Assault Hel Co	Young, Ralph 54 Gen Suppt Gp, 1968-69
119 Assault Hel Co	Brader, Carl 119 AHC, CE, 1970
119 Assault Hel Co	Braum, Dave 119 AHC, CE, 1963-64
119 Assault Hel Co	Carroll, Eugene 119 AHC, 1968-69
119 Assault Hel Co	Coombs, Ed 119 AHC, P, 1965-66
119 Assault Hel Co	Corbin, Ron 119 AHC, P, 1967
119 Assault Hel Co	Cosgriff, Joe 119 AHC, P, 1969-70
119 Assault Hel Co	Curran, Mike 119 AHC, 1968-69
119 Assault Hel Co	Doucette, Al, 81 TC, DG, 1962
119 Assault Hel Co	Drury, Doug 119 AHC, P, 1967-68
119 Assault Hel Co	Dunstan, Simon author: THE MAD IRISHMAN
119 Assault Hel Co	Fisher, Harry 81 TC, 1962-63
119 Assault Hel Co	Hayes, Larry 119 AHC, 1968-69
119 Assault Hel Co	Harrison, Richard 119 AHC, CE, 1967-68
119 Assault Hel Co	Herring, Mark 119 AHC, CE, 1969-70
119 Assault Hel Co	Kilpatrick, Bob 119 AHC, CE, 1969
119 Assault Hel Co	Kline, Joe B-101, CE, 1970-71
119 Assault Hel Co	Leirer, Richard 170 AHC, DG, 1967-68
119 Assault Hel Co	Lumpkin, Tom, 119 AHC, Avionics, 1970
119 Assault Hel Co	Lundh, Lennart author: THE MAD IRISHMAN
119 Assault Hel Co	McGarrett, Buddy 81 TC, CE, 1962-63
119 Assault Hel Co	Mixer, Al 119 AHC, CE, 1969-70
119 Assault Hel Co	Olive, Merv 119 AHC, P, 1969-70
119 Assault Hel Co	Olson, Rich 119 AHC, P, 1967
119 Assault Hel Co	Pilat, George 119 AHC, P, 1967-68
119 Assault Hel Co	Ramirez, Fidencio 119 AHC, P, 1969-70
119 Assault Hel Co	Saufley, Jim 119 AHC, P, 1969-70
119 Assault Hel Co	Schmitz, Paul 119 AHC, CE, 1968
119 Assault Hel Co	Taylor, Rob 119 AHC, P, 1966-67
119 Assault Hel Co	Torres, Jose 119 AHC, P, 1969-70
119 Assault Hel Co	Touchstone, Gene 119 AHC, 1969
119 Assault Hel Co	Walter, Bill 119 AHC, DG, 1965-66
119 Assault Hel Co	Wright, Robert 119 AHC, P, 1965-66
12 Combat Avn Bn	Drendel, Lou author: WHISPERING DEATH
120 Assault Hel Co	Arruda, Larry 120 AHC, CE, 1964-65
120 Assault Hel Co	Brown, Dave 120 AHC, CE, 1967-68
120 Assault Hel Co	Davis, Larry author: TIKI #2, WIMPS
120 Assault Hel Co	Iglesias, Pete 120 AHC, CE, 1968
120 Assault Hel Co	Kanakaris, George 120 AHC/98 TC, DG, 1965-66
120 Assault Hel Co	Lundh, Lennart author: CHERRY BOY, CHICKEN RUNNER
120 Assault Hel Co	McDougal, John 120 AHC, CE, 1965-66
120 Assault Hel Co	Miller, Bob 120 AHC, 1967-68
120 Assault Hel Co	Mutza, Wayne author: TIKI #2
120 Assault Hel Co	Patterson, Lynn A/101 Avn Co, 1965-66
120 Assault Hel Co	Schaefer, Wil 145 CAB Medic, 1964
121 Assault Hel Co	Bajc, Marko VN War researcher
121 Assault Hel Co	Beech, Mike 121 AHC, P, 1965
121 Assault Hel Co	Burke, Ray 121 AHC, CE, 1970
121 Assault Hel Co	Chinnery, Philip author: THE GOOD WIDOW MRS JONES, TIGER SURPRISE

U.S. ARMY HELICOPTER NAMES IN VIETNAM

121 Assault Hel Co	Chenoweth, Bob author: BLITZ-KRIEG	128 Assault Hel Co	Angeles, Dan 128 AHC, DG, 1969-70
121 Assault Hel Co	Cunningham, Dave 121 AHC, P, 1966-67	128 Assault Hel Co	Bajc, Marko VN War researcher
121 Assault Hel Co	Davis, Larry author: CHERRY BUSTER, THE GOOD WIDOW MRS JONES, THUMPER, THE YELLOW ROSE OF TEXAS	128 Assault Hel Co	Bary, Victor 11 CAB, 1967
		128 Assault Hel Co	Bowser, Dan 128 AHC, P, 1970-71
		128 Assault Hel Co	Brimmer, Vic 128 AHC, P, 1969-70
121 Assault Hel Co	Dowler, Gary 121 AHC, P, 1966-67	128 Assault Hel Co	Coffman, Wes 128 AHC, P, 1970-71
121 Assault Hel Co	Drendel, Lou author: CHERRY BUSTER, THE GOOD WIDOW MRS JONES, THUMPER, THE YELLOW ROSE OF TEXAS	128 Assault Hel Co	Cox, Jeff 57/114 AHC, P, 1968-69/70-71
		128 Assault Hel Co	Davis, Larry author: BITS + PIECES
		128 Assault Hel Co	Decker, Charles 128 AHC, P, 1966-67
121 Assault Hel Co	Drone, Chuck 121 AHC, CE, 1967-68	128 Assault Hel Co	Doud, Jerry 128 AHC, DG, 1969
121 Assault Hel Co	Eastman, David author, 175 AHC, P, 1967: VIKING SURPRISE	128 Assault Hel Co	Drendel, Lou author: BITS + PIECES
		128 Assault Hel Co	Dubaj, Paul 128 AHC, CE, 1970
121 Assault Hel Co	Eneix, Lowell 121 AHC, P, 1967-68	128 Assault Hel Co	Ewing, Ed 128 AHC, P, 1968-69
121 Assault Hel Co	Hogan, Jeremy, professional photographer	128 Assault Hel Co	Ferrigan, Tom 128 AHC, P, 1969-70
121 Assault Hel Co	Huffman, Bill 121 AHC, CE, 1966	128 Assault Hel Co	Gladwell, Herbert 128 AHC, CE, 1968-69
121 Assault Hel Co	Jackson, Don 121 AHC, CE, 1966-68	128 Assault Hel Co	Gray, Charles 128 AHC, 1969-71
121 Assault Hel Co	Koening, Dick 565 TC, P, 1965-66	128 Assault Hel Co	Grimm, Barry 128 AHC, P, 1967
121 Assault Hel Co	Koone, Mike 121 AHC, P, 1968-69	128 Assault Hel Co	Harlem, Pete author: WITCHDOCTOR II
121 Assault Hel Co	Lammers, Fred 121 AHC, CE, 1968	128 Assault Hel Co	Hinson, Bud 539 TC, 1970
121 Assault Hel Co	Lohman, Jim 121 AHC, 1964-65	128 Assault Hel Co	Honara, Mike 128 AHC, P, 1971-72
121 Assault Hel Co	Lowden, Milton 121 AHC, 1964	128 Assault Hel Co	Janiec, Jerry 128 AHC, CE 1969-70
121 Assault Hel Co	McCullough, Tim 121 AHC, 1966-68	128 Assault Hel Co	King, Larry 128 AHC, CE, 1967-69
121 Assault Hel Co	McGregor, Wayne 121 AHC, DG, 1969-70	128 Assault Hel Co	Kriegsmann, Karl 128 AHC, P, 1969-70
121 Assault Hel Co	McQuade, Julie daughter of Bill, 121 AHC, P, 1966-67	128 Assault Hel Co	Layton, Russ 128 AHC, CE, 1968-69
		128 Assault Hel Co	Lundh, Lennart USS *Tripoli*, 1968-69
121 Assault Hel Co	Muccianti, George 121 AHC, 1964	128 Assault Hel Co	Mann, Jim 128 AHC, P, 1966-67
121 Assault Hel Co	Mutza, Wayne author: THE YELLOW ROSE OF TEXAS	128 Assault Hel Co	McDonald, Bill 128 AHC, CE, 1966-67
		128 Assault Hel Co	Perry, Jim 15 MB, Avionics, 1967-68
121 Assault Hel Co	O'Neil, Joe 93 TC, 1962-63	128 Assault Hel Co	Rackley, Lawrence 128 AHC, CE, 1967-71
121 Assault Hel Co	Quackenbush, George 121 AHC, P, 1968-69	128 Assault Hel Co	Riseden, Jay 128 AHC, P, 1967-68
121 Assault Hel Co	Radabaugh, Dana 121 AHC, CE, 1967-68	128 Assault Hel Co	Sabatini, Joe 128 AHC, CE, 1971
121 Assault Hel Co	Schmied, John 121 AHC, 1966-67	128 Assault Hel Co	Shields, Alan 128 AHC, CE, 1967-68
121 Assault Hel Co	Shakocius, Mike 121 AHC, P, 1967-68	128 Assault Hel Co	Tracey, Johnson 128 AHC, CE, 1971
121 Assault Hel Co	Smith, John 121 AHC, DG, 1967-69	128 Assault Hel Co	Trumper, Gerry128 AHC, CE, 1966-67
121 Assault Hel Co	Thomas, Rick 121 AHC, P, 1968-70	128 Assault Hel Co	Ulrich, Don 128 AHC, P, 1971-72
121 Assault Hel Co	Tunnell, Rodger 121 AHC, P, 1969-70	128 Assault Hel Co	Vanbenthusen, Eric 128 AHC, 19 65-67
121 Assault Hel Co	Verebely, Bill 93 TC, 1963-64	128 Assault Hel Co	Ward, Dennis 128 AHC, CE, 1968-70
121 Assault Hel Co	West, Gary 121 AHC, 1968	128 Assault Hel Co	Waugh, Mike 128 AHC, P, 1971-72
121 Assault Hel Co	Wilhite, Ray USAAM	128 Assault Hel Co	Wilks, Jim 128 AHC, CE, 1967-68
121 Assault Hel Co	Young, Ralph author: DROOPY	128 Assault Hel Co	Williams, James 128 AHC, 1965-67

Unit	Contributor
128 Assault Hel Co	Zubrinic, Ed 128 AHC, CE, 1968-70
129 Assault Hel Co	Adams, Leo 129 AHC, CE, 1970
129 Assault Hel Co	Alexander, Jack 129 AHC, P, 1970
129 Assault Hel Co	Alvis, Fred 129 AHC, DG, 1971
129 Assault Hel Co	Barbee, Karl 129 AHC, P, 1967
129 Assault Hel Co	Buller, Larry 129 AHC, CE, 1972
129 Assault Hel Co	Burnett, Randy 129 AHC, CE, 1966-68
129 Assault Hel Co	Casey, Matt 129 AHC, CE, 1970
129 Assault Hel Co	England, Rick 129 AHC, CE, 1968-69
129 Assault Hel Co	Foster, Arthur 129 AHC, CE, 1970-7
129 Assault Hel Co	Jackson, Larry 129 AHC, CE, 1968-69
129 Assault Hel Co	Jeanes, Bill 129 AHC, P, 1972-73
129 Assault Hel Co	Lackey, Larry 129 AHC, P, 1971-72
129 Assault Hel Co	Loveday, Frank 129 AHC, CE, 1969-70
129 Assault Hel Co	Masencup, Jim 129 AHC, P, 1970-71
129 Assault Hel Co	McCort, Don 129 AHC, CE, 1971-72
129 Assault Hel Co	Mount, Gary 129 AHC, CE, 1970-71
129 Assault Hel Co	Mutza, Wayne author: FREE AND EASY
129 Assault Hel Co	Nicolich, Joe 129 AHC, CE, 1965-66
129 Assault Hel Co	Powers, Dave 129 AHC, CE, 1971
129 Assault Hel Co	Ragonese, Lou 129 AHC, Svc Plt, 1970
129 Assault Hel Co	Redmon, John 129 AHC, P, 1966-67
129 Assault Hel Co	Reese, George personal website
129 Assault Hel Co	Reeves, George 335 TC, 1966-67
129 Assault Hel Co	Robinson, Lloyd 129 AHC, CE, 1969-70
129 Assault Hel Co	Sale, David 128 AHC, P, 1966-67
129 Assault Hel Co	Sartor, John 129 AHC, CE, 1969-70
129 Assault Hel Co	Smith, Ron 129 AHC, P, 1969-70
129 Assault Hel Co	Stokes, Larry 129 AHC, CE, 1972-73
129 Assault Hel Co	Stymerski, John 483 CAMS, USAF, 1968-69
129 Assault Hel Co	Swanson, Barry 129 AHC, CE, 1972-73
129 Assault Hel Co	Vega, Tony 129 AHC, CE, 1971
129 Assault Hel Co	Wilhite, Ray USAAM
129 Assault Hel Co	Wolf, Bill 129 AHC, CE, 1969-70
129 Assault Hel Co	Woodward, Gary 129 AHC, CE, 19 71-72
13 Combat Avn Bn	Bell, Carl C-3-17, P, 1972
131 Surveillance Avn Co	Davis, Larry author: THE IRISH-EAGLE, IRON SPUD
131 Surveillance Avn Co	Love, Terry, 1 Sig Bde, 1966-68
131 Surveillance Avn Co	Lundh, Lennart author: THE IRISH EAGLE, IRON SPUD
132 Assault Support Hel Co	Aleshire, Gordon 132 ASHC, FE, 1970
132 Assault Support Hel Co	Brackendoff, Robert 174 AHC/409 TC, 1970-71
132 Assault Support Hel Co	Chesser, Ben 132 ASHC, 1968
132 Assault Support Hel Co	Davis, Clarke 132 ASHC, 1970-71
132 Assault Support Hel Co	Davis, Larry author: FOXY LADY, THE VIRGIN HUNTER
132 Assault Support Hel Co	Gatliff, Ben 132 ASHC, CE, 1970-71
132 Assault Support Hel Co	Heminger, Dave 132 ASHC, P, 1969-70
132 Assault Support Hel Co	Hines, Les A-123 Avn Bn, CE, 1968-70
132 Assault Support Hel Co	Holbert, Craig 132 ASHC, 1970-71
132 Assault Support Hel Co	Lien, Terry 132 ASHC, FE, 1968-69
132 Assault Support Hel Co	McDonald, Monte 132 ASHC, FE, 1970
132 Assault Support Hel Co	McRae, Bill 132 ASHC, P, 1970-71
132 Assault Support Hel Co	Moist, Gary 132 ASHC, FE, 1968
132 Assault Support Hel Co	Mutza, Wayne author: THE VIRGIN HUNTER
132 Assault Support Hel Co	Nawrot, Bill 132 ASHC, 1969-70
132 Assault Support Hel Co	Nichols, Dave 610 TC, DG, 1969
132 Assault Support Hel Co	Pearlstein, Mark 132 ASHC, DG, 1969-70
132 Assault Support Hel Co	Seeger, Larry 132 ASHC, P, 1970-71
132 Assault Support Hel Co	Semanek, Jim 132 ASHC, P, 1970
132 Assault Support Hel Co	Taglauer, Richard A-4-77 ARA, 1970-71
132 Assault Support Hel Co	Van Rope, Jeff 132 ASHC, P, 1968
132 Assault Support Hel Co	Wadginski, Francis 132 ASHC, P, 1971
134 Assault Hel Co	Berg, Jerry 134 AHC, CE, 1968-69
134 Assault Hel Co	Blankenship, Ken 134 AHC, P, 70-71
134 Assault Hel Co	Cowan, Jean 134th AHC Assn Associate
134 Assault Hel Co	Dye, Roger 134 AHC, DG, 1970-71
134 Assault Hel Co	Fusilier, Phil 134 AHC, P, 1971
134 Assault Hel Co	Gano, Steve 134 AHC, CE, 1967-68
134 Assault Hel Co	Gorsky, John 134 AHC, CE, 1969-71
134 Assault Hel Co	Heath, Stan 134 AHC, P, 1969-70
134 Assault Hel Co	Kline, Joe B-101, CE, 1970-71
134 Assault Hel Co	Lauritsen, Corky 134 AHC, DG, 1969-70
134 Assault Hel Co	McClain, Nat 134 AHC, CE, 1968-69

134 Assault Hel Co	Merricks, Joe 134 AHC, CE, 1968-69
134 Assault Hel Co	Pettit, Danny 134 AHC, CE, 1968-69
134 Assault Hel Co	Pierce, Roger 134 AHC, CE, 1969-70
134 Assault Hel Co	Poarch, Ron 134 AHC, CE, 1969-70
134 Assault Hel Co	Pointer, Randy 134 AHC, DG, 1968
134 Assault Hel Co	Renz, Karl 134 AHC, CE, 1968-69
134 Assault Hel Co	Rovig, Joe 134 AHC, P, 1970-71
134 Assault Hel Co	Seesions, Dee 134 AHC, CE, 1969-70
134 Assault Hel Co	Smith, James 134 AHC, DG, 1970-71
134 Assault Hel Co	Snyder, Frank 134 AHC, DG, 1968-69
134 Assault Hel Co	Sutphen, Ed 134 AHC, CE, 1970-71
134 Assault Hel Co	Swank, Dan 134 AHC, CE, 1970-71
134 Assault Hel Co	Swickard, Jack 134 AHC, P, 1967-68
134 Assault Hel Co	Torres, Ray 134 AHC, CE, 1969-70
134 Assault Hel Co	Underwood, Hans 134 AHC, CE, 1970-71
134 Assault Hel Co	Webb, John 134 AHC, CE, 1968-69
134 Assault Hel Co	Whitaker, George 134 AHC, P, 1969-70
134 Assault Hel Co	Wilhite, Ray USAAM
134 Assault Hel Co	Wilson, Lucky 134 AHC, P, 1970-71
134 Assault Hel Co	Yerden, Art 134 AHC, DG, 1967-68
135 Assault Hel Co	Abels, Jerry 135 AHC, CE, 1967-68
135 Assault Hel Co	Andreasen, Russell 135 AHC, CE, 1969-7
135 Assault Hel Co	Bratkovic, Robert 135 AHC, P, 1970-71
135 Assault Hel Co	Coleman, Rick 135 AHC, DG, 1967-68
135 Assault Hel Co	Ford, Bob 135 AHC, DG, 1968-69
135 Assault Hel Co	Guard, Mike 135 AHC, CE, 1969-70
135 Assault Hel Co	Mounts, Bob 135 AHC, CE, 1967-68
135 Assault Hel Co	Mowery, Scott 135 AHC, DG, 1969-71
135 Assault Hel Co	Peterson, Mike 135 AHC, CE, 1971-72
135 Assault Hel Co	Ralph, Joe 135 AHC, CE, 1969-70
135 Assault Hel Co	Rogers, John 135 AHC, P, 1968-69
135 Assault Hel Co	Steward, Tom 135 AHC, DG, 1969
135 Assault Hel Co	Staadt, Tom 135 AHC, P, 1969-70
135 Assault Hel Co	Wingrove, James 135 AHC, CE, 1971
145 Airlift Plt	Stanfield, Jerry 145 Airlift Plt, DG, 1965-67
145 Airlift Plt	Young, Ralph author: THE THREE A'S

145 Combat Avn Bn	Breyer, Alex 145 CAB, CE, 1969-70
145 Combat Avn Bn	Chase, Dan 145 CAB, CE, 1969-70
147 Assault Support Hel Co	Bray, Bill 147 ASHC, DG, 1967-68
147 Assault Support Hel Co	Call, Jim 147 ASHC, CE, 1967-68
147 Assault Support Hel Co	Choate, James 147 ASHC, FE, 1967-68
147 Assault Support Hel Co	Coryhell, Newt 147 ASHC, FE, 1966-68
147 Assault Support Hel Co	Davis, Richard 147 ASHC, FE, 1967-68
147 Assault Support Hel Co	Gale, David 147 ASHC, FE, 1967-68
147 Assault Support Hel Co	Fernitz, Manfred 147 ASHC, P, 1967-69
147 Assault Support Hel Co	Fitzgerald, Al 147 ASHC, P, 1969-70
147 Assault Support Hel Co	Friend, Ross 147 ASHC, DG/CE, 1966-67
147 Assault Support Hel Co	Kilborn, David 147 ASHC, CE, 1966-67
147 Assault Support Hel Co	Miller, Melvin 147 ASHC, CE, 1969-70
147 Assault Support Hel Co	Nagel, Sam 147 ASHC, P, 1967-68
147 Assault Support Hel Co	Shivley, Mike 147 ASHC, FE, 1969-70
147 Assault Support Hel Co	Smith, Larry 147 ASHC, FE, 1967-68
155 Assault Hel Co	Acker, Ken 155 AHC, P, 1966-67
155 Assault Hel Co	Austin, Steve 155 AHC, CE, 1966-67
155 Assault Hel Co	Bollens, Al 155 AHC, P, 1968-69
155 Assault Hel Co	Brown, Ken 155 AHC, CE, 1968-69
155 Assault Hel Co	Bundage, Herb 155 AHC/165 TC, 1966-67
155 Assault Hel Co	Byrnes, Ken 155 AHC, CE, 1966-67
155 Assault Hel Co	Chido, Bruce 155 AHC, P, 1967-68\
155 Assault Hel Co	Cranford, Floyd 155 AHC, CE, 1965-66
155 Assault Hel Co	Davison, Les 155 AHC, CE, 1969-70
155 Assault Hel Co	Fadz, Paul 155 AHC, CE, 1966-68
155 Assault Hel Co	Fitzgerald, Al 155 AHC, P, 1966-67
155 Assault Hel Co	Gale, Gary 155 AHC, 1965-66
155 Assault Hel Co	Gardner, Bob 155 AHC, P, 1968-69
155 Assault Hel Co	Gliet, Ed 155 AHC/165 TC, CE, 1965-66
155 Assault Hel Co	Goerig, Pat 155 AHC, P, 1965-66
155 Assault Hel Co	Gordon, Jack 155 AHC, 1966
155 Assault Hel Co	Grant, Carl 155 AHC, 1967-68
155 Assault Hel Co	Grow, John 155 AHC, P, 1966-67
155 Assault Hel Co	Harlem, Pete author: ARES, LUKE
155 Assault Hel Co	Harris, John 155 AHC, CE, 1969-70
155 Assault Hel Co	Hedrick, Herman 155 AHC, CE, 1969-70

Unit	Contributor
155 Assault Hel Co	Hunt, Tom 155 AHC, CE, 1968-69
155 Assault Hel Co	Jones, Lacy 155 AHC, 1966-67
155 Assault Hel Co	Kahler, Doug 155 AHC, 1969-70
155 Assault Hel Co	Kinder, Joe 155 AHC, CE, 1966-69
155 Assault Hel Co	Kottler, Jack 155 AHC, P, 1965-66
155 Assault Hel Co	Lajoie, Dennis 155 AHC, CE, 1968-70
155 Assault Hel Co	Lehman, Phil 155 AHC, P, 1967-68
155 Assault Hel Co	Lundh, Lennart USS *Tripoli*, 1968-69
155 Assault Hel Co	Lundh, Lennart author: LUKE, RIDE A SLICK TO HELL + BACK
155 Assault Hel Co	McRee, Burris 155 AHC/165 TC, DG, 1967-68
155 Assault Hel Co	Meadows, Al 155 AHC, DG, 1970-71
155 Assault Hel Co	Morton, Dan 155 AHC, CE, 1966-67
155 Assault Hel Co	Mosher, Craig 155 AHC, CE, 1965-69
155 Assault Hel Co	Mullen, Tom 155 AHC, DG, 1968-69
155 Assault Hel Co	Mutza, Wayne author: LUKE
155 Assault Hel Co	Petersen, Bradley 155 AHC/165 TC, P, 1967-68
155 Assault Hel Co	Roalofs, Ray 155 AHC, P, 1967
155 Assault Hel Co	Schrader, Jeff 155 AHC, P, 1968-69
155 Assault Hel Co	Smith, Warren 155 AHC/165 TC, 1965
155 Assault Hel Co	Stark, Jim 155 AHC, P, 1970-71
155 Assault Hel Co	Thibodeau, Charles 155 AHC/165 TC, P, 1965-66
155 Assault Hel Co	Wussow, Lloyd 155 AHC, CE, 1968
159 Medical Det	Beson, Jim 159 MD, P, 1969-70
159 Medical Det	Blickenstaff, Jon 159 MD, CE, 1970-71
159 Medical Det	Moy, Innis 159 MD, Medic, 1970-71
159 Medical Det	Mutza, author: LORD OF THE FLIES
161 Assault Hel Co	Hastings, John 161 AHC, CE, 1967-68
161 Assault Hel Co	Lasser, Tom 161 AHC, P, 1967
161 Assault Hel Co	Martin, Wes 161 AHC, 1966-67
161 Assault Hel Co	Old, Roger 161 AHC, P, 1967
161 Assault Hel Co	Peecook, Jeff 161 AHC, P, 1967
162 Assault Hel Co	Arcouette, Ron 162 AHC, 1968-69
162 Assault Hel Co	Bell, George 162 AHC, CE, 1971-72
162 Assault Hel Co	Bray, Eric 162 AHC, P, 1970-71
162 Assault Hel Co	Bryan, Tom 162 AHC, CE, 1968
162 Assault Hel Co	Calderon, Gary 162 AHC, DG, 1968-69
162 Assault Hel Co	Carden, Harold 162 AHC, 1968-69
162 Assault Hel Co	Coletta, Mark 162 AHC, P, 1971-72
162 Assault Hel Co	Dike, Leroy 162 AHC, P, 1970
162 Assault Hel Co	Donahue, Jack 162 AHC, P, 1968-69
162 Assault Hel Co	Gallagher, Mike 162 AHC, DG, 1968
162 Assault Hel Co	Greenhalgh, Bill 162 AHC, P, 1968-69
162 Assault Hel Co	Herdon, Dan 162 AHC, P, 1970
162 Assault Hel Co	Lauffer, George 162 AHC, P, 1971-72
162 Assault Hel Co	Layman, Joe A-229, P, 1971-72
162 Assault Hel Co	Lewis, James 162 AHC, CE, 1971-72
162 Assault Hel Co	Malick, Len 162 AHC, CE, 1971-72
162 Assault Hel Co	McCamish, John 162 AHC, P, 1967-68
162 Assault Hel Co	Mockler, Tom 162 AHC, P, 1967-68
162 Assault Hel Co	Nicholson, Don 162 AHC, P, 1970-71
162 Assault Hel Co	Nieto, Dan 162 AHC, CE, 1969
162 Assault Hel Co	Prine, Jim A-7-1, 1971-72
162 Assault Hel Co	Robertson, Gary 162 AHC, 1966-67
162 Assault Hel Co	Salee, Larry 162 AHC, CE, 1968-69
162 Assault Hel Co	Saunders, David 162 AHC, P, 1968-69
162 Assault Hel Co	Seward, William 162 AHC, CE, 1969-70
162 Assault Hel Co	Spears, Steve 162 AHC, 1968-69
162 Assault Hel Co	Stoehr, Bruce 162 AHC, P, 1967-68
162 Assault Hel Co	Stringer, Floyd, 162 AHC, CE, 1969
162 Assault Hel Co	Tibbers, Jackie 162 AHC, CE, 1971-72
162 Assault Hel Co	Walsh, Ed 162 AHC, CE, 1966-67
162 Assault Hel Co	Weatherly, Mitch 162 AHC, P, 1971-72
162 Assault Hel Co	Weddle, Carl 162 AHC, CE, 1967-68
162 Assault Hel Co	Wilhite, Roy USAAM
165 Trans Co	Koonce, Bob 165 TC, 1965
165 Trans Co	Lund, Pat 165 TC, CE, 1971
170 Assault Hel Co	Hooper, David 170 AHC, CE, 1970-71
170 Assault Hel Co	Jaimes, Jose 170 AHC, CE, 1967-69
170 Assault Hel Co	Kernodle, Charles 170 AHC, P, 1969-70
170 Assault Hel Co	Knight, Gary 170 AHC, P, 1969-70
170 Assault Hel Co	Leirer, Richard 170 AHC, DG, 1967-68
170 Assault Hel Co	Leopold, Bob 170 AHC, P, 1967
170 Assault Hel Co	MacDougall, Doug 170 AHC, P, 1968
170 Assault Hel Co	Mutza, Wayne author: CHUCK YOU FARLIE
170 Assault Hel Co	Reese, George personal website
170 Assault Hel Co	Roy, Tom 170 AHC, P, 1967-68
170 Assault Hel Co	Sanders, Ron 170 AHC, CE, 1969-70
170 Assault Hel Co	Summers, Don 170 AHC, CE, 1969

170 Assault Hel Co	Vitale, Vincent 101 Abn, 1970	173 Assault Hel Co	Wolk, Richie 173 AHC, CE, 1968-69
170 Assault Hel Co	Weaver, Roger 170 AHC, P, 1967-68	173 Assault Hel Co	Zanfardino, Tony 173 AHC, CE, 1966-67
173 Airborne Bde	Bono, Lou, 1968-71	174 Assault Hel Co	Alejandro, John F-8 Cav, DG, 1971
173 Airborne Bde	Brown, Jerry 173 Abn Bde, CE, 1970	174 Assault Hel Co	Bailey, John 174 AHC, P, 1969-70
173 Airborne Bde	Charlton, Don 173 Abn Bde, P, 1969-70	174 Assault Hel Co	Benton, Robin 11 Bde, 1969-70
173 Airborne Bde	Hoza, John 173 Abn Bde, P, 1966-67	174 Assault Hel Co	Berry, Russell A-1-20, 11 LIB, 1970-71
173 Airborne Bde	Kinney 173 Abn Bde, 1969	174 Assault Hel Co	Bordeaux, Joe 174 AHC, CE, 1970
173 Airborne Bde	Klinefelter, Lowell 173 Abn Bde, 1966	174 Assault Hel Co	Brackenhoff, Robert 174 AHC/409 TC, 1970-71
		174 Assault Hel Co	Brown, William 174 AHC, CE, 1969-70
173 Assault Hel Co	Buffington, John 173 AHC	174 Assault Hel Co	Bullen, John 174 AHC, CE, 1970
173 Assault Hel Co	Chenoweth, Bob author: MR. LUCKY	174 Assault Hel Co	Carlson, Fred 174 AHC, CE, 1969-70
173 Assault Hel Co	Combs, Jerry 173 AHC, P, 1967-68	174 Assault Hel Co	Chenoweth, Bob author: EASY RIDER
173 Assault Hel Co	Crow, Dick 173 AHC, P, 1970	174 Assault Hel Co	Clement, Ross 174 AHC, P, 1968-69
173 Assault Hel Co	Gaston, Cliff 173 AHC, P, 1971-72	174 Assault Hel Co	Coffman, Wayne 174 AHC, 1969-70
173 Assault Hel Co	Harbison, Joe 173 AHC, P, 1968-69	174 Assault Hel Co	Collins, Bob 174 AHC, P, 1968
173 Assault Hel Co	Harlem, Pete author: MR. LUCKY	174 Assault Hel Co	Conner, Ron 174 AHC, CE, 1967-69
173 Assault Hel Co	Harton, Bud 173 AHC, CE, 1968	174 Assault Hel Co	Cooper, Harry 174 AHC, CE, 1968
173 Assault Hel Co	Hathaway, Kevin 173 AHC, CE, 1967	174 Assault Hel Co	Davis, Sam 174 AHC, CE, 1967-68
173 Assault Hel Co	Jackson, John 173 AHC, CE, 1967-69	174 Assault Hel Co	Decker, Doug 174 AHC, P, 1971
173 Assault Hel Co	Johnson, Larry 173 AHC, P, 1969	174 Assault Hel Co	Drendel, Lou author: EASY RIDER
173 Assault Hel Co	Kovolesky, Arthur, 173 AHC, CE, 1967-68	174 Assault Hel Co	Elam, Danny 11 LIB, 1969-71
173 Assault Hel Co	Malone, Howard 173 AHC, P, 1966-67	174 Assault Hel Co	Elliott, Butch 174 AHC, P, 70-71
173 Assault Hel Co	Mann, Gary 173 AHC, CE, 1966-67	174 Assault Hel Co	Fisher, Mark 174 AHC, P, 1968-69
173 Assault Hel Co	Matriscians, Dan 173 AHC, CE, 1966-67	174 Assault Hel Co	Garza, Albert 174 AHC, CE, 1970
173 Assault Hel Co	Mutza, Wayne author: FRIAR TUCK, MR. LUCKY	174 Assault Hel Co	Gauby, Tom 174 AHC, CE, 1969
173 Assault Hel Co	Padroza, George 173 AHC, DG, 1968	174 Assault Hel Co	Godbold, Randy 174 AHC, CE, 1971
173 Assault Hel Co	Perkins, Clarence 173 AHC, CE, 1967-68	174 Assault Hel Co	Gomes, Abe 174 AHC, CE, 1971
173 Assault Hel Co	Perrin, Wayne 173 AHC, 1969-70	174 Assault Hel Co	Greenhalgh, Bill 162 AHC, P, 1968-69
173 Assault Hel Co	Politi, Vincent 173 AHC, CE, 1966-67	174 Assault Hel Co	Hahn, Roy 174 AHC, DG, 1971
173 Assault Hel Co	Prevost, Frank 173 AHC, CE, 1968-69	174 Assault Hel Co	Harlem, Pete author: WOODSTOCK
173 Assault Hel Co	Reigel, Jay 173 AHC, DG, 1968-69	174 Assault Hel Co	Hodges, Chris 174 AHC, CE, 1970
173 Assault Hel Co	Revels, Jack 173 AHC, P, 1968-69	174 Assault Hel Co	Jarett, Keith 174 AHC, CE, 1971-72
173 Assault Hel Co	Richardson, Rich 173 AHC, CE, 1967-68	174 Assault Hel Co	Kelly, Thad 174 AHC, 1968-70
173 Assault Hel Co	Sullivan, Pat 173 AHC, CE, 1970-71	174 Assault Hel Co	Liebrandt, Geogg digital artist
173 Assault Hel Co	Taylor, Max 173 AHC, 1968-69	174 Assault Hel Co	Lundh, Lennart author: MEXICAN EXPRESS
173 Assault Hel Co	Ward, Doug 173 AHC, CE, 1967	174 Assault Hel Co	Lutgring, Melvyn 174 AHC, CE, 1971
173 Assault Hel Co	Wilhite, Ray USAAM	174 Assault Hel Co	Magee, Art 174 AHC, P, 1970-71
173 Assault Hel Co	Wilton, Mike 173 AHC, P, 1966-67	174 Assault Hel Co	McDaniel, Jim 174 AHC, P, 1967-68
173 Assault Hel Co	Windsand, Doug 187 AHC, 1970	174 Assault Hel Co	Medeiros, Wayne 174 AHC, CE, 1966-67

174 Assault Hel Co	Messinger, Jim 174 AHC, P, 1967-68
174 Assault Hel Co	Miller, Tom 174 AHC, CE, 1966
174 Assault Hel Co	Mumaw, Carl F-8 Cav, 1969
174 Assault Hel Co	Mutza, Wayne author: MEXICAN EXPRESS
174 Assault Hel Co	Newcomer, Ron 174 AHC, P, 1966-67
174 Assault Hel Co	Nunn, Wally 174 AHC, DG, 1967-68
174 Assault Hel Co	Parker, Dale 174 AHC, CE, 1970-71
174 Assault Hel Co	Pelliccia, Dennis 174 AHC, CE, 1967-68
174 Assault Hel Co	Petty, Tom B-3-1, 1969
174 Assault Hel Co	Price, Walter 174 AHC, DG, 1968-69
174 Assault Hel Co	Ratcliffe, Steve 174 AHC, CE, 1969-70
174 Assault Hel Co	Reinshagen, Tom 174 AHC, P, 1968-69
174 Assault Hel Co	Richardson, Don 174 AHC, CE, 1968
174 Assault Hel Co	Rios, Dave 174 AHC, DG, 1970-71
174 Assault Hel Co	Rosenthal, David 174 AHC, P, 1970
174 Assault Hel Co	Schumacher, Rex 174 AHC, CE, 1970-71
174 Assault Hel Co	Shedd, Jim 174 AHC, CE, 1969-70
174 Assault Hel Co	Sieben, James 174 AHC, CE, 1967-69
174 Assault Hel Co	Silva, Mike F-8 Cav, P, 1970-71
174 Assault Hel Co	Thompson, Fred 174 AHC, P, 1970-71
174 Assault Hel Co	Tuerk, Jerry 174 AHC, DG, 1969-70
174 Assault Hel Co	Whalen, Larry 174 AHC, CE, 1969-70
174 Assault Hel Co	Wilder, Billy 174 AHC, CE, 1971
174 Assault Hel Co	Wilhite, Ray USAAM
174 Assault Hel Co	Wood, Charlie FSB 4-11, D Btry, 1970
175 Assault Hel Co	Aldridge, Dan 199 RAC, P, 1967-68
175 Assault Hel Co	Anderson, Roger 175 AHC, CE, 1967-69
175 Assault Hel Co	Andreoff, Steven 175 AHC, DG, 1970-71
175 Assault Hel Co	Anzalone, Tony 114 AHC, CE, 1967-68
175 Assault Hel Co	Armijo, Ross 175 AHC, CE, 1970-71
175 Assault Hel Co	Barter, William 175 AHC, CE, 1969-70
175 Assault Hel Co	Bean, Jerry 28 Sig Det, 1966
175 Assault Hel Co	Bernard, Vernon 175 AHC, CE, 1967-68
175 Assault Hel Co	Berowski, Ken 175 AHC, 1970-71
175 Assault Hel Co	Chenoweth, Bob author: ACE OF SPADES, LUCKY LEITA
175 Assault Hel Co	Chenoweth, Bob 4 TC/120 AHC/58 Avn Det, CE, 1967-68
175 Assault Hel Co	Claymore, Clay 175 AHC, CE, 1969-70
175 Assault Hel Co	Cowart, Jim 175 AHC, P, 1971
175 Assault Hel Co	Cox, Tim 175 AHC, CE, 1969-70

175 Assault Hel Co	Davis, Larry author: MORNING AFTER, REAPER
175 Assault Hel Co	Donnelly, Jim 175 AHC, DG, 1971-72
175 Assault Hel Co	Eastman, Dave author: BA MOUI BA, BIERE 33 EXPORT, CAT BALLOU, CHECKER CAB, MR.LUCKY, MORNING AFTER, NEGATIVE SUPPRESSION, ROADRUNNER, SATAN'S PLAYMATE, SLOPE CAB, YELLOW CAB
175 Assault Hel Co	Eastman, Dave 175 AHC, P, 1966-67
175 Assault Hel Co	Effenberger, Frank 175 AHC, P, 1970-71
175 Assault Hel Co	England, Norm 175 AHC, P, 1971-72
175 Assault Hel Co	Estes, Frank A-502 Avn Bn, 1966
175 Assault Hel Co	Ferland, Roland 175 AHC, P, 1967-68
175 Assault Hel Co	Fryant, Bill 175 AHC, P, 1970
175 Assault Hel Co	Gaston, Cliff 175 AHC, CE, 1970-71
175 Assault Hel Co	Gray, Steve 175 AHC, Svc Plt, 1967-68
175 Assault Hel Co	Greenfield, Tom 175 AHC, DG, 1967
175 Assault Hel Co	Greve, Dan 175 AHC, P, 1970-71
175 Assault Hel Co	Griffin, Robert, Combat Photographer
175 Assault Hel Co	Haley, Mike 175 AHC, P, 1968-69
175 Assault Hel Co	Harlem, Pete author: BLOOD SWEAT + TEARS, RAPE PILLAGE BURN
175 Assault Hel Co	Hayes, Sam 175 AHC, CE, 1970
175 Assault Hel Co	Herrell, Marty 346 Div Avn Supp, DG, 1967-68
175 Assault Hel Co	Hersey, Mike 175 AHC, P, 1966-67
175 Assault Hel Co	Hoder, Andy 175 AHC, DG, 1968
175 Assault Hel Co	Holmes, Alan 175 AHC, CE, 1966-67
175 Assault Hel Co	Hostetler, Tim 175 AHC, CE, 1968-69
175 Assault Hel Co	Howard, Chuck 175 AHC/150 TC, 1968-69
175 Assault Hel Co	Iannazzo, Dennis 175 AHC, P, 1968-69
175 Assault Hel Co	Isenberg, Don 175 AHC, P, 1968-69
175 Assault Hel Co	Johnson, Alan 28/96 Sig Det, 1966-67
175 Assault Hel Co	Kenna, Mike 175 AHC, DG, 1967-68
175 Assault Hel Co	Kennedy, Tom 175 AHC, CE, 1968-69
175 Assault Hel Co	Keeney, Andrew 175 AHC, P, 1967
175 Assault Hel Co	Khachadourian, Harry 175 AHC, TI, 1971-72
175 Assault Hel Co	Kidd, Mike 175 AHC, CE, 1967-68
175 Assault Hel Co	Koenig, Dick 175 AHC, P, 1967-68
175 Assault Hel Co	Koonce, Ed 150 TC/A-502, CE, 1964-65
175 Assault Hel Co	Last, Daniel 175 AHC, P, 1967-68
175 Assault Hel Co	Law, Tony 175 AHC, Armorer, 1967-68
175 Assault Hel Co	McDowell, Terry 175 AHC, P, 1966-67
175 Assault Hel Co	McGuire, Ed 175 AHC, DG, 1969-70

175 Assault Hel Co	Meana, Richard 175 AHC, P, 1970-71
175 Assault Hel Co	Millward, Bob 175 AHC, P, 1967
175 Assault Hel Co	Mirati, Al 114 AHC, P, 1970-71
175 Assault Hel Co	Mutza, Wayne author: DADDY RABBIT
175 Assault Hel Co	Myhre, Jon 175 AHC, P, 1966-67
175 Assault Hel Co	O'Neill, Joe 175 AHC, P, 1967-68
175 Assault Hel Co	Osborne, David 175 AHC, DG, 1966-67
175 Assault Hel Co	Parsley, Larry 175 AHC, DG, 1966-67
175 Assault Hel Co	Pengov, James 175 AHC, 1970-71
175 Assault Hel Co	Peterson, Roger 175 AHC, CE, 1970-71
175 Assault Hel Co	Pratt, Tom 175 AHC, CE, 1969-70
175 Assault Hel Co	Reese, George personal website
175 Assault Hel Co	Robinson, Cindy, sister of Tom Ivey (KIA), 175 AHC, CE, 1970-71
175 Assault Hel Co	Roth, Ray 175 AHC, DG 1966-67
175 Assault Hel Co	Rozanski, Walter 175 AHC, 1966
175 Assault Hel Co	Sala, Ron 1968, unk personal data
175 Assault Hel Co	Scott, John 175 AHC, DG, 1966-67
175 Assault Hel Co	Shearer, Vance 175 AHC, P, 1967-68
175 Assault Hel Co	Sheldon, Stephen Army photog
175 Assault Hel Co	Smith, Larry 175 AHC, DG, 1966-67
175 Assault Hel Co	Smith, Steven 175 AHC, DG, 1969-70
175 Assault Hel Co	Spiers, Jim 175 AHC, P, 1968-69
175 Assault Hel Co	Stowell, Tom 175 AHC, P, 1969-70
175 Assault Hel Co	Sturgill, Enoc 175 AHC, CE, 1965-66
175 Assault Hel Co	Thayer, Ed 175 AHC, DG, 1966-67
175 Assault Hel Co	Tidd, Bob 175 AHC, DG, 1965-67
175 Assault Hel Co	Timmers, Ed 175 AHC, CE, 1969-70
175 Assault Hel Co	Weber, Jeff 175 AHC, CE, 1968-69
175 Assault Hel Co	Wesselman, Gary 175 AHC, P, 1966-67
175 Assault Hel Co	Westburg, Rick 175 AHC, DG, 1969-70
175 Assault Hel Co	Wilhite, Ray USAAM
175 Assault Hel Co	Williams, Dwayne 175 AHC, P, 1966-67
175 Assault Hel Co	Wilson, Doug A/502, CE, 1965-66:
175 Assault Hel Co	Wininger, Roger 175 AHC, Armorer, 1971-72
175 Assault Hel Co	Workman, James, 175 AHC/150 TC, 1964-65
175 Assault Hel Co	Young, Ralph author: ROADRUNNER
175 Assault Hel Co	Zanetti, Al 175 AHC, DG, 1966-67
176 Assault Hel Co	Baker, David 176 AHC, CE, 1969-70
176 Assault Hel Co	Barron, David 176 AHC, CE, 1967
176 Assault Hel Co	Bigelow, Ken brother of Ralph (KIA), 176 AHC, P, 1969-70
176 Assault Hel Co	Boettger, Tim 176 AHC, CE, 1971
176 Assault Hel Co	Brant, Owen 176 AHC, CE, 1970-71
176 Assault Hel Co	Chenoweth, Bob author: OREGON TAXI
176 Assault Hel Co	Clutter, Ron 176 AHC, CE, 1967-68
176 Assault Hel Co	Davis, Larry author: 1%, VC FOR LUNCH BUNCH
176 Assault Hel Co	Deland, George, EBAY dealer
176 Assault Hel Co	Drendel, Lou author: 1%
176 Assault Hel Co	Fatheree, Chuck 176 AHC, P, 1970-71
176 Assault Hel Co	Gross, Joe 176 AHC, P, 1970
176 Assault Hel Co	Harlem, Pete author: 1%
176 Assault Hel Co	Herrington, Tom 176 AHC, P, 1969-70
176 Assault Hel Co	Hilton, Mike 176 AHC, CE, 1968-69
176 Assault Hel Co	Kerchenfaut, Steve 176 AHC, P, 1969-71
176 Assault Hel Co	Ladd, Roger 176 AHC, P, 1970-71
176 Assault Hel Co	Lambie, Brian 176 AHC, P, 1968-6
176 Assault Hel Co	Lipscomb, Henry 176 AHC, DG, 1971
176 Assault Hel Co	Malwiju, David 176 AHC, DG, 1969
176 Assault Hel Co	Mulcahy, Jim 198 LIB, 1971
176 Assault Hel Co	Mull, Don 176 AHC, CE, 1969-70
176 Assault Hel Co	Mutza, Wayne author: 1%
176 Assault Hel Co	Parris, Mike 176 AHC, DG, 1968-69
176 Assault Hel Co	Phillips, Rick 176 AHC, CE, 1970-71
176 Assault Hel Co	Reavill, Rick 176 AHC, CE, 1969-70
176 Assault Hel Co	Reed, Mike 176 AHC, CE, 1966-68
176 Assault Hel Co	Richmond, Murlen 176 AHC, CE, 1970-71
176 Assault Hel Co	Roberts, Garry 176 AHC, CE, 1970-71
176 Assault Hel Co	Scheck, Roland 176 AHC, DG, 1967
176 Assault Hel Co	Shatto, Larry 176 AHC, CE, 1969
176 Assault Hel Co	Silva, Larry 176 AHC, CE, 1967-69
176 Assault Hel Co	Tepper, Art 610 TC, TI, 1968-70
176 Assault Hel Co	Tuttle, Scott, son of Jerry Tuttle, 176 AHC, P, 1969
176 Assault Hel Co	Wiese, Dale 176 AHC, CE, 1967-68
176 Assault Hel Co	Williams, Ron 176 AHC, CE, 1967-68
176 Assault Hel Co	Wilson, William 176 AHC, CE, 1970-71
176 Assault Hel Co	Zipperer, Carl 176 AHC, P, 1970-71

178 Assault Support Hel Co	Baird, Mark 178 ASHC, FE, 1971	179 Assault Support Hel Co	Neckerman, Stan 179 ASHC, FE, 1969-70
178 Assault Support Hel Co	Balmer, Jerry 178 ASHC, FE, 1967	179 Assault Support Hel Co	Rubalcava, Mike 179 ASHC, DG, 1969-70
178 Assault Support Hel Co	Bearley, Ron 178 ASHC, FE, 1967	179 Assault Support Hel Co	Smith, Sam 179 ASHC, FE, 1968-69
178 Assault Support Hel Co	Caeton, Lionel 178 ASHC, 1969-70	179 Assault Support Hel Co	Strand, Phil 179 ASHC, 6198-69
178 Assault Support Hel Co	Calloway, James 178 ASHC, 1968-70	179 Assault Support Hel Co	Swift, Ron 179 ASHC, CE, 1968-69
178 Assault Support Hel Co	Chappell, Ralph 178 ASHC, P, 68-69	179 Assault Support Hel Co	Wilson, Stewart 179 ASHC, CE, 1967-68
178 Assault Support Hel Co	Cribbs, Larry 178 ASHC, P, 1971-72		
178 Assault Support Hel Co	Dameron, Les 178 ASHC, Flt Opns, 1970	180 Assault Support Hel Co	Balmer, Jerry 178 ASHC, FE, 1967
178 Assault Support Hel Co	Davis, Conrad 178 ASHC, P, 1967-68	180 Assault Support Hel Co	Beckenhauer, John 180 ASHC, P, 1968
178 Assault Support Hel Co	Eckelson, Marty 178 ASHC, FE, 1970-71	180 Assault Support Hel Co	Burrow, Roy, 243 ASHC, 1969
178 Assault Support Hel Co	Eoff, William 178 ASHC, P, 1968	180 Assault Support Hel Co	Faddis, Rodger 180 ASHC, FE, 1969
178 Assault Support Hel Co	Evans, Earl 178 ASHC, FE/CE, 1968-69	180 Assault Support Hel Co	Finke, Edward 180 ASHC, FE, 1969-70
178 Assault Support Hel Co	Falloway, Jim 178 ASHC, FE, 1968-70	180 Assault Support Hel Co	Greenawalt, Allen 180 ASHC, CE, 1970
178 Assault Support Hel Co	Hawkins, Joe 178 ASHC, CE, 1966-67	180 Assault Support Hel Co	Lohr, Fred 180 ASHC, P, 1972-73
178 Assault Support Hel Co	Janousek, Richard 178 ASHC, FE, 1967-68	180 Assault Support Hel Co	Molish, Mike 180 ASHC, P, 1971-72
178 Assault Support Hel Co	Kaminski, William, LRRP, 1971	180 Assault Support Hel Co	Neally, Michael 180 ASHC, 1971
178 Assault Support Hel Co	McLenaghan, Joe 178 ASHC, FE, 1969-70	180 Assault Support Hel Co	Nolan, Jim 180 ASHC, P, 1972
178 Assault Support Hel Co	Means, Bob 178 ASHC, FE, 1967-68	180 Assault Support Hel Co	Verity, Rick 180 ASHC, FE, 1972-73
178 Assault Support Hel Co	Mesko, Jim author: WILD THANG	180 Assault Support Hel Co	Watters, Curtis 180 ASHC, CE, 1972-73
178 Assault Support Hel Co	Nelson, Dean 178 ASHC, CE, 1966-67	180 Assault Support Hel Co	Young, Ralph 54 Gen Suppt Gp, 1968-69
178 Assault Support Hel Co	Niedbala, Stephen 178 ASHC, FE, 1965-67		
178 Assault Support Hel Co	Nix, Don 178 ASHC, 1969-70	187 Assault Hel Co	Avery, Dennis 187 AHC, P, 1969
178 Assault Support Hel Co	Novak, Rick 178 ASHC, FE, 1970-71	187 Assault Hel Co	Babb, Mike 187 AHC, P, 1971
178 Assault Support Hel Co	Quigley, Ron 178 ASHC, DG, 1969-70	187 Assault Hel Co	Bellerue, Rik 187 AHC, CE, 1970-72
178 Assault Support Hel Co	Peterson, Larry 178 ASHC, 1970-71	187 Assault Hel Co	Brooker, Dan 187 AHC, DG, 1971
178 Assault Support Hel Co	Reynolds, Dave 178 ASHC, FE, 1970-71	187 Assault Hel Co	Brown, David 187 AHC, CE, 1968-69
178 Assault Support Hel Co	Sanchez, Raul 178 ASHC, FE, 1971-72	187 Assault Hel Co	Damerow, Chuck 187 AHC, P, 1970-71
178 Assault Support Hel Co	Wolak, Steve 178 ASHC, FE, 1970-71	187 Assault Hel Co	Daniel, Richard, 187 AHC, P, 1969-70
		187 Assault Hel Co	Doke, Richard 187 AHC, CE, 1971
179 Assault Support Hel Co	Bearly, Ron 179 ASHC, FE, 1967-68	187 Assault Hel Co	Dougan, Pat 187 AHC, P, 1968-69
179 Assault Support Hel Co	Boyd, Roger 179 ASHC, FE, 1969	187 Assault Hel Co	Drinkwine, Frank 187 AHC, CE, 1970-71
179 Assault Support Hel Co	Finke, Edward 179 ASHC, FE, 1968-69	187 Assault Hel Co	Duquette, Al 187 AHC, P, 1967-68
179 Assault Support Hel Co	Gilmore, Jack 179 ASHC, FE, 1968-69	187 Assault Hel Co	Elliot, Mike 187 AHC, CE, 1970-71
179 Assault Support Hel Co	Jacobs, Roy 179 ASHC, CE, 1968-69	187 Assault Hel Co	Gaffney, Jim 187 AHC, P, 1968-69
179 Assault Support Hel Co	Joyce, Don 179 ASHC, P, 1967-68	187 Assault Hel Co	Gray, Bob 187 AHC, P, 1971-72
179 Assault Support Hel Co	Kremp, Ralph 179 ASHC, DG, 1969-70	187 Assault Hel Co	Greenhalgh, Bill 162 AHC, P, 1968-69
179 Assault Support Hel Co	Luttrell, James 179 ASHC, CE, 1968	187 Assault Hel Co	Guynn, Edward 187 AHC, CE, 1969-70
179 Assault Support Hel Co	Lynch, John 179 ASHC, DG, 1966-67	187 Assault Hel Co	Hodges, Mike 187 AHC, P, 1970-71
179 Assault Support Hel Co	Marriott, Eric 179 ASHC, 1970	187 Assault Hel Co	Hoselton, Douglas 187, CE, 1970-71
179 Assault Support Hel Co	McAdams, Larry 179 ASHC, FE, 1967-68	187 Assault Hel Co	Johnson, Johnny 187 AHC, P, 1971
179 Assault Support Hel Co	Messenger, Tom 179 ASHC, FE, 1970-71	187 Assault Hel Co	Kammers, Tom 187 AHC, CE, 1970-71
179 Assault Support Hel Co	Miller, Terrry 179 ASHC, FE, 1969-71	187 Assault Hel Co	Kittleson, Rob 187 AHC, P, 1966-68

187 Assault Hel Co	Leak, Arnie 187 AHC, P, 1968-69
187 Assault Hel Co	Leith, Bob 187 AHC, P, 1968-69
187 Assault Hel Co	Martin, Tom 187 AHC, P, 1967-68
187 Assault Hel Co	McEntyre, Don 539 TC, 1967-68
187 Assault Hel Co	McKee, Thomas 187 AHC, CE, 1970-71
187 Assault Hel Co	McLeod, Jesse 187 AHC, CE, 1967-68
187 Assault Hel Co	Mercer, Eric 187 AHC, P, 1967-68
187 Assault Hel Co	Monroe, Greg 187 AHC, DG, 1971-72
187 Assault Hel Co	Mullen, Mike 187 AHC, DG, 1967
187 Assault Hel Co	Mutza, Wayne author: KILLER HAWK, PISTOL PETE
187 Assault Hel Co	Nadal, Hector 25 Div Combat Photographer, 1968
187 Assault Hel Co	Nivens, Kirk 187 AHC, P, 1968
187 Assault Hel Co	Reese, George personal website
187 Assault Hel Co	Renaud, Rick 187 AHC, P, 1970-71
187 Assault Hel Co	Scott, Ron 187 AHC, CE, 1970
187 Assault Hel Co	Simpson, Benjamin 187 AHC, CE, 1970-71
187 Assault Hel Co	Smith, Terry 187 AHC, CE, 1970-71
187 Assault Hel Co	Steiger, Jim 187 AHC, CE, 1967-68
187 Assault Hel Co	Stevenson, Glenn 187 AHC, DG, 1967-68
187 Assault Hel Co	Stino, Tom 187 AHC, CE, 1969-70
187 Assault Hel Co	Stowell, Kieth 187 AHC, DG, 1967-68
187 Assault Hel Co	Stratton, Mike 187 AHC, P, 1969-70
187 Assault Hel Co	Strople, Pat 187 AHC, CE, 1971-72
187 Assault Hel Co	Sullivan, George, Lycoming Tec Rep, 1968
187 Assault Hel Co	Thompson, Carroll 187 AHC, CE, 1970-71
187 Assault Hel Co	Tortolano, Vincent 187 AHC, P, 1967-68
187 Assault Hel Co	Wagner, Jerry 187 AHC, P, 1967-68
187 Assault Hel Co	Watford, John 187 AHC, DG, 1971-72
187 Assault Hel Co	Webster, David 187 AHC, P, 1967-68
187 Assault Hel Co	Wilhite, Ray USAAM
187 Assault Hel Co	Windsand, Doug 187 AHC/602 TC, 1970
187 Assault Hel Co	Wise, Alan 187 AHC, DG, 1968-69
187 Assault Hel Co	Woods, Rodney 187 AHC, P, 1970-71
187 Assault Hel Co	Worner, Matt 187 AHC, DG, 1968
188 Assault Hel Co	Alley, Ted 188 AHC, CE, 1968
188 Assault Hel Co	Beebe, Max 188 AHC, P, 1967-68
188 Assault Hel Co	Blankenship, Dennis 188 AHC, DG, 1968-69
188 Assault Hel Co	Clark, Larry 188 AHC, P, 1968
188 Assault Hel Co	Detra, Dick 188 AHC, DG, 1967-68
188 Assault Hel Co	Handel, Geoff 188 AHC, P, 1967-68
188 Assault Hel Co	Linster, Frank 188 AHC, P, 1967-68
188 Assault Hel Co	Matt, Joe 188 AHC, CE, 1967
188 Assault Hel Co	Maurer, Charlie 188 AHC, P, 1966-68
188 Assault Hel Co	Merlock, Ron 188 AHC, CE, 1967-68
188 Assault Hel Co	Murphy, Gilbert 188 AHC, P, 1968-69
188 Assault Hel Co	Mutza, Wayne author: FRIDAY'S CHILD, FTA, LUCY IN THE SKY WITH DIAMONDS, RAGIN CAJIN, SATISFACTION, SUMMER WINE
188 Assault Hel Co	Ogle, Jim 188 AHC, P, 1967-68
188 Assault Hel Co	Pepper, Greg 188 AHC, CE, 1968-69
188 Assault Hel Co	Piecuch, Ron 188 AHC, DG, 1967
188 Assault Hel Co	Sites, Joe 188 AHC, P, 1967
188 Assault Hel Co	Soares, John 188 AHC, P, 1968
188 Assault Hel Co	Stahlkuppe, Joe, 269 CAB, 1967-68
188 Assault Hel Co	Tollefsen, Kjell 188 AHC, P, 1968
188 Assault Hel Co	Walker, Joe 188 AHC, P, 1967-68
189 Assault Hel Co	Anderson, Larry 189 AHC/604 TC, 1968-69
189 Assault Hel Co	Benka, Jim 189 AHC, CE, 1967-70
189 Assault Hel Co	Cockrell, Gordon 189 AHC, P, 1970-71
189 Assault Hel Co	Hoagland, Ray 189 AHC/604 TC, 1968
189 Assault Hel Co	Johnston, Bruce 189 AHC, 1968-69
189 Assault Hel Co	Leary, Pat 189 AHC, P, 1967-68
189 Assault Hel Co	Lomonaco, Jim 189 AHC, P, 1967-68
189 Assault Hel Co	Lundh, Lennart USS *Tripoli*, 1968-69
189 Assault Hel Co	Lundh, Lennart author: BARBIE
189 Assault Hel Co	MacDonald, Harold, 125 ATC, 1970
189 Assault Hel Co	Meeker, George 189 AHC, 1968-69
189 Assault Hel Co	Munsell, David 189 AHC, CE, 1968-69
189 Assault Hel Co	Rutherford, Claude 189 AHC, CE, 1969-70
189 Assault Hel Co	Simmons, Ty 189 AHC, P, 1970-71
189 Assault Hel Co	Steinback, Joe 189 AHC, CE, 1968-69
189 Assault Hel Co	Steinbrunn, Robert, author, 189 AHC, P, 1968: BARBIE
189 Assault Hel Co	Torres, Don 189 AHC, CE, 1968-69
189 Assault Hel Co	Ytsen, Mike 189 AHC, DG, 1968
190 Assault Hel Co	Bajc, Marko VN War researcher
190 Assault Hel Co	Coveney, Bob 190 AHC, P, 1968
190 Assault Hel Co	Dancsecs, Frank 190 AHC, P, 1969

190 Assault Hel Co	Fisher, Joe 190 AHC, CE, 1969-70
190 Assault Hel Co	Harney, Tom 190 AHC, P, 1970
190 Assault Hel Co	Ireland, Danny 190 AHC, CE, 1968
190 Assault Hel Co	Logan, Jon 190 AHC, P, 1969-70
190 Assault Hel Co	Maher, Rom 190 AHC, CE, 1967-69
190 Assault Hel Co	Ouellette, Paul 190 AHC, CE, 1967-68
190 Assault Hel Co	Petra, Eugene 190 AHC, DG, 1968-70
190 Assault Hel Co	Roloff, Raymond 190 AHC, 1968-69
191 Assault Hel Co	Almaraz, Art 191 AHC, CE, 1967-68
191 Assault Hel Co	Barkley, Roger 191 AHC, CE, 1967-68
191 Assault Hel Co	Burney, Andy 191 AHC, CE, 1967-68
191 Assault Hel Co	Calton, Dick 191 AHC, DG, 1967-68
191 Assault Hel Co	Carlton, Ken 191 AHC, P, 1969-70
191 Assault Hel Co	Cherrie, Stan 191 AHC, P, 1967-68
191 Assault Hel Co	Dunstan, Simon author: FAYE'S LOVE
191 Assault Hel Co	Flores, Bill 191 AHC, CE, 1968-69
191 Assault Hel Co	Francis, Gary 191 AHC, CE, 1969-70
191 Assault Hel Co	Fryant, Bill 191 AHC, P, 1971
191 Assault Hel Co	Gosch, Gordon 191 AHC, DG, 1970-71
191 Assault Hel Co	Hahn, Gordon 191 AHC, CE, 1968-69
191 Assault Hel Co	Healy, Steve 191 AHC, CE, 1970-71
191 Assault Hel Co	Honl, Jim S-1 Advisor, 1968
191 Assault Hel Co	James, David 191 AHC, P, 1968-69
191 Assault Hel Co	Maw, Alan 191 AHC, CE, 1968-69
191 Assault Hel Co	Patnode, Bud 191 AHC, P, 1967
191 Assault Hel Co	Phenicie, Glenn 191 AHC, CE, 1968-69
191 Assault Hel Co	Powers, Dave 191 AHC, 1969
191 Assault Hel Co	Reese, George personal website
191 Assault Hel Co	Sandrock, Don 191 AHC, P, 1967-69
191 Assault Hel Co	Schwartz, Dave 191 AHC, P, 1968-69
191 Assault Hel Co	Stinnett, Roger 191 AHC, 1967-68
191 Assault Hel Co	Stitt, Harold 191 AHC, P, 1967-68
191 Assault Hel Co	Walker, Bob 191 AHC, CE, 1967-68
191 Assault Hel Co	Waugh, Skip 191 AHC, CE, 1967-68
191 Assault Hel Co	Williams, Don 191 AHC, P, 1967-68
192 Assault Hel Co	Allison, Warren 192 AHC, CE, 1967-68
192 Assault Hel Co	Ashley, Art 192 AHC, P, 1970-71
192 Assault Hel Co	Burns, Danny 192 AHC, DG, 1967-68
192 Assault Hel Co	Chenoweth, Bob author: HAVE GUN WILL TRAVEL, THE UGLY AMERICAN

192 Assault Hel Co	Cole, Steve 192 AHC, CE, 1968-69
192 Assault Hel Co	Cope, Bill 192 AHC, P, 1971
192 Assault Hel Co	Crowder, Larry 192 AHC, CE, 1970-71
192 Assault Hel Co	Davis, Robert 192 AHC, CE, 1969-70
192 Assault Hel Co	Frazier, Don 192 AHC, CE, 1971-72
192 Assault Hel Co	Freel, Jon 192 AHC, CE, 1969-70
192 Assault Hel Co	Godfrey, Jim 192 AHC, P, 1969-70
192 Assault Hel Co	Javens, Dennis 192 AHC, P, 1971
192 Assault Hel Co	Klein, Dennis 192 AHC, P, 1971
192 Assault Hel Co	Kuchar, Roman 192 AHC, DG/CE, 1968-70
192 Assault Hel Co	Lavenberg, Mike 192 AHC, CE, 1969-70
192 Assault Hel Co	Lemke, Don 192 AHC, P, 1971
192 Assault Hel Co	Miller, Bob 192 AHC, P, 1968-69
192 Assault Hel Co	Mitchell, Roger 192 AHC, P, 1969-71
192 Assault Hel Co	Noble, Dave 192 AHC, CE, 1970-71
192 Assault Hel Co	Pederson, Mike 192 AHC, CE, 1970-71
192 Assault Hel Co	Rockenstire, Walt 192 AHC, DG, 1970
192 Assault Hel Co	Sellers, Don 192 AHC, P, 1970-71
192 Assault Hel Co	Webb, Rob 192 AHC, CE, 1971
192 Assault Hel Co	Whitney, Bruce 192 AHC, P, 1970-71
192 Assault Hel Co	Zimmerman, Mike 192 AHC, CE, 1970-71
195 Assault Hel Co	Cornell, Curt 195 AHC, P, 1968-69
195 Assault Hel Co	Croley, Chuck 195 AHC, CE, 1970
195 Assault Hel Co	Curtis, Grant B-1-9, P, 1969-70
195 Assault Hel Co	Dan, Tweek Van, 1969
195 Assault Hel Co	Miller, Earl 195 AHC, CE, 1970
195 Assault Hel Co	Nadeau, Thomas 195 AHC, P, 1970
196 Assault Support Hel Co	Alberts, Dan 196 ASHC, FE, 1967-68
196 Assault Support Hel Co	Kastens, Charles 196 ASHC, 1968-69
196 Assault Support Hel Co	Kluge, Stan 196 ASHC, FE, 1969-70
196 Assault Support Hel Co	Massey, Marcel 196 ASHC, FE, 1969-70
196 Assault Support Hel Co	Mikesell, Rich 196 ASHC, CE, 1971
196 Assault Support Hel Co	Oswald, Joe 196 ASHC, FE, 1967-68
196 Assault Support Hel Co	Riley, Joe 196 ASHC, P, 1968-69
196 Light Inf Bde	Aiken, Danny 11 LIB 23 Div, CE, 1970-71
197 Assault Hel Co	Bajc, Marko VN War researcher
197 Assault Hel Co	Greenhalgh, Bill 162 AHC, P, 1968-69

Unit	Person
198 Light Inf Bde	Petrovich, Ron 198 LIB, P, 1971
200 Assault Support Hel Co	Boxley, Joe 200 ASHC, FE, 1967-68
200 Assault Support Hel Co	Bray, Bill 200 ASHC, DG, 1967
200 Assault Support Hel Co	Dwyer, Rodger 200 ASHC, FE, 1967-68
200 Assault Support Hel Co	Ellis, Tom A-228 ASHB, P, 1968-70
200 Assault Support Hel Co	Howlett, David 200 ASHC, FE, 1967
200 Assault Support Hel Co	Ketcham, Jim C-228 ASHB, FE, 1967-68
200 Assault Support Hel Co	Langley, Bob 200 ASHC, FE, 1967-68
200 Assault Support Hel Co	Ledbetter, Garry 200 ASHC, FE, 1967-68
200 Assault Support Hel Co	Miller, George 200 ASHC, P, 1967
200 Assault Support Hel Co	Reese, George personal website
200 Assault Support Hel Co	Roscoe, Phil 200 ASHC, FE, 1967-68
200 Assault Support Hel Co	Seibert, David A-159 ASHB, 1968
200 Assault Support Hel Co	Stogner, Grady, 11 ACR, 1968-69
201 Corps Avn Co	Stogner, Grady, 11 ACR, 1968-69
203 Assault Support Hel Co	Moore, Warren 203 ASHC, DG/CE/FE, 1971-72
205 Assault Support Hel Co	Bray, Bill 205 ASHC, FE, 1967-68
205 Assault Support Hel Co	Chappell, Ralph 205 ASHC, P, 1968-69
205 Assault Support Hel Co	Galo, George 205 ASHC, P, 1967-68
205 Assault Support Hel Co	Hinson, Bud 539 TC, 1970
205 Assault Support Hel Co	Viol, Adolf 205 ASHC, CE, 1968-69
205 Assault Support Hel Co	Veteto, Ricci 205 ASHC, 1968-69
213 Assault Support Hel Co	Brown, Mike 213 ASHC, FE, 1966-67
213 Assault Support Hel Co	Cayze, Bob 213 ASHC, FE, 1968-69
213 Assault Support Hel Co	Corbett, Patrick 213 ASHC, CE, 1970-71
213 Assault Support Hel Co	Craft, Steve 213 ASHC, DG, 1966-67
213 Assault Support Hel Co	Goyea, Rich 213 ASHC, 1967-68
213 Assault Support Hel Co	Hollan, Jesse 213 ASHC, 1967-68
213 Assault Support Hel Co	Hoopes, Tom 213 ASHC, 1966-67
213 Assault Support Hel Co	LeFavor, George 213 ASHC, P, 1971-72
213 Assault Support Hel Co	Posey, Ward 213 ASHC, CE, 1967-68
213 Assault Support Hel Co	Stanley, James 213 ASHC, CE, 1967-68
213 Assault Support Hel Co	Thomsen, Craig 213 ASHC, 1967
215 Composite Service Bn	Cardinal, Patrick 215 Composite Svc Bn, CE, 1971-72
215 Composite Service Bn	Traub, Eric 215 Composite Svc Bn, Medic 1971-72

Unit	Person
222 Combat Aviation Bn	Wilhite, Ray USAAM
222 Combat Support Avn Bn	Thompson, Thomas 222 CSAB, 1967
235 Aerial Weapons Co	Bernstein, Jonathan author: EXECUTIONER
235 Aerial Weapons Co	Curtis, Grant B-1-9, P, 1969-70
235 Aerial Weapons Co	Lundh, Lennart USS *Tripoli*, 1968-69
235 Aerial Weapons Co	Rosenberg, Bob author: WAR WAGON
235 Aerial Weapons Co	Sprinkle, James author: DELTA TO DMZ, SUPER SNAKE
236 Medical Det	Braddock, John 236 MD, Medic, 1971-72
236 Medical Det	Evans, James 91 Evac Hosp, 1970
236 Medical Det	Kearney, Mike VN War researcher
236 Medical Det	Moore, John 571 MD, CE, 1970-71
236 Medical Det	Wills, Dale 236 MD, CE, 1971-72
237 Medical Det	Boyd, Tim 237 MD, CE, 1970-71
237 Medical Det	Gordon, Wayne 237 MD, Medic, 1970-71:
237 Medical Det	Graff, Jerry 237 MD, CE, 1970-71
237 Medical Det	Halliday, Dan 237 MD, Medic, 1971-72
237 Medical Det	Hansen, Dave 237 MD, P, 1970-71
237 Medical Det	Hill, Robert 237 MD, P, 1970
237 Medical Det	Iacobacci, Ed 237 MD, Medic, 1971-72
237 Medical Det	Krol, Joe 142 TC, 1970-71
237 Medical Det	Marcieski, Stan 326 MB, P, 1971
237 Medical Det	Marshall, Phil 237 MD, P, 1969
237 Medical Det	Rhodes, Allen 237 MD, P, 1970-71
237 Medical Det	Simcoe, Paul 237 MD, Medic, 1970-71
237 Medical Det	Sylvester, Ernie 57 MD, P, 1964-65
237 Medical Det	Warner, Ken 571 MD, P, 1971-72
238 Aerial Weapons Co	Bernstein, Jonathan author: PANDORA'S BOX
238 Aerial Weapons Co	Mutza, Wayne author: PANDORA'S BOX
238 Aerial Weapons Co	Russ, Mike 238 AWC, P, 1969-70
238 Aerial Weapons Co	Smith, Larry 238 AWC, P, 1968-69
238 Aerial Weapons Co	Stiefel, David 238 AWC, DG, 1969
240 Assault Hel Co	Bay, Frank 240 AHC, CE, 1967-68
240 Assault Hel Co	Cooper, Bob 240 AHC, P, 1969-70:
240 Assault Hel Co	Drendel, Lou author: PABST BLUE FLIGHT, KENNEL KEEPER
240 Assault Hel Co	Fox, Dave 240 AHC, CE, 1968-69

Unit	Contributor
240 Assault Hel Co	Greenhalgh, Bill 162 AHC, P, 1968-69
240 Assault Hel Co	Hoffman, Glenn 240 AHC, P, 1967-68
240 Assault Hel Co	Klann, Martin 240 AHC, CE, 1967-68
240 Assault Hel Co	LaChance, Frenchy 240 AHC, CE, 1967-68
240 Assault Hel Co	Lundh, Lennart USS *Tripoli*, 1968-69
240 Assault Hel Co	Marchetti, Bill 240 AHC, CE, 1969-70
240 Assault Hel Co	Miller, Morris 240 AHC, CE, 1968
240 Assault Hel Co	Mutza, Wayne 240 AHC, CE, 1971
240 Assault Hel Co	Schuckman, Thomas 240 AHC, DG, 1969-70
240 Assault Hel Co	Tarnovsky, Joe 240 AHC, CE, 1969-70
240 Assault Hel Co	Thrift, John 240 AHC, CE, 1967-68
240 Assault Hel Co	Windsor, Greg 240 AHC, 1971-72
242 Assault Support Hel Co	Baker, Wade, 242 ASHC, 1970-71
242 Assault Support Hel Co	Cauley, Bud 242 ASHC, DG, 1968-69
242 Assault Support Hel Co	Clapper, Craig 68 AHC, P, 1970-71
242 Assault Support Hel Co	Dunstan, Simon author: RUNNIN SCARED
242 Assault Support Hel Co	Hinson, Bud 539 TC, 1970-72
242 Assault Support Hel Co	Larce 242 ASHC, 1969-70
242 Assault Support Hel Co	Layton, Russ 128 AHC, CE, 1968-69
242 Assault Support Hel Co	Luttenberger, Ed 242 ASHC, P, 1970-71
242 Assault Support Hel Co	Mahoney, George 242 ASHC, 1967-68
242 Assault Support Hel Co	Miller, Mel 242 ASHC, FE, 1969-70
242 Assault Support Hel Co	Montgomery, Roger 242 ASHC, CE, 1967-68
242 Assault Support Hel Co	Peters, Ron 242 ASHC, FE, 1967-69
242 Assault Support Hel Co	Redburn, J.D. 242 ASHC, 1967-69
242 Assault Support Hel Co	Ross, Don 242 ASHC, 1968
242 Assault Support Hel Co	Smith, Butch 242 ASHC, DG, 1967-68
242 Assault Support Hel Co	Spence, Larry 242 ASHC, CE/FE, 1969-70
242 Assault Support Hel Co	Spillane, John 242 ASHC
242 Assault Support Hel Co	Youtube
242 Assault Support Hel Co	Wetherell, Ron 242 ASHC, FE, 1967-68
242 Assault Support Hel Co	Windsand, Doug 602 TC, 1970
242 Assault Support Hel Co	Witte, Larry 242 ASHC, FE, 1971
242 Assault Support Hel Co	Wittner, Rickey 242 ASHC, CE, 1970
243 Assault Support Hel Co	Beckenhauer, Jon 243 ASHC, CE, 1968-71
243 Assault Support Hel Co	Behn, Dave 243 ASHC, CE/FE, 1968-69
243 Assault Support Hel Co	Bell, William 243 ASHC, CE, 1968
243 Assault Support Hel Co	Bollens, Al 155 AHC, P, 1968-69
243 Assault Support Hel Co	Bunger, Bill 243 ASHC, FE, 1968
243 Assault Support Hel Co	Dickerson, Walt 243 ASHC, 1970-71
243 Assault Support Hel Co	Ferguson, James 243 ASHC, CE, 1968-69
243 Assault Support Hel Co	Foutz, Daryl 243 ASHC, FE, 1968-70
243 Assault Support Hel Co	Green, Curtis 243 ASHC, 1970-71
243 Assault Support Hel Co	Hutson, Bill 243 ASHC, 1968
243 Assault Support Hel Co	Lewis, Lloyd 243 ASHC, FE, 1969-70
243 Assault Support Hel Co	Moenich, Thomas 243 ASHC, 1969-70
243 Assault Support Hel Co	Moser, Tom 243 ASHC, FE, 1967-68
243 Assault Support Hel Co	Rivera, Juan 243 ASHC, 1968-69
243 Assault Support Hel Co	Scheibel, Curt 243 ASHC, CE/FE, 1970-71
243 Assault Support Hel Co	Studer, Mike 243 ASHC, 1968-69
243 Assault Support Hel Co	Vasquez, Carlos 243 ASHC, DG/FE, 1969-70
244 Avn Co	Charlton, Rod 244 Avn Co, P, 1967-68
244 Avn Co	Gaylord, Bruce 244 Avn Co, 1968
247 Medical Det	Crump, Chet 247 MD, Medic, 1969-71
247 Medical Det	Farley, Pat 247 MD, CE, 1970
247 Medical Det	Hartman, Malcomb 247 MD, P, 1970
247 Medical Det	Holcomb, Ron 247 MD, 1969-70
247 Medical Det	Jones, Jerry 247 MD, CE, 1970-71
247 Medical Det	Lacher, Dale 254 MD, Medic, 1969-70
247 Medical Det	Thorson, Richard 247 MD, Flight Opns, 1970-71
247 Medical Det	Zinkeler, William 247 MD, CE, 1969-70
254 Medical Det	Bynum, Jim 254 MD, P, 1966-67
254 Medical Det	Dinsmore, Richard 254 MD, Medic, 1968-70
254 Medical Det	Drendel, Lou author: HELEN SUE
254 Medical Det	Grubbs, Barry 254 MD, Medic, 1967-68
254 Medical Det	Hannon, Ron 254 MD, CE, 1966-67
254 Medical Det	Lacher, Dale 254 MD, Medic, 1969-70
254 Medical Det	McMahan, Waul 254 MD, Medic, 1967-68
254 Medical Det	Roberts, George 254 MD, CE, 1968-69
254 Medical Det	Roberts, Tom 254 MD, Medic, 1970-71
269 Combat Avn Bn	Bagnaschi, Chuck 4th Avionics Co, P, 1967-68
269 Combat Avn Bn	Detra, Dick 188 AHC, DG, 1967-68
269 Combat Avn Bn	Huffman, Steve 269 CAB, Courier, 1968-69
269 Combat Avn Bn	Lundh, Lennart USS *Tripoli*, 1968-69
269 Combat Avn Bn	Schwend, Bill 269 CAB, P, 1967
269 Combat Avn Bn	Walton, Scott 269 CAB, 1968

Unit	Name
271 Assault Support Hel Co	Bjurstrom, Mark 271 ASHC, CE, 1968-69
271 Assault Support Hel Co	Blazina, Tom 271 ASHC, CE, 1968-69
271 Assault Support Hel Co	Brennan, John 114 AHC, 1970-71
271 Assault Support Hel Co	Cabrera, Jess 271 ASHC, DG, 1969-70
271 Assault Support Hel Co	Creamer, Ron 271 ASHC, CE, 1969-70
271 Assault Support Hel Co	Fesmire, Dave 271 ASHC, CE, 1971
271 Assault Support Hel Co	Gatzemeyer, Dwight 271 ASHC, FE, 1969-70
271 Assault Support Hel Co	Herrin, Mike 271 ASHC, CE, 1968-69
271 Assault Support Hel Co	Hood, Dewey 271 ASHC, FE, 1969
271 Assault Support Hel Co	Hope, Tom 271 ASHC, CE, 1970-71
271 Assault Support Hel Co	Hutson, Bill 271 ASHC, FE, 1968
271 Assault Support Hel Co	Lampman, Dan 271 ASHC, FE, 1969-70
271 Assault Support Hel Co	Markell, Dan 271 ASHC, FE, 1968
271 Assault Support Hel Co	Markovich, Craig 271 ASHC, FE, 1969-70
271 Assault Support Hel Co	Massard, Gus 271 ASHC, 1970-71
271 Assault Support Hel Co	McBee, Jerry 271 ASHC, FE, 1967-68
271 Assault Support Hel Co	Miller, Mel 271 ASHC, FE, 1970-71
271 Assault Support Hel Co	Mutza, Wayne author: EASY RIDER
271 Assault Support Hel Co	Patterson, Tom, 1971
271 Assault Support Hel Co	Reichert, Jack 271 ASHC, CE, 1968
271 Assault Support Hel Co	Stone, Eric 271 ASHC, CE, 1968
271 Assault Support Hel Co	Stroud, David 271 ASHC, CE, 1970-71
271 Assault Support Hel Co	Tucker, John 271 ASHC, CE/FE, 1968-70
271 Assault Support Hel Co	Whitaker, Woody 271 ASHC, 1968-69
273 Avn Co (HHC)	Aeilts, Mike 117 AHC, CE, 1969-70
273 Avn Co (HHC)	Humphreys, Jack 273 Avn Co, FE, 1970-71
281 Assault Hel Co	Anderson, Joe 281 AHC, P, 1967-68
281 Assault Hel Co	Bailey, Jim 281 AHC, CE, 1969-70
281 Assault Hel Co	Evangelho, Daryl 281 AHC, CE, 1969
281 Assault Hel Co	Gachich, John 281 AHC, DG, 1968-69
281 Assault Hel Co	Krothe, Trubee, 281 AHC, CE, 1967-68
281 Assault Hel Co	Lewis, Fred 281 AHC, P, 1967-68
281 Assault Hel Co	Sangl, Rudy 281 AHC, P, 1970
281 Assault Hel Co	Stagman, Gary 281 AHC, CE, 1966-70
281 Assault Hel Co	Stanfield, Jerry 145 Airlift Plt/281 AHC, DG, 1965-67
281 Assault Hel Co	Swol, Paul 281 AHC, CE, 1969-70
281 Assault Hel Co	Wetmore, Harry 281 AHC, P, 1967-68

Unit	Name
282 Assault Hel Co	Adams, Tom 282 AHC, CE, 1965-66
282 Assault Hel Co	Atanian, Bud 282 AHC, CE, 1967-68
282 Assault Hel Co	Boyle, Ray 282 AHC, CE, 1969-70
282 Assault Hel Co	Bush, Jim 282 AHC, CE, 1970-71
282 Assault Hel Co	Cano, Jose 282 AHC, CE, 1971
282 Assault Hel Co	Carlson, Kent 282 AHC, DG, 1966-67
282 Assault Hel Co	Gabriel, Kent 282 AHC, DG, 1969-70
282 Assault Hel Co	Hickerson, Larry 282 AHC, P, 1970-71
282 Assault Hel Co	Johnson, Loren 282 AHC, CE, 1968-69
282 Assault Hel Co	Pullen, Tom 282 AHC, P, 1967-68
282 Assault Hel Co	Sauter, Al 282 AHC, 1969-70
282 Assault Hel Co	Somerfield, Bill 282 AHC, P, 1971-72
282 Assault Hel Co	Tallent, Robert 282 AHC, CE, 1967-68
283 Medical Det	Anglin, Tom 283 MD, CE, 1967-68
283 Medical Det	Draper, Gary, 20 Eng Bn, 1970-71
283 Medical Det	Henderson, Dan 283 MD, Medic 1970-71
283 Medical Det	Lovely, Mike, 1-10 Cav, Medic, 1971
283 Medical Det	Rhinehart, Mike 283 MD, P, 1969
283 Medical Det	Smith, Joe 604 TC, 1967-68
283 Medical Det	Tomczak, Roger 283 MD, CE, 1965-66
308 Combat Avn Bn	Jolet, Joe 308 CAB, 1969
326 Medical Bn	Carnes, Ed 326 MB, 1970-71
326 Medical Bn	Casper, John 326 MB, CE, 1968-69
326 Medical Bn	Wilson, Doug 326 MB, CE, 1970-71
334 Aerial Weapons Co	Aretz, James 334 AWC, CE, 1967-68
334 Aerial Weapons Co	Barnett, Jim 334 AWC, CE, 1971
334 Aerial Weapons Co	Carlton, Ken 191 AHC, P, 1969-70
334 Aerial Weapons Co	Harlem, Pete author: JAY
334 Aerial Weapons Co	McCurry, Rick 334 AWC, CE, 1967-68
334 Aerial Weapons Co	Spratt, Greg, 334 AWC, CE, 1967-68
334 Aerial Weapons Co	Sprinkle, Jim 235/334 AWC, CE, 1971-72
334 Aerial Weapons Co	Sprinkle, Jim author: NATURE'S OWN
334 Aerial Weapons Co	Stanley, David 68 AHC, 1967-68
334 Aerial Weapons Co	Stevens, Graham 334 AWC, P, 1969-70

Unit	Contributor
335 Assault Hel Co	Bajc, Marko VN War researcher
335 Assault Hel Co	Chenoweth, Bob author: HORSE THIEF
335 Assault Hel Co	DeCurtis, Dan 335 AHC, P, 1967-68
335 Assault Hel Co	Dupuis, Dennis 335 AHC, P, 1969-70
335 Assault Hel Co	Fields, Joe 335 AHC, DG, 1966-67
335 Assault Hel Co	Gould, Tom 335 AHC, P, 1969-70
335 Assault Hel Co	Harelson, Dave 335 AHC, DG, 1970-71
335 Assault Hel Co	Hoff, Terry 335 AHC, P, 1969-70
335 Assault Hel Co	Hooker, Andy 335 AHC, CE, 1968-70
335 Assault Hel Co	Hoza, John A-82/335, P, 1966
335 Assault Hel Co	Jennings, George 335 AHC, CE, 1968
335 Assault Hel Co	Kendrick, Larry 335 AHC, DG, 1968-69
335 Assault Hel Co	Lawler, John 335 AHC, P, 1969-70
335 Assault Hel Co	Luffman, Ralph 335 AHC, CE, 1969-70
335 Assault Hel Co	Miller, Phil 335 AHC, P, 1969-70
335 Assault Hel Co	Morrison, Larry 335 AHC, P, 1968-69
335 Assault Hel Co	Nesbitt, Tom 335 AHC, P, 1970
335 Assault Hel Co	Poole, John 335 AHC, CE, 1966-67
335 Assault Hel Co	Schimpf, Mark 335 AHC, P, 1969-70
335 Assault Hel Co	Smith, Robert 335 AHC, DG, 1969-70
335 Assault Hel Co	Snyder, Don 335 AHC, CE, 1966-67
335 Assault Hel Co	Souza, Louis 335 AHC, CE, 1969-70
335 Assault Hel Co	Stibbe, Russ 335 AHC, CE, 1967-71
335 Assault Hel Co	Stiles, Howard 335 AHC, P, 1969
335 Assault Hel Co	Tabor, Rick 335 AHC, CE, 1969-70
335 Assault Hel Co	Wilson, Doug 335 AHC, CE, 1969-70
335 Assault Hel Co	Wisell, George 335 AHC, P, 1968-69
336 Assault Hel Co	Amato, Art A-101/336 AHC, CE, 1966-67
336 Assault Hel Co	Beddingfield, Jim 336 AHC, P, 1969-70
336 Assault Hel Co	Benedict, Dan 336 AHC, P, 1969-70
336 Assault Hel Co	Carter, Gary 336 AHC, DG, 1970
336 Assault Hel Co	Chenoweth, Bob author: CHIEF
336 Assault Hel Co	Coleman, Bill 336 AHC, CE, 1969-71
336 Assault Hel Co	Cronan, John 336 AHC, CE, 1969-70
336 Assault Hel Co	Cronin, Earl 336 AHC, P, 1970
336 Assault Hel Co	Curtis, Grant B-1-9, P, 1969-70
336 Assault Hel Co	Drennon, Lloyd 336 AHC, P, 1969-70
336 Assault Hel Co	Feigel, Tom 336 AHC, CE, 1969-70
336 Assault Hel Co	Gustafson, Allan 336 AHC, Flt Opns, 1967-69
336 Assault Hel Co	Jones, Harold 336 AHC, DG, 1967-69
336 Assault Hel Co	Knight, Bob 336 AHC, P, 1965-68
336 Assault Hel Co	Langlois, Lucien 167 TC/336 AHC, 1965-66
336 Assault Hel Co	Leandro, John 336 AHC, P, 1969-70
336 Assault Hel Co	Markley, Butch 336 AHC, CE, 1968-69
336 Assault Hel Co	Martin, Tom 336 AHC, CE, 1968-69
336 Assault Hel Co	Materene, Tom 336 AHC, DG, 1968-69
336 Assault Hel Co	Mitchell, Frank 336 AHC, DG, 1969-70
336 Assault Hel Co	Morris, Crayton 336 AHC, P, 1967
336 Assault Hel Co	Null, Jan C-16 Cav/ 520 TC, 1969-70
336 Assault Hel Co	Olson, Randy 336 AHC, P, 1969-70
336 Assault Hel Co	Proff, Mike A-101+336 AHC, CE, 1965-67
336 Assault Hel Co	Ray, John 336 AHC, P, 1968-69
336 Assault Hel Co	Scates, Lester 167 TC/336 AHC, P, 1968-69
336 Assault Hel Co	Segura, Raul 336 AHC, CE, 1968-70
336 Assault Hel Co	Tunnell, Roger 121 AHC, P, 1969-70
336 Assault Hel Co	VanZilen, Art 336 AHC, CE, 1969-70
336 Assault Hel Co	Wainscott, Tom 336 AHC, CE, 1966-67
336 Assault Hel Co	Wardwell, Robert 336 AHC, CE, 1966-67
336 Assault Hel Co	West, Morris 336 AHC, CE, 1968-69
336 Assault Hel Co	Wills, Dale 336 AHC, DG, 1968-69
336 Assault Hel Co	Woodworth, Scott 336 AHC/167 TC, CE, 1968-69
336 Assault Hel Co	Wilhite, Ray USAAM
336 Assault Hel Co	Yokum, Dennis 336 AHC, DG, 1968-69
339 Trans Co	Baumgartner, Ken 339 TC, CE, 1967-68
339 Trans Co	Davis, Larry author: HANG ON SNOOPY, WOOLYBERGER
339 Trans Co	Ferry, Frank 339 TC, DG, 1963-64
339 Trans Co	Jenkins, Ted 478 HHC, P, 1967-68
339 Trans Co	Keith, Cecil 339 TC, DG, 1963-64
339 Trans Co	Lundh, Lennart author: HANG ON SNOOPY, WOOLYBERGER
339 Trans Co	Woodward, James 339 TC, CE, 1962-63
339 Trans Co	Young, Ralph author: IGOR'S NUMBA WUN, JOHNNY REB JR, SIX PACK TO GO, WAYNE'S WORK HORSE
355 Avn Co (HHC)	Poole, David 1969
355 Avn Co (HHC)	Sheridan, Jim 355 Avn Co, FE, 1968-69
361 Aerial Weapons Co	Sloan, John 361 AWC, CE, 1969-70
361 Aerial Weapons Co	Speer, Steve 361 AWC, CE, 1971-72
362 Assault Support Hel Co	Lawrence, Dan 362 ASHC, FE, 1971-72
362 Assault Support Hel Co	Murtha, Paul, F/9, P, 1971-72

Unit	Name
371 Radio Research Co	Newby, Carl 371 RRC, 1968-69
478 Avn Co (HHC)	Jenkins, Ted 478 Avn Co, P, 1967-68
478 Avn Co (HHC)	Joyce, Don, P, 1965
478 Avn Co (HHC)	Keller, Robert A-227 AHB, 1965-66
478 Avn Co (HHC)	Lundh, Lennart USS *Tripoli*, 1968-69
478 Avn Co (HHC)	Lundh, Lennart author: BIG BAD JOHN
478 Avn Co (HHC)	Mesko, Jim author: BIG MOTHER, OK BABE
478 Avn Co (HHC)	Oden, Jim 478 Avn Co, P, 1968-69
478 Avn Co (HHC)	Strew, Jerrell 1 Cav (Air), 1965-66
498 Medical Det	Allen, Bill 498 MD, CE, 1968-69
498 Medical Det	Bishop, Dennis 498 MD, 1970-71
498 Medical Det	Brackenhoff, Robert 409 TC/174 AHC, 1968-71
498 Medical Det	Condon, Lyle 498 MD, Medic, 1968-70
498 Medical Det	Coogan, Tim 498 MD, Medic, 1969-70
498 Medical Det	Cunningham, Kerry 498 MD, 1968-69
498 Medical Det	Ferg, John 498 MD, Medic, 1967-68
498 Medical Det	Foxworthy, Dennis 498 MD, Medic, 1968-70
498 Medical Det	Gallipeau, Charles 498 MD, CE, 1968
498 Medical Det	Hastie, Mike 1-10 Cav, Medic, 1970-71
498 Medical Det	Hise, Richard 498 MD, Medic, 1969-70
498 Medical Det	Jones, Don 498 MD, CE, 1969-71
498 Medical Det	Jostandt, Gary 498 MD, Medic, 1968-69
498 Medical Det	Kline, Joe B-101, CE, 1970-71
498 Medical Det	Knisely, Ben 498 MD, P, 1968
498 Medical Det	Krause, Gary 498 MD, Medic, 1969
498 Medical Det	Kulik, Gary 61 MB, 1969-70
498 Medical Det	Leepson, Mark VVAArts editor, 1st Log Comm 1967-68
498 Medical Det	McKemey, Tom 498 MD, Medic, 1965-66
498 Medical Det	Messersmith, Emory 498 MD, Medic, 1972
498 Medical Det	Modjeski, Howard 498 MD, P, 1970-71
498 Medical Det	Paul, Jerry 498 MD, CE, 1970-71
498 Medical Det	Roby, Phillip 498 MD, P, 1971-72
498 Medical Det	Talley, Bill 498 MD, CE, 1966-68
498 Medical Det	Taylor, Alan 498 MD, 1969-71
498 Medical Det	Van Horn, James 498 MD, Medic, 1968
498 Medical Det	Young, Jerry 498 MD, CE, 1968-69
539 Trans Co	Balentine, John 539 TC, 1970
539 Trans Co	Erickson, Jim 539 TC, 1967-68
539 Trans Co	Greenhalgh, Bill 162 AHC, P, 1968-69
539 Trans Co	Hinson, Bud 539 TC, 1970-72
539 Trans Co	Null, Jan, C-16 Cav/520 TC, 1969-70
539 Trans Co	Smith, Cameron 539 TC, 67-68
539 Trans Co	Stilwell, Dexter 539 TC, 1968
539 Trans Co	Thies, Mike 20 TC, 1970-71
539 Trans Co	Thompson, Fred 539 TC, DG, 1967-68
571 Medical Co	Bauer, Scott 571 MD, Medic, 1972
571 Medical Co	Bohrman, Ken 571 MD, CE, 1971-72
571 Medical Co	Brown, John 571 MD, Medic, 1972-73
571 Medical Co	Hanson, Scott 571 MD, Medic, 1972
571 Medical Co	Krol, Joe 142 TC, 1970-71
571 Medical Co	Moore, John 571 MD, CE, 1970-71
571 Medical Co	Rhodes, Allen 237 MD, P, 1970-71
571 Medical Co	Shelly, Jay 571 MD, 1969-70
571 Medical Co	Simcoe, Paul 237 MD, Medic, 1970-71
571 Medical Co	Warner, Ken 571 MD, P, 1971-72
571 Trans Co	Sanderlin, Joe 571 TC, 1964-65
605 Trans Co	Parsley, David 605 TC, 1968-69
611 Trans Co	Edson, Chuck 611 TC, P, 1963-64
611 Trans Co	Garcia, Frank 611 TC, 1964-65
611 Trans Co	Griffo, Frank 611 TC, 1966
611 Trans Co	Lowden, Milton 121 AHC, 1964
611 Trans Co	Mutza, Wayne author: HOW SWEET IT IS, SLAVE DRIVER
611 Trans Co	Pike, Douglas, Historian, VN Center + Archives, TX Tech Univ
611 Trans Co	Reese, George personal website
611 Trans Co	Wilhite, Ray USAAM
611 Trans Co	Williams, Earl 121 AHC, 1964
611 Trans Co	Young, Ralph author: DON JUAN, HAVE AXES WILL TRAVEL
937 Combat Engineer Group	Borchin, George 937 Cbt Eng Gp, P, 1965-66

Unit	Contributor
A Battery-2 Bn-20 Artillery ARA	Sullivan, George 15 TC, 1968
A Battery-2 Bn-20 Artillery ARA	Wood, Billy A-2-20 ARA, P, 1966-67
A Battery-4 Bn-77 Artillery ARA	Mack, Dennis A-4-77 ARA, P, 1968-69
A Co-1 Avn Bn-1 Inf	Alioto, Ernie A Co 1 Avn Bn, DG, 1968
A Co-1 Avn Bn-1 Inf	Chenoweth, Bob author: BIG IRON, RED BARON
A Co-1 Avn Bn-1 Inf	Chenoweth, Bob 4 TC/120 AHC/58 Avn Det, CE, 1967-68
A Co-1 Avn Bn-1 Inf	Drendel, Lou author: NANCY
A Co-1 Avn Bn-1 Inf	Lewis, Carl A Co 1 Avn Bn, 1965-66
A Co-1 Avn Bn-1 Inf	Mesko, Jim author: BIG IRON
A Co-1 Avn Bn-1 Inf	Mutza, Wayne author: NANCY
A Co-1 Avn Bn-1 Inf	Myers, Harry A Co 1 Avn Bn, CE, 1966-67
A Co-1 Avn Bn-1 Inf	Nicolich, John 129 AHC, CE, 1965-66
A Co-1 Avn Bn-1 Inf	Patrick, Rod 184 RAC, P, 1966
A Co-1 Avn Bn-1 Inf	Smith, J.T. A Co 1 Avn Bn, CE, 1965-66
A Co-1 Avn Bn-1 Inf	Young, Gary A Co 1 Avn Bn, CE, 1967-68
A Co-4 Avn Bn-4 Inf	Donoghue, Jay A Co 4 Avn Bn, P, 1967-68
A Co-4 Avn Bn-4 Inf	Fuller, Henry A Co 4 Avn Bn, CE, 1968-69
A Co-4 Avn Bn-4 Inf	Gipson, Beck A Co 4 Avn Bn, P, 1968-69
A Co-4 Avn Bn-4 Inf	Hyde, Steven A Co 4 Avn Bn, CE, 1966-67
A Co-4 Avn Bn-4 Inf	Morrison, Frank A Co 4 Avn Bn, CE, 1968-69
A Co-4 Avn Bn-4 Inf	Wells, Bill A Co 4 Avn Bn, CE, 1969-70
A Co-9 Avn Bn-9 Inf	McCullough, Dennis A-9, CE, 1967-68
A Co-9 Avn Bn-9 Inf	Stonner, Dean A-9, P, 1968-69
A Co-25 Combat Avn Bn	Cannizzaro Sal A-25 Avn Bn, DG, 1968-69
A Co-25 Combat Avn Bn	Thompson, Ronnie A-25 Avn Bn, CE, 1967-68
A Co-82 Avn Bn	Ashton, Larry A-82 Avn Bn, CE, 1965
A Co-82 Avn Bn	Champlin, Don A-82 Avn Bn, P, 1965-66
A Co-82 Avn Bn	Chenoweth, Bob author: BIG TRAIN
A Co-82 Avn Bn	Drendel, Lou author: BIG TRAIN
A Co-82 Avn Bn	Hoza, John A-82 Avn Bn/335 AHC, P, 1966
A Co-82 Avn Bn	Mutza, Wayne author: BIG TRAIN
A Co-82 Avn Bn	Schultz, Kurt A-82 Avn Bn, DG, 1965-66
A Co-82 Avn Bn	Woody, Harold A Co 82 Avn Bn, DG, 1965
A Co-101 Assault Hel Bn	Amato, Art A-101 AHB, CE, 1966-67
A Co-101 Assault Hel Bn	Hamilton, Jim A-101 AHB, P, 1971-72
A Co-101 Assault Hel Bn	Klein, Howard A-101 AHB, P, 1967-68
A Co-101 Assault Hel Bn	Milavic, Jack, A-101 AHB, P, 1965-66
A Co-101 Assault Hel Bn	Patterson, Lynn A-101 AHB, 1966-67
A Co-101 Assault Hel Bn	Proff, Mike A-101 AHB, CE, 1965-67
A Co-101 Assault Hel Bn	Tiller, Art A-101 AHB, 1971
A Co-101 Assault Hel Bn	Trujillo, Davis A-101 AHB, P, 1970-71
A Co-101 Assault Hel Bn	Turner, Jerry A-101 AHB, P, 1965-66
A Co-123 Combat Avn Bn	Hogan, Steve A-123 Avn Bn, P, 1970-71
A Co-158 Assault Hel Bn	Franck, Eugene A-158 AHB, P, 1969-70
A Co-158 Assault Hel Bn	Reasoner, John A-158 AHB, P, 1969-70
A Co-158 Assault Hel Bn	Simonson, Frank A-158 AHB, CE, 1969-70
A Co-158 Assault Hel Bn	Smith, Larry A-158 AHB, P, 1969-70
A Co-159 Assault Support Hel Bn	Boxley, Joe A-159 ASHB, FE, 1968
A Co-159 Assault Support Hel Bn	Keller, John A-159 ASHB, P, 1971
A Co-159 Assault Support Hel Bn	Seabourn, Joe A-159 ASHB, FE, 1969-71
A Co-159 Assault Support Hel Bn	Seibert, David A-159 ASHB, 1968
A Co-159 Assault Support Hel Bn	Walters, David A-159 ASHB, CE, 1967-68
Hdqs + Hdqs Co-227 AHB	Beckler, Dennis C-227 AHB, CE, 1968
A Co-227 Assault Hel Bn	Abel, Bill 11 GS, 1969-70
A Co-227 Assault Hel Bn	Appel, Dirk A-227 AHB, 1969-70
A Co-227 Assault Hel Bn	Bateman, Bobby A-227 AHB, P, 1970-71
A Co-227 Assault Hel Bn	Batey, Bill A-227 AHB, P, 1969-71
A Co-227 Assault Hel Bn	Bergeron, Richard A-227 AHB, 1970
A Co-227 Assault Hel Bn	Bridges, Gary A-227 AHB, P, 1970-71
A Co-227 Assault Hel Bn	Burden, Dennis A-227 AHB, CE, 1966-67
A Co-227 Assault Hel Bn	Carder, Ed A-227 AHB, P, 1966-67
A Co-227 Assault Hel Bn	Cooper, James A-227 AHB, CE, 1969
A Co-227 Assault Hel Bn	Cox, Braxton A-227 AHB, CE, 1970-71
A Co-227 Assault Hel Bn	Foster, Bill A-227 AHB, CE, 1967-68
A Co-227 Assault Hel Bn	Friday, Ed A-227 AHB, CE, 1969
A Co-227 Assault Hel Bn	Gailfoil, John A-227 AHB, CE, 1969
A Co-227 Assault Hel Bn	Green, John A-227 AHB, CE, 1971
A Co-227 Assault Hel Bn	Gunter, James A-227 AHB, DG, 1966-67
A Co-227 Assault Hel Bn	Harrison, Tom A-227 AHB, P, 1966-67

Unit	Name	Unit	Name
A Co-227 Assault Hel Bn	Hearne, Maury A-227 AHB, P, 1969	A Co-228 Assault Support Hel Bn	McMillan, Mac, C-2-20 ARA, P, 1970-71
A Co-227 Assault Hel Bn	Henry A-227 AHB/388 TC, 6197-68	A Co-228 Assault Support Hel Bn	Miller, DeWayne A-228 ASHB, FE, 1969-70
A Co-227 Assault Hel Bn	Hill, Stephen A-227 AHB, CE, 1971-72	A Co-228 Assault Support Hel Bn	Moore, Ron A-228 ASHB, FE, 1970-71
A Co-227 Assault Hel Bn	Howell, Dennis A-227 AHB, CE, 1971-72	A Co-228 Assault Support Hel Bn	Morley, Clifford B-228 ASHB, FE, 1968-69
A Co-227 Assault Hel Bn	Jackson, Wayne A-227 AHB, CE, 1969-70	A Co-228 Assault Support Hel Bn	Pepe, Matt A-228 ASHB, DG, 1965-66
A Co-227 Assault Hel Bn	Jefferson, Thom A-277 AHB, CE, 1966-67	A Co-228 Assault Support Hel Bn	Reese, George personal website
A Co-227 Assault Hel Bn	Jester, Jim. A-227 AHB, P, 1970-71	A Co-228 Assault Support Hel Bn	Seelig, Russ A-228 ASHB, FE, 1967-68
A Co-227 Assault Hel Bn	Lachiondo, Steve A-227 AHB, CE, 1970-71	A Co-228 Assault Support Hel Bn	Usry, John A-228 ASHB, FE, 1970
A Co-227 Assault Hel Bn	Ladue, John B-227 AHB, P, 1966-67		
A Co-227 Assault Hel Bn	Lazenby, Ron A-227 AHB, CE, 1968-69	Hdqs + Hdqs Co-229 Assault Hel Bn	Thornton, Mike H+HC-229 AHB, CE, 1971-72
A Co-227 Assault Hel Bn	Lenotte, George A-227 AHB, CE, 1966-67		
A Co-227 Assault Hel Bn	Lietzan, Jim A-227 AHB, CE, 1968-69	A Co-229 Assault Hel Bn	Collier, Sandy A-229 AHB, CE, 1968-69
A Co-227 Assault Hel Bn	Loughlin, Tom A-227 AHB, CE, 1966-67	A Co-229 Assault Hel Bn	Cowan, Sidney A-229 AHB, P, 1965-66
A Co-227 Assault Hel Bn	Lovelace, H.C A-227 AHB, CE, 1969-71	A Co-229 Assault Hel Bn	Foster, Hugh B-1-5 Cav, 1970-71
A Co-227 Assault Hel Bn	Michels, Ben A-227 AHB, CE, 1966-67	A Co-229 Assault Hel Bn	Georger, Tom, A-229 AHB, 1971-72
A Co-227 Assault Hel Bn	Moon, Terry army photog, 1969	A Co-229 Assault Hel Bn	Jorgenson, Doug A-229 AHB, P, 1971
A Co-227 Assault Hel Bn	Moore, Terry A-227 AHB, CE, 1970-71	A Co-229 Assault Hel Bn	Layman, Joe A-229 AHB, P, 1971-72
A Co-227 Assault Hel Bn	O'Connor, Tim A-227 AHB, CE, 1969-70	A Co-229 Assault Hel Bn	Noonan, Dan A-229 AHB, CE, 1968-69:
A Co-227 Assault Hel Bn	Ondrey, Dave A-227 AHB, DG, 1968-69	A Co-229 Assault Hel Bn	Sloniker, Mike A-229 AHB, P, 1971-72
A Co-227 Assault Hel Bn	Paranal, Joe A-227 AHB, CE, 1970-71		
A Co-227 Assault Hel Bn	Pender, Don D-1-10, P, 1971	Hdqs + Hdqs Troop-1-9	Mutza, Wayne author: SANDRA
A Co-227 Assault Hel Bn	Rogers, Bill A-227 AHB, 1969-70		
A Co-227 Assault Hel Bn	Rose, Tom A-227 AHB, CE, 1966-67	A Troop-1 Squad-9 Cav	Anzelmo, George A-1-9, CE, 1969-70
A Co-227 Assault Hel Bn	Schlaudraff, Mike A-227 AHB, CE, 1965-66	A Troop-1 Squad-9 Cav	Bennett, Dan A-1-9, P, 1969-70
A Co-227 Assault Hel Bn	Stevens, Chuck A-227 AHB, CE, 1965-66	A Troop-1 Squad-9 Cav	Black, Ron A-1-9, P, 1969-70
A Co-227 Assault Hel Bn	Tartar, Mike A-227 AHB, DG, 1969	A Troop-1 Squad-9 Cav	Brennan, Matthew, author: QUEER JOHN
A Co-227 Assault Hel Bn	Tobias, P.J. A-227 AHB, 1970-71	A Troop-1 Squad-9 Cav	Chesson, Rick B-1-9, P, 1968-69
A Co-227 Assault Hel Bn	Tonjes, Craig A-227 AHB, CE, 1970-71	A Troop-1 Squad-9 Cav	Craig, John A-1-9, P, 1967-68
A Co-227 Assault Hel Bn	Vogel, Rick A-227 AHB, CE, 1971	A Troop-1 Squad-9 Cav	Cronen, James A-1-9, P, 1966
A Co-227 Assault Hel Bn	Winge, Larry A-227 AHB, CE, 1966-67	A Troop-1 Squad-9 Cav	Erickson, Robert A-1-9, P, 1968-69
		A Troop-1 Squad-9 Cav	Farner, Jim A-1-9, CE, 1968-69
228 ASHB	Gunbroker.Com Forum	A Troop-1 Squad-9 Cav	Ficker, Gene A-1-9, CE, 1969-70
		A Troop-1 Squad-9 Cav	Frazer, Bill A-1-9, P, 1970-71
A Co-228 Assault Support Hel Bn	Bartlett, Robert A-228 ASHB, FE, 1967	A Troop-1 Squad-9 Cav	Geiger, Robert unk unit, 1970
A Co-228 Assault Support Hel Bn	Daniel, Garry A-228 ASHB, P, 1968	A Troop-1 Squad-9 Cav	Greenhalgh, Bill 162 AHC, P, 1968-69
A Co-228 Assault Support Hel Bn	Ellis, Tom A-228 ASHB, P, 1968-70	A Troop-1 Squad-9 Cav	Gifford, Mike A-1-9, CE, 1969-70
A Co-228 Assault Support Hel Bn	Fenton, Brian 117 AHC, 1964-65	A Troop-1 Squad-9 Cav	Hendron, Chuck A-1-9, CE, 1970-71
A Co-228 Assault Support Hel Bn	Hughes, Bill A-228 ASHB, CE, 1968-69	A Troop-1 Squad-9 Cav	Horton, Duane A-1-9, 1969-70
A Co-228 Assault Support Hel Bn	Ketcham, Jim C-228 ASHB, FE, 1967-68	A Troop-1 Squad-9 Cav	Kelly, Mike C-1-9, CE, 1965-66
A Co-228 Assault Support Hel Bn	Lee, Neil A-228 ASHB, P, 1969-70	A Troop-1 Squad-9 Cav	Kline, Joe B-101, CE, 1970-71

Unit	Contributor
A Troop-1 Squad-9 Cav	Kurtz, Jim A-1-9, 1970-71
A Troop-1 Squad-9 Cav	Lawless. Matthew A-1-9, P, 1967
A Troop-1 Squad-9 Cav	Lemay, Bruce A-1-9, DG, 1968-69
A Troop-1 Squad-9 Cav	Lentino, Mike A-1-9, DG, 1969-70
A Troop-1 Squad-9 Cav	Lockhart, Ken A-1-9, CE, 1970-71
A Troop-1 Squad-9 Cav	Lundh, Lennart USS *Tripoli*, 1968-69
A Troop-1 Squad-9 Cav	Mader, John A-1-9, DG, 1969
A Troop-1 Squad-9 Cav	Marks, Richard A-1-9, DG, 1967-68
A Troop-1 Squad-9 Cav	Mutza, Wayne author: IRON BUTTERFLY, LIZ, MIGHTY GUN BIRD
A Troop-1 Squad-9 Cav	Newby, Claude A-1-9, Chaplain, 1969-70
A Troop-1 Squad-9 Cav	Rochat, Lou A-1-9, P, 1970
A Troop-1 Squad-9 Cav	Senkowski, Glen A-1-9, P, 1969-70
A Troop-1 Squad-9 Cav	Sullivan, George 15 TC, 1968
A Troop-1 Squad-9 Cav	Swain, Robert A-1-9, P, 1966-67
A Troop-1 Squad-9 Cav	Tepper, Art 610 TC, TI, 1968-70
A Troop-1 Squad-9 Cav	Washburn, Jack A-1-9, 1967-69
A Troop-1 Squad-9 Cav	Woolwine, Don A-1-9, 1968-70
A Troop-1 Squad-9 Cav	Wright, Larry A-1-9, CE, 1965-66
A Troop-2 Squad-17 Cav	Bernstein, Jonathan author: HAVE GUN WILL TRAVEL
A Troop-2 Squad-17 Cav	Smith, Dan 326 Med Bn, P, 1969-70
A Troop-3 Squad-17 Cav	Billow, Mike A-3-17, P, 1970-71
A Troop-3 Squad-17 Cav	Cannon, Dan A-3-17, 1971
A Troop-3 Squad-17 Cav	Connor, John A-3-17, 1968
A Troop-3 Squad-17 Cav	Farrier, Craig A-3-17, 1969-70
A Troop-3 Squad-17 Cav	Greenhalgh, Bill 162 AHC, P, 1968-69
A Troop-3 Squad-17 Cav	Hays, John A-3-17, CE, 1968-69
A Troop-3 Squad-17 Cav	Kickarek, Ed, CE, 1971
A Troop-3 Squad-17 Cav	Marshall, John A-3-17, CE, 1970-71
A Troop-3 Squad-17 Cav	McCalister, Bill A-3-17, P, 1969
A Troop-3 Squad-17 Cav	Mesko, Jim author: ANACRONISTIC
A Troop-3 Squad-17 Cav	Mills, Robert A-3-17, P, 1970-71
A Troop-3 Squad-17 Cav	Montana, Paul A-3-17, 1967-68
A Troop-3 Squad-17 Cav	Murphy, Dan A-3-17, P, 1969-70
A Troop-3 Squad-17 Cav	Nickel, Dave A-3-17, P, 1970-71
A Troop-3 Squad-17 Cav	Platner, Mike A-3-17, P, 1970
A Troop-3 Squad-17 Cav	Preston, James A-3-17, CE, 1967-68
A Troop-3 Squad-17 Cav	Richardson, Tom A-3-17, P, 1970-71
A Troop-3 Squad-17 Cav	Sherrer, Larry A-3-17, P, 1970-71
A Troop-3 Squad-17 Cav	Smith, Bill A-3-17, P, 1969-70
A Troop-3 Squad-17 Cav	Strickland, Larry A-3-17, 1971
A Troop-3 Squad-17 Cav	Swartz, Gary A-3-17, CE, 1969-70
A Troop-3 Squad-17 Cav	Swinford, Marvin A-3-17, P, 1971
A Troop-3 Squad-17 Cav	Talmich, Ben A-3-17, 1969-70
A Troop-3 Squad-17 Cav	Tela, Dave A-3-17, P, 1969-70
A Troop-3 Squad-17 Cav	Young, Roger A-3-17, CE, 1970
Hdqs + Hdqs Troop-7 Squad-1 Cav	Bracewell, Jim H+HT-7-1, P, 1970
Hdqs + Hdqs Troop-7 Squad-1 Cav	Walker, Ed H+HT-7-1, P, 1968-69
A Troop-7 Squad-1 Cav	Brewer, Gary D-1-4/C-16, CE, 1969-70
A Troop-7 Squad-1 Cav	Brown, Larry A-7-1, CE, 1971-72
A Troop-7 Squad-1 Cav	Cattilini, Jack A-7-1, P, 1970-71
A Troop-7 Squad-1 Cav	Cupp, Paul A-7-1, CE, 1969-70:
A Troop-7 Squad-1 Cav	Gibbons, Will A-7-1, P, 1970-71
A Troop-7 Squad-1 Cav	Hinton, Mel A-7-1, P, 1971-72
A Troop-7 Squad-1 Cav	Hesselbein, Bob A-7-1, P, 1972
A Troop-7 Squad-1 Cav	Huss, J.D. 370 TC, P, 1970-71
A Troop-7 Squad-1 Cav	Larcher, Ken A-7-1, CE, 1970-71
A Troop-7 Squad-1 Cav	Little, John A-7-1, P, 1968-69
A Troop-7 Squad-1 Cav	Mills, Hugh, D-3-5, P, 1971-72
A Troop-7 Squad-1 Cav	Nelson, Rob A-7-1, P, 1969-70
A Troop-7 Squad-1 Cav	Null, Jan C-16 Cav/520 TC, 1969-70
A Troop-7 Squad-1 Cav	Prine, Jim A-7-1, CE, 1971-72
A Troop-7 Squad-1 Cav	Putnam, Tom A-7-1, P, 1971-72
A Troop-7 Squad-1 Cav	Searcy, Roger B-3-17, P, 1971-72
A Troop-7 Squad-1 Cav	Turnbull, Jack A-7-1, P, 1967-69
A Troop-7 Squad-1 Cav	VanZilen, Art A-7-1, CE, 1971-72
A Troop-7 Squad-1 Cav	Willis, Randy A-7-1, P, 1969-70
A Troop-7 Squad-17 Cav	Anthony, Jeff A-7-17, P, 1971-72
A Troop-7 Squad-17 Cav	Brinn, Joe A-7-17, P, 1968-69
A Troop-7 Squad-17 Cav	Johnson, Lawrence author: OLD GLORY
A Troop-7 Squad-17 Cav	Lyons, Walter A-7-17, DG, 1968-69
A Troop-7 Squad-17 Cav	Pender, Don D-1-10, P, 1971
A Troop-7 Squad-17 Cav	Shepard, Steve A-7-17, P, 1971-72
A Troop-7 Squad-17 Cav	Young, Bob A-7-17, P, 1967-68
B Battery-2 Bn-20 Artillery ARA	Nalty/Neufeld/Watson authors: CANNED HEAT
B Battery-2 Bn-20 Artillery ARA	Bogue, Jeff B-2-20 ARA, P, 1970-71
B Battery-2 Bn-20 Artillery ARA	Chenoweth, Bob 4 TC/120 AHC/58 Avn Det, CE, 1967-68

Unit	Entry
B Battery-2 Bn-20 Artillery ARA	Cole, Mike B-2-20 ARA, CE, 1969-70
B Battery-2 Bn-20 Artillery ARA	Drendel, Lou author: BAD NEWS, CANNED HEAT, PANDORA'S BOX
B Battery-2 Bn-20 Artillery ARA	Geiger, Robert, unk unit, 1970
B Battery-2 Bn-20 Artillery ARA	Huckleberry, Paul B-2-20 ARA, P, 1970-71
B Battery-2 Bn-20 Artillery ARA	Jetter, Art C-2-20 ARA, P, 1970-71
B Battery-2 Bn-20 Artillery ARA	Richardson, Wayne B-2-20 ARA, P, 1970-71
B Battery-2 Bn-20 Artillery ARA	Shemley, Larry C-229 AHB, P, 1969-70
B Battery-2 Bn-20 Artillery ARA	Stedman, Craig 595 Sig Co, 1969
B Battery-2 Bn-20 Artillery ARA	Teetsel, John B-2-20 ARA, P, 19 70-71
B Battery-2 Bn-20 Artillery ARA	Walowicz, Les 128 AHC, 1969-70
B Battery-82 Artillery	Skinner, William, 1969
B Co-1 Avn Bn-1 Inf	Rosenburgh, Bob author: EXECUTIONER
B Co-4 Avn Bn-4 Inf	Polman, Gerald B Co 4 Avn Bn, DG, 1967
B Co-4 Avn Bn-4 Inf	Simmons, Mike B Co 4 Avn Bn, DG, 1967
B Co-9 Avn Bn-9 Inf	Bernstein, Jonathan author: HAPPINESS IS A WARM GUN
B Co-9 Avn Bn-9 Inf	Jones, Dale 9 Inf Div, Medic, 1968-69
B Co-9 Avn Bn-9 Inf	Reese, George personal website
B Co-15 Trans Bn	Lundh, Lennart USS *Tripoli*, 1968-69
B Co-25 Combat Avn Bn	Adessa, Tony B-25 Avn Bn, P, 1966
B Co-25 Combat Avn Bn	Asberry, Andy B-25 Avn Bn, CE, 1968-69
B Co-25 Combat Avn Bn	Bernstein, Jonathan author: GHOST RIDER IN THE SKY
B Co-25 Combat Avn Bn	Burnett, Chuck B Co 25 Avn Bn, DG, 1966-67
B Co-25 Combat Avn Bn	Chenoweth, Bob 4 TC/120 AHC/58 Avn Det, CE, 1967-68
B Co-25 Combat Avn Bn	Chinnery, Philip author: SNOOPY
B Co-25 Combat Avn Bn	Edwards, JP B-25 Avn Bn, P, 1970
B Co-25 Combat Avn Bn	Farren, Dan B-25 Avn Bn, CE, 1967-70
B Co-25 Combat Avn Bn	Ferris, Norm B-25 Avn Bn, Svc Plt, 1969-70
B Co-25 Combat Avn Bn	Footer, Joe B-25 Avn Bn, P, 1968
B Co-25 Combat Avn Bn	Gant, Chuck B-25 Avn Bn, P, 1970
B Co-25 Combat Avn Bn	Garrity, Mike B-25 Avn Bn, 1965-66
B Co-25 Combat Avn Bn	Kimm, Mark B-25 Avn Bn, CE, 1968
B Co-25 Combat Avn Bn	Leonard, Ron B Co 25 Avn Bn, CE, 1968-69
B Co-25 Combat Avn Bn	Lyons, Ed B-25 Avn Bn, DG, 1968-69
B Co-25 Combat Avn Bn	Mikulan, Mik 116 AHC/269 CAB, P, 1969-70
B Co-25 Combat Avn Bn	Montana, Jim B Co 25 Avn Bn, CE, 1966-68
B Co-25 Combat Avn Bn	Moorhead, Bob B-25 Avn Bn, CE, 1967
B Co-25 Combat Avn Bn	Parham, Jim B-25 Avn Bn, P, 1969
B Co-25 Combat Avn Bn	Schmuck, Earl B-25 Avn Bn, DG, 1967-68
B Co-25 Combat Avn Bn	Shea, Pat B-25 Avn Bn, DG, 1966
B Co-25 Combat Avn Bn	Simons, Tom B-25 Avn Bn, CE, 1966-67
B Co-25 Combat Avn Bn	Taylor, Don B-25 Avn Bn, DG, 1966-67
B Co-25 Combat Avn Bn	Whitey, Eugene B-25 Avn Bn, 1968-69
B Co-101 Combat Avn Bn	Everhart, Tom B-101 Avn Bn, P, 1968-69
B Co-101 Combat Avn Bn	Wood, Thomas B-101 Avn Bn, P, 1967-68
B Co-123 Combat Avn Bn	Bajc, Marko VN War researcher
B Co-123 Combat Avn Bn	Brakenhoff, Robert 174 AHC, 1968-71
B Co-123 Combat Avn Bn	Barnett, Jim 334 AHC, 1971
B Co-123 Combat Avn Bn	LaPointe, Ray B-123 Avn Bn, P, 1971
B Co-123 Combat Avn Bn	Lundh, Lennart USS *Tripoli*, 1968-69
B Co-123 Combat Avn Bn	Lynn, Walter B-123, CE, 1969-71
B Co-123 Combat Avn Bn	Mahler, Cloudy B-123 Avn Bn, DG, 1971-72
B Co-123 Combat Avn Bn	Mangano, Steve B-123 Avn Bn, CE, 1971
B Co-123 Combat Avn Bn	Mills, Hugh D-3-5, P, 1971-72
B Co-123 Combat Avn Bn	Mutza, Wayne author: CAPTAIN AMERICA, CHALLENGER
B Co-123 Combat Avn Bn	Summey, Paul B-123 Avn Bn, P, 1970-71
B Co-123 Combat Avn Bn	Wilson, Chuck, B-123 Avn Bn, 1970-71
B Co-158 Assault Hel Bn	Mussey, Dave B-158 AHB, CE, 1968-69
B Co-158 Assault Hel Bn	Taylor, Tommy B-158 AHB, CE, 1969
B Co-159 Assault Support Hel Bn	Bass, Norm B-159 ASHB, DG, 1970-72
B Co-159 Assault Support Hel Bn	Clarke, Wayne B-159 ASHB, DG, 1969
B Co-159 Assault Support Hel Bn	Hendrickson, John B-159 ASHB, P, 1969-70
B Co-159 Assault Support Hel Bn	Maddock, John B-159 ASHB, FE, 1969
B Co-159 Assault Support Hel Bn	Taylor, Tom B-159 ASHB, FE, 1970
B Co-159 Assault Support Hel Bn	Voss, James B-159 ASHB, 1968
B Co-159 Assault Support Hel Bn	Zednick, George B-159 ASHB, FE, 1968-69

Unit	Contributor
B Co-227 Assault Hel Bn	Anderson, Paul 2 BDE 1 CAV, P, 1969-70
B Co-227 Assault Hel Bn	Cramer, Gary C-5-7, Medic, 1970
B Co-227 Assault Hel Bn	Goosman, John B-227 AHB, DG, 1970-71
B Co-227 Assault Hel Bn	Lander, Jack D-1-9, 1970-71
B Co-227 Assault Hel Bn	Lipford, Bob C-227 AHB, 1970-71
B Co-227 Assault Hel Bn	Lunde, Bob B-227 AHB, P, 1969-70
B Co-227 Assault Hel Bn	Mellquist, John B-227 AHB, DG, 1969-71
B Co-227 Assault Hel Bn	Moon, Terry, 1 Cav Div PIO, Army Photographer, 1969
B Co-227 Assault Hel Bn	Mooney, Kevin B-227 AHB, CE, 1969-70
B Co-227 Assault Hel Bn	Mullinax, Bobby B-227 AHB, DG, 1970-71
B Co-227 Assault Hel Bn	White, Chris B-227 AHB, CE, 1968-69
B Co-228 Assault Support Hel Bn	Buzzell, Hugh B-228 ASHB, FE, 1968-69
B Co-228 Assault Support Hel Bn	Davis, Larry author: WAR WAGON
B Co-228 Assault Support Hel Bn	DeRouchey, Louis B-228 ASHB, FE, 1970-71
B Co-228 Assault Support Hel Bn	Ellis, Tom A-228 ASHB, P, 1968-70
B Co-228 Assault Support Hel Bn	Glass, Pat B-228 ASHB, P, 1970-71
B Co-228 Assault Support Hel Bn	Gozier, Juan B-228 ASHB, CE, 1969-70
B Co-228 Assault Support Hel Bn	Kee, Bill B-228 ASHB, FE, 1966-67
B Co-228 Assault Support Hel Bn	Ketcham, Jim C-228 ASHB, FE, 1967-68
B Co-228 Assault Support Hel Bn	Komich, Lee B-228 ASHB, P, 1968-69
B Co-228 Assault Support Hel Bn	Labriola, Mike B-228 ASHB, FE, 1966-67
B Co-228 Assault Support Hel Bn	Lawless, Bill B-228 ASHB, 1965-66
B Co-228 Assault Support Hel Bn	Lippert, John B-228 ASHB, CE, 1970-71
B Co-228 Assault Support Hel Bn	McClain, Bill B-228 ASHB, FE 1967-68
B Co-228 Assault Support Hel Bn	Morley, Clifford B-228 ASHB, FE, 1968-69
B Co-228 Assault Support Hel Bn	Mutza, Wayne author: WAR WAGON
B Co-228 Assault Support Hel Bn	Redmon, Paul B-228 ASHB, 1967-69
B Co-228 Assault Support Hel Bn	Rex, Robert B-228 ASHB, FE, 1966-67
B Co-228 Assault Support Hel Bn	Scott, Bill B-228 ASHB, FE, 1967-69
B Co-228 Assault Support Hel Bn	Sheridan, Scott B-228 ASHB, CE, 1969-70
B Co-228 Assault Support Hel Bn	Stefanini, Gary B-228 ASHB, FE, 1968-69
B Co-228 Assault Support Hel Bn	Tepper, Art 610 TC, TI, 1968-70
B Co-229 Assault Hel Bn	Bracewell, Jim, B-229 AHB/HHT-7-1, P, 1966-67/1970
B Co-229 Assault Hel Bn	Breyer, Harry B-229 AHB, 1970
B Co-229 Assault Hel Bn	Carr, Ron B-229 AHB, CE, 1969-70
B Co-229 Assault Hel Bn	Eggert, Wayne B-229 AHB, DG, 1969-70
B Co-229 Assault Hel Bn	Emerson, Chuck B-229 AHB, P, 1970-71
B Co-229 Assault Hel Bn	Evans, Robert B-229 AHB, P, 1968-69
B Co-229 Assault Hel Bn	Keele, Mike B-229 AHB, CE, 1967-68
B Co-229 Assault Hel Bn	Leathers, Jack B-229 AHB, CE, 1968
B Co-229 Assault Hel Bn	Martin, John B-229 AHB, CE, 1969-70
B Co-229 Assault Hel Bn	Mason, Robert B-229 AHB, P, 1965
B Co-229 Assault Hel Bn	McMillin, Larry B-229 AHB, CE, 1968-69
B Co-229 Assault Hel Bn	Osborne, Dennis B-229 AHB, CE, 1967-68
B Co-229 Assault Hel Bn	Packham, Bob B-229 AHB, CE, 1966-67
B Co-229 Assault Hel Bn	Rose, Mike B-229 AHB, CE, 1969-70
B Co-229 Assault Hel Bn	Sim, William B-229 AHB, DG, 1965-66
B Co-229 Assault Hel Bn	Weber, Bill B-229 AHB, CE, 1965-66
B Troop-1 Squad-9 Cav	Allman, Darrell B-1-9, P, 1970-71
B Troop-1 Squad-9 Cav	Anderson, Jere B-1-9, P, 1967-68
B Troop-1 Squad-9 Cav	Bajc, Marko VN War researcher
B Troop-1 Squad-9 Cav	Breski, Joe B-1-9, P, 1969
B Troop-1 Squad-9 Cav	Brown, Larry B-1-9, P, 1967-68
B Troop-1 Squad-9 Cav	Burgess, Chris B-1-9, P, 1968-69
B Troop-1 Squad-9 Cav	Caine, Vaughn E-1-9, P, 1970-71
B Troop-1 Squad-9 Cav	Davis, Larry author: PEACEMAKER
B Troop-1 Squad-9 Cav	Elliott, Richard B-1-9, P, 1966-67
B Troop-1 Squad-9 Cav	Flanagan, John B-1-9, P, 1967-68
B Troop-1 Squad-9 Cav	Hale, Dick B-1-9, P, 1966-67
B Troop-1 Squad-9 Cav	Hogan, Jeremy, son of Jerry Hogan, B-1-9, DG, 1969-71
B Troop-1 Squad-9 Cav	Hogan, Jerry B-1-9, DG/CE, 1969-71
B Troop-1 Squad-9 Cav	Holland, Howard B-1-9, DG, 1968-69
B Troop-1 Squad-9 Cav	Hnizdil, James B-1-9, 1969-70
B Troop-1 Squad-9 Cav	Hraben, Robert B-1-9, 1969
B Troop-1 Squad-9 Cav	Johnson, Lawrence author: DONNA
B Troop-1 Squad-9 Cav	Jones, Mike B-1-9, CE, 1969-70
B Troop-1 Squad-9 Cav	Kenerson, Ron B-1-9, CE, 1969-70
B Troop-1 Squad-9 Cav	Kurtz, Jack B-1-9, P, 1970-71
B Troop-1 Squad-9 Cav	Lundh, Lennart author: PEACEMAKER
B Troop-1 Squad-9 Cav	Luse, Glen brother of Ken Luse (KIA), B-1-9, P, 1969
B Troop-1 Squad-9 Cav	Maanao, Robert B-1-9, CE, 1969-71
B Troop-1 Squad-9 Cav	Minda, George B-1-9, CE, 1970-71
B Troop-1 Squad-9 Cav	Murtha, Paul B-1-9, P, 1971
B Troop-1 Squad-9 Cav	Mutza, Wayne author: DIXIE BELL, PEACEMAKER
B Troop-1 Squad-9 Cav	Nash, Stan B-1-9, P, 1966-67
B Troop-1 Squad-9 Cav	O'Grady, Steve B-1-9, CE, 1968-69
B Troop-1 Squad-9 Cav	Phipps, Wayne B-1-9, CE, 1967-68
B Troop-1 Squad-9 Cav	Pratt, Jim B-1-9, P, 1967
B Troop-1 Squad-9 Cav	Rago, A.J., B-1-9, DG, 1968-69

Unit	Name	Unit	Name
B Troop-1 Squad-9 Cav	Smith, Russell B-1-9, P, 1968-69	C Battery-2 Bn-20 Artillery ARA	Bernstein, Jonathan author: MURDER INC, SOUND OF SILENCE
B Troop-1 Squad-9 Cav	Snow, Roger B-1-9, DG, 1969-70		
B Troop-1 Squad-9 Cav	Sullivan, George 15 TC, 1968-69	C Battery-2 Bn-20 Artillery ARA	Bogue, Jeff C-2-20 ARA, P, 1970
B Troop-1 Squad-9 Cav	Wilkerson, Richard B-1-9, 1967	C Battery-2 Bn-20 Artillery ARA	Brewer, Gary D-1-4/C-16, CE, 1969-70
B Troop-1 Squad-9 Cav	Wright, Larry B-1-9, 1965	C Battery-2 Bn-20 Artillery ARA	Brown N.G. C-2-20 ARA, P, 1968-69
		C Battery-2 Bn-20 Artillery ARA	Chenoweth, Bob author: HAVE GUN WILL TRAVEL, SNOOPY
B Troop-2 Squad-17 Cav	Allen, Larry B-2-17, 1969-70		
B Troop-2 Squad-17 Cav	Garrett, Don B-2-17, 1969-70	C Battery-2 Bn-20 Artillery ARA	Doudna, Dean C-2-20 ARA, CE, 1971-72
B Troop-2 Squad-17 Cav	Kincaid, John B-2-17, P, 1969-70	C Battery-2 Bn-20 Artillery ARA	Hendrickson, Bruce C-2-20 ARA/F-79 AFA, CE, 1971-72
B Troop-2 Squad-17 Cav	Knight, Ray B-2-17, P, 1969	C Battery-2 Bn-20 Artillery ARA	Jackson, James F-79 AFA, P, 1972
B Troop-2 Squad-17 Cav	Moore, Larry B-2-17, CE, 1969-70	C Battery-2 Bn-20 Artillery ARA	Jetter, Art C-2-20 ARA, P, 1970-71
B Troop-2 Squad-17 Cav	Russell, Bill B-2-17, P, 1969	C Battery-2 Bn-20 Artillery ARA	Marling, Pat D-1-12 Cav, Medic, 1971
B Troop-2 Squad-17 Cav	Ryan, Gary B-2-17, P, 1970-71	C Battery-2 Bn-20 Artillery ARA	Martin, Jerry C-2-20 ARA, P, 1970-71
		C Battery-2 Bn-20 Artillery ARA	Mather, Don C-2-20 ARA, CE, 1970-71
B Troop-3 Squad-17 Cav	Berthel, George B-3-17, CE, 1969-70	C Battery-2 Bn-20 Artillery ARA	McMillan, Mac C-2-20 ARA, P, 1970-71
B Troop-3 Squad-17 Cav	Brownell, Steve B-3-17, CE, 1969	C Battery-2 Bn-20 Artillery ARA	Medlock, Rick 15 Med Bn, 1970-71
B Troop-3 Squad-17 Cav	Camp, Ken B-3-17, P, 1969-70	C Battery-2 Bn-20 Artillery ARA	Mesko, Jim author: HAVE GUN WILL TRAVEL
B Troop-3 Squad-17 Cav	Duff, Art B-3-17, 1969	C Battery-2 Bn-20 Artillery ARA	Moran, Jim C-2-20 ARA, P, 1970-71
B Troop-3 Squad-17 Cav	Earhart, Donivan, B-3-17, 1972	C Battery-2 Bn-20 Artillery ARA	Mutza, Wayne author: HAVE GUN WILL TRAVEL
B Troop-3 Squad-17 Cav	Gray, Carl B-3-17, P, 1968-69	C Battery-2 Bn-20 Artillery ARA	Palkow, John C-2-20 ARA, 1970-71
B Troop-3 Squad-17 Cav	Heinlein, Greg B-3-17, DG, 1970	C Battery-2 Bn-20 Artillery ARA	Reese, George personal website
B Troop-3 Squad-17 Cav	Hinson, Bud 539 TC, 1970	C Battery-2 Bn-20 Artillery ARA	Rickenbacker, Ernest, C-2-20 ARA, P, 1971
B Troop-3 Squad-17 Cav	Pierce, Robert B-3-17, 1969	C Battery-2 Bn-20 Artillery ARA	Sloniker, Mike A-229 AHB, P, 1970-71
B Troop-3 Squad-17 Cav	Rogers, Peter B-3-17, P, 1969	C Battery-2 Bn-20 Artillery ARA	Sprinkle, Jim 235/335 AWC, CE, 1971-72
B Troop-3 Squad-17 Cav	Searcy, Roger B-3-17, P, 1971-72	C Battery-2 Bn-20 Artillery ARA	Tyler, Dan C-2-20 ARA, P, 1970
B Troop-3 Squad-17 Cav	Simmons, Bill B-3-17, P, 1971-72	C Battery-2 Bn-20 Artillery ARA	Weaver, Randolph D-227 AHB, 1967-68
B Troop-3 Squad-17 Cav	Sprinkle, Jim 235/334 AWC, CE, 1971-72		
B Troop-3 Squad-17 Cav	Ward, Jay B-3-17, P, 1971-72	C Battery-4 Bn-77 Artillery ARA	Smith, Robert C-4-77 ARA, P, 1969
B Troop-3 Squad-17 Cav	Witte, Larry B-3-17, CE, 1972		
		C Co-101 Assault Hel Bn	Detra, Dick 188 AHC, DG, 1967-68
B Troop-7 Squad-1 Cav	Farber, Barry B-7-1, CE, 1968	C Co-101 Assault Hel Bn	Heidtke, Lonnie C-101, CE, 1968-69
B Troop-7 Squad-1 Cav	Granby, Jon 611 TC, 1968-69	C Co-101 Assault Hel Bn	Journeycake, Mike C-101, CE, 1969-70
B Troop-7 Squad-1 Cav	Thompson, Rich B-7-1, P, 1969-70	C Co-101 Assault Hel Bn	Linster, Frank 188 AHC, P, 1967-68
B Troop-7 Squad-17 Cav	Hefferman, Richard, B-7-17, CE, 1968	C Co-159 Assault Support Hel Bn	Brady, Jim C-159 ASHB, FE, 1971
B Troop-7 Squad-17 Cav	Haler, Ron B-7-17, 1970	C Co-159 Assault Support Hel Bn	Brown, J.C. C-159 ASHB, DG, 1968
B Troop-7 Squad-17 Cav	Maker, Don B-7-17, 1968-69	C Co-159 Assault Support Hel Bn	Holdings, David C-159 ASHB, FE, 1971
B Troop-7 Squad-17 Cav	Renfro, Doug B-7-17, 1970	C Co-159 Assault Support Hel Bn	Ianniello, Bill C-159 ASHB, CE, 1969-70
		C Co-159 Assault Support Hel Bn	Patterson, Dave C-159 ASHB, CE, 1968-69
C Battery-2 Bn-20 Artillery ARA	Barnes, Jerry C-2-20 ARA, P, 1966-67	C Co-159 Assault Support Hel Bn	Sexton Jerry C-159 ASHB, FE, 1967-68

Unit	Contributor
C Co-159 Assault Support Hel Bn	Stanley, Cleve C-159 ASHB, CE, 1970
C Co-159 Assault Support Hel Bn	Walters, David C-159 ASHB, FE, 1967-68
C Co-159 Assault Support Hel Bn	Wuthrich, 3-187-101 Abn, 1968-69
C Co-227 Assault Hel Bn	Beckler, Dennis C-227 AHB, CE, 1968-69
C Co-227 Assault Hel Bn	Belkin, Howie C-227 AHB, DG, 1969-70
C Co-227 Assault Hel Bn	Buehler, Dick C-227 AHB, CE, 1967
C Co-227 Assault Hel Bn	Faux, Tom C-227 AHB, 1967
C Co-227 Assault Hel Bn	Fifield, Tom C-227 AHB, CE, 1971
C Co-227 Assault Hel Bn	Griffin, Robert Army photographer, 1968
C Co-227 Assault Hel Bn	Hogan, Jerry photographer
C Co-227 Assault Hel Bn	Lesemann, Milton C-227 AHB, P, 1968-69
C Co-227 Assault Hel Bn	Lipford, Ben C-227 AHB, 1970-71
C Co-227 Assault Hel Bn	McCarty, Chuck 15 Med Bn, 1968
C Co-227 Assault Hel Bn	Mellquist, John B-227 AHB, DG, 1969-71
C Co-227 Assault Hel Bn	Parra, Frank C-227 AHB, CE, 1968-69
C Co-227 Assault Hel Bn	Perry, Jim 15 Med Bn, Avionics, 1967-68
C Co-227 Assault Hel Bn	Roy, Andy C-227 AHB, DG, 1968
C Co-227 Assault Hel Bn	Williams, Phil C-227 AHB, CE, 1971-72
Co-228 Assault Support Hel Bn	Chappell, Mel C-228 ASHB, FE, 1968-69
Co-228 Assault Support Hel Bn	Cornwell, Jim A-2-7 Cav, 1968-69
Co-228 Assault Support Hel Bn	Duke, Philip C-228 ASHB, FE, 1970
Co-228 Assault Support Hel Bn	Goodknight, Mike C-228 ASHB, FE, 1969-71
Co-228 Assault Support Hel Bn	Hadgkiss, Robert C-228 ASHB, FE, 1967
Co-228 Assault Support Hel Bn	Morley, Clifford C-228 ASHB, FE, 1970
Co-228 Assault Support Hel Bn	Schweitzer, Bob C-228 ASHB, CE, 1968
C Co-229 Assault Hel Bn	Anderson, Tom C-229 AHB, 1969-70
C Co-229 Assault Hel Bn	Atkinson, Gary C-229 AHB, CE, 1969-70
C Co-229 Assault Hel Bn	Baker, Dale F/8, CE, 1970
C Co-229 Assault Hel Bn	Baker, Roger C-229 AHB, P, 1969-70
C Co-229 Assault Hel Bn	Baldwin, Reg, C-229 AHB, P, 1968-69
C Co-229 Assault Hel Bn	Bargala, Sonny C-229 AHB, CE, 1970
C Co-229 Assault Hel Bn	Bridges, Roy C-229 AHB, DG, 1970-71
C Co-229 Assault Hel Bn	Brouwers, Dan C-229 AHB, DG, 1970-71
C Co-229 Assault Hel Bn	Buchheister, Bill B-2-5, 1968-69
C Co-229 Assault Hel Bn	Crawford, Bernie F/8, 1970
C Co-229 Assault Hel Bn	Flam, Mike C-229 AHB, CE, 1968-69
C Co-229 Assault Hel Bn	Griffiths, Ed C-229 AHB, CE, 1969-70
C Co-229 Assault Hel Bn	Head, Wayne C-229 AHB, P, 1970-71
C Co-229 Assault Hel Bn	Holt, John D-229, 1965-66
C Co-229 Assault Hel Bn	Holte, Dave C-229 AHB, CE, 1969-70
C Co-229 Assault Hel Bn	Hubbs, John C-229 AHB, DG, 1971-72
C Co-229 Assault Hel Bn	Peatross, Rob C-229 AHB, CE, 1970-71
C Co-229 Assault Hel Bn	Pritchett, Ron C-229 AHB, CE, 1967
C Co-229 Assault Hel Bn	Rhoades, Alan C-229 AHB, CE, 1968-69
C Co-229 Assault Hel Bn	Rittman, David C-229 AHB, P, 1966-67
C Co-229 Assault Hel Bn	Shemley, Larry C-229 AHB, P, 1969-70
C Co-229 Assault Hel Bn	Simonett, Kelly C-229 AHB, CE, 1969-70
C Co-229 Assault Hel Bn	Sites, Ron C-229 AHB, DG, 1970
C Co-229 Assault Hel Bn	Sloniker, Mike A-229 AHB, P, 1971-72
C Co-229 Assault Hel Bn	Sullivan, George 15 TC, 1968
C Co-229 Assault Hel Bn	Thomas, Craig 229 AHB surgeon, 1969-70
C Co-229 Assault Hel Bn	Tyler, Dan C-229 AHB, P, 1970-71
C Co-229 Assault Hel Bn	Wisbith, Stan C-229 AHB, CE, 1967-68
C Troop-1 Squad-9 Cav	Askew, Mike C-1-9, CE, 1967-68
C Troop-1 Squad-9 Cav	Bajc, Marko VN War researcher
C Troop-1 Squad-9 Cav	Bernstein, Jonathan author: THE CRYSTAL SHIP, CINDY ANN, HEATHER DAWN, BETTY K
C Troop-1 Squad-9 Cav	Brennan, Matthew, author: FAMILY CAR
C Troop-1 Squad-9 Cav	Brooks, Bill, 1970
C Troop-1 Squad-9 Cav	Cairns, Ernest C-1-9, CE, 1966-67
C Troop-1 Squad-9 Cav	Campbell, Bruce C-1-9, P, 1970-71
C Troop-1 Squad-9 Cav	Carlton, Ken 191 AHC, P, 1969-70
C Troop-1 Squad-9 Cav	Chinnery, Philip author: CINDY ANN
C Troop-1 Squad-9 Cav	Craig, John C-1-9, P, 1970-71
C Troop-1 Squad-9 Cav	Delarosa, Lionel C-1-9, 1969-70
C Troop-1 Squad-9 Cav	Harlem, Pete E-1-9, CE, 1970
C Troop-1 Squad-9 Cav	Hiservia, Frank C-1-9, 1966
C Troop-1 Squad-9 Cav	Hinch, Sam C-1-9, P, 1970-71
C Troop-1 Squad-9 Cav	Jacobsen, Gary C-1-9, P, 1969-70
C Troop-1 Squad-9 Cav	Jones, Gordon C-1-9, DG, 1966-67
C Troop-1 Squad-9 Cav	Jones, Walker C-1-9, P, 1970-71
C Troop-1 Squad-9 Cav	Kekar, Randy C-1-9, DG, 1970-71
C Troop-1 Squad-9 Cav	Kelley, Mike C-1-9, CE, 1965-66
C Troop-1 Squad-9 Cav	Knowlen, Chuck C-1-9, 1965-66
C Troop-1 Squad-9 Cav	Lemaster, Bob C-1-9, P, 1970-71
C Troop-1 Squad-9 Cav	Lipford, Ben C-227 AHB, 1970-71
C Troop-1 Squad-9 Cav	Maring, Marshall C-1-9, CE, 1970-71
C Troop-1 Squad-9 Cav	McWaters, John C-1-9, P, 19 70-71
C Troop-1 Squad-9 Cav	Miller, Harold C-1-9, CE, 1966-67
C Troop-1 Squad-9 Cav	Mutza, Wayne author: IRON BUTTERFLY

Unit	Name
C Troop-1 Squad-9 Cav	Powell, John C-1-9, P, 1968-69
C Troop-1 Squad-9 Cav	Rainwater, Ross C-1-9, P, 1970-71
C Troop-1 Squad-9 Cav	Rochat, Lou A-1-19, P, 1970
C Troop-1 Squad-9 Cav	Salazar, Rolando bro of Leo Salazar, C-1-9, CE, 1968-69
C Troop-1 Squad-9 Cav	Schillereff, John C-1-9, P, 1970-71
C Troop-1 Squad-9 Cav	Shaffer, Nate C-1-9, DG, 1970-71
C Troop-1 Squad-9 Cav	Smith, Mike C-1-9, P, 1970-71
C Troop-1 Squad-9 Cav	Sot, Wayne 13 Sig Bn, 1969-70
C Troop-1 Squad-9 Cav	Sprinkle, Jim 235/334 AWC, CE, 1971-72
C Troop-1 Squad-9 Cav	Stedman, Craig 595 Sig Co, 1969
C Troop-1 Squad-9 Cav	Verner, Larry C-1-9, CE, 1970-71
C Troop-1 Squad-9 Cav	Wright, Grover C-1-9, P, 1969-70
C Troop-1 Squad-9 Cav	Zahn, Randy author, C-1-9, P, 1970-71
C Troop-2 Squad-17 Cav	Caughlin, Sonny, CE, 1969-70
C Troop-2 Squad-17 Cav	Garrett, Bob C-2-17, P, 1969-70
C Troop-2 Squad-17 Cav	Miller, Ricky C-2-17, CE, 1971
C Troop-2 Squad-17 Cav	Wilhite, Ray USAAM
C Troop-3 Squad-17 Cav	Bell, Carl C-3-17, P, 1972
C Troop-3 Squad-17 Cav	Bonevich, Art C-3-17, DG, 1969-70
C Troop-3 Squad-17 Cav	Brown, Gary 25 Avn Bn, 1968-69
C Troop-3 Squad-17 Cav	Chapman, Ralph C-3-17, CE, 1971
C Troop-3 Squad-17 Cav	Gooch, Rex C-3-17, P, 1971-72
C Troop-7 Squad-1 Cav	Chenoweth, Bob author: PATRICIA ANN
C Troop-7 Squad-1 Cav	Chinnery, Phil author: PATRICIA ANN
C Troop-7 Squad-1 Cav	Davidson, Van 1968
C Troop-7 Squad-1 Cav	Dike, Joe C-7-1, CE, 1968-69
C Troop-7 Squad-1 Cav	Goodowens, Fowler C-7-1, P, 1968
C Troop-7 Squad-1 Cav	Groth, Jim C-7-1, CE, 1970-71
C Troop-7 Squad-1 Cav	Holder, Rick C-7-1, P, 1970-71
C Troop-7 Squad-1 Cav	Mesko, Jim author: PATRICIA ANN
C Troop-7 Squad-1 Cav	Nalty/Neufeld/Watson authors: PATRICIA ANN
C Troop-7 Squad-1 Cav	O'Connell, Richard C-7-1, CE, 1970-71
C Troop-7 Squad-1 Cav	Peacock, Lindsay author: PATRICIA ANN
C Troop-7 Squad-1 Cav	Peterson, Mike C-7-1, CE, 1968-69
C Troop-7 Squad-1 Cav	Smith, Dayne C-7-1, P, 1971-72
C Troop-7 Squad-1 Cav	Sprinkle, Jim author: PATRICIA ANN
C Troop-7 Squad-1 Cav	Strait, Clyde C-7-1, CE, 1967-68
C Troop-7 Squad-1 Cav	Wikoff, Al C-7-1, CE, 1971-72
C Troop-7 Squad-1 Cav	Young, Billy C-7-1, P, 1968-69
C Troop-7 Squad-17 Cav	Alexander, Charles, P, 1969-71
C Troop-7 Squad-17 Cav	Haines, Clint C-7-17, CE, 1969-70
C Troop-7 Squad-17 Cav	Shepard, Steve C-7-17, P, 1972
C Troop-16 Cav	Bernstein, Jonathan author: GLADIATOR
C Troop-16 Cav	Brewer, Gary D-1-4/C-16, CE, 1969-70
C Troop-16 Cav	Burk, Wayne C-16, P, 1970-71
C Troop-16 Cav	Gallardo, Orlando C-16, 1970-71
C Troop-16 Cav	Hawkins, George C-16, P, 1970-71
C Troop-16 Cav	Hodges, Don C-16, P, 1971-72
C Troop-16 Cav	King, Mike C-16, P, 1971-72
C Troop-16 Cav	Lundh, Lennart USS *Tripoli*, 1968-69
C Troop-16 Cav	Lundh, Lennart author: LE DISIPLE DU PAIX, LOVE AMERICAN STYLE, MISS CLAWD IV, TUBBERS TIGER
C Troop-16 Cav	Mills, Hugh C-16, P, 1972
C Troop-16 Cav	Mutza, Wayne author: ELECTRIC OLIVE I+II, SUZIE Q III
C Troop-16 Cav	Peacock, Lindsay author: PALE RIDER
C Troop-16 Cav	Reese, Bob C-16, CE, 1970-71
C Troop-16 Cav	Sprinkle, Jim 235/334 AWC, CE,1971-72
C Troop-16 Cav	Thacker, Greg C-16, DG, 1972
C Troop-16 Cav	Vick, Jack C-16, CE, 1970-71
C Troop-16 Cav	Washburn, Woody, 1970
C Troop-16 Cav	Willis, Rod C-16, P, 1970-73
D Co-227 Assault Hel Bn	Aamot, Leif A-5-7, 1968-69
D Co-227 Assault Hel Bn	Anderson, Paul 2 Bde 1 Cav, P, 1969-70
D Co-227 Assault Hel Bn	Barber, Lou C-227 AHB, P, 1966-67
D Co-227 Assault Hel Bn	Beckman, Martin D-227 AHB, P, 1969-70
D Co-227 Assault Hel Bn	Belkin, Howie, C-227 AHB, DG, 1969-70
D Co-227 Assault Hel Bn	Bernstein, Jonathan author: HULK
D Co-227 Assault Hel Bn	Bishop, Chris author: LEPRECHAUN
D Co-227 Assault Hel Bn	Bowling, Richard D-227 AHB, 1967-68
D Co-227 Assault Hel Bn	Bridges, Jim D-227 AHB, CE, 1966-67
D Co-227 Assault Hel Bn	Buchanan, Bobby 174 AHC, P, 1969

Unit	Contributor
D Co-227 Assault Hel Bn	Carlton, Ken 191 AHC, P, 1969-70
D Co-227 Assault Hel Bn	Chenoweth, Bob, author: AVENGER, GREMLIN, HULK, TIMUJIN SHIP
D Co-227 Assault Hel Bn	Dirnberger, Jay A-227 AHB, P, 1967-68
D Co-227 Assault Hel Bn	Francis, Jim A-227 AHB, 1969
D Co-227 Assault Hel Bn	Friday, Ed A-227 AHB, CE, 1969
D Co-227 Assault Hel Bn	Gates, Alan D-227 AHB, CE, 1968-69
D Co-227 Assault Hel Bn	Hankins, Randy A-227 AHB, CE, 1968-70
D Co-227 Assault Hel Bn	Harlem, Pete author: AVENGER
D Co-227 Assault Hel Bn	Jones, Dave D-227 AHB, 1968-71
D Co-227 Assault Hel Bn	Korbel, Rick, CE, A-227 AHB, 1968-69
D Co-227 Assault Hel Bn	Levengood, Joe D-227 AHB, CE, 1967-68
D Co-227 Assault Hel Bn	McMahan, Guy D-227 AHB, CE, 1968-69
D Co-227 Assault Hel Bn	Mesko, Jim author: LEPRECHAUN
D Co-227 Assault Hel Bn	Mills, Hugh D-1-4, P, 1969
D Co-227 Assault Hel Bn	Moon, Terry Army photog, 1969
D Co-227 Assault Hel Bn	Mutza, Wayne author: AVENGER, MISTER OLDS, PANDORA'S BOX
D Co-227 Assault Hel Bn	Obrecht, Mike D-227 AHB, CE, 1968-69
D Co-227 Assault Hel Bn	O'Neil, Mike D-227 AHB, P, 1970
D Co-227 Assault Hel Bn	Rochat, Lou A-1-9, P, 1970-71
D Co-227 Assault Hel Bn	Sprinkle, Jim 235/334 AWC, CE, 1971-72
D Co-227 Assault Hel Bn	Tepper, Art 610 TC, TI, 1968-70
D Co-227 Assault Hel Bn	Weaver, Randolph D-227 AHB, 1967-68
D Co-229 Assault Hel Bn	Bernstein, Jonathan author: THE MAGICAL MYSTERY TOUR
D Co-229 Assault Hel Bn	Carlton, Ken 191 AHC, P, 1969-70
D Co-229 Assault Hel Bn	Covert, Charles D-229 AHB, CE, 1970-71
D Co-229 Assault Hel Bn	Godden, Glen D-229 AHB, DG, 1971-72
D Co-229 Assault Hel Bn	Holt, John D-229, CE, 1965-66
D Co-229 Assault Hel Bn	Lundh, Lennart USS *Tripoli*, 1968-69
D Co-229 Assault Hel Bn	Moon, Terry Army photog, 1969
D Co-229 Assault Hel Bn	Okken, Wayne H-75 Inf, 1971-72
D Co-229 Assault Hel Bn	Roberge, Norm 15 Med Bn, 1968
D Co-229 Assault Hel Bn	Rosenburgh, Bob author: THE MAGICAL MYSTERY TOUR
D Co-229 Assault Hel Bn	Sullivan, George 15 TC, 1968
D Co-229 Assault Hel Bn	Walton, Bill D-229 AHB, CE, 1970-71
D Co-229 Assault Hel Bn	Wilhite, Ray USAAM

Unit	Contributor
D Troop-1 Squad-1 Cav	Adams, David D-1-1, P, 1969-70
D Troop-1 Squad-1 Cav	Ayers, Dave, D-1-1, P, 1972
D Troop-1 Squad-1 Cav	Bauman, Mike D-1-1, P, 1967-68
D Troop-1 Squad-1 Cav	Barrett, James D-1-1, 1969
D Troop-1 Squad-1 Cav	Bernstein, Jonathan author: DDAP
D Troop-1 Squad-1 Cav	Brittingham, Al D-1-1, CE, 1968-69
D Troop-1 Squad-1 Cav	Elderbaum, Russ D-1-1, 1969
D Troop-1 Squad-1 Cav	Gustin, Mike D-1-1, CE, 1970-71
D Troop-1 Squad-1 Cav	Harris, John D-1-1, 1970-71
D Troop-1 Squad-1 Cav	Johnson, Russell D-1-1, P, 1971
D Troop-1 Squad-1 Cav	Kane, Gary D-1-1, CE, 1971
D Troop-1 Squad-1 Cav	Kerchenfaut, Steve 176 AHC, P, 1969-71
D Troop-1 Squad-1 Cav	Klein, Jay D-1-1, 1970
D Troop-1 Squad-1 Cav	Lappos, Nick D-1-1, P, 1969-70
D Troop-1 Squad-1 Cav	Mahoney, Jim D-1-1, P, 1969-70
D Troop-1 Squad-1 Cav	McCue, Jim D-1-1, P, 1970-71
D Troop-1 Squad-1 Cav	Phillipson, Charles E-123 Avn Bn, 1970-71
D Troop-1 Squad-1 Cav	Timberlake, Ron D-1-1, 1971
D Troop-1 Squad-1 Cav	Tucker, Bill D-1-1, DG, 1970-71
D Troop-1 Squad-1 Cav	Walker, Mel D-1-1, P, 1968-70
D Troop-1 Squad-1 Cav	Wargi, Don D-1-1, P, 1969-70
D Troop-1 Squad-4 Cav	Bernstein, Jonathan author: SQUATTER SWATTER, WIDOW MAKER
D Troop-1 Squad-4 Cav	Brewer, Gary D-1-4/C-16, CE, 1969-70
D Troop-1 Squad-4 Cav	Caraker, Robert D-1-4, P, 1967-68
D Troop-1 Squad-4 Cav	Dunstan, Simon author: SQUATTER SWATTER
D Troop-1 Squad-4 Cav	Hudson, Kelly D-1-4, AC, 1967-68
D Troop-1 Squad-4 Cav	Kelly, Colin D-1-4, DG, 1965-66
D Troop-1 Squad-4 Cav	Lundh, Lennart USS *Tripoli*, 1968-69
D Troop-1 Squad-4 Cav	Mills, Hugh D-1-4, P, 1969-70
D Troop-1 Squad-4 Cav	Mong, Don commercial artist
D Troop-1 Squad-4 Cav	Peoples, Ken author: SQUATTER SWATTER
D Troop-1 Squad-4 Cav	Tenney, Bob D-1-4, P, 1967-68
D Troop-1 Squad-4 Cav	Willis, Rod D-1-4, P, 1969-70
D Troop-1 Squad-4 Cav	Witter, Tom D-1-4, 1968-69
D Troop-1 Squad-10 Cav	Belis, Mike D-1-10, 1969-70
D Troop-1 Squad-10 Cav	Bramuchi, David D-1-10, CE, 1969-70
D Troop-1 Squad-10 Cav	Cambo, Pablo C-7-17, 1969-70

D Troop-1 Squad-10 Cav	Eaton, Chuck D-1-10, 1970-71
D Troop-1 Squad-10 Cav	LaTour, Tim D-1-10, P, 1969-70
D Troop-1 Squad-10 Cav	Maas, Doug D-1-10, P, 1970-71
D Troop-1 Squad-10 Cav	Melvin, Brad D-1-10, DG, 1969-70
D Troop-1 Squad-10 Cav	Pender, Don D-1-10, P, 1971
D Troop-1 Squad-10 Cav	Snyder, Jim D-1-10, P, 1969-70
D Troop-2 Squad-1 Cav	Cron, Mike D-2-1, 1970
D Troop-2 Squad-1 Cav	Lohr, Fred D-2-1, P, 1968-69
D Troop-3 Squad-4 Cav	Allen, Stan D-3-4, 1969-70
D Troop-3 Squad-4 Cav	Atkinson, Dave D-3-4, DG, 1970
D Troop-3 Squad-4 Cav	Betsill, Carl F-4, 1971
D Troop-3 Squad-4 Cav	Blackmon, Billy D-3-4, DG, 1969-70
D Troop-3 Squad-4 Cav	Brethen, Eric D-3-4, P, 1969-70
D Troop-3 Squad-4 Cav	Burns, Carl D-3-4, P, 1966-67
D Troop-3 Squad-4 Cav	Coles, Dan D-3-4, 1970-71
D Troop-3 Squad-4 Cav	Drendel, Lou author: PEACE MAKER
D Troop-3 Squad-4 Cav	Eastes, Pat D-3-4, P, 1967-68
D Troop-3 Squad-4 Cav	Favata, Chris D-3-4, CE, 1968-69
D Troop-3 Squad-4 Cav	Fleming, Tom D-3-4, P, 1967
D Troop-3 Squad-4 Cav	Fluharty, Tom D-3-4, CE, 1969-70
D Troop-3 Squad-4 Cav	Greenhalgh, Bill 162 AHC, P, 1968-69
D Troop-3 Squad-4 Cav	Hoag, Jim D-3-4, CE, 1970-71
D Troop-3 Squad-4 Cav	Jones, Gary D-3-4, P, 1969
D Troop-3 Squad-4 Cav	Kirker, Jim D-3-4, CE, 1969-70
D Troop-3 Squad-4 Cav	Kloppel, Ken D-3-4/F-4, 1970-71
D Troop-3 Squad-4 Cav	Maxey, Robert D-3-4, 1971-72
D Troop-3 Squad-4 Cav	Mutza, Wayne author: BORROWED TIME, PEACE MAKER
D Troop-3 Squad-4 Cav	Nemeyer, Jack D-3-4, CE, 1969-70
D Troop-3 Squad-4 Cav	Odom, Jerry D-3-4, P, 1968-69
D Troop-3 Squad-4 Cav	Parks D-3-4, CE, 1968-69
D Troop-3 Squad-4 Cav	Preqent, Tom D-3-4, 1969
D Troop-3 Squad-4 Cav	Schmidt, Gary D-3-4, CE, 1970-71
D Troop-3 Squad-4 Cav	Sprinkle, Jim 235/334 AWC, CE, 1971-72
D Troop-3 Squad-4 Cav	VanZilen, Art A-7-1, 1971-72
D Troop-3 Squad-4 Cav	Walt, Jim D-3-4, 1968-69

D Troop-3 Squad-5 Cav	Bonevich, Art C-3-17, DG, 1969-70
D Troop-3 Squad-5 Cav	Branigan, George D-3-5, Ce, 1971-72
D Troop-3 Squad-5 Cav	Callison, Don D-3-5, P, 1970-71
D Troop-3 Squad-5 Cav	Chapman, Ralph D-3-5, CE, 1971-72
D Troop-3 Squad-5 Cav	Feltner, James D-3-5, CE, 1968-69
D Troop-3 Squad-5 Cav	Frady, Larry D-3-5, CE, 1968
D Troop-3 Squad-5 Cav	Garrison, Bill D-3-5, CE, 1971-72
D Troop-3 Squad-5 Cav	Hyler, Jim D-3-5, 1968-69
D Troop-3 Squad-5 Cav	Lovell, Wayne D-3-5, P, 1967
D Troop-3 Squad-5 Cav	Marsden, Russ D-3-5, CE, 1970-71
D Troop-3 Squad-5 Cav	Mills, Hugh D-3-5, P, 1971-72
D Troop-3 Squad-5 Cav	Minney, Mel D-3-5, CE, 1967-68
D Troop-3 Squad-5 Cav	Mitchell, Bruce D-3-5, CE, 1968-69
D Troop-3 Squad-5 Cav	Mong, Don commercial artist
D Troop-3 Squad-5 Cav	Norman, Billy D-3-5, DG, 1967-68
D Troop-3 Squad-5 Cav	Reeves, Kinsey D-3-5, 1971
D Troop-3 Squad-5 Cav	Rokey, D-3-5, P, 1970-71
D Troop-3 Squad-5 Cav	Stonner, Dean A-9, P, 1968-69
D Troop-3 Squad-5 Cav	Zavis, Joe D-3-5, CE, 1970-71
D Troop-17 Cav	Mahoney, Ray, 28/96 Sig Det, 1972-73
D Troop-17 Cav	Neely, Rich, D-17, P, 1972-73
D Troop-17 Cav	Robinson, John D-17, P, 1972-73
E Battery-82 Artillery	Lemp, Ed E Btry 82 Arty, CE, 1965-66
E Battery-82 Artillery	Liebrandt, Geoff digital artist
E Battery-82 Artillery	Mutza, Wayne author: DOUCHE BAG III
E Co-123 Avn Bn	Atkins, Gaylord E Co 123 Avn Bn, CE, 1970-71
E Co-704 Maint Bn	Brown, Danny E-704 Mnt Bn, CE, 1969-70
E Co-709 Maint Bn	Foss, Ken 709 Mnt Bn, P, 1966-67
E Co-723 Maint Bn	Hines, Les A-123 Avn Bn, CE, 1968-70
E Troop-1 Squad-9 Cav	Caine, Vaughn E-1-9, P, 1970-71
E Troop-1 Squad-9 Cav	Carlton, Ken 191 AHC, P, 1969-70
E Troop-1 Squad-9 Cav	Lundh, Lennart author: AS YE SOW SO SHALL YE REAP

Unit	Contributor
E Troop-1 Squad-9 Cav	Mutza, Wayne author: DOCTOR DEATH, LITTLE GREEN KILLING MACHINE, MONTANA MERCENARY
E Troop-1 Squad-9 Cav	Rochat, Lou E-1-9, P, 1970-71
E Troop-1 Squad-9 Cav	Snow, Roger E-1-9, CE, 1970-71
F Troop-4 Cav	Bernstein, Jonathan author: #1 DU ME MI
F Troop-4 Cav	Betsill, Carl F-4, 1971
F Troop-4 Cav	Cooper, Bill F-4 Cav, P, 1971-72
F Troop-4 Cav	Dillon, Frank F-4, 1971-72
F Troop-4 Cav	Drendel, Lou author: #1 DU ME MI
F Troop-4 Cav	Keirsey, Dan F-4 Cav, P, 1972-73
F Troop-4 Cav	Schmidt, Gary, D-3-4, CE, 70-71
F Troop-4 Cav	Wall, Tim F-4 Cav, 1972
F Troop-8 Cav	Baker, Dale F-8, CE, 1970
F Troop-8 Cav	Kudel, Leo F-8, 1971
F Troop-8 Cav	Mumaw, Carl F-8/570 TC, 1968-70
F Troop-8 Cav	Peacock, Lindsay author: HAMMERHEAD
F Troop-8 Cav	Sloniker, Mike A-229, P, 1971-72
F Troop-8 Cav	Thompson, Neal F-8, P, 1972
F Troop-9 Cav	Hostetler, Mark F-9 Cav, CE, 1972
F Troop-9 Cav	Murtha, Paul F-9, P, 1972
F Troop-9 Cav	Timberlake, Ron, 1972
F Battery-79 Artillery AFA	Cav Banicki, John C-2-8 Cav, 1972
F Battery-79 Artillery AFA	Brown, Mike F-79 AFA, P, 1971-72
F Battery-79 Artillery AFA	Doudna, Dean F-79 AFA, CE, 71-72
F Battery-79 Artillery AFA	Ferris, Bob C-2-8 1st Cav, 1972
F Battery-79 Artillery AFA	Harnett, Steve C-2-20/F-79 AFA, CE, 1971-72
F Battery-79 Artillery AFA	Hendrickson, Bruce C-2-20/F-79 AFA, CE, 1971-72
F Battery-79 Artillery AFA	Hubbs, John C-229 AHB, DG, 1971-72
F Battery-79 Artillery AFA	Jackson, Jet F-79 AFA, P, 1972
F Battery-79 Artillery AFA	Jetter, Art C-2-20 AFA, P, 1970-71
F Battery-79 Artillery AFA	Mather, Don F-79 AFA, CE, 1971-72
F Battery-79 Artillery AFA	Rickenbacker, Ernest F-79 AFA, P, 1971
F Battery-79 Artillery AFA	Sloniker, Mike A-229 AHB, P, 1971-72
F Battery-79 Artillery AFA	Sprinkle, Jim 235/334 AWC, CE, 1971-72
F Battery-79 Artillery AFA	Stotler, Bruce F-79 AFA, CE, 1971-72
COBRA NET TEAM	Bary, Victor 11 CAB, 1967
COBRA NET TEAM	McFarland, Tom COBRA NETT, P, 1970
COBRA NET TEAM	Mesko, Jim author: VIRGINIA ROSE I
COBRA NET TEAM	Mutza, Wayne author: VIRGINIA ROSE I
Utility Tactical Transport Hel Co-UTT	Ashton, Larry A-82 Avn Bn, CE, 1965
Utility Tactical Transport Hel Co-UTT	Chenoweth, Bob author: OLE HOTBOX
Utility Tactical Transport Hel Co-UTT	Wilhite, Ray USAAM
Utility Tactical Transport Hel Co-UTT	Young, Ralph author: BIG BERTHA, KATHRYN, LITTLE RUDY, PANDORA

Donna Sue II: *254 Med Det, UH-1H, Phan Thiet, 1967*. Jump doors were not commonly utilized for painted copter names. Seated pilot is James Ihli. Photo by Waul McMahan.

BIBLIOGRAPHY / RESOURCES

Numbers correspond to Contributor notations in the Helicopter Names A-Z section.

Unit History Photo Books

3000	4 Aviation Battalion: 1968-69
3025	14 Combat Aviation Battalion, CAB: 1967
3050	16 Combat Aviation Group, CAG: 1970
3075	57 Assault Helicopter Company, AHC: 1971, 1973
3100	114 Assault Helicopter Company, AHC: 1965, 1966, 1967, 1970, 1971
3125	119 Assault Helicopter Company, AHC: 1970
3150	123 Aviation Battalion: 1969
3175	132 Assault Support Helicopter Company, ASHC: 1969, 1970
3200	135 Assault Helicopter Company, AHC: 1969
3225	162 Assault Helicopter Company, AHC: 1972
3250	174 Assault Helicopter Company, AHC: 1969, 1970
3275	176 Assault Helicopter Company, AHC: 1969
3300	187 Assault Helicopter Company, AHC: 1971
3325	189 Assault Helicopter Company, AHC: 1971
3350	335 Assault Helicopter Company, AHC: 1970
3375	A Troop, 7 Squadron, 1 Cavalry: 1971
3400	C Company, 229 Assault Helicopter Battalion, AHB: 1970
3425	C Troop, 16 Cavalry: 1972
3450	D Troop, 1 Squadron, 1 Cavalry: 1968-69, 1969-70, 1970-71
3475	D Troop, 3 Squadron, 4 Cavalry: 1970, 1971-72
3500	F Troop, 4 Cavalry: 1971-72
3525	F Troop, 8 Cavalry: 1969

Internet Reference Resources

3540   Air War Vietnam: Darkhorse, AH-1G named "PALE RIDER" *(airwarvietnam.com/16cavctroopstory)*

3550   All The World's Rotorcraft Directory *(aviasrat.org)*

3575   Army Air Crews KIA Database *(armyaircrews.com)*

3600   Army Helicopter Units Vietnam War, in-country videos *(militaryvideo.com)*

3625   Aviation Art and Helmet Painting *(gunfightergrafx.com/huey)*

3650   Aviation Enthusiasts Corner *(aero-web.org)*

3675   Barbara Gluck, combat photographer, personal website *(barbaragluck.com/about_barbara.html)*

3680   Bill Frazer, A-1-9 pilot, personal website: OH-6A named "QUEER JOHN" news article *(angelfire.com/tx3/page3)*

3700   Billy Norman, D-3-5 Cav, personal website *(billynorman.com/Vietnam)*

3710   Brian Lambie, 176 AHC pilot, UH-1D named "PATCHES" *(vhpa.org/stories/wreckage)*

3725   Brothers of Nam website *(closed or moved?)*

3750   Bruce "Sarge" Holzhauer, 2 Bn,12 Inf Reg, personal website *(community2.webtv.net/@HH!D8!C7!358EEE307F99/infantry2bn12th/2ndBATTALION12th)*

3775   Can Tho-Delta, extensive IV Corps area website *(cantho-rvn.org)*

3800   Cavalry, dedicated to preserving the history and traditions of the Cavalry *(cavhooah.com)*

3850   Combat Helicopter Pilots Assn, CHPA *(chpa-us.org)*

3875   Dan Cannon, A-3-17 Cav, personal website *(coyoteroadkill.com/events/vietnam-3rdof17th/vietnam-pictures)*

3900   David Parsley, 605 TC, in-country photos *(pbase.com/character/svietnam68)*

3925   Drew's World of Choppers *(slick-net.com)*

3950   Ed Lyons, B-25 Avn Bn, personal pic album *(combatveteranonline.net/vietnam002)*

3975   Former In-Country Huey Smoke Ship, Smithsonian Institution collection: *(nasm.si.edu/collections/artifact.cfm?id=A19960005000)*

4000   Fred Lohr, D-2-1 Cav and 180 ASHC pilot, personal website *(fredlohr.com)*

4025   Gary Brown, 25 Avn Bn, personal pic album: *(picasaweb.google.com/GaryK4GPB/19681969Vietnam#)*

4050   George Reese, 25 Avn Bn/117 AHC, extensive in-country Army helo photo archives *(flyarmyair.com)*

4075   HAWK, 1 Avn Bde, in-country magazine,'67-'72 index *(1stavnbde.com/Hawk/Hawk_index_visual)*

4100   Hector Nadal, Combat Photographer, personal website *(namvet-malambo.com)*

4125   In The Shadow of The Blade *(intheshadowoftheblade.com)*

4150   Int'l Plastic Modelers Assn, Memphis Chapter, 170 AHC nose art *(ipmsmemphis.com/page15/page15)*

4175   Jerry Hogan, B-1-9 Cav, via son Jeremy *(searchingfortheblues.com/Searching_for_the_Blues/Home)*

4200   Jim Bracewell, B-229 and HHT-7-1 Cav pilot, personal website *(jimbro.org)*

Internet Reference Resources (cont.)

4225	Joe Baugher, U.S. Aircraft Serial # Database *(joebaugher.com/usaf_serials/usafserials)*
4250	Joe Kline, personalized aviation and military art *(joekline.com)*
4275	Larry Sherrer, A-3-17 Cav pilot, book review *(amazon.com/Zigzag-Men-Larry-Sherrer/dp)*
4280	Milton Lowden, 121 Avn Co, personal website *(121stavnco.com)*
4300	MSN Groups, online communities *(closed)*
4325	N.G. Brown, C-2-20 Aerial Rocket Artillery (ARA) pilot, personal website *(bluemax69q1.com)*
4350	Online Auction Website *(ebay.com)*
4400	Profile Illustrations of Vietnam War Hueys *(vietnam-hueys.tripod.com)*
4425	Quigley's Down Under, personal website dedicated to all U.S. Nam vets *(docmelson.com/quig's)*
4450	Radio Controlled Model Aircraft *(rcwarbirds.com)*
4460	Rick Lester, 48 AHC pilot, UH-1C named "BROTHER LOVE'S TRAVELIN' SALVATION SHOW", American Legion Post 134, March 2009 newsletter story *(www.alpost134.org/index.php?option=com_content&task=view&id=120&Itemid=1)*
4475	Robert Fischer, 9th Division, 1969, personal website *(gingerb.com/Vietnam)*
4480	Robert Mason, B-229 pilot, personal website *(robertcmason.com)*
4500	Shoebox Photos *(shoeboxphotos.net)*
4510	Stan Cherrie, 191 AHC pilot, UH-1C named "MOTHER GOOSE", Vietnam magazine article, February 2009 issue: *(historynet.com/a-hueys-wild-duel-with-a-50-cal-gunner-during-tet)*
4525	Terry Moon, 1st Cav PIO Photographer, 1969, personal website *(1stcavphotog.tripod.com)*
4530	Thomas Nadeau, 195 AHC pilot: UH-1H '210, "DEUCE AND A DIME" *(vhpa.org/stories/deuce)*
4550	Tom Martin, 187 AHC pilot, personal website *(rvnair.info/?p=68)*
4575	U.S. Army Attack Helicopter *(incolor.inebraska.com/iceman)*
4600	U.S. Army Aviation Museum, USAAM *(armyavnmuseum.org)*
4625	U.S. Military Community Heritage Websites *(togetherweserved.com)*
4650	Veterans Lost and Found Search Engine *(vietvet.org/lostfnd)*
4675	Vets With A Mission *(vwam.com)*
4700	Vietnam Helicopter Artifacts and Images *(vhpamuseum.org/defaultmenu)*
4725	Vietnam Helicopter Crew Members Assn, VHCMA *(vhcma.org)*
4750	Vietnam Helicopter Crew Members Assn, VHCMA, Links Page *(vhcma.org/unit)*
4775	Vietnam Helicopter Flight Crew Network, VHFCN *(vhfcn.org)*

Internet Reference Resources (cont.)

4800	Vietnam Helicopter Flight Crew Network, VHFCN, Links Page *(vhfcn.org/unitlinks)*
4825	Vietnam Helicopter Pilots Assn, VHPA *(vhpa.org)*
4850	Vietnam Helicopter Pilots Assn, VHPA, Calendar: 2000, 2004, 2010, 2011 *(vhpaphoto.org/calendars)*
4875	Vietnam Helicopter Pilots Assn, VHPA, Links Page *(vhpa.org/prod01)*
4900	Vietnam Veterans of America, VVA *(vva.org)*
4925	Vietnam Veterans of Korea *(cafe3.ktdom.com/vietvet/us/us)*
4950	Vietnam Vets Home Page *(vietvet.org)*
4975	Vietnam War Helicopter Veterans Assn *(heli-vet.net)*
5000	Vintage Film Arsenal, VFA, in-country videos *(vintagef.startlogic.com)*
5025	Virtual Vietnam Archives, TX Tech Univ *(vietnam.ttu.edu/virtualarchive)*
5050	Wayne "Cappy" Capps, 13 CAB, personal website *(gemini65.tripod.com/index-2.html)*
5075	Yahoo Groups, online communities *(groups.yahoo.com)*

Periodicals, Newsletters and Newspapers

5100	Andrews, Paul. "Seventeen Bits And Pieces: Boeing's B-17 F's and G's Assigned To The 8th U.S Army Air Force, August 1942-May 1945: *AAHS Journal*, Fall, 1979
5150	Chenoweth, Bob. "Bell's Early Hueys And The Vietnam Connection," *Air Enthusiast*, Dec '84-Mar '85
5175	Chenoweth, Bob. "Chenoweth's Choppers," *Pri-Fly*, Wash DC Chapter, IPMS, #39, 1981
5200	Chenoweth, Bob. "Guns A-Go-Go," *Aviation News*, 15-28 July, 1983
5225	Chenoweth, Bob. "Helicopter War," *Aviation News*, 20 Nov-3 Dec, 1981
5250	Chenoweth, Bob. "Huey Delta's And Hotel's," *Air Enthusiast*, Mar-Jun, 1986
5275	Chenoweth, Bob. "Vietnam: The Helicopter War," *Scale Aircraft Modeling*, Vol. 4, # 9, June, 1982
5300	Griffith, James S. Dr. "Military Aircraft Nose Art: An American Tradition," Univ of Arizona (on-line also)
5325	Lacdan, Joe. "Vietnam Veteran, Helicopter Reunited," *Warrenville Press*, Oct 30, 2008, pg 12. Paul Goodwin, former CE on UH-1H "CHICAGO II," 117 AHC, 1972
5400	Sprinkle, James D. "Naming The Bell AH-1G," *AAHS Journal*, Summer, 1974, pgs 157-158
5425	Sprinkle, James D. "The HueyCobra in Vietnam," *AAHS Journal*, Fall, 1975, pgs 162-170
5427	*AAHS Journal*: American Aviation Historical Society periodical (on-line also)

Periodicals, Newsletters and Newspapers (cont.)

5430   *Army Magazine*: February 1965

5433   *The Army Reporter*: in-country newspaper: May 1969, August 31, 1970, September 1971

5436   *Aviation Week and Space Technology*: periodical, February 22, 1965

5440   *Life*: magazine, Larry Burrows photograph, 1963

5444   *Pacific Stars and Stripes*: military newspaper: July 17, 1968 and late 1970

5446   *Straight Scoop*: newsletter, Pacific Coast Air Museum, June 2009 (on-line also)

5448   *The VVA Veteran*: newsletter, Vietnam Veterans of America, VVA, Feb 2009 (on-line also)

Books

5450   Bernstein, Jonathan: *US Army AH-1 Cobra Units In Vietnam*, 2003

5475   Bishop, Chris: *Huey Cobra Gunships*, 2006

5500   Bows, Ray: *Vietnam Military Lore, 1959-73: Another Way To Remember*, 1988

5525   Bows, Ray: *Vietnam Military Lore: Legends, Shadows And Heroes*, 1997

5550   Brandt, Robert: *Thunderbird Lounge*, 2006

5560   Brennan, Matthew: *Hunter-Killer Squadron*, 1990

5575   Chenoweth, Bob: *Army Gunships In Vietnam*, 1987

5625   Chinnery, Philip: *Vietnam: The Helicopter War*, 1991

5650   Cook, John: *Rescue Under Fire: The Story Of Dust Off In Vietnam*, 1998

5675   Davis, Larry: *Planes, Names and Dames, Vol III*, 1995

5700   Drendel, Lou: *Gunslingers In Action*, 1974

5725   Drendel, Lou: *Huey*, 1983

5750   Dunstan, Simon: *Vietnam Choppers: Helicopters In Battle*, 1950-75, 1988

5775   Eastman, David: *Outlaws In Vietnam, 1966-67 In The Delta*, 2001

5800   Ethel, Jeff: *History of Aircraft Nose Art*, 1991

5825   Ford, Dan: *The Only War We've Got*, 2001

5850   Forman, Wallace: *B-17 Nose Art Name Directory*, 1996

5875   Forman, Wallace: *B-24 Nose Art Name Directory*, 1996

5900   Harlem, Pete: *The UH-1C Huey*, 1985

5925   Johnson, Lawrence: *Winged Sabers: The Air Cavalry In Vietnam*, 1990

Books (cont.)

5950   Jones, W. Bailey: *Year Of The Snake: One Helicopter Pilot's Story Of A Year In Vietnam's Mekong Delta*, 1999

5975   Kelley, Michael: *Where We Were In Vietnam*: 2002

6000   Lucas, Jim: *Dateline, Viet Nam*, 1966

6025   Lundh, Lennart: *U.S. Army Aviation Color Schemes and Markings*, 2000

6050   Mesko, Jim: *Airmobile: The Helicopter War In Vietnam*, 1984

       Mutza, Wayne:

6075   ——— *UH-1 Huey In Action*, 1986

6100   ——— *Chinook In Action*, 1989

6125   ——— *Huey In Color*, 1992

6150   ——— *Bent and Battered Rotors, Vol 3*, 1993

6175   ——— *AH-1 Cobra in Action*, 1998

6200   ——— *Walk Around AH-1 Cobra*, 2002

6225   ——— *Walk Around UH-1 Huey Gunships*, 2004

6250   ——— *Loach: The Story Of The H-6/Model 500 Helicopter*, 2005

6275   ——— *U.S. Army Aviation In Vietnam*, 2009

6300   ——— *Helicopter Gunships*, 2010

6325   Nalty, B, Neufeld, J, Watson,G: *The Air War Over Vietnam*, 1981

6350   Peacock, Lindsay: *AH-1 Huey Cobra*, 1987

6375   Peoples, Kenneth: *Bell AH-1 Cobra Variants*, 1988

6400   Rosenburgh, Bob: *Snake Driver: Cobras In Vietnam*, 1993

6425   Stanton, Shelby: *Vietnam Order Of Battle*, 1986

6450   Steinbrunn, Bob: *Vietnam Scrapbook: An Army Pilot's Combat Tour*, 2008

6475   VHPA: *Vietnam Helicopter Pilots Association* (Vol II), 2007

6500   Young, Ralph: *Army Aviation In Vietnam, 1961-63*, 1999

6525   Young, Ralph: *Army Aviation In Vietnam, 1963-66*, 2000

6550   Zahn, Randy: *Snake Pilot: Flying The Attack Cobra Helicopter In Vietnam*, 2005

Self Published, Limited Edition

6625 Callaghan, Bob: *Wee Luck'ed Out (2 Signal Group)*: in-country diary, Jan-Dec 1966

6650 Marzen, Claus: *114th Avn Co Armament Section: A Partial History, 1963-66*, 1998

Military Associations: Archives, Directories, CD-ROM, Reunions and Unit Histories

6700 114 Aviation Company Association: *Knights Over The Delta: An Oral History Of The 114th Avn Co in Vietnam, 1963-72*, 2002

6725 114 Aviation Company Association: *Membership Directory*: 1993-2008

6750 114 Aviation Company Association: Reunions, 1993-2007

6775 114 Aviation Company Association: Unit Archives

6790 Vietnam Helicopter Crew Members Assn, VHCMA: *Membership Directory, '03, '07, '08, '10*

6805 Vietnam Helicopter Crew Members Assn, VHCMA: Reunion, 2009

6820 Vietnam Helicopter Pilots Assn, VHPA: *Historical Reference Directory, Vols 1 and 2*, 1993

6835 Vietnam Helicopter Pilots Assn, VHPA: *Membership Directory*: 1989 – 2009

6850 Vietnam Helicopter Pilots Assn, VHPA: *Vietnam Helicopter History CD-ROM*, 2002

6865 Wolf, Bill: *Bite & Strike: The History, Stories, And Images Of The 129th AHC*, 2007

Military Unit and Unit Association Newsletters, Newspapers, Periodicals: In-Country and Post-VN War

6875 *The Aviator*: VHPA newsletter

6900 *The Cavalair*: 1st Air Cavalry Division, in-country newspaper, Vol. 4, # 16, April 22, 1970, pg 7, "Graffiti Gives Birds Colorful Personality" (re: C Co, 229 AHB)

    Hawk: 1 Aviation Brigade, in-country magazine (on-line also):

6925 —— Sept 1967, Vol 1, # 1

6950 —— Apr 1968, Vol 1, # 8

6975 —— July 1968, Vol 1, # 11, pg 6: "Tiger Ships Are Works of Art" (re: 121 AHC)

7000 —— Apr 1969, Vol 2, # 8

7025 —— May 1969, Vol 2, # 9

7050 —— Aug 1970, Vol 3, # 12

7075 —— Sum-Fall 1971, Vol 5, # 2

7085 *Hawk Talk*: 7 Armored Sqdn 1 Air Cav, Blackhawk Assn Newsletter

7090 *Knight Cap*: 114 Avn Co, in-country newsletter

7095 *The Knight Letter*: 114 Avn Co Assn newsletter

Military Unit and Unit Association Newsletters, Newspapers, Periodicals: In-Country and Post-VN War (cont.)

7125   *LZ Home*: VHCMA newsletter

7150   *The Straphanger Gazette*: Aerial Rocket Artillery (ARA) Assn, Jan-Mar 2010 (on-line also)

7200   *U.S. Army Vietnam, Aviation Pamphlet, USAV Avn Pamphlet*, August 1970

Dustoff – Medevac Reference Resources

7375   15 Med Bn *(15thmedassociation.com)*

7400   15 Med Bn, MSN Group *(closed)*

7425   45 Med Co *(vietnamdustoff.com)*

7450   45 Med Co Richard Cunnare, Crew Chief *(war-stories.com/aspprotect/dustoff-cunnare-1967-2.asp)*

7475   45 Med Co Steve Vermillion *(dustoff40.com/aboutdustoff40)*

7500   57 Med Det *(psysim.www7.50megs.com/html/dustoff)*

7525   57 Med Det *(xmission.com/~doug/VietNam)*

7550   57 + 82 Med Det *(deltadustoff.com)*

7575   82 Med Det *(82ndmedicaldetachment.bravehost.com)*

7600   159 Med Det *(159thdustoff.com)* (closed))

7625   159 Med Det *(159thdustoff.net)*

7650   237 Med Det *(dmzdustoff.org)*

7675   498 Med Co *(498airamb.citymax.com/home)*

7700   498 Med Co *(498thdustoff.com)*

7725   Dustoff Assn *(dustoff.org)*

7750   Dustoff Photo Project *(home.swbell.net/robmock)*

7775   Dustoff and Medevac KIA List + Memorial Register *(psysim.www7.50megs.com/html/dustkia)*

7780   Hansen, Dave, 237 Med Det pilot: "The Final Flight Of 'CURIOUS YELLOW'" *(vhpa.org/stories/yellow)*

CH-47 Chinook Websites

Hyperlinks to numbered units can be found via the VHPA, VHCMA, VHFCN and 1st Avn Bde websites.

7800	132 ASHC	7950	200 ASHC	8100	271 ASHC (closed)
7825	147 ASHC	7975	205 ASHC	8125	362 ASHC
7850	159 ASHB	8000	213 ASHC	8150	A-159 ASHB
7875	178 ASHC	8025	228 ASHB	8175	B-159 ASHB
7900	179 ASHC	8050	242 ASHC	8200	C-159 ASHB
7925	180 ASHC	8075	243 ASHC		

8225	*CH47.org* (The Ol' Hooker Hangout)
8250	*Chinookcrews.com*
8275	*Chinook-Helicopter.com*
8300	*Gunsagogo.org*
8325	*Members.tripod.com/frenchys_205* (205 ASHC, Adolf Viol)
8350	*Muleskinners.net* (242 ASHC)
8360	A Different Kind of Military Reunion ("GRANNY TWITCHETT", 178 ASHC) *(theboxcar.org/savannah_news/index)* Aug 10, 2001
8365	The Crash of "THE PUSHER" in Cambodia (C/228 ASHB) *(vhpa.org/stories/pushercrash)*
8370	"THE ODYSSEY": Chinook Bomber of C/228 ASHB *(vhpa.org/stories/update)*
8375	"THE ODYSSEY": Strafed In A Jungle Shootout (C/228 ASHB) *(vhpa.org/stories/jungle)*

Internet Forums

8400	*ArcAir.com*	Aircraft Resource Center (ARC), Helicopter Modeling Forum
8425	*Armchairgeneral.com*	VN War Forum
8450	*Finescale.com*	Fine Scale Modeler (FSM), Helicopter Forum
8475	*Gunbroker.com*	VN War Forum
8500	*Helikitnews.com*	Helicopter Models, Books, Articles, Decals
8525	*Military.com*	VN War Forum; Unit Pages
8550	*Patriotfiles.com*	VN War Forum
8575	*Scale-Rotors.com*	Helicopter Modeling Forum
8600	*USmilitariaforum.com*	Mil-Aviation Forum

Internet Photo Hosting Sites

8625	*Facebook.com*	8775	*Picasa.google.com*	8925	*Youtube.com*
8650	*Flickr.com*	8800	*Smugmug.com*		
8675	*Metacafe.com*	8825	*Snapfish.com*		
8700	*Military.com*	8850	*Togetherweserved.com*		
8725	*Pbase.com*	8875	*Vetfriends.com*		
8750	*Photobucket.com*	8900	*Webshot.com*		

Source Websites For In-Country Army Unit Helicopter Info and Images

Hyperlinks can be found via the links pages on the VHCMA, VHFCN, VHPA and 1st AVN BDE websites.

8950	1 AVN BDE *(1stavnbde.com/companies_index)*	9160	51 LRRP *(elitebastards.org)*
8975	1 BDE 1 CAV	9170	52 CAB
9000	1 BN 1 INF	9180	57 AHC
9010	1 BN 6 INF *(a-1-6.org/1-6th Site/1st Bn 6th Inf Web Site Off Line/0HomePage1-6Inf)*	9190	62 AHC
		9200	68 AHC
9020	1 BN 50 INF *(ichiban1.org/index)*	9210	71 AHC
9030	1 CAV DIV	9220	92 AHC
9040	1-4 QUARTER CAV	9230	114 AHC
9050	2 BN 60 INF 9 INF DIV *(closed)*	9240	116 AHC
9060	4 AVN BN	9250	117 AHC
9070	8 TC *(8thtrans.com)*	9260	118 AHC
9080	9 INF DIV *(9thinfdivsociety.org)*	9270	119 AHC
9090	11 ACR *(11thacraviation.com)*	9280	120 AHC
9100	12 CAG	9290	121 AHC *(121avn.org)*
9110	17 *(closed)*	9300	128 AHC
9120	25 AVN BN	9310	129 AHC
9130	28-96 SIG DET *(testequipland.com)*	9320	134 AHC
9140	37 SIG BN *(the37thsignalbn-rvn.org)*	9330	135 AHC
9150	48 AHC	9340	142 TC *(home.comcast.net/~jshebert142)*

Source Websites For In-Country Army Unit Helicopter Info and Images (cont.)

9350	145 CAB	9630	388 TC
9360	155 AHC	9640	390 TC *(390tc.com)*
9370	161 AHC	9650	391 TC
9380	161 RECCE *(161recceflt.org.au)*	9660	539 TC
9390	162 AHC *(162ahc.ning.com)*	9670	604 TC
9400	170 AHC	9680	A-101 AVN BN
9410	173 ABN Caspar	9690	A-1-9 CAV
9420	173 AHC	9700	A-227 AHB
9430	174 AHC	9710	A-229 AHB
9440	175 AHC	9720	A-3-17 CAV
9450	176 AHC	9730	A-7-17 CAV
9460	184 RAC *(184rac.com)*	9740	B-1-9 CAV
9470	187 AHC	9750	B-123 AVN BN
9480	188 AHC	9760	B-2-17 CAV
9490	189 AHC	9770	B-227 AHB
9500	191 AHC	9780	B-229 AHB
9510	192 AHC	9790	B-3-17 CAV
9520	199 RAC *(swampfox199thrac.com)*	9800	B-7-17 CAV
9530	238 AHC	9805	C-1-9 CAV
9540	240 AHC	9810	C-16 CAV*(darkhorsevietnam.com)*
9550	281 AHC	9815	C-16 CAV, 1972-73 photos
9560	282 AHC		*(82ndmedicaldetachment.bravehost.com/Viet Nam*
9570	334 AHC *(334th-awc.com)*		*1972-73/index)*
9575	334 AHC *(deanmcgaha.tripod.com)*	9820	C-2-17 CAV
9580	334 AHC photos *(flyhuey.com)*	9825	C-227 AHB
9590	335 AHC	9830	C-229 AHB
9600	335 TC	9835	D-1-1 CAV
9610	336 AHC	9840	D-1-10 CAV
9620	339 TC	9842	D-2-1 CAV

Source Websites For In-Country Army Unit Helicopter Info and Images (cont.)

9845	D-227 AHB
9850	D-229 AHB (closed)
9855	D-3-4 CAV
9860	D-3-5 CAV
9865	F-4 CAV
9870	F-8 CAV
9875	A Battery, 6 Battalion, 27 Field Artillery *(quanloi.org)*
9880	Aerial Rocket Artillery, Blue Max *(aerial-rocket-artillery.org)*
9885	Americal *(americal.org)*
9890	Army Rangers, CO H, 75 Inf, 1 Cav Div *(lrrprangers.com/f-PicIndex)*
9895	Blackhawk Assn, 7-1 *(sandersusa.com)*
9900	Blue Max MSN Group *(closed)*
9905	Bullwhip Squadron Assn, 1-9 *(bullwhipsquadron.org)*
9910	Camp Holloway *(52dcab.org)*
9915	Caribou Assn *(c-7acaribou.com/album)*
9920	Centaurs MSN Group *(closed)*
9925	Firebase Phu Loi *(home.comcast.net/~jbenner411/benner)*
9930	HHB Battery, 6-27 Arty *(quanloi.org)*
9935	Lighthorse, C-3-17 and D-3-5 *(lighthorseaircav.com)*
9940	LZ Betty, Phan Thiet *(lzbetty.com)*
9945	Pleiku Air Base Vietnam Assn *(pleikuab.com)*
9950	Pleiku Pals *(pleikupals.org)*
9955	Quan Loi AAF *(quanloi.org)*
9960	Tan Son Nhut Assn *(tsna.org/mainpage)*

Under Dog*: A Co 158 AHB, (sn 67-17632), 1969.* Frank Simonson, pictured, is quick to point out that before the AC adopted this name as his personal call-sign it existed as a bona-fide, visible copter name, something rarely seen in this unit, or for that matter, any 101st Airborne Division unit. Photo courtesy Frank Simonson.

ABBREVIATIONS INDEX

Symbols

*	v-nn	Verbal Name
**	v-nnp	Verbal Name Relating to Nose Art
***	pv-nnp	Partial Verbal Name Relating to Nose Art
^	callsign	Pilot, Crew, Platoon or Unit Callsign
^^	slogan	Platoon or Unit Slogan
^^^		Platoon Name
#		Number

Configurations/Abbreviations

AO	Art Only
NO	Name Only
N+A	Name + Artwork
NAA	Name as Art
ABN	Airborne
A/C	Aircraft
AC	Aircraft Commander
ACR	Armored Cavalry Regiment
AFA	Aerial Field Artillery
AHB	Assault Helicopter Battalion
AHC	Assault Helicopter Company
AKA	Also Known As
ARA	Aerial Rocket Artillery
ARTY	Artillery
ASHB	Assault Support Helicopter Battalion
ASHC	Assault Support Helicopter Company
ASSN	Association
ATC	Air Traffic Control
AVN	Aviation
AWC	Aerial Weapons Company
BDE	Brigade
BK	Book

BN	Battalion
BPW	Below Pilot Window
BTRY	Battery
BUG	Helicopter equipped with powerful Xenon searchlight and night vision gear
C+C	Command + Control
CAB	Combat Aviation Battalion
CAC	Corps Aviation Company
CAG	Combat Aviation Group
CARGO	CH-47 Chinook: heavy lifter, troop and cargo carrier
CAV	Cavalry
CBT	Combat
CE	Crew Chief
CHUNKER	Grenade launcher in nose turret
CLAMSHELL	Engine access doors on the OH-6A
CO	Company
C. O.	Commanding Officer
COL	Colonel
COMD	Command
CONFIG	Configuration
CP	Co-Pilot
CPT	Captain
CSAB	Combat Support Aviation Battalion
CSBN	Composite Services Battalion
DD	Date Destroyed
DEROS	Date Estimated Return from Overseas Service
DET	Detachment
DG	Door Gunner
DIV	Division
DOGHOUSE	Rotor housing area
DR	Door
DUSTOFF	Air Ambulance
ENG	Engineer
EVAC	Evacuation

FE	Flight Engineer
FIREFLY	Helicopter equipped with powerful Xenon searchlight and night vision
FLT	Flight
FROG	UH-1B/C with 14 rockets, grenade launcher and M-60 machine-guns
GN	General
GP	Group
GS	General Support
GUN	Gunship, armed helicopter: ACH-47A, AH-1G HueyCobra, UH-1B, C, M
HEL/HELO	Helicopter
H+HC	Headquarters + Headquarters Company
HHC	Heavy Helicopter Company
H+HT	Headquarters + Headquarters Troop
HOG	UH-1B/C with 48 rockets and M-60 machine guns
HUEY	UH-1A, B, C, D, H, M
INF	Infantry
KIA	Killed In Action
LIB	Light Infantry Brigade
LIFT	CH-21 Shawnee, predecessor to the UH-1 troop carrier
LIGHTSHIP	UH-1 mounted with seven landing lights for night missions
LOACH	OH-6, a light observation helicopter
LOG	Logistical
LRRP	Long Range Reconnaissance Patrol
LT	Lieutenant
LTC	Lieutenant Colonel
LZ	Landing Zone
MAD	Mortar Aerial Delivery
MAINT	Maintenance
MAJ	Major
MB	Medical Battalion
MC	Medical Company
MD	Medic
MD	Medical Detachment
MED	Medical
MEDEVAC	Air Ambulance, 1st Cavalry Division
MNT	Maintenance Battalion
NETT	New Equipment Training Team
NIGHTHAWK	UH-1 with spotlight and Starlight capabilities
NN	Name
NWSLTR	Newsletter
NVA	North Vietnamese Army
OPNS	Operations
P	Pilot
PG	Page
PIC	Photograph
PIO	Public Information Office
PITOT	Exterior mounted device on an aircraft that measures air speed
PLT	Platoon
RAC	Reconnaissance Aviation Company
RECOVERY	Heavy lifters: CH-37 Mojave, CH-54 Sky Crane
RED-X	Indefinitely grounded
RRC	Radio Research Company
SAC	Surveillance Aviation Company
SAPPER	Enemy commando infiltrator who often targeted U.S. aircraft
SCOUT	Observation helicopters: OH-6 Cayuse, OH-13 Sioux, OH-23 Raven, OH-58 Kiowa
SGN/SIG	Signal
SHIP	Helicopter
SLICK	UH-1 Huey helicopter with only protective armaments
SMOKE	Smoke Ship: UH-1 utilized for laying down a billowing screen of smoke to blind the enemy to trailing troop carrying aircraft

SN	Serial Number
SQD	Squadron
SVC	Service
TB	Transportation Battalion
TC	Transportation Company
TI	Tech Inspector
TRP	Troop
UNK	Unknown
USAAM	U. S. Army Aviation Museum (Ft. Rucker, AL)
UTT	Utility Tactical Transport
VC	Viet Cong
VN	Vietnam
WIA	Wounded In Action

ACKNOWLEDGMENTS

Reconstructing history where they are no written records requires an alternative methodology for gathering data. These individuals and institutions helped me meet that challenge each in their own unique way.

Harley Patrick, who saw the potential where others didn't, and engineered a platform at Hellgate Press to display all my findings; **Bob Chenoweth**, my old Smithsonian buddy, who to this day always finds the time to walk me through the intricacies of in-country Army helicopter markings and rotorcraft nomenclature; **Jim Gosnell**, fellow 114th vet, friend, and computer mentor who employed an ingenious methodology for finding former VN vets and VN War data vital to this project; **Jeremy Hogan**, who selflessly lent his professional photography expertise to the project, and whose relentless pursuit to preserve a bit of family aviation history is an inspiration to us all; **Greg Kleven**, good friend these past fifty-five years whose strength and will to survive three bullets on Oct 17, 1967 near the Ho Chi Minh Trail is not only an inspirational story, but more importantly, emblematic of a determined soul who would not rest until he found an alternate way home, and in the process constructed bridges where none existed before; **Geoff Liebrandt**, digital artist extraordinaire whose talent is most evident on the book cover graphic which captures the expressive spirit as practiced by American helicopter crews in Vietnam; **Tom Payne** and **David Adams** of the VHPA for alerting the membership about this project and for their help in publishing a two-part Copter Name Quiz in their superb bi-monthly Association periodical; **John Hastings**, for his generosity in getting the word out about this project via the VHCMA newsletter; **Doug Wilson**, impassioned collaborator and # 1 benefactor of images and data relating to Army helicopter activities in Vietnam; the late **George Young**, who after offering me the position of Unit Historian in the 114 Aviation Company Association would become an equal partner in all subsequent tasks, and in so doing thoroughly redefined the qualities reflective of a Master mentor. His resolute devotion to his men and his sense of equality and recognition of those under his command, regardless of rank, was his hallmark, and became the inspiration for the very structure of this book; **Ray Wilhite**, for unhesitatingly sharing the riches of the USAAM photo archives, thank you; to **Janet, Andrew and Josie Brennan**, for maintaining a domestic environment conducive to my 5,000+ hours of deep computer searches and data entry, where the back of my head was seemingly more in view these past few years than my glassy-eyed front; to those post-WW II fantasy palaces known as **Army-Navy Surplus** stores which dotted the S.F. Bay Area of my youth. The tactile, olfactory, and visionary experience rivaled many an aeronautical museum for capturing that X-factor component known as the magic of flight; my two favorite haunts for aviation literature in my hometown of Oakland, CA were **Holmes Books** and **De Lauer's News Stand**, both historical downtown icons and institutions of their day. Their uncanny ability to know what I liked and needed, mind you without any input from me, for building a foundation of knowledge went a long way to helping me gain employment at the National Air and Space Museum in Washington, DC; finally, there have been many heralded aviation milestones connected with my hometown, both military and civilian. Names such as Lindbergh, Earhart, Doolittle and Hiller are legendary in these parts. Then, to my astonishment, the realization came to me that another milestone was in the making and it was all due to two giants in their own right. You see, I was tutored by the best flight instructors a kid could have, **Herbert and Margaret Brennan** of Oakland, California.

Other Contributors

I also wish to express my thanks to the following non-copter name contributors for miscellaneous data and images, and other information not associated with a particular copter name:

Akridge, Jim 116 AHC, P, 1967-68; Ausdemore, Jim 119 AHC, 1969; Barati, Steve B-1-9, P, 1965-66; Berg, Doug 170 AHC, 1969-70; Boothe, Riley 117 AHC, P, 1968-69; Bullington, Amos B-101 Avn Bn, 1970-71; Chapman, George 176 AHC, P, 1967; Cook, Riley 114 AHC, 1967-68; Cotton, Mike 162 AHC, 1967-69; Dunlap, 48 AHC, 1970; Duvall, Joe 116 AHC, P, 1968-69; Fetters, Roger 179/213 ASHC; Fitzpatrick, Gerard 611 TC, 1970-71; Foster, Arthur 129 AHC, 1970-71; Frigstad, Ron 57 AHC, 1969-70; Garrett, Gene A-7-1, 1972; Garza, Oscar Medic, 1967-68; Gillies, Lynn B-228 ASHB, 1968-69; Grisanti, Mike A-1-5 Cav, 1968-69; Hamilton, Jim A-101 AHB, P, 1971-72; Hannan, Mark 1 Bn-50 Inf; Haskins, Dan 540 TC/604 TC, 1970-71; Hiltbrand, Lance E-82 Arty, 1968-69; Juliot, Steve 610 TC, CE, 1969-70; Kerr, John A-229 AHB, CE, 1970-71; Kinter, Jim USAF, 1961-64; Knowlen, Chuck C-1-9, 1965-66; LaCroix, Tom 117 AHC, 1969; Lama, Tony C-1-12, 1968-69; LeBuhn Bob 195 AHC, DG, 1968; Lewis, Steven 199 LIB, 1968-70; McGarrett, Buddy 81 TC, 1962-63; Moore, James 117 AHC, 1966-68; Nagle, Steve 12 CAG, 1971-72; Newton, Tom A-228 ASHB; Noziska, Mike 117 AHC, 1969-71; Nunn, Lowen 11 ACR, CE, 1969-70; O'Guin, Philip 4 Avn Bn, 1968-69; Pesnicak, Thomas 125 ATC, 1967-68; Powell, Bruce D-3-4, P, 1967-68; Riley, Bill, 197 AHC, 1965; Rock, Thom 4 Mil Intel Bn, 1968-70; Rohlfing, Bill, 189 AHC, CE, 1968-69; Ron Serafinowicz, Ron 175 AHC, 1970-71; Salitore, Fred 117 AHC, 1965-66; Schubert, Gene 116 AHC, 1968-69; Schuckman, Thomas 240 AHC, 1968-70; Sedey, Allen bro of John Sedey, 114 AHC; Shipes, Joe 281 AHC; Smith, Clyde 312 Avn Support Det; Sot, Wayne 13 Sig Bn, 1969-70; Stem, Tim 129 AHC, CE, 1965-66; Titchenell, Walt C-1-9, CE, 1965-66; Tinay, Stanley B-7-1; Tramp, Tom 57 Med Det, CE, 1962; Trumper, Gerry 128 AHC, CE, 1966-67; Van Dine, Howard C-159, ASHB, 1969; Wadsworth, Jack B-123 Avn Bn; Wagner, Travis A-228 ASHB 1967-68; Walker, Al 610 TC, 1967; Walsh, Mike B-4 Avn Bn, P, 1967-68; Wixom, Larry C-3-17; Womack, Gene 189 AHC, DG, 1970; and Zolnoski, Harry A-2-20 ARA, 1967-68.

SPECIAL THANKS

I was fortunate beyond measure in having availed to me a multitude of sources that acted as helpers in creating this book. The quality and quantity of their contributions were beyond priceless, and in return deserve a note of recognition for teaming up to unbury a time capsule that was never meant to be buried. My sincere gratitude is extended to each and every one.

Adams, David VHPA
Bajc, Marko VN War researcher
Baugher, Joe A/C SN Database
Bennett, Allen 117 AHC
Bishop, Dennis 498 Med Det
Bodkin, Jim 145 CAB
Bows, Ray author
Boyne, Walter author
Brewer, Gary D-1-4
Brown, Rod 147 ASHC
Bruss, Al 390 TC
Callaghan, Bob 2 Sig Gp
Callison, Don D-3-5
Carlton, Ken 191 AHC
Cathey, George 116 AHC
Chenoweth, Bob author
Cherrie, Stan 191 AHC
Clark, Larry VHPA
Conway, John VHPA
Cope, Bill 192 AHC
Cowan, Jean 134 AHC Associate
Cox, Larry 1 Avn Bde
Cummings, Phil 179 ASHC
Davison, Les 155 AHC
Dell, Terry 114 AHC
Deperro, John 15 TC
Detra, Dick 188 AHC
Donnelly, Jim 175 AHC
Dorr, Robert author
Dowler, Gary 121 AHC
Eastman, Dave 175 AHC

Forman, Wallace author
Frankenfield, Tom VHCMA
Fritz, Ken VHPA
Galloway, Joe author
Gibbs, Murray 15 Med Bn
Goodwin, Paul 117 AHC
Gosnell, Jim 114 AHC
Green, Dave 68 AHC
Greenhlagh, Bill 62 AHC
Gregory, Ed Pleiku Pals
Griffin, Robert photographer
Grubbs, Barry 254 Med Det
Gustin, Mike D-1-1
Hansen, Dave 237 Med Det
Harlem, Pete author
Hastie, Mike 4 Inf Div
Hastings, John VHCMA
Haws, Curtis 48 AHC
Heikkila, Dave 56 TC
Hines, Les A-123 Avn Bn
Hogan, Jeremy son of B-1-9 Jerry Hogan
Horton, Glenn 199 LIB
Hubbard, Rollie 62 CAC
Hubbs, Johnny 229 AHB
Iacobacci, Ed 237 Med Det
Jackson, Don 121 AHC
Janes, Bill 191 AHC
Jetter, Art C-2-20 ARA
Jones, John VN War researcher
Jones, Walker C-1-9
Kelley, Mike author

Ketchum, Jim 228 ASHB
Kleven, Greg USMC
Kline, Joe B-101 Avn Bn
Koch, Jim 92 AHC
Koenig, Dick 175 AHC
Koo, Tony MS Excel troubleshooter
Lampman, Dan 271 ASHC
Larkins, William author
Law, Mike VHPA
Ledbetter, Garry 200 ASHC
Leepson, Mark VVA
Leonard, Ron 25 Avn Bn
Lester, Richard 48 AHC
Liebrandt, Geoff digital artist
Love, Terry 1 Sig Bde
Lundh, Lennart author
Marshall, Phil 237 Med Det
Marzen, Claus 114 AHC
Maxham, Steve USAAM
McDaniel, Jim 174 AHC
McDonald, Bill 173 AHC
McRae, Bill 132 ASHC
Miller, George 200 ASHC
Miller, Marty 17 AHC
Miller, Mel 147/242 ASHC
Miller, Robin 114 AHC
Mills, Hugh D-3-5
Moon, Terry photographer
Mounts, Robert 135 AHC
Mutza, Wayne author
Nelson, Dean 178 ASHC

Nichols, John 114 AHC
O'Reilly, Mike C-7-1
Oakes, Hiawatha 8 TC
Papapietro, Joe 114 AHC
Paranal, Joe A-227 AHB
Payne, Tom VHPA
Peterson, Mike C-7-1
Pullen, Tom 282 AHC
Pystor, Richard 114 AHC
Raczon, Don 336 AHC
Rains, Charlie VHCMA
Reese, George 25 Avn Bn
Rhoades, Alan C-229 AHB
Rhoades, Rock 11 ACR
Riseden, Jay 128 AHC
Robie, Bill 92 AHC
Rochat, Lou A-1-9
Roush, Gary VHPA
Sanderlin, Terry 213 ASHC
Schmidt, Gary D-3-4
Schwanebeck, Gene 114 AHC
Schwartz, Richard author
Seabolt, Ron 71 AHC
Skarda, Joe 116 AHC
Sloniker, Mike VHPA
Sprinkle, Jim 235/334 AWC
Stanton, Shelby author
Stino, Tom 187 AHC
Stogner, Grady 11 ACR
Sullivan, George 15 TC
Swickard, Jack VHPA

Tarnovsky, Joe 240 AHC
Tepper, Art 610 TC
Underwood, Hans 134 AHC
Vanderwedge, Phil 114 AHC
Vermillion, Steve 45 Med Co
White, Frank Guns A-Go-Go
Wilhite, Ray USAAM
Wilson, Doug 175 AHC
Windsand, Doug 187 AHC
Wolf, Bill 129 AHC
Woods, Rodney 187 AHC
Young, George 114 AHC
Young, Ralph author
Young, Roger A-3-17
Zipperer, Carl 176 AHC

1st Cavalry Division Assn
114 Aviation Company Assn
Aerial Rocket Artillery Assn
American Legion
Bullwhip Squadron Assn,1-9 Cav
Combat Helicopter Pilots Assn, CHPA
Disabled American Veterans, DAV
Dustoff Assn
Veterans of Foreign Wars, VFW
Vietnam Helicopter Crew Members
  Assn, VHCMA
Vietnam Helicopter Flight Crew
  Network, VHFCN
Vietnam Helicopter Pilots Assn, VHPA
Vietnam Veterans of America, VVA

Wargasm*: F Troop 4 Cav, OH-6A, (sn 66-17795), 1972.* Entering country on August 1968, it went on to amass 2,280 flight hours before returning to the States in May 1972. Today it flies for the Army Aviation Heritage Foundation in Hampton, GA. Photo by Carl Betsill.

www.ingramcontent.com/pod-product-compliance
Lightning Source LLC
Chambersburg PA
CBHW080249030726
47593CB00009B/2419